sociology
for pleasure

edited by

MARCELLO TRUZZI

New College

PRENTICE-HALL, INC., *Englewood Cliffs, New Jersey*

Library of Congress Cataloging in Publication Data

TRUZZI, MARCELLO, comp.
   Sociology for pleasure.

   Bibliography: p.
   1. Sociology-Addresses, essays, lectures.
I. Title.
HM51.T753   301'.08   73-18070
ISBN 0-13-821256-2

© *1974 by PRENTICE-HALL, INC., Englewood Cliffs, N.J.*

Printed in the United States of America

10 9 8 7 6 5 4 3

Cover design by Pat Truzzi

PRENTICE-HALL INTERNATIONAL, INC., London
PRENTICE-HALL OF AUSTRALIA, PTY. LTD., Sydney
PRENTICE-HALL OF CANADA, LTD., Toronto
PRENTICE-HALL OF INDIA PRIVATE LIMITED, New Delhi
PRENTICE-HALL OF JAPAN, INC., Tokyo

contents

iii

7

problems and change, 327

further readings, 421

1
introduction

Sociology has been called the "Littlest Science."[1] Since its origin about 1830, promulgated by the sometimes mad Frenchman August Comte as the positivistic science of society (the "social physics"), it has had many detractors. Many critics have been sadly ignorant of the real content of the discipline, but some have been well acquainted with its very real fads and foibles.[2] Like most of man's memorable accomplishments, sociology has had excesses and vanities as well as glories.

Recent responses to critics of modern sociology have cited the relevance of the discipline to human affairs through scientific promise. All the defenses of sociology picture it as an important *instrument,* a means toward social planning, change, or amelioration.[3] They neglect the value of sociology in and for itself. In our struggle to predict, explain, and control society, we sociologists have largely ignored the descriptive function of our discipline. The foremost function of any science, including sociology, is to tell, through validated observations, the true state of the empirical world—in the case of sociology, the social world. Description is the backbone of any science. Only after we know what is "out there" can we begin to look for intercorrelations, generalizations, and causalities.

Unfortunately, sociologists are at a disadvantage when they merely describe reality, for the general public is not likely to interpret such activity

[1] Allan Mazur, "The Littlest Science," *The American Sociologist,* 3, 3 (1968), 195–200. For responses to Mazur's analysis, see *The American Sociologist,* 3, 4 (1968), 292–96.

[2] For example, Pitirim A. Sorokin, *Fads and Foibles in Modern Sociology and Related Sciences* (Chicago: Henry Regnery Co., 1956); C. Wright Mills, *The Sociological Imagination* (New York: Oxford University Press, 1959); and Alvin W. Gouldner, *The Coming Crisis of Western Sociology* (New York: Basic Books, Inc., 1970).

[3] For example, see Jack Douglas, ed., *The Relevance of Sociology* (New York: Appleton-Century-Crofts, 1970). For consideration of the varieties of relevance, see the introductory essay in Marcello Truzzi and Philip B. Springer, *Is Sociology Relevant?* (Pacific Palisades, Calif.: Goodyear Publishing Co., in press).

as scientific. Other sciences usually are not subject to this problem. For example, if a biologist spends his lifetime in the field studying the mating habits of bumblebees, he is considered to be doing scientifically legitimate work. An anthropologist who describes the curious sexual customs of the Bongo Bongo is considered to be doing legitimate ethnography. But a sociologist who writes a paper on the sexual practices of middle Americans is likely to be called a journalist at best, a voyeur at worst. It seems that if a scientist describes something objectively, most laymen will consider it scientific only if the scientist reveals something they would otherwise not be able to learn.[4] For this reason critics have called sociology a search for truisms. Thus, most of us would consider the study of special or unusual interactions among midgets or transsexuals "respectable"; however, the same kind of observation about everyday matters would probably not impress us as being especially scientific. The layman expects science to reveal something new. Merely validating something he already knows (for example, a physicist stating that spectrographic analysis reveals that most people will see apples as red) is not judged scientifically important.

Two factors account for much of the problem. First, most people do not understand that science is merely refined common sense; it is a method, not a body of knowledge per se. Many people expect sociology to produce what approximates magical results (such as predicting the outcome of an election)—results like the wonders of physics. Second, much observation done by nonscientists is, in fact, in accord with scientific method. Good journalists often gather data just as a good sociologist might.[5] Science is merely a method of examining the objective world, an attempt to obtain intersubjectively verifiable knowledge, usually through empiricism. Yet, if we sociologists are to legitimate sociology among laymen, we should try to tell them something new about the social world. Just as we would expect a biologist to tell us more than that fish live in water and do not secretly gulp a lung-full of air at night, we should seek the expansion as well as the validation of knowledge. Going beyond description to obtain prediction, explanation, and control of human affairs clearly performs that service. But

---

[4] Obviously, whether information is considered informative depends on who is receiving the information. The Bongo Bongo kinship pattern would hardly seem a piece of scientific news to a native of Bongo Bongo, but it might greatly surprise and enlighten nonnatives. Similarly, a Martian scientist might consider it an important breakthrough to discover that people dominate the planet earth, rather than pets, which might superficially seem to be in control of the people insofar as pet-owners tend to their needs and seem even to worship them.

Sociology has often been guilty of inventing special technical language—jargon—to make sometimes trivial findings appear less so to the uninitiated.

[5] For an excellent example of this sort of parallelism, see Clarice S. Stoll, "George Plimpton: The Journalist as Social Observer," in Marcello Truzzi, ed., *The Humanities as Sociology* (Columbus, Ohio: Charles E. Merrill Publishing Co., 1973), pp. 181–94.

descriptive studies have similar virtues.[6] Sociological description can give us (1) information about aspects of the social world not normally encountered or observed by most of us (for example, descriptive studies of other societies, various subcultures and strata of our society, or different analytic dimensions of common social life);[7] (2) information about aspects of our everyday world not normally examined by us (such as the ethnographic and ethnomethodological studies of everyday life interaction in much of what is now called microsociology);[8] and (3) surprising, contrary information about things we thought we had knowledge about, thus debunking folk wisdom about social life (for example, the fact that the general economic position of blacks in the United States is worse today than it was just after World War II,[9] although most people think it has been improving steadily since then).

The readings in this volume are intended to revive interest in sociological description. This is not to deny the scientific promise of sociology as a discipline capable of more advanced functions. Actuarial prediction ("x people will be killed on the highway next Memorial Day weekend" or "z percentage of the population q will vote in the next election") has become a sophisticated part of social science, as the financial success of insurance companies, which base their existence on extrapolation from today's social patterns into the future, demonstrates. Sociology has been far less successful in developing true covering-law theories that could explain social behaviors. The search for theoretical prediction (knowing *why* something will happen, not just *that* it happened for unknown reasons several times before) and explanation remains a major concern of sociologists, and rightly so. But the failure of contemporary sociology to match scientifically the advanced stages of the natural sciences like physics should not blind us to the excellence of the equally legitimate descriptive accomplishments of soci-

[6] See Gideon Sjoberg, "A Rationale for Descriptive Sociology," *Social Forces*, 29, 3 (1951), 251–57.

[7] Many of the descriptive foundations of many advanced formulations rest on studies done several decades ago. The intervening social change makes much of this foundation obsolete as an explanation for current events which are likely to be the results of new variables that have entered the scene or old ones that have lost importance. For example, it is questionable how much one could explain about a modern factory or union, using even the best descriptive study of an organization examined during the Depression.

[8] See especially Erving Goffman, *The Presentation of Self in Everyday Life* (Garden City, N.Y.: Doubleday & Company, Inc., 1959), *Behavior in Public Places* (New York: The Free Press, 1963), and *Relations in Public* (New York: Basic Books, Inc., 1971). For a review of the literature in one area of microsociology, see Donald W. Ball, *Microecology: Social Situations and Intimate Space* (Indianapolis: The Bobbs-Merrill Co., Inc., 1973).

[9] See Thomas Mayer, "The Position and Progress of Black America," in Steven Duetsch and John Howard, eds., *Where It's At: Radical Perspectives in Sociology* (New York: Harper & Row, Publishers, 1970), pp. 398–411.

ology. This collection of articles unapologetically emphasizes description. Because the articles are therefore usually less technical and sophisticated (quantification is certainly not absent but is usually minimized in descriptive studies), they should be easily and enjoyably read by the beginning student of sociology. In fact, this anthology is frankly intended to present what some might call "sociology for people who hate sociology."

I hope that the student will experience some of the basic pleasure of sociology as he reads some of its less methodologically aspiring and less pretentious work—work which is still good science, and which most sociologists enjoy reading even though they may find little reason to cite it in their specialized research. Because my goal is entertainment as well as enlightenment, I have not chosen the articles in this volume with any great concern for achieving methodological variety or distributional coverage of many social institutions.[10] My primary consideration was that they bring enjoyment while still teaching something important about the content or method of sociology. I believe that the articles encompass all the dimensions of pleasure derived from description, as described above. But in the final analysis the selection was largely based on my subjective judgment, often intuitive but sometimes reinforced by the comments of my students and colleagues. I hope that students will find these articles as pleasing as I did.

[10] For a similar collection which did attempt more representative coverage, see Marcello Truzzi, ed., *Sociology and Everyday Life* (Englewood Cliffs, N.J.: Prentice-Hall, Inc., 1968). On the problem of what constitutes "interesting" sociological work of the sort focused on in this collection, see Murray S. Davis, "That's Interesting! Toward a Phenomenology of Sociology and a Sociology of Phenomenology," *Philosophy of Social Science,* 1 (1971), 309–44.

2
interactions

PIERRE VAN DEN BERGHE

The Game Sociologists Play

THE PROTECTIVE MYTHS

The Ivory Tower is unquestionably the most pleasant microcosm in American society. Fortunately for its academic fauna, few of the other subspecies of Homo sapiens know it. And the reason for this widespread ignorance is not accidental. Like all privileged guilds, academics restrict entry into their group and wrap themselves in shrouds of protective secrecy. The first and the most important line of defense against the massive intrusion of outsiders is a set of elaborate and highly successful myths about the nature of academic life. Briefly, there are three principal myths:

1. An academic career requires superior ability.
2. The rewards, especially the material rewards, of academic life are meager.
3. Academic life is dull.

The first myth does not stand scrutiny. The distribution of academic talent, as in all professions, follows a normal curve—i.e., most professors are mediocre, a few are incompetent, and a few are intellectually superior. It is highly questionable that college professors have greater average ability than physicians, lawyers, watchmakers, plumbers, secretaries, or perhaps even army officers. Mediocrity should be no deterrent to a university career because, combined with lengthy and semiesoteric training, it ensures a sufficient level of competence to pass for erudition and profundity of thought.

Since college professors are scrutinized mostly by undergraduates (themselves a mediocre group and one which does not have the additional benefit of esoteric training), they have little to fear, except perhaps at a few selective places like Harvard or Princeton where students are often brighter than the staff. Generally, however, students cannot tell the difference between pedantry and scholarship, between glib facility and profound insight. Indeed, neither can most academics. Consequently, the myth of college professors as a formidable brain trust of eggheads is secure. The great mass of college graduates, who, more than anything else, fear being made fools of, shrink from the audacity of even contemplating an incursion into the august groves of academe after getting their sheepskins and having their photographs taken in silly flat-topped hats.

It may be argued that professors are recruited from the best students, and hence that professors are a select group. However, since professors themselves do the selection, and since school grades at any level show a perverse lack of correlation with anything else except other school grades, the validity of this argument is highly questionable. At best, it can be argued that those students with a gift for mental mimicry become professors.

The second myth—that an academic career condemns one to a life of quasi-monastic material penury—is the most ingenious of the three. In American society, where the pecuniary criterion of excellence is so important, this myth is a powerful deterrent. As many myths, this one originated in fact. In Medieval Europe, in Imperial China, and in other preindustrial societies, scholars were often reduced to the status of respectably indolent mendicants. Even in 19th century Europe and America, scholarship was not a self-supporting way of life. It was still a luxury for gentlemen with both leisure and means to invest in the pursuit of a seat in the academy, a chair at a top university, or some other mark of prestige, all the more valuable for not being *directly* purchasable like a title of nobility, a commission in the army, or a diplomatic post.

Today, however, professors need not have inherited wealth or live in garrets. They earn as good a living as other professionals with similar amounts of training, if one considers the numerous fringe benefits and the four months of annual vacation. The president of Harvard earns only a fraction of what his counterpart at General Motors does, but at that level, differences in income are almost purely symbolic. The successful professor at a major university can easily earn $25,000 to $30,000—some three times the national average. His professional income includes, besides his regular salary, consulting and lecturing fees, book and article royalties, extra salary for summer teaching or research, not to mention opportunities for free trips to exotic places, scholarships for his children, and numerous tax deductions for professional expenses. Even the young assistant professor is hardly impecunious with a starting salary of $10,000 to $12,000. In fact, he roughly *begins* life at the national average, with good prospects of doubling his income in a decade or less.

University professors earn less than physicians, but then they do not have to work as hard or as long for their money. No other profession gives one so much security and material comfort to do what one likes at one's own pace and in nearly complete independence. As to security of tenure, it is nearly unparalleled in any other job. Academia combines the security of a large and affluent bureaucracy with the independence of "free" entrepreneurship. It is the surest road to a life of comfortable indolence if one feels so inclined, and of serene dedication to one's harmless manias if one chooses to "work."

How then, one may ask, does the myth of the indigent professor survive? The answer lies largely in the behavior of professors who, unlike most of their fellow citizens, compete with each other in *in*conspicuous consumption. Through a peculiar kind of reverse snobbery, the display of wealth is held by most professors to be a vulgar expression of material mass culture, a trap of the advertising industry and the "consumer society." They leave the flashy Chryslers and Cadillacs to low-brow prizefighters and real estate agents, and sport dusty Volkswagens or Volvos, or at least motorcars which do not *look* flashy and expensive. They would not dream of buying their wives mink stoles; they sneer at television (the "idiot box"), and if they have color sets they hide them in their bedrooms; they dress in drab, baggy clothes, cherish shoes with holes in the soles, and visit the barber at most once a month. Thus the careful affectation of a seedy look gets mistaken by the layman for financial need.

The luxuries of professors have relatively low visibility: private schools for their children, cultural trips to Europe (staying at inconspicuous hotels), theater and concert tickets, French wines, art books, record collections, recorder lessons, and other paraphernalia of the "high culture" of which academics regard themselves as the custodians. The affectation of poverty protects professors from the envy and competition of laymen, flatters their self-perception of superiority over the mass of uncouth philistines, and allows the more politically conscious among them the thrill of vicarious identification with the oppressed. They can have their cake, eat it, and yet pretend not to eat it.

The third protective myth concerns the alleged dullness of university life. Unlike the first two myths, the third one is perpetuated by laymen rather than academics. The stereotype of the professor as a dull, pedantic bookworm spending his life ruining his eyes in a dingy library or over a microscope, or boring his students in the classroom, is, of course, a caricature of reality. The professor is held to be a paragon of impracticality, removed from the "real" world of action. "Those who can, do; those who can't, teach." Although this stereotype is difficult to reconcile with the picture of the academic as a person of staggering intellect, the two views are often simultaneously held by the same laymen. Academics are disliked for their aloofness, ridiculed for their absent-mindedness, feared for their radicalism. The important thing is that to most red-blooded American boys and girls, the red-minded professor is a fairly repulsive figure. Consequently, competition for the few born into the academic caste is not very keen.

The degree to which professors succeed in shielding the mass of their compatriots from knowledge about their way of life is little short of amazing. One might suppose that undergraduates after spending four years on a campus might catch a few glimpses of what kind of animals their teachers are, but in fact very few students see through the protective myths. Professors know a good deal about student culture, but the reciprocal is not true. Teachers and students live side by side in two groups separated by a symbolic one-way window such as sociologists and social psychologists devise for their small-group experiments. Professors can observe the students, but the students see only the faintest shadows behind the metallic glare of the glass. The two groups live in different worlds, have different interests and values, and interact only in the most ritualized circumstances. . . .

A few students, through the intimacy of the laboratory, the office, or the bedroom penetrate the screens and get to know their teachers as persons. By emulating the behavior, tastes, and idiosyncracies of their mentors, they catch their attention, and soon get recognized as "good" students and potential recruits to academia. However, they will still have to undergo a lengthy and tedious novitiate before they are finally admitted into the priesthood. They will have to undergo the hazing and rites of passage of graduate school, the second line of defense against lay intruders. . . .

THE ACADEMIC PECKING ORDER

The ingenuity displayed by man in making invidious distinctions between himself and his fellows is sufficiently great as to provide a field of specialization, and hence a livelihood for a substantial number of sociologists. The academic game cannot be played successfully without an adequate understanding of the status hierarchy or pecking order of the players. Hierarchies are the consequence of competition for scarce resources. The more you get, the higher you rank; and the higher you rank, the more you are allowed to take. Subhuman species, and some human groups, compete for basic necessities like food and sex. However, professors are too well fed to regard food as a scarce resource. Prescriptive monogamy in American society has seriously interfered with man's harem-building propensities, though, of course, modest and clandestine little ventures in that direction may occasionally be indulged in. Unlike baboons, professors cannot openly fight over the right to mount coeds on the campus green. In fact, any attempt to do so outside the privacy of one's office would be regarded as moral turpitude and a cause for dismissal.

There remain three basic commodities over which most men spend most of their lives fighting: power, wealth, and prestige. Academics fight over all three, but most of all over the last. Universities and colleges are, first and foremost, institutions in which positions are gained or improved by patting your colleagues' backs, or by deprecating their efforts, or by a judicious combination of both techniques.

This is not to say that professors are indifferent to power and wealth, but the scope for invidious distinctions on these two dimensions is not very great. The salary ratio of a full professor to a beginning assistant professor is only about two to one. How unsatisfying for a Nobel Prize winner in Physics to think of himself as only twice as good as the young Ph.D. from Kansas State who may never get anything worthwhile published. (By comparison, the head of a corporation can regard himself as twenty or thirty times as valuable as a junior executive or production engineer.)

Power also does not differentiate well enough among professors. The basic power of professors is to flunk students, and hence to affect adversely their life chances. This power is jealously guarded and shared equally by all teachers, from the most junior assistant professor to the most senile full professor. Under the guise of protecting academic freedom and professional autonomy, every teacher has despotic power over students. In the British system, this power is mitigated by external examiners and reviewed by academic Senate, but in America, the judgment of the teacher is final. A student may cajole, bribe, or seduce his or her teacher to change a grade; a dean may drop a discreet hint over the telephone that the star football player should be given a D instead of an F so that he can stay in school; but in last analysis, there is no effective redress against the arbitrary judgment of the teacher.

The trouble with this power, however, is that, since it is equally shared by all professors, it cannot serve as a basis for making invidious distinctions among them. The only kind of power that can serve that gratifying function is power over one's colleagues. Some measure of it can be acquired by becoming a departmental chairman, a dean, a provost, or a university president. By and large, the more academically mediocre a college or university is, the more powerful its administration is, and the more valued administrative posts are. The poorer community colleges and religiously affiliated schools are almost undistinguishable from high schools in this respect. In big-league academia, however, to become an administrator often entails a loss of prestige and leisure, a vast amount of uninteresting work, and only a modicum of power.

At good schools, a department chairman or a dean can have a certain amount of nuisance value to his colleagues; he can retard their promotion or deny them a "merit" increase in salary. But, actually, his power is limited because the opportunities for professors to move to a better job at another university are so great. In fact, the mere threat of resignation, judiciously used, frequently suffices to obtain what one demands. . . . Once a professor has tenure, there is little a chairman or dean can do to him, except be an irritant, and even that is very much a two-way affair.

Luckily, there remains prestige as a basis of differentiation among professors. Here the possibilities are limitless, and professors have developed a pecking order of such scope, complexity, and subtlety as to deserve admiration. Vanity, a trait ascribed to certain male birds of bright plumage and to females of the human species who display varying portions of their epidermis on the screen or stage, is likewise the dominant characteristic of college and university teachers.

This little book cannot do justice to the intricacies of academic rankings; it can only provide a modest introduction to an extremely immodest world. Every academic belongs to at least three discrete status systems: he is a member of the larger society, of his college or university, and of the group of people who share his specialty.

In the larger society, the professor is ascribed a solid place in the upper middle class, though his unkept lawn, unwashed car, black friends, or long-haired progeny may occasionally attract the ire of his neighbors. However, even withal his status is sufficiently secure that he can afford such harmless eccentricities. In any case, most professors could not care less what their neighbors think of them, because their social life is almost exclusively confined to other academics. Whether professorial homes are grouped in a gilded ghetto as is the case in some small college towns, or physically dispersed over large metropolitan areas, professors constitute something close to an occupational caste with strict rules of commensality. There are exceptions of course. Some bored wives of civic-minded professors will canvass for the League of Women Voters or engage in some other form of do-good-ism. And the more radical academics will occasionally rub shoulders with the oppressed in protest marches. But, for most academic families, the supermarket and department store are the only significant links with the outside world.

Occasionally, a professor gains notoriety in the larger society by climbing Mount Everest,[1] writing a salacious book, inventing a bigger and better bomb, murdering his wife, stirring up the students, transplanting a heart, naming his dog after the president of the republic to which he has been temporarily sent as ambassador, or some such noteworthy action. Celebrity among laymen, however, is frowned upon in academia and often can only be purchased at the cost of prestige loss in the other two status systems, the ones that really count.

Professors belong to two large groups of colleagues: the staff of their college or university, and all fellow specialists in their discipline. Only the members of a given department at a given university share common membership in both of these larger groups. Thus the department is the academic habitat par excellence, the principal scene for the enactment of competition for prestige. Only fellow specialists can fully evaluate one's prestige, and one regularly interacts only with those specialists who teach at the same university. Yet, both of the larger groups contribute to a scholar's sum total of prestige in a complex and partly reciprocal fashion.

[1] With apologies to my friend and colleague Richard Emerson, who was crazy enough to do just that.

Universities and colleges, as even laymen know, are ordered in a hierarchy of prestige. The layman's hierarchy does not necessarily correspond to the academic person's evaluations. Thus, it may be socially prestigious to go to an "elite" liberal arts college tucked away in the hills of New Hampshire or Connecticut, but such places do not rank high in the preference of most academics, except for a few snobs and eccentrics who genuinely enjoy teaching. With a remarkable degree of consensus, professors rank institutions of higher learning into a number of pyramidal categories. At the top, there are ten or twelve great universities, with the twin giants of Harvard and Berkeley among them; then one finds a further fifteen or so distinguished institutions trembling on the edge of greatness but lacking the aura of the great ones. Following is roughly a score of highly respectable schools, which however begin to show certain weaknesses especially in graduate training and facilities; then come some fifty to seventy-five colleges that do a decent job of educating undergraduates and to whose staff one can belong without having to apologize or explain where the school is located; a further 200 to 250 schools might still perhaps be described as on the right side of academic respectability, but one would rather not be there if one had a choice. Finally there is the great dismal mass of the 2000-odd institutions that are of "higher learning" only by the most charitable of definitions.[2]

The large university, whether private or public, with a well-established graduate program, a good library and research facilities, low teaching loads, and a selected undergraduate body is the most desirable. The small isolated college with heavy teaching, a poor library, and no research facilities or graduate students stands at the other extreme, especially if it is a vocationally oriented community college or a religiously affiliated one. The "elite" liberal arts college stands somewhere in between. To join a given institution automatically places one on a prestige ladder according to the rank of the institution, and, more specifically, of one's own department among the others in the nation. Indeed, not only are colleges and universities given an over-all ranking, but in each discipline an academic will, with considerable consistency, be able to establish a rank order of departments in his field. Thus University A might have a "top ten" over-all ranking, but its chemistry department might only rank "top twenty but not top ten."

One's university affiliation pegs one at a certain level vis à vis colleagues on other campuses, but within one's institution many finer status distinctions are made. First, in a given college or university, the various departments are placed on a rough scale of intellectual distinction, and, interest-

---

[2] This last category has been termed "academic Siberia," a designation unfair to Siberia, whose institutions of higher learning are undoubtedly of better quality. Perhaps one should speak of academic Alaska instead. The reader should excuse my refusal to name any schools (beyond the reference to Harvard and Berkeley), as doing so might adversely affect the sale of this book.

ingly, the order is much the same everywhere: medicine, mathematics, and the natural sciences are high status subjects, while education, agriculture, social work, and nursing rank low; the social sciences and humanities have intermediate status with yet finer distinctions between the specific fields, e.g., economics frequently ranks higher than sociology. As a general rule, the more quantitative and the less "applied" a subject is, the higher its status; and as the higher status subjects tend to attract the better students and vice versa, this prestige order frequently does reflect real qualitative differences in both staff and students.

This prestige ranking of subjects is also related to the students' assessment of the difficulty of a course. Courses known to be "gut," "snap," or "mickey mouse" have low status; thus one way a professor can enhance his status as a lecturer is to be a stiff grader. Alternatively, he can try to be a popular lecturer, a policy which calls for lenient grades and a certain histrionic flair. . . . It should be noted that the opinions of students, especially of undergraduates, have relatively little direct bearing on the teacher's prestige. Nevertheless, the person who has a reputation for being a good teacher is the object of a certain amount of envy on the part of his colleagues. (This envy is reflected in sneering remarks that X is a "crowd pleaser.") Interestingly, most professors are unwilling to grant that students are legitimate judges of their performance, yet teachers *do* compete for students, especially for graduate ones. Ability to attract a coterie of sycophantic graduate students is an important prestige symbol. And, recently, student ratings of teachers have somewhat increased the relevance of undergraduate opinion to academic prestige within the university.

On the whole, however, in conformity with Veblen's theory of conspicuous leisure, a top prestige symbol in academia is how little one teaches. The higher one's rank and the more exalted one's reputation, the fewer defiling "contact hours" one has with students, and the more senior the students. Lecturers and assistant professors typically spend nine to twelve hours a week with freshmen and sophomores; full and associate professors spend six or fewer hours with seniors and graduate students. And a few prima donnas manage to get research professorships that entail no teaching at all beyond an occasional graduate seminar.

Academic title (instructor, lecturer, assistant professor, associate professor, etc.) is perhaps the most visible determinant of prestige within the university. To each rank belong certain rights and privileges. Tenure usually comes with promotion to an associate professorship; salary and power increase with rank though not very steeply, while work load decreases. Office space, especially where scarcity forces some "doubling up," is generally proportional to rank, and so is access to secretarial assistance. In short, the less one has to do, the better the facilities one has to do it, and the more one gets paid for it. . . .

So much for the main factors making for prestige competition within the university. Let us now turn to the external prestige system—the prestige determined by the recognition of colleagues in your discipline. The overwhelming majority of them are attached to other institutions and are thinly spread all over the world. Each discipline thus constitutes a vast network of people isolated from each other except during the brief ritual of the annual convention when scholars converge on some large city's Hilton Hotel for three or four days of inebriated gossip, frantic job-hunting, and unashamed prestige-mongering. The national, indeed the international, nature of this prestige system, as well as the imputed expertness of the judgments passed makes the body of fellow specialists the ultimate measure of a scholar's worth. Unless your work is known and discussed by other experts in your field, you are a strictly local figure. It is immaterial that most criticisms be adverse, as they most typically are; the important thing is that you be spoken and written about, preferably by people you have never met.

One of the surest indices of academic prestige is the frequency with which your name is cited in colleagues' publications. As important as frequency is the context in which you are quoted. It may range from an incidental footnote, to a critical paragraph, an entire article, or even a doctoral thesis or a biography. Of course, you get quoted to the extent that you publish. . . .

Apart from printed evidence of scholarly status, the annual convention or meeting of the professional association is the greatest prestige show in the academic world. Conventions mean many things to many people. Ostensibly, they are a forum for the exchange of ideas and the presentation of papers on the latest advances in the discipline. In fact, this is little more than a pretext to justify the university's paying your travel expenses. To graduate students, conventions are a slave market for academic employment. More senior academics have a chance to peddle their manuscripts to publishers' representatives. Old classmates exchange gossip over cocktails. Various committees transact business. Foundation and government agents are solicited for support. All these varied and useful functions are overshadowed, however, by the fact that the annual meetings are first and foremost rituals of prestige competition. Professors strut around on the soft carpets of hotel lobbies with the assiduousness of birds of paradise in their display dances, but without even the excuse of a tangible reward such as the favors of females.

Unknown young scholars attend conventions to court the favor of the nationally known ones, and the latter in order to receive the homage of the nonentities, to bask in the sunshine of their glory, and to defend their territory against challengers. Regular attendance at conventions can actually be a substitute for publishing as a method for achieving a reputation. If the people who matter have seen you often enough, your name will be bandied about and suggested for editorial boards, offices in your professional society, and the like. After a decade of diligent attendance and proper courting of the mighty, you may find yourself an established star of a magnitude quite disproportional to your scholarly accomplishment. You will then be one of these people about whose accomplishments colleagues are understandably hazy, but whose name will nevertheless appear on a great many committees and boards. You will in fact have become the recipient of an unearned academic reputation, but as relatively few people can tell the difference between that and the *bona fide* article, the sources of your recognition are of little consequence.

Meetings are excellent barometers of professional standing. You know that you are leaving the drab herd of mere teachers of undergraduates when the following things begin to happen with increasing frequency:

1. People whom you cannot remember having ever seen claim to have met you at such and such a place.
2. Important colleagues recognize you on sight without having to cast a furtive glance at the name tag on your lapel.
3. Colleagues who have never met you read your name tag and exclaim: "Oh! I have long wanted to meet you," or "I am using your book in my class," or "I have just read your article in such-and-such journal."
4. People whom you only know slightly approach you and say: "The grapevine has it that you are unhappy at X. Would you be interested in coming to Y?"
5. Graduate students deferentially approach you as the authority on the subject on which they are writing their thesis, and ask for advice or for clarification of a fine point in your thinking.
6. You accidentally overhear your name mentioned in colleagues' conversations.
7. Your name is formally cited by colleagues reading papers. (It doesn't matter whether their comments are positive or negative.)
8. Rumors and anecdotes circulate about you. (Their nature is unimportant.)
9. Publishers' agents ask you: "Won't you write a textbook for us?"
10. Your feuds with colleagues become notorious.
11. A slight expectant hush follows your appearance in a group.
12. People approach you with greater frequency than you approach others.
13. Your own former classmates become openly envious.

If these flattering things do not begin to occur between five and ten years after getting your Ph.D., they will probably never happen. You might as well stop attending professional meetings and withdraw to the security of your college, where you can at least cut something of a figure at the faculty club and make students laugh at your jokes.

These two academic prestige systems—the one rooted in the local university and the other based on national recognition in the professional association—are intricately interconnected. Thus, in order to gain the respect of your professional peers, you must be affiliated with a respectable institution. If you are located at Apache Creek Junior College,[3] you have obviously fallen by the wayside, and no self-respecting school will condescend to pull you out of the hole. Conversely, tenure and promotion at the better universities depend in good part on publication and on some test of professional recognition outside the home campus.

The principal ground on which these two forces meet is, of course, the academic department. And, since the national system is paramount, day-to-day prestige competition between members of a department consists mostly in impressing upon others how much better known than your colleagues you are outside the home university. There are several ways to do this, such as discreetly attracting your colleagues' attention to quotations from your work in the publications of others. You may even resort to some such ruse as asking your secretary to drop into a departmental meeting to let you know that you have a person-to-person call from the Under-Secretary of Defense or the Chancellor of the University of Chicago.

By far the most effective way of establishing prestige is to be frequently away from the campus on long-distance trips. The top dogs in any department are the ones who are constantly attending international conferences, giving lectures at other universities, or consulting with government or industrial firms—in short, the professorial jet set. The jet-propelled professor does almost everything except that for which he draws his salary. His undergraduates have to be content with lecture notes hastily scribbled on the back of airline menus between the martini and the crab cocktail; the university that pays his way to give a prestigious public lecture will have to be satisfied with a few associations of ideas hastily thrown together between planes to the accompaniment of saccharine music at O'Hare airport. Some professors even keep a mental note of their annual air mileages. The truly big-league log at least 100,000 miles (about fifteen transcontinental round-trips). Meanwhile, the graduate teaching assistants get valuable experience, and the undergraduates get what is known in polite society as the short end of the stick but what in student culture goes by a more vivid (but alas, unprintable) simile. The airborne professor is no longer simply absent-minded, he is also absent-bodied, a fleeting shadow that can occasionally be sighted picking up his mail in the departmental mail room.

Short of being physically absent from campus, prestige competition calls for at least being inaccessible, ostensibly in order to engage in prestigious work, namely research or writing. The device of the secretary to answer the phone and screen visitors is of course widely used inside and outside of aca-

---

[3] The name is meant to be fictitious, but such a place probably does exist, in which case I proffer my apologies in advance.

demia. But only a few of the more senior professors who are departmental chairmen or have large research grants have private secretaries. So professors have devised other ways of making themselves unavailable, especially to students. They can stay at home where they can keep a nice little tax-deductible study. More ingeniously, they can have unnamed office doors where only the initiated can find them. Or else they can get lost between their multiple offices. Thus a professor can belong to both an institute and a department and have an office in each; or he can abscond to the entrails of the library where he has a cozy cubicle and cannot even be reached by telephone.

GARY S. FELTON

Psychosocial Implications of the Coffee Break

Now whither shall a person, wearied with hard study, or the laborious turmoils of a tedious day, repair to refresh himself? or where can young gentlemen, or shopkeepers, more innocently and advantageously spend an hour or two in the evening, than at a coffee house? . . . To read men is acknowledged more useful than books; but where is there a better library for that study, generally than here; among such a variety of humours, all expressing themselves on diverse subjects according to their respective abilities?[1]

Out of the liberalized puritanism existing beneath the babel of the early coffee houses grew a new man—Man who became interested in the other person, his ideas, thoughts, and manners; Man who showed respect for differing opinions, who experienced a heightened alertness to the sensitivity and rights of others, and who maintained a consideration of courtesy for others; Man who scorned ridicule and learned tolerance. These gatherings opened vistas for the exploration into communication, expression, the formation of opinion, and the exchange of ideas and prejudices. They af-

Reprinted from the *Journal of Human Relations*, 14, 3 (1966), 434–49, by permission of the publisher, Central State University, Wilberforce, Ohio.

[1] Harold V. Routh, "The Advent of Modern Thought in Popular Literature," in *Cambridge History of English Literature*, VII, p. 442.

forded the opportunity to show openness and seriousness, to grow intellectually, to examine personal difficulties, and to converse. In this regard, it is
believed by this writer that there are many close parallels between the vitalization of Man in the coffee houses of old, and the vitalization of the
worker in contemporary business and industrial work settings. As the ". . .
movement was so inchoate that the middle classes themselves were hardly
conscious of it,"[2] so, indeed, a great number of contemporary workers and
their employers are not conscious of these interpersonal elements of the coffee break. Nevertheless, there does exist a realm of psychological values, the
effects of social and personal interchange at the coffee break which contributes significantly to the betterment of the worker in his occupational setting. The interpretation of this worker satisfaction by the employer, in
terms of production, efficiency, morale, absenteeism, accidents, turnover,
and fatigue, must be expanded such that greater insight into employee
dynamics may be forthcoming. One important reason for this need is depicted poignantly in the statement of one company representative: "Many
of our people keep working during the break, just taking intermittent sips
of their coffee."[3] The elements of time lost and cost involved may be minimized or reduced markedly under such conditions, but one must question
whether the over-all effect of depriving the worker of his opportunity for
relaxation from work and for social-personal interchange over coffee is
more beneficial from the standpoint of employee satisfaction and vitalization. Is the elimination of interaction at a coffee break away from the work
setting not destructive and limiting? Are business and industry so concerned with economic conservation that the beneficial outgrowths of the
coffee break are all but eliminated? These issues merit much serious inquiry, for the attempt to reduce economic expenditures and to maximize
man-hours of work may be depriving the employee of the opportunity to
reflect on his integrity as an individual, thus creating a potentially serious
employee dissatisfaction.

It is felt by this writer that a revitalization of approach and restructuring
of thinking must be undertaken in order to provide a more dynamic, less
parochial understanding of the meaning and implications of the coffee
break. In addition, this writer believes that the heightened sense of individuality as well as the increased humanization of values, perspectives, and
ideas provided by personal interchange in the coffee break plays a very significant role in the motivation and satisfaction of the employee. A thorough
examination of these factors in the context of a daily coffee respite may offer
a wealth of material to the employer which will provide further insight in-

---

[2] Harold Routh, "Steele and Addison," in *Cambridge History of English Literature,*
IX, p. 37.

[3] "Buns and Coffee," *New York Times,* May 5, 1960, p. 50.

to employee dynamics and therefore will result in more than the stimulus-response approach (coffee break → increased production) currently viewed in so many work settings.

Within the scope of the contemporary coffee break structure, the time allowance is of such limited duration that for the worker, development of a sense of personal integrity and identity—the matrices of truly solid morale and concomitant social values—is precluded. In this regard, such that a full and meaningful integration of interpersonal and psychosocial need considerations be realized to maximum levels, it is felt by this writer that introduction of a more substantial, less restricted coffee respite be effected and considered seriously by management in industry and business. Such an operation, self-constituted and of liberal time designation, e.g., one-half hour or more in both morning and afternoon work segments, could offer to management an enhanced worker satisfaction, performance, and realization of personal or self-worth. The full implications and ramifications of such a change of order in the currently functioning business and industrial framework would be understood clearly over an extended period of operation, offering to the sponsor a vitalized work effort, the impact of which heretofore has been considered only a distant possibility.

PSYCHOSOCIAL IMPLICATIONS

One can see a common meaning through developmental stages of the coffee break; namely, the presence of psychosocial or personal-interactive need considerations. From the sharing of the news of the day in the Middle Eastern *kaveh kanes* to English coffee-house dialogues to intimate conversations carried out in the German *kaffee klatsch* some 300 years later to the contemporary coffee breaks characterized by personal interchange, the psychosocial element has played a key role in the successful development of the coffee-drinking phenomenon.

THE HAWTHORNE PROJECT

In order to grasp more fully the meaning and implications of the coffee break, one might continue by examining one of the most significant psychological research efforts to date; namely, that conducted by the Western Electric Company at its Hawthorne Works in Chicago in 1927.[4] This research effort was among the first studies to indicate that as long as rest pauses were interpreted in the light of providing only physical effects, it

[4] F. J. Roethlisberger and W. J. Dickson, *Management and the Worker* (Cambridge, Mass.: Harvard University Press, 1946).

was difficult to furnish an explanation for the findings that was not in accord with reduction of fatigue. If one were to examine the social meaning of the environment to the worker, it would follow that an explanation of the positive results of rest pauses could well be based on their social function. In this regard, the worker sensed, on the part of management, an interest in the health and satisfaction of the employee when rest pauses were granted. The workers were able to congregate and converse, to relax and relieve tension—normal social interaction was permitted. These respites and their accompanying consideration from management were interpreted as sentiments favorable to maintenance of individual integrity. The researchers concluded that the significance of rest pauses lies in the meaning of the respites rather than the respites themselves. That meaning largely is determined by the social milieu within which the rest pauses occur. If these breaks are interpreted by the employee as a concealed form of attempt to expedite employee work patterns, the respites will be viewed with apprehension and resistance. Should he feel, in contradistinction, that these represent genuine expression of interest in the well-being of the employee, and that the environmental-social milieu provides reinforcement of this view, then there likely will follow a favorable response to the innovations, reflected, in part, in heightened motivation toward the work.[5]

From their research findings, these investigators concluded that ". . . these operators were at all times working well within their physical capacity. There is no evidence in support of the hypothesis that the increased output rate of all these operators during the first thirteen experimental periods was due to relief from fatigue. This hypothesis, which at first seemed most plausible, had to be abandoned."[6]

PAN-AMERICAN COFFEE BUREAU REPORT

The Pan-American Coffee Bureau, in 1955, sponsored a comprehensive study of consumer motivations toward coffee; this project was conducted by the Institute for Motivational Research, Inc. From several points of view, the findings reflect a recognition of the importance of coffee to psychosocial considerations. What those interviewed stated about coffee indicates the significant role that it plays in preserving and assisting their emotional health. Furthermore, along this line coffee is viewed by the employee as playing an important role in one's achieving independence and self-control. Recognition of the psychosocial importance of drinking coffee is reflected in one of the six recommendations made by the Institute for Motivational Research, Inc.; namely, "Dramatize Coffee's Role of Helping People to Meet Every-

[5] *Ibid.*
[6] *Ibid.*, pp. 183–84.

day Problems."[7] In another section of the report all the findings are consolidated into the popularized picture of coffee in the mind of the consumer. Here coffee is seen as representing intimacy. In describing the meeting with another person over coffee, such terms as "close," "closer together," and "feeling warmer towards people" frequently are used.[8] In addition, coffee is associated with adjuncts favorable to the development of comradeship; namely, the intimacy and sureness of well-defined, comfortable settings.[9]

A second major psychosocial function of coffee, as stated by interviewees, is that coffee removes barriers and promotes understanding. These workers feel that coffee stimulates one to talk; this talk represents flexible conversation through which one learns to know other people, thereby humanizing business by removing the competitive coldness of business conversation.

UNIVERSITY OF CALIFORNIA RESEARCH

A more recent investigation of the psychological and sociological implications of the coffee break was carried out at the School of Medicine, University of California, Los Angeles. Among considerations dealt with, the following relevant points were discussed:

> . . . experiences are exchanged, tensions are loosened by not too hostile a form of raillery, plans are made for point activities, romances are given nourishment, and low-level counselling is executed. . . . As a focal site for ventilation of restrained expression, voicing of group opinions, and general forum for the exchange of beefs and gripes, the coffee-break setting serves as a steam-head reducer in keeping pressures at a tolerable level. Rumors and grapevine products are brought in . . . and group thinking gives impetus to what eventually may become a change in company policy . . . it represents a lone form of democracy in the culture of bigness—big industry, big unions, big market, and big government.[10]

ATTITUDES TOWARD THE COFFEE BREAK

The worker's point of view. The coffee break is considered by the worker to be a fundamental right, and as such, one which must be recognized by the employer. This feeling is evidenced, in part, by the fact that in work situations where these rest breaks are not provided or authorized by man-

---

[7] E. Dichter, *New Horizons for Coffee Promotion* (New York: Pan-American Coffee Bureau, 1955), p. 5.

[8] *Ibid.*

[9] *Ibid.*

[10] Pan-American Coffee Bureau, *The Coffee Break* (New York: The Bureau, 1959), p. 4.

agement, the workers will take them anyway.[11] This consideration was recognized forty years ago when, in efforts to urge the establishment of authorized rest periods and instruction of the worker in the art of complete relaxation, Hersey observed that "industrial workers doing routine or monotonous work will steal time to rest on the job whether or not management makes provision for rest periods."[12] In this regard, management recognized shortly thereafter that rest periods are an essential part of the work schedule; on the part of management, early efforts to deal with this facet were directed toward providing the rest periods, for those workers who had earned them, as unpaid times off from work. This approach to satisfying worker demands was not successful, however, as management learned quickly that workers who are paid for resting will perform better while working.[13]

Subsequent experience with provisions for paid rest periods has led to the more extensive adoption of such considerations to the extent that in recent years the paid rest period has received attention as a principal agent in collective bargaining agreements for labor contracts.[14] In this regard, several factors have contributed to the formalization of rest periods; namely, from the viewpoint of those interested in the worker, attention must be given to the psychological and physiological demands of modern industry. They argue that unrelieved physical or mental fatigue may have marked effect on the safety of employees as well as on the magnitude and quality of worker effort. They contend, in addition, that monotonous, routine tasks will decrease one's alertness on the job. Furthermore, they believe that the worker in the area of manual labor feels that a respite from the job is needed.

The most favorable reaction toward or interpretation of the coffee break by the worker is in terms of its serving as a symbol of "creative considerateness" by management. Here, the response of the worker is in terms of the intention of the employer rather than the coffee break per se. The employer is viewed as being "creatively considerate" of the needs of the worker by any attempts on his part to satisfy the employee. At the same time, the worker constantly is attuned to the interpretation given to the coffee break by management; in this regard, he particularly is sensitive to a negative employer attitude. If he believes that the coffee break is viewed as a necessary evil, he is resentful.[15]

[11] L. Lieber, "The Inside Story of the Coffee Break," *This Week Magazine*, April 2, 1961; W. McGehee and E. B. Owen, "Authorized and Unauthorized Rest Pauses in Clerical Work," *Journal of Applied Psychology*, 24 (1940), 605–14.

[12] "Rest Periods for Factory Workers," *Science*, August 28, 1925, xiv.

[13] R. Presgrave, "Frequent Rest Periods for Workers Prevent Fatigue and Increase Productivity," *Textile World*, October 17, 1931, 40–41.

[14] D. G. Weiss and E. M. Moore, "Paid Rest Periods in Major Union Contracts, 1959," *Monthly Labor Review*, 80 (1960), 958–63.

[15] *Ibid.*

On the part of the worker, other interpretations have been forthcoming; some of these may be exemplified in the employee's feeling he ". . . is getting something for nothing from his boss"[16] in his viewing the coffee break as indulgence in legitimate time out from discipline and as a safety valve for controlling possible rebellion against monotony or routine, and in his recognizing that the coffee break is related to the excuse of escaping or delaying work.

The management point of view. As a permanent part of the American business and industrial scene, the coffee break also has become an item of great concern to the employer. In this regard, one might examine why he has accepted the coffee break and will continue to operate with it. First, the employer associates the coffee break with subsequent increased worker efficiency, increased production, increased morale of workers, decreased absenteeism, and reduction of fatigue and accidents. As understood by him, the theory behind the coffee break is based on experimental findings stemming from research conducted in the 1920's and subsequently, which showed that the worker's mental and physical efficiency wanes at certain midmorning and midafternoon time segments and that "coffee, if properly prepared, has a remarkable stimulating and fatigue-relieving effect . . . increases the power of concentration of mental efforts, and therefore is an aid to sustained brain work."[17] Psychologists, in this regard, maintain that the improvement in efficiency and morale on the part of the worker more than compensates for time lost.

In a survey of 304 city-manager operated cities, sponsored by *The American City* (1957), it was learned that in general the coffee break is seen as worthwhile, the major reason being the subsequent improvement in worker morale. Furthermore, this survey indicated that the respite serves as a symbol that the employee is a person who can be trusted in the carrying out of his work operations to such proportions as to merit a brief respite. Great importance was given by the managers to the role of coffee breaks in the reduction of fatigue. Many other factors were indicated as playing significant roles; namely, increased work production, greater accuracy of work, reduction of absenteeism, and lower turnover of employees.[18]

Although he has been attuned to the psychosocial-dynamic considerations, the employer has viewed the coffee break primarily in terms of cost and time involvements. In this regard, not every employer interprets the respite as an inalienable employee right, many arguing that the ten-minute break often is extended to thirty or forty minutes or possibly longer; they complain that the employee, in anticipation of the respite, begins to abate

[16] Dichter, *New Horizons for Coffee Promotion*, p. 5.
[17] "In Praise of Coffee," *Literary Digest*, November 24, 1923, 26.
[18] "The Municipal Coffee Break," *The American City*, 72 (February, 1957), 18.

his work output some fifteen minutes prior to it and frequently spends another fifteen minutes following the respite to reestablish work levels.[19]

The employer also objects to the high costs which are associated with the
granting of coffee breaks. First, the productive-economic effects of coffee
breaks can be quite marked when an entire industrial production line must
be halted in order that workers may take their morning and afternoon respites for coffee.[20] Second, the coffee break adds approximately two weeks
per year to paid time off, supplementing the paid time taken from work annually in the form of vacations and other fringe benefits.[21]

It is quite clear to management that the worker is unwilling to do without coffee breaks, irrespective of other inducements offered. In this regard,
the employer has attempted to devise efficient methods by which coffee
might be brought to the worker at the job setting; e.g., hiring in-plant ca-
terers, such that there is reduction of time spent preparing for, engaging in,
and cleaning up from coffee breaks. Other considerations rest on the employer's desire to maintain coffee break facilities at in-plant localities;
namely, there is decreased chance of the worker's receiving injury while
traveling by automobile, etc., to a distant locale for the coffee break and
thereby a lessening of the possibility of having to award workman's compensation.

As one means of legislating some control over and minimizing disputes
about the union-demanded coffee breaks, management frequently has been
successful in inserting into collective bargaining agreements the right for it
to specify the time, place, and mode of carrying out the coffee breaks. In
this regard, for those contracts containing references to scheduling of the
coffee break, frequently the details are left to the company for policy making or are to be established such that there is no interference with opera-
tional requirements.[22]

Thus, contemporary efforts to adopt the coffee break in business and industrial settings as a paid respite for the worker, initially meeting reluctance and question by the employer, came to be associated with a most
advantageous consideration; namely, that provisions allowing the worker
to take the brief respites seemingly resulted in and accounted for noticeable
beneficial modifications of levels of efficiency, production, morale, absenteeism, turnover, accidents, and fatigue. These advantages, although not
always recognized by employers as stemming from psychosocial dynamic
considerations, have assisted in allaying the hesitations of management to-

---

[19] R. Rutter, "The Coffee Break, Asset or Liability, Seems Here to Stay," *New York Times*, February 10, 1956, p. 29.

[20] "The Cost of Tea," *The Economist*, 200, 1237.

[21] "Time Out for Coffee—A New 'Fringe Benefit,'" *U.S. News and World Report*, January 18, 1957, 61–63.

[22] Weiss and Moore, "Paid Rest Periods in Major Union Contracts, 1959."

ward acceptance of the coffee break and have provided for managerial personnel a nearly solid rationale for instituting the coffee breaks and for allowing their continuation. These understandings, on the part of the employer, have come from empirical observations, research procedures, and through the efforts of coffee manufacturers and retailers to promote their product.

HISTORICAL DEVELOPMENT

To incorporate the entire perspective on the meaning and implications of the coffee respite, a complete evaluation, rooted in an examination of the significant historical developments of coffee drinking, must be undertaken. The most diligent research has shown that coffee, first mentioned in the literature by Rhazes, an Arabian physician, had its development in the classical period of Arabian medicine.[23]

MIDDLE EASTERN COFFEE DRINKING

In the early 1500's ". . . the inhabitants of Mecca became so fond of the beverage that, disregarding its religious associations, they made of it a secular drink to be sipped publicly in *Kaveh Kanes,* the first coffee houses."[24] In these spots the idle gathered to drink coffee, to play chess and other games, to discuss the day's happenings, and to find amusement through singing, dancing, and music. Also, this drink precipitated social, political, and religious discourse and was helping to liberate a heightened meaning of life for those frequenters of the public meeting houses.[25]

The *Kaveh kanes* soon became a common meeting ground for members of all social classes. Above the din of conversation and celebration, argumentation always could be heard, as could discussions of the latest scandal. Such gatherings for social intercourse were welcomed, received, and carried out with marked enthusiasm.[26]

COFFEE DRINKING IN ENGLAND

In England, it was not until the end of the Civil War that as a whole, the middle classes began to find themselves restless with medieval modes of rea-

---

[23] W. H. Ukers, *The Romance of Coffee* (New York: The Tea and Coffee Trade Journal Company, 1948).

[24] *Ibid.,* p. 24.

[25] *Ibid.*

[26] *Ibid.*

soning and expression; they were beginning to develop and refine more modern amenities. In part, this growth was a reaction of sentiment, but more significantly it reflected a certain change in the manner of life with which the people were familiar. The citizenry of Old London were sociable, communicative persons, and as the Civil War had provided the battleground for disagreement of opinion, the necessity for discussion which emerged from this period of conflict seemed a logical outgrowth. As a people alerted to maintenance of sound health and solid means, these citizens of London were not frequenters of the taverns. Instead, they began to congregate in the newly discovered and recently established coffee houses which offered an unknown Turkish beverage that could be quaffed for one penny and which, supposedly, was a cure for minor infirmities.[27]

From this curiosity about Man suddenly emerged a literature grounded in the ways of life in the coffee houses. For the writer of dialogues, the freedom of conversation and unchecked expression of personality, adjuncts of the republican equality extant among the clientele of the coffee houses, provided an entirely new area with which to deal and in which to explore. This form of expression was regarded as the means of communicating ideas to the people. The dialogues in essence represented studies of character, the arguers having much more significance than the topic of discussion.[28]

The citizens of Old London congregated in the coffee establishments, and through continued social intercourse began to sense a genuine personal interest in the attitudes, thoughts, actions, and manners of others. The shallow-witted distractions offered in the city were little cared for. Rather, these citizens were interested in examining and experiencing the enjoyment of news and conversation, such that by the early 1700's the coffee houses had become the focal point of life in London. But those who assembled daily in the coffee houses were concerned not only with their friends' thoughts and bearing, "they cultivated an eye for trivial actions and utterances, a gift for investigating other people's prejudices and partialities, and they realized the pleasures of winning their way into the intricacies of another man's mind."[29] From this orientation a new feeling about and openness toward one's companions developed. Persons who previously would have been ridiculed or disliked now were viewed as intellectual enigmas. The eccentric was afforded sympathetic attention, and the intellectual learned tolerance.

---

[27] According to *Brewer's Dictionary of Phrase and Fable* (New York: Harper & Brothers, 1953), the coffee house first was introduced into England in 1650 at Oxford. The first London coffee house dates from the following year. These London coffee houses, the centers of wit and learning, were referred to as "penny universities," as they served as schools for conversation supported by a one-penny fee. See also Routh, "The Advent of Modern Thought in Popular Literature."

[28] Routh, "The Advent of Modern Thought in Popular Literature."

[29] *Ibid.*, p. 35.

The closeness provided by these resorts resulted in the establishment of a new code of manners. In order to benefit from daily personal interchange, men learned to value each other's expression and to promote self-suppression. In essence, a respect and consideration for others was developed, and the middle class came to view courtesy as playing an integral role in civilization.

The coffee houses provided more than an exposure to the civilities of social living; the effects of these resorts on the citizenry was such that nearly all men of intelligence had a favorite coffee house to which they went frequently. This element consisted primarily of those who read and wrote the literature of the day and those who created the standards of taste and ignited the thinking. The meaningful simplicity of true personal interchange, through the act of conversation, seldom had been experienced to such an extent prior to this half-century of intellectual vitalization.[30]

In this regard, men learned to bring forth intellectual concepts in a fresh, natural manner, one which awakened and provided heightened sensitivity to thought. Thus, the middle classes were

> . . . accomplishing their own education. They were becoming thinkers with a culture and a standard of manners born of conversation and free from pedantry of thought or expression. Coffee houses had given them a kind of organization; a means of exchanging ideas and forming the public opinion of their class. . . . Coffee houses had unconsciously become fraternities for the propagation of a new humanism. This movement was so inchoate that the middle classes themselves were hardly conscious of it.[31]

USE OF COFFEE IN GERMANY

One might consider the *kaffee klatsch* a phenomenon which developed in Germany one hundred and fifty years later in the early 1800's. The term *kaffee klatsch* (coffee + scandal) was coined by husbands of the socializing women as a way of teasing their wives who gossiped at coffee parties. Although the event was the butt of amusement, there was an accompanying uneasiness on the part of these men; for the first time, the housewife had something to participate in away from the immediate domestic setting. The *kaffee klatsch* provided the opportunity for Woman to share Man's world of ideas and to vie for her position in society; she could carry out the role of the free thinker and free talker. This activity, then, played a significant role in the obtaining of social equality for women. The burgher's wife was experiencing part of the radical social revolution that was occurring in Eu-

---

[30] *Ibid.*
[31] *Ibid.*, pp. 36–37.

rope; namely, the elevation of the middle class. In this experience, the wife became a social personality, one whose feelings and thoughts were verbalized in the *kaffee klatsch*. Prior to this radical change, coffee had been a drink limited to the nobility and the educated classes. With the social revisions, coffee became a drink that the housewife could serve to her friends at any time.[32]

A second factor underlying the establishment of the *kaffee klatsch* was the urge to play a role in elements of society more expansive and challenging than those offered within the limitations of the home. These factors, allied with other considerations, allowed the development of a custom of drinking coffee in spontaneous meetings with housewives where intimate conversation and exchange of ideas could be furthered.[33]

THE COFFEE BREAK IN THE UNITED STATES

The coffee break first was experienced as an on-the-job event during the early years of World War II when it was introduced and maintained by the federal government in defense plants. There was general belief, on the part of management, that the respite could serve successfully as an inducement to attract needed workers, as a means by which flagging energy levels could be elevated, and as a builder of morale. This practice of drinking coffee in business and industry has developed from its wartime inception in the United States to the position of a contemporary, universalized occurrence and its present status as an almost inalienable employee right.[34]

Review of statistics. To appreciate the extent to which the coffee break has become engrained in the daily activity of the American work force, one might examine, summarily, some statistics of coffee drinking habits. In this regard, several evaluations and research surveys have been carried out. One of the first such undertakings, in 1950, indicated that an estimated 49 per cent of this country's employees were participating in the practice of drinking coffee at work.[35]

That the coffee break, involving nearly 50 million workers, has made noteworthy inroads into the complexities of the work setting is indicated by the fact that currently between 80 per cent and 90 per cent of all companies, industries, and corporations provide the worker with the opportunity to take the respite. The duration of these rest periods ranges from five to ninety minutes per day. In cases where maximum time limits are imposed,

[32] The Coffee Brewing Institute, Inc., *There's a Story in Your Coffee Cup* (New York: The Institute, 1963).

[33] *Ibid.*

[34] "On the Wagon," *The Economist,* 91 (1959), 529–30; Rutter, "The Coffee Break, Asset or Liability."

[35] "Topics of the Times," *New York Times,* December 30, 1957, p. 22.

nearly one-half of the companies investigated by the Bureau of Labor Statistics granted twenty minutes. This survey showed, also, that companies most commonly provide two rest periods of ten or fifteen minutes per day, one during each half shift.[36]

As a ritualized gathering of workers, then, the daily coffee break, demanded by workers and often challenged by management, has provided additional humanized elements to the increasingly mechanized occupational setting, affecting many aspects of all relationships between employee and employer. When this psychosocial phenomenon is interpreted by the worker experiencing it as a contribution by the employer toward the strengthening and solidification of his individual integrity, an over-all picture of worker vitalization and beneficial modification of such work parameters as production, efficiency, morale, absenteeism, accidents, fatigue, and turnover is evidenced. In an historical-developmental, psychosocial context, this paper emphasizes the need for management to broaden its perspectives on the coffee break, from viewing it as a respite which "produces" for management to one which promotes a heightened sense of personal satisfaction of worker toward himself and toward others with whom he interacts in this daily hegira to the coffee drinking area, and with whom he works.

Heretofore, in the context of a coffee break or work respite, researchers and interested management have emphasized the key role of coffee as a multifaceted, psychophysiological stimulant. Contemporary, ongoing research, however, brought to focus in a psychosocial dynamic framework, indicates that the full meaning and implications of this rest pause only have begun to be investigated and understood. In this regard, further examination is needed to clarify and delineate the full scope and far-reaching ramifications of the coffee break.

[36] Weiss and Moore, "Paid Rest Periods in Major Union Contracts, 1959."

PAUL CAMERON

Frequency and Kinds of Words in Various Social Settings, or What the Hell's Going On?

One does not need a high degree of sensitivity to notice that profanity is not necessarily the "mark of the uneducated" or even that it is not necessarily socially taboo. In our society "profane" or "taboo" words fulfill many functions—if you don't know someone or only know him to a modest degree, calling him an "old bastard" is apt to elicit a sore nose; on the other hand, the same phrase many constitute endearment to a friend. Situationally we well know that taboo words *are* taboo on the airways, in formal or quasi-formal gatherings (such as professional or religious assemblies), or in most written communication. At the same time taboo words are often *demanded* if one is to be "one of the boys" at a party, or on an assembly line, or a comedian at night clubs. Then, too, if special force or emphasis is to be given to an utterance in a formal gathering, nothing will do quite as well as a profanity. On the assembly line floor a similar contrast is often effected by a "straight" statement.

Examples as the above illustrate the importance of verbal behavior, including profanity, in social research. In fact, verbal behavior is probably the most frequent kind of behavior, and profanity a commonplace in many situations. Yet, for three decades psychologists, sociologists, teachers, and philologists have been using the Thorndike-Lorge (1944) word frequency count—even though it includes almost no profanity and is based entirely on written English—as "gospel." Although it is obviously a serious methodological error to assume the equivalence of written and spoken English, even the more recent efforts to sample spoken English have betrayed such a bias.

In the most ambitious undertaking to date, French, Carter, and Koenig (1930) sampled 80,000 words used over the phone in New York business conversations in the year 1929. Though the expenditure of time and energy had to be considerable to produce such an array of data, the investigators

"Frequency and Kinds of Words in Various Social Settings, or What the Hell's Going On?" by Paul Cameron, is reprinted from *Pacific Sociological Review*, Volume 12, No. 2 (Fall, 1969), pp. 101–104 by permission of the Publisher, Sage Publications, Inc.

deliberately excluded 25 per cent of the words heard from their sample and yet had the temerity to claim that their sample was ". . . a good representation of the main body of telephone conversation [p. 292]." More recently, an English professor (Berger, 1968) collected a sample of words spoken by college students in predominantly mixed groups in his or a female associate's presence and, having found his sample in major agreement with the Dewey (1923) and French *et al.* (1930) studies, concluded that ". . . printed and oral English are generally alike in word frequency . . . [p. 71]." It seems highly probable that these and other (Fairbanks, 1944; Haggerty, 1930; Uhrbrock, 1935) word-samples were gathered in such pristine situations and/or in such a biased manner that they couldn't possibly represent typical U. S. speech patterns; hence this study.

METHOD

SAMPLE I: COLLEGE STUDENT USAGE

If you want a *representative* sample of college students' word-usage,[1] you must sample their speech proportionate to the amount of time they spend in each segment of their life space. It is highly improbable that a professor or a female associate can gather a representative sample by wandering about the campus "listening-in" on what students say. The very presence of either would change the range of vocabulary. Further, unlike the Berger (1968) study, you cannot allow the sampling to depend on your judgment of what you will record (*i.e.,* at what moment you will start and stop recording), because you will not be sure whether the data was "out there" or a function of your selective process. To solve the first sampling problem, we utilized 47 Stout State student "overhearers" (25 were female, a third upperclassmen) who were instructed to carry out their normal activities over a week's time while surreptitiously recording the speech they overheard. Great emphasis was put upon remaining undetected and keeping the sampling proportionate to actual behavior. By having a relatively large number of overhearers we assured ourselves that any one person's life-space pattern would not unduly influence our results. We largely eliminated the measurement of personal selective process by having the overhearers record the first three words they heard during the conversation at 15-second intervals as determined by the sweep-second hand on their watches. In the choosing of conversations to record from, it was further stipulated that overhearers were to sample speech: *(a)* in as many locations as possible, *(b)*

---

[1] The author would like to thank Cindy McElwain and Fred Smith for their dedicated efforts in the compilation of the great mass of data.

to spend no more than 10 minutes sampling from the same conversation, *(c)* to attempt to listen in on conversations between members of the same sex about two-thirds of the time (which a pre-sample had suggested would approximate normal speech patterns), *(d)* to spend about half their time listening to members of the opposite sex, and *(e)* to choose the moment of first sampling *before* entering into the vicinity where recording would take place.

SAMPLE II: ADULTS AT WORK

As we wanted a sample of non-college-student words-at-work we had 22 Wayne State University students (2/3 male, all upperclassmen) sample speech on their part-time jobs.[2] Only employee–employee conversation out of ear-shot of customers was sampled. All of the previous strictures were applied where possible, although the student was allowed to adjust the interval between time samples to his particular job with consideration to retaining it and remaining an unknown recorder. Part-time jobs being what they are, we oversampled white collar situations. (Samples were from two factories, three eating establishments, seven retail stores and a clinic.)

SAMPLE III: ADULTS AT LEISURE

The adult leisure sample was drawn in Detroit by seven Wayne students from shoppers, telephone conversations of their parents, a party, and a pool hall.

We attempted to guard against data-contamination in two ways: *(a)* by checking each list of collected words for "reasonableness" and *(b)* anonymous polls as to honesty and faithfulness-to-method. The latter check turned up two students who inflated their contribution by a total of 60 words; their list had already "passed" the reasonableness check and a previous poll and is included in the job-words list.

RESULTS

We got a sample of 48,912 words of college student-usage; 16,323 adult on-the-job-between-employees usage, and a 1,532 word sample of adults-at-leisure. The number of different words from each sample was 1668, 668, and 404, respectively. Table 1 lists the 30 most frequent words for each of the three samples. Comparing our top 30 with any of the previous investigator's

[2] With thanks to Jeffry Zaks, John Wolfe, and Greg Tighe in the compilation of the data.

Table 1   30 Most Frequently Used Words

College Students at Leisure		Adults at Work		Adults at Leisure	
Word	Times Used	Word	Times Used	Word	Times Used
a	1341*	the	1154**	I	77**
you're	1226	school	801	you	43**
you	1212**	please	781	she	33**
I	896**	book	799	it	31**
the	866**	tomorrow	673	damn	31**
is	633**	and	648**	your	30*
what	517**	you	570**	shit	26
that's	509*	a	505**	motherfucker	26
it	500*	was	452*	Christ	25
I'll	481**	people	452	to	25**
to	434**	to	398**	of	25**
damn	404**	really	327*	and	25**
he	397**	these	290	that	24**
I'm	395	he	271**	the	21**
and	391**	that	245**	a	21**
don't	380*	she	215**	bitch	20
hell	378*	damn	212**	know	19
do	369**	your	208*	fuck	18**
in	358*	I	204**	Jesus	17*
beer	347	stamp	199	so	15
no	340**	broad	175	God	15*
of	339**	what	172**	he	14**
did	328*	oh	158*	son	14*
Jesus	321*	me	139*	for	13
fuck	311**	there	128	no	13*
have	306	of	128**	get	12*
was	305	fuck	127**	have	12**
we	305	think	125	is	12**
not	304	shit	120**	do	12**
they	302	kids	119		

** in most frequent 50 of both other lists
 * in most frequent 50 of one other list

top 30 leaves little doubt that there are significant discrepancies. The most obvious is the almost complete lack of profanity-taboo words, or whatever you choose to call them, in all the other published lists. Taking Berger's (1968) recent list, for instance, we find no such words in his top 50, yet our college sample had the following profanities in their top 50: damn, hell, Jesus, fuck, shit, bastard, and God! Profanity accounted for 8.1 per cent of the college, 12.7 per cent of the adult-leisure, and 3.5 per cent of the on-the-job samples! This is further pointed up in Table 2 where the profanities are grouped by type and frequency of each noted for the three samples.

Table 2   FREQUENCY OF KINDS OF PROFANITY FOR THE THREE SAMPLES

Sexual		Sacred		Excretory	
Word	Times Used	Word	Times Used	Word	Times Used
College Leisure Sample					
fuck	311	damn	404	shit	266
bastard	234	hell	378	bull	176
bitch	189	Jesus	321	piss	115
prick	136	God	218	ass	100
horny	112	Christ	94	B.S.	63
screw	82			fart	61
ass	78			hole	57
hole	59			cram	52
queer	57			crap	48
cock	52			asshole	16
boob	51			shitting	10
piece	42			crock-of-shit	10
butt	26			shitty	1
blow	22				
fucker	18				
fern	16				
son-of-a-bitch	13				
pussy	10				
sucks	9				
dink	6				
jack-off	5				
balls	4				
dic	3				
screwed	3				
tit	3				
box	2				
dong	2				
cunt	2				
bitchy	1				
friging	1				
Totals	1554		1415		975
Adult Work Sample					
fuck	127	damn	212	shit	120
bastard	19	hell	47	ass	12
blow	11	God damn	2		
fucking	5	Christ	2		
nuts	2	Jesus Christ	1		
mother-fucking	2				
mother-fucker	1				
fuzznuts	1				
bitch	1				
boob	1				
Totals	170		264		132

Table 2   (Continued)

Sexual		Sacred		Excretory	
Word	*Times Used*	*Word*	*Times Used*	*Word*	*Times Used*
Adult Leisure Sample					
mother-fucker	26	damn	31	shit	26
fuck	18	Christ	25	asshole	8
son-of-a-bitch	14	Jesus	17	ass	3
bitch	6	God	15	piss	2
ass	3	hell	5		
lay	2				
Totals	69		93		39

The obvious decrement of profanity on-the-job is highlighted by inter-viewer Joe Klotz' sample of the same medical professionals working and at a party. The incidence of profanity was 1.1 per cent at the clinic and 3.3 per cent at the party. Although our sample is as yet too small for the parameters to have normative weight, overhearers estimated the profanity rate on-the-job at about 1 per cent for white-collar proletarians; about 5 per cent for common service occupations, and around 10 per cent for blue-collar workers.

"Damn" is apparently the most popular profanity, possibly among the 15 most frequent words in spoken English. "Shit," "fuck," "Jesus," "hell," and "God" probably fall in the 75 most frequently spoken words. In all three samples the excretory profanities (shit, piss, bull, crap, fart) were sur-passed in frequency by the sacred (God, Jesus, damn, hell) and sexual (fuck, screw, mother-fucker, balls, cunt).

In the college sample a sub-sample of about 5,000 words was drawn ex-clusively from female–female conversation with the finding that the words they used did not seem to differ appreciably from a like sub-sample of male–male interaction.[3] (A somewhat lower incidence of "fuck" was made up for by a higher incidence of "shit.")

DISCUSSION

The explanation for the differences between our and the other published spoken-English word lists is not hard to find. The studies of Haggerty (1930) and Uhrbrock (1935) were performed upon the speech of children

---

[3] Which seems in harmony with Stoke and West's (1931) finding that Ohio Univer-sity female students told about the same proportion of "shady" stories in bull sessions as male students.

under the age of six—we really wouldn't expect children to use the same vocabulary as adults. The French *et al.* (1930) study suffers from a representative standpoint in *(a)* sampling business conversation 89 per cent of the time, *(b)* choosing a phone sample in 1929 when a majority of the population didn't have a phone, *(c)* the deliberate exclusion of 25 per cent of the words overheard, and *(b)* a strange method of gathering words to be counted (all the nouns one time, all the verbs the next). There is every reason to believe that the kind of vocabulary one would record under such a regimen would approximate written English. Again we would expect a close match between the kind of vocabulary employed and written English for the Fairbanks (1944) sample of words used by university freshmen in an extemporaneous speech situation. Such a situation could hardly be called "informal." The recent Berger (1968) study which purports to sample the "conversational English of university students [p. 65]," suffers representatively in: *(a)* the deliberate exclusion of "many" samples because they were not complete sentences (an admittedly common occurrence), *(b)* the choice of a professor and female graduate student as samplers, *(c)* the very long recording time necessary most of the time (he reports that the average sentence was 7.8 words, a difficult recording task compared to our 3-word samples), and *(d)* the lack of a control against selection-bias.

Explanations for discrepancies aside, what the hell's been going on in the study of real people's speech? Something is decidedly off-kilter among sociolinguistic scientists when they allow the peculiar conventions of a society to blind them to an actual situation. And we are not talking here about some mystical, ethereal, subliminal, subconscious event, but honest-to-goodness objective, countable, observable human behavior. We are reminded that recently a team of social scientists "discovered" starvation down in Mississippi. Perhaps we might reserve a goodly number of the snide remarks about Soviet social science for ourselves.

REFERENCES

Berger, K., "Conversational English of University Students," *Speech Monographs* 34 (July 1968), 65–73.

Dewey, G., *Relative Frequency of English Speech Sound.* Cambridge: Cambridge University Press, 1923.

Fairbanks, H., "The Quantitative Differentiation of Samples of Spoken Language," *Psychological Monographs* 56 (1944), 19–38.

French, N. R., and C. W. Carter, Jr., "The Words and Sounds of Telephone Conversations," *Bell System Technical Journal* 9 (April 1930), 290–324.

Haggerty, L. C., "What a Two-and-one-half-year-old Child Said in One Day," *Journal of Genetic Psychology* 37 (January 1930), 75–101.

Stoke, S. M., and E. D. West, "Sex Differences in Conversational Interests," *Journal of Social Psychology* 2 (February 1931), 120–26.

Thorndike, E. L., and I. Lorge, *The Teacher's Word Book of 30,000 Words.* New York: Columbia Teachers College Press, 1944.

Uhrbrock, R. S., "The Vocabulary of a Five-year-old," *Educational Research Bulletin* 14 (January 1935), 85–92.

LOUIS A. ZURCHER, JR.

The "Friendly" Poker Game: A Study of an Ephemeral Role

Games, forms of play with consensually validated sets of rules, assist in the socialization and personality formation of the individual. The structure and dynamics of various games often reflect specific traits, values, expectations, and kinds of social control within a given culture. For adults, games may maintain existing societal forms, or resolve perceived conflicts and threats in the social world (cf. Caillois, 1961; Erikson, 1950; Huizinga, 1955; Piaget, 1951; Robbins, 1955; Strauss, 1956; Sutton-Smith and Roberts, 1963).

Card playing apparently continues to be a favorite American game. Though recent statistics are not available, an American Institute of Public Opinion poll (1948), with a national sample, revealed that *56* percent of the respondents played cards either regularly or occasionally, and *19* percent preferred poker. There have been several studies of gamblers, gambling, and gaming behavior (cf. Bergler, 1957; Herman, 1967a; Edwards, 1955), but few studies which seek to determine the social-psychological functions of card playing (cf. Crespi, 1956), and fewer such studies of poker playing (cf. Lukacs, 1963; Martinez and LaFranci, 1969) despite the fact that poker and many of its terms are prominent in our culture. There is no previous study, to the author's knowledge, of the "friendly game" of poker,

Reprinted from *Social Forces,* 49, 2 (1970), 173–86, by permission of the publisher.

The author expresses his appreciation to William Key, William Bruce Cameron, Erving Goffman and James Henslin, and to Frank Bean, Ivan Belknap, Richard Curtis, Russell Curtis, Robert Cushing, Dale McLemore, and Susan Lee Zurcher for their helpful comments. For the opportunity to have known and interacted with the poker group members, and for the insights they generously offered during interviews, the author is profoundly grateful.

that regularly scheduled game "among the boys" held alternately in one of their houses for relatively low stakes.

The participants of the friendly game are not gamblers in the social-problem sense of the word. Their game is not part of a commercial enterprise, yet they are drawn together regularly, take their participation seriously, and usually thoroughly enjoy themselves. What social-psychological functions does the friendly game serve for the participants? What is its attraction? What aspects of society-at-large are reflected in its dynamics?

The structure and some of the social-psychological functions of a friendly game were observed by a participant, yielding an analytical ethnography of the poker group and highlighting the theoretical concept "ephemeral role." An ephemeral role is a temporary or ancillary position-related behavior pattern *chosen* by the enactor to satisfy social-psychological needs incompletely satisfied by the more dominant and lasting roles he regularly must enact in everyday life positions.[1]

PROCEDURE

For twelve months the author attended the twice-monthly friendly game of a long-established poker group. He was a "complete participator" in Gold's (1958) classification. That is, he played and the other players did not know they were being observed. No notes were taken during the game, nor were any recording devices used. Though such techniques would have enhanced reliability, they may have disrupted the game. The author did, however, outline his observations immediately following adjournment of the session, and dictated a narrative based on the outline within eight hours.

Recreation, and not detached research was the primary reason for the author's joining the friendly game. However, after the first session he felt that the social dynamics of the game and the manifest benefits of participation for the players were important to record and analyze.

The day after his last game (the day before his departure to a job in another state), the author conducted semistructured individual interviews with all of the regular players concerning their reasons for playing, criteria for selecting new players, socialization processes, group rituals, and group argot.

THE PLAYERS

The seven "core" players who attended almost every game during the period of observation were all college educated, married, professional men: a

[1] For an earlier definition and example of the concept, see Zurcher (1968).

lawyer, a college coach, a high school coach, an engineer, a sociologist, a so-cial-psychologist (the author), and an insurance broker. Four had been playing poker together for over ten years, and two others for over five years. They ranged in ages from early thirties to late forties, and all were in the middle, salaried, socioeconomic bracket. Four had been reared and edu-cated in the midwestern city (population *125,000*) where the game took place, and where all of the players presently resided. When the friendly game first formed, the players had been associated with a small local col-lege. Three of the current players still were employed by the college, each in a separate department. A second common characteristic of the founding members and four of the current members was experience in coaching scho-lastic athletic teams.

Since three core players, because of job transfers or time conflicts, were going to leave the group, members were actively recruiting "new men." Those new men invited during the course of the observation included, after the author: an accountant, a rancher, a sports writer, a high school teacher, and a purchasing agent. The author had been brought into the group by the sociologist, who was a co-worker at a local psychiatric research facility.

THE SETTING AND STRUCTURE
OF THE GAME

The games were held twice monthly, between *7:30* p.m. and *12:00* p.m. on Monday nights, in rotation at each of the core players' homes. One of the players hosted the game in a den; the others in dining rooms, kitchens, or spare rooms. Three had purchased commercially produced, green felt cov-ered, poker tables; the others used whatever large table was available. The playing table was surrounded by smaller tables containing ashtrays, and bowls of chips and pretzels. Hot coffee and soft drinks were available throughout the game, but no alcoholic beverages were allowed during the game. Then, after the completion of the "last deal around the table," which started at *12:00* p.m., the hosting player was responsible for a meal of hors d'oeuvres, sandwiches, and desserts.

The evening's leisure was divided into three major components: (1) the informal discussion while waiting for all the players to arrive and the poker chips to be distributed; (2) the game itself; (3) the meal following the game. During the game it was understood that there were to be no "outside" inter-ruptions. There were no radios or television sets playing, no wives serving beverages, no children looking over shoulders. The atmosphere was quite relaxed and the dress casual (although on occasion a member arrived in suit and tie following a business meeting). There was no apparent seating pref-erence around the table except that if there was an empty chair, it generally would be next to a new man.

At the beginning of the game each player purchased *$3.00* worth of chips (blue, *25* cents; red, *10* cents; white, *5* cents). One had the option to buy additional chips at any time, although frequently cash was introduced in place of chips. The host player was responsible for being the banker, and also for dragging a dime or so out of each pot to defray the cost of the post-game meal. The betting limit was established at *25* cents, with a three-raise limit. Drawing "light" (borrowing money) from the pot or purchasing chips by check was tolerated.

The general rules of poker were closely followed, but the games played under "dealer's choice" were more varied than in a commercial poker setting. Use of the joker or naming of wild cards was forbidden. Often the "draw" and "stud" games were dealt with the stipulation that the high hand split with the low hand, or the high hand split with the low spade. Rarely, low ball (where low hand wins) was played. Each player seemed to have one or two favorite games which he dealt regularly and which were called "his" games.

BECOMING A MEMBER: SELECTION AND ROLE SOCIALIZATION

The criteria by which a new man was judged for membership revealed much about the group dynamics and functions. The core players, when being interviewed by the author, reflected about these criteria:

> A fellow coming into the game almost must feel like he's walking into a closed group, because we've been playing together for quite a while. I guess some newcomers leave the game sometimes feeling 'will they ever ask me back again' or 'I don't want to play with that bunch of thieves again.' Sometimes we have fellows join us who we decide we don't want to come back. In particular, we don't like people who slow up the game, or bad players who get wiped out. They have to be capable of playing with the other players, or we don't want them.

> In our game the group is the thing. We invite people in who we think are nice persons, and who we can be friends with. That's the important thing. But he has to be more than a nice person. He has to be able to play poker with the rest of us. It's no fun to sandbag a sucker! So to get invited to sit in regularly, we've got to like the person, and he's got to know what he's doing so that he adds to the game and doesn't subtract from it. The group has to be kept in balance. One dud can throw the whole thing out of focus. Another thing, too. In our group, he has to be able to take a lot of teasing, and maybe give out some too. We have a good time teasing each other.

The new man therefore had to be friendly and experienced enough to learn, compete, and to maintain the pace and stability of the game.

Lukacs (1963:58) has observed that "there are a thousand unwritten rules in poker, and continuous social standards and codes of behavior." The new man, as a prerequisite to invitation was expected to know the basic rules and etiquette of poker. He was to be socialized, however, in accordance with the group's idiosyncratic expectations. He was to learn the local rules of the game, the style and tempo of play, and the patterned interactions. In other words, he was not going to be taught how to play poker, but how to be a member of this poker group.

Many of the socialization messages were verbal instructions from the core members, particularly with regard to betting rules, games allowed, quitting time, and borrowing money. Other socialization messages were more subtle, though no less forceful. The player who slowed the pace of the game might hear the drum of fingers on the green felt or an annoyed clearing of the throat. The player who talked too lengthily about a topic unessential to the game might be reminded that it was his deal, or his turn to bet.

The new man would be strongly reinforced for behavior that conformed to the group's expectations by verbal compliment, camaraderie, or a simple but effective "now you've got it!" One new man, for example, unwittingly disrupted the group's unwritten strategy, that of killing large raises from a strong hand by exhausting the three-raise limit with nickel bets. Three of the core players immediately made pleasant comments about the "lack of insurance" in that particular hand. They did not directly admonish the new man for not having enacted his part of the "insurance." When on a later occasion he did carry out the strategy, he was immediately reinforced by a hearty, "good play!" from two core players.

At no point during the entire period of observation did any of the core players show overt anger at a new man's violation of group expectations. They did on a few occasions invoke what appeared to be their most severe sanction, an absence of response cutting the errant player momentarily from group interaction. When, for example, a new man challenged a dealing core player's choice of game, the dealer dealt and the rest continued to play their cards as if the new man had not said a word. On another occasion, when a new man angrily threw down his cards in disgust, two of the core players quietly gathered them up, handed them to the dealer, and there was otherwise a total absence of response.[2] If someone suggested a game be played which was not in the group's repertoire, he would be met with a lack of enthusiasm that was more crushing than any verbal negation could have been.

One of the core players commented about the "silent communication that takes place" within the group:

---

[2] See Goffman (1956) for a description of emotionally "flooding out" from group interaction.

We've been playing together for so long that we can read each other's expressions for the opinion that we have about something. If one of the fellows who's new or who is just sitting in for the night does something out of line, there's a quick and silent communication that takes place, and almost simultaneously we know what to do about it. We tease him or we give him instruction or something.

Sometimes the core players united in humorously expressed sanctions of a player's behavior. One new player had committed the cardinal sin of criticizing the play of core members. He had also lectured on the "right way to play poker." As if on cue, a core player deliberately checked his bet and, when the bet came around to him again, laughingly announced he was going to raise (an act which actually was forbidden by the group, as the bettor knew). The new man exploded:

You can't do that! You can't check and then raise! What kind of a game is this! Where did you learn to play poker!

A second core member with straight face replied,

We always do that! We do some strange things in our group!

A third added,

Yes, sometimes we allow ourselves to take back our discards if we think they can improve our hand.

A fourth added,

Well, but we have to match the pot first!

Shortly thereafter, when the man won his first pot, a core member again with straight face asked for 25 percent of the pot to put into the kitty, since "it is a custom that you always donate one-fourth of your first pot in this game." The new man, who was not asked to return, was effectively excluded from the group interaction, even though he was present for the remainder of the evening.

One core player told how novices were covertly appraised:

It's hard to put your finger on it, but there's a secret evaluation of a new player during the game. You know, we look at each other, and seem to be able to come to a conclusion about whether or not we want him to come back and play with us again, even before the game is over. Sometimes we talk about the player after the game, or during the week if we see each other before the next game. But most of the time we know even before that.

Of six new men, including the author, invited to "sit in for a night" three were asked to return. Each of these had manifested during their first night, behavior which corresponded to group expectations and which was openly reinforced. In two cases, the new men at the end of the session were welcomed to "our group" and told where the game would be held two weeks hence. The third man was informed by telephone after some of the core members had "talked it over," and agreed to invite him back. When core members felt unsure about inviting a new man back, or when they were certain that they did not want to invite him back, there was no post-game discussion of the next meeting.

A new man who was being accepted could be observed increasingly identifying himself as a member. During the early hours of the game he would ask questions about specific rules that "you fellows have." In the later hours he might phrase his questions differently, asking what "we" do in certain situations.

The core players clearly seemed to enjoy instructing a new man, overtly and covertly, about their expectations. In fact, his receptivity to those socialization messages was a key criterion for acceptance. A core player expressed how he felt about the socialization process:

> I think there is a certain enjoyment in teaching the rules of our game to people that can learn them. It's a kind of pride. Maybe it's a simple pride, but it's still a matter of pride to be able to show other people how to play in our game, when you know all the rules, but they don't.

Once accepted as a core member the individual retained that status even if circumstances precluded his regular participation. This was clearly illustrated when three core members terminated regular attendance. The author was present when the first member announced he was being transferred to a job in another state. The players were eating their post-game meal, when he said:

> I may as well tell you fellows this before you find out from somewhere else. I won't be able to play anymore because I got orders to go to Wisconsin. I hate to tell you this, because I hate to leave my contacts here with all my friends, and especially I hate to leave the poker club.

The group was silent for several seconds, and a few players stopped eating. Finally, one said, sadly, "That's too bad." Several inquiries were made about the specifics of his transfer, and players commented that he would be missed. One added that "the gang won't be the same without you." They talked briefly about the "breaking up of the group," and discussed the importance of starting to recruit new men for permanent positions. As they left, they warmly said goodbye to the departing member, and several of them earnestly asked him to "get in touch" whenever he visited the city. "Remember," encouraged one, "there will always be a chair open for you in the game." The offer of "an open chair" was similarly made to two core members who subsequently had to terminate regular attendance; one of them has played while in town at the time of a scheduled session.

A returning core member was not immune from socialization, however. During the author's participation one returned to "sit in for a night" after an absence of two years. Throughout the evening he inadvertently violated some of the group norms. He started to bet beyond the limit, and he began to deal a game not in the repertoire. One of the core members smilingly reminded him of the norms, and said, "You've been away so long you've forgotten our standing rules." The visitor was gently being resocialized.

BENEFITS OF MEMBERSHIP: SATISFACTIONS FROM THE EPHEMERAL ROLE

Participation in the friendly game seemed to provide the individual with several rewarding social-psychological experiences, including opportunities for: scripted competition; self- and situation control; event brokerage; normative deception and aggression; micro-institutionalizing; and retrospective conquest.

SCRIPTED COMPETITION: "KNOCKING HEADS"

The criteria for acceptance as a core member included one's ability to "hold his own" in the game. He was not to be "easy" or a "pigeon," but rather should be able to "put up a fight" and maintain the "balance" of the play. The new man was expected to be a competitor, to have "guts" and not be a "feather merchant."

Zola (1964) has pointed out that the importance and relevance of competition to gambling varies with the social context in which it occurs. Competition among the players seemed to be a carefully scripted and central dynamic in the friendly game. Competition involved money, but more importantly accomplishments of skill, daring, and bluffing, as two core players indicated:

> We cut each other's throats while the game is going on. We forget about it after the game, but it's that very competitive part of the game that I enjoy so

much. Maybe it's a carry-over from my sports days, but I just like to compete. There aren't many places anymore where I can really get eye to eye with someone and "knock heads." A hand starts and you try get other players to drop out. Then there's just two or three of you left, and you really start putting the pressure on. You can really slug it out, but it's only a game, and you forget about it when you leave the table.

It's sort of like when you were a kid, and you were testing yourself all the time. Poker is like the good old days; you get a chance to test yourself.

Several other observers have reported that competition in gambling, whether against others or "the system," provides individuals with opportunities to demonstrate self-reliance, independence, and decision-making abilities which for some reason or other are unavailable to them in their major life roles (cf. Herman, 1967b; Bloch, 1951; Crespi, 1956; Goffman, 1967). All of the core players were employed in bureaucracies. It may have been that their jobs made impossible the kind of competition, the kind of "testing" that they desired—particularly in the case of those members who had histories of athletic competition. Within the friendly game they could carefully and normatively script for themselves satisfactory and safe competitive experiences.

SELF- AND SITUATION CONTROL: "SHOWING SKILL"

Each of the players was expected to possess considerable skill in dealing, betting, playing his hand, and bluffing. A player who noticeably showed skill was pleased with his accomplishment, whether or not he won the hand. Core members rewarded his demonstration of skill with compliments and verbal recounting ("instant replay") of the action.

Skill was closely related to competition, as illustrated by the following:

I like to keep a mental file about the way people play. I like to think about how a person acts when he has something, and how I might act myself when I have something, and try and change that periodically. I think about how someone played a hand last time, and then try to figure out what he has by the way he's playing this time. You decide how to play your hand by the way you see others playing. That's the real skill in the game.

It's a beautiful thing to see a guy play a hand of poker well. It's better, of course, if you are the one who's doing it, but it's still nice to watch somebody else make a good bet, play his cards right, and then win. I don't like to lose, but if I've got to lose, I'd much rather lose to someone who's showing some skill in the game than to somebody who just steps into it.

Crespi (1956) pointed out that "skill players of necessity play frequently and by preference with others who are also highly skilled," and that they "seek to demonstrate their mastery of the necessary skills and, if possible, their skill superiority." Zola (1964: 255) concurred when he observed in the horse parlor that "the handicapper gains and retains prestige not because of monetary profits or preponderance of winners, but because he demonstrates some techniques of skill enabling him to select winners or at least come close."

Skill, as it appeared in the friendly game, seemed also to be related closely to control over other players, over self (e.g., "poker face"; resisting temptations to bet or draw cards impulsively), and to a large extent over luck. Lukacs (1963:57) considered "the uniqueness of poker to consist of its being a game of chance where the element of chance itself is subordinated to psychological factors, and where it is not so much fate as human beings who decide." Zola (1964:260) extrapolated this interpretation to gambling in general, and felt that it "occasionally allows bettors to beat the system through rational means, and thus permits them to demonstrate to themselves and their associates that they can exercise control, and for a brief moment that they can control their fate . . . (it) denies the vagaries of life and gives men a chance to regulate it." Skill in this sense indeed has a rational character, but also seems to have a kind of magical quality.

EVENT BROKERAGE: "FEELING THE ACTION"

The poker group did not tolerate disruption of the "pace" of the game. Some players commented about the rapid series of "thrills" that were strung together in a night's playing—the thrill of the "chance" and the "risk." Gambling, according to Bloch (1951:217–18), allows the player to "escape from the routine and boredom of modern industrial life in which the sense of creation and instinctive workmanship has been lost. Taking a chance destroys routine and hence is pleasurable." Bergler (1957:117) wrote of the "mysterious tension" that is "one of the pivotal factors in deciphering the psychology of gambling . . . This tension is a mixture, part pleasurable, part painful. It is comparable to no other known sensation."

Goffman (1967:155, 185) saw gambling as being most thrilling when it requires "intense and sustained exercising of relevant capacity," and when, as "action," "squaring off, determination, disclosure and settlement occur over a period of long enough time to be contained within a continuous stretch of attention and experience." Each hand of poker met the criteria for "action" and the requirement for "intensive and sustained exercising of relevant capacities" (skill and competitiveness). Central to this process was the opportunity for the player to make decisions concerning his participation in the play, decisions which were perceived to influence the outcome of his "action." Herman (1967b:101) wrote that the function of money, in the context of the gambling institution, is primarily to reify the decision-making process, establishing "the fact of a decisive act" and "verifying the involvement of the bettor in the action."

Both Goffman and Herman, in their discussions of "action" and "decision-making," referred to commercial gambling establishments. However, these factors, particularly as they relate to the stimulation of players and their experiencing of "thrill," were clearly manifested in the friendly game. A core member explained, when the author first joined, "We don't eat sandwiches and things like that during the game, and we don't shoot the bull, because it causes a break in the action." Another remarked, "It's like a new game every hand. There's a new dealer, you get a new set of cards, and it's a whole new ball game. You get your new cards dealt to you and you've got to think all over again what you are going to do with this hand." Each player was a broker of events potentially thrilling to himself and his colleagues.

NORMATIVE DECEPTION AND AGGRESSION: "YOU'RE A LIAR!"

To "bluff" in poker is to attempt by a pattern of betting, physical cues, and playing the cards to deceive other players about the quality of your hand. In poker the bluff is

> not only occasional but constant, not secondary but primary. Like certain other games of chance, poker is played not primarily with cards but with money; unlike other games the money stakes in poker represent not only our idea of the value of cards, but our idea of what the other player's idea of the value of cards might be (Lukacs, 1963:57).

Goffman (1961:38–39) observed that, "assessing a possible bluff is a formal part of the game of poker, the player being advised to examine his opponents' minor and presumably uncalculated expressive behavior."

Bluffing is related to the dynamics of competition, skill, decision-making, and action. Each player attempts to "fake out" the others. By giving the appearance that the cards randomly dealt to him are really something other than what they appear to be, he tries symbolically to control fate. With each succeeding hand the player must decide whether to try to "run one by" or to "play them straight."

Shortly after the author joined the group, he was shown a cartoon sketch of the players that one had drawn. The drawing caricatured the core members at play. They were addressing one another, and strikingly every comment referred to self, others, or the whole group "lying." In the friendly game, to "lie" or "speed" meant to bluff, and the performance of this act, successful or not, brought great pleasure to all, as indicated by the following interview responses:

> I really enjoy slipping one by the other guys . . . Putting one over on them
> —that's *really* a great feeling. I get a kick out of that.

> I like the teasing that goes on in the game. You can say things there to people that you couldn't say elsewhere. I tell one of the other players he's a damned liar, for example, and he might take offense at that under other circumstances. But here it's almost a form of endearment. You'll say something to the rest like "nobody here is telling the truth. Everybody is a phony." Well, some of the guys may hit you on the head with something if you said that anywhere else.

To be called a "liar" or to be accused of speeding was a compliment, a sign that one could engage in the intense personal interaction that bluffing stimulated. The game, and particularly the bluff established the kind of "focused gathering" that Goffman (1961:17–18) described as providing "a heightened and mutual relevance of acts; an eye to eye ecological huddle" quite generative of a gratifying "we rationale."

Core members often discussed their ability to catch one another "speeding," and the cues that would give fellow players away:

> When he puts a big stack of chips on his cards like that, I know he's bluffing. . . .
> When he puffs his pipe like that, he's trying to speed. . . . He's got that funny
> look in his eye. . . . When he says, "I don't know why I'm doing this" or "I
> must be stupid to stay in this," you better look out!

Lukacs (1963:57) commented, "Since the important thing to poker is not the cards but the betting, not the value of the player's hands but the player's psychology, as one gets to know the habits, the quirks, the tendencies, the strengths, the weaknesses of the other players, the play becomes increasingly interesting."

To be caught speeding and then teased as a liar seemed to be a *rite de passage* for a new man. On his first night, a new player was caught attempting to bluff and lost to a better hand. The men burst into laughter, and a core player loudly commented, "Now you're a member of this thieving group! You've been caught lying! Trying to speed, huh? Now you're one of us!" The new man was asked to return for subsequent sessions.[3]

On the other hand, not to have the capacity or inclination to bluff, or to

---

[3] The "liar" in the poker group seems honorifically similar to the "handicapper" in horse playing (cf. Zola, 1964:255).

be considered "honest," was flatly an insult. A new man in exasperation asked during his first and only night why it was that everyone dropped out whenever he initiated a bet or a raise. A core player shook his head and responded, "because you are too honest." This was said unsmilingly, and was based upon the new man's tendency to bet only when he had cards to validate the size of his bet. He was not inclined to bluff or lie. He was *too* predictable. One didn't have to read subtle cues or study the pattern of his play in order to approximate whether or not he was speeding or "for real." Potentially, he was a "pigeon" who would destroy the group "action."

Ironically, a player had to be caught bluffing if others were to know that he was a "speeder." Once caught and appropriately teased, he established his potential for speeding and further stimulated the intense personal interaction, competition, and opportunity for cue-reading skill that generated from the bluff. In essence, the speeder contributed to the uncertainty in the game and to cognitive imbalance for the players. The resolution of this uncertainty and cognitive imbalance seemed to be pleasurable and thus rewarding.

When a core player was caught in a particularly gross bluff, there were comments from others about historically memorable "lies," and the former culprit, if present, was again teased for his attempt. Usually someone would add, "Well, that's a time we caught him. Nobody knows how many times his lying is successful!" The uncalled winner does not have to show his hand in poker, so players are never really certain when he was bluffing. A common poker strategy used occasionally in the group is deliberately to be caught bluffing so that on subsequent occasions the relation between betting and hand strength is less clear.

The lie can also be interpreted as an opportunity to engage safely in behavior which might be considered "deviant" according to norms outside the friendly game.[4] "Honesty" became a negative attribute and "dishonesty" became a positive attribute. A fellow player could be called a liar and he would laugh. To have called him such in public would probably have invited anger. Within the game, delimited aggression and deception were normative and functional.

MICRO-INSTITUTIONALIZING: "ALMOST A LAW"

Ritual, magic, and tradition, complexly interrelated, have often been described as central components in human play. That component complex is present in poker, and was dramatically apparent in the friendly game. In addition to the more explicit rules governing play discussed above, there were instances of at least implicit "rules of irrelevance." According to Goff-

---

[4] For a relevant treatment of group norms for deviance, see Erikson (1962).

man (1961:19–21), rules of irrelevance are an important aspect of focused interactions. They strengthen idiosyncratic norms and the cohesion and "separateness" by declaring irrelevant certain characteristics of the participants or setting which may have considerable saliency in the world "outside."

In the friendly game, even though a player's occupational status may have had some influence in his being invited, that status became irrelevant. The author was, for example, asked by a new man what his occupation was. Before he could answer, a core player laughingly but nonetheless forcefully exclaimed, "Right now he's a poker player, and it's his deal!"

Although all the core players were married, family roles were also deemed irrelevant. One might talk about family problems or items of mutual interest in the "socializing" before the game began or during the meal after the game but certainly not in the game. The mere presence of wives or children was prohibited, and even the thought of allowing wives to play was, as one core player summarized it, "horrible!" Another commented, "My son would like to come and watch us, but I won't let him. It's kind of an invasion of privacy, and you don't want *people* to be butting in at times like that."

During the game virtually all topics of conversation not appropriate to the action were deemed irrelevant. "My wife asked me what we talk about when we play cards," observed a core player. "I tell her we don't talk about anything, we play cards. She can't understand that, because they gossip when they play bridge. But they aren't really playing a game them." On one occasion a core player worriedly interjected, "My God, how about this war in Viet Nam!" The others were silent for a few seconds, then one answered, "Whose deal is it?" The player who had commented about the war continued his statements, and quickly was interrupted by another who somewhat sternly though not angrily advised, "I didn't come here to hear you give a speech. I came here to play poker. I could give a speech myself you know." "Who will sell me some chips," inquired another, and the game continued.

Along with the accepted and expected verbal interactions of teasing and "game talk," the players enjoyed, indeed institutionalized, a core member's occasional references to the sagacity of his grandfather as a poker player. Whenever he was facing a particularly difficult decision, he would lean back in his chair, puff on a cigar (all but one of the players smoked either pipes or cigars during the game), and reflectively comment, "Well, my grandfather used to say," (for example) "never throw good money after bad." Often other players would make similar statements when they were faced with problem situations. The "grandfather" quotes had reference to betting, bluffing, soundness of decision, or competition. The content of the messages might accurately be described, as suggested by an interviewee, as "a poker player's Poor Richard's Almanac." The quotes seemed to be an important mechanism for bringing into the friendly game, as a lesson of a wise, "pioneer" man, considerations of the Protestant Ethic. The advice of grandfather was often cited to new men, thus serving a socialization function.

The verbal rituals, rules of irrelevance, and various behavioral taboos seemed to support valued group dynamics. The no-alcohol rule, for example, was adopted early in the group's history when an inebriated player had disrupted the pace. Similarly, the no-eating rule was inaugurated when players were observed to drop cards, or get them sticky. A number of specific games or methods of playing split-pot games were outlawed because they had in the past caused anger among players.

Although the players stressed the use of skill, particularly as a manifestation of control over fate, they also invoked what Malinowski (1948:38, 88) called "practical magic," primarily in an attempt to control the flow of cards or to change their luck. They would, for example, talk to the deck, urging it to give them good cards; rap the table with their knuckles just before receiving a card; slowly "squeeze out" a hand dealt to them, particularly after having drawn another card or cards, in order to "change the spots"; make a "fancy cut" as a luck changer; bet a hand "on the come" or "like you had them," as a means of guaranteeing getting the card or cards desired; deal a different game in order to "cool off" or "heat up" the deck; get up and stretch, or get a cup of coffee, in order to "change the way the money is flowing on the table"; stack their chips in a "lucky" way. On one occasion a player reached over and disordered another's chips, laughingly saying, "That should change your luck! You're winning too much!"[5]

The most striking example of magical behavior within the friendly game was the clearly understood and always followed rule that a player must bet fifteen cents, no more and no less, on the first face-up ace he received in a hand. It was agreed that if one did not follow this rule he would "insult the ace" and would inevitably lose. No one seemed to know where the "rule" originated, but all followed it and made a point of instructing new men to do likewise. Three members specifically referred to the fifteen-cent rule when interviewed about "specific rules." "I don't know why we do that," commented one, "but that's our precious ritual. I do remember one time I forgot to bet in that way, and by God I lost!" The second member thought betting fifteen cents on the ace was "a funny rule, but still a rule." The third man referred to the fifteen-cent bet as "almost a law. It's stupid, I guess, but it makes the game more fun." In this case, the magic served not

---

[5] For a fascinating discussion of such behavior among craps shooters, see Henslin (1967).

only the function of insuring against possible loss but also as another contributor to group cohesion. It may have been a "stupid" law, but it was "our" law.

The meal following the game might be considered a ritual feast. The strict poker rules and interactions were loosened, and the players discussed various topics deemed inappropriate during the game itself.

RETROSPECTIVE CONQUEST: "IF I HAD ONLY . . ."

In the friendly game, winners necessitate losers. Unlike forms of betting games in which the participants play against the "house," not every player in poker can win.

The most a member could win or lose was approximately $30.00. Generally, there was one "big winner," one "big loser," and the rest were distributed in between. One core player was a "big winner" more often than the others, but not enough to disrupt the balance of the group. There was no consistent "big loser." All of the members were in approximately the same income bracket, and thus winning or losing $30.00 had a similar impact upon them. Goffman (1961:69) pointed out that if betting is low relative to the financial capacities of the players, interest may be lacking in the game and they may not take it seriously. If conversely players feel that betting is too high then interest may be "strangled" by concern for the money they could lose. The core members understood the impact of someone who "couldn't afford to lose" or "didn't care about losing." In their view the former "makes you feel guilty if you win," and the latter "is no challenge, because if he's not really losing anything, you're not really winning anything." It was important that the financial conditions of the players be such that they maintained the dynamic equilibrium of the group.

The players knew that someone had to lose and inevitably at times it would be themselves. All agreed it was better to win than lose, but losing was not a disgrace so long as one did so through no lack of skill. For the member who had "played well" but nonetheless ended up a loser at the end of the evening the group offered and accepted several rationalizations, most commonly sympathizing about a plague of "second-best hands." This meant that the loser had played his cards well, "knocked heads" to the very end, and then come up with a slightly inferior hand. In essence, the cards were being blamed for his loss. It was no fault of his, because he "played well." When a player of this quality lost, luck was the culprit. But, when he won, it was by virtue of his skill; luck had nothing to do with it.

The core members looked with disfavor upon anyone who won by luck alone. A skillful player might invest some money early in a hand, but should not consistently "ride the hand out" hoping subsequently to be dealt some good cards. He should assess the odds, appraise through observation of cues and actions the quality of others' hands, and if evidence warranted he should decide to drop out and take his temporary loss.

Those who had lost a hand were often seen to "relive" the play. They would utter such statements as: "I figured that you . . ."; "If I hadn't thrown away those . . ."; "All I needed was another spade and . . ."; "I thought you had three of a kind because you were betting . . ." Zola (1964: 256) observed this phenomenon, which he called "the hedge," in the horse parlor, and described it as a means of maintaining some status even when losing. The loser would give a series of reasons why he lost, and how he wouldn't have if he had done some minor thing differently.

Goffman (1967:247) pointed out instances where in competitive interactions "both parties can emerge with honor and good character affirmed." This opportunity was clearly provided in the friendly game for those players who would "knock heads." There was potential in that situation for a "good winner" and one or more "good losers."

If a core player clearly had made a blunder, he would be teased by the others. Often the blunderer, in defense, would narrate a blunder historical for the group, whether made by himself or some other player. "Remember the time when Joe bet like crazy on his low hand because he thought the game was high-low split, and it was a high hand take all!" Considerable detail would be shared about the nature of the epic mistake. The current blunderer effectively would have anchored his own current error on a point somewhere less gross than a historical one. The core players appreciated and were comforted by the fact that all of them made mistakes. As one interviewee pointed out, "Nobody likes to play poker against a machine."

The player who had lost despite his skill might choose some other form of rationalization. He might consider the evening to have been "cheap entertainment," or "the cost of some lessons in poker." He might indicate that it was "his turn to lose tonight," or he had "let the host win." Nobody ever really complained about losing (although frustration was expressed concerning "second-best hands"). "I have more fun *losing* in this group," commented a core member, "than I do *winning* at roulette, or something like that."

The amount of money won or lost was discussed only in the most offhand manner. Specific figures were seldom mentioned, only estimates given, and then only sporadically and without pattern by different players. A core member reflected,

> At the end of the evening the game is over. Who cares how much you win or lose on one evening because each of us wins or loses, and it balances it out. It's each hand during the game that counts, and whether you win or lose that hand. The overall thing doesn't mean as much.

The money, out of the context of group interaction, seemed unimportant.

CONCLUSIONS: THE EPHEMERAL ROLE

The core members perceived themselves to be in a "different world" when they were playing. The friendly game, with its idiosyncratic roles, norms, rituals and rules of irrelevance, maintained clearly established boundaries. New men were selected carefully, and anyone or anything that disrupted the group dynamics or reduced the satisfactions experienced was eliminated or avoided. The players testified to their awareness that the poker group was "separate" from their other, broader, day-to-day social relationships:

> I look forward every other Monday to getting away from it all. I can do that when I'm playing poker with the guys. I forget about my job, and other problems that I have, and I can just sort of get lost in the game.

> It's a chance to get away from our wives and families. Every man needs a chance to get away from that once in awhile.

> When that first card hits the table, it's like we're on an island, you know, all to ourselves. Nobody bothers us. You're your own man! I miss it whenever we have to cancel a game for some reason or another.

In this sense, the friendly game seemed, as did Zola's (1964:248–49) horse parlor, to allow the players to effect "disassociation from ordinary utilitarian activities."

Goffman (1961:36, 67–68) described a "gaming encounter" as having social participants deeply involved in a focused interaction, and as such has "a metaphorical membrane around it." When the core players had all arrived, they formed the metaphorical membrane, and the friendly game became "a little cosmos of its own" (Riezler, 1941:505). Within the group boundaries, each member enacted the "ephemeral role" of core member, providing him the opportunity for scripted competition, self- and other-control, event brokerage, normative deception and aggression, micro-institutionalizing, and retrospective conquest. More specifically it provided him with the following opportunities for satisfaction: to share in the establishing and/or maintaining of a personally relevant group structure and interaction pattern; to compete vigorously but safely with equals; to bluff, tease, or otherwise "one-up" equals; to demonstrate and be admired for skill in betting and playing; to become deeply involved in intense but controlled personal interaction; to read, analyze, and utilize cues emitted from other players; to control and become immersed in action, including a series of thrills and the exhilaration of "pace"; to enjoy the fellowship of a chosen and mutually developed primary group; to exert control over self, others and luck or fate; to capture or relive some of the competencies and freedoms of youth; to reaffirm one's masculinity; to enjoy legitimized deviancy; to implement, in rapid succession, a great number of significant decisions; to declare as irrelevant, norms and roles which society-at-large deems mandatory in favor of idiosyncratic group norms and roles; and to escape the routine and "ordinary" social dynamics of everyday life.

The core member appeared to enter and leave the metaphorical membrane and ephemeral role through two buffer zones structured in the friendly game. The first buffer zone was the pre-game socializing period during which players waited and discussed various topics until all had arrived. The transition from everyday social interaction to the contrived interaction in the game, the "easing" into the ephemeral role, was facilitated by this short delay. Players who had arrived late and thus missed the socializing period were heard to comment, for example, "give me a second to shift gears," or "let me put on my poker hat."

The other buffer zone, the meal after the game, served a similar function. The players then were behaving as members of any other group sitting down to have a snack together. The topics of conversation were unrestricted, and only rarely and briefly were any comments made concerning the game itself. During that period of the evening, the players were being "eased back" into their day-to-day complex of social roles.

Those who could not make the transition into the ephemeral role were disruptive to the group. This happened on only two occasions observed by the author. The first occasion involved a new man whose home had some months before been destroyed by a severe tornado. Shortly before the game had begun a tornado watch had been announced for the area; the sky was heavy with clouds and the wind was noticeably increasing. The new man kept looking over his shoulder and out of the window, rose several times to walk to the front porch and look up at the sky, and twice dropped out of the game to phone his wife. A core player commented, in an uncriticizing manner, "Your mind is wandering, isn't it." The distracted man commented that since he was "so nervous" it might be a "good idea" for him to go home. The group quickly agreed with him, and he left. A minute or so later a core player announced, "Okay, let's settle down and play some poker," and the game went on.

In the second incident, a core player seemed to be distracted throughout the game. He told short jokes, talked about "irrelevant" topics, and generally slowed down the pace. "What the hell's the matter with you!" inquired another, "Why are you so talkative tonight?" The reasons for his behavior were not clear until later, during the meal, when he announced that he was being moved to another area and would no longer be able to participate.

He apparently had found it difficult to enact fully the ephemeral role, since he realized he would no longer be part of the friendly game. His distraction by the world "out there" had distracted the other players. As Goffman (1957) observed, in a gaming encounter "the perception that one participant is not spontaneously involved in the mutual activity can weaken for others their own involvement in the encounter and their own belief in the reality of the world it describes."

Core member of the friendly game is only one example of an ephemeral role. Other examples might include such diverse behavioral patterns as LSD "tripper," encounter "grouper," adulterer, volunteer work crew member (Zurcher, 1968), vacationer, weekend fisherman, or whatever is intense and intermittent and defined in contrast to one's day-to-day social world. Hopefully, we may see more systematic and comparative studies showing why people choose to develop or enact specific ephemeral roles, the satisfactions they gain, and the relation between ephemeral roles and major "life" roles.

REFERENCES

AMERICAN INSTITUTE OF PUBLIC OPINION, "The Quarter's Polls," *Public Opinion Quarterly* 12 (Spring 1948), 146–76.

BERGLER, E., *The Psychology of Gambling*. New York: Hill & Wang, 1957.

BLOCH, H. A., "The Sociology of Gambling," *American Journal of Sociology* 57 (November 1951), 215–21.

CAILLOIS, R., *Man, Play and Games*. New York: Free Press of Glencoe, 1961.

CRESPI, I., "The Social Significance of Card Playing as a Leisure Time Activity," *American Sociological Review* 21 (December 1956), 717–21.

EDWARDS, W., "The Prediction of Decisions Among Bets," *Journal of Experimental Psychology* 50 (September 1955), 201–14.

ERIKSON, E., *Childhood and Society*. New York: Norton, 1950.

ERIKSON, K., "Notes on the Sociology of Deviance," *Social Problems* 9 (Spring 1962), 307–14.

GOFFMAN, E., "Embarrassment and Social Organization," *American Journal of Sociology* 62 (November 1956), 264–71.

———, "Alienation from Interaction," *Human Relations* 10 (February 1957), 47–60.

———, *Encounters: Two Studies in the Sociology of Interaction*. Indianapolis: Bobbs-Merrill, 1961.

———, *Interaction Ritual*. Chicago: Aldine, 1967.

GOLD, R., "Roles in Sociological Field Observation," *Social Forces* 36 (March 1958), 217–23.

HENSLIN, J. M., "Craps and Magic," *American Journal of Sociology* 73 (November 1967), 316–30.

Herman, R. D., ed., *Gambling*. New York: Harper & Row, 1967.

———, "Gambling as Work: A Sociological Study of the Race Track," pp. 87–104 in R. D. Herman, ed., *Gambling*. New York: Harper & Row, 1967.

Huizinga, J., *Homo Ludens, The Play Element in Culture*. Boston: Beacon Press, 1955.

Lukacs, J., "Poker and American Character," *Horizon* 5 (November 1963), 56–62.

Malinowski, B., *Magic, Science and Religion*. New York: Doubleday, 1948.

Martinez, T. M., and R. LaFranci, "Why People Play Poker," *Transaction* 6 (July-August 1969), 30–35, 52.

Piaget, J., *Play, Dreams and Imitations in Childhood*. New York: Norton, 1951.

Riezler, K., "Play and Seriousness," *The Journal of Philosophy* 38 (September 1941), 505–17.

Robbins, F. G. *The Sociology of Play, Recreation and Leisure Time*. Dubuque, Iowa: Brown, 1955.

Strauss, A., *The Social Psychology of George Herbert Mead*. Chicago: University of Chicago Press, 1956.

Sutton-Smith, B., and J. M. Roberts, "Game Involvement in Adults," *Journal of Social Psychology* 60 (1963), 15–30.

Zola, I. K., "Observations on Gambling in a Lower Class Setting," pp. 247–60 in H. Becker, ed., *The Other Side*. New York: Free Press, 1964.

Zurcher, L. A., "Social Psychological Functions of Ephemeral Roles," *Human Organization* 27 (Winter 1968), 281–97.

LEON MANN

Queue Culture: The Waiting Line as a Social System[1]

This paper deals with the kinds of formal and informal arrangements made in queues to regulate behavior, to recognize the priority of

Reprinted from *The American Journal of Sociology*, 75, 3 (1969), 340–54, by permission of The University of Chicago Press. Copyright 1969 by The University of Chicago Press.

[1] This study was supported by a grant from the Comparative International Program of the Department of Social Relations, Harvard University. The helpful suggestions of Thomas Cottle, George Homans, Alex Inkeles, Irving Janis, and Gerald Platt are gratefully acknowledged. I wish to express my gratitude to Ruth Chaplin and Frank Nordberg for their assistance in collecting and analyzing the data.

early-comers, and to inhibit the growth of conflict. The study of queues is an attempt to describe the patterns of behavior which attend waiting in lines where a great deal of time, discomfort, and risk of disappointment must be endured before the desired commodity is obtained. Our focus is on the forms of etiquette developed to regulate life in the queue and to minimize the amount of suffering experienced while waiting. The queue culture provides direction on such matters as place-keeping privileges, sanctions against pushing in, and rights of temporary absence from the waiting line. Evidence that the queue constitutes an embryonic social system is based primarily on the study of long, overnight lines for football tickets in Melbourne, Australia.

THE STUDY

Every Saturday afternoon in the month of September, over 100,000 spectators crowd into a stadium in Melbourne, Australia, to watch the "world series" of Australian rules football.

On August 15, 1967, approximately 10,000 people formed twenty-two queues outside the Melbourne Football Stadium to buy 14,000 sets of tickets for the four games. It was the last opportunity to get tickets because mail applications for the bulk of the tickets had been oversubscribed weeks before. A great many of the 10,000 faced disappointment because most queuers usually buy the full allotment of two adult and two children's tickets.

From 6 A.M. until 8 A.M., when the selling windows opened, a team of nine research assistants, male psychology majors from the University of Melbourne, conducted short, standard interviews with 216 people in ten of the twenty-two queues. Each interviewer was randomly assigned a queue. Starting with the first person in line, the procedure was to approach every tenth person. The request was brief and informal: "I am from the University, and we are doing a study of how people feel about the queues. Would you care to answer a few questions?" Only two refusals were encountered; with the exception of one queue, all interviews were completed by 8 A.M. when the lines began to move. Questions covered attitudes toward the system of queueing, evidence of pushing in and place keeping, arrangements to make the task of queueing more pleasant, as well as estimates of position in line and chances of getting a ticket. Interviewers also made notes on their observations of the physical shape of the queues and on their impressions of the mood and morale of the people in them. Data from the Melbourne stadium are the main source of evidence cited in this paper.

Members of the research team also conducted interviews and made observations in the club queues at suburban Collingwood, Carlton, and Richmond, each of which had allocations of 1,000 tickets for club members. Data gathered from the club queues provide additional evidence presented in this paper.

THE QUEUE TRADITION

The system of selling seat bookings for the football finals several weeks before the start of the series was first introduced in 1956. Before 1956, people queued outside the stadium on the day of the game, and "first in" took the best seats. Over the years, because of the large increase in the number of football followers, the queue system became accepted as the only workable method for selling tickets. Although there were complaints from the public, the great overnight queues became a regular event at the end of a Melbourne winter. And as the queues took on an institutional character, increasing numbers of veterans began to regard them as a kind of cherished tradition or ritual. For example, even during the regular season, although it was possible to get choice seats two hours before the commencement of most Saturday games, long queues formed outside stadiums on Friday, perhaps to train for the big one in August.

The queue of 1965 was perhaps the most remarkable, for in that year 25,000 people waited for 12,500 tickets, some of them for over a week, in mud and drizzling rain. Queuers erected a shanty town of tents and caravans outside the stadium, and conditions, according to the Melbourne town clerk rapidly became "squalid and unhygienic." In 1966, to prevent a recurrence of the shantytown, the Melbourne City Council banned tents and camping equipment from the queues and prohibited the lighting of fires. Also, queues or assemblies were not allowed outside the stadium until twenty hours before ticket sales started. The city council regulations made the wait for tickets colder, but much shorter, and accordingly it was decided to retain them the following year.

In the 1967 queues, our interviewers noted that people improvised tents by tying tarpaulins to the side of barricades, and brought stretchers, sleeping bags, and supplies of liquor to make themselves comfortable during the wait. Even after a cold night in the open, 26 percent of the respondents claimed they were happy with the queue system. Only the aged and those who had to go straight to work felt very unhappy about their night out. In 1966, when a sample of 122 queuers were interviewed on a mild afternoon before the ticket windows opened, 47 percent reported satisfaction with this method of selling tickets.

At Collingwood, the Melbourne City Council regulations did not apply, and accommodations in the first part of the queue resembled a refugee camp. The first three families in line, numbering approximately thirty men, women, and children, pitched a bedouin tent on the sidewalk fronting the ticket box, and settled down to a six-day wait around a blazing camp fire. Some enthusiasts moved out of their homes and took up formal residence in the queue. Five days before tickets went on sale, the general secretary of Collingwood, Gordon Carlyon, received a letter addressed to "Mr. Alfred McDougall, c/o Queue outside Collingwood Football Ground, Collingwood, 3066." The *Melbourne Herald* of August 8, 1967 reported that Mr. Carlyon threaded his way through beds and tents on the sidewalk outside the stadium to deliver the letter. Melbournians had not only started to tolerate queues but actually seemed to be enjoying them. One woman outside the Melbourne stadium was heard to remark: "People are always knocking queues, what I would like to know is what people like myself would do without them" (*Melbourne Age*, August 16, 1967).

It seems that the means behavior, that is, lining up to get tickets for the event, almost becomes an end in itself, with its own intrinsic rewards and satisfactions. What does queueing mean, and why has it become an important occasion in the lives of these people? The answer lies partly in the publicity and recognition given to the queuers and partly in the challenge and excitement. For several days in August the attention of Melbourne and its mass media is focused on the brave queues outside its stadium. To be able to claim, in football-mad Melbourne, that one has stood through the night and obtained tickets earns the kind of kudos and respect that must have been given to those who fought at Agincourt. And there are other pleasures. Outside the stadium something of a carnival atmosphere prevails. The devotees sing, sip warm drinks, play cards, and huddle together around the big charcoal braziers. If he has come as part of a large group, or a cheer squad, the aficionado enjoys a brief taste of communal living and the chance to discuss and debate endlessly the fine points of the game. Above all, football fans regard the great queue as an adventure, an unusual and yet traditional diversion at the end of a Melbourne winter, as the football season approaches its exciting climax.

PROFILE OF THE QUEUER

The typical queuer is male, not yet twenty-five years of age, lives in a working-class suburb, and probably has absented himself from work to wait in line. Together with three friends, he has waited for at least fifteen hours to get tickets to watch his club play in the finals. He cannot explain why he likes football, but he has followed his team faithfully since childhood. He claims he would still be queueing even if his team were not playing, but the scarcity of supporters of nonfinals teams in the queue indicates that this is not likely. He has not counted the number of people ahead of him and has no real idea of the number of tickets for sale to the queue. He is fairly confident that he will get tickets, and he does not seem very unhappy about the queue system.

THE PROFESSIONAL QUEUER

When demand exceeds supply, it is inevitable that ticket speculators move into the queue in search of supplies for the flourishing market in hard-to-get tickets.

The Australian football queue contains two kinds of speculators: groups of highly organized people, hired at a fee to wait and buy tickets for large business concerns; and small-time operators, who resell their two tickets to the highest bidder. Often the speculators are university students, whose earnings help to pay tuition fees. Two days before ticket sales opened at the Melbourne stadium, twenty students flew from Tasmania to the mainland to join the queue. The airline company, which hired them to buy the tickets, also provided free return flights, accommodation at a leading hotel, and taxis during their stay (*Melbourne Herald,* August 12, 1967). An advertising agency engaged Melbourne University students to stand in line for one dollar an hour each, the tickets to be given away as prizes. Other students, operating as free-lance scalpers, asked an outraged public fifty dollars for $5.60 tickets, and had no difficulty getting their price.[2]

It is difficult to estimate the number of speculators in the football queues, as most people would be reluctant to admit to this kind of activity, but it was apparent from the number of advertisements for tickets in the "Wanted to Sell" columns of the Melbourne newspapers that a large proportion of queuers turned professional in the week following the ticket sales.

In the Melbourne stadium lines, very few people actually counted their position, perhaps because they believed there was no point in it since there was no accurate information available about the number of tickets available to each line (see Mann and Taylor 1969). In club queues, however, a different set of conditions obtained. There was usually a single mammoth queue (at Richmond it included over 3,000 people and ringed the perimeter of the stadium). More important, the number of tickets on sale was well publicized, and therefore it was possible to make a fairly accurate estimate of the chances of getting tickets, if the person had accurate information

---

[2] Speculation in the physical position itself is not found in Australian queues, as it is in waiting lines for Broadway hit shows. At smash hits it is not unusual for people to make a business of getting in line early in order to sell their advanced positions to latecomers for a large fee (see *Life,* September 24, 1956).

about his position in line. Accordingly, the estimates of position in the club queues were somewhat more accurate than at the stadium because people either had taken the trouble to count the number ahead or had consulted with a queue "counter." Queue counters are boys who count the queue at regular intervals, if it is long and winding. Queue counters, like ticket speculators, "invent" business to go along with what began simply as a necessary social act. At Carlton a group of boys went backward and forward during the night, counting the queue, and at Richmond the counters turned professional and, for a fee (ten cents), gave each customer up-to-date information on the number of people ahead and behind, as well as topical news and gossip.

THE PRE-QUEUE

A queue is a line of persons waiting in turn to be served, according to order of arrival. But the act of queueing involves more than the acquisition of a right to prior service because of early arrival. To validate this priority, the person must also spend time in the queue, not only to show latecomers that he occupies a given position, but also to demonstrate that his right to priority is confirmed by an unquestionable willingness to undergo further suffering to get the commodity.

If all that is required to reserve a place in a queue is the act of registering order of arrival, everyone would make an effort to be present at the time of queue formation. This would either lead to uncontrolled competition and hostility at the time of registration, or more probably, the formation of pre-queues to establish recognition of the right to priority in the official queue.

The pre-queue is an unofficial line which forms spontaneously before the official, recognized queue is allowed to form. The Melbourne football queues were not allowed to form until 3 P.M. of the afternoon before the sale of tickets. To enforce this regulation, police erected a perimeter of barricades around the wall of the stadium. Nevertheless, hundreds of people gathered in the park hours before queueing was officially allowed to start and, without police direction or intervention, spontaneously formed lines outside the barricades. At 3 P.M., when the barricades were removed, they folded their chairs, and keeping the lines intact, filed in perfect order to the ticket windows to commence the official seventeen-hour wait. The formation of a pre-queue, in this instance, almost certainly functioned to prevent an explosive situation which could have occurred had people failed to sort themselves into some kind of recognized order before the official line started. The lack of competition for positions among the early-comers can be explained in terms of the reward-cost structure in the first part of the line. There is little to be gained from being first, rather than twentieth or fiftieth (all are virtually guaranteed a ticket), but there is much to be lost if aggressive competition leads to physical damage and general disorder.

SERVING TIME IN QUEUES

There is a curious dilemma in the overnight queue. If there is a unanimous willingness to respect the order of arrival, it is pointless to require everyone to spend an uncomfortable night in the open. But if large numbers absent themselves, those remaining to protect the queue from outsiders will feel that their greater inputs of time and suffering now outweigh the merits of early arrival and entitle them to priority of service. Also, they will feel no responsibility for minding the places of people who, by their absence, are in no position to offer reciprocal place-minding services. In recognition of the conflicting considerations of unnecessary suffering caused by continuous occupancy, and the necessity to validate one's position by spending some time in residence, various arrangements are made which function to lessen the ordeal while protecting the rights of early-comers. Usually the arrangements represent a compromise which allows the queuer to take brief leaves of absence while retaining undisputed rights of reentry.

In Australian football lines, "time-out" is accomplished by two informal arrangements. Early-comers, who usually come in groups of four or five, often organize a "shift system," in which members spend one hour on with four hours off. One person can hold up to four places until the relief reports back to take over as group custodian. In our survey, an average of 39 percent of respondents in the first 100 of every queue reported that they had organized a shift system; in the latter part of the queue only 24 percent reported participation in a shift system. Sometimes the system involves a large group of people who share not only place-keeping duties but also facilities for eating, sleeping, and entertainment. The *Melbourne Herald* of August 15, 1967 described a seventeen-year-old girl, one of twelve people who took turns to leave the queue to eat and sleep in one of the few trailers found outside the Melbourne stadium. The same newspaper carried a story of a young scalper who combined business with pleasure: "I was one of a group of 20 students who stood together all night in the queue outside the ground. We were well organized. A couple of us kept our positions, and the others went out on the town" (*Melbourne Herald*, August 22, 1967).

It is rare for queuers at the head of the line to come alone; 94 percent of the respondents questioned in the first 100 of every line reported that they had come with others (see table 1). However, a large minority toward the end of each line came alone; while their need for time-outs was less pressing, they also made arrangements to cover brief absences if necessary. It is an accepted practice to "stake a claim" in a queue by leaving some item of

personal property. One can keep a place in a line with a labeled box, fold-
ing chair, haversack, or sleeping bag for quite long periods. The object
stands for the person and his place, symbolism reminiscent of burial customs of the ancient Egyptians.[3] During the early hours of waiting, when
many people were enjoying a carefree game of football in the surrounding
park, the queues often consisted of one part people to two parts inanimate
objects. The norm in leaving position markers is that one must not be absent for periods longer than two to three hours. In the Collingwood queue
of 1966, irate latecomers, who noticed that many people in the middle of
the queue had not made an appearance for most of the day, spontaneously
seized their boxes and burnt them. The latecomers were protesting the violation of the principle of serving time to earn occupancy of a position. In
the ensuing melee, scores of people made significant advances in their positions. Because arrangements for absence from the football queue are of
necessity extremely informal, inefficiency and abuse often occur. To ensure
protection of their valued positions, some do not trust the shift or marker
systems but prefer to keep a constant vigil which lasts the entire life of the
queue.

Table 1   PATTERNS OF QUEUE-RELATED BEHAVIOR AS A FUNCTION OF POSITION
IN LINE: MELBOURNE FOOTBALL QUEUES, 1967

Actual Position in Line	Member of an Organized Shift System		Came with Others		Observed Hostile Response to Push-in Attempt		Consider Place-keeping Permissible	
10–100 ($N = 95$)	39%	$Z = 1.91$ $P < .05$	94%	$Z = 2.81$ $P < .01$	46%	N.S.	25%	N.S.
110–200 ($N = 82$)	23%	N.S.	78%	$Z = 1.41$	33%	N.S.	35%	N.S.
210–330 ($N = 39$)	25%		64%	N.S.	27%		24%	

Note: Number of respondents varies slightly for each question.

First come, first served, the fundamental concept of queueing, is a basic
principle of the behavior referred to as distributive justice (Homans 1961).
There is a direct correspondence between inputs (time spent waiting) and
outcomes (preferential service). Generally, if a person is willing to invest
large amounts of time and suffering in an activity, people who believe there
should be an appropriate fit between effort and reward will respect his
right to priority. We have seen, however, that the principle of distributive

---

[3] Markers such as notebooks, coats, newspapers, and umbrellas are often used to
defend a "reserved" space in public places, such as a crowded cafeteria or study hall
(see Sommer 1969).

justice is elaborated to encompass the need for leaves of absence in marathon queues. In recognition of the fact that continuous residence in the line imposes great hardship, members come to an agreement on the minimum inputs of time necessary to validate occupancy of a position. It is reasonable to claim that rules regulating time spent in and out of the line are the essential core of the queue culture.[4]

QUEUE JUMPING

Placekeeping and pushing in violate the principle of first come, first served. When people at the end of a queue feel certain that the violation does not jeopardize their own chances of obtaining the commodity, there is likely to be some irritation but no attempt to eject the offender. Stronger measures are likely, however, if people at the tail end believe that the lengthening of the line worsens their prospect of receiving service.

Since there is a great deal at stake, football queuers are especially annoyed by any attempt to jump the queue, and they adopt a variety of physical and social techniques to keep people in line. At certain times in the life of the queue when police supervision was minimal, queuers had to devise their own constraints. The most extreme constraint was physical force. During the early hours of August 15, five men were taken to hospital after four separate brawls broke out in the ticket lines (*Melbourne Herald*, August 15, 1967). The strategic placement of barriers acts as a constraint against would-be infiltrators. It was observed that people in the middle of the queue worked together to erect barricades from material left in the park. Keeping close interperson distance also serves to maintain the "territory" in the face of would-be intruders. At times of maximum danger, and in the hour before the ticket windows opened, there was a visible bunching together, or shrinkage, in the physical length of the queue, literally a closing of the ranks. The exercise of effective social constraints depends on the capacity for cohesive action on the part of the queuers. At the stadium, whenever outsiders approached the head of the queue, they were intimidated by vociferous catcalls and jeering. Ordinarily, this mode of protecting the queue was successful during daylight, the pressure of concerted disapproval inhibiting all but the boldest. During the hours of darkness,

---

[4] Queue systems with inbuilt guarantees of distributive justice are to be found in both the United States and USSR. At the weekly line for tickets to the Metropolitan Opera in New York, an unofficial "keeper of the list" registers applicants in order of arrival, assigns numbers, and checks names when the queuers appear for roll call every three hours (see *New Yorker*, January 14, 1967). In Moscow, when scarce goods go on sale, a series of queue custodians take turns "standing guard" and list the names of interested customers as they arrive throughout the night (see Levine 1959, pp. 338–39).

social pressure proved less effective; the knowledge that one cannot be seen easily undermines social pressure and shaming as a technique.

Despite these constraints, many latecomers attempted to push in, and it was apparent that some succeeded. Letters to the newspapers by disappointed queuers testified to the activity of queue jumpers. One man who missed out in the Carlton queue claimed that he had been dislodged from 185th to 375th place in the span of two hours. When asked, "Has anyone tried to push in?" respondents in every part of each queue reported that they had witnessed attempts to jump the queue, but only in a minority of cases had the intruder been ejected. According to the reports of our respondents, the act of intrusion was usually met with passivity rather than a physically hostile response, especially toward the end of the line, where people came alone and were not organized for dealing with intruders (see table 1). Yet, when asked what they would do if someone tried to crash the queue immediately in front of them, respondents were almost unanimous in claiming that they would resort to physical force.

According to our respondents' reports, pushing in occurred most often near the tail of the queue. This seems puzzling at first, for, if someone is going to risk pushing in, it seems sensible to try at the front, where there is a greater certainty of getting tickets. However, we must bear in mind the more effective policing at the front, as well as the decreased risk toward the rear of the queue, where, in absolute numbers, fewer people are put out by the violation and hence there is less likelihood of concerted action. In brief, opposition to a queue jumper decreases as a function of the number of people whose chances of getting tickets are affected by the intrusion; at the end of the line there are very few such people. Ironically, however, it is these people, regardless of where pushing in occurs, who stand to lose most by the infraction because their chances of getting tickets are put in even greater jeopardy.

Why does the queue fail to act in unison to dismiss the queue jumper? To some extent, the varying interests of people in different parts of the queue provide an answer. People at the front of the queue do not care particularly about pushing in which occurs behind them because they do not suffer from the intrusion. Of course, if queue jumping becomes widespread, the early-comers show concern because their positions may be threatened by latecomers who realize that the entire line is vulnerable. But usually they have nothing to gain and much to lose from becoming involved in policing the queue. It is surprising, however, that people after the point of intrusion do not act together to expel the violator, since they all suffer equally by the loss of a place. It seems that responsibility for evicting a trespasser falls squarely on the shoulders of the person who is the immediate victim of the violation, that is, the person directly behind the violator. Those further back may jeer and catcall, but the immediate victim is expected to take the initiative in ejecting the queue jumper. The reasoning seems to be that the victim, either through his passive looks or careless surveillance of his territory, must have given some encouragement to the queue jumper, so he is now obliged to handle the situation without causing unpleasantness for other people.

The reluctance of queuers to exert physical action against queue jumpers may also be related to the nature of informal versus formal organization of the queue. In any informal queue, there are many signs of organizational control, role prerogatives, and orderly behavior, which are almost exactly the same as those in well-organized queues, where there is real policing and monitoring of the line. Therefore, people will assume that the informal queue will function in much the same way as the organized queue. When acts of pushing in and disorder occur, members of the queue realize they were mistaken and jeer spontaneously, exert informal pressure, and make threats to preserve their positions. If verbal constraints fail, physical violence emerges as a last resort. At this point there is a reluctance to pursue the matter further because more may be lost from physical action than from a small loss in position. The person who jumps the queue could be desperate, and the immediate victim anticipates the possibility that a struggle could cause injury and damage. If the police action is unsuccessful, the person is made to look foolish in the eyes of the onlookers. It is also possible that, if the struggle sets off a widespread melee, he stands to lose more than face and position. Therefore, if verbal censure fails, members of the queue fall back on a conspiracy of silence to ignore minor violations. Resorting to physical violence seems to represent a kind of public acknowledgment that the queue is no longer organized and under control. Once this happens, a grave danger exists that people in less favorable positions, as well as outsiders, will take advantage of what is then recognized to be a helpless, unorganized queue. To prevent this, occasional minor infractions, if they are not met successfully by verbal threats and jeering, are seldom handled by physical threats and violence. The use of physical methods, especially if they prove unsuccessful, is a signal to others that the queue organization is about to disintegrate completely, and this may actually serve to encourage an epidemic of queue jumping.

One reason for the prevalence of pushing in, and the failure to exert effective action against it, is the confusion which exists between illegal acts of entry and the somewhat more acceptable act of place keeping. Because place keeping occurs fairly frequently, it is not always clear whether an individual who moves boldly into a line is attempting to crash the queue or is merely joining his group. Therefore many are reluctant to challenge the entry of outsiders during the early hours of the queue. Although the custom of place keeping is a cause of friction, only informal rules have been formulated to regulate its practice. Of the respondents, 29 percent believed that it is permissible to keep a place for someone, and that people behind would not care (see table 1). However, only a handful of queuers admitted to actually keeping a place for someone. People do not admit freely to place keeping because the newcomer usually makes his appearance only in the last hour before tickets go on sale, and people already in line are likely to be very resentful.

THE QUEUE AS A SOCIAL SYSTEM

The queue, although made up of numerous groups of strangers gathered together temporarily, emerges as an embryonic social system with a set of norms for controlling conflict.

Parsons (1951) maintains that social systems develop spontaneously whenever two or more people come into some stabilized, patterned mode of interaction. He lists three properties of any social system: (1) two or more actors occupying differentiated statuses or positions and performing differentiated roles; (2) some organized pattern governing the relationships of the members, describing their rights and obligations with respect to one another; and (3) some set of common norms and values, together with various types of shared cultural objects and symbols.

The long, overnight queue has all three characteristics of a social system. While the queue may not directly allocate different statuses or roles to its members, the members themselves assume different roles. In and around every queue there is a host of people: professional and hired speculators, queue counters, custodians, vigilantes, police, and officials, performing a variety of queue-related tasks.

The other two properties of a social system—an organized pattern of relationships and a set of common norms—are readily identifiable in the queue. Order of arrival governs the relationship among members, while the shift system and the practice of time-outs controls the network of rights and obligations. Moreover, there are shared norms about the desirability of distributive justice, as reflected in the set of rules regulating place keeping and pushing in.

Interactive systems, such as the queue, develop within the matrix of a long-established sociocultural system which defines roles, normative standards, and goals. When a large number of people gather together and priority of service has value, a line is formed. All members bring to the new queue a host of ideas about the roles they should play, and develop firm notions about the way in which deviant behavior should be punished. Roles in the queue are drawn from and are molded by the institutional system of the larger society. The precise form of social organization, the sharing and division of labor inherent in the shift system, the preferred modes of policing the queue, the development of businesses and ticket speculation, the notion that one must earn one's place in line by spending time in it, even the very reason for queueing itself, reflect the character of the surrounding society.

The culture of the queue also draws upon and incorporates elements in the broader culture. The importance of time as a value in Western society is reflected in the emphasis placed on serving time, and restrictions on time-outs. The way in which people orient themselves toward a scarce commodity, their preference for cooperation, the entrepreneurial zeal they display in scalping tickets and charging fees for counting the queue, is a function of broad culture patterns, as well as the way society has taught them to behave.

The queue, moreover, is subject to sanctioning pressure from outside officials and onlookers, who try to bring it into conformity with societal expectations. Ultimately, of course, each queue has to work out its own final set of mutual adjustments in which socially prescribed rules about queueing are modified and embellished in various ways. A prime example of these adjustments is to be found in the various interpretations of the rules governing leaves of absence from the line.

While the queue system is embedded in a larger social matrix, it is also composed of many subsystems—groups, cliques, and coacting individuals —whose physical presence reinforces the very idea or concept of a line.

According to Parsons and Smelser (1957), there are four functional problems, or imperatives, faced by every social system: goal attainment, adaptation, integration, and latency. The queue, even though it is a relatively minor, short-lived social system, must confront these four problems.

The problem of goal attainment is to keep the system moving steadily toward the collective goal of its members, in this case, the purchase of tickets in an orderly manner with a minimum of unpleasantness. Before the system can move toward this goal, however, a host of instrumental and technical problems must be solved. Many of the problems are external to the queue, in the sense that they are not under the control of its members; for example, the seller (not the customer) must decide when and where people should be allowed to queue, how many lines should be formed, how many tickets will be made available, what limitation will be placed on the number of tickets sold to each customer, and so on. But the question of how to begin the queue, especially if people have gathered before the official starting time, is a problem left to the members themselves. As we have seen, the football fans solved this difficulty by forming a pre-queue, which became the officially recognized queue when the barriers to the ticket boxes were lowered.

Adaptation is the problem of bringing facilities and resources to the system which enable it to come to terms with the environment. One aspect of adaptation is the active manipulation of the environment. Thus queuers formed their line along concrete paths, constructed barriers out of material found in the park, erected shelters by tying tarpaulins to the barriers, built fires, and even brought in trailers, to make their temporary living quarters as comfortable as possible.

Manipulation of the system itself to blend with the environment is another aspect of adaptation. For the most part, the queue, rather than a single file of people, consisted of numerous knots of people, two and three abreast, who sat side by side to facilitate efficient communication and social interaction.

The integrative problem, perhaps the most distinctive in any social system, is concerned with the maintenance of appropriate emotional and social ties among members of the system. In order to achieve its goals, the system must establish and maintain a high degree of solidarity and cohesion. In the queue, cohesion is achieved by establishing informal rules which are kept sufficiently general to allow individual members to adjust to the normative pattern. Those who stay out too long, and therefore are unable to make the line viable, are sanctioned, or lose their place. In a sense this represents a form of turn taking; if the queue structure is to be preserved, only some members can be permitted to take leaves of absence at any one time.

The group or clique, by means of the shift system, regulates turn taking for its members, and this ensures continuity of the line. The group, since it is the carrier of queue culture, brings a high level of solidarity to the line.

At the head of the line, the group takes on the characteristics of a community. Large family groups share eating, rest, and recreational facilities, and time spent together serves to strengthen the feelings of community. It is likely that the major factor underlying the effective policing of the head and middle regions of the line is the presence of large, coordinated groups. The breakdown of defense against intruders in the end part of every line can be attributed primarily to the fragmented, isolated nature of the membership.

But even in parts of the line where organized groups are less prominent, individuals trade on a mutual trust which allows them to ask one another to "mind my place" and feel confident that they will be vouched for when they return from a brief leave of absence.

The latency function is reflected in two related but different problems— pattern maintenance and tension management.

Pattern maintenance is the problem faced by an individual in reconciling the conflicting norms and demands imposed by his participation in the queue. Many members experience role conflicts arising out of their obligations to the queue and to their family or work roles. As we have seen, some queuers solve the problem by moving their entire family into the line.

Others are faced with a different kind of dilemma: whether or not to keep a place for friends. The member who fails to commit himself to the queue norms is subject to considerable social pressure. If rules governing leaves of absence are not observed, the member is likely to find himself no longer part of the queue.

Tension management is the related problem of maintaining a level of commitment sufficient to perform the required role. To cope with tension and fatigue, members introduce a variety of entertainments in and around the line, such as pick-up games, story and joke telling, and beer parties. Time-out from the queue is, however, the major mode of tension management.

The queue system is mostly concerned with the problem of pattern maintenance and tension management because these are the most significant from the viewpoint of continuous participation and control. Of course, at critical times in the life of the queue, the other three functional problems require attention. Indeed, all four must be solved if the system is to continue in the state of equilibrium necessary for control and order.

CULTURAL VALUES AND QUEUEING

How do rules of etiquette develop in queues, and how do people come to recognize and respect them? To some extent, the answer lies in attitudes toward queues in general, which reflect broad cultural differences in sensitivity to queue norms, as well as the individuals' history of experience in waiting lines. Behavior in queues is a function of many variables: kind and length of queue; the importance of inputs and the value of the commodity; cultural and subcultural differences in respect for time, order, and the rights of others; and individual differences in such personality characteristics as aggressiveness and assertiveness.

The anthropologist Hall (1959) has suggested that a cultural value of egalitarianism is responsible for the manner in which queues and queueing are treated with deference in Western society. In *The Silent Language* Hall (1959, p. 157) writes: "As a general rule, whenever services are involved we feel that people should queue up in order of arrival. This reflects the basic equalitarianism of our culture. In cultures where a class system or its remnants exist, such ordinality may not exist. That is, where society assigns rank for certain purposes, or whenever ranking is involved, the handling of space will reflect this. To us it is regarded as a democratic virtue for people to be served without reference to the rank they hold in their occupational group. The rich and poor alike are accorded equal opportunity to buy and be waited upon in the order of arrival. In a line at the theater Mrs. Gottrocks is no better than anyone else."

While there is merit in the thesis that a strain of equality in a culture is related to the orderliness of public behavior, it would seem that egalitarianism alone does not explain respect for priority in queues. Consider the English, a people famous for their strictly democratic queueing behavior. It is safe to say that the English have a more rigid social structure and are more class conscious than Americans, and yet their public behavior is probably more orderly. The relationship between cultural equality and public orderliness is attenuated in the area of queueing because waiting in line is not a habit of all social classes in Western society. It is reasonable to suppose that if Mrs. Gottrocks joined a theater or a football line in the United States, Australia, or England, she would not be treated differently than anyone else, but it would be a rare event for someone of Mrs. Gottrocks's status to use a line. Ordinarily, in both class-conscious and relatively class-free societies, the privileged classes circumvent the line altogether and get their tickets through agents or other contacts. Our point, then, is that queueing is confined largely to the less-privileged groups in society. It might be more accurate to speak of a subcultural value of equalitarianism in public behavior.

In his recent book, *The Hidden Dimension,* Hall (1964) continues his examination of the basis of public behavior and makes the assertion that respect for queues can also be attributed to a cultural value of orderliness. Presumably, culture patterns in different societies emerge on a continuum of order–disorder, and, like the value of equality, a strain of orderliness runs through life in a society.

One difficulty with the orderliness hypothesis is that the principle of queueing is not always maintained in situations where there are no officials or police present to scrutinize and control the outbursts of unruly behavior. Only if the principle is supported religiously under these conditions, can one speak of a culturally ingrained disposition toward orderliness.

In brief, to seek an explanation for organized cooperative behavior in queues, we cannot appeal only to cultural values of egalitarianism and orderliness. Answers must also be sought with reference to the queue as a social system in which these values often receive only token or symbolic acknowledgment. The main concern of the queue membership is maintenance of a state of control and order while the system moves toward its goal. Indeed, values of orderliness, egalitarianism, and distributive justice are invoked to help maintain that order, but they are primarily used and modified to make life in the queue tolerable, rather than obeyed in a rigid and mechanical manner.

CONCLUSION

This paper described how patterned regularities in behavior and attitudes emerge to regulate life in an overnight football queue. Although arrangements made to control behavior in the queue are informal, they are clearly identifiable, and it is appropriate to regard them as constituting a kind of culture. The queue, which possesses the characteristics of a social system, attempts to solve the set of functional problems confronted by every social system.

Our major findings were: (a) the growth of a queue tradition in which large numbers of people return annually to share the experience of waiting for tickets overnight in the open; (b) an increasing professionalization of the queue, marked by an influx of speculators and middlemen who profit by the increased demand for tickets; (c) the formation of unofficial pre-queues to recognize the priority of people who arrived before the start of the official queue; (d) elaboration of the principle of first come, first served to control the amount of time spent in and out of the queue ("shift" and "marker" systems, which control "time-outs," were developed to regulate leaves of absence from the line); (e) social constraints, and less often physical constraints, used to control queue jumping and to govern the practice of place keeping.

It is appropriate to conclude that queueing behavior, a neglected area of social research, could be a rich source of ideas for students of crowd behavior, judgmental processes, cross-national differences, and the influence of cultural values on public behavior.

REFERENCES

HALL, E. T., *The Silent Language*. New York: Doubleday, 1959.

——, *The Hidden Dimension*. New York: Doubleday, 1964.

HOMANS, G. C., *Social Behavior: Its Elementary Forms*. New York: Harcourt, 1961.

LEVINE, I. R., *Main Street, U.S.S.R.* New York: Doubleday, 1959.

MANN, L., and K. F. TAYLOR, "Queue Counting: The Effect of Motives upon Estimates of Numbers in Waiting Lines," *Journal of Personality and Social Psychology* 12 (1969), 95–103.

PARSONS, T., *The Social System*. New York: Free Press, 1951.

PARSONS, T., and NEIL J. SMELSER, *Economy and Society*. New York: Free Press, 1957.

SOMMER, R., *Personal Space*. Englewood Cliffs, N.J.: Prentice-Hall, 1969.

BARRY SCHWARTZ

The Social Psychology of Privacy

Patterns of coming and staying together imply counterpatterns[1] of withdrawal and disaffiliation which, as modalities of action, are worthy of analysis in their own right. Simmel makes the identical point in his essay, "Brücke und Tür": "Usually we only perceive as bound that which we have first isolated in some way. If things are to be joined they must first be separated. Practically as well as logically it would be nonsense to speak of binding that which is not separate in its own sense. . . . Directly as well as symbolically, bodily as well as spiritually, we are continually separating our bonds and binding our separations."[2] Simmel, however, ignores the question of how separation subserves integration—of how men are bound by taking leave of one another as well as by their coming together. One sociologically relevant approach to this problem is through the analysis of privacy, which is a highly institutionalized mode of withdrawal.

THE GROUP-PRESERVING FUNCTIONS
OF PRIVACY

Withdrawal into privacy is often a means of making life with an unbearable (or sporadically unbearable) person possible. If the distraction and relief of privacy were not available in such a case, the relationship would have to be terminated if conflict were to be avoided. Excessive contact is the condition under which Freud's principle of ambivalence most clearly exercises itself, when intimacy is most likely to produce open hostility as well as affection.[3] Issue must therefore be taken with Homans' proposition, "Per-

Reprinted from *The American Journal of Sociology,* 73, 6 (1968), 741–52, by permission of The University of Chicago Press. Copyright 1968 by The University of Chicago Press.

[1] The initiation of a social contact generally entails a withdrawal from a preceding one. Therefore, men may withdraw into new social circles as well as into seclusion. In this particular sense it would be most exact to employ the term "contact-withdrawal," as opposed to a single term for engagement and another for disengagement. However, this distinction does not apply to movements into privacy.

[2] Georg Simmel, "Brücke und Tür," in *Brücke und Tür* (Stuttgart: K. F. Koehler, 1957), p. 1.

[3] Sigmund Freud, *Group Psychology and the Analysis of the Ego* (New York: Bantam Books, Inc., 1960), pp. 41–42.

sons who interact frequently with one another tend to like one another" (providing the relationship is not obligatory).[4] The statement holds generally, but misses the essential point that there is a threshold beyond which interaction is unendurable for both parties. It is because people frequently take leave of one another that the interaction-liking proposition maintains itself.

Guarantees of privacy, that is, rules as to who may and who may not observe or reveal information about whom, must be established in any stable social system. If these assurances do not prevail—if there is normlessness with respect to privacy—every withdrawal from visibility may be accompanied by a measure of espionage, for without rules to the contrary persons are naturally given to intrude upon invisibility. "Secrecy sets barriers between men," writes Simmel, "but at the same time offers the seductive temptations to break through the barriers."[5] Such an inclination is embodied in the spy, the Peeping Tom, the eavesdropper, and the like, who have become its symbols.

"Surveillance" is the term which is generally applied to institutionalized intrusions into privacy. And social systems are characterizable in terms of the tension that exists between surveillant and anti-surveillant modes. Much of our literature on the anti-utopia, for example, George Orwell's *1984*, which depicts the dis-eases of excessive surveillance, is directed against the former mode. But dangers of internal disorder reside in unconditional guarantees of invisibility against which many administrative arms of justice have aligned themselves. On the other hand, surveillance may itself create the disorder which it seeks to prevent. Where there are few structural provisions for privacy, social withdrawal is equivalent to "hiding." For Simmel, "This is the crudest and, externally, most radical manner of concealment."[6] Where privacy is prohibited, man can only imagine separateness as an act of stealth.[7]

Since some provisions for taking leave of one another and for removing oneself from social observation are built into every establishment, an individual withdrawal into privacy and the allowance of such a withdrawal by other parties reflects and maintains the code that both sides adhere to. Leave taking, then, contains as many ritualistic demands as the act of coming together. Durkheim, like Homans, is not altogether correct in his insistence that the periodic gatherings of the group are its main sources of

[4] George C. Homans, *The Human Group* (New York: Harcourt, Brace & Co., 1950), p. 111.

[5] Georg Simmel, "The Secret and the Secret Society," in Kurt Wolff, ed., *The Sociology of Georg Simmel* (New York: Free Press, 1964), p. 334.

[6] *Ibid.*, p. 364.

[7] *Ibid.*

unity.[8] After a certain point the presence of others becomes irritating and leave taking, which is a mutual agreement to part company, is no less a binding agent than the ritual of meeting. In both cases individual needs (for gregariousness and isolation) are expressed and fulfilled in collectively indorsed manners. The dissociation ritual presupposes (and sustains) the social relation. Rules governing privacy, then, if accepted by all parties, constitute a common bond providing for periodic suspensions of interaction.

If privacy presupposes the existence of established social relations its employment may be considered as an index of solidarity. Weak social relationships, or relationships in the formative stage, cannot endure the strain of dissociation. By contrast, members of a stable social structure feel that it is not endangered by the maintenance of interpersonal boundaries. This point is of course well reflected in the Frostian dictum, "Good fences make good neighbors."

PRIVACY HELPS MAINTAIN STATUS DIVISIONS

It is also well known that privacy both reflects and helps to maintain the status divisions of a group. In the armed forces, for example, the non-commissioned officer may reside in the same building as the dormitoried enlisted man but he will maintain a separate room. The officer of higher rank will live apart from the non-commissioned, but on the same base, often in an apartment building; but officers of highest status are more likely to have private quarters away from the military establishment.

In organizational life the privacy of the upper rank is insured structurally; it is necessary to proceed through the lieutenant stratum if the top level is to be reached. In contrast, the lower rank, enjoying less control over those who may have access to it, find their privacy more easily invaded. Even in domestic life persons of the lower stratum lack "the butler" by means of whom the rich exercise tight control over their accessibility to others.

Privacy is an object of exchange. It is bought and sold in hospitals, transportation facilities, hotels, theaters, and, most conspicuously, in public restrooms where a dime will purchase a toilet, and a quarter, a toilet, sink and mirror. In some public lavatories a free toilet is provided—without a door.

Privacy has always been a luxury. Essayist Phyllis McGinley writes: "The poor might have to huddle together in cities for need's sake, and the frontiersman cling to his neighbor for the sake of protection. But in each

---

[8] Émile Durkheim, *The Elementary Forms of the Religious Life* (Glencoe, Ill.: Free Press, 1947), pp. 214–19.

civilization, as it advanced, those who could afford it chose the luxury of a withdrawing place. Egyptians planned vine-hung gardens, the Greeks had their porticos and seaside villas, the Romans put enclosures around their patios. . . . Privacy was considered as worth striving for as hallmarked silver or linen sheets for one's bed."[9] In this same respect Goffman comments upon the lack of front and back region differentiation in contemporary lower-class residences.[10]

The ability to invade privacy is also reflective of status. The physician's high social rank, for instance, derives perhaps not only from his technical skill but also from his authority to ignore barriers of privacy. However, this prerogative is not limited to those of high status. We must not forget the "non-person" who lacks the ability to challenge the selfhood of his superiors. Goffman cites Mrs. Frances Trollope: "I had indeed frequent opportunities of observing this habitual indifference to the presence of their slaves. They talk to them, of their condition, of their faculties, of their conduct exactly as if they were incapable of hearing. . . . A young lady displaying modesty before white gentlemen was found lacing her stays with the most perfect composure before a Negro footman."[11] In general society the assumption of the social invisibility of another is looked upon as indecency, that is, as a failure to erect a barrier of privacy between self and other under prescribed conditions.

The general rule that is deducible from all of this is that outside of the kinship group an extreme rank is conferred upon those for whom privacy shields are voluntarily removed. The prestige afforded the physician is exaggerated in order to protect the self from the shame which ordinarily accompanies a revelation of the body to a stranger, particularly if he is of the opposite sex. Likewise, the de-statusing of the servant is necessary if he is to be utilized for purposes of bathing, dressing, etc.

Persons of either high or low rank who have access to the private concerns of their clients are subject to definite obligations regarding both the manner in which secret knowledge is to be obtained and, most importantly, the way in which it is treated once it has been obtained. Explicit or implicit guarantees of confidentiality neutralize the transfer of power which would otherwise accompany the bestowal of private information. Both the possession of an extreme rank and the assurance of confidentiality thus legitimize the "need to know" and the intrusions which it makes possible.

---

[9] Phyllis McGinley, "A Lost Privilege," in *Province of the Heart* (New York: Viking Press, 1959), p. 56.

[10] Erving Goffman, *The Presentation of Self in Everyday Life* (Edinburgh: University of Edinburgh, 1958), p. 123.

[11] *Ibid.,* p. 95.

PRIVACY AND DEVIATION

Up to this point we have tried to indicate privacy's stabilizing effect upon two dimensions of social order. Withdrawal subserves horizontal order by providing a release from social relations when they have become sufficiently intense as to be irritating. Privacy is also a scarce social commodity; as such, its possession reflects and clarifies status divisions, thus dramatizing (and thereby stabilizing) the vertical order. But we must recognize that privacy also opens up opportunities for such forms of deviance as might undermine its stabilizing effects. However, privacy admits of *invisible* transgression and therefore serves to maintain intact those rules which would be subverted by the public disobedience that might occur in its absence.

Moore and Tumin, in their discussion of the function of ignorance, stated: "All social groups . . . require some quotient of ignorance to preserve esprit de corps."[12] And Goffman has made it clear that every establishment provides "involvement shields" for its members wherein "role releases" may take place, particularly deviant ones.[13] As Merton puts it:

> Resistance to full visibility of one's behavior appears, rather, to result from structural properties of group life. Some measure of leeway in conforming to role expectations is presupposed in all groups. To have to meet the strict requirements of a role at all times, without some degree of deviation, is to experience insufficient allowances for individual differences in capacity and training and for situational exigencies which make strict conformity extremely difficult. This is one of the sources of what has been elsewhere noted in this book as socially patterned, or even institutionalized, evasions of institutional rules.[14]

Thus, each group has its own "band of institutionalized evasion" which expands and contracts as conditions change. Rose L. Coser, in this connection, has considered observability in terms of the social status of the observer. She indicates that persons of high rank tend to voluntarily deprive

[12] Wilbur E. Moore and Melvin M. Tumin, "Some Social Functions of Ignorance," *American Sociological Review*, 14 (December, 1949), 792. See also Barney Glaser and Anselm Strauss, "Awareness Contexts and Social Interaction," *American Sociological Review*, 29 (October, 1964), 669–79, in which social interaction is discussed in terms of "what each interactant in a situation knows about the identity of the other and his own identity in the eyes of the other" (p. 670). A change in "awareness context" accompanies acquisitions of knowledge, provisions of false knowledge, concealment of information, etc.

[13] The "involvement shield" and Everett C. Hughes' concept of "role release" are elaborated in Erving Goffman's *Behavior in Public Places* (New York: Free Press, 1963), pp. 38–39.

[14] Robert K. Merton, *Social Theory and Social Structure* (New York: Free Press, 1964), p. 343.

themselves of visibility by signaling their intrusion with a prior announcement.[15] The deviation band, then, is normally condoned by both the upper and lower strata.

Moore and Tumin stress the importance of preventing deviation from being known to the group as a whole.[16] No doubt, a publication of all of the sins, crimes, and errors that take place in a social unit would jeopardize its stability. The preoccupation of the press with sensational deviations from norms might be considered from this point of view. Similarly, the more one person involves himself with another on an emotional basis the more both will need private facilities to conceal nasty habits and self-defaming information from each other. If the child, for instance, became suddenly aware of all the non-public performances of his father, and if the latter were aware of all the perversions that are privately enacted by his off-spring, a father–son relationship characterized by mutual admiration would be impossible. This same point is illustrated in well-adjusted marriages which depend not only upon mutually acceptable role playing but also upon the ability of both parties to conceal "indecent" performances. This presupposes a modicum of physical distance between husband and wife. Simmel, in addition, adds that a complete abandon of one's self-information to another "paralyzes the vitality of relations and lets their continuation really appear pointless."[17]

Privacy enables secret consumption. We observe, for example, the adolescent practices of smoking or drinking in their locked rooms. Similarly, "women may leave *Saturday Evening Post* on their living room table but keep a copy of *True Romance* ('something the cleaning woman must have left around') concealed in their bedroom."[18] However, some modes of secret consumption have come into the public light. The erotic "girlie magazines," for example, no longer need be employed privately by the middle-class male since the advent of the *Playboy* magazine. As some activities emerge from secrecy others go underground. Thus, the person who nowadays finds pleasure in the Bible will most likely partake of it in private rather than in a public place or conveyance. These new proprieties are perhaps specific instances of a general rule set down by Simmel, that "what is originally open becomes secret, and what was originally concealed throws off its mystery. Thus we might arrive at the paradoxical idea that, under otherwise like circumstances, human associations require a definite ratio of

[15] Rose L. Coser, "Insulation from Observability and Types of Social Conformity," *American Sociological Review*, 26 (February, 1961), 28–39.

[16] Moore and Tumin, "Some Social Functions of Ignorance," 793.

[17] Simmel, "The Secret and the Secret Society," p. 329.

[18] Goffman, *The Presentation of Self in Everyday Life*, p. 26. Needless to say, many instances of the employment of privacy for "secret production" could be given.

secrecy which merely changes its objects; letting go of one it seizes another, and in the course of this exchange it keeps its quantum unvaried."[19]

Incidentally, just as the person must employ proper language for the public situations in which he finds himself, he is required to maintain an appropriate body language as well. Differing postures must be assumed in his public encounters. But public postures do not exhaust the many positions of which the human body is capable. Anyone who has maintained a single position over a long period of time knows that the body demands consistent postural variation if it is to remain comfortable and capable of good role performance. Privacy enables the person to enact a variety of nonpublic postures and thus prepares him physically for public life.

It should be stressed that the absence of visibility does not guarantee privacy. The hypertrophied super-ego certainly makes impossible the use of solitude for deviant objectives. The person who is constantly in view of an internalized father, mother, or God leads a different kind of private life than those possessed by a less demanding conscience. This reveals an interesting paradox. Privacy surely provides for some measure of autonomy, of freedom from public expectation; but as Durkheim so persistently reminded us, the consequences of leaving the general normative order are moral instability and social rootlessness. (It is for this reason that secret societies compensate for the moral anarchy inherent in pure autonomy by means of ritual.)[20] Is it then possible that through privacy the ego escapes the dominion of the public order only to subordinate itself to a new authority: the super-ego? In some measure this is certainly the case, but one may also venture the suggestion that the super-ego, like the social structure whose demands it incorporates, has its own "band of institutionalized evasion." The super-ego cannot be totally unyielding, for if every deviation of the ego called into play its punitive reaction the consequences for the self would be most severe.

PRIVACY AND ESTABLISHMENTS

It was earlier noted that rules or guarantees of privacy subserve horizontal and vertical order. Such rules are embodied in the physical structure of social establishments. Lindesmith and Strauss, for instance, have noted that proprieties concerning interpersonal contact and withdrawal are institutionalized in the architecture of buildings by means of a series of concentric circles. Specific regulations permit or forbid entry into the various parts of this structure, with a particular view to protecting the sacred "inner cir-

---

[19] Simmel, "The Secret and the Secret Society," pp. 335–36.
[20] *Ibid.*, pp. 360–61.

cle."[21] A more specific instance of the physical institutionalization of norms is found in the case of the bathroom, whose variation in size and design is limited by the requirement that body cleansing and elimination be performed privately.[22] This norm is reinforced by the architectural arrangements in which it is incorporated. The fact that the bathroom is only built for one literally guarantees that the performances which it accommodates will be solos. However, this normative-physical restriction admits of more complicated, secondary proprieties. Bossard and Boll write:

> The fact that the middle-class family rises almost together, and has few bathrooms, has resulted in a problem for it, which has been resolved by a very narrowly prescribed ritual for many of them—a bathroom ritual. They have developed set rules and regulations which define who goes first (according to who must leave the house first), how long one may stay in, what are the penalties for overtime, and under what conditions there may be a certain overlapping of personnel.[23]

[21] Alfred R. Lindesmith and Anselm L. Strauss, *Social Psychology* (New York: Henry Holt & Co., 1956), p. 435. However, in an interesting statement, McGinley announces the death of the very idea of the "inner circle": "It isn't considered sporting to object to being a goldfish. On the same public plan we build our dwelling places. Where, in many a modern house, can one hide? (And every being, cat, dog, parakeet, or man, wants a hermitage now and then.) We discard partitions and put up dividers. Utility rooms take the place of parlors. Picture windows look not onto seas or mountains or even shrubberies but into the picture windows of the neighbors. Hedges come down, gardens go unwalled; and we have nearly forgotten that the inventor of that door which first shut against intrusion was as much mankind's benefactor as he who discovered fire. I suspect that, in a majority of the bungalows sprouting across the country like toadstools after a rain, the only apartment left for a citadel is the bathroom" ("A Lost Privilege," pp. 55–56).

In contrast, Edward T. Hall observes: "Public and private buildings in Germany often have double doors for soundproofing, as do many hotel rooms. In addition, the door is taken very seriously by Germans. Those Germans who come to America feel that our doors are flimsy and light. The meanings of the open door and the closed door are quite different in the two countries. In offices, Americans keep doors open; Germans keep doors closed. In Germany, the closed door does not mean that the man behind it wants to be alone or undisturbed, or that he is doing something he doesn't want someone else to see. It's simply that Germans think that open doors are sloppy and disorderly. To close the door preserves the integrity of the room and provides a protective boundary between people. Otherwise, they get too involved with each other. One of my German subjects commented, 'If our family hadn't had doors, we would have had to change our way of life. Without doors we would have had many, many more fights. . . . When you can't talk, you retreat behind a door. . . . If there hadn't been doors, I would always have been within reach of my mother'" (*The Hidden Dimension* [Garden City: Doubleday & Co., 1966], p. 127. For a discussion of the norms regulating privacy among the English, French, Arab, and Japanese, see pp. 129–53).

[22] Alexander Kira, *The Bathroom* (New York: Bantam Books, Inc., 1967), pp. 178–84. The requirement of complete privacy for personal hygiene is only a recent phenomenon (see pp. 1–8).

[23] J. H. S. Bossard and E. S. Boll, *Ritual in Family Living* (Philadelphia: University of Pennsylvania Press, 1950), pp. 113–14 (cited by Kira, *The Bathroom*, pp. 177–78).

The very physical arrangement of social establishments thus opens and shuts off certain possibilities for interaction and withdrawal and creates a background of sometimes complex ritual in support of a foreground of necessary proprieties. Needless to say, the form taken by such ritual is always subject to modification by architectural means.

Charles Madge also urges the architect to take explicit account in his designs of the ambivalences of social life. Men, for example, are given to both withdrawal and self-display. This duality, notes Madge, requires an "intermediate area" in housing projects, such as a backyard or garden which separates the home or inner circle from the "common green."[24] But it is one thing to so divide our physical living space as to insure ourselves of interactional options; it is another to regulate the interactional patterns that the division of space imposes upon us. The latter task is most efficiently met by the door.

Doors. McGinley has referred to the door as a human event of significance equal to the discovery of fire.[25] The door must surely have had its origin among those whose sense of selfhood had already developed to the extent that they could feel the oppression of others and experience the need for protection against their presence. Continued use of the door very probably heightened that feeling of separateness to which it owed its creation. Doors, therefore, not only stimulate one's sense of self-integrity, they are required precisely because one has such a sense.

The very act of placing a barrier between oneself and others is self-defining, for withdrawal entails a separation from a role and, tacitly, from an identity imposed upon oneself by others via that role. Therefore, to waive the protection of the door is to forsake that sense of individuality which it guarantees. As Simmel points out, some measure of de-selfing is characteristic of everything social.[26]

I would like now to discuss various kinds of doors, including horizontal sliding doors (drawers) and transparent doors (windows). I shall also treat of walls, as relative impermeable interpersonal barriers, in contrast to doors, which are selectively permeable.

Doors provide boundaries between ourselves (i.e., our property, behavior, and appearance) and others. Violation of such boundaries imply a vio-

[24] Charles Madge, "Private and Public Places," *Human Relations,* 3 (1950), 187–99. F. S. Chapin (in "Some Housing Factors Related to Mental Hygiene," *Journal of Social Issues,* 7 [1951], 165) emphasizes that the need for relief from irritating public contact must be consciously and carefully met by the architect. On the other hand, Kira writes: "There are problems which cannot be resolved by architects and industrial designers alone, however; they also pose a challenge to the social scientists and to the medical and public health professions. This is an area in which the stakes are enormous and in which little or no direct work has been done." (*The Bathroom,* p. 192).

[25] See n. 21 above.

[26] Simmel, "The Secret and the Secret Society," p. 373.

lation of selfhood. Trespassing or housebreaking, for example, is unbearable for some not only because of the property damage that might result but also because they represent proof that the self has lost control of its audience; it can no longer regulate who may and who may not have access to the property and information that index its depths.[27] The victim of a Peeping Tom is thus outraged not only at having been observed naked but also for having lost control of the number and type of people who may possess information about her body. To prove this we note that no nakedness need be observed to make Peeping Tomism intolerable.

"Alone, the visual feeling of the window," writes Simmel, "goes almost exclusively from inward to outward: it is there for looking out, not for seeing in."[28] This interdiction insures that the inhabitants of an establishment may have the outside world at their visual disposal, and at the same time it provides for control over their accessibility to this world. But, whereas the shade or curtain may be employed to regulate accessibility between the private and public spheres of action, situational proprieties are depended upon for protection in public. One such norm is that of "civil inattention" which has been elaborated by Goffman.[29]

Unlike the window, "the door with an in and out announces an entire distinction of intention."[30] There must be very clear rules as to who may open what doors at what times and under what conditions. The front and back doors are normally the only doors that any member of a family may enter at any time and under any circumstances. A parent may enter a child's room at any time and may inspect and replenish drawers, but visiting friends may not. But the parent must learn that some private doors (drawers) may not be opened (although they may be to friends); if they are, new receptacles for ego-indexes will be found, for example, the area between mattress and spring. The child, however, must never inspect the contents of the drawers of his parents nor enter their room at night. Thus the right of intrusion is seen to be an essential element of authority, whose legitimacy is affected by the degree to which it is exercised. Correspondingly, authority is dependent upon immunity against intrusion. Cooley notes

---

[27] The law recognizes the psychological effect of such criminal acts and provides additional penal sanction for them. Wolfgang and Sellin report that "the chain store is more outraged by theft from a warehouse, where the offender has no business, than from the store where his presence is legal during store hours." Moreover, "the victim of a house burglary is usually very disturbed by the fact that the offender had the effrontery to enter the house illegally. . . . For these and similar reasons, breaking and entering as well as burglary carry more severe sanctions in the law" (Marvin E. Wolfgang and Thorsten Sellin, *The Measurement of Delinquency* [New York: John Wiley & Sons, 1964], pp. 219–20).

[28] Simmel, "Brücke und Tür," p. 5.

[29] Goffman, *Behavior in Public Places*, pp. 83–88.

[30] Simmel, "Brücke und Tür," p. 4.

that "authority, especially if it covers intrinsic personal weakness, has always a tendency to surround itself with forms and artificial mystery, whose object is to prevent familiar contact and so give the imagination a chance to idealize . . . self concealment serves, among other purposes, that of preserving a sort of ascendency over the unsophisticated."[31] In this same connection, Riesman writes:

> As compared with the one room house of the peasant or the "long house" of many primitive tribes, he (the inner directed child) grows up within walls that are physical symbols of the privacy of parental dominance. Walls separate parents from children, offices from home, and make it hard if not impossible for the child to criticize the parents' injunctions by an "undress" view of the parents or of other parents. What the parents say becomes more real in many cases than what they do. . . .[32]

Moreover, it is possible to map personal relations in terms of mutual expectations regarding intrusion. The invasion of various degrees of privacy may be a duty, a privilege, or a transgression, depending upon the nature of the interpersonal bond. And, clearly, expectations regarding such impositions may not be mutually agreed to.

Parental obligations concerning the care of a child override the child's rights to seclusion and place him in a position of social nakedness wherein he has no control over his appearance to others. However, to be subject to limitless intrusion is to exist in a state of dishonor, as implied in the rule against "coming too close." This point is made in Simmel's discussion of "discretion" as a quality which the person-in-private has a right to demand of another who is in a position to invade his seclusion.[33] Compromises between child and parent are therefore necessary and generally employed by the manipulation of the door. For example, the bedroom door may be kept half open while the child sleeps, its position symbolic of the parents' respect

[31] Charles Horton Cooley, *Human Nature and the Social Order* (New York: Schocken Books, Inc., 1964), p. 351.

[32] David Riesman, *The Lonely Crowd* (Garden City, N.Y.: Doubleday & Co., 1953), p. 61. Another characteriologist, William H. Whyte, suggests that "doors inside houses . . . marked the birth of the middle class" (*The Organization Man* [Garden City, N.Y.: Doubleday & Co., 1956], p. 389).

[33] Simmel, "The Secret and the Secret Society," pp. 320–24. Similarly, Erving Goffman writes, "There is an inescapable opposition between showing a desire to include an individual and showing respect for his privacy. As an implication of this dilemma, we must see that social intercourse involves a constant dialectic between presentational rituals and avoidance rituals. A peculiar tension must be maintained, for these opposing requirements of conduct must somehow be held apart from one another and yet realized together in the same interaction; the gestures which carry an actor to a recipient must also signify that things will not be carried too far" ("The Nature of Deference and Demeanor," *American Anthropologist*, 58 [June, 1956], 488).

for the youngster's selfhood. Furthermore, a general temporal pattern might emerge if a large number of cases were examined. During infancy the door to self is generally fully open;[34] it closes perhaps halfway as a recognition of self development during childhood, it shuts but is left ajar at prepuberty, and closes entirely—and perhaps even locks—at the pubertal and adolescent stages when meditation, grooming, and body examination become imperative. Parents at this time are often fully denied the spectatorship to which they may feel entitled and are kept at a distance by means of the privacy that a locked door insures.

There are also certain situations wherein husband and wife must remain separate from one another. A spouse, for example, must generally knock before entering a bathroom if the other is occupying it. This is a token of deference not to nudity but to the right of the other party to determine the way he or she wishes to present the self to the other. This rule insures that the self and its appearance will remain a controllable factor, independent of the whims of others, and it contributes to self-consciousness as well. This is seen most clearly in total institutions like the armed forces where open rows of toilets are used first with some measure of mortification and later with a complete absence of consciousness of self. In such doorless worlds we find a blurring of the distinction between "front and back regions," between those quarters where the self is put on and taken off and those in which it is presented.[35] In conventional society those who confuse these two areas are charged with vulgarity.

In contrast to the door, the wall symbolizes "separation" rather than "separateness" and denies the possibility of the encounter and withdrawal

---

[34] The absence of ability among infants and children to regulate the appearance and disappearance of their audience does not mean that privacy or separateness is not an important feature of their development; the privacy need is simply expressed differently. The infant, for example, can sometimes remove himself from the field of stimulation by going to sleep or wriggling away from the adult who holds him. This is probably why pathology resulting from overcontact is less likely than that due to undercontact, for the former is far more easily regulated by the infant than the latter. At a later stage of development, the infant learns that he can hold back and let go in reference not only to sphincters but to facial expressions and general dispositions as well. He comes to view himself as a causal agent as he inherits the power of voluntary reserve. When the child is locomoting he first confronts privacy imposed against him by others and begins to define himself in terms of where he may and may not go. On the other hand, his ambulatory ability gives him enormous control over his audience, a power in which he delights by "hiding." Espionage is practiced as well and suspected in others—whereby the condition of shame begins to acquire meaning for the child. These incomplete comments suffice to illustrate the point that the privacy impulse is not at all inactive in infancy and childhood. They further suggest that each stage of development has its own mode of privacy, which may be defined in terms of the ego's relationship to those from whom privacy is sought and the manner in which withdrawal is accomplished.

[35] Goffman, *The Presentation of Self in Everyday Life*, pp. 66–86.

of social exchange. It strips away that element of freedom which is so clearly embodied in the door. "It is essential," notes Simmel, "that a person be able to set boundaries for himself, but freely, so that he can raise the boundaries again and remove himself from them."[36] In privacy, continues Simmel, "A piece of space is bound with himself and he is separated from the entire world."[37] But in enforced isolation man is bound *to* space. While the door separates outside from inside, the wall annihilates the outside. The door closes out; the wall encloses. Yet doors are converted into walls routinely, as is seen in the popular practice of "sending a child to his room" for misdeeds and the like. In this sense, many homes contain private dungeons or, rather, provisions for transforming the child's room into a cell—which forces upon us the distinction between formal and informal imprisonment.

Privacy is not dependent upon the availability of lockable doors. Goffman, for example, discusses "free places" in the institution where inmates may, free of surveillance, "be one's own man . . . in marked contrast to the sense of uneasiness prevailing on some wards."[38] In addition there is "personal territory" established by each inmate: for one a particular corner; for another a place near a window, etc. "In some wards, a few patients would carry their blankets around with them during the day and, in an act thought to be highly regressive, each would curl up on the floor with his blanket completely covering him; within the covered space each had some margin of control."[39] Thus do men withdraw from others to be at one with themselves and to create a world over which they reign with more complete authority, recalling Simmel's observation that "the person who erects a refuge demonstrates, like the first pathfinder, the typically human hegemony over nature, as he cuts a particle of space from continuity and eternity."[40]

In summary, islands of privacy exist in all establishments and throughout even the most intimate household. These islands are protected by an intricate set of rules. When these rules are violated secret places are sought after, discovered, and employed as facilities for secret action. These places and their permeability constitute one type of map, as it were, of interpersonal relationships and reveal the nature of the selves participating in them.

[36] Simmel, "Brücke und Tür," p. 4.

[37] *Ibid.*, p. 3.

[38] Erving Goffman, "The Underlife of a Public Institution," in *Asylums* (Garden City, N.Y.: Doubleday & Co., 1961), p. 231.

[39] *Ibid.*, p. 246. For more on norms regulating territorial conduct in face-to-face encounters, see Nancy Felipe and Robert Sommer, "Invasions of Personal Space," *Social Problems*, 14 (May, 1966), 206–14; and Robert Sommer, "Sociofugal Space," *American Journal of Sociology*, 72 (May, 1967), 654–60.

[40] Simmel, "Brücke und Tür," p. 3.

Privacy, property and self. Implied in any reference to a private place is its contents, personal property. One perhaps more often than not withdraws into privacy in order to observe and manipulate his property in some way, property which includes, of course, body and non-body objects.

There are two types of objects: those which may be observed by the public (and which may be termed personal objects) and those which are not available to public view (private property). Private property, as we are using the term, may be further delineated in terms of those intimate others who may have access to it in terms of visibility or use. Some private objectifications of self may be observed by family members, but some may be observed by *no one except the self*. There is no doubt that these latter objects have a very special meaning for identity; some of these are sacred and must not be contaminated by exposing them to observation by others; some are profane, and exposure will produce shame, but both are special and represent an essential aspect of self and, from the possessor's point of view, must not be tampered with.

It is because persons invest so much of their selves in private and personal things that total institutions require separation of self and material objects. When individualism must be minimized private ownership is always a vice worthy of constant surveillance. In such situations the acquisition and storage of personal things persist in the form of the "stash," which might be anything from a long sock to the cuff of one's pants.[41]

It follows that those who have direct or indirect access to the belongings of others or to articles which have been employed by them in private ways enjoy a certain amount of power which, if judiciously employed, may serve their interests well. Hughes observes:

> It is by the garbage that the janitor judges, and, as it were, gets power over the tenants who high-hat him. Janitors know about hidden love affairs by bits of torn-up letter paper; of impending financial disaster or of financial four-flushing by the presence of many unopened letters in the waste. Or they may stall off demands for immediate service by an unreasonable woman of whom they know from the garbage that she, as the janitors put it, "has the rag on." The garbage gives the janitor the makings of a kind of magical power over that pretentious villain, the tenant. I say a kind of magical power, for there appears to be no thought of betraying any individual and thus turning his knowledge into overt power.[42]

But, certainly, power need not be exercised to be effective. The mere knowledge that another "knows" invokes in the treatment of that other a certain amount of humility and deference.

---

[41] Goffman, *Asylums*, pp. 248–54.

[42] Everett C. Hughes, *Men and Their Work* (Glencoe, Ill.: Free Press, 1958), p. 51.

DEPRIVATIZATION

We have attempted to show that the possibility of withdrawal into well-equipped worlds which are inaccessible to others is that which makes intense group affiliations bearable. But we have also seen that men are not always successful in protecting their invisibility. Accidental leakages of information as well as the diverse modes of espionage threaten the information control that privacy is intended to maintain. But information control also consists of purposeful information leakage and even of the renunciation of secrecy. Just as men demand respite from public encounter they need periodically to escape themselves, for a privacy which lacks frequent remissions is maddening. The over-privatized man is he who is relieved of public demand only to become a burden to himself: He becomes his own audience to performances which are bound for tedium. Self-entertainment is thus a most exhausting business, requiring the simultaneous performance of two roles: actor and spectator. Both tire quickly of one another. When privacy thereby exhausts itself new and public audiences (and audience-ships) are sought.

Moreover, we are led to relinquish our private information and activities by the expediencies and reciprocities routinely called for in daily life. We all know, for example, that in order to employ others as resources it is necessary to reveal to them something of ourselves, at least that part of ourselves which for some reason needs reinforcement. When this occurs (providing support is forthcoming), two things happen. First, we achieve some degree of gratification; second, and most important, our alter (or resource) reveals to us information which was heretofore withheld, for self-revelation is imbued with reciprocal power: It calls out in others something similar to that which we give of ourselves. There is both mutual revelation and mutual gratification. It is easy to see that when stress or need is prolonged this process may become institutionalized: Intimacy is then no longer an alternative; it is enforced, and private activity becomes clandestine and punishable. The deprivatization process approaches completion when we are not only penalized for our withdrawals but feel guilty about them. A housewife who had probably undergone the deprivatization process confided to Whyte: "I've promised myself to make it up to them. I was feeling bad that day and just plain didn't make the effort to ask them in for coffee. I don't blame them, really, for reacting the way they did. I'll make it up to them somehow."[43]

But loss of privacy among conventional folk is free of many of the pains of social nakedness which are suffered by inmates and by others undergoing total surveillance. The civilian voluntarily subjects himself to publicity and is relatively free of the contamination of unwanted contacts. His

---

[43] Whyte, *The Organization Man*, p. 390.

unmaskings are selective and subject to careful forethought. The intruder is chosen rather than suffered; indeed, his resourcefulness depends upon his ability to "know" his client-neighbor. Therefore, in civil life, we find valid rationalization for our self-revelations. The demand that we "be sociable" is too compelling and too rewarding to be ignored by any of us.

But a substantial self-sacrifice is made by those who actually believe themselves to be what they present to public view. An awareness of the masquerades and deceptions that are part of good role performance is necessary to recall ourselves to our *own* selfhood and to our opposition to that of others. We must indeed deceive others to be true to ourselves. In this particular sense privacy prevents the ego from identifying itself too closely with or losing itself in (public) roles. Daily life is therefore sparked by a constant tension between sincerity and guile, between self-release and self-containment, between the impulse to embrace that which is public and the drive to escape the discomfort of group demands. Accordingly, our identities are maintained by our ability to hold back as well as to affiliate. Thus Goffman writes:

> When we closely observe what goes on in a social role, a spate of sociable inter-action, a social establishment—or in any other unit of social organization—embracement of the unit is not all that we see. We always find the individual employing methods to keep some distance, some elbow room, between himself and that with which others assume he should be identified.
>
> Our sense of being a person can come from being drawn into a wider social unit; our sense of selfhood can arise through the little ways in which we resist the pull. Our status is backed by the solid buildings of the world, while our sense of personal identity often resides in the cracks.[44]

For Goffman, privacy is one of "the little ways in which we resist the pull" of group commitments and reinforce our selfhood.

[44] Goffman, *Asylums,* pp. 319–20.

3
culture
patterns

TERRANCE L. STOCKER, LINDA W. DUTCHER,
STEPHEN M. HARGROVE, and EDWIN A. COOK

Social Analysis of Graffiti[1]

Graffiti, as an aspect of culture, can be used as an unobtrusive measure to reveal patterns of customs and attitudes of a society. Observing graffiti will reveal changes in customs and attitudes. Through studying graffiti, Lindsay was able to reconstruct much about life in ancient Pompeii.[2] To date, many projects have used the thematic content of graffiti to posit certain motivational hypotheses about the individuals and the societal attitudes that produced it, but few studies have approached graffiti by problem testing. There have been no diachronic studies devoted to problem testing. This article is a midway report of a longitudinal study testing three problems that were formulated in earlier studies.

LITERATURE ON SOCIAL ATTITUDES

Lomas and Weltman conducted in 1966 a cross-sectional study of graffiti in the Los Angeles metropolitan area.[3] Correlating the type of graffiti, for instance, outdoors as opposed to indoors, and the thematic content with the class and ethnic composition of the community in which the graffiti were written, they concluded that graffiti "reflect shared attitudes and values as well as ethnocentric variations on main cultural themes."[4] Sechrest and Flores in 1969 chose graffiti as an unobstrusive measure of attitudes toward homosexuality in the United States and the Philippines.[5] Public restroom graffiti with homosexual content were almost non-existent in the Philippines, which coincides with the relatively tolerant attitudes toward homo-

Reprinted from the *Journal of American Folklore,* 85, 338 (1972), 356–66, by permission of the American Folklore Society.

[1] Grateful acknowledgment is made to Margaret Horton, Bernard Lazerwitz, and Bruce MacLachlan for their aid in directing this research. We also thank Milton Altschuler and Michael Robbins for commenting on this paper.

[2] J. Lindsay, *The Writing on the Wall* (London, 1960).

[3] H. Lomas and G. Weltman, "What the Walls Say Today: A Study of Contemporary Graffiti," paper presented at the meeting of the American Psychiatric Association, Atlantic City, New Jersey (1966).

[4] *Ibid.,* p. 5.

[5] L. Sechrest and L. Flores, "Homosexuality in the Philippines and the United States: The Handwriting on the Wall," *The Journal of Social Psychology,* 79 (1969) 3–12.

sexuality found there. In the United States, where homosexuality is more socially condemned, there was a high proportion of homosexual graffiti. Most of Sechrest and Flores' American sampling took place on the University of Chicago campus. In 1971 Sechrest and Olson reported a study of graffiti involving trade schools, junior colleges, four-year colleges, and professional schools. In the latter two types of schools, there was a relatively greater incidence of Semite-Gentile graffiti, and in the former there was a higher proportion of Negro-White racial inscriptions. This statistic correlated with the socioeconomic background and education of the individuals attending the schools.[6]

The less systematic studies of Reisner[7] and Read[8] have suggested that graffiti can be used to reveal changes in customs. Yet, Rudin and Harless contend that graffiti cannot be used as a measure of social and political issues.[9] They collected graffiti at a Texas college before the 1968 national elections. They found a preponderance of racial items, but very few graffiti relating to the national election. Collins and Batzle placed blackboards and chalk in men's washrooms on a college campus to increase the number of responses; they concluded the graffiti collected did not reflect important social issues.[10]

LITERATURE ON GRAFFITI WITH
HOMOSEXUAL CONTENT

Kinsey's 1953 data indicated 75 percent of graffiti was homosexual in content.[11] He hypothesized that many graffiti concerned with male genitalia and male function were produced by males who were not conscious of homosexual reactions and who may never have had homosexual experiences. Males who wrote and read these graffiti presumably expressed unsatisfied homosexual desires.[12] Kinsey does not list a source for his data. Lomas and Weltman tentatively suggest that all sexually arousing graffiti in men's restrooms are homosexual since they are not intended for a mixed audience.[13] Sechrest and Olson found that trade schools and junior colleges

[6] L. Sechrest and K. Olson, "Graffiti in Four Types of Institutions of Higher Education," *The Journal of Sex Research,* 7 (1971), 62–71.

[7] R. Reisner, *Graffiti* (New York, 1967).

[8] A. W. Read, *Lexical Evidence from Folk Epigraphy in Western North America: A Glossarial Study of the Low Element in the English Language* (Paris, 1935).

[9] L. Rudin and M. Harless, "Graffiti and Building Use: The 1968 Election," *Psychological Reports,* 27 (1970), 517–18.

[10] T. Collins and P. Batzle, "Method of Increasing Graffito Responses," *Perceptual and Motor Skills,* 31 (1970), 733–34.

[11] A. Kinsey, W. Pomeroy, C. Martin, and P. Gebhard, *Sexual Behavior in the Human Female* (Philadelphia, 1953).

[12] *Ibid.,* pp. 674–75.

[13] Lomas and Weltman, "What the Walls Say Today," 9.

had the highest frequency of heterosexual inscriptions. The trade schools had the lowest level of homosexual graffiti, while the other three types of schools had a high and approximately equal frequency of homosexual graffiti. Sechrest and Olson considered these differences to reflect the "preoccupation and interest of the groups involved."[14] They maintain, following Kinsey, that lower socioeconomic groups are more likely to have had more and earlier heterosexual experience than the higher socioeconomic groups, while the converse is true for homosexual experience. However, Sechrest and Flores feel that most homosexual inscriptions are written by "normal" males, and it is the societal conflict over homosexual behavior that causes it to be used as an insult device.[15]

LITERATURE ON SEX DIFFERENCES OF GRAFFITI

According to Kinsey, women are not aroused by the same stimuli that arouse men; therefore, women produce less graffiti and that which they do produce are not of a sexual content.[16] Dundes, using a Freudian framework, feels the difference in the amount of latrinalia in men's and women's washrooms can be explained by the lack of pregnancy envy in women.[17] Dundes defines latrinalia as that subset of washroom graffiti which is traditional. He breaks traditional graffiti down into five types, only one of which will be considered here—that concerning defecation. At least two studies have noted the greater incidence of smoking in female restrooms than in male restrooms. Landy and Steele suggest that smoking is the woman's substitute for the male's graffiti, which they consider a form of phallic expression.[18] Rudin and Harless note that women's graffiti occurs in quantity only in restrooms that have no smoking lounges, and suggest that equating men's and women's restrooms for function might reveal that no significant sex difference in graffiti production exists. Horton reports a great many documented studies which reveal that the difference between male and female behavior is a result of different childhood socialization practices.[19] Although she makes no reference to graffiti, we feel that differences in socialization processes between sexes can best account for the differences in amount and kind between men's and women's graffiti. Furthermore she re-

[14] Sechrest and Olson, "Graffiti in Four Types of Institutions of Higher Education," 69.

[15] Sechrest and Flores, "Homosexuality in the Philippines and the United States," 9.

[16] Kinsey, et al., *Sexual Behavior in the Human Female,* p. 12.

[17] A. Dundes, "Here I Sit—A Study of American Latrinalia," *Kroeber Anthropological Society Papers,* 34 (1966), 91–105.

[18] E. Landy and J. Steele, "Graffiti as a Function of Building Utilization," "*Perceptual and Motor Skills,* 25 (1967) 711–12.

[19] M. Horton, "The Development and Implications of Sex-Role Stereotypes," presented to St. Louis University Psychology Department Colloquium (January 13, 1971).

ports that aggressive behavior (like graffiti) "is probably the most reliable and durable dimension of sex-typed behavior."[20] Sixteen of twenty observational and experimental studies concluded boys to be more aggressive than girls. Four showed no differences, but those four dealt with verbal behavior.

PROBLEMS

From this literature, three problems were formulated to be tested: (1) graffiti are an accurate indicator of the social attitudes of a community, and their thematic content will discriminate similar communities with different sociopolitical ideation; (2) most homosexual graffiti are a result of societal condemnation of homosexual behavior, which permits this behavior to be used as an insulting device; and, with Gay Liberation as a liberalizing influence, homosexual graffiti will decrease; and (3) the difference between men's and women's graffiti is due to childhood socialization; and, if there is a change in amount and kind of women's and men's graffiti, then there has been a change in some aspect of women's socialization patterns.

DATA ON SCHOOLS

These problems were tested by comparing graffiti from three universities over a two-year period. The universities were chosen on the assumption that they ranged from the more liberal to the more conservative in sociopolitical attitudes. Southern Illinois University, Carbondale, was assumed to be the most liberal; Western Kentucky University, Bowling Green, the most conservative; and the University of Missouri, Columbia, somewhere between the two, but closer to Southern Illinois University. Hereafter, these will be referred to as SIU, WKU, and MU, respectively. The respective enrollment of each school is 23,000, 10,000, and 20,000. To validate the supposition of liberality at each school an unobtrusive measure as outlined by Webb and colleagues was employed.[21] News reports were compared of students' reactions at each school to the Kent State University incident and the United States military incursion into Cambodia in the spring of 1970. These reactions were taken from the files of each town's major newspaper. Data were taken from the front page of issues from May 1 to May 17.

In general, crowds at demonstrations were upward of 3,500 at SIU. Riots resulted in one building being burned and considerable property damage both on and off campus, which was estimated at $100,000. There were four hundred arrests, and a state of civil emergency was declared. The National

---

[20] Ibid., p. 18.

[21] E. Webb, D. Campbell, R. Schwartz, and L. Sechrest, *Unobtrusive Measures: A Survey of Nonreactive Research in Social Sciences* (Chicago, 1966).

Guard was called onto campus twice, and the university was shut down twenty-four days before the end of the term. At MU, crowds were upward of 2,000. Minor incidents of property destruction occurred. Local law enforcement officers were on campus for one afternoon. There were thirty-five arrests, and a brief state of emergency was declared. At WKU there were crowds of around 500, but demonstrations were peaceful.

Another factor that must be considered in the SIU riots is the presence of an AID-funded Vietnamese Center on the Carbondale campus. The presence of this center was presumably a point of crystallization for the riots.

COLLECTING OF GRAFFITI

Graffiti collecting was done during the last two weeks of December through the first two weeks of January to control for national political variables. In 1970 graffiti were collected from all the stalls in men's rooms in classroom buildings at all three universities. Women's graffiti were not collected in 1970. In 1971 the men's stalls were randomized, and data were gathered from 25 percent of all stalls on the SIU and WKU campuses. At MU 25 percent of the stalls in each building were sampled, producing a stratified sample. The difference in sampling was due to a misunderstanding between the authors. Graffiti from all women's stalls were collected in 1971.

Each graffito was recorded verbatim and drawings duplicated. The only aspect of concern was the thematic content. Other factors, such as size of inscription, mode of inscription, and so on, were not recorded. In categorizing the graffiti, the major aspect of concern was the explicit intent of the writer. Thus, "All music majors are queer" was considered nonsexual hostile, since the homosexual aspect was a mechanism to insult music majors. We realize that some graffiti may have a latent meaning of which we were not aware, for instance, "The balloons are coming"; this is possibly a remark concerning inflation. Each inscription was recorded under a single category, except those which were responding to another graffito. For example, "Fuck you" was a reply to "Kennedy in '72," and in this case "Fuck you" was categorized as a political graffito since its existence was dependent upon a political graffito. At the same time it was separately categorized as response graffito.

The graffiti were coded and tabulated in a method as similar as possible to that of Kinsey's and Sechrest and Flores' material. That is, they were categorized according to percentages in major categories of homosexual, heterosexual, and nonsexual. Each of these categories was further subdivided (see tables and appendix). However, certain modifications were made to accommodate our data. For example, racist remarks—"All whites must die now"—would normally have been classified as nonsexual hostile (a classification that includes such graffiti as "Hippies suck Aggies wife's tits"), but racist graffiti were so frequent at SIU in 1970 that a separate racist category was formed and further subdivided (Table 1), though in 1971 only eight racist inscriptions were found at all three universities.

In 1971, we felt that greater insights into the community attitudes could be gained by breaking down the statement category into "statements," "social statements," and "drug statements." "Stanford 14–Missouri 10" would be a statement; a social statement would be "Beautiful people! Hear my song, think what I'm speakin' of, anyone can let their hair grow long, but few take the time to love"; and a drug statement would be "STP will get you free."

Our "trite" category is what Dundes terms "traditional." Trite is repetitious or inherited rather than having been taught in some systematic manner. An example of graffiti in this category would be the following:

> "Those who write on shithouse walls
> Roll their shit in little balls
> Those who read those words of wit
> Eat those little balls of shit."

A "love" statement category was added for the women's graffiti. It includes remarks like "Bob loves Alice"; and, to add comparability of sex differences, this category was added to the male data in 1971.

Table 1   MALE GRAFFITI

	SIU		MU		WKU		Total	
	1970	1971	1970	1971	1970	1971	1970	1971
Number of Graffiti	(306)	(181)	(710)	(474)	(172)	(115)	(1188)	(770)
Heterosexual	9.8%	11.7%	8.1%	9.0%	7.5%	9.6%	8.7%	9.7%
1. Invitations and Requests	2.0	1.1	.4	.2	1.2	1.7	.9	.6
2. Accusations of Others' Behavior	1.0	.6	2.8	2.3	2.3	.9	2.3	1.7
3. Drawings of Female Genitalia	2.3	1.7	.4	1.9	0	.9	.8	1.7
4. Humor	1.3	1.7	2.3	2.5	0	0	1.7	1.9
5. Drawings of Intercourse	0	0	.8	.4	0	0	.5	.3
6. Statement or Question	3.3	6.6	1.4	1.1	4.1	5.2	2.3	3.0
7. Love Statement		0		.6		.9		.5
Homosexual	14.3%	13.9%	13.3%	12.9%	32.5%	20.0%	16.1%	14.0%
1. Invitations and Requests	7.5	1.7	4.9	4.9	10.5	12.2	6.1	5.1

Table 1 (Continued)

Number of Graffiti	SIU 1970 (306)	SIU 1971 (181)	MU 1970 (710)	MU 1971 (474)	WKU 1970 (172)	WKU 1971 (115)	Total 1970 (1188)	Total 1971 (770)
2. Accusations	0	0	1.5	.2	9.3	0	2.3	.1
3. Drawings of Male Genitalia	2.0	3.3	.1	2.7	.6	4.3	.7	3.1
4. Hostile Comments	2.3	.6	1.3	0	1.7	0	1.6	.1
5. Humor	.3	.6	2.0	.2	0	0	1.3	.3
6. Masturbation	1.0	0	1.7	1.5	.6	3.5	1.3	1.4
7. Statement or Question	1.3	7.7	1.8	3.4	9.9	0	2.9	3.9
Nonsexual	53.9%	55.3%	65.3%	69.9%	47.7%	61.0%	59.7%	65.5%
1. Other Humor	5.6	8.3	15.2	11.8	5.2	9.6	11.7	10.6
2. Cosmic and Religious	2.6	1.7	4.9	3.0	.6	0	3.7	2.2
3. Philosophical	2.6	3.9	1.5	.6	0	0	1.6	1.3
4. Political	15.7	6.6	10.8	10.3	8.1	3.5	11.7	8.4
5. Social Satire	6.5	0	2.1	.4	1.7	0	3.3	.3
6. Hostile	2.3	11.0	5.1	7.4	0	13.0	3.6	9.1
7. Word	2.6	3.9	1.8	10.1	5.2	7.0	2.4	8.2
8. Statement	10.1	9.4	18.0	10.3	20.9	15.7	16.4	11.4
9. Social Statement		2.2		8.0		2.2		5.4
10. Drug Statement		4.4		1.9		.9		2.3
11. Play-on-Words	2.6	1.7	3.4	1.5	1.2	3.5	2.9	1.8
12. Drawing	3.3	2.2	2.3	4.6	4.7	7.8	2.9	4.5
Racist	10.4%	1.7%	1.1%	1.0%	1.2%	0%	3.6%	1.0%
1. Racist Elimination	3.3	0	0	0	0	0	1.0	0
2. Racist Hostile	4.6	1.7	.3	.8	1.2	0	1.5	.9
3. Racist Derogatory	2.0	0	.3	.2	0	0	.7	.1
4. Racist Sexual	.7	0	.6	0	0	0	.5	0
Undecided Sex	.7	3.9	.8	.2	0	2.6	.7	1.4
Humor of elimination	2.6	8.8	7.7	4.2	2.3	3.5	5.6	5.2
Trite	2.9	0	1.3	.4	5.2	.9	2.3	.4
Fuck	.7	2.2	1.1	.4	1.7	.9	1.1	.9
Fuck you	2.3	2.8	.1	1.5	1.7	.9	1.0	1.7
Responses	20.8	26.5	27.5	27.2	11.1	27.0	23.3	26.8

Table 2 FEMALE GRAFFITI

Number of Graffiti	SIU 1970	SIU 1971 (243)	MU 1970	MU 1971 (18)	WKU 1970	WKU 1971 (0)
Heterosexual		26.9%		0%		0%
1. Invitations and Requests		.4		0		0
2. Accusations of Others' Behavior		1.2		0		0
3. Drawings of Male Genitalia		1.6		0		0

Table 2   (Continued)

Number of Graffiti	SIU 1970	SIU 1971 (243)	MU 1970	MU 1971 (18)	WKU 1970	WKU 1971 (0)
4. Humor		.8		0		0
5. Drawings of Intercourse		0		0		0
6. Statement or Question		2.9		0		0
7. Love Statement		19.3		0		0
Homosexual		10.7%		5.6%		0%
1. Invitations and Requests		4.9		5.6		0
2. Accusations		0		0		0
3. Drawings of Female Genitalia		.8		0		0
4. Hostile Comments		.4		0		0
5. Humor		.4		0		0
6. Musturbation		0		0		0
7. Statement or Question		4.9		0		0
Nonsexual		50.3%		83.4%		0%
1. Other Humor		2.1		0		0
2. Cosmic and Religious		4.5		0		0
3. Philosophical		2.9		16.7		0
4. Political		4.5		0		0
5. Social Satire		0		0		0
6. Hostile		.4		0		0
7. Word		9.5		16.7		0
8. Statement		9.1		0		0
9. Social Statement		9.9		22.2		0
10. Drug Statement		0		0		0
11. Play-on-Words		.4		0		0
12. Drawing		7.0		16.7		0
13. Scribbling		0		11.1		0
Racist		3.7%		5.6%		0%
1. Racist Elimination		0		0		0
2. Racist Hostile		2.9		5.6		0
3. Racist Derogatory		.8		0		0
4. Racist Sexual		0		0		0
Undecided sex		2.1%		0%		0%
Humor of elimination		.4		0		0
Trite		0		5.6		0
Fuck		4.1		0		0
Fuck you		0		0		0
Responses		19.3		22.2		0

DISCUSSION

With regard to the first problem, we felt that in a liberal community accusations of homosexuality, such as "Billy Jones is a queer," would have a low frequency since it would have very little impact. A high amount was expected in a conservative community. These suppositions were correct, with no such accusations at SIU, 9.3 percent at WKU, and 1.5 percent at MU. Similar reasoning was applied to the political category, for instance, "Assassinate Spiro Agnew and become a national hero"; the social satire category, for instance, "Fuck Censorship"; and the philosophical category, as in "The essence of love is unselfishness." A liberal school was expected to have the highest percentage in each category. Again, SIU had the highest percentage in each category, and WKU the lowest in the 1970 results.

The category most difficult to interpret was the racist, for instance, "Black plus white equals zero." SIU, rated the most liberal campus, had the highest amount of racist graffiti in 1970. Four factors are proposed to account for this. SIU is thirty miles north of Cairo, Illinois, which is afflicted with heavy racial strife. SIU has the highest enrollment of blacks of the three schools, it has a Black Studies Center, and in the fall of 1970 there were frequent encounters between blacks and law enforcement agencies in Carbondale. Sechrest and Olson also found the greatest proportion of Negro-White racial graffiti in the trade schools that also had a greater proportion of Negro students compared to the other four schools—a situation analogous to the population of SIU as compared to MU and WKU.

Excluding the racial factor, MU had the highest percentage of hostile statements reflecting a high proportion of interest groups. Besides the common "aggie–non-aggie" syndrome and "long hair vs. non–long hair" rivalries, MU has a school of religion and a law school, which the other two universities do not have. Yet, this problem is not easily assessed by merely listing the number of interest groups; the intensity of their rivalry is obviously more important as was manifest by the racial category. At MU there is a relatively high proportion of "aggies" enrolled, which intensifies the rivalry with "non-aggies." Also, interest group rivalries probably enter into the different percentages of the response category, for instance, "I feel like homemade shit," is responded to with, "Oh, you must be an Aggie." Rivalries contribute to the other humor category, "How do you tell an Aggie from an engineer? Answer: One has shit on his boots; the other has shit in his head."

The 1971 results present a somewhat more complex picture. Judging from the decrease in homosexual accusations, one would be inclined to say that liberalness is increasing at MU and WKU. However, the amount of social satire and philosophical and political graffiti has dropped at all three schools, and MU has a greater percentage of political and social satire than SIU. Racist graffiti have dropped at SIU, which is concomitant with a decline in racial confrontations in both Cairo and Carbondale as reported in local newspapers. In the two new categories, which were incorporated in 1971, MU had a greater percentage of social statement than SIU, and SIU had a greater percentage of drug statement than MU. The shifting percentages between SIU and MU would indicate that the social attitudes of the two schools are converging with reference to liberality. It should also be kept in mind that two new freshman classes have enrolled since the Kent State and Cambodia incidents. Any interpretation of the 1971 results must be viewed with the fact in mind that nonsexual hostile rose at all three schools, with very substantial rises at SIU and WKU. This last point is difficult to assess.

The frustration-aggression hypothesis, as outlined by Dollard and his colleagues, suggests that an increase in aggressive responses derives from an increase in frustrating conditions.[22] When attack cannot be directed against the frustrating agent, aggression may be transferred to another, more accessible, target. As Feshbach has pointed out, the displacement hypothesis is limited by its failure to specify the dimensions along which the frustrator and ultimate target must resemble each other.[23] It is possible that recent cutbacks in government spending for education have had a direct and frustrating impact on student welfare, thus contributing to outgroup hostility. The continuation of the present longitudinal study will shed light on this problem.

The objection may be raised here that random sampling and differences in sampling techniques may have skewed our results, since different buildings on any given campus may produce different types of graffiti. Landy and Steele, at the University of Oklahoma, found that building utilization did affect the type of graffiti written therein. However, we suspect that the difference in our sampling of male graffiti has skewed our results. For example, of the twelve stalls in the library at SIU, graffiti were collected from only two. The graffiti in the library tend to be liberal. On the other hand, three out of seven stalls were sampled in the agriculture building where the graffiti tend to be conservative. Unfortunately, the structure of the study to date as well as time constraints for each of us did not permit a reevaluation of this problem. In 1973, stratified sampling will be employed at all three schools to test the variability of graffiti on each campus.

When Rudin and Harless' study is considered in light of these data, one can see that two factors operated to produce their results. The first was the sociopolitical attitude of the community. If their Texas school was similar to WKU, one might reasonably expect a small amount of political graffiti. Second is the need for a time lag. Our results show a great fluctuation in political graffiti. The impact of any government administration seems to follow a curvilinear function throughout the term of office. Thus, the graffito "This is a Spiro Agnew Memorial Shithouse" was more often found two years after the administration took office than in either election year. The

[22] J. Dollard, L. Doob, N. Miller, O. Mowrer, and R. Sears, *Frustration and Aggression* (New Haven, 1939).

[23] S. Feshbach, "Aggression," in *Carmichael's Manual of Child Psychology*, ed. P. Mussen (New York, 1970).

longitudinal study is slowly bearing out a curvilinear function explanation for the fluctuation of political graffiti. Rudin and Harless' study also tends to confirm this stance. Botkin has pointed out a similar trend for jokes satirical of cars, for instance, "The Edsel of Government Policy."[24]

Thus, this study supports the idea that graffiti are an accurate indicator of the social attitude of a community.

In considering graffiti of homosexual content in a diachronic framework, there is a considerable drop from Kinsey, with 75 percent in 1953 (publishing date), to Sechrest and Flores with 42 percent in 1966 (published in 1969), Sechrest and Olson with 36 percent at the four-year colleges in 1971 (publishing date), and the present study with an overall total of 16 percent in 1970 and still less in 1971. We feel, as Sechrest and Flores maintained, that homosexual graffiti are produced by societal conflict.

The largest discrepancy between the Sechrest and Flores' study and ours is the invitations-and-requests category. This type of solicitation is perhaps no longer necessary due to the impact of Gay Liberation, but there is little evidence to prove that such inscriptions are a valid type of solicitation. Members of Gay Liberation interviewed at MU and SIU maintain that such graffiti are not a means of actual solicitation. Also, our data would indicate that they are not actual solicitation devices, since one often finds "Blow job here at nine on May 5" and the reply, often in apparently the same handwriting, "I was here, where were you"; they are often carried out further to "I couldn't make it; I'll see you on May 10," and so on. Thus, we maintain that the decrease through time of homosexual graffiti is a result of more liberal attitudes toward homosexual behavior.

However, this alone does not actually negate the hypothesis that those who write this type of graffiti are not latently homosexual, since one would expect that, with a liberalizing of attitudes toward homosexuals, there would also be a concomitant adjustment of socialization practices by parents. That is, whatever factors may have been producing latent homosexuality may also have been altered. However, it appears from the literature that Gay Liberation has been responsible for overturning attitudes toward homosexuals, and it was not changes in attitudes toward homosexuals that produced Gay Liberation.[25] This is not to say that there was no precedent for Gay Liberation. Certainly the Matachine Society and the influence of the Wolfenden Report in liberalizing the laws concerning homosexuality in England could be logically assumed to have influenced the development of Gay Liberation.[26] However, there does not appear to have been any fa-

[24] B. Botkin, "Automobile Humor: From the Horseless Carriage to the Compact Car," *Journal of Popular Culture*, 1 (1967), 395–402.

[25] See Donn Teal, *Gay Militants* (New York, 1971).

[26] *The Wolfenden Report: Authorized American Edition.* Introduction by K. Menniger (New York, 1963).

vorable nationwide sentiment in the United States that gave the impetus for Gay Liberation; rather it was an unfavorable sentiment that prompted it. Therefore, we join Sechrest and Flores in maintaining that homosexual inscriptions are written by "normal" males, and it is the societal conflict over homosexual behavior that is the causal factor for its being used as an insulting device. We predict that within five to ten years homosexual graffiti on the college campus will be almost non-existent.

The difference in the amount of trite and humor-of-elimination category in the men's and women's graffiti appears, at first, to quantitatively support Dundes' stance that men write such graffiti due to pregnancy envy. However, the great fluctuation in the men's data for these categories indicates that causal factors other than pregnancy envy may be operating to produce such differences. One hypothesis we advance is that, when there is a lull in local and national sociopolitical events such that they do not exist to be parodied in graffiti, then there will be an accompanying increase in humor-of-elimination graffiti, which entails the breaking of a taboo, discussing defecation. A final consideration concerning latrinalia is that we may have misclassified some traditional graffiti. We agree with Dundes that it is difficult to determine what is traditional because of a lack of data on graffiti.

By far the bulk of women's graffiti at SIU was collected from a restroom-smoking lounge area in the main library. Since there are no smoking facilities or restrooms on the first floor, the restroom-smoking lounge area on the second floor is heavily used. There was ample evidence of smoking and a great amount of graffiti (132), which required over an hour and a half to copy from the lounge area alone. However, there was not an unusual amount of graffiti in the restroom stalls. Landy and Steele's hypothesis of smoking as a phallic substitute for graffiti would not appear supported by these observations. A point that should be considered is that, traditionally, smoking in public by women was not socially acceptable.

We feel that, when and where graffiti in women's washrooms thematically approach those of men's, their socialization processes are approaching men's. With the liberality of SIU, we assume that part of the liberalizing effect is the decline of non-aggressive patterns in women's socialization, whereby it is more closely approaching men's socialization. A more probable interpretation is that the SIU campus has been the liberalizing influence on the females attending that school. This is given tentative support by the increase in "male type" graffiti in women's restrooms at SIU. A valid comparison of the women's data at MU and SIU cannot be made since there were only 18 women's graffiti at MU. We also maintain that the total lack of female graffiti at WKU is due to non-aggressive socialization processes of the female student body. This conclusion is of course purely hypothetical, and we intend to test our hypothesis in the future with a project designed to measure indices of women's socialization at all three schools.

APPENDIX

HETEROSEXUAL

Invitations and Requests: I want a good piece of ass. Leave a girl's name on that wall that will fuck. (M___ W___ C___)[27]

Accusations of Others' Behavior: D_____ F_____ will fuck. Tell her J_____ sent you.

Humor: Virginity is not an incurable disease.

Statement or Question: Pussy sure is good.   (How would you know)

HOMOSEXUAL

Invitations and Requests: M_____ J_____ would like to meet horny guy, large prick; call 00–0000. (Send him to XXX)[28]
(   )

Accusations: W_____ J_____ sucks dicks.

Hostile: Screw Homos.

Humor: John, love you, Jim.   (But John doesn't love you, John)

Masturbation: Masterbate Now! You'll never know what you missed. (See what it does? Beat off and you lose the ability to spell and write)

Statement: Hi H_____; Love, M_____ M_____.

NONSEXUAL

Other Humor: Robbie S. eats eagle shit. Oh a patriot.

Religion: God is dead; but don't worry, Mary is pregnant again.

Philosophical: Hope exceeds Reality.   (There is no hope)

Political: Nixon pisses fresca.

Social Satire: Ag-new's in 1984.

Hostile: Pop music sucks. Yankee turds like pop music; therefore, Yankees suck.
    (They also don't wear socks)   (They also ride hondas)

Single Words: R.O.T.C.

Statement: Zorro was here this year 1970.

Social Statement: Sisters remember you are women not men.

Drug Statement: I ain't going to sell drugs no more.

Play-on-Words: Women should be obscene not heard.

RACIST

Elimination: Niggers shit dog shit.

Hostile: All whites must die now.

Derogatory: Niggers smell white.

Sexual: Black + White = 0.

---

[27] Statements in parentheses are responses to graffiti.
[28] X's signify a designated fraternity.

Undecided sex: Use your cock; it's there for a purpose.

Humor of Elimination: We here at SIU would like to know . . .: how was your shit?

good	bad	wow	indifferent
□	□	□	□

Trite: Some come here to sit and think; others come here to shit and stink.
(But I come here to scratch my balls and read the writing on the walls)

JACK LEVIN and JAMES L. SPATES

Hippie Values: An Analysis of the Underground Press

There is little doubt by this time that the hippie phenomenon of the late 1960s is a social movement of some consequence for American society (see Yablonsky, 1968: 290 ff.). Whatever its greater significance, the movement has already contributed to a revolution in modern dress, hairstyles, music, art, and youth culture.

Since 1966, the mass media have analyzed, scrutinized, supported, and condemned the movement, so that almost all Americans, whether or not they have had direct experience with the hippies, presently hold some opinion regarding the merits of this group of young people.

Why have the hippies attracted so much attention? It is doubtful that the answer lies solely in the number of hippies: percentagewise, they are a very small proportion of the American population—numbering, at highest estimate, only 200,000 full-time participants (Yablonsky, 1968: 36). Nor does it seem likely that the concern is a direct product of the much publicized generation gap. Despite ample evidence that most hippies are young (under thirty) and that most of their critics are old (over thirty), support

"Hippie Values: An Analysis of the Underground Press," by Jack Levin and James L. Spates is reprinted from *Youth and Society*, Volume 2, No. 1 (Sept. 1970) pp. 59–73 by permission of the Publisher, Sage Publications, Inc.

We wish to especially thank Herbert J. Greenwald for his many helpful suggestions. We are also grateful to Stephen R. Marks, Kingsley H. Birge, and William F. Macauley for their critical review of earlier versions of this paper and we gratefully acknowledge the coding assistance of Ann MacConnell, Kenneth Sweezey, and Marilyn Thomas.

for the movement ranges far beyond age lines: many of the hippies' most ardent admirers, if not participants, are over thirty; many of their detractors, under thirty.

After this widespread popularization, social scientists have recently attempted to account for the American reaction to the hippie phenomenon (see Berger, 1967; Davis, 1967; Simon and Trout, 1967; Brown, 1969; Marks, 1969; Yablonsky, 1968). Some have specifically focused upon the value gap between the hippies and the middle class—a gap which has been characterized as an attempt by the hippie movement to substitute a viable alternative in place of the traditional American value pattern (see Marks, 1969). From this standpoint, the hippie problem becomes distinctly ideological, being directly related to those values or ideals which serve as the most general guidelines for action within society (such as the general American ideal that everyone, in order to be an American in good standing, must achieve individual success through his own occupational efforts).

The value argument raises an important aspect of the problem—that of conflict between different values as an expression of the basic gap between the hippie and middle-class views of life. Values are the most general directives for action in society, in that they are the most generally shared ideas about the correct way to behave. A challenge to the values of a social system is therefore regarded by the members of that system as a basic threat to the very raison d'être of their social structure. Hence, one might expect the expression of strong concerns regarding the challenging elements of the hippie phenomenon.

THE MIDDLE-CLASS PATTERN

The hippie mode of existence cannot be understood apart from the value structure of American society as a whole. More specifically, hippie culture has arisen directly out of the middle-class value system within which the majority of hippies were initially socialized. It has been estimated that over seventy percent of all hippies come from this middle- (or upper-) class orientation (Yablonsky, 1968: 26).

Characteristically, middle-class values tend to specify acts which are oriented to the future and normally require the individual to inhibit emotional expression in order for his resources to be fully directed toward the cognitive or rational solution to life tasks (see Parsons, 1951; Parsons and White, 1964: 196 ff.).

In the American case, the middle-class pattern typically manifests itself in the pursuit of economic concerns—that is, in rationally constructed efforts to increase economic production, profits, and occupational status by means of extended formal education and hard work. The achievement dimension of this pattern cannot be overemphasized: the middle-class value structure places major demands upon each individual to achieve occupational success, not merely in terms of personal wealth, power, or status, but as a moral obligation to contribute to the building of the good society (Parsons and White, 1964: 196). In other words, middle-class achievement cannot be purely utilitarian: a person cannot use any means to a particular end, but must use instead socially legitimized (normatively sanctioned) means to ends. Basic success, then, is defined in social as well as personal terms, and rewards are commensurate. Thus, from the middle-class perspective, the hard-working businessman who makes $10,000 a year is much more respectable than the gangster who makes ten times that amount, and, all things being equal, it is the businessman who will be given the upstanding position in the society.

These essential features of the middle-class pattern, that is, its economic, cognitive, and achievement dimensions, all of which denote the goal-oriented nature of activity within the system, can be summarized for convenience under the term "instrumentalism." (See Parsons and White, 1964: 196 ff.; Zelditch, 1955: 309–12.)

THE HIPPIE PATTERN

The hippies contend that their subculture offers a radical departure from the dominant American value structure which they see as thoroughly materialistic, dehumanizing, inauthentic, and alienating (Yablonsky, 1968: 361–66). This point of view is reflected in the hippies' "almost total rejection of economic individualism and the 'dog eat dog' or 'do unto other before they do unto you' attitude that is seen by them as the driving force behind contemporary American society" (Yablonsky, 1968: 358). The following responses (Yablonsky, 1968: 350, 351, 358, 365) are illustrative of the hippies' rejection of middle-class values:

[A hippie drop-out since 1960] To me, dropping-out means to reject the dominant moral, economic, and social values of one's society. I dropped out because the values in our society have become obsolete. . . . Our society is simply full of internal contradictions between its values and the reality of what people actually think and do. . . . Forty percent of America is terribly poor and yet we have tried to hide this from ourselves and the world because the dominant American middle-class has interests in perpetuating the myth.

[A hippie] In order to act with freedom, one must not be constrained by the oppressive systems of orientation and the selfish meaningless goals that were learned while a member of the uptight, plastic society.

[A 23-year-old hippie] We [America] have reached a high level of material development, many people have become hypnotized and obsessed with a desire for material good. There is a strong feeling of "us" and "them." . . . This is a negative part of contemporary American life and is blocking people from seeing the essence of one another.

In sum, then, it would appear that the hippie views the instrumental values of American society, whatever their original purpose, as presently generating dehumanized life styles, even to the point where human beings themselves, in the active quest for success, have become objects of manipulation to one another.

Such a negative reaction to his own society's dominant values (and to his own original values) has led the hippie to form a life style that is quite at odds with the typical American ideal of the hard-working, self-denying, rational businessman or professional. Yablonsky (1968: 29–31) has set forth what he sees as the basic elements of the ideal hippie: he is a philosopher who claims to be "tuned-in to the cosmic affinity of man"; he thus loves all men (the love ethic); "he has achieved this insight, at least in part, from the use of drugs [marijuana, LSD] as a sacrament"; he is a role model for new hippies to look up to; he is creative; he does not work in the traditional sense of American culture, rather preferring to do his own thing, whatever that may be; he is, in a word, "totally dropped out of the larger society," which he regards as plastic, and is actively engaged in "fostering another mode of existence."

This other mode of existence is, for the hippie, an alternative which completely deemphasizes the economic and achievement criteria of American society, and focuses instead upon all objects and actions as ends in themselves, as valuable and necessary foci of immediate gratification and present (rather than future) time orientation. More specifically, rather than attempting to deal with their affairs on a cognitive-rational level, or in terms of economic value, the hippie's ideals (see Greeley, 1969: 14–28) stress nonmaterial or spiritual concerns (such as participation in cosmology, mysticism, and the occult), as well as the search for love and intimacy in human relationships (Yablonsky, 1968: 358, 366). In addition, the achievement aspects of the middle-class pattern are replaced by the quest for self-expression as experienced in the immediate ongoing situation (that is, by grooving on or getting into music, art, psychedelic drugs, and the like). Whereas the middle-class individual is rewarded for following socially legitimized paths to achievement, the hippie is expected to follow his own personal path to wherever it leads him. That is, whatever his thing is, he does it.

The essential components of the hippie value pattern—as indicated by self-expression, affiliation, concern for others, and religious philosophical interests—can be conveniently characterized under the term "expressivism" (see Zelditch, 1955: 311).

The value gap between the hippies and the middle class, though often suggested by previous investigations of the hippie phenomenon, has, for the most part, lacked systematic, quantitative substantiation.[1] For this reason, it was the central purpose of the present study to test the hypothesis that, *contrary to the middle class pattern, hippie values stress expressive concerns and deemphasize instrumental concerns.*

METHOD

To delineate the value structure of the hippie movement, a sample was taken from Underground Press Syndicate (UPS) periodicals published in 1967 and 1968—a recent period during which hippie literature was available. The UPS (1969: 17–18) has an estimated, combined circulation of one million and, as self-described, consists of an "informal association of publications of the 'alternative press' . . . produced in storefronts and basements by feelthy hippies, distributed by unorthodox channels and free-thinking bookstores and from curbs." Ron Thelin, the editor of a representative underground newspaper, has expressed the purpose of his publication in the following manner (1968: 143–44):

> [to] provide an organ for the hip community, an evolution of communications consciousness and group consciousness to reflect the universal spirit and the miracles of light in this community [Haight-Ashbury] . . . . To show that LSD provides a profound experience. . . . To provide communication of the historical and ancient discoveries that are coming out of the hip culture, to spread the word, to get everyone to turn on, tune in, and drop out.

Most hippie underground papers appeared in the mid-sixties, many of them after the publicity of 1967, and many of them were short-lived. But their common components were an emphasis on hippie argot, psychedelic lettering and art, the glorification of folk rock, flower power, and love-ins— all, as Thelin says, in an attempt to describe the hip experience to their readers.

To obtain a representative sample of underground newspapers, the following most widely circulated periodicals were selected from major centers of recent hippie activities including both eastern and western regions: *Avatar* (Boston), *Distant Drummer* (Philadelphia), *East Village Other* (New York), *Los Angeles Free Press, San Francisco Oracle,* and *Washington Free Press.* A single issue of each UPS periodical from every second month in the

---

[1] See Berger (1967), Davis (1967), Simon and Trout (1967), Brown (1969), Marks (1969), and Yablonsky (1968). One major exception is Yablonsky, whose methods include lengthy participant observation and a questionnaire approach (n=600). However, the study has been severely criticized on methodological grounds, particularly in its participant observations aspect—see, for example, Berger (1969).

period from September 1967 to August 1968 was selected on a random basis. Every second nonfictional article appearing in this sample of issues, excluding poetry and letters to the editor, was subjected to analysis (n = 316).

To provide a comparable sample of articles representative of middle-class values, an analysis was also conducted of concurrently published issues of the *Reader's Digest,* selected for its variety of middle-class articles from diverse sources (see Ginglinger, 1955: 56–61). Excluding fiction and poetry, each article appearing in every other issue of *Reader's Digest* was studied (n = 162).

The major value-theme of articles in both samples was coded by means of a modified version of Ralph K. White's *Value Catalogue* (1951). All materials were coded using a detailed set of definitions of the value-themes and appropriate coding sheets.

The central hypothesis regarding expressive and instrumental values was tested in the following manner. On the basis of the theoretical discussion above, the categories Self-Expression, Concern for Others, Affiliation, and Religious-Philosophical were treated as aspects of Expressivism, while the categories Achievement, Cognitive, and Economic became the basis for Instrumentalism. Categories of the value analysis are listed below:

INSTRUMENTAL

a. Achievement: Values which produce achievement motivation for the individual in terms of hard work, practicality, or economic value are often expressed by means of contributions to society through occupation and high regard for ownership.

b. Cognitive: These represent the drive for learning as an end in itself as well as the means for achieving success, welfare, or happiness.

c. Economic: Economic values are at the collective level (such as, national, state, industrial), thus differing from individual goals such as achievement.

EXPRESSIVE

d. Self-expressive: This area includes all the self-expressive values and goals. The main ones are humor, play, and fun in general, relaxation, or exciting new discoveries, and travel. Art and beauty are included as well as other creative-expressive activities.

e. Affiliative: These may be the product of social conditioning, or a result of the need to belong to a group, to affiliate with another person. This category focuses upon the gregariousness of individuals and the friendships which they develop. These affiliative aims may be expressed as conformity, loyalty to the group, friendship, or other-directedness.

f. Concern for others: Concern for others does not depend upon a drive to interact. Unlike the affiliative values, this category focuses upon attitudes and feelings toward particular groups or toward humanity in general. Therefore, this category tends to include more abstract objectives than those associated with affiliation.

g. Religious-philosophical: This category includes goals dealing with ultimate meaning in life, the role of deity, concerns with after-life, and so on.

OTHER

h. Individualistic: This category is concerned with values which stress the importance of the individual, the development of his unique personality, individual independence, and the achievement of individualized personal fulfillment including rebellion.

i. Physiological: These are goals created by simple physiological drives such as hunger, sex, physical health, and physical safety.

j. Political: This category includes collective goals (such as, state, community, national, international objectives) in their central reference to group decision-making processes.

k. Miscellaneous: Any other goals not covered above (such as, hope, honesty, purity, modesty, and manners).

The reliability of the value analysis was tested by having three coders independently code thirty articles from both the UPS and the *Digest* samples. Using a two-out-of-three criterion (that is, where two of three coders agreed), agreement reached 90%. Total agreement was 78%.

RESULTS AND DISCUSSION

Results obtained in any analysis of UPS and *Reader's Digest* value-themes suggest that expressivism occupies a central position in the hippie value structure, whereas instrumentalism occurs only peripherally. As shown in Table 1, expressive concerns accounted for 46% of the value-themes in the underground press, while instrumental concerns were the major focus of only 10% of the articles. In sharp contrast, instrumental concerns represented the major value-theme in the *Reader's Digest* sample (42%), while expressive concerns were substantially less important (23%).

Within the expressivism of the hippie sample, the dominant emphasis appeared to be Self-Expression (28%). For example, typical articles in the underground press dealt with the mind-blowing psychedelic properties of drugs, the relationship of early rock and roll music to contemporary rock groups (such as, the Beatles and the Rolling Stones), the influence of such figures as Ken Kesey, Timothy Leary, and Lenny Bruce on the hippie movement.

In the *Reader's Digest* sample, Achievement was the dominant compo-

Table 1   VALUE-THEMES IN THE UNDERGROUND PRESS AND READER'S DIGEST[a]

Value-Theme	Underground Press		Reader's Digest	
Expressive	46%	%	23%	%
self-expressive		28		9
concern for others		8		6
affiliative		4		3
religious-philosophical		6		5
Instrumental	10		42	
achievement		3		28
congnitive		5		7
economic		2		7
Other	44		35	
individual		20		10
political[b]		19		12
physiological[c]		4		12
miscellaneous		1		1
TOTAL		100		100
(n = 478)		(316)		(162)

[a] A chi-square analysis was conducted by comparing the Underground Press and *Reader's Digest* on the two major value-themes, Expressive and Instrumental ($x^2 = 61.17$, $df = 1$, $p < .001$).

[b] The distribution of political values reveals an important aspect of the nature of the underground press: a secondary appeal of these newspapers is often to politically radical or New Left types, though most of the material is designed for hippie consumption (see Wolfe, 1968: 135–44)—a group known for its apolitical stance (see Yablonsky, 1968).

[c] In the *Reader's Digest*, this category consisted primarily of health-related topics such as methods of weight reduction, physical diseases such as cancer, and aging. In the Underground Press, it contained references to physiological sex.

nent of instrumentalism, representing 28% of all value-themes. Typically, *Reader's Digest* articles emphasized methods for occupational achievement, including business enterprises created by college students, advice concerning financial investments and taxes, the careers of well-known persons who had achieved occupational success, and so on.

An independent analysis of a random sample of underground press advertisements appearing in our sample yielded the following supportive data: almost 90% of the hippie advertisements focused on expressive-related products, that is, on products which are designed either for expressive behavior or expressive consumption, such as music (rock, folk, blues, soul, and the like), movies, plays, psychedelic shops, clothing (mod), and coffee and tea houses. The most important of these expressive categories contained music-related products such as concerts, records, recording artists, and stereophonic equipment; these products accounted for 25% of all hippie advertisements. These results lend support to the suggestion that expressive concerns are a staple of great magnitude for the readers of the underground press, and more generally for the hippie movement as a whole.

An examination of the relationship of individualism to the expressive-instrumental dichotomy may shed additional light on the above findings. As is well-known, social scientists have long been concerned with the position of individualism in the American value structure. In the middle-class case, individualism has the major task of locating responsibility for contributions to the building of the good society. Thus, each individual must actively strive to accomplish those objectives which society has defined as legitimate concerns.

Similarly, the hippies show a characteristic American concern for the individual. As shown in the present study, 20% of the articles appearing in the underground press contained an individualistic value-orientation. However, the hippie version may indicate an individualism of a different order: an individualism closely tied to the expressive value-orientation. It is here that the hippie phrase, "Do your own thing!" has particular relevance, in that it essentially directs attention to the immediate gratification of needs by means of creative self-expression—an expressive individualism which stands in sharp contrast to the dominant middle-class pattern (Marks, 1969).

The hippies form a unique phenomenon in contemporary America—a large-scale movement which has arisen out of the mainstream of American life to form a contraculture within its societal boundaries. Results obtained in the present study support the contention that the hippies are attempting to stress values of an expressive nature—values which they feel have been neglected by the highly instrumental middle class.

From the sociological point of view, this is where the concern of Americans about the hippies comes home to roost: a way of life is being criticized, and sides are being taken. The ideology of the hip movement attempts to cut to the core of the instrumental view of things. The middle-class ideology, the hippies are saying, neglects the personal needs of the individual to be a human being; it neglects his need to be affective, loving, and trustful of other people; it neglects his need for self-realization by following his own individual needs; in a word, it neglects his need to be expressive.

Yet, how expressive can a social system be? There is increasing evidence that the strongly reactive nature of the hippie value system may in large part account for the general failure of the movement to form viable communities or other social structures.[2] The perceived overemphasis of the

_____

[2] Because of harassment by various agencies of the dominant culture, a significant number of hippies have literally taken to the woods to form communes. While some of these social systems have existed for a number of years, their long-term stability has not yet been confirmed. In addition, even if successful, the price of their success may be more instrumentally oriented behavior. Such groups are in the minority if one takes

middle class on instrumentalism seems to have been matched by a similar overemphasis by the hippies on pure expressivism. In structural terms, extreme expressivism poses a significant problem for long-term, stable patterns of interaction—that is, the basic tasks of maintaining the system are not performed on a regular basis, which, in the extreme, can result in social disorganization and decay. Indeed, the literature on the hippies is replete with examples of community and group termination because food was not taken in, rent was not paid, and so on. Clearly, for a stable society, everyone doing his own thing has its limitations.

It is just this system dissolution that the middle-class American intuitively—and, we think, rightly—feels may be a consequence of a purely expressive mode of existence. Knowing this, he, like the hippie, takes a stance in defense of his life style. Though the ideological stance of each group often becomes a battle of ego defenses (that is, "My way of life is right because it is *my* way of life"), there seems to be objective merit in both positions; extreme instrumentalism does appear to neglect the necessities of personality and organismic expression, while extreme expressivism appears to neglect the requirements of stable social systems. For this reason, it may well be that neither the expressive nor instrumental value structures may come to be dominant in this ideational conflict. Rather, the solution may be in the form of systems which combine elements of both these systems—systems which are already in the process of formulation.

It already appears that the hippie's purely expressive solution to life is considered too radical as a viable solution for the society as a whole. Very few people completely drop out (which the totally expressive solution necessitates). But there is evidence that fewer and fewer people are taking the straight life in its extreme sense as their life style either. Rather, some sort of balance is apparently being worked out on both sides of the fence.

From a more general perspective, the hippie emphasis on expressive values could be regarded as partially illustrative of a process of widespread balancing in American society as a whole, whereby the social system, being pushed more and more to an instrumental extreme, is reintroducing various modes of expressivism at all levels of its structure. If this is the case, then the societywide trend toward expressivism, exemplified in its most extreme form by the hip movement, could be seen as part and parcel of other strong trends in contemporary America—civil rights, freedom of speech, representation, life style, and the like. Though the end result will most likely not be the extreme expressivism found dominant in many hip subcultures, it may very well be, over time, that an expressivism suitable to all age levels and classes of American society will become part of the American

the hippie population as a whole: most hippies still reside in major urban centers and exist in extremely loose confederations. See Brown (1969: 37).

ideology. It is in this sense that the hippie movement may have its most profound influence on the character of the American value system.

REFERENCES

BERGER, B. M., "Sociologist on a Bad Trip," *Trans-action* 6, 4 (February 1969), 54–56.

——, "Hippie Morality—More Old than New," *Trans-action* 5, 2 (December 1967), 19–27.

BROWN, M. E., "The Persecution and Condemnation of Hippies," *Trans-action* 6, 10 (September 1969), 33–46.

DAVIS, F., "Why All of Us May Be Hippies Someday," *Trans-action* 5, 2 (December 1967), 10–18.

GINGLINGER, G., "Basic Values in Readers Digest, Selection, and Constellation," *Journalism Q.* 32, 1 (Winter 1955), 56–61.

GREELEY, A. M., "There's a New Time Religion on Campus," *New York Times Magazine* (June 1, 1969), 14–28.

MARKS, S. R., "The Hippies and the Organism: A Problem for the General Theory of Action," Dept. of Sociology, Boston Univ. Unpublished, 1969.

PARSONS, T., *The Social System*. New York: Free Press, 1951.

—— and W. WHITE, *Social Structure and Personality*. New York: Free Press, 1964.

SIMON, G. and G. TROUT, "Hippies in College—From Teeny-boppers to Drug Freaks," *Trans-action* 5, 2 (December 1967), 27–32.

UNDERGROUND PRESS SYNDICATE, *Directory*. Phoenix: Orpheus, 1969.

WHITE, R. K., *Value-Analysis: The Nature and Use of the Method*. New York: Society for the Psychological Study of Social Issues, 1951.

WOLFE, B. H., *The Hippies*. New York: Signet, 1968.

YABLONSKY, L., *The Hippie Trip*. New York: Pegasus, 1968.

ZELDITCH, M., JR., "Role Differentiation in the Nuclear Family: A Comparative Study," pp. 309–12 in T. Parsons and R. F. Bales, et al., *Family: Socialization and Interaction Process*. New York: Free Press, 1955.

WALTER M. GERSON and SANDER H. LUND

Playboy *Magazine: Sophisticated Smut or Social Revolution?*

Since publication of the Kinsey reports, much commotion has been raised about the so-called "American Sexual Revolution." Many social scientists and laymen alike claim that recent American social history has witnessed a marked, revolutionary, general relaxation of the restrictive cultural norms governing human sexual behavior. This general loosening of American sexual norms, it is claimed, is manifested in both the findings of scientific research and in the operation of the contemporary popular cultural milieu. It is often asserted that the "decline" in American sexual morality is reflected in both sociological and social psychological research and in such areas of American popular culture as fashion (the bikini and miniskirt), mass entertainment (topless dancers and "sexy" movies), and the mass media ("raw," uncensored books and nudie magazines).

Those who contend that the "sexual revolution" is but a popular myth, however, have pointed out many weaknesses in this argument. They have noted, for example, that the conclusions drawn by Kinsey may have been biased, since his sample came from volunteers who may have over-represented that portion of American society which is sexually active. Critics of a "sexual revolution" have also pointed out that the term has never been adequately defined. There is no absolute and necessary relationship between verbal statements and actual behavior.

However one reacts to the notion of a "Sexual Revolution," one point is clear, obvious, and indisputable: there has been a massive increase, at least at the verbal level, in popular concern with sex and sex-related topics.

This increase is clearly manifest in the continuing rise to eminence of sophisticated men's magazines—magazines which, to a greater or lesser extent, are oriented toward sex and the glorification of scantily clad beautiful young women. The magazine perhaps most representative of this field is *Playboy,* owned and edited by Hugh Hefner. Before the advent of *Playboy,* sexuality and sophistication occupied opposite ends of a continuum. Sexual magazines for men had been aimed at the lower classes and were consequently rather crude. Sophisticated men's magazines apparently deemed it

Reprinted from the *Journal of Popular Culture*, 1, 3 (Winter 1971), 218–27, by permission of the publisher.

117

impolite and improper to allude to sex overtly. Into the gap thus generated moved Hugh Hefner and *Playboy* in the early 1950's. *Playboy* allowed the more urbane men of the middle and upper classes—who tended to be repelled by the raw and often adolescent level of other men's magazines—to indulge their desire for sexual material at a more sophisticated level. In a real sense, the magazine was a response to a new demand in the popular cultural milieu. Overt interest in sex was no longer defined by higher-status men as a sign of immorality and degeneracy.

Moreover, *Playboy* accelerated this acceptance of sex as healthy by dispensing with crude, suggestive pictures and stories of rape and murder, and substituting urbane and literate essays, intellectual articles, and "artistically sensual" drawings and photographs. Burgeoning *overt* masculine interest in sexuality precipitated by an increasingly permissive moral climate (at the verbal level) was satisfied then by *Playboy*. The magazine was a first venture, so risky, in fact, that the first issue was not dated, with the expectation that there might not be another. Today, however, supported by accelerating popular interest in sexuality, it is one of the nation's most popular magazines.

Playboy serves one significant function today—socialization, as a largely informal content analysis of randomly sampled issues published during the period December 1965 through June 1967 will demonstrate. In this analysis it has been necessary to rely, perhaps inordinately, on some form of "sociological imagination" rather than purely quantitative methodology. The conclusions, therefore, are tentative and exploratory and are hypotheses for further study.

When one speaks of a magazine's functions, one must answer the question: "Functional for whom?" Obviously the way a magazine is used varies from reader to reader, and one publication can serve different purposes for different people. *Playboy's* main function is the socialization process. Not all of *Playboy's* readers use the magazine for these purposes. But analysis of *Playboy,* even a very informal analysis, reveals certain regularities and consistencies in style and content which when compared to the magazine's impressive success, appear functional in at least a minimal sense.

Playboy seems to supply its readers a goal to achieve, a model of behavior to emulate, and an identity to assume. In essence, the reader is taught how to become a "Playboy." Throughout the magazine—in advertisements, editorials, pictorial essays, cartoons, articles, and works of fiction—the Playboy model, or what we shall call the "Playboy Stereotype" is pounded into the reader. This stereotype generally consists of a sophisticated, cosmopolitan, urbane, diverse, affluent, intellectual, promiscuous (if that is the word), mature bachelor. This goal is, perhaps, what most American men have long desired as a perfect style of life. *Playboy* was not only the first magazine to delineate the stereotype in a systematic and explicit

Table 1 Classification of Factual-Informative Articles in Playboy Magazine from June, 1966, to June, 1967

Topic	No. of Articles	% of Total
Fashion	13	15.9
Grooming	3	3.7
Interior Decorating	2	2.4
Cars	2	2.4
Music (Jazz)	2	2.4
Food	5	6.1
Drink	3	3.7
Parties ("how to . . .")	6	7.3
Travel ("where to go; what to do")	3	3.7
Sports	4	4.8
Entertainment	13	15.9
Modern Society—Human Problems	10	12.2
Popular Culture	7	8.5
Business—Money	5	6.1
Women—Sexual Freedom	3	3.7
Cameras	1	1.2
TOTALS	82	100.0

form, but also the first systematically to suggest means for achieving the ideal.

The single most salient concrete representation of the "Playboy Stereotype" is the *Playboy* Rabbit, self-acknowledged symbol of the magazine. The rabbit is almost inevitably shown in the company of one or more beautiful and adoring young women. He is always dressed impeccably (and expensively) in the latest styles, which range from formal dinner-wear to Bermuda shorts and cashmere sweaters, and is frequently depicted engaging in such diverse and sophisticated activities as skin diving, mountain climbing, yachting, or driving a foreign sports car. One of the rabbit's most striking and revealing characteristics, however, is his sophisticated blasé attitude. Although he appears to lead the life of an ideal Playboy (which includes being in intimate surroundings with spectacularly beautiful and alluringly unclad young women), his expression never changes. His eyes are always half-closed in a bored fashion and his mouth is constantly turned up at the corners in an almost smug smile of self-satisfaction. Every aspect of his style of life reflects sophistication. He is, in every sense of the word, a man (or rabbit) of the world.

It is reasonable to hypothesize that a good many of *Playboy's* readers are men who for one reason or another (typically youth and inexperience) do not meet the levels established by the *Playboy* criteria. Hypothesizing further that these men accept the stereotype standards, then the second aspect of the *Playboy* socialization process begins to operate. *Playboy* at this stage begins to serve as a means of educating its readers in how to achieve the stereotype. It teaches them how to look, think, and act like Playboys. This instruction takes two forms: (1) formal or overt and (2) informal or covert.

Readers of *Playboy* are instructed on the formal level through such conventional channels as informative articles, advice columns, and certain kinds of advertisements. The instruction is often quite straight-forward and direct, seemingly consciously aimed at teaching its readers some aspect of Playboy living. From June 1966 through June 1967, there appeared in *Playboy* 82 factual-informative articles (features defined as "articles" in the magazine's table of contents). A rough classification of the articles by topic appears in Table 1.

Each article was classified according to the primary subject topic the article dealt with; hence, each article is tabulated only once in the table. Note that the vast majority of the articles are in some manner instructive. They show the reader what to wear and how to wear it, what cars to drive, what food and drink to consume, how to throw parties, and where to travel. For the young, the socially ignorant, the uninitiated, *Playboy* functions as an operating manual. It teaches them how to achieve the "Playboy Stereotype." For the more blasé and cosmopolitan, *Playboy* functions to reinforce or validate what they already know about being a playboy.

A high standard of quality typifies the "Playboy Stereotype." The food and drink, for example, are exceptional and of gourmet quality (old Cognac and exotic foods); the cars are inevitably sports models; and the clothes are expensive and in the latest fashion. In other words, the stereotype is consistent with the image of an upper-class playboy.

Another source of formal instruction can be found in the "Playboy Advisor," an institutionalized feature in the magazine. Confused and troubled readers can find therein information to solace their troubles and advice to solve their problems. The questions raised (and apparently answered) range from moral problems ("Should I have sexual intercourse with girls other than my fiancee?") to fashion and etiquette ("When is it proper to wear a white dinner jacket?") to gourmet matters ("What is the difference between imported and domestic wine?").

Other avenues of formal instruction are exemplified by features such as "The Playboy Forum," where readers debate and discuss salient issues such as sexual morality and exchange ideas and pieces of important information, and various other regular editorial features such as "Playboy After Hours," and "The *Playboy* International Datebook." *Playboy* also regularly reviews books, records, movies, Broadway plays, nightclubs, and other such attractions. All of these features, in some manner or other, demonstrate to the reader how a "Playboy" should behave—what books he should read, records he should listen to, movies and plays he should attend, where he should travel, what food and drink he should consume, where he should be entertained, and so on. . . .

Examples of informal avenues of instruction are such features as cartoons, fictional stories, and certain aspects of advertisements. It may be that the key difference between the formal and informal avenues of instruction, besides their degree of manifestness, is that the formal avenue teaches the reader *what* to do, and the informal teaches him *how* to do it. In other words, on the formal level *Playboy* teaches its readers the symbols, artifacts, and rituals which proclaim a Playboy's status, and on the informal level it teaches him the subtle actions, the attitudes, the beliefs, and the style of living which goes with them. The two categories are not mutually exclusive. Both are found pervasively throughout the magazine. Some aspects of formal instruction are found in works of fiction, and some aspects of informal instruction are found in informative articles. In terms of emphasis, however, the formal means of instruction is generally most salient in the direct and straight-forward informative article, while the informal means of instruction is most salient in the more subtle and indirect works of fiction.

The style of living which *Playboy* seemingly attempts to teach could probably be best described as "cool but active sophistication." The other traits implicit in the "Playboy Stereotype" (i.e., sexuality and intellectuality) are oriented to this basic value theme. Since there are so many traits associated with the stereotype, however, and since they are interrelated, it is unfortunately difficult to extract the value's essence in a clear and unconfounded manner. Fortunately, at least an indication of its existence can often be seen in the content of many of the magazine's cartoons, advertisements, and works of fiction. A typical cartoon, for example, shows a husband suavely serving his wife and her lover cocktails in bed. The wife's reaction is: "Henry, I think you're taking this like a cad." The husband, true to the highest *Playboy* tradition, has "kept his cool," and effectively demonstrated his unruffled sophistication.

The subtle influence of the "Playboy Stereotype" is also reflected in many of the magazine's advertisements. As with the *Playboy*'s symbol, the rabbit, the men depicted inevitably appear to behave in a suave, cool, and sophisticated fashion. They are always impeccably dressed in the latest style. Their female companions are usually lovely, adoring, and pliant. They are always in diverse but sophisticated surroundings (from sky diving to skin diving, from formal dinners to intimate bedrooms). Their most significant characteristics are their sublime "coolness," their self-assurance, their command of the situation. They do not represent the "man next door" who drives a Ford station wagon and has two children. They are self-assumed, inimitably cool, and elite. As with the rabbit, they represent to some readers both a goal and a means of achieving that goal.

In addition to cartoons and advertisements, a third vehicle for indirect socialization in *Playboy* is, of course, the works of fiction. The process of learning is essentially the same as with other indirect avenues: instruction through identification and imitation on the part of the reader. With works of fiction, however, it is slightly more complex and diverse. The stereotype is generally the same. But works of fiction allow the Playboy's intellectuality and personality to be brought forth and rounded out. The stereotyped Playboy becomes multidimensional. He can quote Ibsen, Sartre, and Mailer. He is at home at formal dinner parties and "hippie" beer bashes, and as a consequence he seduces with equal facility sophisticated debutantes and female bohemians. Sarcasm and a "cool" sense of social awareness are his weapons. His morality and intellectuality are cool; he is the true individualist making his way towards some sort of secular nirvana.

The essential process involved in indirect socialization is, first, identification with the "Playboy Stereotype" and, second, imitation of the stereotype's behavior as presented in the advertisements, cartoons, and works of fiction. Therefore, as one assimilates the essential features of the "Playboy" image through identification and imitation, one tends to develop a "Playboy" self-conception and becomes, in essence if not in fact, a Playboy.

A third facet of *Playboy's* socialization process is the dual function of motivation-reinforcement. That is, having given its readers a goal and providing them with a method of achieving that goal, *Playboy* provides them with some motivation for starting the process and reinforces them for continuing it. We shall consider these two functions as one, for the stimuli which initiate the reader into the socialization process are the same stimuli which keep him going.

The obvious initial desire which probably motivates many of *Playboy's* readers to embark upon the socialization process is sexual interest. Much of the intent in adopting the "Playboy Stereotype," aside from increases in status, prestige, and the like, appears to be to increase one's sexual activity. Overall, nonmarital sexual intercourse is still probably largely disapproved of in American society. Social punishment, in the form of legal sanctions and/or adverse public opinion, and psychological punishment, in the form of anxiety and guilt, are often the result for those who violate the traditional norms. *Playboy* functions to motivate the adoption of its stereotype and reinforces its continued assimilation by attempting to create among its readers the belief that not only is nonmarital sexual intercourse all right, but that it is good, healthy and desirable. Once the readers have largely accepted this contention, *Playboy* further facilitates the adoption of its stereotype by fostering the impression that belief in the morality of nonmarital sexual intercourse is a widely held opinion by people of high status.

The first stage in this motivation-reinforcement process, creation of the belief that nonmarital sexual activity is both healthy and normal, is manifest in the "Playboy Philosophy," a regular feature of the magazine. The essence of the morality found therein is that *it is indeed morality*. Sex is taken out of the gutter, cleaned off, and put back in its rightful place in "polite society." The unhappiness caused by Victorian repression is depicted, and at the same time it is demonstrated that a more liberal moral atmosphere is conducive to a happier, more well-adjusted society.

The "Playboy" morality is a logical, well thought out, possibly valid rationalization for the existence of the "Playboy Stereotype." The psychological punishment of guilt is alleviated by the demonstration that nonmarital sexual activity is in most cases moral, and that it is the traditional morality which is wrong. Thus it functions to motivate and reinforce the acceptance of the "Playboy Stereotype" by freeing the reader from the grasp of the traditional moral code.

The second stage of the motivation-reinforcement process (creation of the belief that the "Playboy" morality is widely accepted by high status people) can be found in such features as "Dear Playboy" (Letters to the Editor) and the "Playboy Forum." In the first place, it can be seen that an unusually high number of high status individuals (psychologists, psychiatrists, heads of citizens' committees, ministers, and professors of sociology) write to the magazine heartily praising the "Playboy Morality." Such feedback may tend to create in the reader the impression that the "Playboy Stereotype Morality" is largely accepted by the elite, people whom they know they can trust. In the second place, although *Playboy,* in the interest of impartiality, does print the letters of some of those who disagree concerning its morality, the vast majority of letters published do in fact support it. Moreover, as an aside, it seems that somehow letters supporting *Playboy* are always literate and logical, while critical letters often tend to be irrational and fanatical (depicting Victorian reasoning at its worst). Be that as it may, however, the main point is that the large number of pro-*Playboy* letters create a feeling of "we-ness," a sort of abbreviated ethnocentrism. The person who adopts the *Playboy* morality and through it, the "Playboy Stereotype," is supported by the impression that he is a member of a large, high status group. This is functional for him in two ways: First, the high status of his supporters tends to legitimize and strengthen his belief in the "Playboy" morality, which decreases the effects of guilt. Second, the large number of his supporters enhances his impression that belief in the morality of nonmarital sexual intercourse is increasing in American society which, in turn, tends to convince him that the social and legal sanctions elicited by violations of the traditional norms will be less painful. In any case, the supporter of the "Playboy" morality is freed to a certain extent to pursue the "Playboy Stereotype."

Another source of reinforcement-motivation is *Playboy's* treatment of women. Since, as we have noted, the "Playboy" morality is presented as morality, women cannot be shown being manipulated and exploited in this magazine, as they are in the lower class media. They must enjoy sex;

it must be good for them. The contention that sex should be and is moral and healthy for women is a cornerstone of the "Playboy" morality. Rape and manipulative seduction are totally absent in *Playboy*. Those women who are seduced are usually experienced and of age, but even if they are not, the seduction is "for their own good," they enjoy it, and afterwards are grateful it was performed. The essence of this attitude is reflected in a statement of one foldout "Playmate": "I am my own woman . . . I lead my life according to my own standards, . . . [which is] the pursuit of intellectual pleasure."

A fourth facet of the *Playboy* socialization process, what we refer to as the safety valve function, is also a form of reinforcement. Although the readers may be motivated to accept the "Playboy Stereotype," many are simply not able to live up to all its standards. Some men are not affluent enough, or intellectual enough, or "cool" enough (they might have some rather permanent personality characteristic which is not consistent with the "Playboy Stereotype"). Furthermore, there may be those who do not wish overtly to become Playboys. They may be insufficiently socialized, or they may implicitly realize that the stereotype is beyond their reach. At any rate, for those who accept at least minimally the "Playboy Stereotype," but refuse to pursue it overtly, *Playboy* provides them with potential vicarious satisfactions. It provides an imaginary world in which they can be Playboys without having to be intellectual, sophisticated, and affluent. They can do exciting things, go to exotic places, and seduce voluptuous young women, all in their imaginations, without having to risk the ego-shattering experience of failure and rejection.

The center page foldout, a monthly feature which depicts various beautiful young women in gaping stages of nudity, is a key factor in the safety valve function. The young Aphrodites function to a certain extent as the reader's vicarious lovers. The pictures easily convince the viewer that the girl could be his sexually and he could be in the picture. Thus, for example, the young women always stare directly into the camera and their expressions are intimate and willing. An example is the November 1966 foldout which reveals a young girl lying completely nude on the floor, gazing expectantly into the camera which looms directly above her. The impression is of a man looking down at his lover who reclines at his feet. This impression is enhanced by the *two* glasses of wine in the picture. One for the girl, the other apparently for the viewer, her lover. Another example, in the December 1965 issue, shows a nude young woman lying in a mussed-up double bed. There are two pillows, the one on which she rests and one beside her which is indented as though it had been slept on. The reader can easily feel that he has just arisen from bed, and is now looking back at the woman with whom he has spent the night.

Between the December 1964 and the June 1967 issues, *Playboy* published thirty centerfold "Playmate" pictorials. Of twenty-six of these photographs (February, March, April and July 1965 being unavailable), fifty per cent (13) depicted a girl either in or near a bed or wearing a negligee. Another thirty per cent (8) showed a girl in the process of undressing, and seven per cent (2) revealed a young woman emerging from a shower or bath. The latent and overt sexuality of many of the poses demonstrates graphically that the playmate may easily function as more than mere sensual art.

The safety valve function is also somewhat of a reinforcer for those who perhaps intend to adopt the "Playboy Stereotype" morality in their overt behavior. The centerfold and other pictorial features foster the impression that many respectable and lovely young girls are willing to engage in nonmarital sexual activities. The reader is motivated, firstly, by the graphic depiction of the sensual pleasures that await him if he adopts the stereotype morality. Secondly, he is reinforced by the apparent willingness of the girls. He discovers he will not be forced to try to manipulate or exploit them, and he therefore knows he will be able to avoid the potential guilt of success and potential anxiety of failure. Thirdly, he is reinforced because the girls are respectable. They are assumedly on his level socially, so he will not have to experience the discomfort of a sordid and "raw" affair.

Thus, we have *Playboy* magazine, a contemporary American phenomenon. To most observers, reasons for the magazine's instant and continuing success are probably self-evident. However, all too often, books, movies, and magazines are examined only in terms of their entertainment value while their latent functions remain relatively unnoticed. Social phenomena like *Playboy* are significantly part of the popular culture of contemporary American society. Serious students of American culture and social life cannot afford to continue to ignore them as unworthy of scholarly investigation.

JAMES T. RICHARDSON, MARY HARDER,
and ROBERT B. SIMMONDS

Thought Reform
and the Jesus Movement[*]

Back in the 1950s many Americans were taken aback and appalled by psychologically and physically coercive methods used against prisoners of war in the Korean conflict. This indignation was compounded by information concerning similar methods used against Chinese intellectuals and Western prisoners in mainland China.[1] Apparently most Americans believed that any good American soldier should be able to withstand the pressures brought to bear on the POWs. When it became public knowledge that such was not the case, a great hue and cry arose from educated and lay public alike. Scapegoats were sought, and simplistic explanations were proffered in order to "explain" how otherwise fine young American soldiers succumbed to the techniques used against them. A favored explanation was that of Pavlovian psychology, with its emphasis on the reduction of the human organism to its animal nature through the use of physical-psychological pressures. Even today, this explanation seems to be generally accepted, especially among the lay public. Scientists who were involved in research into the brainwashing phenomenon were nearly unanimous in their debunking of this popular theory, mainly because it deemphasized the very important group influences involved in thought reform or, as it is popularly called, brainwashing.

We wish to examine these group influences, apparently the essential elements in thought reform, in relation to the contemporary Jesus Movement. We have chosen to apply the findings of the thought reform literature to the Jesus Movement because of the striking similarities between this

"Thought Reform and the Jesus Movement," by James T. Richardson, Mary Harder, and Robert B. Simmonds is reprinted from *Youth and Society*, Volume 4, No. 2 (Dec. 1972) pp. 185–202 by permission of the Publisher, Sage Publications, Inc.

[*] A version of this paper was read at the annual meeting of the Rocky Mountain Social Science Association in Salt Lake City in 1972.

[1] There is a fairly large literature on brainwashing, which separates logically into two unequal portions. Most research has been done on the experience of POWs in the Korean War. See, for example, Schien (1957a, 1957b, 1956), Segal (1957), Bauer (1957), Miller (1957), and Kinkead (1957). Less work has been done on the experiences of Western prisoners in China and of Chinese "intellectuals," but this work is a major focus of this paper (see Lifton, 1963, 1957, and 1956).

contemporary phenomenon and the brainwashing that took place in China and Korea during the early 1950s. The similarities include the dramatic changes in "world view" for some of the individuals in both situations and the methods whereby these changes are made. A look at these methods will reemphasize the earlier findings of the brainwashing research that elements of group structure and process were keys to thought reform. This reemphasis occurs because it is evident that few, if any, of the Jesus Movement groups use anything like the Pavlovian methods attributed to the Chinese. The thought reform, however, has been nearly as drastic in some cases—from activist radicalism to voluntaristic fundamentalism.[2]

The idea of applying the thought reform findings to the Jesus Movement grew out of some extensive and systematic research on the Jesus Movement with which the authors have been involved (Harder and Richardson, 1971; Simmonds et al., 1972; Harder, 1972; Harder et al., 1972).[3] This research focused on one particular group that is part of the movement and has been in existence for some four years. The longevity of the group indicates that it has been successful in recruiting members and that its techniques of "conversion" have been fairly well worked out in practice. This brief paper will not allow a thorough description of the group studied. Other papers will give more information concerning the group itself and its members. Suffice it to say that, during an initial two-week stay at a branch of the group studied, a thirty-page questionnaire (mostly open-ended) and a personality instrument were administered to 88 of about 93 members of the commune. The data focused on a thorough description of the participants (including the effects of joining the group) and on testing some ideas concerning the conversion process.[4] Two subsequent visits have

[2] There is little systematic evidence concerning the number of individuals so markedly changed. The popular treatments of the Jesus Movement would have one believe that this is a regular occurrence. However, evidence gathered by the authors indicates that only a minority of those involved ever participated greatly in political activism (although a good portion do classify themselves as liberal or radical before joining; see Harder et al., 1972). The implication of this finding is that the political activist and Jesus Movement groups have less overlap of membership than we have been led to believe. This suggestion does not vitiate the need for our study of brainwashing in the Jesus Movement, for something noteworthy is happening when large numbers of society's children are made into proselytizing Christians in an age that is supposed to be secular.

[3] There is a vast and growing popular literature on the Jesus Movement that also contributed to the paper. While little of this reporting presents systematic evidence, it is highly suggestive. See Adams and Fox (1972), which is one of the best discussions of research on the movement. Other treatments include Time (1971 and 1970), Commonweal (1970), Ramparts (1971), and Newsweek (1971). Two fairly good treatments in book form are Stricker (1971) and Enroth et al. (1972).

[4] The authors were testing an extended model of the conversion and disaffiliation processes which derived directly from the work of Lofland (1966), Cantril (1941), Toch (1965), and Gerlach and Hine (1970). Results of this examination will be presented in a later paper.

allowed the gathering of even more information on the group and its members.

BRAINWASHING AND RELIGION

Before we proceed into a direct application of some of the thought reform findings, we would like to point out that we are certainly not the first to note the similarities between brainwashing and the techniques used by some religious groups. Lifton (1963: 454–61), whose work will be a major focus in this paper, has pointed out the similarities. He notes that "religious totalism" has often been associated with "revitalizing enthusiasm," and he cites as examples post-Reformation fundamentalist and revivalistic cults—directly anticipating our analysis. Also, he notes the fundamental relationship of thought reform to religion in general. This similarity has also been noted by Brown (1963: 223–43). Of direct interest, too, is the application of the ideas of Lifton to the religious community of Bruderhof offered by Zablocki (1971: 239–85). Many other passing references to the relationship of religion and brainwashing could be noted, but these are the major ones of which we are aware.

One other important point that should be made prior to the specific analysis is that we do *not* intend our comments to be considered normative in nature. In other words, we are not saying that the similarities between thought reform as practiced by the Chinese and conversion processes as practiced by religious groups mean ipso facto that such religious groups are bad. We make no evaluations at all, for as Lifton (1963) and others have pointed out, the goodness or badness of applying the principles involved depends completely on one's point of view. The Chinese felt that they were helping people "see the light," which is also the perspective adopted by most persons attempting to convert others to a given religion.[5]

THE JESUS MOVEMENT

As indicated, the work of Lifton (1963, 1957, 1956) will be the primary source for the examination of the Jesus Movement. Most readers will recall his theorizing derived from interviews with Chinese intellectuals and Western prisoners who had experienced thought reform during incarceration in Communist China. His work will be used because it is more relevant

---

[5] As noted in Harder et al. (1972), there is some very strong evidence that joining the Jesus Movement can be "good" (aids in getting participants off drugs, and so on), but there are also drawbacks. One such negative influence (to some) is the fact that, upon joining the movement, many of the participants become completely apolitical and henceforth care only about converting others to the movement.

than that of those who studied only POWs, a situation less comparable to the experience of most adherents to the Jesus Movement than that of Western prisoners and particularly Chinese intellectuals who were subjected to thought reform. The experience of Western prisoners led Lifton (1963) to develop an eleven-part process of resocialization,[6] which is used by Zablocki (1971) in his study of the Bruderhof commune. The process, with three major subheadings supplied by Zablocki, is as follows:

A. The stripping process
   1. the assault upon identity
   2. the establishment of guilt
   3. the self-betrayal
   4. the breaking point

B. Identification
   5. leniency and opportunity
   6. the compulsion to confess
   7. the channeling of guilt
   8. reeducation: logical dishonoring
   9. progress and harmony

C. Death and rebirth of the self
   10. final confession
   11. rebirth

This model has many aspects that recommend it to an analysis of the recruitment processes used in the Jesus Movement. However, it also has major deficiencies, as noted by Zablocki (1971). Chief among the problems is the lack of direct physical coercion in most Jesus Movement groups. Some groups have apparently made strong efforts to separate members from their parents, attempting to disallow any meaningful contact between members and their families. Dart (1971) describes some of these difficulties associated with the Children of God group (see also St. Louis Post Dispatch, 1971; Newsweek, 1971). Leaders in the group have been accused by parents of participants of practicing hypnosis (although this is strongly denied by group leaders); this is the nearest thing to the kinds of coercion used on Western prisoners or on Chinese intellectuals (who were forced to denounce their fathers) that one can find in the literature concerning the movement.

---

[6] Lifton (1956) presented an earlier version of this model that has some interesting features. We particularly like his earlier emphasis on the "recording of reality," which was the last step in his eleven-part process.

Another problem with the model is that it stresses the "stripping process" through which the identity of the individual is destroyed. Jesus Movement groups reemphasize identity destruction to the extent that it was practiced by the Chinese. A strong degree of overt coercion is not used in the movement for two major reasons: (1) such tactics are considered immoral by many and, perhaps more importantly, (2) the tactics are not necessary. Overt coercion is not necessary because most of the participants are characterized in terms of lack of identity or low self-concept.[7] Put simply, for many of the participants described in the popular press and for those encountered by the authors of this paper, there is no strong identity to destroy, and the methods used by the Chinese to destroy the often very strong personalities of incarcerated prisoners (e.g., priests, doctors, diplomats, and the like) are superfluous. Although most of the Jesus Movement participants were strongly affiliated with aspects of the contemporary drug culture prior to affiliation, anecdotal evidence from many of the members studied indicates that their previous life styles were maladaptive (e.g., one member said, "If I had not come to the Lord, I would either be in jail or in an institution, or maybe dead by now"). Thus, conversion to Christianity seems to represent a more adaptive decision for the participants, and this, in conjunction with the "weak" personalities of the members, eliminates an emphasis on the stripping process in Jesus Movement groups.

It can also be said that a stripping process is unnecessary to establish guilt in the majority of members of the movement. As with the case of Zablocki's analysis of the Bruderhof, most of the individuals come to the movement with a well-established sense of personal guilt. Perhaps this is the case with participants in the movement because of their involvement in many activities not condoned by their background values. Many have a history of heavy involvement with drugs, drinking, and premarital sex, and some have taken part in political activities of a disruptive nature. This type of activity from persons with predominantly religious backgrounds (see Harder and Richardson, 1971) could be guilt-producing, particularly if it were defined by the individuals as unrewarding in the long run. Possibly because of these past activities, which have not led to the utopia that was sought, many of the persons are at "the breaking point" before they

[7] Some evidence for this point is presented in the paper by Simmonds et al. (1972). The members as a group do not seem to have "strong" personalities, a finding that could result both from a selection bias and from effects of group membership. We would suggest both these facets play an important part in the finding. Using the theorizing of Fromm (1950), in his classic statement about the effects on an individual of participating in an authoritarian religion, we would expect to find "weaker" personalities among people whose early religious socialization was into such groups, and also among persons who had experienced adult socialization into such a group. One might even expect an additivity of effect, something that is partially testable from the data that have been gathered.

come into contact with the movement (an important element in Lofland's [1966] model of conversion). Some even seek out the movement as a way of alleviating an impossible situation. Their self-betrayal is readily obtained, without the coercion needed by the Chinese.

The "identification" and "death and rebirth" sections of the sequence do seem to have more application in the Jesus Movement—as they also do with the Bruderhof. An identity is offered as the initiates are led into accepting a definition of themselves as sinners in need of confession. This new definition is facilitated both by many of their backgrounds and by their activities prior to joining the movement. Their backgrounds also aid greatly in the process of reeducation into the fundamentalist Christian world view. As this view is accepted, they move into a state of "progress and harmony" in which they learn what roles to occupy, what ideas to hold, what language to use. In short, they learn what is rewarding in their new social milieu.

The eventual outcome of staying in contact with a group of the Jesus Movement is Lifton's final phase, rebirth, which involves a radical affirmation of the fundamentalist world view and is an important part of the initiate's required changes. For some, this culminating action is rather drastic, in that they have had little meaningful contact with such a view in the past. These individuals are somewhat analogous to Western prisoners in China. They are having to learn something relatively new and to incorporate it into their self-concepts. As noted earlier, however, *many* of the members of the Jesus Movement are from fundamentalist backgrounds. Thus, the rebirth they experience can (and perhaps should) be viewed as a "rededication" or reaffirmation of an earlier, discarded world view and thus of the society based on the old world view.

It must be understood, however, that this reaffirmation of society does not have to be (and probably seldom is) a conscious act on the part of the participants. On the conscious level, most of the participants are *withdrawing* from society (which they rapidly come to define as non-Christian or pagan). Many of them have experienced great failure in trying to cope with society, and they are seeking a more rewarding existence within a subsegment of society that offers them "success" (conversion to status of "saved") and rewards (acceptance and concern). The overt rejection of society is evidenced by the fact that an overwhelming majority of the persons we interviewed expected the "end of the world" during their generation, and they wanted this to occur. The *latent* function of this explicit rejection of society is the maintenance of the very society that is so strongly rejected and withdrawn from. Thus, Berger's (1969) theorizing about the function of religion as the chief sanctioning agent of any society seems to be evidenced by the Jesus Movement.

In some ways, the experience of these "returning fundamentalists" can be thought of as parallel to that of the Chinese intellectuals. The Jesus Movement members are "flipping back into their society" in a sense, because the values of American society are, to a large extent, derived directly from the fundamentalist tradition. Many or most of the Jesus Movement members do not view their experience in this way, but it seems somewhat apparent that they are affirming their society in general when they enter seriously into the Jesus Movement. (Why else would so many segments of society have applauded the growth of the movement and even aided directly in its support? See Dart [1971] and other discussions.) This "moving back into society" is similar to the experience of some of those Chinese intellectuals Lifton describes. Many apparently sought out the "Revolutionary Universities" in order to learn how to adapt to the changes in their society. One of Lifton's most prominent cases (Mr. Hu) fits this pattern. It seems that many members of both the Chinese intellectual groups and the Jesus Movement may be thought of as persons wanting to reenter society, since they have found their personal situation such that they can no longer cope with life's experiences outside the mainstream of society.

Because of the apparent similarities between the situations and experiences of the Chinese intellectuals and many members of the Jesus Movement, it seems efficacious to apply more directly Lifton's theorizing concerning the Chinese intellectuals (we would suggest that Zablocki could have also done this in his study of Bruderhof). Lifton (1957) presents three major elements in his analysis of the thought reform of the intellectuals:

1. The great togetherness: group identification
2. The closing in of the milieu: the period of emotional conflict
3. Submission and rebirth

His analysis is taken from an examination of the activities associated with the Revolutionary Universities set up in China between 1948 and 1952. These universities were quite large, sometimes involving up to four thousand persons in a highly organized and authoritarian situation. At the start of a session (which lasted approximately six months), participants were brought together in an austere but friendly atmosphere. They were warmly greeted and told to spend several days getting to know members of a small group of about six to ten persons to which they were assigned. Lifton points out that there very rapidly developed a high esprit de corps, as members openly exchanged personal information and discussed the reasons for their attendance at the "university." Thus, we see the development of a new reference group for the persons involved, something similar to what happens upon first contact with most Jesus Movement groups. They are friendly, open, and seem to express genuine concern for prospective members. Perhaps the movement convert is allowed to "crash" at a group's place of residence, and he is treated as an important person by group members.

The "great togetherness" is further exemplified by the close personal ties that begin to develop between prospects and members. Many of the prospects have been in situations where close relationships were not fostered (i.e., in the dog-eat-dog world of drug-oriented communities or simply in moving around the country), and this new experience becomes very meaningful for them. We think that they quite often stay because of the primary relationships that develop, and, in order to do this successfully, they must begin to show interest in the group's ideology. As has been noted in many reports about the movement, much time is spent in participating in such activities as Bible studies, prayer groups, and group-sharing sessions. These activities serve as vehicles whereby the prospect can demonstrate an interest, and they also furnish information about how to act and believe if one is to remain in the group. The activities are very similar to the formal courses and group discussions held by members of the Revolutionary Universities. In both situations, group leaders present the acceptable views and help others to rationalize them during the group discussions.

It is just a matter of time, however, before the harmonious situation that prevails changes drastically. In Lifton's terms, there is a "closing in of the milieu." Prospects are expected to make progress toward the goal of "committed Christian," and this follows a fairly regular timetable. Pressure, both subtle and overt, is brought to bear on the novice. This pressure is designed to let him know what is expected of him. If he continues to respond properly, the pressure forces the prospect to eventually adopt the group ideology as his own. One "house" of the group examined for this research allowed persons to remain in the house for three to four days with no indication from the individual that he was "accepting Christ." After this period, however, the person was asked to leave if his activities and discussion gave no indication that he was seriously considering "taking Jesus." The group members justified this in terms of their goal, bringing people closer to Christ, and rationalized that the nonaccepting person would not feel comfortable for any long period of time unless he shared the beliefs of the others.

The pressure is often successful because of the high value that the prospect has placed on the primary relationships he has developed. (This situation is perhaps illustrative of the rather profound definition of conversion as "coming to agree with your best friend.") However, if anything impedes "normal progress," then sanctions are brought to bear. Group members explain over and over the value in taking Christ (happiness, and implicit acceptance) and the reasons for the difficulty (pride, sinfulness, pleasures of this world, and so on). The person is expected to respond appropriately. When he does, there is celebration, and social rewards (warmth, acceptance, being addressed as "brother" or "sister") are offered. If he does not eventually respond properly, then as a last resort he is asked to leave. Zablocki cites several illustrations of this cutting of ties. Another illustration is the experience of Lofland (1966), who was asked to convert or leave (he left).

A simple way of describing the process of milieu closure is to say that the prospect, after a certain length of time, is no longer allowed the privilege of occupying the newcomer status (even if he is a researcher). He is forced to occupy a new role of "interested person," which, if occupied for any length of time, leads to the eventual role of "convert" (see Zetterberg [1952] for a discussion of conversion as a change of roles). This last stage of the process is accomplished through submission and rebirth. The prospect decides either not to submit (and leaves) or submits to the group pressures and gradually accepts the world view of the group. This world view, of course, contains many elements that aid him in a proper self-definition and in knowing what actions to take as a consequence of being in this state. He is told that he should confess, and perhaps he even has some role models who demonstrate this ritual to him. Thus, the prospect is led to a confession that has the effect of confirming his new world view. The confession primarily involves an oral denial of the past and a commitment to the new future.

RELIGIOUS TOTALISM

Earlier in the paper, we mentioned that Lifton had related thought reform to religion through his discussion of "religious totalism." It is apparent that the ideology of much of the Jesus Movement, including the segment we studied, adheres strongly to something that can best be characterized as religious totalism. Lifton notes that religious totalism is just one of several possible forms of the more general ideological totalism. He describes ideological totalism as situations of "the coming together of immoderate ideology with equally immoderate individual character traits" (Lifton, 1963: 419). Our comment will not focus upon the individuals involved as much as it will the things they come to believe. This paper has suggested that group forces and processes in the Jesus Movement cause a person to accept ideas and behaviors quite foreign to or previously rejected by the person.

This is perhaps not the place for a full-blown analysis of the elements of fundamentalism. However, since forms of fundamentalism have gained so many adherents in some parts of the United States and because the elements of fundamentalism may be unfamiliar to some readers, a brief look at the phenomenon seems in order.

Lifton mentions eight separate elements that are all part of ideological totalism. These include: (1) milieu control, (2) mystical manipulation, (3) the demand for purity, (4) the cult of confession, (5) the "sacred science," (6) loading the language, (7) doctrine over person, and (8) the dispensing of existence. Since some of these are not readily understandable, a few comments will be made about each.

Milieu control, which Lifton defines as "control of human communication," was nearly complete in the group we studied, although the degree of such control varies across the movement as a whole. At one extreme are groups like the Children of God and at the other are groups of "teenie boppers for Jesus" who live at home and attend regular schools. In the group we examined, none but leaders could go into town or even talk on the phone without permission. We were unable to find out if there was any censorship of mail. There was also control of intragroup communications, but this will be examined as a part of "loading the language."

Mystical manipulation is the term Lifton used for the sense of higher purpose or calling felt in ideological totalism. Members are told that they are part of some great plan that has been revealed; they have been "chosen" by forces outside themselves to carry on some mystical imperative. All those we interviewed shared the view that they had been selected by God for the work and witnessing they were doing. Most made it very plain that they had "given themselves up to God." Thus, they would work for ten hours in the fields or go into town to witness if God, through one of the pastors, would only so direct them. All life's major decisions were made with the "great plan" in mind, and most members were possessed by the "psychology of the pawn," as Lifton terms it.

The *demand for purity* refers to the dichotomous picture of the world that is adopted by believers. Everything is in black and white. "He who is not for me is against me" is the rule. This includes old friends and loved ones, who are simply defined away as significant others (except perhaps as potential converts). It should also be noted that a major emphasis of the demand for purity is to bring out feelings of guilt on the part of participants. The rigorous standards can seldom be met; the individual nearly always falls short and is left remorseful and repentant (and thus more easily manipulable). But the problem goes even to a deeper level. If the individual is successful at some task, credit is to go to the higher power. Thus we found respondents who would blame themselves when they did something wrong, but accept no credit when they did something properly. Fromm (1950) suggests that such an ideology is very destructive of viable personalities.

The *cult of confession* appears not as strong an element in most Jesus Movement groups, although there are some elements of similarity. The compulsive nature of confession that occurred in the Revolutionary Universities was not noted in our research. However, we did note that most major and even minor decisions were discussed openly with pastors, and there was also an emphasis on discussing "trials" (temptations or fleshly desires) with pastors.

All adherents seemed to treat their brand of Christianity as a very explicit *sacred science*. They believed their basic dogma was completely true and did not question it. Contained within this dogma was an implicit view of the moral vision for ordering human existence. In the case of fundamentalism, the sacred science is even blatantly anti-scientific and anti-intellectual, but it is still a sacred science in Lifton's terms. One important element of a sacred science is that, in the totalist environment, there is no distinction made between the sacred and the profane or secular. All things have a meaning, and nothing is frivolous. Even the most apparently casual action or thought has a greater meaning in the plan of God.

Loading the language means that a "language of non-thought" is developed and used. Such was the case with the group we studied. A few "thought-terminating clichés" were used in many different types of situations. "Praise God," "Thank you, Lord," "Are you a Christian," and "Pray about it" are examples. No situation was too complex for one of these or a similar phrase. The members were "linguistically deprived" by the acceptable language norms in the group.

Doctrine over person occurs when there is a "subordination of human experience to the claims of doctrine." Such is certainly the case in fundamentalism—including that practiced by most of the Jesus Movement. Ideas are held to be of ultimate importance, and people must conform to them. If they refuse, then they are asked to leave or are treated as deviant. Eventually members learn that their own experiences are inconsequential in relation to the doctrine of the group.

Closely related to the notion of "doctrine over person" is the *dispensing of existence* of those that are not doctrinally pure. All things human are subjugated to the doctrine, and this includes friends, family, loved ones, and even oneself. Individuals are either believers or nonbelievers. There is no middle ground of compromise on doctrinal points. The "dispensing" is not as literal in the case of the Jesus Movement as it was in the thought reform practiced in China, but it still has profound effects. Young people are taught to believe that their parents or friends are basically evil and not to be even talked to except in a witnessing situation. They are also led to believe that they themselves are evil if they disagree on major points of doctrine.

Lifton suggests that the more these eight elements combine in a situation, the more the situation can be used to change peoples' thought and behavior patterns. Certainly the Jesus Movement is not as extreme an example as was the brainwashing that went on in China. However, many of the same elements are present, and the backgrounds of many participants make them quite susceptible to adopting such a totalistic view of everything.

SUMMARY

Hopefully, the preceding discussion has evidenced the initial point that there are some rather important similarities between the thought reform of Western prisoners and Chinese intellectuals and the conversion processes of the Jesus Movement. We would particularly emphasize the group structure and process elements present in both situations. As we can verify, the group pressures brought to bear on persons having contact with the movement are quite often extremely intense. Coauthors of this paper who were involved in the interviewing of members of one Jesus Movement group were under such pressure that they felt a need to withdraw daily in order to reaffirm their own world view through "the thin thread of conversation" (Berger, 1967: 17). If trained and fairly objective observers such as these began to succumb to the group influences, then the effect on participants without "strong" personalities and with few viable alternative reference or primary groups must indeed be great. Also, we have noted similarities between the types of thought systems possessed by each movement. The fundamentalism of the Jesus Movement seems to be a good example of Lifton's concept of ideological totalism.

REFERENCES

ADAMS, R. L., and R. J. Fox, "Mainlining Jesus: The New Trip," *Society* 9 (February 1972), 50–56.

BAUER, R. A., "Brainwashing: Psychology or Demology? *J. of Social Issues* 13, 3 (1957), 41–47.

BERGER, P., *The Sacred Canopy*. Garden City, N.Y.: Doubleday, 1969.

BROWN, J. A. C., *Techniques of Persuasion*. Baltimore: Penguin, 1963.

CANTRIL, H., *The Psychology of Social Movements*. New York: John Wiley, 1941.

Commonweal, "Jesus Freaks: Savagery and Salvation on Sunset Strip," 93 (October 30, 1970), 122–25.

DART, J., "Youth Commune Religion Upsets Parents," *Los Angeles Times* (October 10, 1971).

ENROTH, R. M., E. F. ERICSON, JR., and C. B. PETERS, *The Jesus People: Old Time Religion in the Age of Aquarius*. Grand Rapids, Mich.: Ferdmans, 1972.

FROMM, E., *Psychoanalysis and Religion*. New Haven, Conn.: Yale Univ. Press, 1950.

GERLACH, L. P., and V. H. HINE, *People, Power, Change: Movements of Social Transformation*. Indianapolis: Bobbs-Merrill, 1970.

HARDER, M. W., "The Role of Women in a Fundamentalist Religious Sect," presented at the annual meeting of the Rocky Mountain Social Science Association, Salt Lake City, 1972.

———, and J. T. RICHARDSON, "The Jesus Movement: Some Preliminary Empirical Evidence," presented at the annual meeting of the Society for the Scientific Study of Religion, Chicago, 1971.

————, and R. B. SIMMONDS, "The Jesus People," *Psychology Today* (December 1972).

KINKEAD, E., "The Study of Something New in History," *New Yorker* 33, 36 (1957), 102–53.

LIFTON, R. J., *Thought Reform and the Psychology of Totalism.* New York: W. W. Norton, 1963.

————, "Thought Reform of Chinese Intellectuals: A Psychiatric Evaluation," *J. of Social Issues* 13, 3 (1957), 5–20.

————, "Thought Reform of Western Civilians in Chinese Communist Prisons," *Psychiatry* 19, 2 (1956), 173–95.

LOFLAND, J., *Doomsday Cult.* Englewood Cliffs, N.J.: Prentice-Hall, 1966.

MILLER, J. G., "Brainwashing: Present and Future," *J. of Social Issues* 13, 3 (1957), 48–55.

Newsweek, November 22, 1971, 89–90.

Ramparts, "Jesus Now: Hogwash and Holy Water," 10 (August 1971), 24–26.

SALZMAN, L., "The Psychology of Religious and Ideological Conversion," *Psychiatry* 16, 3 (1953), 177–87.

SEGAL, J., "Correlates of Collaboration and Resistance Behavior Among U. S. Army POW's in Korea," *J. of Social Issues* 13, 3 (1957), 31–40.

SIMMONDS, R. B., J. T. RICHARDSON, and M. W. HARDER, "The Jesus Movement: An Adjective Check List Assessment of Members of a Fundamentalist Religious Community," presented at the annual meeting of the Western Psychological Association, Portland, Oregon, 1972.

SCHIEN, E. H., "Epilogue: Something New in History," *J. of Social Issues* 13, 3 (1957a), 56–60.

————, "Reaction Patterns to Severe, Chronic Stress in American Army Prisoners of War of the Chinese," *J. of Social Issues* 13, 3 (1957b), 21–30.

————, "The Chinese Indoctrination Program for Prisoners of War," *Psychiatry* 12, 2 (1956), 149–72.

STRIEKER, L. D., *The Jesus Trip: Advent of the Jesus Freaks.* Nashville: Abingdon, 1971.

St. Louis Post Dispatch, "Parents Protest Jesus-Freak Movement," October 17, 1971.

Time, "New Rebel Cry: Jesus Is Coming," 97 (June 21, 1971), 56–63.

————, "Street Christians: Jesus as the Ultimate Trip," 96 (August 3, 1970), 31–32.

TOCH, H., *The Social Psychology of Social Movement.* Indianapolis: Bobbs-Merrill, 1965.

ZABLOCKI, B. D., *The Joyful Community.* Baltimore: Penguin, 1971.

ZETTERBERG, H., "The Religious Conversion as a Change of Social Roles," *Sociology and Social Research* 36, 3 (1952), 159–66.

4
social
relationships

KINGSLEY DAVIS

Jealousy and Sexual Property

I

Descartes defined jealousy as "a kind of fear related to a desire to preserve a possession." He was, if we look at what is customarily called jealous behavior, eminently correct. In every case it is apparently a fear or rage reaction to a threatened appropriation of one's own, or what is desired as one's own, property.

Conflicts over property involve four major elements: Owner, Object, Public, and Rival (or Trespasser). These have a slightly different nature and a slightly different relation according to whether the conflict situation is one of regulated and legitimate competition or of illegitimate trespass. In the former case Ego is a *would-be* owner and his enemy a rival. A popular fallacy has been to conceive the jealous situation as a triangle. Actually it is a quadrangle, and the failure to include the public or community element has led to a failure to grasp the social character of jealousy. The relationships between the four elements are institutionally defined. They constitute the fixed traditional constellation of rights, obligations, and neutralities called property, and are sustained by interacting attitudes.

Since property, however, is not always actually in the hands of the owner, ownership must be distinguished from possession, the one being a matter of law and mores, the other a matter of fact. Possession by a person other than the owner may be either licit or illicit. Illicit possession shows that institutions of property are susceptible of evasion; licit possession by one not the owner, as with a borrowed or rented piece of property, emphasizes their strength.

Acquisition of property proceeds usually according to socially established rules of competition, and, in many cases, by stages. In the initial stage the field is generally open to a class of persons, anybody in this class being free to put in a claim. The qualifying rounds of an amateur golf tournament or the sudden entrance of a strange but attractive young woman are cases in point. Gradually a few competitors take the lead. Social order then requires that others recognize the superiority of these, quit struggling, and turn their attention elsewhere. Finally, after continued competition

Reprinted from *Social Forces*, 14, 3 (1936), 395–405, by permission of the publisher.

among the favored few, one competitor wins. This is the signal for everyone who was initially interested to drop all pretense of a claim and take his defeat in good spirit. Competition for this particular piece of property is now, by social edict, either temporarily or permanently over. It is owned by one man, behind whose title stands the authority of the community.

Values, however, do not invariably change hands in any such orderly fashion. The unscrupulous stand always ready to take possession in defiance of the rules, to replace the orderliness of rivalry with the disarrangement of trespass. They may at any stage, under peril of organized retaliation, upset the procedure and seize physical possession of the property.

There are thus two dangers which beset any person with regard to property. The first is that somebody will win out over him in legitimate competition. This is the danger of superior rivalry. The second is that somebody will illegitimately take from him property already acquired. This is the danger of trespass.

Most malignant emotions are concerned with these two dangers, being directed either at a rival or trespasser or at someone who is helping a rival or trespasser. Such emotions may be suppressed by the group culture or utilized for maintaining the organized distribution of property. In general fear and hatred of rivals is institutionally suppressed; fear and hatred of trespassers encouraged.

In the initial stages of acquisition fear of rivals is frequently paramount. Such fear is merely the obverse side of strong desire to win. In so far as a society fosters the desire to win and builds up an emotional drive in the individual to that end, it inevitably fosters the fear of losing. By the same token, when defeat actually occurs it implies a frustration of strong desire, hence an inevitable emotion. This emotion, since most competitors cannot win, occurs frequently. Yet social organization requires that such emotions, once the property is in the winner's hands, be curbed. Society tends necessarily to suppress them, and to encourage one-time rivals to be "good sports," "graceful losers."

The successful rival, however, need not suppress these emotions. Once established as owner, he is encouraged by the culture to express them toward any trespasser. Free expression of malevolent emotion against a trespasser protects the established distribution of property and maintains the fixed rules for its competitive acquisition.

II

Can the relationship of affection between two persons be conceived as a property relationship? This is a question not to be answered too glibly. The affectional relationship is certainly not identical with *economic* property, although sheer sexual gratification, as in prostitution, may be. Affection assumes that the object is desired in and for itself. It therefore cannot be bought and sold; it is not a means to something else, not an economic thing. Yet the affectional relationship has features that are characteristic of property in general. It is regulated, highly institutionalized; and involves some sort of institutionalized exclusiveness, hedged about with rights and obligations. There is competition for possession, a feeling of ownership on the part of the successful competitor, a "hands-off" attitude on the part of the public, and a general resentment against anyone who endeavors to break up the relationship by "stealing" the object. In view of these considerations I feel justified in applying the term property to the institutionalized possession of affection. There exists no other term, apparently, which will describe those types of sanctioned possession which are not economic. Nevertheless the distinction between economic and non-economic property must be made clear. This can be accomplished by a more detailed consideration of types and sub-types of property.

Economic property is that type in which the object possessed is a means to an ulterior end. Non-economic property is that type in which the object is an end in itself. Several sub-types can be distinguished under each head, but I shall rest content with distinguishing three kinds of economic and one kind of non-economic property, calling them by the attitude which Ego has in each case towards the object—respectively, *need, vanity, pride,* and *love*.

1. *Need*. Some objects of property satisfy organic needs. Food, shelter, prostitute, or servant may fall into this category. The object is not valued for itself, but simply as a means of satisfying the need; it may be bought, sold, and substituted. The attitude of the public is subsidiary. A person desires the public to regard the object as his property, but solely because he needs it.

2. *Vanity*. When an object is valued not for the satisfaction of a need but for the response it elicits in one's neighbors, and when the only connection between owner and object is mere possession, a new property situation is apparent. The attitude of the public is no longer subsidiary but paramount. An expensive diamond, a top-hat, a long automobile are useless except as tokens and instruments of the owner's social status. The ulterior end is the envious approval of the community.

Whereas in the need situation a rival or trespasser could proceed only by gaining possession of the actual object, he may in the vanity situation employ an additional procedure. He may gain the ulterior end by possession of a different but superior object.

Vanity is often condemned on moral grounds because there is no necessary relationship between merit and possession of an enviable object. A fool may inherit a crown; an ignorant farmer acquire riches in oil; a silly girl possess incomparable beauty. When such people attribute merit to themselves for such possessions, they are vain, and such vanity, for the public, is thin and unlovely.[1]

3. *Pride*. This type is characterized by an intrinsic relation between owner and object. The object is some form of accomplishment, and reflects professional ability. There is thus a necessary connection, recognized by the public, between the qualities of the owner and the nature of his possession. The ownership is indeed more a matter of accomplishment than of legal technicality. All that law or the public can do is to recognize and protect it when it comes; it cannot create it.

4. *Love*. In the three previous cases the object, while not necessarily inanimate or completely passive, takes no dynamic part in the equilibrium. In the present case, however, the object consists in a personal attitude—an attitude of affection. Since affection is a phenomenon of will, the question of possession is thereby placed largely in the hands of the object.

Out of this peculiarity grow the other idiosyncrasies of love-property. We find, for instance, that a jealous lover often attacks the love object herself, seeking to restrain or retaliate. Having control of the vital element in the situation—affection—she is in a position to decide the issue. She can bestow affection either on Ego or on his rival, as she chooses. A man might destroy his food in order to keep another from getting it; he might destroy his jewels or other emblems of prestige; he might even renounce and forsake his profession—but unless indulging in an anthropomorphic extravaganza he would not do this out of resentment toward the object itself. Yet in the case of sexual jealousy the resentment may be more against the object of love than against the rival.

In the situations both of vanity and of pride we noted that the thing really desired was the envy or admiration of the public—in other words, an attitude. The same is true of the love situation, where an attitude of affection is desired. To this extent the three property situations are similar, and we do find that jealousy has been applied to all of them—especially to the pride situation as "professional jealousy." (Only to the need situation does jealousy seem totally inapplicable.) Yet in spite of similarities we have to separate the love-property situation from the others, because the object possessed in this situation is purely an end in itself. This is a peculiarity which it shares with other forms of property. Moreover, the affectional relationship implies a reciprocal, mutual interchange between owner and object

[1] This type, like the others, is of course an abstraction—an ideal-type. Motives and attitudes in actual life situations are nearly always mixed. Need, vanity, pride, and love will be present in practically every concrete situation. Rarely, for example, is sheer possession the reason for the public's envy and respect. Usually the secret of such envy and respect is that possession conveys power. Such power may be valued merely for the envy it commands, in which case the relationship remains within the vanity type. Or it may be valued because it enables one to satisfy needs, to succeed in love, or to acquire skills, in which case it falls by implication into one of the other three types. In actual life, however, several or all of these attitudes are present in the same situation.

which is not true of the other forms. Thus the relationship, in addition to being an end in itself, gives the object a dynamic rôle in determining the direction of the conflict situation. It may be, too, that conflicts over love generate more emotion than other kinds. When the object possessed is another person the universal process by which the owner identifies himself with the thing possessed (transmuting "mine" into "I") is perhaps more complete than when the object is not a person. Still this identification, simply because the object is not inert but willful, is probably most tenuous of all. The relationship thus being unusually close and at the same time unusually tenuous, becomes doubly intense.

III

In depicting the four types of property relationship we have stopped four processes in mid-air. They are not static but dynamic—instable conflict situations tending inevitably toward their own solution. Fidelity to fact would require that some notion be given of their processual sequence from *début* to *dénouement*.

A complete sequence in love-property conflict would begin with the rivalry phase. It would depict the changing attitudes of the rivals, and of the object and the public, as some are eliminated and one finally wins. The next phase would show the winner in secure possession at some level of ownership such as the "sweetheart," the "fiancée," or the "spouse" level. He is no longer jealous because rivalry is finished and no trespasser is in sight, and the public has an attitude of "don't disturb." The third phase, trespass, would describe the attitude of Ego as he becomes aware of an enemy—his attitudes toward the trespasser, the love object, and the public. It would describe also the attitudes of the trespasser; and since the direction of the sequence hinges largely upon the woman, her attitudes toward lover, rival, and public. If she favors the trespasser and is willing to risk Ego's and the community's wrath, Ego may lose. On the other hand if she does not favor the trespasser, or if he, himself, is not willing to take the risk, or if Ego or the public uses irresistible force, Ego may win. The complexity of attitudes between the four interacting agencies grows amazingly complex. Innumerable combinations are possible. To describe them all, though a fascinating adventure into the anatomy of dramatic reality, would require a tome.[2]

---

[2] One attitude that seems dependent upon the stage of conflict is envy. Envy is the attitude not of the owner but of either the public or a potential rival. It implies that a person would like to have a possession that another owns but that he is at the time making no effort to wrest it away from the owner. It can hardly be present in one's mind at the same time as jealousy, because the latter implies some claim to possession or at least a right to compete. Envy is the obverse side of the desire for the valuables of a community, and since it usually cuts across the institutional distribution it is frowned upon by the group culture.

IV

Since in love-property the object of possession is the affection of another person we may expect jealousy to have direct bearing upon the sociology of intimacy. Only when there is a presumption of *gemeinschaft* or *primary* association in past, present, or future can jealousy, apparently, appear.

Yet jealousy signifies at least a partial negation of that rapport between persons which we commonly ascribe to intimacy. It admits that affection has strayed in the direction of a rival. Even where affection has not strayed jealousy shows on the lover's part a mistrust inimical to the harmony of perfect intimacy.

What, then, is the function of jealousy with regard to intimate association? As a fear reaction in the initial stages of rivalry it is simply the obverse side of the desire to win the object. The desire to win being institutionally cultivated, the fear of losing is unavoidably stimulated also, though its expression is publicly frowned upon. But after ownership has been attained, jealousy is a fear and rage reaction fitted to protect, maintain, and prolong the intimate association of love. It shelters this personal relationship from outside intrusion. This is not to say that it never defeats its own purpose by overshooting the mark. So deeply emotional is jealousy that it appears in the midst of modern social relationships, which are most profitably manipulated by self-composed shrewdness, as a bull in a china shop. Nonetheless its intention is protective. It is a denial of gemeinschaft only in so far as its presence admits a breach; and is destructive of it only in so far as it muddles its own purpose.

Jealousy stresses two characteristics of gemeinschaft relationship: its ultimate and its personal qualities. The relationship is for the jealous person an ultimate end in itself, all other considerations coming secondary. This explains the bizarre crimes so frequently connected with jealousy—crimes understandable only upon the assumption that for the criminal the affection of a particular person is the supreme value in life. It also explains the connection between extreme jealousy and romantic love. The "personal" quality of the relationship is manifested by the unwillingness of the jealous person to conceive any substitute for the "one and only." He insists upon the uniqueness of personality. Were the particular person removed, the whole relationship and its accompanying emotion of jealousy would disappear.

An old debate poses the question whether or not affection is divisible. Is it possible to love two people sincerely at the same time? Most sexologists answer that it is possible, and cite cases as proof. Iwan Bloch, for example, asserts that simultaneous passion for several persons happens repeatedly.[3]

---

[3] *Sexual Life of Our Time*, pp. 206–207. Havelock Ellis, *Studies in Psych. of Sex*, VI, 568–69, agrees. Also Joseph K. Folsom, in his *Social Psychology*, pp. 154–55.

He adds that the extensive psychic differentiation between individuals in modern civilization increases its likelihood, for it is difficult to find in a single person one's complement. He gives numerous examples from history and literature, particularly cases where one aspect of a person's nature is satisfied by one lover, another aspect (usually the sensual) by a different lover.

The conclusion invariably deduced from this is that jealousy is harmful and unjustified. But to end the discussion with this ethical argument is to miss the point. Even though love, like any other distributive value, is divisible, institutions dictate the manner and extent of the division. Where exclusive possession of an individual's entire love is customary, jealousy will demand that exclusiveness. Where love is divided it will be divided according to some scheme, and jealousy will reinforce the division.

V

While the love-property situation contains a relationship of intimacy and throws light upon the sociology of gemeinschaft association, it also contains a diametrically opposite kind of relation—namely, that of power—which concerns the sociology of dominance and subordination. This relationship, which obtains between the lover and his rival or trespasser, is not a value in itself but a means to an ulterior end; and it connotes an absolute opposition of purpose, in the sense that if one succeeds the other fails. The rival or trespasser may be a stranger or a close friend; in either event, so far as the common object is concerned, he is an enemy.

Here, as elsewhere in the discussion, it makes a difference whether the enemy is a trespasser or a rival. Rivalry is most acute in the early stages of acquisition, and jealousy is at this point a fear of not winning the desired object. Toward one's rival one is supposed to show good sport and courtesy, which is to say that society requires the suppression, in this context, of jealous animosity. Regulated competition constitutes the *sine qua non* of property distribution and hence of stable social organization. But as one person gets ahead and demonstrates a superior claim, his rivals, hiding their feelings of jealous disappointment, must drop away. If any rival persists after the victor has with institutional ritual fortified his claim he is no longer a rival but a trespasser.

Jealousy toward the trespasser is encouraged rather than suppressed, for it tends to preserve the fundamental institutions of property. Uncles in our society are never jealous of the affection of nephews for their father. But uncles in matrilineal societies frequently are, because there is a close tie socially prescribed between uncle and nephew. The nephew's respect is the property of the uncle; if it is given to the father (as sometimes happens because of the close association between father and son), the uncle is jealous.

Jealousy does not occur in the natural situations—and the "natural situations" are simply those defined in terms of the established institutions. Our malignant emotions, fear, anger, hate, and jealousy, greet any illicit attempt to gain property that we hold. They do not manifest themselves when a licit attempt is made, partly because we do not then have the subjective feeling of "being wronged," and partly because their expression would receive the disapprobation of the community. The social function of jealousy against a trespasser is the extirpation of any obstacle to the smooth running of the institutional machinery.

Discussions of jealousy usually overlook the difference between rivalry and trespass. A case in point is the old problem of whether one can be jealous of a person not one's equal. If the person is a trespasser the answer is that he can be at any social distance away. But if he is a rival he cannot be too far distant. Rivalry implies a certain degree of equality at the start. Each society designates which of its members are eligible to compete for certain properties. While there are some properties for which members of different classes may compete, there are others for which they may not compete. In such cases the thought of competition is inconceivable, the emotions reserved for a rival fail to appear, and the act is regarded not as rivalry but as a detestable thrust at the class structure. Thus it happens that for a given lover some people cannot arouse jealousy as of a rival. If the love-object yields to a member of a distinctly inferior social class, jealousy will turn into moral outrage, no matter if the lover himself has no claim on the love-object. It is inconceivable, for this reason, that a Negro could be the rival of a southern white man for the hand of a white girl. The white man would have him lynched. Southern society does not permit Negroes as a class to compete for the affection of white girls. It is almost equally inconceivable that a white man could be a Negro's rival for the hand of a colored girl. The Negro has either too much advantage in the likelihood of social ostracism for the white man, or too little advantage in that the white man, if immune to ostracism, can take the property by force.

But jealousy against a trespasser is another matter. A trespasser being by definition a breaker of customary rules, the more he breaks, including the rules of class structure, the more of a trespasser he is. A violator of property rights may for this reason occupy any position on the social scale.

The fact that men of native races sometimes prostitute their wives to civilized men without any feeling of jealousy, while they are extremely jealous of men of their own race,[4] is sometimes pointed out as showing that men are jealous only of their equals. This is true only in so far as jealousy of rivals is meant. The civilized man is not conceived by the natives as a rival, nor as a trespasser. He may be conceived as a trespasser—if, for exam-

[4] Malinowski, *Sexual Life of Savages*, p. 271.

ple, he attempts to retain the wife without paying anything. Yet in the case mentioned he is not a trespasser, but merely one who has legitimately paid for the temporary use of property. His very payment recognizes the property rights of the husband. The following case is much more illustrative: "A Frenchman of position picks for his mistress a girl who is not his social equal. You can see for yourself that his wife is not jealous. But let him choose a woman of his own social rank—then you'd see the fur fly; . . ."[5] Among some social spheres in France, if we are to believe what we hear, women of different classes customarily exercise proprietary rights in the same man, and no jealousy is felt. But since it is not customary for members of the same rank to share a man, such a condition is either rivalry or trespass, and arouses intense jealousy.

One may argue that the nearer two people are in every plane, the more intense will be the jealousy of rivalry; while the further apart they are, the greater the jealousy of trespass.

But between the lover and the object of his love the relationship is not one of power. If a woman is regarded simply as a pawn in a game for prestige the pattern is No. 2 in our typology, not No. 4. It is a question of vanity rather than jealousy. In the love situation the jealous person values the affection for itself. It is his fear of losing this intrinsically valuable affection to a rival or a trespasser, rather than his fear of losing prestige in the eyes of his public and his rival, that paralyzes him.

VI

Into every affair of love and battle for power steps society. It has an inherent interest in love not only because future generations depend upon it but because social cohesion rests upon the peaceful distribution of major values.

A question that all authorities feel compelled to settle concerns the social or anti-social character of jealousy. Forel declares that jealousy "is only the brutal stupidity of an atavistic heritage, or a pathological symptom,"[6] while Havelock Ellis calls it "an anti-social emotion."[7] The chief arguments are that it is an inheritance from animal ancestors, a hindrance to the emancipation of women, and an obstacle to rational social intercourse.

The hasty readiness to praise or condemn prevents a clear understanding of the relation of jealousy to institutional structure. Careful analysis is cut short by the quick conclusion that jealousy is instinctive, the assump-

---

[5] Reported by Ben. B. Lindsey, *Companionate Marriage*, p. 88.

[6] *The Sexual Question*, pp. 118–119.

[7] *Studies in Psychology of Sex*, VI, 564.

tion being that certain stimuli call forth a stereotyped, biologically ingrained response. Jealousy is therefore regarded as an animal urge, and since biological nature and sociological nature are assumed to be eternally at odds, jealousy is denounced as anti-social.[8]

This view fails to analyze jealous behavior into its different components —to distinguish between the stimulus (with its physical and meaningful aspects) and the physical mechanism of response. It puts all constituents into the undifferentiated category of instinct.

Doubtless the physiological mechanism is inherited. But the striking thing about this mechanism is that it is not specific for jealousy, but operates in precisely the same manner in fear and rage. The sympathetic nervous system plays, apparently, the usual rôle: increased adrenal activity speeding the heart, increasing the sugar content of the blood, toning up the striated and staying the smooth muscles.

If we are to differentiate jealousy from the other strong emotions we must speak not in terms of inherited physiology but in terms of the type of situation which provokes it. The conflict situation always contains a particular content, and the content varies from one culture to the next. The usual mistake in conceiving jealousy is to erect a concrete situation found somewhere (often in the culture of the author) into the universal and inherent stimulus to that emotion. This ignores the fact that each culture distributes its sexual property and defines its conflict situations in its own way, and that, therefore, the concrete content cannot be regarded as an inherited stimulus to an inherited response.

This mistake is made, I think, by those theorists who seek to explain certain human institutions on the basis of instinctive emotions. In the field of sexual institutions Westermarck is the outstanding theorist who has relied upon this type of explanation. He disproves the hypothesis of primeval promiscuity and proves the primacy of pair marriage largely on the basis of allegedly innate jealousy.[9] He assumes, indeed, that all types of sexual relationship other than monogamy, as he knows it in his own culture, are native stimuli to instinctive jealous retaliation.

As soon, however, as we admit that other forms of sexual property exist, and that they do not arouse but instead are protected by jealousy, the ex-

---

[8] The logic of social ethicists at times becomes badly scrambled. Frequently it is clear that what they call "instinctive" is merely the institutions to which they are habituated and to which they lend their approval. The biological basis of the institutions is thus assumed to justify them, for, if a thing is instinctive, like love, it should be given free expression, not suppressed. On the other hand the inveterate propensity to derive all social phenomena from the genetic qualities of the individual leads the ethicists to infer that certain disapproved behavior, like criminality, war, or jealousy, is also instinctive. In this case the assumption that it is biological becomes, not a justification, but a reason for condemnation. It is "atavistic," "barbaric," "animal-like."

[9] *History of Human Marriage,* Ch. 9.

planation of monogamy breaks down. Whether as the obverse side of the desire to obtain sexual property by legitimate competition, or as the anger at having rightful property trespassed upon, jealousy would seem to bolster the institutions where it is found. If these institutions are of an opposite character to monogamy, it bolsters them nonetheless. Whereas Westermarck would say that adultery arouses jealousy and that, therefore, jealousy causes monogamy, one could maintain that our institution of monogamy causes adultery to be resented and, therefore, creates jealousy.

Had he confined himself to disproving promiscuity instead of going on to prove monogamy, Westermarck would have remained on surer ground. Promiscuity implies the absence of any sexual property-pattern. Yet sexual affection is, unlike divine grace, a distributive value. To let it go undistributed would introduce anarchy into the group and destroy the social "system." Promiscuity can take place only in so far as society has broken down and reached a state of anomie.

The stimulus to jealousy, moreover, is not so much a physical situation as a meaningful one. The same physical act will in one place denote ownership, in another place robbery. Westermarck appears to believe that it is the physical act of sexual intercourse between another man and one's wife that instinctively arouses jealousy. But there are cultures where such intercourse merely emphasizes the husband's status as owner, just as lending an automobile presumes and emphasizes one's ownership of it.

We may cite, for example, the whole range of institutions whereby, in some manner, the wife is given over to a man other than her husband. These run from those highly ritualized single acts in which a priest or a relative deflowers the wife, to the repeated and more promiscuous acts of sexual hospitality and the more permanent and thorough-going agreements of wife-exchange; not to mention the fixed division of sexual function represented by polyandric marriage. In societies where any institution in this range prevails, the behavior implied does not arouse the feeling of jealousy that similar behavior would arouse in our culture. Jealousy does not respond inherently to any particular situation; it responds to all those situations, no matter how diverse, which signify a violation of accustomed sexual rights.

VII

Possession of a thing of value without any right to it is a prevalent condition in sexual behavior, affection being evidently difficult to govern. The converse—ownership without custody—appears equally prevalent. At least in our culture the instances are countless in which there is no overt transgression of convention and yet affection has strayed. Wives and husbands abound who have little or no affection for their mates, but who would not actually sully the marriage tie. Their affection is owned by their mates, but not possessed.

Our discussion seems to have associated jealousy exclusively with ownership, with outward conformity, rather than with actual possession. This has not been due to ignorance of possible discrepancy between the two, or to ignorance of the fact that many lovers, especially the romantic variety, profess to care only for the possession of affection, and nothing at all for conformity to senseless tradition. It has been due, rather, to a conviction that so-called outward conformity, either through speech or overt behavior, is always the symbol of the inward state. If a woman never, by word or deed, let the fact appear that she did not love her husband, he would never have cause to feel jealous. She must say or do something contrary to a wife's institutionally sanctioned rôle before jealousy will be justified. If she says she loves her husband and yet does things contrary to the mores, such as have intercourse with a prohibited man, actions will be presumed to speak louder than words, and jealousy will be in order.

To us who conform outwardly to many meaningless and secretly detested conventions, and perform an even greater number of routine technological acts which try our patience, a close correspondence between inner feeling and external act seems questionable. Yet if we analyze the less conspicuous because less conscious aspects of our behavior, we find the correspondence frequently quite close. In situations where we are supposed to feel ashamed, we feel ashamed—and prove it by our outward embarrassment. In situations where we are supposed to show respect, we usually feel respect. In only a few civilizations is the distinction between external act and internal feeling sharply realized, and even then they are not far apart. In any case action which conforms to the institutions of property is the symbol of genuine possession, and contrary action the symbol of lack of possession.

It is true that conformity at any particular time may be a deception, but the deception is hardly significant unless it manifests itself at some time in non-conformist outward behavior. Whether or not it is a deception depends, of course, upon the internal state, which is the motivating factor. So the aim of the lover is always to control the inner state of affection, not simply to enforce a present conformity which guarantees nothing concerning future behavior. This in spite of the fact that his only clue is the loved one's outward conformity or non-conformity.

Unless through each stage of progressive ownership actual possession also progresses, inconvenience will result. A girl who becomes engaged to a man without caring for him and without intending to marry him is in an uncomfortable position. She cannot complain if her fiancé's legitimate jealousy and the public's interest in morality restrict her actions. She knows that when she breaks her engagement she must have a good excuse wherewith to avoid social censure. At all times she is constrained to feign an affection she does not feel. On the whole the inconvenience of a hiatus between real feeling and institutional status is in this case greater than the advantage. Moreover, most girls are trained to think of such a thing as not only unwise but also unfair and immoral. In this way ownership tends to approximate genuine possession.

VIII

Unfortunately our treatment has been couched entirely in terms of the stable and integrated culture, and there is not space to treat the complications arising when society has reached a state of anomie. As the institutions of property in general disintegrate, sexual property follows suit. In extreme cases, apparently, ownership may disappear and be replaced entirely by sheer possession.

Juxtaposition of contrary mores and rapid change have given our culture a certain amount of anomie, which is reflected in the emotions surrounding the distribution of sexual favor. None of our sexual institutions is sanctioned by all groups. Consequently, no matter how customary the sexual behavior, somebody can be found who is made jealous by it. For example, those who are not used to dancing and who disapprove of it are apt to grow extremely jealous if a wife or sweetheart indulges. This, coupled with other traits such as our individualism and romanticism, has tended, in the eyes of our intelligentsia, to give jealousy a negative value. Yet among the juries of the land the "unwritten law" is still a sanctioned reality.

GALE PETER LARGEY and DAVID RODNEY WATSON

The Sociology of Odors[1]

Universally, human animals are simultaneously emitting and perceiving odors. Ethologists, psychoanalysts, and biologists have seriously

Reprinted from *The American Journal of Sociology*, 77, 6 (1972), 1021–34, by permission of The University of Chicago Press. Copyright 1972 by The University of Chicago Press.

[1] We thank Michael Farrell, D. C. Morton, W. W. Sharrock, Gunhilde Werrick, and Robert Snow for their helpful suggestions and encouragement.

studied the phenomenon. Yet, with the exception of Georg Simmel (1908, pp. 646–60), sociologists have either ignored odors or regarded them as an insignificant dimension of human interaction—a curious fact for the sociology of knowledge.

The sociological approach to odors might ask: What effects do differences in culture and life style have upon the perception and generation of odors? What social meanings are attributed to such perceived and generated odors? What social functions do such meanings fulfill? More specifically: Why are Negroes and lower-class persons often stereotyped as being "foul smelling"? To what extent are alleged malodors used as grounds for avoiding interaction? What is the social significance of the fart taboo? What are the dynamics of odor manipulation? Why, for instance, do people perfume? And does the use of incense during religious services have a sociological relevance?

In this essay, the authors will attempt to examine these questions and point out that odors, though long neglected by sociologists, do indeed have a significant bearing upon human interaction.

ODORS AND MORAL STATUS

Much of the moral symbolism relevant to interaction is expressed in terms of olfactory imagery. An untrustworthy person may be described as a "stinker," a "stinkoe," or a "stinkpot." In contrast, a holy or ritually pure person may be metaphorically described as emitting the "odor of sanctity" (see Wright 1967, pp. 23–24). At the same time, groups may be termed "smelly and slovenly" or, on the other hand, "clean and orderly." In any case, particular odors, whether real or alleged, are sometimes used as indicants of the moral purity of particular individuals and groups within the social order, the consequences of which are indeed real.

For example, E. T. Hall (1969, p. 119) has observed that when intermediaries arrange an Arab marriage they often take great care to smell the girl, and will reject her if she "does not smell nice." In the same vein, Havelock Ellis (1928, 4:64) cites a variety of situations where priests claim they are able to perceive whether a woman is a virgin by her odor. And, likewise, Pearl Buck (1946, p. 159) describes the association of odors with purity in the Oriental culture. In *Pavilion of Women* she portrays the Chinese reaction to Westerners: they are "rank from the bone because of the coarseness of their flesh, the profuseness of their sweat, and the thickness of their woolly hair." And later (1946, p. 262) she depicts Madame Wu assessing the character of one of her girls, Rulan: " 'Open your mouth' . . . from it came a sweet, fresh breath . . . she noted that all of the girl's skirts and inner garments were scented. She lifted the girl's hands and smelled the palms. They were scented, and her hair was scented, and from the body came a delicate scent. 'You will do well, my child,' Madame Wu said kindly."

Historians (Bacon 1957, 3:248) inform us that during the Middle Ages perfumers were suspected of "moral laxity," and it is pointed out that "although it hardly mattered to them they were held ineligible for service as kings." Also, it was commonly believed that "sorcerers and heretics could be detected by their foul and fetid odor (see Summers 1956, p. 44); and it was widely held that deeply religious persons could generally ascertain the specific virtues and vices of those they met by the odor that was emanated. A particular vice at the time was being a Jew, and Jews were noted for emitting an unusually foul odor which was believed to miraculously disappear upon conversion and baptism into the Christian faith (Golding 1938, p. 59; Klineberg 1935, p. 130). Apart from illustrating the moral relevance of odors, the belief is interesting in that it drew much of its meaning from an additional belief that at Passover Jews would themselves sacrifice criminally obtained Christian children (in parody of the Passion of Jesus) and consume the blood in order to rid themselves of their fetid odor—an act intrinsic to only a fiendish faith, that is, an immoral group (see Hecker 1859, pp. 38, 70–74).

Anthropologists have also afforded some fascinating examples of the association of odors with "purity" in the moral order. For instance, Reynolds (1963, p. 126) reports the activities of a diviner within the Nguni tribe: "Where he seeks out cannibals and necrographers he does so with his nose for they have the smell of flesh on their fingers . . . the diviners frequently sniff vigorously when in the company of other people." Similarly, the nose-kissing practices of the Eskimoes and many other so-called primitive groups is usually associated with the mutual expression and assessment of character.

In modern societies there are many comparable examples. For instance, many males of the labor class associate the odor of cologne on a male with effeminacy—"he smells pretty." Consequently, it would be rare to find a steelworker who dabbed himself with cologne before going off to work. By the same token, a white-collar worker may be heard expressing a repugnance toward those who emit a "stinky sweat" or those who "smell like a farmer"—dirty and unclean. And his before-work ritual is more likely to include odorizing himself with cologne.

There are also echoes of the Middle Ages: "she smells like a whore," the implication being that a heavily perfumed woman is likely to be promiscuous. At the same time, advertisers are continuing to create a social consciousness that "bad breath," "ugly perspiration," or the "feminine odor" are signs of a contaminating character, a women who rudely affronts others.

The linkage between one's olfactory identity and one's moral state is referred to in the so-called scientific, as well as the fictional, accounts of human life. For example, the British social psychologist Ronald Goldman

(1969, p. 95), in writing of a youth club, strikingly describes a "problem member": "In personal terms . . . Tim was always smelly and dirty, and many teachers reported the obnoxious nature of the smell that came from him during school hours. Very few people who dealt with him could dissent from the judgment that he was sly, vicious, and totally unreliable." In this case, Tim, the individual, stank physically and therefore morally.

Likewise, many alleged odors of groups are related with stereotyped notions about their moral laxity. For example, Pakistanis in Britain are described by a London dockworker (*Time*, May 20, 1970, p. 38) in the following way: "They seem passive and weak. They smell, don't they?" Similarly an American white may be heard to speak of the "stench of niggers," suggesting that it arises necessarily from their failure to bathe and to follow "decent human standards," and because they "live like pigs" (see Faulkner 1948; Dollard 1957; Brink and Harris 1969, pp. 138–40).

Finally, there is the "fart taboo," that is, the rule of etiquette which restricts flatus. It is so widely agreed upon that formal etiquette books do not even discuss it, and certainly anyone who "lets go a fart" in public is usually considered somewhat crass and undisciplined.

Curiously, social scientists have not touched upon the taboo, but its significance in human interaction is often vividly portrayed in novels. For example, in *The Catcher in the Rye*, J. D. Salinger (1951, p. 48) describes a situation: "All of a sudden this guy sitting in front of me, Edgar Marsalla, laid this terrific fart. It was a very crude thing to do in chapel and all." Again, in *The Sotweed Factor*, John Barth (1967, p. 371) describes the indignation that such a fart may evoke: "But this was a hard matter, inasmuch as for everrie cheerie wave of the hand I signalled them, some souldier of Gentleman in my companie must needs let goe a fart, which the Salvages did take as an affront, and threwe more arrowes." One might also note that the stigmatization of an individual for so "letting go" often involves an attempt by the "crass one" to convince others that it was someone else.

In short, odors, whether real or alleged, are often used as a basis for conferring a moral identity upon an individual or a group. And certainly such moral imputations bear upon the processes of human interaction. Let us next consider olfactory boundaries and the patterns of avoidance and attraction as they are generated through olfactory definitions of individuals, groups, and settings.

ODOR-AVOIDANCE AND ODOR-ATTRACTION

A skunk is a symbol of avoidance, whereas a rose is a symbol of attraction. Upon encountering a skunk most persons carefully maintain distance and warn others nearby of potential contamination. On the other hand, if one smells a rose he is attracted toward it, and he invites others to smell it and admire its aroma.

AVOIDING THE SKUNK

From the sociological standpoint, the "skunk" we avoid may be an individual, a group, or even a setting, that is, a physical environment. If we encounter an individual "skunk" (e.g., a person with "bad breath"), it is commonly accepted that we may step back from the person so as to prevent further violation of our sense of smell. Usually, we mentally label such a person, and we may extend our discreditation by informing others that the person has a "problem." Strangely enough, the person himself is seldom directly confronted about his "problem" because of the embarrassment it would cause the dishonored self to embarrass the dishonoring one. Nonetheless, it is quite clear that if sensorial involvement were disrupted repeatedly, then social involvement would become sharply jeopardized—particularly in modern societies in which there appears to be a growing consciousness of odors.

The "skunky group" has more sociologically interesting aspects. As indicated previously, stereotypes and the dynamics of prejudice often derive from alleged, as well as real, odors given off by particular groups. Indeed, odors are often referred to as the insurmountable barrier to close interracial and/or interclass interaction, and they are repeatedly referred to in order to account for avoidance patterns and segregated ecological niches. In Poland, for instance, anti-Semitism is often expressed in terms of the odor of garlic. The novelist Prus (1969, p. 68) presents a graphic example of this association in his work *Lalka* [The puppet]: "The new assistant set to work immediately, and half an hour later Mr. Lisiecki murmured to Mr. Klein: 'What the hell is it that smells of garlic?' And a quarter of an hour later, he added: 'To think that the Jewish rabble are pushing toward the Cracow suburb! Can't the damned nasty Jews stick to Nalewki or St. George street?' Schlangbaum kept quiet but his red eyes trembled!"

Like the hostile stereotype of the Jews, racial prejudices, too, seek credence by reference to the malodor of the minority group. In fact, both Dollard (1957, p. 381) and Klineberg (1935, p. 29) have pointed out that alleged malodor is a crucial component in the white racist's conception of Negroes—so much so, Dollard suggests, that a hypersensitivity to or fastidiousness about body odors may become evident.

Class prejudices are equally supported by imputations that those of the lower class are "foul smelling" and must be avoided if one is sensitive to such odors. As Simmel (1908, p. 658) observed: "no sight of the proletarian's misery, much less the most realistic account of it, will overwhelm us

so sensuously and directly . . . that we can smell the atmosphere of somebody is the most initimate perception of him . . . and it is obvious that
with the increasing sensitiveness toward impression of smelling in general,
there may occur a selection and a taking of distance, which forms, to a certain degree, one of the sentient bases for the sociological [*sic*] reserve of the
modern individual."

It might also be added to Simmel's statement that given (*a*) the extremely subjective nature of olfactory perception, (*b*) the simultaneous process
of social interpretation of these perceptions, and (*c*) socially generated and
maintained stereotypes influencing (*a*) and (*b*), the allegation of the malodor of a group member can be imputed a priori rather than "accurately"
perceived, and our interpretation of the meaning of the odor may not reflect the condition or the customs of either the individual or his group.
Hence, social distance may be maintained by conventionally imputed,
rather than "actually perceived," impressions of malodor. An example of
this is contained in a pamphlet (National Renaissance Bulletin 1963) that
urged white parents to keep their children away from youth camps allegedly dedicated to miscegenation: "How would you like it if an exquisitely-
formed white child was no longer white? . . . Its sensitive mind no longer
sensitive but apelike? Its beautiful body no longer beautiful but black and
evil-smelling?"

Finally, there are the urban-rural stereotypes. In Western societies ur-
banites may be heard identifying farmers with manure or "earthy-dirty"
work, while the farmer may label the urbanite as "artificial-smelling," perfumed, or factory-smelling.

A poignant description of similar urban-rural antagonisms in Chinese
society is offered by Pearl Buck (1931, pp. 110–11):

> Wang Lung and his wife and children were like foreigners in this southern city
> . . . where Wang Lung's fields spread out in leisurely harvest twice a year of
> wheat and rice and a bit of corn and beans and garlic, here in the small cultiva-
> tions about the city men urged their land with stinking fertilizing of human
> wastes. . . .
>
> In Wang Lung's country a man, if he had a roll of good wheat bread and a
> sprig of garlic in it, had a good meal and needed no more. But here the people
> dabbed with pork balls and bamboo sprouts and chestnuts stewed with chicken
> and goose giblets and this and that of vegetables, and when an honest man came
> by smelling of yesterday's garlic, they lifted their noses and cried out, "Now here
> is a reeking, pig-tailed northerner." The smell of the garlic would make the very
> shopkeepers in the cloth shops raise the price of blue cotton cloth as they might
> raise the price for a foreigner.

As with individuals and groups, we are also prone to identify certain settings or physical environments in terms of real, as well as alleged, odors; and, we thereby seek to avoid them. Consider, for example, the avoidance feelings and patterns generated by the odor of a dental surgery,[2] an unkempt greasy-smelling restaurant, or a smoke-filled tavern. Note the tendency to associate mental hospitals and wards for the elderly with the odor of urine (see Henry 1966, pp. 406–8). Likewise, it may be observed that land use and development may be impaired in communities where the odors of a cannery, glue factory, brewery, tannery, or paper mill dominate the setting. Too often in their concern with the political and economic institutions of a community, social scientists overlook its sensorial aspects— whether they be visual, auditory, or olfactory.

SMELLING LIKE A ROSE

While "skunks" are to be avoided, "roses" suggest intimacy; and the individual who emits attractive odors relates effectively on at least one sensorial level. This fact is evidenced by the importance placed on odorizing and deodorizing rituals, as well as such practices as sending flowers or scented letters to one's lover.

Smelling, however, is not restricted to individual "roses." We also like bouquets. In other words, there are grounds for hypothesizing that group intimacy or alignments are at least partially established or recognized through olfactory stimuli. As pointed out by Herbert Spencer (1896, 2:15–16), the practices of nose-kissing and sniffing among the Eskimoes, Samoans, and Phillipine Islanders are not simply salutary gestures. More important, they are means of group identification and cohesion. And, quite possibly, those very odors that serve as indicants for avoidances by outgroups simultaneously generate a we-feeling in the in-group. In this regard, one may hypothesize that the odor of garlic which constitutes a component of the anti-Pakistani complex among the British, may nonetheless contribute to an in-group identification among the Pakistanis themselves.

Finally, there is the "rose garden," that is, the odor setting that attracts and facilitates interaction. While we tend to have avoidance feelings toward urine-smelling asylums, we are drawn to pine-scented parks; while we

---

[2] Also, it should be noted that the distinctly different odors of dental surgeries and taverns help express the primary function of those settings. A dental surgery smelling of beer, whiskey, and stale cigarette smoke would conceivably cause a certain amount of suspicion or anxiety among the clients. The odors would undermine implicit social expectations involving the social meanings of trust in the dentist's professional responsibility, integrity or competence (e.g., his solicitude for hygiene). Thus, odors function partly to maintain the boundaries of social settings or the appropriateness of the relationships engendered within the setting. If the perceived odors in a setting clash with its routine definition, an individual would probably feel "dissonance anxiety" and difficulty in sustaining any bona fide identification with his setting.

are disgusted by canneries, we are enticed by bakeries; while we find cess-pools and polluted streams repugnant, we delight at beaches permeated by the smell of salt and sand. In short, an odor is often a crucial component in the definition of, and orientation to, an environment and is instrumental in generating appropriate activity. While odor settings may be taken for granted in an unreflective manner, they are nonetheless cues to particular modes of involvement within the setting.

IMPRESSION MANAGEMENT THROUGH ODORS

Since odors do indeed bear social meaning, it is not surprising that various practices have developed by which olfactory identity and odor settings may be manipulated. Cross-culturally and historically one may observe efforts by actors to insure that they "give off" a creditable odor. Likewise, there are numerous examples of efforts to create a desirable odor setting.

To establish and maintain a socially accepted olfactory identity, actors engage in two basic practices: deodorizing and odorizing. The first practice usually entails the removal of socially discreditable odors through such activities as washing, gargling, and cleansing of teeth. There is usually a particular concern about the removal of perspiration. Odorizing, on the other hand, involves presentation of self with accreditable odors through the "art" of perfuming.[3] The existent rationales for deodorizing include "health" and "cleanliness," while those for odorizing include "being fresh and pleasing to others." Through the use of deodorants and odorants an actor may anticipate his identifying label to be that of a "good, clean, and decent person" rather than a "stinker" or a "stinkpot." Through these practices an actor attempts to avoid moral stigmatization and present an olfactory identity that will be in accord with social expectations, in turn, gaining moral accreditation: he who smells good is good.

One's olfactory identity is particularly associated with racial, class, and sexual identification; and, as noted earlier, perfuming is closely related to the presentation and manipulation of those identifications. It has already been observed that racial minority groups are often stigmatized in terms

[3] In regard to perfuming, Theodor Rosebury (1969, p. 208) has raised an interesting and basically sociological question: "Maybe we ought to stop at times to wonder why we like flowers or coconuts or little Asiatic deer or the guts of a sperm whale; couldn't we learn to love the smell of healthy sweat of men and women?" He is, of course, referring to man's almost universal historical concern to change and manipulate his personal odors in order to smell like a flower, tree, or animal. Why does the smell of lilac suggest an accreditable moral status while human sweat suggests a discreditable status? Does the discreditable social meaning almost always associated with human odors alienate human actors from their bodily selves?

of odors, and, as Dollard (1957, p. 380) pointed out, the allegation that a minority group is "foul-smelling is an extremely serviceable way of fixing on him an undesirable lower-caste mark and by inference justifying superiority behavior." Likewise, Myrdal (1944, 1:107) noted that "the belief in a peculiar 'hircine odor' of Negroes, like similar beliefs concerning other races, touches a personal sphere and is used to justify denial of social intercourse and the use of public conveniences which would imply close contact, such as restaurants, theatres, and public conveyances."

Dollard (1957, p. 381) found that in order to cope with their stigmatization Negroes engage in a widespread use of perfume: "Perfume is an effort to avoid the odor-stigma of being ill-smelling which Negroes know to be one of the beliefs of white people about them."[4] Unfortunately it might well be that the perfuming is seldom effective in the avoidance of the stigma. Instead, it may reinforce the white racist's belief that Negroes stink: If they didn't stink, they wouldn't have to cover themselves with perfume.

Like racial identity, class identity is often imputed in terms of odors. On the basis of reactions to forty-three different odors, Brill (1932, p. 40) reported that respondents "disliked most" the odor of perspiration; and he concluded that "this was not only because of its very sour smell, but, because it was associated with people of the lower class." Likewise, novelists and literary critics have noted that the odor of perspiration denotes lower class or status.

In a perceptive observation about Western society in the early twentieth century, Somerset Maugham (1930, p. 140) asserted: "The matutinal tub divides the classes more effectively than birth, wealth, or education . . . the cesspool is more necessary to democracy than parliamentary institutions. The invention of sanitary conveniences has destroyed the sense of equality in men. It is responsible for class hatred much more than the monopoly of capital." In addition, Maugham thought it was significant that "writers who have risen from the ranks of labor are apt to make the morning tub a symbol of class prejudice" (see Brill 1932, pp. 41–42).

The observation of Maugham may have been grossly exaggerated; nonetheless, deodorizing-odorizing practices to avoid being "foul-smelling" and thus being associated with the lower class remain widespread. And, as with racial minority groups, it appears that the lower class often utilizes a great deal of perfume to avoid stigmatization—so much so that the lower class is sometimes described as being "scent smothered" or "daubed in cheap perfume," "cheap" being a term used to imply lower class.

---

[4] Brink and Harris (1969, p. 141) have pointed out that one of the white stereotypes about "better-educated Negroes" is that they take pills to avoid the odor they carry as a race.

At the same time, the middle and upper classes attempt to support their status position by the appropriate use of "expensive perfumes," perfumes that symbolize high status. These perfumes are known through their advertisements in middle- and upper-class magazines: *Fete,* "a really distinguished, sophisticated, classic perfume"; *Amalie,* "expensive"; and, *Joy,* "the costliest perfume in the world." Often, too, these advertisements are associated with an aristocratic tradition, suggesting for instance, that Cleopatra or Queen Elizabeth used the perfume, and thereby appealing to a potential consumer's concern with class identity or status.

In short, one may observe that actors manipulate their olfactory identity to establish and/or to maintain their class identity. Often, too, they attempt to follow class rules set forth by etiquette books regarding the amount and type of perfume worn by those of the "proper class."

Historically, perfuming has also been associated with the enhancement of one's sexual attractiveness; and the belief that perfumes are erotic stimulants persists in most societies. For example, Beach (1965, pp. 183–84) has described a Southwest Pacific society where there is an aphrodisiac based upon the similarity of vaginal odor to that of fish: "Men use a red ground cherry attached to the leader of a trolling line to attract fish. After having caught a fish in this way the ground cherry is believed to have the power to attract women in the same way as it attracted fish. Their vaginas, like elusive fish, will be attracted to the possessor of the ground cherry." Beach continues: "Other odors are also thought to be seductive. Most potent of these is a very musky aromatic leaf worn only by men when they dance and another is the somewhat astringent odor of coconut oil mixed with tumeric. Women rub this mixture in their hair."

In modern Western societies, the perfuming practices are quite similar. Perfumes themselves are widely used by both men and women, and odorants are usually added to toothpastes, shaving lotions, hand lotions, and soaps, as well as hair oils (see Aikman 1951). Moreover, if advertising appeals indicate the legitimating motives for their use, then odorants are worn very often to enhance sexual identification. Consider the following advertisements of men's colognes: *Old Spice,* "Starts the kind of fire a man can't put out"; *Kent of London,* "It can't talk but women get the message"; *Pub,* "Uncorks the lusty life"; *By George,* "She won't? By George, she will!"; *007,* "007 gives any man license to kill . . . women." These types of advertisements are very often featured with nude or "sexually suggestive" women. They appeal to male desires to manipulate their olfactory identity so that it is sexually attractive.

Though less direct in approach, many advertisements for women's perfumes express a similar message: *Emeraude,* "Want him to be more of a man? Try being more of a woman"; *Tabu,* "The forbidden fragrance"; *Intimate,* "What makes a shy girl intimate?"; *Chanel No. 5,* "The spell of Chanel"; *L'Air du Temps,* "To summon a man, push this button"; *Maja,*

"Maja is Woman. Genteel, earthy, provocative, poignant. The very mystique of a woman"; *Ambush,* "Wait for him in Ambush."[5]

The extent to which a motive offered in an advertisement serves as a legitimating rationale for the use of a particular perfume needs further study; nonetheless, it can be hypothesized that a relationship does indeed exist. It is suggested that often the manipulation of an olfactory identity is related to a sexual identity.[6]

Social actors realize, too, that the context within which they act sometimes influences behavioral patterns. They know that an odor often defines a setting. Thus, like olfactory identity, odor settings are subjected to manipulation. As previously mentioned, the odor of whole communities is sometimes described as "stinky"; and the label may be detrimental to the image and development of the community. It is therefore understandable that efforts have been made to control or alter the odor of communities.

In 1969, Washington, D.C., adopted an air pollution code which outlawed odors injurious to the public welfare, the definition of welfare including reasonable enjoyment of life and property. To enforce the case the city acquired a scentometer, a scientific device for calibrating "stink" (reported in *Time,* October 19, 1970, p. 12). Other communities have adopted similar procedures, particularly to force industries and sewage treatment plants to deodorize.[7] Each time the essential argument was: "Getting rid of the odor will stimulate a growth of the community through a more pleasant and healthy environment."[8]

While communities are often concerned with deodorizing a setting to create a more aesthetic environment, other efforts have been made to odor-

---

[5] Taylor (1968, p. 135) has suggested that if aphrodisiacs are effective, perhaps anaphrodisiacs may also be developed. "Such a course might be convenient for explorers, astronauts, and others cut off from the society of the opposite sex. In prisons where abnormal sexual behavior commonly occurs, as a result of such isolation, the use of such anaphrodisiacs might be justifiable, paralleling the alleged use of flowers of sulfur in the past for the same purpose."

[6] One may also want to consider the relationship of smoking and identity. Smoking itself conceals personal odors, and the smoking of various types of tobacco—which have different odors—is often associated with different identities; cigars, with businessmen; pipes, with intellectuals or sportsmen; cigarettes, with bookmakers or cardplayers.

[7] See McKenzie (1966). For a discussion of scentometers, see "How to Trace Bad Odors," *American City* 82 (June 1967): 144.

[8] There have been various newspaper and magazine reports concerning odors and community development. For example: "A proposed site at William and Babcock has been judged unsuitable for a school because of industrial and stockyard odors" (*Buffalo Courier-Express,* January 14, 1970, p. 3); "Citizens of Escabana, Michigan, have formed a group to resist building of sulfate pulp mill in their community" (Associated Press release, August 29, 1970); "In Selbyville, Delaware, the Bishop Processing Co. has been ordered to de-odorize because an obnoxious atmosphere envelops the town with the consistency of a damp blanket and the aroma of rotting flesh. . . . Mayor A. B. Carey thinks that getting rid of the odor will stimulate the growth of other industry" ("War on Smell: Bishop Processing Company, Selbyville, Delaware Ordered to Deodorize," *Newsweek,* January 31, 1966, pp. 23–24).

ize settings. For example, odorants were applied extensively in the Roman Colosseum during gladiatorial games, the intent being to create a communal or we-group feeling (McKenzie 1930, p. 56). Likewise, the Chicago White Sox baseball organization has attempted to spray the scent of hot buttered popcorn in its stadium because that "makes people feel good"; and at the 1964–65 New York World's Fair, the India exhibition was presented with the manufactured scent of curry and cows (Hamilton 1966, p. 84).

The use of incense is another example of the management of an odor setting. Religious groups have traditionally used incense to create an "odor of sanctity," an atmosphere of "sacredness" among the followers. It is burned so that the group may share a common experience. As each follower introjects "particles of the odor" within himself, he is believed to more nearly achieve unity with the others. Boulogne (1953, p. 95) has noted that the use of incense "provides for the senses a symbolic representation of the invisible action (communion) that is taking place" (see also Frazer 1951, 1:379–84). In the Durkheimian sense, the use of incense generates a truly social phenomenon.[9]

The deodorizing and/or odorizing of other settings such as theatres, supermarkets, home, and rooms might also be considered. Again, each setting has a socially expected or desirable odor. Thus we find widespread use of aerosols, for example, the seasonal application of pine and spruce scents in homes to convey "the spirit of Christmas." As Hark (1952, p. 152) describes Christmas eve: "Throughout the room, intangible but definite, the faint perfume of spruce and moss and beeswax hovered like a benediction."

Finally, odors are sometimes used to control, rather than please, a group within a setting. The use of tear gas to disperse a crowd is one such example—though at the same time it creates a common or shared experience by which a we-feeling may be generated within a group, thus only reinforcing the crowd's further unity: "Did you get gassed by the cops?"[10]

CONCLUSION

While much of this paper has of necessity been truncated and impressionistic, we feel that it nevertheless points to a need for the study of a

---

[9] From the psychoanalytic perspective, it is understandable why odors and the act of smelling have been used to achieve a sense of communion with god (society, in the Durkheimian sense). Odors and the act of smelling suggest a more personal and intimate identification with the other. In contrast, visual and auditory experiences are seen as more alienating acts than those of smelling, tasting, and touching. In the former experiences, the self does not consume or take in the stimulating particle.

[10] In this regard, Taylor (1968, p. 53) has speculated that further development of aerosols to regulate crowd behavior may be expected.

much-neglected field of sociological analysis. Simmel (1908) and Berger and Luckmann (1967, p. 203) are just about the only sociologists who even mention the possibility of a sociology of the senses, or "sociology of the body" (e.g., considerations of the alienation from one's "bodily self," social projection of the "bodily self," etc.). The sociology of odors and olfaction should, ideally, develop as one part of a more general sociological concern with the senses.

Possible areas for further research include the following, which, of course, is not an exhaustive list: What is the relation between life style, bodily state, and odors? What sociocultural conditions function to repress and which to elicit a consciousness of olfactory stimuli? What are some of the historical and cross-cultural differences and similarities in "odor consciousness"? What are the relations between "odor consciousness" and social development? What are the psychosocial dynamics involved in the definitions and/or identifications of olfactory stimuli? What are the social dynamics supportive of odor control and manipulation? Why do interactants perfume themselves? What taboos operate in the area of odor control and manipulation?

What are the relations between perceived odors and "labeling" or "social typing" (e.g., "stereotyping")? Under what conditions, if any, do olfactory perceptions involve a more personal and intimate identification with others? Under such conditions, how effective are odors in the generation of an intersubjective "we-feeling," or a less detached, atomized, or objectified awareness of others?

What effect, if any, does a negatively defined olfactory perception have upon spatial considerations such as the establishment of personal space and spatial arrangements of interactants? Following from this, what effect, if any, do olfactory perceptions have upon ecological processes and land-use patterns within the larger society?

In short, how do interactants become conscious of how to feel about or define a given odor perceived to emanate from a given other in a given social setting at a given time?

REFERENCES

AIKMAN, LONNELE, "Perfume, the Business of Illusion," *National Geographic* 99 (April 1951), 531–50.

BACON, S. W., *A Social and Religious History of the Jews.* New York: Columbia University Press, 1957.

BARTH, JOHN, *The Sotweed Factor.* New York: Doubleday, 1967.

BEACH, FRANK, ed., *Sex and Behavior.* New York: Wiley, 1965.

BERGER, PETER, and THOMAS LUCKMANN, *The Social Construction of Reality*. London: Allen Lane, 1967.

BOULOGNE, CHARLES D., *My Friends the Senses*. New York: Kenedy, 1953.

BRILL, A. A., "The Sense of Smell in the Neuroses and Psychoses." *Psychoanalytic Quarterly* 1 (Spring 1932), 7–42.

BRINK, WILLIAM, and LOUIS HARRIS, *The Negro Revolution in America*. New York: Simon & Schuster, 1969.

BUCK, PEARL, *The Good Earth*. New York: Grosset & Dunlap, 1931.

———, *Pavilion of Women*. New York: John Day, 1946.

DOLLARD, JOHN, *Caste and Class in a Southern Town*. New York: Doubleday, 1957.

ELLIS, HAVELOCK, *Studies in the Psychology of Sex*. Philadelphia: Davis, 1928.

FAULKNER, WILLIAM, *Intruder in the Dust*. New York: Modern Library, 1948.

FRAZER, JAMES G., *The Golden Bough*. New York: Macmillan, 1951.

GOLDING, LOUIS, *The Jewish Problem*. London: Penguin, 1938.

GOLDMAN, RONALD, *Angry Adolescents*. London: Routledge & Kegan Paul, 1969.

HALL, E. T., *The Hidden Dimension*. New York: Doubleday, 1969.

HAMILTON, ANDREW, "What Science Is Learning about Smell." *Science Digest* 55 (November 1966), 81–85.

HARK, ANN, *Blue Hills and Shoofly Pie*. Philadelphia: Lippincott, 1952.

HECKER, J. F. D., *The Epidemics of the Middle Ages*. Translated by B. G. Babington. London: Trubner, 1859.

HENRY, JULES, *Culture against Man*. London: Tavistock, 1966.

KLINEBERG, OTTO, *Race Differences*. New York: Harper, 1935.

MCKENZIE, DAN, *Aromatics and the Soul: A Study of Smells*. New York: Hoeber, 1930.

———, "Burn Up Those Life Station Odors: Crystal, Minnesota." *American City* 81 (November 1966), 80–82.

MAUGHAM, SOMERSET, *On a Chinese Screen*. New York: Doran, 1930.

MYRDAL, GUNNAR, *An American Dilemma*. New York: Harper & Row, 1944.

National Renaissance Bulletin, Youth Movements. Pamphlet. New York: National Renaissance Party, ca. 1963.

PRUS, B., *Lalka*. Warsaw: Governmental Publishing House, 1969.

REYNOLDS, BARRIE, *Magic, Divination, and Witchcraft among the Barotse of Northern Rhodesia*. Berkeley: University of California Press, 1963.

ROSEBURY, THEODOR, *Life of Man*. New York: Viking, 1969.

SALINGER, J. D., *The Catcher in the Rye*. New York: Harper & Row, 1951.

SIMMEL, GEORG, *Sociologie*. Leipzig: Duncker & Humblot, 1908.

SPENCER, HERBERT, *The Principles of Sociology*. New York: Appleton, 1896.

SUMMERS, MONTAGUE, *The History of Witchcraft and Demonology*. New York: University Books, 1956.

TAYLOR, GORDON RATTRAY, *The Biological Time Bomb*. New York: World, 1968.

WRIGHT, LAWRENCE, *Clean and Decent*. Toronto: University of Toronto Press, 1967.

BARRY M. DANK

Coming Out in the Gay World

In spite of the recent sociological interest in the study of the transition from primary to secondary deviance,[1] few empirical studies have been addressed to this question.[2] It is in essence posited that at one point in time the actor can be described as being at the "primary stage," in which he engages in rule-breaking behavior and still regards himself as "normal"; at a later point in time he may reach the secondary stage, in which he may engage in overtly the same behavior but regard himself as "deviant," or at least in some way different from the average, ordinary person. For example, at one point in time a person may furtively take goods from a store and regard himself as a borrower, but at a later time he may take similar goods and regard himself as a thief (Cameron). This paper is devoted to exploring the emergence of a particular deviant identity—the male homosexual identity.

There is almost no sociological literature on "becoming" homosexual. There is a vast literature on the etiology of homosexuality—that is, the family background of homosexuals[3]—but little is known concerning how the actor learns that he is a homosexual, how he decides that he is a homosexual. In terms of identity and behavior, this paper is concerned with the transition to a homosexual identity, not in the learning of homosexual behavior per se, or the antecedent or situational conditions that may permit an actor to engage in a homosexual act. One may engage in a homosexual act and think of oneself as being homosexual, heterosexual, or bisexual. One may engage in a heterosexual act and think of oneself as being heterosexual, homosexual, or bisexual, or one may engage in no sexual

Reprinted from *Psychiatry*, 34 (1971), 180–97, by permission of the William Alanson White Foundation, Inc., and the author.

[1] See Becker, 1963; Erikson; Goffman, 1961, 1963; Lemert, 1951, 1967; Lofland; Matza; Scheff.

[2] See Becker, 1953; Bryan; Cameron; Chambliss; Feldman; Goffman, 1961; Lemert, 1962; Scheff; Wertham and Piliavin.

[3] See Bergler; Bieber; Freud; Gebhard et al.; Hooker, 1969; Krich; Ovesey; Ruitenbeek; Schofield; West; Westwood.

acts and still have a sexual identity of heterosexual, homosexual, or bi-sexual. This study is directed toward determining what conditions permit a person to say, "I am a homosexual."[4]

RESEARCH METHOD

This report is part of a study that has been ongoing for over two years in a large metropolitan area in the United States. The analysis is based on data obtained from lengthy interviews with 55 self-admitted homosexuals, on observations of and conversations with hundreds of homosexuals, and on the results of a one-page questionnaire distributed to 300 self-admitted homosexuals attending a meeting of a homophile organization. The statistical data are based on the 182 questionnaires that were returned.

The 4- to 5-hour interviews with the 55 self-admitted homosexuals were generally conducted in the subject's home, and in the context of a "participant-observation" study in which the researcher as researcher became integrated into friendship networks of homosexuals. The researcher was introduced to this group by a homosexual student who presented him correctly as being a heterosexual who was interested in doing a study of homosexuals as they exist in the "outside world." He was able to gain the trust of the most prestigious person in the group, which enabled him, on the whole, to gain the trust of the rest of the group. The guidelines employed in the study were based on those outlined by Polsky for participant-observation studies.

There is no way of determining whether the sample groups studied here, or any similar sample, would be representative of the homosexual population. Thus it remains problematic whether the findings of this study can be applied to the homosexual population in general or to other samples of homosexuals.[5] Since age is a critical variable in this study, the questionnaire sample was used in the hope that the replies to a questionnaire would represent a fairly wide age range. The age distribution of the questionnaire sample is shown on Table 1.

---

[4] It should also be pointed out that from the subjective viewpoint of the actor, it becomes problematic exactly at which point a "homosexual" act should be viewed as such. A male actor may have a sexual contact with another male, but fantasize during the sexual act either that the other male is a female or that he himself is a female; in either case he may view the act as being heterosexual. Or a male actor may have a sexual contact with a female, but fantasize the female as being a male or himself as being a female; in such a case he might view the act as being homosexual (Stoller).

[5] In addition, it should be pointed out that the sample employed may be skewed in an unknown direction since the questionnaire response rate was approximately 60%. In the interview sample, the researcher received excellent cooperation from both those who viewed themselves as being psychologically well-adjusted and those who did not; those more reluctant to participate tended to occupy high socioeconomic positions.

Table 1   AGE CHARACTERISTICS OF SAMPLE

Age	Age Distribution		Age of First Sexual Desire Toward Same Sex		Age at Which Decision Was Made That Respondent Was a Homosexual	
	N	(%)	N	(%)	N	(%)
0–4	0	(0)	1	(0.5)	0	(0)
5–9	0	(0)	28	(15)	1	(0.5)
10–14	0	(0)	83	(46)	27	(15)
15–19	13	(7)	54	(29)	79	(44)
20–24	36	(20)	14	(8)	52	(29)
25–29	39	(22)	1	(0.5)	11	(6)
30–34	28	(16)	1	(0.5)	4	(2)
35–39	21	(12)	0	(0)	3	(2)
40–44	18	(10)	0	(0)	1	(0.5)
45–49	6	(3)	0	(0)	0	(0)
50–59	11	(6)	0	(0)	0	(0)
60–69	8	(4)	0	(0)	1	(0.5)
Total	180	(100)	182	(99.5)	179	(99.5)
	$\bar{X} = 32.5,\ S = 11.3$		$\bar{X} = 13.5,\ S = 4.3$		$\bar{X} = 19.3,\ S = 6.4$	

COMING OUT

The term "coming out" is frequently used by homosexuals to refer to the identity change to homosexual. Hooker states: "Very often, the debut, referred to by homosexuals as the coming out, of a person who believes himself to be homosexual but who has struggled against it will occur when he identifies himself publicly for the first time as a homosexual in the presence of other homosexuals by his appearance in a bar" (p. 99). Gagnon and Simon refer to coming out as that ". . . point in time when there is self-recognition by the individual of his identity as a homosexual and the first major exploration of the homosexual community" (p. 356).

In this study it was found that the meaning that the informant attached to this expression was usually directly related to his own experiences concerning how he met other gay[6] people and how and when he decided he was homosexual. For purposes of this study the term "coming out" will mean identifying onself as being homosexual.[7] This self-identification as being homosexual may or may not occur in a social context in which other gay

[6] In homosexual argot, "gay" means homosexual and "straight" means heterosexual. These terms are acceptable to homosexuals whether used by gay or straight persons.

[7] Sometimes homosexuals use the expression "to bring out" or "bringing out." The meaning attached to these expressions varies; they are sometimes used interchangeably with "coming out." However, as used by my informants, they usually refer to the first complete homosexual act which the subject found enjoyable. The statement, "He brought me out," usually means, "He taught me to enjoy real homosexual acts."

people are present. One of the tasks of this paper is to identify the social contexts in which the self-definition of homosexual occurs.

THE SOCIAL CONTEXTS OF COMING OUT

The child who is eventually to become homosexual in no sense goes through a period of anticipatory socialization (Merton); if he does go through such a period, it is in reference to heterosexuality, not homosexuality. It is sometimes said that the homosexual minority is just like any other minority group (Cory; Westwood); but in the sense of early childhood socialization it is not, for the parents of a Negro can communicate to their child that he is a Negro and what it is like to be a Negro, but the parents of a person who is to become homosexual do not prepare their child to be homosexual—they are not homosexual themselves, and they do not communicate to him what it is like to be a homosexual.[8]

The person who has sexual feelings or desires toward persons of the same sex has no vocabulary to explain to himself what these feelings mean. Subjects who had homosexual feelings during childhood were asked how they would have honestly responded to the question, "Are you a homosexual?," at the time just prior to their graduation from high school. Some typical responses follow:

> SUBJECT 1: I had guilt feelings about this being attracted to men. Because I couldn't understand why all the other boys were dating, and I didn't have any real desire to date.
> INTERVIEWER: Were you thinking of yourself as homosexual?
> SUBJECT 1: I think I did but I didn't know how to put it into words. I didn't know it existed. I guess I was like everybody else and thought I was the only one in the world. . . . I probably would have said I didn't know. I don't think I really knew what one was. I would have probably asked you to explain what one was.
> SUBJECT 2: I would have said, "No. I don't know what you are talking

---

[8] Some homosexuals are parents. In the homosexual social networks that I am involved in, there are many persons who once played the role of husband and father—generally before they decided they were homosexual (Dank). In addition, there are homosexual couples who are raising children they adopted or children from a former heterosexual marriage; however, such couples tend to be lesbian. In some cases one parent has decided that he or she is homosexual, but both parents have remained together as husband and wife. "Front" marriages also occur, in which a male homosexual marries a female homosexual and they adopt children or have children of their own; such marriages are generally for purposes of social convenience. What the effects are, if any, of being raised by at least one homosexual parent have not been determined. In this sample, there were no cases in which a subject had a homosexual mother or father.

about." If you had said "queer," I would have thought something about it; this was the slang term that was used, although I didn't know what the term meant. SUBJECT 3: I don't think I would have known then. I know now. Then I wasn't even thinking about the word. I wasn't reading up on it.

Respondents were asked the age at which they first became aware of any desire or sexual feeling toward persons of the same sex; subsequently they were asked when they decided they were homosexual. Results are presented in Table 1. On the average, there was a six-year interval between time of first sexual feeling toward persons of the same sex and the decision that one was a homosexual. The distribution of the differing time intervals between a person's awareness of homosexual feelings and the decision that he is homosexual is presented in Table 2. As Table 2 indicates, there is considerable variation in this factor.[9]

Table 2 TIME INTERVAL BETWEEN FIRST HOMOSEXUAL DESIRE AND THE DECISION THAT ONE IS A HOMOSEXUAL

Time Interval	Distribution	
(years)	N	(%)
0	29	(16)
1–4	66	(37)
5–9	49	(27)
10–14	21	(12)
15–19	7	(4)
20–29	5	(3)
30–39	1	(0.5)
40–49	0	(0)
50–59	1	(0.5)
Total	179	(100)
	$\bar{X} = 5.7, \ S = 6.4$	

The fact that an actor continues to have homosexual feelings and to engage in homosexual behavior does not mean that he views himself as being homosexual. In order for a person to view himself as homosexual he must be placed in a new social context, in which knowledge of homosexuals and homosexuality can be found; in such a context he learns a new vocabulary

[9] First sexual desire toward persons of the same sex was chosen instead of first sexual contact with persons of the same sex since it is quite possible for one to have homosexual desires, fight against those desires, and have no homosexual contacts of any type for an extensive period of time. The mean age of first homosexual contact of any type was 13, which was not significantly different at the .01 level from age of first homosexual desire. In reference to which came first, homosexual act or homosexual desire, 31% (56) had desire before the act; 49% (87) had act before desire; 20% (36) had first homosexual desire and first homosexual act at approximately the same time.

Table 3   SOCIAL CONTEXTS IN WHICH RESPONDENTS CAME OUT

Social Contexts	N*	(%)
Frequenting gay bars	35	(19)
Frequenting gay parties and other gatherings	46	(26)
Frequenting parks	43	(24)
Frequenting men's rooms	37	(21)
Having a love affair with a homosexual man	54	(30)
Having a love affair with a heterosexual man	21	(12)
In the military	34	(19)
Living in a YMCA	2	(1)
Living in all-male quarters at a boarding school or college	12	(7)
In prison	2	(1)
Patient in a mental hospital	3	(2)
Seeing a psychiatrist or professional counselor	11	(6)
Read for the first time about homosexuals and/or homosexuality	27	(15)
Just fired from a job because of homosexual behavior	2	(1)
Just arrested on a charge involving homosexuality	7	(4)
Was not having any homosexual relations	36	(20)

* Total N of social contexts is greater than 180 (number of respondents) because there was overlap in contexts.

of motives, a vocabulary that will allow him to identify himself as being a homosexual. This can occur in any number of social contexts—through meeting self-admitted homosexuals, by meeting knowledgeable straight persons, or by reading about homosexuals and homosexuality. Knowledge of homosexuals and homosexuality can be found in numerous types of physical settings: a bar, a park, a private home, a psychiatrist's office, a mental hospital, and so on (see Table 3). It is in contexts where such knowledge tends to be concentrated that the actor will be most likely to come out. It is therefore to be expected that an actor is likely to come out in a context in which other gay people are present; they are usually a ready and willing source of knowledge concerning homosexuals and homosexuality. In the questionnaire sample, 50 percent came out while associating with gay people.

It is also to be expected that a likely place for an actor to come out would be in one-sex situations or institutions. Sexually segregated environments provide convenient locales for knowledge of homosexuality and homosexual behavior. Examples of these one-sex environments are mental institutions, YMCAs, prisons, the military, men's rooms, gay bars, and school dormitories. The first six case histories below illustrate the influence of such milieux.

The first example of an actor coming out in the context of interacting with gay persons concerns a subject who came out in a mental hospital. The subject was committed to a mental hospital at age 20; his commitment did not involve homosexuality and the hospital authorities had no knowledge that the subject had a history of homosexual behavior. Prior to commitment he had a history of heterosexual and homosexual behavior, thought of himself as bisexual, had had no contact with self-admitted homosexuals, was engaged to marry, and was indulging in heavy petting with his fiancée. In the following interview excerpt the subject reports on his first reaction to meeting gay persons in the hospital:

SUBJECT: I didn't know there were so many gay people, and I wasn't used to the actions of gay people or anything, and it was quite shocking walking down the halls, going up to the ward, and the whistles and flirting and everything else that went on with the new fish, as they called it.

And there was this one kid who was a patient escort and he asked me if I was interested in going to church, and I said yes . . . and he started escorting me to church and then he pulled a little sneaky to see whether I'd be shocked at him being gay. There was this queen[10] on the ward, and him and her, he was looking out the hall to see when I'd walk by the door and they kissed when I walked by the door and this was to check my reaction. And I didn't say a word. So he then escorted me to the show, and we were sitting there and about half-way through the movie he reaches over and started holding my hand, and when he saw I didn't jerk away, which I was kind of upset and wondering exactly what he had in mind, and then when we got back to the ward, he wrote me a long love letter and gave it to me; before we knew it we were going together, and went together for about six months.

[After 3 weeks] he had gotten me to the point where I'd gotten around the hospital, where I picked up things from the other queens and learned how to really swish and carry on and got to be one of the most popular queens in the whole place. [About that same time] I'd gotten to consider myself—I didn't consider myself a queen. I just considered myself a gay boy; we sat down, a bunch of us got together and made out the rules about what was what as far as the joint was concerned, drew definitions of every little thing . . . if someone was completely feminine, wanted to take the female role all the time, then they were a "queen," if they were feminine but butchy, then they were a "nellie-butch," and I was considered a "gay boy" because I could take any role, I was versatile.

INTERVIEWER: Before this bull session were you considering yourself gay?

SUBJECT: Yes, I had definitely gotten to be by this time; after three months my folks came down to see me and I told them the whole thing point blank.

INTERVIEWER: What would you say was the most important effect the hospital had on you?

SUBJECT: It let me find out it wasn't so terrible. . . . I met a lot of gay people that I liked and I figured it can't be all wrong. If so and so's a good Joe, and

[10] In gay argot, the meaning of the term "queen" is variable. Depending on the context, it can mean any homosexual or a homosexual on the feminine side.

he's still gay, he can't be all that bad. . . . I figured it couldn't be all wrong, and that's one of the things I learned. I learned to accept myself for what I am —homosexual.

This subject spent a year and a half in the mental hospital. After release he did not engage in heterosexual relations, and has been actively involved in the gay subculture for the past four years.

The above example clearly demonstrates how a one-sex environment can facilitate the development of a homosexual identity. Although some one-sex environments are created for homosexuals, such as gay bars, any one-sex environment can serve as a meeting and recruiting place for homosexuals, whether or not the environment was created with that purpose in mind.

The YMCA is a one-sex environment that inadvertently functions as a meeting place for homosexuals in most large urban areas in the United States.[11] The following subject came out while living and working at a YMCA. He was 24 when he first visited a Y, never had had a homosexual experience, and had just been separated from his wife.

I became separated from my wife. I then decided to go to Eastern City. I had read of the Walter Jenkins case and the name of the YMCA happened to come up, but when I got to the city it was the only place I knew of to stay. I had just $15.00 in my pocket to stay at the Y, and I don't think I ever had the experience before of taking a group shower. So I went into the shower room, that was the first time I remember looking at a man's body and finding it sexually enticing.[12] So I started wondering to myself—that guy is good-looking. I walked back to my room and left the door open and the guy came in, and I happened to fall in love with that guy.

After this first experience, the subject became homosexually active while living and working at the Y and became part of the gay subculture that existed within the Y.

. . . I found that the kids who were working for me, some of them I had been to bed with and some of them I hadn't, had some horrible problems and trying to decide the right and wrong of homosexuality . . . and they would feel blunt enough or that I had the experience enough to counsel them along the lines of homosexuality or anything else. . . . Part of this helped me realize that one of

[11] YMCAs have not been studied in their relation to homosexual society. It appears that YMCAs function as meeting places for homosexuals and for those desiring homosexual relations but defining themselves as straight. This is not a regional phenomenon but is, according to my informants, true for almost all YMCAs in large metropolitan areas. YMCAs are often listed in gay tourist guides.

[12] This subject later admitted that he had previously been attracted to other males.

the greatest things that you can do is to accept what you are and if you want to change it, you can go ahead and do it. . . .

This subject spent six months living in this Y; by the end of three months he had accepted himself as being homosexual and has been exclusively homosexual for the last two years.

The prison is another one-sex environment in which homosexual behavior is concentrated. Although there have been studies of situational homosexuality in prison (Giallombardo; Sykes; Tittle; Ward and Kassebaum), and of how homosexual activities are structured in prison, there have been no studies that have looked at the possible change of the sexual identity of the prisoner. In the following case the subject was sentenced to prison on a charge of sodomy at the age of 32, and spent five years in prison. He had been homosexually active for 22 years, and before his arrest he had been engaging predominantly in homosexual behavior, but he had not defined himself as being a homosexual. He had had only peripheral contacts with the gay subculture before his arrest, largely because he was married and held a high socioeconomic position.

> INTERVIEWER: In prison did you meet homosexuals?
> SUBJECT: Yes.
> INTERVIEWER: I'm not talking about people who are just homosexual while in prison.
> SUBJECT: People who are homosexual, period. I became educated about the gay world, how you can meet people and not lay yourself open to censure, and how to keep from going to prison again. And still go on being homosexual. While in prison I definitely accepted myself as being homosexual. . . . I had frequent meetings with psychiatrists, various social workers. We were all pretty much in tacit agreement that the best thing to do would be to learn to live with yourself. Up until then, I rationalized and disillusioned myself about a lot of things. As I look back on it, I was probably homosexual from ten years on.

After his release from prison, this subject became involved in the gay subculture and has been exclusively homosexual for the last eight years.

The military is a one-sex environment that is a most conducive setting for homosexual behavior. In the military, a large number of young men live in close contact with one another and are deprived of heterosexual contacts for varying periods of time; it is not surprising that a homosexual subculture would arise. Given the young age of the military population, it should also be expected that a certain proportion of men would be entering military service with homosexual desires and/or a history of homosexual behavior, but without a clearly formulated homosexual identity. Approximately 19 percent of the sample came out while in military service. The following subject had a history of homosexual desires and behavior previous to joining the Navy, but came out while in military service.

> INTERVIEWER: How did you happen to have homosexual relations while in the Navy?
> SUBJECT: We were out at sea and I had heard that one of the dental technicians was a homosexual, and he had made advances toward me, and I felt like masturbation really wouldn't solve the problem so I visited him one night. He started talking about sex and everything. I told him I had never kissed a boy before. And he asked me what would you do if a guy kissed you, and I said you mean like this and I began kissing him. Naturally he took over then. . . . There were other people on the ship that were homosexual and they talked about me. A yeoman aboard ship liked me quite a bit, was attracted to me; so he started making advances toward me, and I found him attractive, so we got together, and in a short period of time, we became lovers. He started to take me to the gay bars and explain what homosexuality was all about. He took me to gay bars when we were in port.
> INTERVIEWER: Did you start to meet other gay people aboard ship?
> SUBJECT: The first real contact with gay people was aboard ship. . . .
> INTERVIEWER: Was it while you were in the Navy that you decided you were a homosexual?
> SUBJECT: Yes. Once I was introduced to gay life, I made the decision that I was a homosexual.

Public restrooms, another part of society which is sexually segregated, are known in the gay world as T-rooms, and some T-rooms become known as meeting places for gay persons and others who are looking for homosexual contacts (Humphreys). Sex in T-rooms tends to be anonymous, but since some nonsexual social interaction also occurs in this locale, some homosexuals do come out in T-rooms. In the sample studied here 21 percent came out while frequenting T-rooms for sexual purposes. The following subject came out in the context of going to T-rooms when he was 15. Previously he had been homosexually active, but had not thought of himself as being a homosexual.

> I really didn't know what a homosexual was. In the back of my mind, my definition of a homosexual or queer was someone who wore girls' clothes and women's shoes, 'cause my brothers said this was so, and I knew I wasn't.

At the age of 15 this subject had a sexual relationship with a gay man.

> And he took me out and introduced me to the gay world. I opened the door and I went out and it was a beautiful day and I accepted this whole world, and

I've never had any guilt feelings or hang-ups or regrets. . . . I was young and fairly attractive and I had men chasing me all the time. . . . He didn't take me to bars. We went to restrooms, that was my outlet. He started taking me to all the places they refer to in the gay world as T-rooms, and I met other people and I went back there myself and so on.

After meeting other gay persons by going to T-rooms, this subject quickly discovered other segments of the gay world and has been exclusively homosexual for the last nine years.

Gay bars are probably the most widespread and well-known gay institutions (Achilles; Hooker, 1965). For many persons who become homosexual, gay bars are the first contact with organized gay society and therefore a likely place to come out. In this sample 19 percent came out while going to gay bars. Since gay bars apparently are widespread throughout the nation, this could be viewed as a surprisingly low percentage. However, it should be remembered that generally the legal age limit for entering bars is 21. If the age limit is enforced, this would reduce the percentage of persons coming out in gay bars. T-rooms and gay private parties and other gatherings perform the same function as gay bars, but are not hampered by any age limit. Thus, it is not really surprising that the percentages of persons who came out in several other ways are higher than the percentage coming out in gay bars.

The following subject came out in the context of going to gay bars. He had been predominantly homosexual for a number of years and was 23 at the time he came out.

SUBJECT: I knew that there were homosexuals, queers and what not; I had read some books, and I was resigned to the fact that I was a foul, dirty person, but I wasn't actually calling myself a homosexual yet. . . . I went to this guy's house and there was nothing going on, and I asked him, "Where is some action?," and he said, "There is a bar down the way." And the time I really caught myself coming out is the time I walked into this bar and saw a whole crowd of groovy, groovy guys. And I said to myself, there was the realization, that not all gay men are dirty old men or idiots, silly queens, but there are some just normal-looking and acting people, as far as I could see. I saw gay society and I said, "Wow, I'm home."
INTERVIEWER: This was the first time that you walked into this gay bar that you felt this way?
SUBJECT: That's right. It was that night in the bar. I think it saved my sanity. I'm sure it saved my sanity.

This subject has been exclusively homosexually active for the last 13 years. Even after an introduction to gay bars, labeling oneself as homosexual does not always occur as rapidly as it did in the previous example. Some persons can still, for varying periods of time, differentiate themselves from the people they are meeting in gay bars. The following subject came out when he was 22; he had been predominantly homosexual before coming out. He interacted with gay people in gay bars for several months before he decided he was a homosexual. He attempted to differentiate himself from the other homosexuals by saying to himself, "I am not really homosexual since I am not as feminine as they are."

> Finally after hanging around there for so long, some guy came up to me and tried to take me for some money, and I knew it, and he said, "You know, you're very nellie."[13] And I said I wasn't, and he said, "Yes, you are, and you might as well face facts and that's the way it is, and you're never going to change." And I said, "If that's the case, then that's the way it's going to be." So I finally capitulated.

This subject has been predominantly homosexually active for the last 21 years.

It should be made clear that such a change in sexual identity need not be accompanied by any change in sexual behavior or any participation in homosexual behavior. It is theoretically possible for someone to view himself as being homosexual but not engage in homosexual relations just as it is possible for someone to view himself as heterosexual but not engage in heterosexual relations. Approximately 20 percent of this sample came out while having no homosexual relations. The following subject is one of this group; he came out during his late twenties even though he had had his last homosexual experience at age 20.

> I picked up a copy of this underground newspaper one day just for the fun of it . . . and I saw an ad in there for this theatre, and after thinking about it I got up enough nerve to go over there. . . . I knew that they had pictures of boys and I had always liked boys, and I looked at the neighborhood and then I came home without going in. . . . I went back to the neighborhood again and this time I slunk, and I do mean slunk through the door . . . and I was shocked to see what I saw on the screen, but I found it interesting and stimulating and so I went back several more times.

Eventually this subject bought a copy of a gay publication, and subsequently he went to the publication's office.

---

[13] In gay argot, "nellie" means feminine or feminine-appearing. The word is not usually used in a complimentary manner.

I visited with the fellows in the office and I had time on my hands and I volun-
teered to help and they were glad to have me. And I have been a member of
the staff ever since and it was that way that I got my education of what gay life
is like. . . . For the last ten years, I had been struggling against it. Back then if
I knew what homosexuality was, if I had been exposed to the community . . .
and seen the better parts, I probably would have admitted it then.

This subject has been very active socially but not sexually in the gay subculture for the last year.

In contrast to the previous examples, there are cases in which the subject
has no direct contact with any gay persons, but yet comes out in that context. Fifteen percent (27) of the sample came out upon first reading about
homosexuals or homosexuality in a book, pamphlet, etc.; ten of these
(about 6 percent of the sample) were not associating with gay people at the
time they came out. The following subject came out in this context. He was
14 at the time, had just ended a homosexual relationship with a person who
considered himself to be straight, and had had no contact with gay society.

I had always heard like kids do about homosexuals and things, but that never
really entered my mind, but when I read this article, when I was in the 8th
grade, and it had everything in it about them sexually, not how they looked and
acted and where they go. It was about me and that was what I was thinking. I
just happen one day to see a picture of a guy, and thought he was kind of cute,
so I'll read the article about him. But before that I didn't realize what was happening. I didn't even realize I wasn't right as far as heterosexuals were concerned. I didn't realize that what I was thinking wasn't kosher. . . . If people
don't like it I'll keep my mouth shut. The article said people wouldn't like it,
so I decided to keep my mouth shut. That's the way I was, so I accepted it.

This subject has been active sexually and socially in the gay subculture for
the last five years.

Another context in which a subject can come out is that of having a homosexual relationship with a person who defines himself as being heterosexual; 12 percent (21) of the sample came out in such a context. Of these,
12 (about 7 percent of the sample) had never met any self-admitted homosexuals and had never read any material on homosexuality. The following
case involves a subject who came out in such a context. At the age of 21 he
was having an intense love affair with a serviceman who defined himself as
straight. The subject also became involved in a triangular relationship with
the serviceman's female lover.

This got very serious. I told him I loved him. . . . He wanted me for a sex
release; I didn't admit it then, but now I see, through much heartbreak. He

liked me as a person. . . . At the same time he was dating a married woman; he was dating her and having sex with her. . . . She couldn't admit to having a relationship with him 'cause she was married, but he told me and I was extremely jealous of her. [We worked together] and privately she was a very good friend of mine. So I started feeling hatred toward her because she was coming between he and I, competition. I was strong competition, 'cause I frankly dominated it, and she sensed this; so one day she said, "I bet he'd be very good in bed." So I said, "You know he is." She said, "What did you say?" and I said, "Oh, I guess he would be." And I wanted to tell her; so I finally acted like I just broke down and I told her everything in order to make her not like him. So she got on his tail and told him to stop seeing me or she wouldn't have anything to do with him. . . . I taped all their phone conversations and told her if she wouldn't leave him alone, I'd play them for her husband. She got furious, so she said if I tried to blackmail her she would go to the police with the whole thing . . . it all backfired on me and I really didn't want to hurt her, but my love for him was so strong; I'd hurt anybody to keep him, so I erased the tape. And later I bawled and bawled and cried about it to her because I was very sensitive at this time and I told her I was sorry, didn't want to hurt her, but I loved him so much. . . . After I fell in love with him I knew I was homosexual. I talked to my brother about it and he said I wasn't really in love. He said, you're just doing it 'cause you want to; it's not right, boys don't fall in love with boys. He wasn't nasty about it . . . I really loved him; he was my first love; I even dream about him once in a while to this very day. . . . It was during this time that I came out, and I was extremely feminine, not masculine in any way. I wore male clothing, but dressed in a feminine way, in the way I carried myself, the way I spoke. . . . I realized that I was homosexual because I loved him. I was afraid of gay people; heard they did all kinds of weird things from straight people talking about them.

Before this relationship, the subject had engaged in both homosexual and heterosexual petting. Shortly after the relationship terminated the subject became involved in the gay subculture and has been almost exclusively homosexual since that time.

COGNITIVE CHANGE

What is common to all the cases discussed is that the subject placed himself in a new cognitive category (McCall and Simmons), the category of homosexual. In some cases, such placement can occur as soon as the person learns of the existence of the category; an example of this is the boy who placed himself in that category after reading about homosexuals in a magazine. However, probably most persons who eventually identify themselves as homosexuals require a change in the meaning of the cognitive category *homosexual* before they can place themselves in the category.

The meaning of the category must be changed because the subject has learned the negative stereotype of the homosexual held by most heterosexuals, and he knows that he is no queer, pervert, dirty old man, and so on (Simmons). He differentiates himself from the homosexual image that straight society has presented to him. Direct or indirect contact with the gay subculture provides the subject with information about homosexuals that will challenge the "straight" image of the homosexual. The subject will quite often see himself in other homosexuals, homosexuals he finds to be socially acceptable. He now knows who and what he is because the meaning of the cognitive category has changed to include himself. As one subject said: "Wow, I'm home"; at times that is literally the case since the homosexual now feels that he knows where he really belongs.

A person's identification of himself as being homosexual is often accompanied by a sense of relief, of freedom from tension. In the words of one subject:

> I had this feeling of relief; there was no more tension. I had this feeling of relief. I guess the fact that I had accepted myself as being homosexual had taken a lot of tensions off me.

Coming out, in essence, often signifies to the subject the end of a search for his identity.

IDENTIFICATION AND SELF-ACCEPTANCE

Identifying oneself as being homosexual and accepting oneself as being homosexual usually come together, but this is not necessarily the case. It can be hypothesized that those who identify themselves as being homosexual, but not in the context of interacting with other homosexuals, are more likely to have guilt feelings than those who identify themselves as being homosexual in the context of interacting with other homosexuals. Interaction with other homosexuals facilitates the learning of a vocabulary that will not simply explain but will also justify the homosexual behavior.

Identifying oneself as homosexual is almost uniformly accompanied by the development of certain techniques of neutralization (Sykes and Matza).[14] In this self-identification, it would be incorrect to state that the homosexual accepts himself as being deviant, in the evaluative sense of the term. The subject may know he is deviant from the societal standpoint but often does not accept this as part of his self-definition. Lemert (1951) has defined secondary deviation as the situation in which ". . . a person begins

---

[14] Particularly, denial that there is a victim and denial of injury.

to employ his deviant behavior or a role based upon it as a means of defense, attack or adjustment to the overt and covert problems created by the consequent societal reaction to him" (p. 76). Once the subject identifies himself as being homosexual, he does develop means, often in the process of the change in self-definition, of adjusting to the societal reaction to the behavior. The means employed usually involve the denial, to himself and to others, that he is really deviant. Becker (1963) explained the situation when he stated:

> But the person thus labeled an outsider may have a different view of the matter. He may not accept the rule by which he is being judged and may not regard those who judge him as either competent or legitimately entitled to do so. [pp. 1–2]

The societal reaction to homosexuality appears to be expressed more in a mental health rhetoric (Bieber; Hadden; Ovesey; Socarides; Szasz), than in a rhetoric of sin and evil or crime and criminal behavior. In order to determine how the subjects adjusted to this societal reaction to homosexuality, they were asked to react to the idea that homosexuals are sick or mentally ill. With very few exceptions, this notion was rejected.

> SUBJECT 1: I believe this idea to be very much true, if added that you are talking from society's standpoint and society has to ask itself why are these people sick or mentally ill. . . . In other words, you can't make flat statements that homosexuals are sick or mentally ill. I do not consider myself to be sick or mentally imbalanced.
> SUBJECT 2: That's a result of ignorance; people say that quickly, pass quick judgments. They are not knowledgeable, fully knowledgeable about the situation.
> SUBJECT 3: I don't feel they are. I feel it's normal. What's normal for one person is not always normal for another. I don't think it's a mental illness or mental disturbance.
> SUBJECT 4: Being a homosexual does not label a person as sick or mentally ill. In every other capacity I am as normal or more normal than straight people. Just because I happen to like strawberry ice cream and they like vanilla, doesn't make them right or me right.

It is the learning of various ideas from other homosexuals that allows the subject to in effect say, "I am homosexual, but not deviant," or, "I am homosexual, but not mentally ill." The cognitive category of *homosexual* now becomes socially acceptable, and the subject can place himself in that category and yet preserve a sense of his self-esteem or self-worth.

It should be emphasized that coming out often involves an entire transformation in the meaning of the concept of homosexual for the subject. In these cases the subject had been entirely unaware of the existence of gay bars or an organized gay society, of economically successful homosexuals, of homosexually "married" homosexuals, and so on. In the words of one subject:

> I had always thought of them as dirty old men that preyed on 10-, 11-, 12-year-old kids, and I found out that they weren't all that way; there are some that are, but they are a minority. It was a relief for me 'cause I found out that I wasn't so different from many other people. I had considered consulting professional help prior to that 'cause at the time I thought I was mentally ill. Now I accept it as a way of life, and I don't consider it a mental illness. It's an unfortunate situation. . . . I consider myself an outcast from general society, but not mentally ill.

PUBLIC LABELING

It should be made clear that the self-identification as a homosexual does not generally take place in the context of a negative public labeling, as some labeling theorists imply that it does (Garfinkel; Lemert, 1951; Scheff). No cases were found in the interview sample in which the subject had come out in the context of being arrested on a charge involving homosexuality or being fired from a job because of homosexual behavior. In the questionnaire sample, 4 percent (7) had just been arrested and 1 percent (2) had just been fired from a job. A total of 8 respondents or 4.5 percent of the sample came out in the context of public exposure.

It can be hypothesized that the public labeling of an actor who has not yet identified himself as being homosexual will reinforce in his mind the idea that he is not homosexual. This is hypothesized because it is to be expected that at the time of the public labeling the actor will be presented with information that will present homosexuals and homosexuality in a highly negative manner. For example, the following subject was arrested for homosexual activities at the age of 11. Both before and after the arrest he did not consider himself to be a homosexual. His reaction to the arrest was:

> SUBJECT: The officer talked to me and told me I should see a psychiatrist. It kind of confused me. I really didn't understand any of it.
> INTERVIEWER: And were you thinking of yourself at that time as a homosexual?
> SUBJECT: I probably would have said I wasn't. 'Cause of the way the officer who interrogated me acted. I was something you never admit to. He acted as if I were the scum of the earth. He was very rude and impolite.

If the actor has not yet identified himself as being homosexual, it can probably be assumed that to a significant degree he already accepts the negative societal stereotype; the new information accompanying the public labeling will conform to the societal stereotype, and the actor consequently will not modify his decision not to place himself in the homosexual category. This is not to say that public labeling by significant others and/or official agents of social control does not play a significant role in the life of the homosexual; all that is hypothesized is that public labeling does not facilitate and may in fact function to inhibit the decision to label oneself as being homosexual.

THE CLOSET QUEEN

There are some persons who may continue to have homosexual desires and may possibly engage in homosexual relations for many years, but yet do not have a homosexual identity. Self-admitted homosexuals refer to such persons as "closet queens."[15] Such persons may go for many years without any contact with or knowledge of self-admitted homosexuals. The subject previously cited who came out in prison was a closet queen for 20 years.

An interval of 10 or more years between first awareness of sexual attraction toward males and the decision that one is a homosexual, would probably classify one as having been a closet queen. As Table 2 shows, the questionnaire sample included 35 respondents (20 percent of the sample) who at one time were closet queens.

It is the closet queen who has most internalized the negative societal stereotype of the homosexual. It is to be expected that such persons would suffer from a feeling of psychological tension, for they are in a state of cognitive dissonance (Festinger)—that is, feelings and sometimes behavior are not consistent with self-definition.

The following subject was a closet queen for over 50 years. He had his first homosexual experience at the age of 12, has had homosexual desires since that time, and has been exclusively homosexual for 53 years. At the time the subject was interviewed, he expressed amazement that he had just come out during the last few months. Over the years, his involvement with the gay subculture was peripheral; at the age of 29 for about one year he had some involvement with overt homosexuals, but otherwise he had had only slight contact with them until recently. During that earlier involvement:

[15] In gay argot, the meaning of the term "closet queen" varies, but usually it is applied to one who does not admit to being homosexual. However, the term is sometimes used to refer to a self-admitted homosexual who does not like to associate with other homosexuals, or who may be trying to pass as being straight most of the 24 hours of the day.

I was not comfortable with them. I was repressed and timid and they thought I was being high hat, so I was rejected. It never worked out; I was never taken in. I felt uncomfortable in their presence and I made them feel uncomfortable. I couldn't fit in there, I never wanted to, never sought to; I was scared of them. I was scared of the brazen bitches who would put me down.

During the years as a closet queen he was plagued with feelings of guilt; for varying periods of time he was a patient in over twenty mental hospitals. His social life was essentially nil; he had neither gay friends nor straight friends. His various stays in mental hospitals relieved continuing feelings of loneliness. At the age of 65 he attended a church whose congregation was primarily homosexual. It was in the context of interacting with the gay persons who were associated with this church that after 53 years this subject came out.

SUBJECT: I had never seen so many queens in one place; I was scared somebody would put me down, somebody would misunderstand why I was there. I had this vague, indescribable fear. But all this was washed away when I saw all were there for the one purpose of fellowship and community in the true sense of the term. . . . I kept going and then I got to be comfortable in the coffee hour. . . . Then out in the lobby a young fellow opened his heart to me, telling me all his troubles and so forth, and I listened patiently, and I thought I made a couple of comforting remarks. Then I went out to the car, and when I got in the car I put my hand out to shake hands and he kissed my hand. . . . it's hard for you to understand the emotional impact of something like this— that I belong, they love me, I love them.

Until the last few weeks, in all my life I had never been in a gay bar for more than a few minutes, I was acutely uncomfortable. But now I can actually go into it; this is the most utterly ludicrous transformation in the last few weeks . . . there's no logic whatsoever. I'm alive at 65.

It's a tremendous emotional breakthrough. I feel comfortable and relieved of tensions and self-consciousness. My effectiveness in other fields has been enhanced 100 percent. I have thrown off so many of the prejudices and revulsions that were below the surface. . . . I'm out of the closet. In every way, they know, where I work, in this uptight place where I work; I've told them where I live; I've written back east. What more can I do?

INTERVIEWER: Do you think you are now more self-accepting of yourself?

SUBJECT: Brother! I hope you're not kidding. That's the whole bit. How ironical it would come at 65. The only thing that I wouldn't do now is to go to the baths. I told the kids the other day; it's the only breakthrough I cannot bring myself to.

One can only speculate why after all these years this subject came out. The reason may have been that he had had a very religious upbringing and could not conceive of homosexuals in a religiously acceptable manner. The church he attended for the first time at age 65 presented homosexuals as being religiously acceptable, and presented to the subject highly religious homosexuals.[16] Contact with this church may have helped change the meaning of the category homosexual so that he could now include himself.[17]

In a sense the closet queen represents society's ideal homosexual, for the closet queen accepts the societal stereotype of the homosexual and feels guilt because he does the same sort of things that homosexuals do, yet believes he is really different from homosexuals in some significant way. This inability of the closet queen to see himself in other homosexuals prevents him from placing himself in the cognitive category of *homosexual,* and he will not come out until some new information is given to him about homosexuals which permits him to say, "There are homosexuals like myself" or "I am very much like them."

There may be significant differences between ex-closet queens and those closet queens who never come out. Of course, I had contact only with ex-closet queens, and they uniformly reported that their own psychological adjustment has been much better since coming out. Their only regret was that they had not come out sooner. Possibly the closet queen who remains a closet queen reaches some sort of psychological adjustment that ex-closet queens were unable to reach.

THE ROLE OF KNOWLEDGE

The change of self-identity to *homosexual* is intimately related to the access of knowledge and information concerning homosexuals and homosexuality. Hoffman has observed:

[16] It may be that among closet queens, or those who have been closet queens for many years, one would find a disproportionately high number of very religious persons; the traditional negative religious reaction would probably prevent highly religious persons from easily placing themselves in the homosexual category. It would therefore be expected that clergymen who have homosexual feelings would tend to be closet queens for many years. Not only do clergymen have a more difficult time in resolving problems of guilt, but also interaction with other homosexuals could lead to their losing their jobs. In this sample, there were 10 respondents who were ministers or who were studying for the ministry at the time they came out. Their mean age for coming out was 22, and the mean time interval between first homosexual desire and the homosexual self-identification was 10.4 years. I hope to publish a report in the near future on the social life of homosexual ministers.

[17] There have been some recent actions that challenge the traditional religious reaction against homosexuality and homosexuals. Particularly, see: John Dart, "Church for Homosexuals," *Los Angeles Times,* Dec. 8, 1969, Part 2, pp. 1–3; Edward B. Fiske, "Homosexuals in Los Angeles . . . Establish Their Own Church," *New York Times,* Feb. 15, 1970, Sec. 1, p. 58; "The Homosexual Church," *Newsweek,* Oct. 12, 1970, p. 107. Some churches have openly accepted homosexuals; I am currently preparing an article on such a church.

Society deals with homosexuality as if it did not exist. Although the situation is changing, this subject was not even discussed and was not even the object of scientific investigation until a few decades ago. We just didn't speak about these things; they were literally unspeakable and so loathsome that nothing could be said in polite society about them. . . . [p. 195]

The traditional silence on this topic has most probably prevented many persons with homosexual feelings from identifying themselves as being homosexual. Lofland has noted that the role of knowledge in creating a deviant identity is an important one. If significant others or the actor himself does not know of the deviant category, his experience cannot be interpreted in terms of that category; or if his experience appears to be completely alien from that category he will not interpret his experience in terms of that category. If the societal stereotype of homosexuals is one of dirty old men, perverts, Communists, and so on, it should not be surprising that the young person with homosexual feelings would have difficulty in interpreting his experience in terms of the homosexual category.

The greater tolerance of society for the freer circulation of information concerning homosexuality and homosexuals has definite implications in reference to coming out. The fact that there is greater overt circulation of homophile magazines and homophile newspapers, that there are advertisements for gay movies in newspapers, and that there are books, articles, and movies about gay life, permits the cognitive category of homosexuals to be known to a larger proportion of the population and, most importantly, permits more information to be circulated that challenges the negative societal stereotype of the homosexual.

Since there has been a freer circulation of information on homosexuality during the past few years, it can be hypothesized that the development of a homosexual identity is now occurring at an increasingly earlier age. Indeed, older gay informants have stated that the younger homosexuals are coming out at a much earlier age. In order to test this hypothesis, the sample was dichotomized into a 30-and-above age group and a below-30 age group. It can be seen in Table 4 that the below-30 mean age for developing a homosexual identity was significantly lower (at the .01 level) than the above-30 mean age; the drop in mean age was from approximately 21 to 17.[18]

Indications are that the present trend toward greater circulation of information that is not highly negative about homosexuals and homosexuality will continue. The fact that a mass circulation magazine such as *Time* gave its front cover to an article entitled "The Homosexual in America"

---

[18] It can be argued that this was not a meaningful test because of sample bias, since the sample could not include subjects of the younger generation who had still not come out. However, the age of 30 was chosen as the dividing point because only 9 respondents (5%) had come out after the age of 30. Any remaining bias in the sample from this source should presumably be insignificant.

Table 4 RELATIONSHIP OF RESPONDENT AGE TO AGE AT HOMOSEXUAL SELF-IDENTIFICATION

Age at Homosexual Self-Identification	Age of Respondents			
	30 and above		Below 30	
	N	(%)	N	(%)
5–9	0	(0)	1	(1)
10–14	8	(9)	19	(22)
15–19	35	(38)	44	(50)
20–24	29	(32)	23	(21)
25–29	10	(11)	1	(1)
30–39	7	(8)	0	(0)
40–49	1	(1)	0	(0)
50–59	0	(0)	0	(0)
60–69	1	(1)	0	(0)
Total	91	(100)	88	(100)
Mean	21.4*		17.2*	
Standard Deviation	7.7		3.8	

* Means significantly different at .01 level.

(Oct. 31, 1969) and that this article was not highly negative represents a significant breakthrough. The cognitive category of homosexual is now being presented in a not unfavorable manner to hundreds of thousands of people who previously could not have been exposed to such information through conventional channels. This is not to say that more information about homosexuals and homosexuality will lead to a significantly greater prevalence of persons engaging in homosexuality. What is being asserted is that a higher proportion of those with homosexual desires and behavior will develop a homosexual identity, and that the development of that identity will continue to occur at an increasingly younger age.

CONCLUSION

This study has suggested that the development of a homosexual identity is dependent on the meanings that the actor attaches to the concepts of homosexual and homosexuality, and that these meanings are directly related to the meanings that are available in his immediate environment; and the meanings that are available in his immediate environment are related to the meanings that are allowed to circulate in the wider society. The commitment to a homosexual identity cannot occur in an environment where the cognitive category of homosexual does not exist. Hoffman in essence came to the same conclusion when he hypothesized that the failure to develop a homosexual identity is due to a combination of two factors:

> . . . the failure of society to make people aware of homosexuality as an existent way of life (and of the existence of the gay world), and the strong repressive forces that prevent people from knowing what their real sexual feelings are. One might consider this a psychological conspiracy of silence, which society insists upon because of its belief that it thereby safeguards existent sexual norms. [p. 138]

In an environment where the cognitive category of homosexual does not exist or is presented in a highly negative manner, a person who is sexually attracted to persons of the same sex will probably be viewed and will probably view himself as sick, mentally ill, or queer.

It can be asserted that one of the main functions of the viewpoint that homosexuality is mental illness is to inhibit the development of a homosexual identity. The *homosexuality-as-mental-illness* viewpoint is now in increasing competition with the *homosexuality-as-way-of-life* viewpoint. If the homosexuality-as-way-of-life viewpoint is increasingly disseminated, one would anticipate that the problems associated with accepting a homosexual identity will significantly decrease, there will be a higher proportion of homosexually oriented people with a homosexual identity, and this identity will develop at an earlier age.[19]

If the homosexuality-as-way-of-life philosophy does become increasingly accepted, the nature of the homosexual community itself may undergo a radical transformation. To have a community one must have members who will acknowledge to themselves and to others that they are members of that community. The increasing circulation of the homosexuality-as-way-of-life viewpoint may in fact be a self-fulfilling prophecy. It may lead to, and possibly is leading to, the creation of a gay community in which one's sex life is becoming increasingly less fragmented from the rest of one's social life.

REFERENCES

ACHILLES, NANCY. "The Development of the Homosexual Bar as an Institution," in John H. Gagnon and William Simon (Eds.), *Sexual Deviance;* Harper & Row, 1967.

[19] Weinberg has recently reported that younger homosexuals have on the whole a worse psychological adjustment than older homosexuals. As the age for the development of a homosexual identity drops, the psychological adjustment of younger homosexuals may significantly improve.

BECKER, HOWARD S. "Becoming a Marihuana User," *Amer. J. Sociology* (1953) 59: 235–42.

BECKER, HOWARD S. *Outsiders: Studies in the Sociology of Deviance;* Free Press, 1963.

BERGLER, E. *Neurotic Counterfeit-Sex;* Grune & Stratton, 1951.

BIEBER, IRVING, et al. *Homosexuality, A Psychoanalytic Study of Male Homosexuals;* Vintage Books, 1965.

BRYAN, J. H. "Apprenticeships in Prostitution," *Social Problems* (1965) 12:287–97.

CAMERON, MARY O. *The Booster and the Snitch: Department Store Shoplifting;* Free Press, 1964.

CHAMBLISS, WILLIAM J. "Two Gangs: a Study of Societal Response to Deviance and Deviant Careers," unpublished manuscript, 1967.

CORY, DONALD W. *The Homosexual in America;* New York, Greenberg, 1951.

DANK, BARRY M. "Why Homosexuals Marry Women," in *Medical Aspects of Human Sexuality,* in press.

ERIKSON, KAI T. "Notes on the Sociology of Deviance," *Social Problems* (1962) 9: 307–14.

FELDMAN, H. W. "Ideological Supports to Becoming and Remaining a Heroin Addict," *J. Health and Social Behavior* (1968) 9:131–39.

FESTINGER, LEON. *Theory of Cognitive Dissonance;* Harper & Row, 1957.

FREUD, SIGMUND. *Three Contributions to the Theory of Sex;* Dutton, 1962.

GAGNON, JOHN H., and SIMON, WILLIAM. "Homosexuality: The Formulation of a Sociological Perspective," in Mark Lefton et al. (Eds.), *Approaches to Deviance,* Appleton-Century-Crofts, 1968.

GARFINKEL, HAROLD. "Conditions of Successful Degradation Ceremonies," *Amer. J. Sociology* (1956) 61:420–24.

GEBHARD, PAUL, et al. *Sex Offenders, An Analysis of Types;* Hoeber-Harper, 1965.

GIALLOMBARDO, ROSE. *Society of Women: A Study of a Women's Prison;* Wiley, 1966.

GOFFMAN, ERVING. *Asylums;* Doubleday Anchor, 1961.

GOFFMAN, ERVING. *Stigma;* Prentice-Hall, 1963.

HADDEN, SAMUEL B. "A Way Out for Homosexuals," *Harper's Magazine,* March, 1967, pp. 107–20.

HOFFMAN, MARTIN. *The Gay World, Male Homosexuality and the Social Creation of Evil;* Basic Books, 1968.

HOOKER, EVELYN. "Male Homosexuals and Their 'Worlds'," in Judd Marmor (Ed.), *Sexual Inversion: The Multiple Roots of Homosexuality;* Basic Books, 1965.

HOOKER, EVELYN. "Parental Relations and Male Homosexuality in Patient and Non-Patient Samples," *J. Consulting and Clin. Psychology* (1969) 33:140–42.

HUMPHREYS, LAUD. *Tearoom Trade;* Aldine, 1970.

KRICH, A. M. (Ed.). *The Homosexuals;* Citadel Press, 1954.

LEMERT, EDWIN M. *Social Pathology;* McGraw-Hill, 1951.

LEMERT, EDWIN M. "Paranoia and the Dynamics of Exclusion," *Sociometry* (1962) 25:2–20.

LEMERT, EDWIN M. *Human Deviance, Social Problems and Social Control;* Prentice-Hall, 1967.

LOFLAND, JOHN. *Deviance and Identity;* Prentice-Hall, 1969.

MATZA, DAVID. *Becoming Deviant;* Prentice-Hall, 1969.

McCALL, C. J., and SIMMONS, J. L. *Identities and Interactions;* Free Press, 1966.

MERTON, ROBERT. *Social Theory and Social Structure* (rev. ed.); Free Press, 1957.

OVESEY, LIONEL. *Homosexuality and Pseudohomosexuality;* Science House, 1969.

POLSKY, NED. *Hustlers, Beats and Others;* Aldine, 1967.

RUITENBEEK, HENDRIK (Ed.). *The Problem of Homosexuality in Modern Society;* Dutton, 1963.

SCHEFF, THOMAS. *Being Mentally Ill.;* Aldine, 1966.

SCHOFIELD, MICHAEL. *Sociological Aspects of Homosexuality;* Little, Brown, 1965.

SIMMONS, J. L. "Public Stereotypes of Deviants," *Social Problems* (1965) 13:223–32.

SOCARIDES, CHARLES W. "Homosexuality and Medicine," *J. Amer. Med. Assn.* (1970) 212:1199–1202.

STOLLER, ROBERT. *Sex and Gender;* Science House, 1968.

SYKES, GRESHAM M. *Society of Captives;* Princeton Univ. Press, 1958.

SYKES, GRESHAM M., and MATZA, DAVID. "Techniques of Neutralization: A Theory of Delinquency," *Amer. Sociol. Review* (1957) 22:664–70.

SZASZ, THOMAS. *The Manufacture of Madness;* Harper & Row, 1970.

Time. "The Homosexual in America," Oct. 31, 1969, pp. 56, 61–62, 64–67.

TITTLE, CHARLES R. "Inmate Organization: Sex Differentiation and the Influence of Criminal Subcultures," *Amer. Sociol. Review* (1969) 34:492–505.

WARD, DAVID A., and KASSEBAUM, GENE G. *Women's Prison: Sex and Social Structure;* Aldine, 1965.

WEINBERG, MARTIN S. "The Male Homosexual: Age-Related Variations in Social and Psychological Characteristics," *Social Problems* (1970) 17:527–37.

WERTHMAN, C., and PILIAVIN, I. "Gang Members and the Police," in David Bordua (Ed.), *The Police: Six Sociological Essays;* Wiley, 1967.

WEST, DONALD J. "Parental Figures in the Genesis of Male Homosexuality," *Internat. J. Social Psychiatry* (1959) 5:85–97.

WESTWOOD, GORDON. *A Minority: A Report on the Life of the Male Homosexual in Great Britain;* London, Longmans Green, 1960.

MICHELE S. MATTO

The Transsexual in Society

Because transsexuals possess bodies that their minds cannot accept, they are trapped between society's demand to conform to the anatomical self thrust on them by birth and their own desire to conform to a different interior self. Although the transsexual dresses and behaves as a member of the morphologically opposite sex, this is neither a case of transvestism nor homosexuality. Psychologically, the transsexual is a female within a male body, or a male within a female body. In the past these distinctions were virtually ignored by the medical world. Recently, however, attempts have been made, particularly at The Johns Hopkins Hospital, to determine precisely what constitutes transsexualism and to treat surgically those suffering from it. As important as the need to identify and treat the problem itself is the need to combat the emotionalism and prejudice surrounding the subject, which hamper serious research [Green and Money, 1969: Inside cover notes].

The above excerpt and the 500-page book which follows it are examples of a new perspective on a not-so-new problem: cross-gender identity. Richard Green, assistant professor of psychiatry in residence and director of the Gender Identity Research and Treatment Clinic at UCLA School of Medicine, and coauthor of the book *Transsexualism and Sex Reassignment,* says that evidence for what is today called transsexualism can be found in records back throughout history. "Descriptions from classical mythology, classical history, Rennaisance, and nineteenth-century history plus cultural anthropology point to the long-standing and widespread pervasiveness of the transsexual phenomenon" (Green and Money, 1969: 13).

THE TRANSSEXUAL PHENOMENON

Homosexuality, transvestism, and transsexualism were not "catalogued" and differentiated even up until very recent times—in fact, the term "transsexualism" was used for the first time in 1953 by Dr. Harry Benjamin, a physician who has treated and counseled transsexuals since the early 1920s and who has been referred to as their "patron saint" because of the influ-

"The Transsexual in Society," by Michele S. Matto is reprinted from *Criminology,* Volume 10, No. 1 (May 1972) pp. 85–109 by permission of the Publisher, Sage Publications, Inc.

ence he has asserted upon other professional people toward the recognition of transsexualism as, indeed, an entity unto itself.

Because of the term's recent origin, then, it is not found in historical accounts, and inferences must be made in examining reference material. One interesting case is that of the Chevalier d'Eon de Beaumont, from whose name comes our word "eonist," meaning a male with a compulsion to dress as *and be socially accepted as a woman*. At the time of his death, he had lived 49 years as a man and 34 years as a woman. Another person who throughout her adulthood had been known as Mlle. Jenny Savalette de Lange died at Versailles in 1858 and was discovered to be a man. He had gotten a birth certificate designating himself female, was engaged to men six times, and was given a yearly pension by the King of France with a free apartment in the Chateau of Versailles (Green and Money, 1969: 17).

DISTINCTION AMONG HOMOSEXUALITY, TRANSVESTISM, AND TRANSSEXUALISM

In earlier years and even still today for those unfamiliar with the subject, the greatest confusion was between transvestism and what is now called transsexualism. The line between the two is a fine one.

The transvestite is a person who feels compelled to "cross-dress"; that is, to dress in the clothes of the opposite sex.[1] Most writers treat this as basically a sexual deviation and relate it to the transvestite's desire for sexual arousal and attainment of orgasm while so dressed. The "true" transvestite then, is content with this cross-dressing; he basically "feels" like a man and knows he is a man, content with his morphological sex. He does not wish to have his masculinity, as evidenced by the presence of his external sex organs, taken from him, and he would probably like most of all to be left alone to get his sexual pleasures from dressing, while otherwise leading life as a man.

In contrast to the "true" transvestite, there are borderline cases where, perhaps, a person's desire to cross-dress is a result of "gender discomfort," rather than conscious sexual stimulation. On a linear spectrum showing transvestism at one end and transsexualism at the other, this individual would be placed more toward the transsexual side. However, he does not wish to relinquish his male organs nor live life "completely" as a woman. His sex organ means something to him and gives him pleasure, but to the extent that he feels uncomfortable in the role of a man, he becomes a "borderline" case between transvestism and transsexualism.

The true transsexual, on the other hand, feels he *is* a woman; he identi-

---

[1] Because the ratio of male transsexuals to female transsexuals is about 4:1, I shall discuss only male transsexualism in this article to avoid confusion. Feelings, attitudes, and characteristics are exactly reversed in the female transsexual.

fies with women, is deeply unhappy with his maleness and all of its evidence, particularly the genitalia, which he wishes changed surgically to conform with his psychological sex. "Dressing," which satisfies the transvestite, is not sexually exciting to the transsexual. It only temporarily appeases him and has been likened by one doctor to the taking of aspirin for a brain tumor headache. The transsexual wishes to be and function as a member of the opposite sex, not just to dress as one. To this end, self-castration and other mutilations are quite common, and suicide threats as well as actual attempts are not rare. While the transvestite sees his sex organ as one of pleasure, the transsexual is disgusted by it, as well as his secondary sex characteristics, and wishes them all removed or altered.

Thus, even though a clear cut scientific distinction between the two syndromes cannot be made, the person's attitudes toward the physical sex organs as signs of masculinity seem to be the main point of distinction between them. It is quite possible that a great many transvestites are actually transsexuals, but in lesser degrees. For the remainder of this article, however, the term "transsexual" will refer to the "full-fledged" transsexual, for whom the need for the sex reassignment operation is his end goal and means to future happiness—his passport to acceptance into society as the woman he really is.

The confusion between transsexualism and homosexuality centers around the preference of both types of individuals for a sex or living partner of the same anatomical sex. The difference is, however, that while the homosexual knows and feels he is a man, the transsexual knows and feels he is a woman. To him, the desire or preference for men is purely a heterosexual interest and he is, in fact, "turned off" by the thought of or reference to any relationship with other women. Even though he may have married a woman at some time in his life, biographies and autobiographies typically indicate that such actions were attempts to "make a man of myself" or conform to society's demand in order to appease relatives.

Is, then, a transsexual a homosexual? If one considers the anatomy, yes; but if one believes a transsexual's feelings as evident in his comments ("Men are all the same—they just want one thing from us women"), then the answer must be no.

Although transsexuals do not feel they are homosexual, they often know that they are regarded as such by most people who know them. A remark that would be of interest to readers of Scheff and Becker was made by "K" in her autobiography: "If all the world thinks of you as being homosexual, it is very difficult not to have that image imposed upon you, to resist it in your own mind" (Benjamin, 1966: 279). Even while socially labeled a homosexual, however, if such is the case, the homosexual life is no answer to the transsexual's problems. I must agree with Gagnon and Simon that, "This prepossessing concern on the part of nonhomosexuals with the purely sexual aspect" of life is not a totally adequate way in which to categorize people. Transsexuals must also "come to terms with the problems that are attendant upon being a member of society" and those problems go much deeper than just sexual activity (Gagnon and Simon, 1968: 352, 355).

PREVALENCE OF AND LIMITATIONS ON THE STUDY OF TRANSSEXUALISM

There are an estimated 2,000 transsexuals in this country, and, if the "borderline" cases described as transvestites are included, the figure runs over 10,000. Probably the most accurate minimal estimate of the prevalence of transsexualism is a ratio reported by Dr. Ira B. Pauly in 1968 of 1:100,000 of the general population, the rate for men to women being approximately 4:1.

By March of 1969, Dr. Harry Benjamin, who pioneered much of the work done with transsexuals, had observed nearly 500 male transsexuals and 100 females, and diagnosis and observation is now being conducted or contemplated at medical centers and in universities throughout the country, including not only at Johns Hopkins, where it began in 1966, but at the University of Minnesota, Stanford University, University of Washington, University of Oregon and UCLA.

Opportunities in reseach clinics here are limited, however; subjects selected must meet certain requirements (typically they must be 21 or over, must have a clean police record except for impersonation violations, must agree to follow-up treatment, and the like) in order to be accepted into the programs. Because of these requirements and because the conversion process is a long and involved one, including extensive interviews with psychologists, psychiatrists, gynecologists, and plastic surgeons, many transsexuals go abroad for the operation, which has meant the loss of much scientific data that could have been compiled had they been treated here.

CHARACTERISTICS OF THE TRANSSEXUAL

Childhood cross-gender identification. Many of the "symptoms" of transsexualism are also characteristic of the normal child growing up, and the following is not intended to be interpreted as a list of characteristics common only to transsexuals. Any one of these singly and of itself would not necessarily be cause for concern on a parent's part; the transsexual, however, typically has a great many or all of these traits. A son growing up with manifestations of all these characteristics would cause the average parent a great deal of concern.

The most obvious cross-gender symptoms relate to female clothing preferences, although this is one of the most common expressions of normal childhood role-playing as well. The point at which this behavior is construed as a symptom of cross-gender orientation is when it is done in fulfillment of a definite need, done excessively, done in secret, or done over the protest of the parents. The child may become very angry if denied the pleasure of dressing. He is also often overly concerned with his mother's appearance in terms of what she wears, how she looks, and so on. One boy insisted at 22 months that he was a girl, and from the moment he learned to walk wore his mother's shoes. He liked dressing in girls' clothing as often as he was allowed and stuffed animals inside his clothes to look pregnant.

Another symptom of transsexualism is feminine behavior as it shows in speech inflections, mannerisms, and hand gestures. This is also an index used in "diagnosing" homosexuality and, again, not completely reliable by itself.

Childhood play patterns are probably better indicators of real feelings of gender orientation. Typically, transsexuals play the mother or sister when "playing house" and the nurse when "playing doctor."

The Draw-A-Person test is a device which is felt to be revealing in the measurement of attitudes. The gender of the first person drawn is supposed to reflect the child's gender identity. A study in 1966 by Money and Wang showed that almost two-thirds of a group of "juvenile effeminates" drew a girl first, in contrast to the usually recorded one-fourth for that age group.

Many of the transsexuals even preferred cross-gender household duties to those associated with their own sex. One preferred washing dishes and hanging clothes to even playing outdoors with the boys. The following is from an autobiography of a man now in his early thirties:

> I hated feeding the chickens because I was afraid of them. I didn't want to feed the pigs because they smelled so bad. I didn't like bringing in wood for the fireplace because I got dirty carrying it. I kept envying the girls who seemed always to be helping with the cooking and sewing and playing little games [Benjamin, 1966: 202].

Another trait characteristically feminine was the refusal to fight, even to defend oneself physically. As this same man recalls later:

> Soon I was being chased home from school every night, and if caught up with was usually given a beating. When my stepfather learned about this, and how I refused to fight and would just shake with fear and cry, he told me that the next time I was chased home from school and didn't stand up and make a fight of it, and win, he would whip me with a strap. So instead of one beating a day I began getting two. Mother realized that nothing would ever make me stand up for myself, and so she arranged to have me transferred to a public school. In this new school, as in all previous schools, I got along fine for awhile. Then the

same thing started all over again and I was regularly chased home and beaten. Finally this got so bad that my teacher would send me home fifteen minutes earlier, so that I could avoid the other boys [Benjamin, 1966: 208, 209].

Another transsexual said in her autobiography, "my mannerisms . . . were probably more feminine than those of most of the 'real' girls" (Benjamin, 1966: 221–22).

Several authors indicate that probably the best detectors of cross-gender identity are other children. Just as in the example above, children can sense when one of them is different, and they are quick to label those boys as sissies. Another example from Benjamin (1966: 201–2):

My heart cried out to wear the pretty dresses that the other girls were wearing and it was a torture to watch them laughing and being so happy. At the same time the boys, realizing that I was a little odd, began tormenting me. They seemed to get a lot of pleasure out of pushing me around, and even the smallest boys would bully me because they knew I would never fight back. Then it wasn't long before the girls began staying away from me too, and I was completely alone. I got to the point that going to bed at night was my only escape. I wasn't yet seven years old, and I wanted to die.

The peer groups' influence in the development of a psychologically healthy child is made very clear.

Adult Manifestations. The single most distinguishable manifestation of transsexualism in the adult male (other than the psychological feeling that he is a woman) is probably the complete disgust for and hatred of the male sex organs. He expresses bitterness at being "cheated" by God, and wants to be rid of all semblances of maleness.

Finally, a most convincing hospital report on a transsexual shows the following:

After being carried to the level of corneal anesthesia during narco-synthesia with sodium amytal, his first reaction upon slow recovery was feminine. His feminine affections including voice, defensive gestures, were even more prominent than on a waking level. He repeated his story [details of his life up to that time] as before, adding only that at the age of three, he felt that his older sisters were getting more toys and prettier clothes and were loved more by his parents because they were girls [Benjamin, 1966: 272].

PROCESS OF SEX REASSIGNMENT

The term "sex reassignment" refers to the entire process of changing one's sex over to that of the opposite sex, to the extent to which this can be done. This includes not only the conversion operation itself, which in the case of the male transsexual is the actual penectomy, castration, and subsequent construction of an artificial vagina, but the hormone treatments which take place over a considerable period of time prior to the operation itself. The results of hormone (estrogen) and other therapy are: an often very satisfactory breast development; change in voice pitch; shrinking of the prostate and some testicular atrophy, resulting in fewer involuntary erections; decrease in body hair except pubic and beard growth where distribution remains the same, and scalp growth which often accelerates; and redistribution of weight from shoulders to hips to a more womanly appearance overall. The extent to which any or all of these take place varies according to the dosage, the duration of the treatment period, and the individual response. Generally, the onset of any of the above, and in the cases of prolonged treatment, *all* of the above, is of great psychological benefit to the transsexual patient. Frame of mind improves at each new sign of womanhood.

The legal status of the sex conversion operation itself varies from state to state. Generally legal writers have concluded that it would not be illegal, since, in states which have maiming or "mayhem statutes," it must be shown that there was "malicious intent" on the part of the perpetrator. In addition, there would be considerable room for question in states with mayhem statutes (laws originally derived from feudal England barring soldiers from disabling themselves so as to be rendered incapable of defending themselves in war) as to whether the genitalia come within the intent of such laws.

The fact is, nevertheless, that the legality of the sex conversion operation has never been tested in court. The traditional conservatism of the research institutions engaged in the study and treatment of transsexualism and the high standards and reputations which are associated with them will certainly help protect the entire operation from stirring such disapproval as to come to the courts' attention; and clinics such as Johns Hopkins are taking all the necessary precautions to avoid the possibility of civil suits as well.

THE TRANSSEXUAL AS A DEVIANT TYPE: SOCIAL "PROCESSING"

HOW HE BECOMES A TRANSSEXUAL

It is not yet apparent exactly what causes transsexualism. The more research that has been done on sex and what determines sex, the less we have ended up being able to definitively set forth. To the "man on the street," there are males and females and it is as simple as that. But recent research and thought has determined that there are several "components" to maleness and femaleness. Money and Hampsons (Green, 1969: 97) have set forth six criteria of sex: chromosomal, gonadal, external reproductive, internal reproductive, hormonal, and psychological. Many possible sexual anomalies could arise out of such a matrix, but the transsexual's plight is that of being originally "male" in all but the last criterion (psychological). Even the sex reassignment operation will not technically transform him into a "true" woman, because he will always retain the first criterion,—he will remain chromosomally a male.

The etiology of transsexualism is thought to be more psychologically related than somatically related, although some do feel that eventually some genetic abnormality or "biological reason" for the transsexual phenomenon will be discovered. For now, much emphasis is placed on psychological and social learning factors centering around childhood experiences.

The typical pattern of family life shows a fairly masculine mother who dominates an often-absent or fairly passive father, and who maintains a long-term "too close" relationship with the son, both physically and psychologically. The criticism, of course, of attributing causation to childhood backgrounds and parent-types such as this is that there are also many more people whose parents fit the described molds but who did not become transsexuals. It appears there must then be constitutional or some other contributing factors.

Another interesting theory is that males who tend toward transsexualism are simply trying to escape the responsibilities of the male role—people who "didn't make it" as a man so are looking for the only other alternative which is to become a woman. Case histories such as the boy who at 22 months declared he was a girl, and the like, cast some doubt on the acceptability of this explanation, however.

Finally, there is a position which says that all people, male or female, naturally tend toward femaleness when growing up, largely due to the fact that the people who surround them at early ages (mother, teachers, babysitters) are women, and that in the absence of strong influence from a dominant male figure somewhere along the way in those early years, it is predictable that a boy will be somewhat feminized (Sexton, 1970).

Whatever the cause is discovered to be, the condition of transsexualism is at present psychologically incurable. Two conclusions have been made based on patients studied: most transsexuals have been found to be nonpsychotic by standard diagnostic criteria, and the transsexual's state is, as one psychiatrist put it, "inaccessible to psychotherapy" (Benjamin, 1966: 102).

Concerning this latter point, I would like to suggest the possibility that the psychiatrists' individual and personal attitudes and predispositions toward the subject may play a very important part in the failure of psychiatric treatment in the plight of the transsexual. As Szasz (1968: 84) points out,

> Problems in human relations can be analyzed, interpreted, and given meaning only within given social and ethical contexts. Accordingly, it does make a difference—arguments to the contrary notwithstanding—what the psychiatrist's socioethical orientations happen to be; for these will influence his ideas on what is wrong with the patient, what deserves comment or interpretation, in what possible directions change might be desirable, and so forth.

A case in point here was cited by Benjamin (1966: 72–74) in *The Transsexual Phenomenon:*

> When H. told me that he had been under psychiatric treatment in his home town, I suggested that I consult with the psychiatrist by phone to get his psychiatric diagnosis and see what possibly could be done to calm his emotional turmoil with estrogen in addition to the psychotherapy he was receiving. The doctor did phone me, but to my astonishment he took a non-medical strictly moralistic stand. "This man wants an operation," he said priestlike, "and naturally we cannot tamper with our God-given bodies. His wife should leave him, children or no children. H. is a degenerate and a no-good scoundrel" or something to that effect. The doctor had no psychiatric diagnosis to give me. A letter in which I asked again his medical (psychiatric) opinion remained unanswered. H., a deeply disturbed and bewildered young man, then told me that his sessions with this psychiatrist had been expensive hours of nothing but argumentation and berating on the part of the doctor without any psychological benefit to him. After every session he was worse than before.
>
> Another psychiatrist examined H. later at my suggestion, found him to be non-psychotic, of superior intelligence, a greatly disturbed transsexual for whom psychotherapy in present available forms would be useless, as far as any cure might be concerned. Operation was suggested and performed in 1965.
>
> [She wrote me in November of 1965]: "I have found happiness that I never dreamed possible. I adore being a girl and would go through 10 operations if I had to, in order to be what I am now. . . . The whole world looks so beautifully different."

Another handicap for the transsexual is, in Scheff's (1966: 127) terms, the "payoff" (or lack of it) for the patient or physician. He is not referring to a necessarily just financial payoff, but political or ideological "payoff" as well. That is, on the one hand, if a psychiatrist feels he may come under fire by a conservative local medical or professional association, this is certain to have a bearing on his recommendations. On the other hand, the patient's high degree of motivation to obtain the sex conversion operation —his "payoff"—will likely influence his answers to the psychiatrist's questions, particularly since the transsexual, who is often extremely intelligent, sees the interview as a hurdle to be gotten over and the psychiatrist as a sort of judge on whom his future happiness rests.

HOW SOCIETY PERCEIVES HIM

There are several ways of examining how "society" looks at the transsexual, depending upon what part of society is considered.

The subject of sexuality and sex role identification is practically a sacred matter for the average person. The "man on the street" (who is either unaware of or does not care about the various sexual anomalies) has no tolerance for those individuals with a dissonance in their sexuality; this includes homosexuals, transvestites, and hermaphrodites, as well as transsexuals.

> In our society, the stage, carnival, or masquerade are the only places where a male is by custom tolerated to play the female role or a female the male role. A dichotomous distinction between male and female, with no allowance for a possible spectrum of variation, makes it impossible for the transsexual to maintain his or her self-respect [Green and Money, 1969: 253–54].

One's maleness must be flawless, and even from very early ages, playmates and parents condition boys to "be a man" with admonitions like, "boys don't cry," and "stand up and fight like a man." Any violation of sexuality such as an effeminate walk, vocal lisp, and the like is strongly resented, and such people are frequently ostracized. Emotions run high, even among doctors (recall H.'s psychiatrist) who, regardless of what they learn in the study of medicine, were reared in the same social environment. Thus, to the average person, any man who wants to turn into a woman "has got to be nuts!"

Basically, then, we would have to say that the transsexual does possess an undesirably unique characteristic which is negatively sanctioned by society in general, although like homosexuality, transsexualism will probably be tolerated more now than in years past because it does not represent any real threat to the status quo as do other current types of deviance such as drug addicts, pushers, or the "campus radicals." Transsexuals are basically introverted and nonaggressive, and, in short, there are more threatening forms of deviance for society to concern itself with.

Finally, that part of "society" which has been made aware of the transsexual's plight with an intelligent and thorough explanation of the syndrome has responded sympathetically and with tolerance. Johns Hopkins issued a press release in 1966 explaining transsexualism, its symptoms, etiology to the extent it was known, and their work with transsexuals. "By treating the public maturely and in confidence, the medical profession received in turn a vote of public endorsement that made the pursuance of its new work feasible without legal or pressure group harassment" (Green and Money, 1969: 266).

Benjamin, in his introduction to *Transsexualism and Sex Reassignment*, cites two instances of apparently more tolerant attitudes emerging since the time of the Johns Hopkins press release:

> Early in 1967, a rather striking symptom of progress in attitude occurred in San Francisco. A number of transsexuals in female clothes were repeatedly picked up by the police as prostitutes. Officer Elliot R. Blackstone, with the consent of the Police Department, decided to do something about it. He started procuring legitimate jobs for these transsexuals as women, and was signally successful with some of them.
>
> Also, early in 1967, a Center for Special Problems was started by the San Francisco Health Department, at the suggestion of Dr. Joel Fort. One of these problems was gender-role disorientation. Twenty to twenty-five transsexuals were accepted for counseling and even endocrine treatments. They met once a week, dressed as women, in group therapy [Green and Money, 1969: 8].

Transsexualism may then begin to follow the path of decriminalization toward a mental health context, just as homosexuality and alcoholism have begun to do.

HOW THE TRANSSEXUAL PERCEIVES HIMSELF

Regardless of any tolerance or sympathy shown the transsexual today, the fact remains that during the years when those transsexuals who are now being treated were growing up, they were ostracized, beaten up, labeled sissies, and generally accorded lower social status by their classmates. Usually their differences were first made publicly visible at the time they entered school, and these were painful years for them. Their autobiographies may reveal that they were aware of themselves as "different" before beginning school, but all of them reveal an unhappy life once the "degradation ceremonies" attendant to school life (beatings, name-calling) were begun. Given the visibility of his feminine feelings and the consequent labeling as a "sissy," the transsexual experienced in a very real way Goffman's "spoiled identity"—low self-esteem, fear, shame, frustration, despair, while at the same time feeling disgust for his male body and resentment and bitterness, especially in later adolescence at God's having "done this" to him.

> I was a freak of a girl, one who had to look like a boy. . . . I think that no pain on this earth can equal the pain that I experienced at that time of my life.

If I was forced by the teachers to participate in games, I was always the last one chosen when sides were being picked. The side that was unlucky enough to be last in choosing was stuck with me. I can't really blame them for not wanting me, since I was always doing something wrong or was unable to hold up my part of the game, so that my side would always lose.

I remember that behind the school there was a graveyard and I would go there to hide and cry. I was so confused and unhappy that I was crying much of the time.

Life has played a dirty trick on me, forcing me to live with the outer appearance of a man but the inner feelings and emotions of a woman [Benjamin, 1966].

It is around this time in the chronology of the patient's life that he is likely to attempt self-castration, suicide, penectomy, or other physical mutilation.

The transsexual's next move—one of trying to "unspoil" his identity—is probably one of three alternatives, depending on his age.

His first option is that of withdrawal; he may not only withdraw from school activities but from family relationships as well, spending time off in a secret woods, in his room, or in the attic trying on dresses stored there. Because of his isolation, he does not develop further interpersonally and as a result may handicap himself in obtaining help later, both in finding a doctor who will operate or recommend surgery and, if he does get the operation, in his subsequent resocialization attempts. Personality studies reveal all sorts of objectionable traits which are undoubtedly a result of eary maladaptive interpersonal behavior caused by the transsexual's feelings of rejection by parents and peers.

Secondly, some transsexuals have at some point tried to rejoin the members of their morphological sex—to "make a man of myself." They have joined the Navy or married and fathered children, the latter of which was often only possible by assuming the female position during intercourse and perhaps wearing a nightgown—by fantacizing.

One individual who joined the Army said that throughout his period of service he always felt himself to be a male impersonator. Another, who joined the Navy, said, "My first six weeks of boot camp were the worst weeks of my life. Learning to adjust to Navy life was probably difficult even for the most masculine of men. For me, a person who had lived for so long as a woman, it was pure misery" (Benjamin, 1966: 218).

The path of least resistance and often the period of greatest happiness for many a transsexual is his joining of a female impersonator show where, in the company of other transsexuals (as well as transvestites and homosexuals), he is at last not only accepted but paid for being himself. Although his entrance into this subculture will serve to reinforce his deviance, he accepts this role as the only alternative since it provides him (at least temporary) peace of mind and money to save toward the expensive conversion operation he longs for.

> Perhaps the most rewarding part of those first few weeks of training was the physical presence of so many boys with the same temperament and feelings that I had. Never before had I experienced such total acceptance. Never before had I been with so many people who understood how it felt to be a woman and be saddled with the body of a man. . . . After my first two or three days among the other impersonators, I think I knew that never again would I feel so very much alive and a part of the world around me [Benjamin, 1966: 215].

CONCOMITANT OCCUPATIONAL-ECONOMIC STATUS DEPRIVATION

The question of lower occupational and economic status is an interesting one in that the transsexual faces *two* types of discrimination.

Preoperative Discrimination. In the preoperative period, if he is living as a male, he faces much the same treatment in securing a job that a homosexual does. In fact, he would probably be considered a homosexual by those people for whom and with whom he worked. Thus his feminine manner, speech, or other visible characteristics *may* force him into occupations where homosexuals are accepted because they are known to excel; for example, in one study of 51 patients, 10 were in show business and 6 were hairdressers at the time of their operations.

Postoperative Discrimination. In the postoperative period, and if he is living as a female in the preoperative period, he faces the same kinds of job discrimination all women face: namely, a lower pay scale regardless of type of work performed and less opportunity for upward mobility, including a lower "ceiling" on top potential position. Such discrimination, as today's feminists would be quick to point out, is hard enough to face when one has been "conditioned" for it all through life, but to have once worked as a male in perhaps a high-paying job (some were engineers, stockbrokers, attorneys, or architects) and then to start over as a woman in a new locality (which is not necessarily the only choice, but a wise decision if the social transition is to be made most painlessly) can work real financial hardship on an individual who at that point is accustomed to a higher living standard.

LEGAL AND QUASI-LEGAL DISCRIMINATION

It is interesting that the law, which has no definition of sex (what constitutes maleness or femaleness) concerns itself anyway with the disposition of cases involving such. We know that there are at least six criteria that must be considered in deciding or judging questions that arise as to one's "legal sex." However, in a 1966 New York Supreme Court ruling, a converted male-to-female transsexual had applied to the New York Department of Health for a new birth certificate to be issued showing only the designation of sex as "female," and in this case the request was turned down because sex chromosomes were assumed to be the ultimate criterion for the determination of sex. This decision has been criticized not only by doctors but by legal writers as well (Syracuse Law Review, 1966: 394–95).

Other states vary with regard to handling of birth certificate change requests. Only Illinois has a provision for issuance of a new one; other states have "alteration" statutes which allow for amendments of sex designation to be made to birth certificates. A few states allow only corrections to be made, in cases where a mistake was made at the time of birth. These hamper the transsexual a great deal in his postoperative attempts at resocialization, since the birth certificate is the basic legal record of a person's sex, age, and so on and is needed for proof of at least the latter on occasion.

The most frequent type of encounter the transsexual might have with the law is arrest for impersonating a female, an act which may come under various catchall "vagrancy" statutes, disorderly conduct statutes, or several others. One on the books in New York[2] and used against transsexuals is a 100-year-old law which states that a person must not appear in public "disguised in a manner calculated to prevent his being identified." This law was originally passed to protect law officers from farmers who masqueraded as Indians and attacked them as they tried to enforce unpopular rent laws. Such a law might serve today to protect the unwary from helpless-looking purse snatchers or bank robbers—actually very able-bodied men disguised as women—but these involve quite different motives from the transsexual who dresses as a woman out of psychological need. The presence or absence of fraudulent intent should enter the picture, but it apparently does not in many cases. The transsexual takes a chance if he persists in going out on the street "dressed."

Finally, the transsexual's normal legal rights, to which we are all entitled, are at least indirectly or potentially jeopardized. Irate relatives might contest a will on grounds that anyone who changed his sex must not have been of sound mind. Also, the transsexual's credibility might be challenged in a civil suit where the defendant might attempt to convince the jury that the transsexual plaintiff is dishonest anyway, changing sex, creating a new life, erasing the past, and so forth, surreptitiously. It may not be true exactly as alleged, but it would put the transsexual on the defensive, and he would again face embarrassment and possibly unwanted publicity. Generally, he would be better off to avoid litigation by going out of his way to prevent the occurrence of situations which might lead to lawsuits.

[2] See New York State Code of Criminal Procedure, Section 887, Subdivision 7.

PROSPECTS FOR RESOCIALIZATION

Resocialization of the postoperative transsexual is a complex topic, for, in some respects, the sex reassignment operation has solved his problems and, in other respects, it has created new ones.

First of all, on the problem side, he has the tremendous task of creating a new identity while trying to quash the former identity. Change of *sex designation* on the birth certificate is not easy, as discussed above. Even in the states where it can be "amended," the old information is kept on file even if sealed separately or just attached to the new certificate.

Legal change of name, like change of name on the birth certificate, is on the one hand no trouble to acquire and, on the other hand, not much help to have. First of all, one need not receive the court's permission to change his name, providing his intent is not fraudulent. The purpose which a legal change of name serves is to have a permanent "legal" record of the fact that Jon Horo is, really, John Horowicz. This is precisely what the transsexual is trying to avoid; it does Marilyn Wimperly no service to have a permanent legal record showing that she is, in fact, Mervin Wimp.

The best tack to take in establishing a new identity, according to Robert Sherwin, L.L.B., in "Legal Aspects of Male Transsexualism," (Green and Money, 1969: 417–30) is to appeal to the transsexual's former school or university officials to forward an amended transcript of her grades received while a (male) student. Compliance with this request would be contingent upon the transsexual's attorney's furnishing three affidavits to the school: one assuring officials that Mervin Wimp who graduated from there is the Marilyn Wimperly who is making this request today; another submitted by the physician explaining what took place (the nature of the transsexual phenomenon and the results of the operation); and the third, a sort of biography submitted by the transsexual to evidence good faith and seriousness of purpose in making the request.

Compliance with the request would depend upon the mercy as well as the size, I suspect, of the school or university. Obtaining this transcript is a perfect first step in creating a new identity for the transsexual and has apparently been accomplished by some to date, resulting in a link with the past but with no mention of the transsexual's former status. It also serves as proof of identity and often includes date of birth, which then may be used to change driver's license and social security information.

Gradually, step by step, and by revealing the past to only the necessary and appropriate officials, a new identity emerges and firms up. By making appointments and having an attorney explain the request at each point rather than simply popping up to the window clerk, sincerity of intent is more firmly established, and the objectives are probably more easily attained.

Another problem, not so materially profound, perhaps, as psychologically so, is the effect that the change-of-sex procedure has on relatives. The
transsexual is in many instances an "ex-husband" and "ex-father." It takes
a great deal of empathy on a child's or wife's part to understand that one's
father or husband is now a woman. At a young age, it is understandable
what a damaging effect this may have on a son or daughter. Then, of
course, there is the dissolution of the marriage and property division before the operation takes place.

The new female must be able to pass as a woman in many more situations now, and this requires electrolysis in many patients for the removal
of beard growth, which can be an expensive, as well as a lengthy process.
Also, most postoperative transsexuals at first overdo the dress and makeup
of their new role. One physician stated that a newly operated-upon woman
might come into his office for counseling in a cocktail dress more appropriate for the theatre.

On the plus side of the picture, the transsexual now will probably experience more acceptance on the part of both males and females than she
has ever known before. This makes her "deliriously happy," and she typically feels that all the pain and suffering endured in order to have the
operation were well worth it.

A study of the results of 51 operations[3] showed that 17 rated their operations' success "good" (total life situation including sex life had to be successful and a good integration into the world of women with acceptance by
society and their families was essential), and 27 rated them "satisfactory"
(here the results were lacking in some area above, but otherwise fulfilled
the patient's wishes).

As Gagnon and Simon (1968) point out, the sexuality aspect is only one
part of life's total experience, and, in the transsexual's life up until the
time of the operation, this has completely dominated his existence. How
can a person who is so preoccupied with gender disorientation concentrate
on the everyday problems of growing up and become a productive member
of society—the normal "problems of living"? As mentioned previously, he
cannot very well, and often ends up with a rather "inadequate" personality
from a non-gender perspective. Given the transsexual's greatly improved
mental state, his potential for successful integration back into society—a
sort of rebirth—while restricted by the new problems created, is nevertheless good. His acceptance in the new role is often much greater than acceptance of him as he was, and the degree to which he successfully integrates
into society as a woman is in many respects up to him. There will not be a
blank on a job application which asks, "Were you ever of another sex than

[3] The results of these operations, as well as the descriptions under the categories
"good" and "satisfactory" are taken from Benjamin (1966: 135–36).

your present one?" but if he chooses to offer this information to his coworkers over lunch, he is hampering his chances for success by his own hand.

While some transsexuals are disillusioned by the life of a woman, in that it does not materialize into their fantasized world of white horses and charming princes, and some express disappointment specifically in their sex life (not being able to achieve orgasm as a woman 100% of the time or at all in some cases), for the most part they appear to be happy with their decision and better off than before the operation. The following describes one patient's before-and-after adjustment to others.

At the time of K's psychiatric examination preliminary to surgery, he was described as having a "somewhat restricted range of affectual response," and as leading "a rather isolated existence with no evidence throughout of any warm interpersonal relationships." His psychological-emotional condition subsequent to "sex-change" would seem, therefore, to be much improved: Today, K gives the impression of a warm and friendly personality. She exhibits unusual tolerance and compassion for the problems of others, and is, as indicated, a source of strength for some others who are less stable. Her own stability has definitely increased during the period since her surgery, and she continues to function in society far more effectively as a woman than she ever was able to do as a man [Benjamin, 1966: 282–83].

Prospects for resocialization, then, are good, if the patient shows foresight into the problems that lie ahead and can exercise keen perception in handling new and unfamiliar situations. In short, a great deal depends upon the individual.

REFERENCES

BENJAMIN, H., *The Transsexual Phenomenon*. New York: Ace, 1966.

BERG, R. H., "The Transsexuals—Male or Female?" *Look* (January 27, 1970), 28–31.

Duke Law Review, "Sex Offenses." Durham, N.C.: Duke University, 1960.

GAGNON, J. H. and W. SIMON, "Homosexuality: The Formulation of a Sociological Perspective," in M. Lefton et al. (ed.), *Approaches to Deviance*. New York: Appleton-Century-Crofts, 1968.

GREEN, R., "Change of Sex," *Medical Aspects of Human Sexuality* (October 1969), 96–113.

———, and J. MONEY, *Transsexualism and Sex Reassignment*. Baltimore: Johns Hopkins Press, 1969.

SCHEFF, T., *Being Mentally Ill*. Chicago: Aldine, 1966.

SEXTON, P., "How the American Boy Is Feminized," *Psychology Today* (January 1970), 23–29, 66–67.

SZASZ, T., "The Myth of Mental Illness," in M. Lefton et al. (eds.), *Approaches to Deviance.* New York: Appleton-Century-Crofts, 1968.

Syracuse Law Review, 18 (1966–67), Syracuse: Syracuse University.

EDWARD SAGARIN

Autoeroticism: A Sociological Approach

In recent years, many aspects of sexual behavior have been sub-jected to the analysis of sociologists. The latter have examined prostitu-tion, male and female homosexuality, illegitimacy, premarital patterns, differences in the behavior of members of various social classes and ethnic groups, and other aspects of the erotic life of man. Sociologists have sought to isolate the nature of the social structure that brings forth a specific atti-tude towards various activities; the roles that are carried out by the parti-cipating parties; and not only the source of social disapproval (where it exists), but its effect on people who are involved in a given form of non-normative behavior. Sociology is a relative newcomer to the study of sexu-ality, formerly the domain of biologist and psychologist; but having turned its attention to the world of the erotic, there is hardly an aspect of the com-plex sexual life of mankind that has escaped its searching view.

Nevertheless, autoeroticism has by and large remained free from soci-ological study and analysis. This may be accounted for in several ways. First, by its nature and by definition self-stimulation is not an *inter*per-sonal but an *intra*personal activity, whereas sociology is largely a study of *group* behavior, of how people act in a *social* setting. This setting may be society as an entity or a small subgroup contained therein. It is apparent, at least on the surface, that autoeroticism does not lend itself to the usual type of sociological analysis that seeks to isolate the reciprocal role develop-ment between two persons (the dyad) or between a person and his group or society.

Furthermore, because it is intrapersonal, autoeroticism is particularly prone to psychological (and especially psychoanalytic) study, with the em-phasis on fantasy life, inner fulfillment or frustration, the sense of identity, self-image, and unconscious drives and meanings for the individual. Now,

Reprinted from R. E. L. Masters, ed., *Sexual Self-Stimulation* (Los Angeles: Sher-bourne Press, 1968), by permission of Edward Sagarin.

it is true that each of these and many other elements are influenced by the surrounding environment, and may even be suggested by it; but by and large, one studies the individual, not large groups of people, and this tends to become the domain of psychological investigation.

Finally, autoeroticism is perhaps the most private (although not always the most secret) of sexual activities. In fact, it may be considered as the ultimate in privacy, in that literally no one is usually present; Dearborn does point out that there may be dual masturbation or group masturbation, in which two persons or several, respectively, are present, each performing the stimulation only on himself.[1] With such activity carried out largely in private, and with a taboo surrounding the public discussion of the matter, this has been an area of activity not easily brought to the arena of study of the sociologist.

Nevertheless, some of the gaps in the sociological literature have been filled, particularly by Kinsey[2] and by Ford and Beach,[3] although the latter should more specifically be considered anthropological and crosscultural.

Before Kinsey, it had been believed by many that masturbation was universal or well-nigh universal among males, and some observers felt that it was very high among females as well, although on this point there was dispute. On the basis of a study of some 5600 white American males, Kinsey specifically laid to rest the notion that such activity was universal in the literal sense of the word, but he did find that the incidence was high, ranging from about 85 to 95 per cent of all males, depending upon educational level and other factors. Of the relatively small percentage of males who never masturbate, Kinsey accounted for their failure in several ways, including a very low sex drive among some, and early induction into heterosexual activities among others, particularly in the lower socioeconomic group. Among his other very important data, Kinsey found some differences in the three major religious groups and between the devout and the nondevout, but when one examines the data, one is struck not by the magnitude of such differences but by the very reverse. The devout did show less masturbators than the secular, but both showed a very high percentage, and there is no indication, in fact, that the difference would be significant, at a high level of probability, if subjected to statistical analysis.

When one turns from Kinsey to Ford and Beach, one encounters a description of numerous societies that range from severely restrictive to completely permissive with regard to masturbation. Of the latter, the authors write:

[1] Dearborn, L. W.: "Autoerotism," in Ellis, A. and Abarbanel, A., eds., *The Encyclopedia of Sexual Behavior*, New York, Hawthorn Books, 1961, vol. 1, pp. 204–15.

[2] Kinsey, A. C., Pomeroy, W. B., and Martin, C. E.: *Sexual Behavior in the Human Male*, Philadelphia, W. B. Saunders, 1948.

[3] Ford, C. S. and Beach, F. A.: *Patterns of Sexual Behavior*, New York, Harper & Bros. and Paul B. Hoeber, 1951.

Among the Pukapukans of Polynesia where parents simply ignore the sexual activities of young children, boys and girls masturbate freely and openly in public. Among the Nama Hottentot no secret is made of autogenital stimulation in early childhood. Young Trobriand children engage in a variety of sexual activities. In the absence of adult control, typical forms of amusement for Trobriand girls and boys include manual and oral stimulation of the genitals and simulated coitus. Young Seniang children publicly simulate adult copulation without being reproved; older boys masturbate freely and play sexual games with little girls, but the boys are warned not to copulate on the grounds that this behavior would weaken them. Lesu children playing on the beach give imitations of adult sexual intercourse, and adults in this society regard this to be a natural and normal game. On Tikopia small boys induce erections in themselves through manual manipulation, and this is ignored or at most mildly reproved by adults. Little girls also may masturbate in this society without being punished for such behavior.[4]

However, lest one obtains the impression that the young among the "noble savages" lived in a sexually libertarian garden of Eden, the authors show that many societies were rigidly restrictive in their attitudes towards masturbation:

The severity of restrictions and punishments associated with sexual transgressions in childhood varies from one restrictive society to another. Among the Apinaye, for example, boys and girls are warned from infancy not to masturbate and a severe thrashing awaits the child suspected of such behavior. In Africa, Ashanti boys are told by their fathers at an early age not to masturbate or engage in any sexual play. In New Guinea, Kwoma boys are constantly warned not to finger their genitals; if a woman sees a boy with an erection she will beat his penis with a stick, and boys soon learn to refrain from touching their genitals even while urinating.[5]

Many writers have commented on the harm that may have been caused to people indulging in masturbation, not by the act itself, but by performance of a socially disapproved act, bringing with it shame and sometimes guilt. This may be seen as a specific example of a more general theme that is described by Lemert under the heading of secondary deviation. As stated by Lemert:

Secondary deviation refers to a special class of socially defined responses which people make to problems created by the societal reaction to their deviance. These problems are essentially moral problems which revolve around stigmatization, punishments, segregation, and social control. Their general effect is

[4] *Ibid.,* p. 189.
[5] *Ibid.,* p. 180.

to differentiate the symbolic and interactional environment to which the person responds, so that early or adult socialization is categorically affected.[6]

If, in a highly restrictive society, one were to define masturbation as being a form of deviance (in that there is stigmatization and social disapproval, although the ease of secrecy makes it possible for most individuals to escape the consequences of being labeled deviant by others), then one could think of the strong condemnation as being the societal reaction to the act, and the socially defined responses as being the self-hatred and self-doubt plaguing some performers. In this view, it is neither the act that causes difficulty nor even the condemnation of the act, but it is the response of the individual to this condemnation.[7]

Masturbation is only one of several types of activities that provide sexual gratification and that have been condemned in Western society. The antisexual mores of the Western world are generally traced to its Judeo–Christian heritage, with the emphasis on sex for procreation and not for pleasure. The need to expand rather than to contract or hold in check the population, and the need to provide for the care of the child during the period of helplessness (his economic care, his socialization) led to the dictum: be fruitful, multiply—but do so within the framework of a family. This in turn made it functional for Western society to take a strongly negative attitude towards all sexual relations not directed towards procreation, whether these be extracoital with a marriage partner, coitus interruptus, masturbation, or some other.

Within this framework, one can readily understand the hostile attitudes of society towards prostitution, illegitimacy, homosexuality, noncoital marital sexuality, and birth control. All such activities divert the sex urge in a direction that permits release of tension without fulfilling the needs of the society for procreation and for care of the child. It is but one step, and not a difficult one to make, to travel from condemnation of sexuality that is not procreation oriented and family oriented to condemnation of all sex for pleasure.

Nevertheless, despite the proscription of sex for pleasure and of sex that is not directed towards fulfilling the procreative needs of the society, many forms of socially disapproved sexuality do thrive. Prostitution is but one example, and Davis[8] described the function of prostitution under such cir-

[6] Lemert, E. M.: *Human Deviance, Social Problems, and Social Control*, Englewood Cliffs, N.J., Prentice-Hall, 1967, p. 40.

[7] For an examination of the manner in which psychological disturbance arises, not from an act nor from the manner in which people respond to the act, but from what people tell themselves about the responses of others, see Ellis, A.: *Reason and Emotion in Psychotherapy*, New York, Lyle Stuart, 1962.

[8] Davis, K.: "Prostitution," in Merton, R. and Nisbet, R., eds., *Contemporary Social Problems*, New York, Harcourt, Brace & World, 1961.

cumstances; later, his description was modified somewhat and extended by Polsky,[9] who analyzed the function of pornography. Davis found that prostitution was complementary to the family, because it provided a form of sexual outlet sufficiently transitory and impersonal to be nonthreatening to the family, at the same time serving as a safety valve for the strong and nonsuppressible sexual drive of the male. Pornography, in the view of Polsky, fulfills the same function as does prostitution, but in addition, he points out, both prostitution and pornography permit "polymorphous perverse" and other sexual behaviors "so highly stigmatized as to be labeled deviant even within the intimacy of marriage and morally inhibited from expression therein." Polsky continues:

> In other words, sex is socialized by being placed in a double bind—the marital relationship on the one hand and a specified selection of possible sex acts on the other. It is important to see that the function of prostitution and pornography in alleviating the latter constraint is clearly distinct from their providing merely for coitus *per se* (real or imaginary) in an impersonal and transitory relationship.[10]

Nevertheless, an analogous effort to locate the function of masturbation would beg the question. For it is entirely possible that a society that seeks to keep sexuality within the bounds of the family, and at the same time to provide for an outlet of the "overflow" of energy in a nonthreatening and transitory manner, would welcome masturbation, at least for the youth for whom that society is not yet able (or willing) to provide a heterosexual partner. Masturbation, in an anti-sexual society, might be useful to reinforce the reproduction-oriented, family-oriented sexual drive by offering the youth and other single people a means of gratifying their desires without forcible violence, adultery, and other socially unacceptable modes of behavior.

Adolescence, in the restrictive societies of Western man, is a period of prolonged sexual deprivation, and it is difficult to imagine a form of gratification less likely to be complicating for the society than autoeroticism. The question, then, is not, as it is with prostitution and pornography, to determine the function of masturbation, but rather to determine the function of the antimasturbatory heritage, the accumulation of myth, legend, and superstition that has dominated Western thought on this subject, and that still survives to a certain extent, albeit in modified form, in America.

If one asks the purpose of masturbation, the answer is quite obvious: some people (and particularly adolescents, prisoners, members of the armed forces while separated from camp followers, and others) do not have

[9] Polsky, N.: *Hustlers, Beats, and Others,* Chicago, Aldine Publishing Co., 1967.
[10] *Ibid.,* p. 192.

normatively accepted outlets and must either turn to one another, repress their sex drives completely, or find outlet in self-stimulation. (This does not exhaust the logical possibilities, but it covers the major ones.) For the aid of these deprived or isolated people, masturbation serves a useful purpose; so useful, in fact, that if society did not have it, there would be serious dislocations, and a substitute for it would have to be discovered or invented.

Furthermore, despite countless tracts condemning "the solitary sin" and "the vice," masturbation may have assisted many youths. Kinsey writes, "For the boys (in this study) who have not been too disturbed psychically, masturbation has, however, provided a regular sexual outlet which has alleviated nervous tensions; and the record is clear in many cases that these boys have on the whole lived more balanced lives than the boys who have been more restrained in their sexual activities."[11]

Why, then, the hostility towards masturbation in Western society, if it serves so excellent a need? I suggest that this hostility is first and foremost a consequence of the need for an antagonistic attitude towards *all* nonmarital, nonreproductive sexuality. In order to turn sexual energy towards the family-building reproductive process, it becomes necessary (or at least appears to be necessary, and certainly appears to be desirable) to condemn all other types of sexual expression. In other words, all sexual outlet is condemned where the purpose is pleasure giving and release obtaining rather than reproductive.

It would have been difficult (but not impossible) for a society to devise a set of mores in which all nonreproductive sexuality was condemned for adults, and then some forms of such outlet permitted for the young. Most societies did not condemn coital relations between husband and wife during the period of pregnancy, although it was learned early in human history that this would not result in another conception and hence could serve no purpose except pleasure; and in the same way, societies, having banned all nonfamilial and nonreproductive activities, would not single out one such type because it was useful, for doing so would break the moral code created around sex.

According to such a moral code, all nonreproductive sexuality must be condemned, and this must include even such a harmless and useful act as would serve the function of offering youths, prisoners, and others the outlet of self-stimulation when no partner is available.

A society which makes such condemnation then finds it possible to discover all sorts of arguments to support its view; and it is not difficult to understand how it came to be believed, on absurd and meager evidence, that masturbation left one weakened and poorly equipped to go on to a mature

---

[11] Kinsey *et al., Sexual Behavior in the Human Male,* p. 514.

sexual relationship—that is, one socially defined as mature—that would result in progeny. Masturbation had to be condemned because, failing such condemnation, the principle of denial of sex for pleasure, devoid of reproductive aim, would be tainted. The seed must not fall upon the ground.

But the condemnatory attitude towards masturbation can be understood in still another light. No other type of activity can so easily be hidden from the community; when the story is known only by the one who commits the act, it can effectively be concealed. So that it is possible to fulfill the needs of the society by having strong condemnation, and at the same time provide a mechanism whereby the functional value of masturbation as a release for adolescents and others is not lost, because it becomes an act so widely accomplished that the condemnation is almost universally transgressed.

Along this line, Ford and Beach write:

> There are, however, many societies in which the adult attitudes towards sex play in children or towards premarital affairs in adolescents are characterized by formal prohibitions that are apparently not very serious and in fact are not enforced. In such cases sexual experimentation may take place in secrecy without incurring punishment, even though the parents know perfectly well what is going on.[12]

This passage might describe the attitudes towards masturbation in Western societies, particularly when the act is performed by young persons. The formal prohibitions serve to reinforce the general condemnation of nonreproductive sex and the ascetic tradition in America; the facade and the reality could exist side by side, as a mutually complementary and mutually reinforcing system; and the activity could become so widespread as to be useful, without incurring punishment, so long as it was not openly acknowledged.

Under such conditions, there are some people who take the formal prohibitions seriously and others who become deeply concerned about the harm that will come to them. They believe the arguments by those who admonish against the act, yet feel themselves "too weak" to resist. They are the victims of the secondary deviance. Nevertheless, damaging as these arguments may have been to some, it seems logical to believe that through human history most people have had the ability to throw off such fears and to have both their autoerotic pleasures and their peace of mind, while at the same time participating in the general condemnation of the society.

---

[12] Ford and Beach, *Patterns of Sexual Behavior*, p. 187.

5

occupations

STEPHEN J. MILLER

The Social Base
of Sales Behavior[1]

The automobile salesman, contrary to popular opinion, is no longer an economic entrepreneur operating without restraint and engaged solely in the pursuit of personal profit. In the past, the automobile sales agency was somewhat of a provisional undertaking in which the salesman-customer relationship was a random, transitory and, in many cases, unrenewable encounter. Today, the increased complexity of the social organization of sales practices has resulted in the development of the manufacturer-authorized agency which depends upon mutually satisfactory relationships with its customers and encourages at least a modicum of continuity of clientele. Consequently, the salesman has evolved from the "wheeler and dealer" of the early post-war period to the agency employee who operates in a more restrained social situation. In addition, increased automobile production and a competitive market have modified the position of the customer, increasing his ability to direct or attempt to direct the conditions and outcome of the sales transaction. The salesman of today, in general, sells under conditions which are similar to those which influence the behavior of members of the service occupations—that is, he is subject to institutional prescription and comes into direct and personal contract with his customer.

The behavior of the salesman in the contemporary sales agency may be analyzed in a number of ways. The economic character of sales endeavors could be compared and contrasted to the service character of other occupations (for example, the physician) which enjoy a more reputable position in the hierarchy of work. However, such an analysis would exaggerate the obvious though not always legitimate distinction between service and business behavior—the altruistic motives of the former and the self-interest or

Reprinted from *Social Problems*, 12 (1964), 15–24, by permission of the author and the Society for the Study of Social Problems.

[1] A revision of "The New Car Salesman and the Sales Transaction," a paper read at the annual meeting of the Midwest Sociological Society, 1963. The research on which the paper is based was supported, in part, by Community Studies, Inc., Kansas City, Mo. The writer is indebted to Robert W. Habenstein for his comments and criticism and to Howard S. Becker and Blanche Geer for their critical reading and suggested modification of the original paper.

profit motives of the latter.[2] A more comprehensive and meaningful approach, allowing for sociological as well as economic bases of sales behavior, would focus on the generality and constancy of sales behavior as affected by the normative patterns of the sales agency. In other words, the behavior of the salesman would be seen as influenced not only by the profit to be gained but also by his efforts to advance his self-interests by adherence to the prescribed patterns of behavior which have become institutionalized in the agency.[3] The analysis of sales behavior as the result of institutionalized patterns, though legitimate, would be somewhat limited in that it would not adequately take into account the influence of the direct and personal contact which occurs between salesman and customer.

The object of this paper is to analyze sales behavior by focusing on the interaction which occurs between the new car salesman and customer during the sales transaction: the "contact," marking the beginning; the "pitch," the middle; and the "close," signifying the end of the social encounter. The sales transaction, as interaction, will be treated as a series of events in which each phase arises logically out of and is influenced by the preceding phase. The underlying concern is with the effect of the course of the interaction on sales behavior rather than the influence of the inherent homeostatic tendencies of the agency. The discussion is based on information and materials gathered during a twelve-month period of observation and limited involvement in the social world of salesmen and operations of sales agencies. Most of the data were collected away from agencies, but frequent visits permitted observation of and actual involvement in more than a dozen completed sales transactions and numerous salesman-customer contacts.[4]

---

[2] For a discussion of such an analytical scheme and its shortcomings, see Talcott Parsons, "The Professions and Social Structure," in *Essays in Sociological Theory,* Glencoe, Ill.: The Free Press, 1954, pp. 34–49.

[3] Talcott Parsons, "The Motivation of Economic Activities," *Canadian Journal of Economic and Political Science,* 6 (1940), pp. 187–200. The analysis of sales behavior in terms of the thesis of Parsons' essay would be based primarily on the assumption that the salesman behaves the way he does because a pattern of sales behavior has become institutionalized in the sales agency.

[4] Initial information regarding the salesman and agency operations came from contacts and interviews with the sales manager and a number of salesmen employed by one of the major, high-volume, manufacturer-authorized agencies located in Kansas City, Mo. It was difficult to arrange lengthy visits to other agencies or to engage salesmen in prolonged conversations while on the agency floor. Therefore, interviews were arranged with salesmen who were contacted informally in restaurants, bars and grills, etc., located on the metropolitan "automobile strip." Informal contact and conversation was the most practical method of gathering information and data. In addition, the writer acted as "bird dog" and "leg man" for a number of salesmen at various agencies. The writer, with few exceptions, was accepted as a person interested in automobiles and, though employed, considering a change in work, possibly employment as an automobile salesman.

THE CONTACT

The initial social contact between the salesman and the customer occurs in one of two ways: 1) a random contact—the customer is interested in or has decided to buy a new automobile and presents himself to a salesman on the floor of the agency; 2) a solicited contact—the customer has been recruited by the salesman or referred to him. In the former case, the customer is either a "suspect" (a person who may need or want a new car but cannot afford or is not interested in making an actual purchase) or a "prospect" (a person who has decided to buy but has not decided on which automobile or where to make the purchase). The recruited customer is more often than not a "buyer" (a person who has decided which automobile to purchase and wishes to enter negotiations).

The unrecruited customer, the "drop in," constitutes a "cold call," a customer contact for which the salesman is not completely prepared and the determining of a proper sales approach is difficult. The majority of "drop ins" are nothing more than "suspects," offering the salesman little anticipation of a potential sale; this partially explains why salesmen prefer to invest as little time as possible in negotiations with unrecruited customers. The "drop in" may also have "shopped the car," gathering information which would "put him one-up on the salesman going into the deal," thereby putting the advantage on the side of the customer and reducing the salesman's control of the situation.[5] If personal profit and agency prescription were the primary motivations for sales behavior, the salesman could be expected to enter negotiations with customers regardless of the circumstances of the contact. A logical rationale would be that the more contacts with customers he has, the greater his opportunity for making a sale, gaining a profit, and meeting the expectations of the agency. However, salesmen are reluctant to enter negotiations if there is little anticipation of making a sale in a manner which affords them the greatest control of the negotiations and the outcome of the transaction.[6]

---

[5] Howard S. Becker, in "The Professional Dance Musician and His Audience," *American Journal of Sociology*, LVII (September, 1951), pp. 136-44, has hypothesized that a desire on the part of the practitioner to control the interaction of the contact is chronic to service relationships. See, also, Eliot Freidson, *Patients' Views of Medical Practice*, New York: Russell Sage Foundation, 1961, in which the dilemma of the doctor-patient relationship is presented in terms of potential conflict for control between the doctor and patient.

[6] These same factors explain what, at times, may appear to be a complete lack of interest on the part of the salesman in making a sale. The writer has observed salesmen who, with amazing accuracy, "size-up" a customer as one who is either attempting to verify the wisdom of a contemplated or completed purchase at another agency, or plans on "keeping the salesman honest" by employing information gathered at another agency. The salesman refuses to engage in conversation with such a customer unless it is to "foul him up" by supplying him with inaccurate or fabricated information. The

If a "drop in" proves promising, that is, accepts the role of "buyer," the salesman commits himself to the sales transaction. Though the agency expects a consistent degree of commitment, the salesman invests the majority of his time and effort in sales transactions which are the result of initiated contracts with recruited customers. The "good" salesman is one who not only can make his "pitch" and "close the deal" but can recruit customers as well. As one sales manager expressed it: "The good salesman does anything to get a customer onto the floor."[7] The recruitment of customers is vital to the occupational role of the salesman since it relates directly to his status as a salesman and increases his control of the transaction.

The means by which the salesman recruits his customers include the usual direct mailings, telephone solicitations, and "would you takes" (throw-aways which are placed on parked automobiles implying a favorable deal if the customer would take a certain amount, usually exaggerated, in trade for his present automobile). However, the most rewarding method of recruitment consists primarily in establishing a system of informants, "bird dogs," located at strategic places in the community (gas stations, repair garages, etc.) who introduce or refer "prospects" to the salesman. Such an informant is paid for his services, but the ideal "bird dog" is the satisfied customer who requires no remuneration.

The advantage of the "bird dog" system is that it assures that the majority of contacts will be with customers who are at least "prospects," thus increasing the chance of becoming involved in a transaction which will result in a sale. The "bird dog" referral system also facilitates the work of the salesman during the transaction by placing the seller-buyer relationship on a more personal basis and providing the salesman with information which will allow him to control negotiations. In addition, the "bird dog" has increased the chances of a sale by influencing the customer in favor of purchase. By doing some of the selling himself, the "bird dog" has increased the salesman's advantage.

THE PITCH

If the customer accepts the role of "buyer," increasing the salesman's anticipation of a favorable outcome, the salesman commits himself to the role of "seller" by "making his pitch." The individual approach of each salesman to his customer has certain unique characteristics but sales behavior,

---

accuracy of the salesmen's judgments were verified by subsequent conversations with customers so rebuked.

[7] A reason, expressed by a salesman: "Play on your home court"—a basketball expression, implying that the home team has the advantage.

once both parties accept their respective roles, is literally a performance, the dialogue and action of which reflects a generic character. The importance of the drama of the situation is well known to the salesman, as the following remarks indicate: "What sells a car? To sell a car it all boils down to this: if I can put a better show on than you had where you been, I stand a chance of selling you a car."

The customer is not simply a spectator but plays an important part in determining the nature of the dialogue and the direction of the action: "You can't sell unless you get the customer to tell you about himself . . . you got to listen and get to know the customer before you can make your pitch." The salesman attempts to develop an understanding of the attitudes and feelings of the particular customer—an understanding from which he can evolve hypotheses about customer reaction to the sales "pitch," and which allows him to modify his sales behavior to increase his control of the situation and the chances of a favorable outcome. The attitudes of the customer constitute a stimulus, the understanding of which and adjustment to necessitates role taking. The anticipation and prediction of response to the role being played is a determinant of the course of sales behavior and the nature of the social activity.[8] Role taking is facilitated by interpretation of symbols and cues presented to the salesman during two essential stages of the sales transaction: 1) the trade-in evaluation, which the salesman attempts to accomplish as early in the transaction as possible ("Let's see what you're driving"), even though the final appraisal of its value is usually done by someone other than the salesman; 2) the demonstration ride; "I ask him how he likes the way it handles, how about the power and a lot of other things . . . by the time we finish the ride, I have a good idea of what he wants in a car."

The automobile presently owned by the customer allows the salesman to "size-up the prospect," in terms of generalized customer categories, and set the stage for further action; for example, the car which is outfitted with dual exhaust pipes places the customer in the category of "kid" or "rod," while personal items in the car or trunk indicate the interests of the customer ("If he's got a fishing pole in his car, you know he's interested in fishing and you got something to talk about"). The salesman employs the demonstration ride to establish a situation in which the customer will communicate to the salesman what he values in an automobile and why, information which can be used to stress the merits of the automobile being considered and influence a decision.

The salesman, knowing that the customer is organizing his buying be-

---

[8] For its theoretical orientation, the analysis of sales behavior draws heavily on the work of George H. Mead; for example, *Mind, Self, and Society,* Chicago: The University of Chicago Press, 1934.

havior to assure a favorable purchase, realizes that if he is to continue anticipating customer response correctly he must know with some degree of accuracy what the customer is thinking at all phases of the transaction. A number of methods are employed to facilitate accurate role ascription, including eavesdropping on the conversation between the customer and any person or persons who may have accompanied him to the agency, but the major means is inducing the customer to talk as much as possible: "By listening and getting you to talk, he [the salesman] is going to find out what you're thinking about . . . unless he does, he's not going to sell you . . . he's got to know what you'll take." A salesman who is a poor listener (for example, one who has a rapid-fire delivery of the merits of the automobile he is attempting to sell) is considered one who "talks himself out of a sale."

In addition to offering him information upon which to base his "pitch," "making the customer talk" allows the salesman to counter efforts by the customer to control the situation or set the terms of the deal: "You never let the customer tell you what you are going to do." The salesman desires to keep control, in fact, achieve mastery of his relationship with the customer. The operations of the salesman, similar to those of practitioners in all service relationships, are designed to control the interaction to his advantage.[9] The general sales opinion is that the customer is free to refuse the product and terms he is offered, but "when he tells you what he wants, all you have to do is find it." The customer is never given the opportunity to withdraw from involvement in the sales transaction since, by constantly being offered alternatives, he is not forced to make a decision to accept or reject the final terms; his anticipation of a favorable outcome is never diminished. On the other hand, the salesman is free to control his investment and involvement in the transaction in terms of his anticipation of future negotiations and their outcome.

THE CLOSE

The salesman brings the customer to the point where he makes the decision to purchase by associating himself with the customer and with the customer's position by taking the customer role and anticipating the reactions to his own sales "pitch." The "close" of the sale, the acceptance of commitment to the terms of the deal by the customer, is accomplished by the salesman communicating to the customer that he has not only negotiated a mutually acceptable outcome to the transaction, but that he has gotten the best of the deal: "Before they buy they got to think they beat you and now you're on their side."

[9] Becker, "The Professional Dance Musician and His Audience."

"Changing sides" is a characteristic of the "close." When a possible deal in mutually acceptable terms has been achieved, the salesman implies that the transaction, if completed, will be greatly in the favor of the customer ("You're really beating me to death"). The salesman now suggests he will have to and well might act on the customer's behalf to convince the sales manager to accept the deal on the customer's terms ("I know the sales manager is going to jump all over me when I go in there but we've come to an agreement . . . let me go in there and work on him and see if I can get that car at your price"). Here is what actually happens, as described by one sales manager: "He [the salesman] comes to me and says, 'Here you are' . . . I OK the deal . . . he ain't going to come to me with a bad one . . . he waits, sits down, smokes a cigarette, then goes back to the customer. In fact, the salesman may well come to the sales manager "with a bad one," at least not the best possible deal for the agency.[10] The salesman considers his negotiations with the customer more or less sacrosanct and wishes the agency only to make clear the limits of his operation; for example, "We need at least _____" or "Don't sell for less than _____." He considers the manner in which he has written the contract and the terms of it his concern and resists any interference as long as he has not blatantly violated the economic limits set by the agency. The salesman, on his return to the customer, says he encountered difficulty in having the deal accepted ("You sure got me in a lot of trouble") but that he managed to convince the sales manager ("I got him to accept your deal"). By further implication, the salesman manages to communicate to the buyer that he is a unique and shrewd negotiator ("I'm glad I don't get many like you"). There are a number of variations in method, but "closing the sale" depends upon the customer feeling his negotiations have resulted in the outcome he anticipated.

COOLING THE BUYER

The sales transaction has been, for the salesman, a process of "selling the prospect" on the automobile, by stressing not only its merits, but also the advantages of a continuing relationship, in terms of service, with the agency. It is only those transactions which are blatantly exploitative or in which the prospect has been obviously victimized that require he be cooled; that is, that the entire transaction be presented to him in such a way that he may accept its outcome without a feeling of personal failure or loss which

[10] The agency attempts, in many cases, to control the salesman by paying him a percentage of the difference between the automobile being purchased and the one being traded in rather than a salary or straight commission. The obvious reason is that this increases the chances of the most favorable deal for the agency being written. However, salesmen admit that they have, at times, allowed more than they had to on a trade-in because they "liked the customer" or to "make the sale."

would end the relationship. The majority of sales transactions that result in purchase require a less intense and continuing process of "cooling" through periodically communicating the wisdom of the purchase to the buyer as long as and in order that he maintain a relationship with the agency. The buyer may feel that there are no appreciable differences between the automobile he has purchased and the others he might have purchased, but he does wish to regard this particular transaction as evidence of his wisdom and judgment. In much the same way as the "mark" in the confidence game, by entering the sales transaction, he has committed himself to a concept of self as a shrewd buyer, a sharp bargainer, a wheeler and dealer, or at least not "an easy mark."[11]

The salesman, having exploited the self-concept of the buyer, realizes that it must be preserved and the buyer must be made to feel that the transaction is satisfactory; that is, the customer must continue to feel he has gotten the best of the deal and perceive himself as shrewd and sharp. Because the value of the buyer as a future prospect ("kept" or steady customer) and "bird dog" depends upon his satisfaction with the transaction, it is to the salesman's advantage to see that the customer's self-conception remain intact, that he continue to be cooled. The salesman states these reasons for the process of "cooling," though not in these terms, and rarely concerns himself with the image of the agency or its possible embarrassment. "What do I care what they [customers] think about them [agency]," said one salesman, "I sold the car and have to get the guy off my back but keep him happy."

Upon completion of the transaction, the salesman realizes that he cannot continue to "cool" the buyer; he must become disengaged from his involvement with the buyer for a number of reasons. Continued involvement requires that he expend his time in behavior which is not appropriate to his role as salesman and, therefore, costly to him in income and status. The more time he must spend "cooling" buyers, the less time he has for the selection and cultivation of "prospects," and involvement in other sales transactions. Involvement with the buyer after the sale may also involve the salesman in the blame for future disappointments which may be encountered with the agency later. By proper disengagement, the salesman is able to keep the good faith of the buyer and maintain his value as a future "prospect," "kept" customer, and/or "bird dog." In his role within the agency, by ending his involvement with the buyer, the salesman is free to act as "cooler" to the buyer-as-owner and make an effort to console him if he encounters any difficulty with the agency or finance company after the purchase. Though salesmen resist such a role, they will comply if they feel

[11] Erving Goffman, "On Cooling the Mark Out: Some Aspects of Adaptation to Failure," *Psychiatry*, 15 (November 1952), pp. 451–63.

it will not subvert their relationship with the customer or if any future relationship has become impossible.

The salesman, knowing for his own reasons that the customer must be "cooled," but that he cannot continue the "cooling," arranges for a formal and complimentary transition from buyer to owner. The buyer is ushered to the service department where he is literally promoted from the role of buyer to that of owner and presented with the purchased automobile. The salesman foists the customer on the agency and the service manager now enters into a relationship with the owner. His role is to see that the owner remains reasonably satisfied with the sales transaction (his role as buyer) by handling any complaints which may arise and by reassuring the owner of the wisdom of the purchase. The "cooling" of the buyer becomes a continuing feature of the service manager's role.

The buyer may resist what amounts to a depersonalization of his relationship with the salesman and resent any attempt to shift responsibility for the outcome of the sales transaction from the salesman to the service manager. Realizing the value of a personalistic approach to the buyer, the salesman attempts to create an atmosphere of comradeship, facilitated by a shift in the nature of the relationship from what was basically antagonistic—the objectives of both parties involved in the transaction were originally opposed—to one which is by implication cooperative. Salesman and buyer, at the salesman's suggestion, now enter into what appears to be a conspiracy against the agency and service manager.

Where the automobile has been oversold or the deal misrepresented by the salesman, the buyer may seek out the salesman and demand satisfaction. The salesman as a last resort then calls in the sales manager, who acts as the final "cooler." The principal technique he employs is to offer the buyer his money back, to rescind the sales transaction. Since the acceptance of the offer would suggest that the buyer himself had negotiated a bad deal, subverting his self-conceptions, it is not surprising that even the most outrageously dissatisfied buyer rarely accepts the offer.

WORK, SELF, AND CUSTOMER

A majority of automobile salesmen admit that their customers regard them as "con men," who attempt to "put one over" on the buyer. In informal conversations regarding what makes a "good salesman," salesmen describe their role in much the same way; for example, "Anybody can sell something they [the customers] want but the real bit is to make them think they need exactly what you got to sell, only more of it." The consensus appears to be that the "good" salesman is highly proficient at manipulating the situation and customer in such fashion as to produce a favorable deal for the salesman. The object of the sales transaction, as an experienced older salesman who was tutoring the writer in the techniques of "making out" expressed it, is to "make them think they are getting something instead of losing anything."

It would be an over-simplification to treat automobile salesmen as if they all operate with the same perspective, but their behavior appears organized around the premise that monetary and social success are the results of opportunistic dealing. Though such an attitude toward work appears harsh and lacking in moral scruples, the salesman protects himself from feelings of guilt and resolves the problems presented by the exploitative aspects of his role by attributing to his customers the same characteristics which mark his own behavior. He sees them as opportunistic, "out to make or save a buck any way they can." The salesman's perception of the customer is clearly revealed in the following remarks directed to newly employed salesmen by a sales manager. "He [the customer] wants to get the most car for the least money and your job is to get the most money for your car . . . if he gets what he wants, you lose." By selectively perceiving and, if necessary, by misinterpreting the behavior of the customer to fit his own pattern of expectations, the salesman is able to rationalize the exploitative and manipulative aspects of his role, making his work acceptable to himself and tolerable to others.

Salesmen insist that the approach to the customer is the most important factor in selling: "The pitch is the whole bit," but when the customer does not buy, thereby reflecting unfavorably on the way the salesman "made his pitch," the salesman blames the customer ("He only wanted to come in out of the rain") or the automobile ("You can't move [sell] that dog"), but rarely his own "pitch." The salesman has, by entering into negotiations with the customer, made a substantial investment in the sales transaction; an unsuccessful outcome is not only a loss of time but a threat to his self-conception and status as a salesman. In developing an appropriate "pitch," he is testing and revising, in terms of customer response, as measured by successful sales transactions, a behavior pattern. The salesman is usually always "on," that is, playing a role.[12] The "pitch" is the salesman's characteristic interpersonal style, his personal formula for adjusting and adapting to the demands of interacting with the customer.

The successful outcome of a sales transaction not only results in a monetary gain for the salesman but, by indicating to him that he has found the formula which enables him to "win friends and influence people," adds to

[12] Sheldon L. Messinger, in his discussion of dramaturgical analysis, explains "to be on" as operating with a self and social perspective that requires a dramatic performance; the world is a theater in which the actor stages his show. Cf. "Life as a Theater: Some Notes on the Dramaturgic Approach to Social Reality," *Sociometry*, 25 (March 1962), pp. 93–110.

his personal feeling of worth and position as a salesman. He has demonstrated that he is highly proficient in manipulating situations and customers to produce an effect which is personally and occupationally desirable. His work satisfaction and occupational prestige are dependent upon successful interaction with the customer. Selling the automobile reflects favorably upon the way the salesman has performed his role and, in turn, adds to his status with his colleagues as a "good" salesman.

CONCLUSION

One type of economic behavior, sales behavior, has been explored by focusing on the relationship which occurs between the automobile salesman and his customer. The sales transaction, as well as sales tactics and the behavioral implications of the salesman's conception of himself, his work, and his customer, are influenced by the sociological circumstances of the sales encounter, as much by the dynamics of the salesman-customer relationship as by agency prescription and the immediate profit for the salesman.

The automobile sales agency expects the salesman to engage in negotiations with customers which will result in at least the minimum profit acceptable to the agency. The salesman, looking at the sales situation from the agency perspective, negotiates sales which are in keeping with the economic conditions and limits imposed by the agency. However, the perspective of the salesman, like the perspectives of members of other occupations who come into direct contact with a customer, client, or patient, includes strong opinions regarding the way the sales transaction should be conducted. If the customer, wishing to make the most advantageous purchase possible, attempts to direct the circumstances, conditions, and outcome of the sales transaction, a conflict results. The salesman either counters such attempts by employing the appropriate tactics or, in some manner, terminates his involvement with the customer. The conflict and the importance of control are substantiated by the attitudes and opinions of salesmen. The "good" salesman, as conceptualized by salesmen, is one who not only sells but is also adept at manipulating the circumstances of the negotiation so as to assure his control of the sales transaction.

The salesman engaged in the sales transaction is, of course, calculating the potential economic return to himself and the agency. However, in addition to economic gain, the salesman is vulnerable to loss in such noneconomic areas as status, work satisfaction, and a personally acceptable and socially supportable concept of self. He protects himself from actual loss in noneconomic areas by at times refusing immediate or ultimate profit and by resisting agency prescription—for example, not entering into negotiations with a customer who may have information which would be to his advantage during negotiations. The salesman would prefer the loss of a profit, both for himself and the agency, to involvement in a situation which is controlled by the customer. The implications of the data are not that profit and agency prescription have no influence on the operations and actions of the salesman. Rather, the data suggest that, in addition to institutionalized patterns of economic behavior, there exist other socially based supports for sales behavior making that behavior more social and less economic than it is usually considered to be. The social circumstances and conflicts of the salesman-customer relationship, similar to those found in the practitioner-client relationships of service occupations, constitute such a social base for sales behavior.

MARY GRAY RIEGE

The Call Girl and the Dance Teacher: A Comparative Analysis

INTRODUCTION

In his introduction to The Taxi Dance Hall, Burgess (1932) states:

> The taxi dance hall is an example of the failure of the traditional devices of social control to function in a culturally heterogeneous and anonymous society. Conventional avenues for forming friendships are deficient in the city, and taxi dance halls, lonesome clubs, and matrimonial advertising bureaus appear.

Burgess might have included the branch studios of national dancing school chains and professional prostitution in his list of examples, since these are also phenomena of large cities and are also a-conventional responses to the felt need for friendship formation.

In this context, this paper is a comparative analysis of the occupational roles of the call girl and the female ballroom dance teacher employed by a

Reprinted from the Cornell Journal of Social Relations, 4, 1 (1969), 58–70, by permission of the publisher.

national dance school chain. Both professions fall under the broad heading of service occupations, defined by Becker (1966) as:

> in general, distinguished by the fact that the worker in them comes into more or less direct and personal contact with the ultimate consumer of the product of his work, the client for whom he performs the service.

Both professions may be considered the upper echelon of their occupational sphere. One typology of prostitution (Minnis, 1963) divides this occupation into seven subgroups of which the pony girl and the call girl are the elites.[1] Although there is no comparable study in the sociological literature describing strata among ballroom dance teachers, it is generally accepted that there is a sharp division between those girls who are employed by national chains of ballroom dance schools, such as Arthur Murray or Fred Astaire, and those who work for independent schools. The Murray or Astaire teacher receives extensive professional training in dancing, teaching, salesmanship, grooming, etc. Her dance training is standardized according to a "dance manual" issued to each branch studio of the national chain, and is extensive in that she is able to dance and to teach a wide range of dances at a standard of excellence ranked by professional judges. She earns an average-to-good salary based on an hourly wage as well as commissions for selling additional lessons to the students assigned to her.

At a lower level are those girls employed by independent dance studios. These are of two types—those that attempt to establish themselves in competition with Murray or Astaire schools (and frequently fail), and the resort-type school, usually in business only for "the season." The primary reasons for distinguishing between teachers in national and independent schools are (1) independent schools generally have a short life, while national chains have been in operation for several decades; (2) the training program for teachers in independent schools is generally catch-as-catch-can, not extensive, and usually confined to teaching "what the student wants" rather than a broad academic-type general knowledge of ballroom

[1] A brief description of the roles of the pony girl and the call girl will indicate why the focus in this paper is on the call girl rather than the pony girl: "The prostitute who considers herself above the ordinary prostitute is the call girl. In some cases, this aristocrat of prostitution considers herself not a prostitute at all. She restricts herself to a limited number of contacts with patrons who she may know over long periods and who pay a high fee. Second to the pony girl, this class is the elite of the prostitution world" (Minnis, 1963). The pony girl actually has two occupations—she is either model-and-prostitute or entertainer-and-prostitute. The prostitution in which she engages is sporadic and not her sole or primary source of income. Thus, she falls into a category which is less comparable to that of the female dance teacher than the call girl who, like the dance teacher, usually has only one occupation from which she derives her entire income.

dances; and (3) the female teachers are sometimes ex-employees of national chains who have been fired for one or another reason, or, sometimes, near-prostitutes—that is, girls who use the contacts they make at the school for personal profit.

Having identified the subgroups among prostitutes and dance teachers whose roles will be compared in this paper, we now turn to a discussion of the foci within which these occupations are to be examined. As stated earlier, both the dance teacher and the call girl are reflections of occupations which have grown up within large cities as a spurious response to the need for friendship formation "in a culturally heterogeneous and anonymous society." In this paper, particular interest is focused on the ideology of both occupations and on how that ideology is manifested in the occupational roles of call girls and dance teachers. Neither of these occupations provides genuine friendship—but both sell, along with their manifest service, a simulated friendship. Further, in both cases there is a sexual component which differentiates these services from non-sexually or a-sexually oriented service occupations.[2] While the sexual component of the call girl's role is obvious, it may not be so apparent in the role of the dance teacher. However as Lopata and Noel (1967) state:

> In our society, one of the forms of interaction in primary relations with members of the opposite sex . . . is ballroom dancing. An important factor distinguishing this form of interaction from others . . . is the fact that it involves physical contact on the part of a man and a woman who are supposedly attractive to each other. . . . Its sexual connotations are implicit in the attitude of members of the society toward two women who dance together and in the refusal of men to dance with each other.

Cottle (1966) also notes that:

> The inherent intimacy . . . makes dancing uniquely different from most other observable social interaction.

How does—or indeed, how can—a professional ideology support the sale of simulated friendship in a sexually oriented occupation? (At first thought, this would seem to be a case of fraud at worst, or hypocrisy at best.) This matter is of special interest since sexual behavior is one common aspect of primary relationships and, as such, is incompatible with the notion of simulated friendship. Lopata and Noel (1967) discuss this situation:

---

[2] Non-sexual or a-sexual service occupations are too numerous to mention. Other sexually oriented service occupations are few. The Playboy Bunny type of cocktail waitress is one example.

"Primary relations" . . . are viewed as involving affection, personality-directed goals, pleasure in the relationship itself, and trust in its symmetry or reciprocity. Partners in a primary relationship are expected to commit themselves to equal involvement and to be concerned over each other's feelings. *The presence of commercial lonely hearts clubs and ballroom dance studios violates this distinction* [between primary and secondary relationships] since they supposedly attract defenseless people who want primary relations so badly that they are willing to use secondarily designed organizations to buy them. (Emphasis added.)

According to Becker and Geer (1966):

It makes some difference in a man's performance of his work whether he believes wholeheartedly in what he is doing or feels that in important respects it is a fraud.

While we can readily agree that the sale of simulated friendship is fraudulent, we may wonder what differences there might be in the occupational behavior of (1) the call girl, around whom there is only minimal organizational framework for support, and whose ideology directly acknowledges the fraud involved in her work, and (2) the dance teacher, surrounded by a complicated organizational framework so structured as to keep her from awareness of the fraud involved in her work. Other similarities and differences, regardless of "official" ideologies found in these two occupations, will also be explored below.

TWO CUTURAL FACTORS

1. *SEX AND SEXUALITY*

While there are many superficial similarities between the roles of dance teacher and call girl (to be illustrated below), there is an essential difference in the area of what Masters and Johnson (1966) have called the disparity in our culture between sex and sexuality. These authors demonstrate that sexuality and sex are not synonymous but that they do lie on a continuum—a fact not recognized in our society. They contend that while we educate our children about sex (largely in the form of "reproduction education") we fail to educate them about sexuality. As a result, they state, we fail to produce mature adults, capable of forming adequate interpersonal relationships including tenderness, intimacy, warmth, or responsible and intelligently managed sex behavior. Using Masters and Johnson's framework, the property space on page 234 illustrates how sex and sexuality are differentially bifurcated in the occupations of the call girl and the dance teacher.

	Call Girl	Dance Teacher
Sex	Provided	Not Provided
Sexuality	Simulated	Genuine

Interestingly, since it is implicit in Masters and Johnson's argument that sex without sexuality is a fraud, as is sexuality without sex, the call girl's culturally disapproved occupation actually comes closer to the desired state of affairs than does the dance teacher's culturally approved occupation. Although simulated sexuality may be a fraud-within-a-fraud, at least it is coupled, however spuriously, with sex itself. This is not the case for the dance teacher, in whose occupation sex and sexuality are totally dichotomized.

2. WORK AND FUN

Both the call girl and the dance teacher view their occupational specialties as providing "fun" for the client. The call girl is consistent in her behavioral implementation of this idea. That is, "success" is not expected or demanded from the client; he does not work, nor is he expected to, to obtain fun. Conversely, she provides the work and he has the fun. The dance teacher, on the other hand, is inconsistent in her behavioral implementation of this idea. Learning to dance is seen by her as hard work, something eminently worth doing well, and something which takes a long time in order to be "successful." (The call girl does not teach her client, except perhaps incidentally, and the provision of fun is immediate.)

The paradoxical attitude of the dance teacher and the consistent attitude of the call girl may be seen as differential reflections of lower-class vs. middle- and upper-class values in our culture. In the latter classes, there is a general trend (if not a manifest predilection) toward making work of everything which would customarily be considered play or fun. In the middle and upper classes, play (including dancing) is not spontaneous. In the lower class, however, there is a countervailing attitude which holds that fun is, by definition, spontaneous. Interestingly, comparisons of dancing styles among lower-class Negroes and middle- and upper-class whites reveal that it is only in the lower-class Negro's style that there is a large element of spontaneity. Cottle (1966) finds that:

> Pure innovation occurs primarily in the lower class, where innovators transmit interpretive findings and readings to their groups, but social norms control this activity as well. A great male dancer, for example, is heralded in lower classes, held suspect in middle classes, and is nonexistent among elites.

It is not surprising, therefore, that it is from the lower-class groups that innovations in dancing steps and styles most frequently arise—which are then "learned" and "perfected" by middle- and upper-class dancers.

These notions lead to the conclusion that the call girl's occupational behavior reflects a consistency of attitude similar to that of the lower-class Negro, i.e., that fun is a spontaneous happening. The dance teacher's occupational behavior reflects, on the other hand, an incongruous attitude similar to the middle- and upper-class feeling that having fun is something to be worked at—i.e., non-spontaneous. This paradox may reflect an over-generalization of the Protestant Ethic in our culture, where success is an important element of all behavior, where work is highly valued for its own sake, and where the impetus to successful work becomes extended to the point that one is expected to be "good at" having fun!

OTHER SIMILARITIES AND DIFFERENCES

1. *SOCIAL CLASS ORIGINS*

In view of the discussion above, it is curious that in one extensive study of call girls (Greenwald, 1958), 85% were found to have middle- or upper-class backgrounds—quite the converse of what might have been expected. While no data are available on the social class background of dance teachers, it is the impression of the present writer that most dance teachers come from middle-class families.[3] There is a relationship between the clientele served and the class origin of the teacher. Clients who can afford lessons at an Astaire or Murray studio are generally middle- or upper-class themselves.[4] Greenwald (1958) points out the relationship between class origins of call girls and their clientele. He states:

> Girls from [middle- and upper-] classes are usually more willing than others to provide the variety of sexual activities frequently required by middle- and upper-class males.

2. *RECRUITMENT, TRAINING, AND ROLE SETS*

Dance teachers are usually recruited through newspaper want-ads. Careful screening eliminates the physically unattractive, unpoised, or in any

---

[3] This impression was gained over a 15-year employment span with the Fred Astaire Dance Studios.

[4] Lessons range in price from $10 to $18 per hour with the mean considerably closer to the upper end of this range. Comparatively, the call girl's average fee for services is not lower than $20.

way undesirable applicants. Those who are considered suitable for training are then given an extensive course of instruction in teaching ballroom
dancing as well as in other skills (see above). When the trainee is considered ready to teach, she is officially hired. However, training continues
after hiring, taking up a large part of the time the teacher spends in the
school.

The new teacher is inculcated with upper-class attitudes toward her
students and toward her own role. The professional stance, as Lopata and
Noel (1967) point out, includes:

> . . . no derogatory or degrading remarks about the activity of ballroom dance
> teaching. . . .The regular or "long course" student who dances well is a source
> of pride. . . . The highly professional studio . . . enforces the rules forbid-
> ding outside, non-studio sponsored contact, demands non-sexual connotations
> in the student-teacher relations, and has a non-cynical attitude toward dancing
> and toward the student. It tends to [have] a high morale and strong skill orien-
> tation on the part of teachers. . . .

During the training period, the novice-teacher becomes acquainted with
members of the studio staff who form her elaborate role set. These are:

1. The studio receptionist, who will book appointments and on whom she is dependent not only for this function but also for "keeping the student happy"
   while he waits for his lesson in the reception room of the studio;
2. The studio manager, who is her direct employer, and who will provide sales
   training and orient her to the value system of the studio;
3. The dance director from whom she receives her ongoing training in both
   dancing and teaching;
4. The senior interviewer(s) who is the first salesperson the incoming student
   encounters in the studio, and on whom the new teacher is thus dependent
   for her clientele;
5. The junior interviewer(s) who teaches the first several lessons of a new student's course, and who is a second-line salesperson, "extending" the course of
   lessons originally purchased into a longer, tailor-made program, before the
   student is assigned a regular teacher;
6. The supervisor whose function is to help the teacher obtain "renewals"—
   i.e., to sell additional courses of lessons;
7. The guest director, who encourages students, teachers, and trainees to bring
   guests to the studio in order to provide opportunities to enroll them for
   courses;
8. Other trainees and regular teachers with whom she will be working, once
   hired, and finally;
9. Students assigned to her, and other teachers' students.

Call girls are usually recruited into the profession by other call girls or by men connected with call girl circles. Bryan (1965) describes the standard structure of the apprenticeship period as follows:

> The novice receives her training either from a pimp or from another more experienced call girl, more often the latter. She serves her initial two to eight months of work under the trainer's supervision and often . . . in the trainer's apartment. The trainer assumes responsibility for arranging contacts and negotiating the type and place of the sexual encounter. . . . The content of the training pertains both to a general philosophical stance and to some specifics (usually not sexual) of interpersonal behavior with customers and colleagues.

Bryan describes the interpersonal techniques as consisting primarily of "pitches," telephone conversations, personal and sometimes sexual hygiene, rules against alcohol or drugs while with clients, how and when to obtain fees, and specifics concerning sexual habits of particular customers, although specific sexual techniques are very rarely taught. He states further:

> It appears that the primary function of the apprenticeship, at least for the trainee, is building a clientele. . . . The novice call girl is acclimated to her new job primarily by being thoroughly immersed in the call girl subculture, where she learns the trade through imitation as much as through explicit tutoring.

During her apprenticeship, the call girl becomes acquainted with other members of her rather small role set.[5] This consists largely of clients and other call girls. An attorney may be a member of the role set, although his services are infrequently used. In some cases there may also be a pimp, though he generally functions as a paid lover rather than as a procurer at this level of prostitution (see Greenwald, 1958).

3. MOBILITY

Upward mobility is quite limited for both the dance teacher and the call girl, but downward mobility is commonplace in both occupations.

Among dance teachers, for instance, former employees of other schools

---

[5] Curiously, while the organization is rather loosely structured around the call girl and rather tightly structured around the dance teacher, Caplow's comment (1954) below would seem to apply more to the call girl than to the dance teacher! He states: "The specifications for the control of behavior in a well organized occupation are exceedingly numerous. Indeed training for such an occupation . . . consists primarily in learning the rules governing the exercise of a function rather than in rehearsing the function itself."

are seldom hired by national chains which prefer to train their teachers themselves. Even between the two major studios (Murray and Astaire), very little cross-hiring is done.

Regarding the call girls, Greenwald (1958) states:

> It should be noted that one does not become a call girl by working one's way up the economic ladder of prostitution. Call girls usually start at that level.

As noted above, in both occupations downward mobility is fairly common among those who do not leave their work for marriage or some entirely different occupation. One factor here would seem to be length of time involved. Both dance teachers and call girls need to be fairly young and at least moderately attractive in order to meet the expectations of their respective publics. If a call girl stays "in the life" too long, she may find her clientele diminishing to the point where she "automatically" moves down the ladder—i.e., becomes a B-girl or, should she lose her attractiveness through excessive drinking, drug use, etc., she may be eventually reduced to the status of a streetwalker. The dance teacher is usually not "in the business" for many years. Most leave the profession to take other kinds of jobs or to marry. However, those who are fired from a national chain and who wish to stay in the business—or those who are interested in a less stable job that may offer more short-range financial reward—may move down the occupational ladder to another type of dance studio.

Within the dance studio, however, upward mobility is possible. That is, the teacher may become a salaried supervisor, interviewer, studio manager, or may purchase a franchise from the national chain (though this is rare for women). Since the role set within the dance studio is a large one, there are many possible within-situs moves. No comparable situation exists for the call girl, since her role set is extremely small, and she is not equipped to occupy any of the other roles within her occupational situs (e.g., pimp, attorney, etc.), although a small percentage may become "madams" when age or unattractiveness limit her earning capacity.

4. COMPARISON OF EARNINGS AND SPECIAL EXPENSES

While the call girl earns a great deal more than does the average dance teacher,[6] her expenses are also much higher though the earnings of both are spent for similar occupational necessities. Both the call girl and the dance teacher must maintain extensive and glamorous or semi-glamorous wardrobes. Laundry and cleaning bills, cosmetics, perfumes and beauty shop expenditures account for a much higher percentage of both the call

---

[6] Greenwald (1958) estimates the average call girl's income at $20,000 per year.

girl's and the dance teacher's earnings than, for example, the average office secretary would spend. As may well be imagined, the dance teacher's expenses for shoes alone is considerably higher than average. In addition to the foregoing, the call girl's expenses include large bills for telephone service, often including an answering service; for maintenance of an attractively furnished apartment in an appropriate location; for medical expenses including not only frequent "regular" checkups but sometimes for abortions and sometimes special treatment for venereal disease. The call girl also pays protection or bribe money to the local police, and has large expenses in the form of tips to elevator men, doormen, etc.

5. ASSOCIATIONS

Dance teachers' contacts with "respectable society" are limited. This is largely a function of the unusual working hours they keep. Customarily, a teacher begins work at one o'clock in the afternoon and leaves the studio after ten o'clock at night. Since this schedule is out of pace with a normal nine-to-five working day, contacts with those working regular hours are restricted. Thus, they necessarily associate with others who have late schedules—i.e., musicians, bartenders, etc. Not infrequently, dance teachers use open-all-night beauty shops and, since these are also often used by prostitutes, the two professions come into contact, however fortuitously. Goffman (1963), commenting on the management of spoiled identity, notes that:

> the prostitute, particularly the call girl, is super-sensitive in polite society, taking refuge in her off hours with . . . artists, writers, actors [etc.]. There she may be accepted as an off-beat personality, without being a curiosity.

Because of the above-mentioned unusual working hours of the dance teacher, she frequently spends her leisure time in places where prostitutes and other "off-beat personalities" gather, and because of the inability of the public to differentiate visually between the call girl and the dance teacher, the latter may be seen as a marginal case of spoiled identity, in Goffman's terms. In the eyes of the layman, she is as off-beat as her associates and thus, is stigmatized.

6. OCCUPATIONAL ATTITUDES TOWARD
THE MOTIVES OF THE PUBLIC

Caplow states (1954):

> It is by consensus and by the sharing of attitudes that occupational groups . . . become sociologically meaningful. . . . Even the most loosely organized occu-

pational group will share certain attitudes toward . . . the motives of the public.

Intra- and inter-occupationally, call girls and dance teachers share the view that their clients feel the need for friendship along with the manifest occupational service. The need for a listening ear, for appreciation, for "romance," for feeling wanted, are frequently attributed to their clients by call girls (McManus, 1960; Greenwald, 1958; Stearn, 1956). Bryan (1966) reports that when his sample of call girls was asked to give what they thought were justifying reasons for the existence of prostitution, one of several stereotypic answers given was that men don't just frequent call girls for sex, but also for companionship. Thus, they feel that they are functioning as "someone to talk over problems with." The dance studio's attitude toward students' needs is summarized by Lopata and Noel (1967):

> The studio sees the student as a lonely person who needs the interaction provided by its activities. . . . The assumption is that the student is in the studio because of his inability to relate to people in a satisfactory manner . . . [and] that the student deeply needs primary relations.

IDEOLOGY AND ITS IMPLEMENTATION THROUGH THE ROLE SET

When Bryan (1966) asked his sample of 52 call girls about their attitudes toward their profession, he found certain responses to be stereotypically frequent. His subjects stated that:

1. Prostitution serves important social functions because of man's varied and extensive sexual needs, protecting individuals and social institutions from destructive ruptures;
2. Prostitution takes care of the socially stigmatized (freaks, isolates, etc.), and prevents rapes, murders, perversions, etc.;
3. Because of prostitution, marriage is made more enduring (the prostitute sees herself as more effective in saving marriages than a marriage counselor) and;
4. Prostitutes serve as important psychotherapeutic agents, giving comfort, insight, and satisfaction to those men too lonely, embarrassed, or isolated to obtain interpersonal gratification in other ways.

Compare the foregoing ideological stance with the following brief description of the ideology of the dance studio, taken from Lopata and Noel (1967):

> The studio sees itself as providing important services, increasing the person's self-confidence and poise, and teaching him or her to relate to others in new ways in addition to providing fun for persons who do not have much of it in

their lives. The ideology of the studio thus stresses multi-level help to students who are [seen as] unhappy without it.

While the parallels in these occupational ideologies are striking, Bryan (1966) finds that call girls do not internalize their professional perspective. He states that once entrance into prostitution has been accomplished, there are many reasons for rejection of such beliefs which, for instance, attempt to justify exploitation of customers on the ground that the role of the prostitute is no more immoral than the role of the "square" and that colleagues are more honest than women outside the profession. Prostitutes, feeling that they perform a necessary, even therapeutic service, state that they should not be stigmatized. However, since prostitution at the call girl level is loosely organized and cooperative interaction with colleagues is required only for short periods of time and usually within restricted circumstances, no critical dependence upon particular individuals is developed. Thus, in spite of ideology, the everyday life of the call girl is to a great extent designed to avoid public revelation and is generally successful in this effort. Moreover, much of the interaction of client and prostitute is specifically oriented toward the reduction of the stigma attached to both roles, according to Bryan (1966), each pretending that the other is fulfilling a role more obscure than that which is apparent. "The call girl rarely experiences moral condemnation through interpersonal relations, thus reducing the need for justification. This may further lessen the impact of attempts at occupational socialization." Bryan finds that the group as a whole fails to identify with colleagues.

Conversely, the elaborate role set and intricate system of interdependency within the dance studio contributes toward an ongoing reinforcement of the ideology of the professional dance studio in the attitude of its teachers.

The role sets of call girl and dance teacher are presented diagrammatically below:

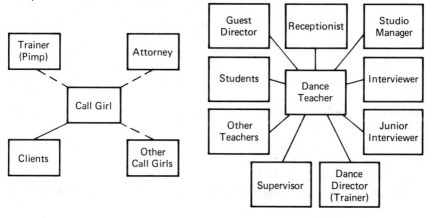

Dotted lines indicate members of the role set who are infrequently and sometimes never encountered. Since, in the dance studio, all role set members interact frequently with all other members, solid lines could be drawn showing all interconnections.

Earlier we noted the *implicit* sexuality involved in ballroom dancing and questioned how the ideology of a profession could support and sustain a condition of "unawareness" of this sexuality. The answer lies in the elaborate system of controls imposed on studio personnel, and in the reinforcing nature of the large role set with its high interaction frequency. The studio controls do not deny the sexual component of the occupation; rather, they impose strong negative sanctions against any *explicit* evidence of it in the behavior of their teachers, either within or outside of the school. Teachers are trained to discourage sexual advances in extremely tactful ways, and to keep the student's attention centered on dancing. Studios forbid teachers to date students, or even to be escorted to or from studio functions by students. For failure to comply, the teacher will be fired. Lopata and Noel (1967) state:

> The constant training of teachers stresses that they must look and act as "gentlemen and ladies." The total atmosphere attempts to be controlled and dignified without involving sexual or deeply personal feelings.

Interdependence on other staff members is deliberately fostered by the studio, and this acts as another form of control. Lopata and Noel (1967) explain:

> Each teacher is encouraged to build up the image of other members of the studio in the eyes of the student. . . . Thus, although the students tend to be relation-oriented at the beginning, increasing participation leads them to become competitively skill-oriented. The studio management is aware of this fact and is probably . . . right in stating that the long-term courses are most likely to produce the best students—not only in terms of money, but in justifying the studio, and maintaining the rationale.

SUMMARY AND CONCLUSIONS

Although there is a large body of sociological literature about the prostitute, including historical background, cross-cultural comparisons, etc., there is little or no comparable data about dance teachers. Therefore, several dimensions of possible comparison or contrast between the professional prostitute and the professional dance teacher have been neglected in this paper. We have not inquired directly into codes of ethics, or possible psychological reasons for recruitment; neither has the aspect of deviance in the roles of either dance teacher or call girl been fully explored; nor has the importance of female attractiveness, so strongly emphasized in our culture, been investigated as it relates to either of the professions of interest here.

We have, however, presented a discussion of:

1. how both the professional prostitute and the professional dance teacher function in their occupational roles as a-conventional responses to the need for friendship formation in the large city—in particular, how both roles are examples of pseudo-primary relationships within secondary relationship systems;
2. how both occupations differentially reflect the bifurcation of sex and sexuality in American culture; and
3. how both occupations differentially reflect class differences in adherence to the Protestant Ethic and its extensions in American culture.

Additionally, we have examined similarities and differences between call girls and dance teachers along the dimensions of social class origins, recruitment, training, role-sets, occupational mobility, associations, occupational attitudes toward motives of the public, stigmatization and its management, and finally, professional ideology.

We have indicated that the professional ideology of call girls, while known to them, does not play a large part in their lives, and that the reason may lie in the very loose organization of the profession, combined with the fairly close internal consistency of the role behavior with certain cultural values. On the other hand, the professional ideology of the dance teacher, in the structural/functional sense, indicates a "need" for an elaborate role set and for a strong system of controls to support it, since it reflects some rather basic inconsistencies. We are not suggesting a causal relationship between relative size of role sets and professional ideologies in any direction, or with any particular level of fraud or hypocrisy involved. However, there does appear to be a revealed correlation in this area, within the two occupations of interest in this paper.

While Becker (1966) was referring to the specific case of the jazz musician in the following quotation, it would seem to have particular relevance to the subject matter of concern here:

It may be suggested that similar conflicts are to be found in other service occupations and that research in such areas could profitably focus on such matters as the professional's conception of his client, the manner in which the client impinges on (or, from the professional's point of view, interferes with) his work, the effects of such conflicts on professional organization, with particular reference to the defensive tactics employed by the profession, and the relation of such dilemmas to thé individual's participation in the life of the larger society.

REFERENCES

BECKER, HOWARD S., "Performing Arts—Music," in *Professionalization*, Howard M. Vollmer and Donald L. Mills, Eds., Englewood Cliffs, N.J., Prentice-Hall, Inc., 1966.

BECKER, HOWARD S., and BLANCHE GEER, "Medicine," in *Professionalization*, Howard M. Vollmer and Donald L. Mills, Eds., Englewood Cliffs, N. J., Prentice-Hall, Inc., 1966.

BRYAN, JAMES H., "Apprenticeships in Prostitution," *Soc. Probl.*, 12, 3 (Winter 1965), 287–97.

——, "Occupational Ideologies and Individual Attitudes of Call Girls," *Soc. Probl.*, 13, 4 (Spring 1966), 441–50.

BURGESS, ERNEST W., quoted in *Sociology*, 3rd Ed., Leonard Broom and Philip Selznik, New York, Harper and Row, 1932, p. 611. (Cressey, Paul G., *The Taxi Dance Hall*, Chicago, University of Chicago Press.)

CAPLOW, THEODORE, *The Sociology of Work*, McGraw-Hill Book Co., University of Minnesota Press, 1954.

COTTLE, THOMAS J., "Social Class and Social Dancing," *Sociol. Quart.* (Spring 1966), 179–96.

GOFFMAN, ERVING S., *Stigma: Notes on the Management of Spoiled Identity*, Englewood Cliffs, N.J., Prentice-Hall, Inc., 1963.

GREENWALD, HAROLD, *The Call Girl: A Social and Psychoanalytic Study*, New York, Ballantine Books, 1958.

LOPATA, HELENA ZNANIECKI, and JOSEPH R. NOEL, "The Dance Studio—Style Without Sex," *Trans-Action* (Jan.–Feb. 1967), 10–17.

MASTERS, W. H., and VIRGINIA E. JOHNSON, "Sex and Sexuality—the Crucial Difference," *McCalls*, Nov. 1966.

McMANUS, VIRGINIA, *Not For Love*, New York, Dell Publishing Co., 1960.

MINNIS, MHYRA S., "Prostitution and Social Class," *Proc. S.W. Sociol. Assoc.* 13 (1963), 1–6.

STEARN, JESS, *Sisters of the Night*, New York, Gramercy Publishing Co., 1956.

ALBERT B. FRIEDMAN

The Scatological Rites
of Burglars

A couple in one of the Southern California beach towns returned late from an evening in Los Angeles to find clothes from the closets heaped neatly on chairs, silver and table top ornaments missing, and drawers ransacked in the wake of a systematic burglary. While the husband phoned the police, he sent his wife into the kitchen to make coffee. A few minutes later he heard her scream. She had gone into hysterics when she caught sight of a pile of excrement left on a porcelain kitchen table by one of the thieves, perhaps the only thief.

The story was told by the wife to a circle of friends some months later. What interested her was her reaction: it was sufficiently upsetting to realize that a stranger had pawed through her intimate possessions, but to find the obscene, gratuitous insult on the kitchen table was completely unnerving. It indicated that a perverse madman had been in the house only a few minutes before, and apparently a madman who knew the couple and hated them. Only one member of the company, which included screen writers, physicians, and academics, some with European backgrounds, had a matching instance, and he too concluded with the others that the burglar's act meant that the culprit was some personal enemy of the victims.

This conversation mildly surprised me, for I had thought it a better known fact that housebreakers once regularly—and still on infrequent occasions—defecate ritually at the scene of their crimes. But apparently the ritual is not a matter of common knowledge, either because it is too unsavory to talk about or because the practice has indeed become rare. There was an allusion to thieves' leaving "visiting cards" in a *Time* magazine article on Theodor Reik over twenty years ago (April 23, 1945), and a whole

© 1968 by The California Folklore Society. Reprinted from *Western Folklore*, Volume 27, Number 3, pp. 171–79, by permission of the Society.

Many of the conclusions in this article derive from interviews with rehabilitated convicts, prisoners, and police officials. I am indebted to Mr. Edwin Meese III, clemency secretary to the governor of California, for arranging access to imprisoned informants. Sgt. James Duffy of the New York Safe, Loft, and Burglary Squad, Lt. Leo T. Crotty of Burglary Area No. 1 of the Chicago Police Department, and Captain Henry O. Mack, Chief of the Burglary Section of the Los Angeles Police Department, were particularly helpful. From Peter Tamony of San Francisco I received an invaluable sheaf detailing modern instances of scatological rites.

chapter (XVIII) is devoted to a burglary of this kind in Paul Goodman's novel *Making Do* (1964). German and French newspapers quite freely print details of such mischievous behavior in describing burglaries,[1] but I have yet to see an American newspaper account which mentions this business, although I know from the detectives I have interviewed that the ritual is not all that rare in American cities. A New York investigator, for example, told me in September 1967 that he had found the "calling card" at least two dozen times in his three and a half years of writing up burglaries on the upper East Side. Yet Susan Black's two brilliant *New Yorker* articles on burglary in that city (December 7 and 14, 1963) notice no such cases. Of the eight folklorists to whom I mentioned the matter during the 1967 American Folklore Society meeting in Toronto, not one had ever heard of the practice. John G. Bourke's classic compendium of scatological rites has not a word on the subject among its thousands of extracts.[2]

That thieves leave *grumi merdae (tumuli excrementi, Einbrecherhaufen, Kothaufen,* piles of feces) is alluded to by Grimmelshausen of *Simplicissimus* fame in the mid-seventeenth century,[3] and the rite is probably much more ancient. A number of nineteenth-century German folklorists (Liebrecht, Wlislocki, Frischbier, Strackerjan, Drechsler, and Jahn, among others) furnish circumstantial reports of this *Diebsglaube;*[4] at the turn of the century, it was known commonly in Rumania, Hungary, Greece, Italy, Switzerland, Holland, France, and England as well.[5] I can find no documentary proof that the *grumus merdae* ritual was practiced in America at that time, but my criminal informants as well as police officials assure me, as I would naturally have supposed, that it is "an old, old custom." Henry Söderman and John J. O'Connell, whose *Modern Criminal Investigation* has been a standard text in this country for over thirty years, observe that "especially in cases of burglary, it is not unusual to find excrements at the scene."[6]

The first folklorist to write discursively on this "superstition," Albert

---

[1] Based on information assembled by Joel and Maggi Busch, West German journalists, and from personal experience.

[2] *Scatologic Rites of All Nations* (Washington, D.C., 1891).

[3] Amersbach's *Grimmelshausen,* II, 62, quoted in *Handwörterbuch des deutschen Aberglaubens,* eds. E. Hoffmann-Krayer and Hanns Bächtold-Stäubli (Berlin and Leipzig, 1930–1931), III, 1178. Hereafter *HddA.*

[4] *HddA,* III, 1178–79; note also synoptic references in the various Hellwig articles cited just below.

[5] Surveyed in the seminal articles of Albert Hellwig: "Einiges über den *grumus merdae* der Einbrecher," *Monatsschrift f. Kriminal-psychologie u. Strafsrechtsreform,* II (1905–1906), 256–57; "Weiteres über den *grumus merdae* der Einbrecher," *ibid.,* 639 ff.; "Die Bedeutung des *grumus merdae* f. den Praktiken," *Archiv. f. Kriminal-anthropologie u. Kriminalistik,* XXIII (1908), 188–191; "Zum Brauch des *grumus merdae,"* *Schweizerisches Archiv f. Volkskunde,* XVIII (1914), 186 ff.

[6] (New York, 1935), p. 241; in the 4th ed. (1951) the passage appears on p. 252.

Hellwig, was absorbed with its possibilities for crime detection.[7] He thought it especially important that the elaboration of the ritual took distinctive national forms. French thieves wrapped their excrement in trousers and left it in the center of the room; German thieves defecated on window sills or tables or in the center of the room, in the latter case covering the product with papers, table scarves or any handy garment; Dutch thieves tended to make their deposits on beds, etc. From the location of the excrement one might thus deduce the thief's national origin, for whatever value that fact might have in identifying him. Hellwig was writing of conditions as of around 1900. To extend and update his data on national styles, one should record that English thieves at this period, like their German counterparts, favored the center of the room,[8] and that in the Orient the thief traditionally defecated not on the premises to be robbed but near them before breaking in, covering the excrement with a pail.[9] Currently in American cities, many thieves who observe the ritual prefer to defecate in a bathtub, on a porcelain table (as in the case with which this paper began), on a tile surface, or in an attic, closet, or some other uncarpeted area, suggesting that they do not wish to harm their victim's property any more than is necessary. The only one of my criminal informants who admitted to committing the ritual insisted that he always used the water closet—but without flushing. Two detectives have written me and an insurance expert has told me that at the present time defecation in the backseats of stolen cars sometimes occurs.

In Moslem countries, Hellwig learned, sperm is left instead of excrement.[10] Hellwig was wrong of course to confound the two practices, since sperm introduces a fetishistic note and implies a different psychological compulsion behind the act. (Evidence that masturbation has taken place during a burglary is not uncommonly met with today by American detectives, pointing to a burglar who, like the collegiate panty-raiders of the 1950's, is perversely stimulated by feminine undergarments. Indeed, such a burglar's primary aim may be to indulge his perversity.) Hellwig's error persists, though moving in a reverse direction; every other American detective with whom I discussed *grumus merdae* insisted on calling it a fetish.

If scatology is not more complex than death, as Norman Mailer would have it,[11] it is certainly a topic that lies under a weightier taboo. Anyone who chooses to peer into this dark and malodorous corner of human behav-

[7] See articles of 1905, 1906, and 1908 cited in n. 6.

[8] Compton Mackenzie, *My Life and Times*, (London, 1963), II, 269, relates an incident from his journal of 1899.

[9] F. S. Krauss and H. Ihm, "Vom Einbrecherhaufen," *Anthropophyteia*, VI (1913), 433.

[10] "Weiteres . . . ," pp. 640 ff.

[11] *Cannibals and Christians* (New York, 1966), p. 273.

ior has his view impeded by those fastidious souls—in my experience they were usually, oddly enough, members of burglary squads—who regard the whole business as an ugly reflection on human dignity (and therefore insist that there is no such thing as a ritual taking place) or who attribute the "excrements left at the scene" to obvious and remarkable causes, hoping by this no-nonsense reductionism to be done with the whole distasteful matter.

Everyone has experienced at some time or another the peristaltic reaction to fright, and one expected explanation of *grumus merdae* is that it is simply the result of the thief's fear and general nervousness. Police investigators lean toward this view, because in police circles burglars are considered among the most timid of criminals. The story is told of a burglar, discovered by a woman in her New York apartment, threatening, "Madam, if you make a noise, I'll scream." Bernhard Kraft argues that the "superstition" is an etiological decoration of the plain physiological fact of nervousness, and Reik accepts Kraft's explanation, building on it uncritically a rather more plausible psychological theory.[12] But if nervousness is the cause, why was it the professional and seasoned burglar who regularly observed the ritual and not the amateur, whom we would expect to be more nervous? For though Kraft, followed by Reik, thinks the "habit" tended to disappear in hardened criminals, all other writers on the subject, even fellow psychologists like Krauss and Ihm,[13] and every criminal informant to whom I have spoken are agreed that it was precisely the old hands and the old-fashioned professionals who were addicted to the practice. And why is the defecation performed in a relatively complicated ritual way[14] if only nature's need is being attended to? It is also peculiar that the burglar robbing a one-room or two-room apartment would choose to defecate uncomfortably on the carpet when normal toilet facilities were only a few feet away. Nor can one easily believe with one writer that the *grumus merdae* is the burglar's precautious lightening of himself in case that flight should be necessary. I am told, however, that prisoners about to attempt an escape always defecate "for good luck," which is probably more an act of prudence than a superstition or rite. (Animal psychologists naturally see an analogy between the *grumus merdae* rite and the instinct many animals have for establishing territorial claims by defecating or urinating on the terrain.)

---

[12] Kraft, "Kotuntersuchung in Kriminalfallen," *Archiv f. Kriminologie*, LXXXIV (1920), 14 ff.; Reik, *The Compulsion to Confess* (New York, 1959), pp. 51 ff.

[13] *Anthropophyteia*, VI, 433; cf. Hellwig, "Einiges . . . ," pp. 256–57.

[14] I have avoided calling *grumus merdae* a superstition, preferring to emphasize the ritual character of the practice, for it is properly a ritual in the strict anthropological sense, i.e., an obsessive action carried out with ceremonial elaboration and technologically extranecessitious.

More troublesome to explain away is the standard police contention that the burglars' excremental mischief is merely vengeance or irrational, unmotivated destructiveness, in which are mixed elements of defiance or mere prankishness. Even when a criminal does not know the absent or sleeping victim and has no premeditated malice, he may become enraged to find fewer portable valuables than he had expected or may in the course of the robbery conceive a hatred, stimulated perhaps by guilt, toward those he is robbing. To defecate or urinate on a person or his possessions or even to say one wishes to do so or intends to do so—a dozen expressions in the tougher strata of speech immediately come to mind—is a universal act of enmity, inflicting a psychological indignity in addition to whatever besmirching or destruction actually takes place. To cite a few miscellaneous illustrations, there is Mencken urinating on Poe's grave "as a mark of respect";[15] Mario Lanza defecating (or so it is alleged) on the doorsteps of his enemies' houses—"an Italian hangup";[16] the SA troopers in Günter Grass's *Tim Drum* leaving "brown sausages" in the shops they loot.[17] But only a few minutes of reflection is necessary to convince one that the carryings-on of Nazi bullies or of a band of adolescent vandals who have broken into a school and smeared the seats and blackboards with excrement are not the same thing as the neat, compulsive, ritual defecation with which we are concerned, although admittedly it is not always easy to tell whether the defecation is ritual or merely vengeful and insulting.

Though doubtless nervousness and vengeance account for many, perhaps most cases of "excrements left at the scene" of burglaries, *grumus merdae* is not a folklorist's illusion. We have the evidence not only of the ritualistic quality of the act as locally elaborated, but also of thieves' own beliefs about it. The latter are crucial though their significance is not unambiguous, so that ultimate interpretation or interpretations of the motives behind *grumus merdae* must remain, finally, conjectural.

One clue to the thieves' belief about the ritual lies in the nomenclature. European folklorists hit upon the perfumed Latin *grumus merdae;* modern criminal investigators refer simply to "excrements at the scene" or to the "defilement" or "befouling of the premises," etc. In Europe at the time when the practice was general, thieves themselves called the ritually deposited feces *Wächter, Soldat* (North Germany), *Posten* (Brandenburg), *Wachtmeister* (Hamburg), *Hirt* (German gypsies), *Schildwacht* (Holland),

[15] Charles Angoff, *Mencken* (New York, 1956), p. 232; W. A. Swanberg, *Dreiser* (New York, 1965), p. 247.

[16] Hedda Hopper and James Brough, *The Whole Truth and Nothing But* (New York, 1963), p. 314.

[17] Tr. Ralph Manheim (New York, 1962), p. 202.

sentinelle (France), *uomini di notte* (Sicily)—all meaning "watchman" or "lookout."[18] The belief here obviously is that the excrement, an intimate product of the thief and an extension of his personality, will in some mysterious way warn him if someone wakes or arrives on the scene unexpectedly, or if the bonafide night watchman chooses to investigate. Possibly, and less fancifully, the *grumus merdae* was called a watchman merely in token of its influence as an amulet. The depositing of the excrement on the window sill, a good position for a lookout, complements the personification theory of course. (Examples of piles of excrement being personified are recorded for the period 1870–1920 in the incantations used at house dedication ceremonies in Central Europe.[19]) Two German commentators thought the window sill deposit a piece of gallows humor, a prankish, symbolic defiance of the actual watchman, but this notion does not seem likely for most cases, since thieves sincerely think of themselves as earning good luck and protection by observing the ritual.

A somewhat contradictory belief—and, in such motive-mongering as this, Lear's "That's true, too" must be our motto—is that the thief is safe from interference or discovery so long as the excrement remains warm. It is for this reason that the *grumus merdae* in so many European instances is covered—a procedure which works against some aspects of the watchman theory—or, as in France, wrapped in a garment or, as in the Orient, enclosed under an inverted pail. The thinking here apparently is that so long as the body heat is in the excrement, it remains magically allied with the producer and protects him. One embellishment of the *grumus merdae* in Latin countries and among Latin-American thieves in New York is the fixing of a lighted candle in the cone of excrement, perhaps to reinforce the warmth principle actually or symbolically, or—more likely—to give the rite a more sacred and thus more binding character by associating it with the lighting of votive candles.

Other possibilities that readily suggest themselves to folklorists get little support from the details of the act or from what thieves themselves say or have said about what they thought they were up to. Since excrement is a common European folk symbol for wealth,[20] the feces could plausibly represent the thieves' ritual compensation for what he was stealing. In Freudian terms, as Reik spells them out, the *grumus merdae* is an "infantile expression of compensation," "a regressive form of restitution," which,

---

[18] See Hellwig, "Weiteres . . . ," pp. 639 ff., *HddA*, III, 1179, Reik, pp. 51 ff.

[19] *HddA;* cf. article on "Kot."

[20] See Bourke, p. 393; cf. Edward Westermarck, *Ritual and Belief in Morocco* (London, 1926), II, 50. In the Siennese ritual horse race, the Palio, it is considered extremely lucky for the *contrado* (the city district) if its representative horse defecates inside the church where the animal has been taken to be blessed.

however, does not preclude its conveying a "sneer" at the same time.[21] Or to follow the Jungian dispensation, the excrement, being an intimate personal product, could ideally serve as a "mineness" sacrificed to propitiate the patron spirits of the despoiled or the guardian genius of the house. So Hellwig argued long before Jung appeared on the scene.[22] Bargheer, however, loftily regards any explanation of *grumus merdae* which brings in the propitiating of deities as pretentious and incredible,[23] contradicting Krauss and Ihm, who think the propitiating idea entirely possible, if only one posits that the *grumus merdae* was originally just one stage in a ceremony that involved incantatory versicles and other hocuspocus now lost.[24] Perhaps the excrement was primarily valued for its stench, which in European folklore is supposed to drive off good spirits in much the way that Roman Catholic apotropaic censing drives off evil spirits. The good spirits the thief would want to put to flight would be the protectors of the place who would obstruct his enterprise. (One should conveniently forget at this point the equally potent European folk belief that stench drives off evil spirits and makes an area safe for good ones.[25])

As these suggestions and countersuggestions demonstrate, one of the oddest things about *grumus merdae* is how the ritual contradicts simultaneously held beliefs in the same belief system; and the bluntest contradiction yet remains to be noted. Our fullest description of *grumus merdae* and the richest literature about it comes from Central Europe of the period 1870–1920. In the same area and period, as in much of the world, it is a tenacious belief among the folk that one attains power over an enemy by obtaining his excrement (or spit or mucus or nail parings, etc.) and performing certain magical acts with it. Thus Mr. Lanza's alleged "Italian hangup" was delivering him into the hands of the very enemies whose doorstep he was defiling in an act of vengeance; and so too the superstitious thief who left his excrement behind would be inviting magical disaster.

But on second thought, there may be no contradiction here; possibly the thief was indeed inviting disaster, if only unconsciously. According to Reik's psychoanalytic interpretation of what he calls the "visiting card" ritual, it may well be prompted by the thief's unconscious compulsion to confess in order to purge himself of guilt. Thus the thief thinks he is doing something for good luck or warding off interruptions or easing his nervousness or avenging himself on his victim, when actually, unconsciously, he wants to betray himself:

[21] Pp. 52–53.
[22] "Einiges . . . ," p. 643.
[23] *HddA*, III, 1179.
[24] *Anthropophyteia*, VI, 633.
[25] See Bourke, p. 386; cf. R. C. Thomson, *Semitic Magic* (London, 1908), p. lviii.

... the superstitious faith in feces as a means of protection is an optimistic interpretation of an opposite belief. It may rest on the criminal's conviction of having paid his "tribute" to justice or to the injured person in this infantile form.[26]

Clearly something like this was at work in the psyche of the notorious Demeter Radek of Czernowitz, who used his prison discharge papers to clean himself after leaving his less revealing *"carte de visite odorante."* Radek was less a ruffian than the unfilial Swiss thief, cited by Hellwig, who *"unvorsichtiger Weise"* used a recent letter from his mother for the same purpose.[27]

Yet the psychoanalytic interpretation of *grumus merdae* is not entirely convincing, even though, since it is based on unconscious motivation, it cannot be refuted. Consciously at least, those thieves who know the practice persist in uniformly regarding it as a protective good luck measure, whether they themselves share the belief or scoff at it as a superstition. And the reason my criminal informants give for the sharp decline in *grumus merdae* in the last thirty or forty years—many of them had never seen it practiced but knew it only as an old-time "kink"—is more consistent with their view than with the psychoanalytic interpretation. In criminology manuals like those of Gross and Sannié, much is made of ways of detecting criminals through sophisticated laboratory analyses of feces. In actual practice, I learn from American detectives, nothing much can be learned from feces beyond the blood type of the thief who left them, and this information is not determinative. The criminal world, however, has a greater respect for forensic medicine than it deserves, apparently, for it believes that feces are as much a give-way as fingerprints and footprints. In the era of scientific crime detection, *grumus merdae* is a good luck measure with unlucky consequences, or so criminals believe, and it is for that reason, my informants assure me, the custom is becoming increasingly rare.[28]

As many criminologists have stressed, burglars are remarkable among criminals for the high degree of specialization they develop and for their compulsive tendencies to rob always the same sort of place of similar goods at the same time of day and in almost precisely the same manner as all their previous jobs. Simply on the basis of M.O.'s *(modus operandi)*, burglary squads become expert at linking crimes and tracing them to their idiosyncratic perpetrators. It must therefore have taken powerful prudential forces to have wrenched the burglar fraternity away from *grumus merdae*,

---

[26] P. 53.

[27] "Die Bedeutung des *grumus merdae* . . . ," p. 190.

[28] German burglars gave the same explanation to criminologists a generation ago—see E. O. G. Künssberg, *Die Volkskunde und ihre Grenzgebiete* (Berlin, 1925), p. 89.

and the fact that ritual defecation occurs at all today testifies to the power of compulsion, perhaps specifically (if Reik is right) to the power of the compulsion to self-betrayal.

GERALD D. ROBIN

The Executioner: His Place in English Society

In view of the voluminous literature on capital punishment, it is surprising that greater attention has not been directed to the executioner. What type of person was the executioner? How did he obtain his position? How was he received by the community which he served? What effect did his work have upon him? Was his position a profitable one? And what, if any, have been the changes over the years in the functions of the executioner and the public's attitude towards him? It is the purpose of this paper to explore these and related phenomena as they apply primarily to the executioner in England.

The role of the executioner has varied with time and place: he was a hangman in England, a guillotiner in France and many German states, a garroter in Spain, and (more recently) an electrocutioner in the United States.[1] Nevertheless, of all methods of administering the death penalty, hanging has been more widely utilized than any other. Accounts of hangings are reported in the earliest literature, and even today hanging is more extensively used throughout the world as a mode of execution than any other device.[2] Unquestionably, England has been the most energetic and persistent supporter of hanging; from England it was introduced to America and became the general method of execution in that country until the electric chair was invented and gradually adopted by several states.[3]

Reprinted from the *British Journal of Sociology*, 15 (1964), 234–253, by permission of Routledge & Kegan Paul Ltd and the London School of Economics and Political Science.

[1] John De Morgan, 'Executions and Executioners', *Green Bag*, XII (1900), 126. These are, more or less, the characteristic types of executioners in these countries.

[2] Harry Elmer Barnes and Negley K. Teeters, *New Horizons in Criminology*, New York: Prentice-Hall, 1943, p. 417.

[3] August Mencken, *By the Neck: A Book of Hangings*, New York: Hasting House, 1942, pp. ix–x.

STATUS OF THE EXECUTIONER

The executioner has never been an esteemed figure. On the contrary, he has been hated, feared, and avoided by those he has served. Even the staunchest advocates of the death penalty rarely commended the man whose duty it was to carry out this grim task; by some strange logic the act itself was justified and defended, while the actor was degraded and ostracized. Among the ancient Romans, the *carnifex*, or public executioner, was held in such contempt that he was not permitted to live within the city; instead, he was required to reside near the place designated for the punishment of slaves, called *Sestertium*, where their bodies were burned on crosses and gibbets.[4] William Ladd informs us that in Spain many years ago 'no man, however low or despicable, would consent to perform the office of hangman; (and) that whoever would dare to suggest such a thing to a decent man would be in danger of bodily injury.' A small fee was allotted to the person willing to perform the execution in that country; since no one would risk touching his hand, the Spanish priest would throw the purse as far as he could, thereby avoiding contamination with the executioner's person. Even the animal that transported the hangman to the gallows was an object of loathing; accordingly, it was cropped and marked so that it might be recognized as the hangman's donkey.[5] In addition, for a time the executioners of Spain were required to have their houses painted red and were not permitted in the streets except in a garment with gallows embroidered on it.[6] Since that time the executioner has been a regularly appointed officer in Spain. A ritualistic procedure follows each of his performances: he is arrested and rushed to prison where a court is in waiting. There he is accused of having killed a man and denounced as a murderer. He responds to the charge, 'It is true that I killed the prisoner, but I deny being a murderer, for though I committed the act charged, I did it in the cause of justice and in pursuance of the law, all of which I was compelled to do by virtue of my office.' The court in turn replies, 'The accused is innocent and is discharged and the formula of Spanish law is satisfied.'[7] In England the dishonouring character of the executioner was legally recognized when a court awarded damages to a gentleman who had been mistakenly identified as the hangman.[8]

[4] George Ryley Scott, *The History of Capital Punishment*, London: Torchstream Books, 1950, p. 139.

[5] Andrew J. Palm, *The Death Penalty*, London: G. P. Putnam's Sons, 1891, pp. 94–95.

[6] John Laurence, *A History of Capital Punishment*, New York: Citadel Press, 1960, p. 89.

[7] Palm, *The Death Penalty*, pp. 95–96.

[8] When a respectable citizen had departed from an Inn in the City of Norwich the night before an execution, one of the bystanders observed a real or imagined resemblance to the executioner of the day, crying loudly, 'You are Jack Ketch.' Although

In early times the accuser was often the executioner. However, this proved unsatisfactory from both a social and legal point of view. From the social point of view there was danger that the accuser might remain silent if he knew that conviction would require that he personally carry out the hanging. It was legally unsatisfactory because it appeared that punishment might be individual vengeance rather than the law of society.[9] Perhaps as a partial solution to this problem, in the medieval period England adopted the practice of appointing hangmen in accordance with the principles of the feudal system. These men were permitted to hold their land provided that they acted as executioner when called upon to do so by an overlord. But with the end of land tenure by service the hereditary principle disappeared, and a different means of securing hangmen was necessitated.[10] As a result, criminals frequently became hangmen because they found it difficult to obtain other work, as a punishment for their offence, or as a condition of a respited death sentence. In the seventeenth century a man named Derrick was sentenced to death but pardoned and employed to hang twenty-three others.[11] In the days of Charles II a father and his two sons were tried at Derby Assizes for horse-stealing. All were found guilty, but the bench of judges offered to pardon any one of them who would consent to hang the other two. The offer was first made to the father, who violently refused it. The elder son was then asked if he would kill his father and brother to save himself, but he also declined. The offer was, however, accepted by the younger brother, John, who apparently showed a certain aptitude for this work for he was eventually appointed to the post of hangman for Derby and a few neighbouring counties, holding this office to a very old age.[12]

In the early days the royal burgh of Wigtown had a public executioner of its own, a distinction which it was permitted under extremely bizarre conditions. The law required that this functionary be a criminal under sentence of death; his doom however was to be deferred until old age inter-

---

the citizen denied it, the bystander persisted in saying that he was, a mob soon gathering and ducking the unfortunate victim in the horsepond. Later, when the victim sued his traducer for damages for slander, the defence asserted that the allegation could not conceivably be considered defamatory: 'The executioner is a public official, necessary to the security of the State, and it is no more a libel to describe a man as an Executioner than to say that he is a Judge.' The court, however, rejected this contention, holding that the charge of being a hangman was intended to bring its victim into 'hatred, ridicule and contempt'. E. Roy Calvert, *Capital Punishment in the Twentieth Century*, London: G. P. Putnam's Sons, 1928, pp. 172–73.

[9] Justin Atholl, *Shadow of the Gallows*, London: John Long Limited, 1954, pp. 134–35.

[10] Ibid., pp. 136–37.

[11] Laurence, *A History of Capital Punishment*, p. 92.

[12] Ibid., p. 98.

fered with his usefulness, at which time he was to be hanged. If the town allowed the executioner to die of natural causes it would lose forever the privilege of possessing a public hangman.[13] The use of criminals as executioners was, of course, not restricted to England. In 1684 a man in Maryland 'of tender years' was convicted of theft and condemned to death. A 'private and secret' pardon was issued by the Assembly, but he was not told of it until he had been conveyed to the place of execution and the rope had been placed around his neck; at this point he was respited on the condition that he would perform for life the role of common hangman, which he did.[14] In 1653 in Virginia a boy of fourteen, having been found guilty of incontinence with an orphan girl, was instructed to appear as the hangman at the gallows in Northampton.[15] Mr. Rich Owens, the Oklahoma hangman who flourished in Macalester until 1952, was acquitted of murder on four occasions.[16] Jimmy Thompson, shortly after being released from the state penitentiary where he was serving a term for highway robbery,[17] became the executioner for Mississippi. He took great delight in travelling about the state killing people in his portable electric chair[18] at $100 a

[13] William Andrews, *Old-Time Punishments*, London: William Andrews & Co., 1890, pp. 214–15. The account of the last official who held the tenure of his life upon these conditions is sufficiently interesting to record. Upon his becoming ill, the people of the town seriously considered hanging him to insure an executioner of their very own in the future. But the hangman's friends, learning of these intentions, propped the dying man up in bed and tricked the townsmen into thinking that he had recovered. The hangman quietly passed away in his bed and the duped burghers found themselves without an executioner and without hope of a successor.

[14] Alice Morse Earle, *Curious Punishments of Bygone Days*, New York: Book League of America, 1929, pp. 66–67.

[15] Philip Alexander Bruce, *Institutional History of Virginia*, London: G. P. Putnam's Sons, 1910, pp. 617–18. Bruce also mentions a case in Virginia occurring in 1676 in which Richard Haines, a servant, was granted his freedom by the General Assembly provided that he assume the duties of a common hangman. But while Haines' master received 2,100 pounds of tobacco for the loss of his slave, Haines himself does not appear to have received a fee for an execution.

[16] Charles Duff, *A New Handbook on Hanging*, London: Andrew Melrose, 1954, p. 74.

[17] Thompson also shot a neighbour for 'talking nasty' to his mother. However, the South's unwritten law concerning the fair sex saved Jimmy from even being tried. Graddock Goins, 'The Traveling Executioner', *American Mercury*, liv (January, 1942), 96.

[18] Through peculiar circumstances, Mississippi became the only state in the Union to establish a portable death chair. As a consequence of a badly managed hanging in the 1930's, shocked citizens demanded the abolition of the noose. For years, however, legal electrocution was blocked by Sunflower County citizens for fear that their area, home of the state penitentiary farm, would be stigmatized as the 'death county'. In 1940 the legislature reached a compromise calling for a special chair that could be transported from one county to the other. The portable electric chair and accessories cost the taxpayers $4,000 and included: a unit consisting of an auto truck, switchboard, death chair, generating equipment, and 600 feet of cable which conveyed the 'juice' from the truck to the county jails' death chambers. Ibid., 93–94.

head.[19] And Wisselus, the Bruges executioner of the sixteenth century, was a convicted murderer, therefore requiring a special pardon before he could begin his duties.[20]

Executioners were frequently guilty of unbecoming behaviour even after assuming office. Indeed, on occasion the hangman would become thoroughly intoxicated in order to insulate himself against public ridicule at the execution and to dull his horror of the task he was about to perform.[21] Moreover, English literature is replete with examples of hangmen who relapsed into or renewed their criminal activities. In 1538 executioner Cratwell was executed at Clerkenwell for robbery.[22] Richard Brandon, who prepared for his calling at a young age by decapitating cats and dogs, was a prisoner in Newgate in 1641 on a charge of bigamy, just one year after he inherited the gallows from his father Gregory.[23] John Price, an ex-seaman of the Royal Navy, was appointed public executioner for the City of London and Country of Middlesex in 1714. Overly fond of good wine and bad women, he soon found himself in debt and was arrested for the embarassingly small sum of 7s. 6d. while he was returning from performing an execution at Tyburn. Price was able to raise the money on the spot and was released from custody; but the publicity caused by the incident prompted his other creditors to seek payment. Unable to meet these demands, he was imprisoned in the debtor's gaol, where he remained for a few years until escaping in the early months of 1718. One evening on his departure from a tavern 'mad drunk' he came upon a poor old apple-seller and attempted

---

[19] In discussing his attitude towards his clients, Jimmy says, 'I told each one of 'em, "Brother, I sho' appreciate your trade. I'm going to show my appreciation by giving you a nice clean job. I'm going to give you the prettiest death a guy can have." You can't imagine how much that helps a poor peckerwood in the death chamber unless you have seen the grateful eyes these men turn upon me when they place themselves in my hands. I guess I just have a talent for this sort of thing. Condemned men seem to trust me, and I never let 'em down.' Ibid., p. 92.

[20] 'Hangmen's Diaries: The Gallows at Close Range', *Living Age*, cccxxx (28 August 1926), 467. The case of Pleil also throws light on the social background of executioners. Pleil was given a life sentence in Brunswick for attempted murder. Unencouraged with his prospects, he applied to the Minister of Justice for the post of executioner, claiming as qualification thirty-three killings. The authorities, upon investigation of Pleil's credentials, discovered that he had exaggerated his previous record: Pleil had only murdered twelve people. Fortunately for Pleil, the investigation of the alleged murders took two years, during which time the death penalty was abolished. Reginald Reynolds, 'A School for Criminals,' *New Statesman and Nation*, xlviii (7 August 1954), 152.

[21] In such condition the executioner's perception is obviously blurred; and the story is told in the *Derby Mercury* for 6 April 1738, that at the execution of Will Summers and Tipping the drunken hangman, supposing that there were three to be disposed of, was about to place the rope around the parson's neck, and was prevented from doing so only with great difficulty. Laurence, *A History of Capital Punishment*, pp. 86–87.

[22] Ibid.

[23] Ibid., pp. 93–94.

to ravish her.[24] In the struggle the old woman was so severely assaulted that she died; and Price was hanged at Bunhill Fields on 3 May 1718.[25] Thomas Turlis, executioner from 1752–71, was apprehended in January of 1763 for stealing coals from a neighbour's cellar, a capital offence in those days.[26] John Thrift, one of the most hated of all executioners because of his sloppy and inefficient work[27]—often requiring two ·or three blows of the axe to decapitate[28] his victims—was found guilty of murder.[29] Edward Dennis, who presided from 1771–86, was condemned to death for larceny, but later respited.[30] James Botting, who loved hanging for hanging's sake, was a resident of the debtor's prison in 1824.[31] William Marvel suffered from the

[24] At his trial Price denied the charge of wilful murder. He explained that while walking in Moorfields he came across something in his path. Moving it with his foot, he realized that it was a woman, whom he lifted, and saw that she was seriously wounded. While holding her in his arms he was arrested. Later, just before he was to be executed, he confessed his guilt to the Ordinary, with the excuse that he committed the crime while he was drunk.

[25] The account of Price is based on ibid., pp. 98–99 and Horace Bleackley, *The Hangmen of England*, London: Chapman and Hall, 1929, pp. 9–19.

[26] When taken before the magistrate, Turlis pleaded poverty as an excuse for his crime, declaring that he was in need of bread for his family. Investigation proved his statement true, for hanging had not been a lucrative business lately. Officialdom, sympathetic to Turlis and obviously ashamed that a valued servant of the state should be compelled to steal to feed his wife and children, obtained a pardon for Turlis and took steps to relieve his financial embarrassment. Bleackley, *The Hangmen of England*, pp. 93–94.

[27] Thrift got off on the wrong foot at his first execution. On 11 March 1735, he had been required to dispose of thirteen malefactors before a Tyburn crowd. Had he followed the ritual, he would have requested that his congregation pull their caps down over their heads. In the excitement of the proceedings he neglected this detail of the ceremony and one of the two carts holding the victims moved away, exposing the faces of several of the men to the crowd. Ibid., p. 72.

[28] The functions of the English executioners were not limited to hanging, which was simply their principal activity and usual means of capital punishment. This point is discussed in detail in a subsequent section of the paper.

[29] In fairness to John Thrift the events surrounding his 'crime' and subsequent developments should be made known. One evening in March of 1750 Thrift was walking to his home when a party of men started to pursue him menacingly, following him to his door. Once there, the crowd increased in number and daring and John, in terror of his life, came forward with a drawn cutlass and ordered his tormentors to disperse. At the sight of the blade, some of the ringleaders fled and John, not now aware of what he was doing, followed them in hot pursuit. It was in the course of this chase that Thrift became involved in the murder of David Farris. Several persons claimed that the hangman was the slayer. Thrift denied the charge, insisting that a friend had snatched the cutlass from him and struck the blow in order to save both of their lives. Despite rather inconclusive evidence Thrift was found guilty and sentenced to death. However, the Mayor and Aldermen of the City of London intervened and so it was that John's life was not only spared but that, upon receiving a free pardon, he was allowed to resume his office as executioner. Ibid., pp. 85–87.

[30] Ibid., pp. 125–28.

[31] Ibid., p. 174. Botting was not one to remain silent about complaints. Within five months after his appointment as assistant executioner, he appealed to the Court of

same vices as John Price; wine and women were his undoing, and despite his increased earnings he fell deeply into debt. On 6 November 1717, a writ was served upon Marvel in Holborn while he was on his way to Tyburn to hang three men. Imagine his embarrassment at being apprehended by the bailiffs just as he was about to carry out the sentence of the court. As a consequence of his unpardonable behaviour and the conduct of the crowd, Marvel was dismissed. From that time onwards he became increasingly destitute, often forced to beg for the price of a piece of bread. But he still managed to maintain his self-respect, bragging of his honesty and protesting that he would rather starve than steal. On 15 October 1719 he was indicted and convicted for stealing ten silk handkerchiefs and sentenced to transportation.[32]

There are also instances of suicide among executioners. Ellis attempted to take his own life shortly after the execution of Mrs. Thompson in 1923, but survived after hospital treatment. He was more successful in 1932 when he killed himself by cutting his throat.[33] John Hulbert, the prosperous state executioner of New York at Auburn and Sing Sing for thirteen years, took his own life in the cellar of his home.[34] According to Charles Duff, the suicide of Herr Schweitz is an example of what might occur if the state neglects to reward properly the public services of great men.[35] The Austrian executioner Herr Lang committed suicide in 1938, and William Bil-

---

Alderman for an increase of salary. Upon becoming chief executioner he petitioned the same court for an assistant and, his request refused, sent in a third petition in 1818 setting forth a list of grievances unlike any ever before submitted by a hangman to the Alderman. Ibid., p. 166.

[32] Ibid., pp. 29–35. Volkel, the Executioner for Berlin and the Soviet Zone after the war, chopped off forty-eight heads at 1,000 marks per head during his two years of employment. But his income, though more than adequate by current standards, was below his aspirations. To remedy this inequity Volkel organized gangs of juvenile delinquents who specialized in robbery. Reynolds, "A School for Criminals."

[33] According to an acquaintance of Ellis, it was not the memories of dead men that drove him to suicide but the slights of the living ones. Ellis complained that 'Conversations cease suddenly when I am about and I can feel people eyeing me as if I am some exhibit in the Chamber of Horrors. Socially it is a sad business being a hangman.' Atholl, *Shadow of the Gallows*, pp. 163–64.

[34] *New York Times,* 23 February 1929, p. 15.

[35] Duff, *A New Handbook on Hanging*, p. 80. The reader's attention is directed to Duff's amazing and amusing little work, *A New Handbook on Hanging*, which should be required reading for anyone concerned with the executioner. The volume contains many interesting and important facts about executions and executioners but also much sarcasm and leg-pulling by the clever Mr. Duff. Two delightful examples of his humour and wit are his suggestions that England's hangmen should be provided with 'a well-trained Public Relations Officer, who would not only relieve them of much tedium, but would see that the right sort of material, whether "human interest", anecdotal, informative, or straight propaganda, was issued to the Press' and his suggestion that a periodical, to be conducted along the progressive lines of *The New Statesman*, should be devoted to the interests of executioners.

lington killed both himself and his family in 1925.[36] When Herr Paul Spaethe decided to kill himself, he prepared the way to infinity by burning one candle for each head that he had severed during his brief term of office.[37]

Enough material has been cited to indicate the origins and destinations of executioners. It is not unreasonable to infer that the employment of condemned criminals as executioners and their behaviour while in office and even afterwards probably reinforced the natural alienation which the people felt towards this functionary.

HEREDITARY HANGMEN

The hereditary descent of the office of executioner has been the subject of much comment. Although it would be impossible to determine with anything resembling precision whether the tendency for the post of executioner to be family-bound exceeded the normal tendency of family-bound occupations, logically there would seem to be strong reasons for such to be the case. Since the executioner's status extended to his family, his sons could not expect to find work easily, while his daughters' opportunity for marriage would be similarly restricted. Faced with the choice between unemployment and becoming a hangman, it is not difficult to understand how the latter alternative might be selected. Nevertheless, despite good reasons—Shakespeare's reference to 'hereditary hangmen' and general impression—there is little evidence to suggest that the office was ever so to any remarkable degree in England.[38] Since the Middle Ages son has rarely followed father as hangman.[39] And of the twenty-eight executioners men-

---

[36] Scott, *The History of Capital Punishment,* p. 120.

[37] Duff, *Shadow of the Gallows,* p. 81.

[38] In other countries and for varying periods of time the job of executioner was strictly hereditary, either by tradition or law. See Phyllis Megroz, 'The Executioner', *Living Age,* cccxi (10 December 1921), 674. In France the office of executioner was hereditary for several centuries; the several families in different areas intermarried, thus presumably overcoming any difficulty that a father might experience about the prospect of giving his daughter to a hangman. It began in 1685 when a young aristocrat fell in love with and married the daughter of the executioner. His family renounced him and the king confiscated much of his property and decreed that the young aristocrat become executioner upon the death of his father-in-law. So it was that the name of Sanson gained a prominent and permanent place in French history through its seven generations of executioners. The decline of capital punishment brought financial ruin to the hereditary executioners since the nature of the calling prevented them from working in other areas of society. Hereditary executioners were abolished in France in 1847, when Henry Sanson was relieved from his position by the government. John De Morgan, "Executions and Executioners," p. 134, and Atholl, *Shadow of the Gallows,* p. 136.

[39] Atholl, *Shadow of the Gallows,* p. 165.

tioned in Laurence's *A History of Capital Punishment* only three had fathers who were executioners.[40]

THE EXECUTIONER'S INCOME

There is little information concerning the pay of English executioners in ancient times, and it seems to have been well into the eighteenth century before the calling carried any prescribed fee, and then it was frequently a small one.[41] However, there were certain 'extras' which, while they lasted, contributed significantly to the executioner's income. They were fondly referred to as 'perks' and included gifts (bribes) from the condemned man or his relatives to insure that the hangman would use all his skill to make the end as painless as possible;[42] the sale of the rope used in the hanging;[43] the confiscation of the victim's clothing, jewellery and other personal property, which could be sold to circus sideshows, museums, and collectors of morbid relics;[44] an occasional fee paid to the executioner by the victim's relatives for his permission to remove the body for burial, or a payment to the hangman by surgeons for corpses that were to be dissected by the Company of Barber-Surgeons;[45] and the possibility of a fee by an inn-keeper in return for the hangman's appearance at his tavern after an execution, the anticipation being that the executioner's presence would attract customers.[46]

At the time of Price, about the beginning of the eighteenth century, the hangman's post was worth about £40 a year.[47] Early in the nineteenth cen-

[40] Laurence, *A History of Capital Punishment*, pp. 86–139.

[41] Scott, *The History of Capital Punishment*, pp. 143–44.

[42] Ibid., pp. 144, 174.

[43] As might be expected, there was a good deal of swindling in the sale of the rope. After the execution of Governor Wall the executioner sold the rope at a shilling an inch. Meanwhile, at the north-east corner of Warwick Lane a woman, reported to be the hangman's wife, was selling the 'same' rope to someone who had witnessed the execution that morning. And in Newgate Street a third 'identical' rope was being sold by another merchant at sixpence an inch. The rope itself was supplied by the executioner and used for several hangings until 1890, when a new rope was required for each execution. Laurence, loc. cit., pp. 54–56. The price a rope would bring depended on the notoriety of the malefactor whose throat it had encircled. Probably the highest price ever paid was for the one which ended the life of William Corder, the murderer of Maria Martin in the Red Barn. The spirited bidding after the hanging reached a guinea an inch—a guinea being worth considerably more in those days (Atholl, *Shadow of the Gallows*, pp. 150–51). There were also some interesting superstitions about the supposed healing power of the hangman's rope. See Atholl, pp. 68–71.

[44] Scott, *The History of Capital Punishment*, p. 145. See also Agnes Repplier, 'The Headsman', *Harper's Magazine*, cv (September 1902), 570.

[45] Atholl, *Shadow of the Gallows*, p. 151.

[46] Ibid., p. 150.

[47] Laurence, *A History of Capital Punishment*, p. 99.

tury the hangman's pay at Old Bailey was £1 a week. Calcraft was appointed executioner in 1829 at a salary of one guinea a week, plus a special fee of a guinea for every execution; he also performed executions in other parts of the country for a fee of £10 each case.[48] For several centuries the public executioner of Dumfries had the curious privilege[49] of receiving remuneration for his services largely in kind, and levies were made by the executioner himself. He would walk through the market place, where the farmers and merchants had their wares displayed, and dip a large iron ladle into the sacks, depositing the contents of each dip into his own sack. This levy was strongly resented by the farmers, particularly since it was made weekly and not just on the occasion of an execution. Despite protests the tax persisted until 1796, at which time the hangman was given the sum of £2 yearly as a compensation for its abolition.[50] In 1874 England abolished the payment of a fixed salary, and the officially recognized hangman was obliged to make his own terms with the High Sheriff of the county in which an execution was to occur. Both Marwood and Binns charged £10 for each execution. James Berry, a methodological man, had cards which clearly stated his terms of employment: £10 for an execution plus all travelling expenses; and £5 and travelling expenses in the event of a reprieve. Berry admits to rarely earning less than £270 a year.[51] At a later date, the hangman's pay seems to have fallen in Great Britain: Ellis (1901–24) received only £2 10s. per execution, with another £2 10s. in 'good conduct money' provided that he did not frequent public houses to attract attention and customers.[52] In North America the fee for executions ranged from $50 to $150 in the twentieth century. Canadian executioner Ellis (who took his name from England's John Ellis) received $100 per execution in 1950;[53] while electrocutioner Hulbert originally earned $50 per job and received an increase to $150 from New York State in 1919.[54]

In England today, according to evidence given before the Royal Com-

---

[48] Scott, *The History of Capital Punishment,* pp. 144–45.

[49] Another 'privilege' the executioner had was that of saving any woman about to be executed if he was able and willing to marry her. It also seems that any member of the crowd witnessing an execution could save the victim by marrying him or her. The story is told of a young girl who offered her hand to a thief who was about to be hanged; he looked at her for some moments and then silently adjusted the rope. 'Hangmen's Diaries: The Gallows at Close Range', pp. 469–70. See also Repplier, "The Headsman."

[50] Laurence, *A History of Capital Punishment,* pp. 89–90.

[51] Scott, *The History of Capital Punishment.*

[52] Atholl, *Shadow of the Gallows,* p. 154.

[53] 'A Night's Work for Mr. Ellis', *Time,* lv (6 March 1950), 38.

[54] *New York Times,* 23 Feb. 1929, p. 15.

mission on Capital Punishment, the average fee paid the hangman is £10, although the Sheriff is authorized to fix the amount; on occasion, therefore, the fee may reach as high as 15 guineas.[55] Even the maximum fee, however, is not overly generous, in view of the lowered purchasing power of the pound today and the reduction in the number of hangees. Hangmen also are no longer entitled to perquisites; the clothes of the condemned man and the rope[56] used to hang him are burned immediately after the execution and the body is buried in the prison graveyard.[57] On the basis of financial reward of English hangmen from the earliest days to the present, there would seem to be little reason for accepting this position. The financial success of Berry[58] and Marwood are clearly exceptional; today the hangman's office is a distinctly part-time one. The same is true of America where capital punishment has been abolished in many states and has fallen into practical disuse in others. Yet, despite the unpopularity of the position and its modest salary there seems to have been no shortage of men to fill the office within the last century. When Berry applied for the job in 1883 he was one of 1,400 rival candidates. In 1949 Major Benke testified that five written applications were received every week.[59] And when H. A. Pierrepoint retired the Home Office received applications from people from all walks of life—clergymen, lawyers, undertakers and doctors, among others.[60] In America, when John Hulbert let it be known that he was going to resign, 800 men were eager to take his place.[61]

---

[55] When Albert Pierrepoint carried out seventeen hangings in one day, the government declined to pay him 'the usual fifteen guineas per drop' but instead 'they offered him a lump sum for the seventeen necks to be broken.' Although the exact sum was not disclosed, Mr. Duff informs us that Albert considered it to be a 'tidy enough sum'. Scott, *The History of Capital Punishment*, pp. 145–46.

[56] The exploitation of ropes was ended as a result of one of Berry's own sales. The purchaser on the train took it out of its case and explained to the passengers that he had bought it from the hangman that very morning. The attitude of the passengers was most unsympathetic and one wrote to the Home Office protesting strongly. The result was a regulation in 1886 that the rope used for hanging would be supplied by the authorities and remain their property. Justin Atholl, *The Reluctant Hangman*, London: John Long Limited, 1956, p. 54.

[57] Scott, *The History of Capital Punishment*, pp. 145, 211.

[58] Berry, in fact, was virtually the last of the true hangmen, in the sense that he depended upon hanging as his one and only source of income. Atholl, *The Reluctant Hangman*, p. 58.

[59] Scott, *The History of Capital Punishment*, p. 141.

[60] Laurence, *A History of Capital Punishment*, p. 139.

[61] Leo W. Sheridan, *I Killed for the Law*, New York: Stackpole Sons, 1938, pp. 22–23. However, when Hulbert formally resigned there were 'only' 100 letters of application to Warden Lawes. Robert G. Elliott and Albert R. Beatty, *Agent of Death*, New York: E. P. Dutton & Co., 1940, p. 97.

MULTIPLE FUNCTIONS OF
'THE EXECUTIONER'

Up to this point no explicit definition of 'the executioner' has been given, and undoubtedly no confusion has resulted from the lack of one. Nonetheless, an analysis of the expression 'the executioner' is in order for it is deceptively simple. There are two distinct areas of explanation involved, one focusing upon *the* executioner, the other upon the *executioner*.

In referring to 'the' or 'common' hangman, the connotation is that of a single executioner, a particular individual that performs all the executions. However, such a person is unknown in either English or American history. Instead, there have always been several people performing the role of 'the' executioner at the same time in different places and in the same place at different times. Consequently the 'hangman of England' does not exist. Moreover, until the introduction of railways, various counties in England had their own executioners, since executions were too prevalent and transportation too slow to make it practical for one man to serve the entire country. To be sure, it was the hangmen of London who received the publicity, but throughout the land there were scores of hangmen 'hanging around,' drawing their pay-cheques and pursuing their profession as best they could. With improved transportation and the decrease in the number of capital offences and sentences, the smaller towns found it more economical to employ one of the executioners by the City of London and pay him on a piece-work basis rather than maintain a permanent hangman of their own.[62] Calcraft was the first executioner to have, geographically speaking, a rather extensive business. But he was only 'the' executioner in the sense that he was the most frequently employed; that there was no obligation on the part of the sheriff to employ Calcraft exclusively was demonstrated in 1856 when the local authorities at Salford used someone else to hang Dr. Palmer.[63] Pushed to its semantic limits, this situation could lead to a hangman (or electrocutioner in the United States) 'resigning' or being 'dismissed' from a position which he does not officially hold since technically he is not employed by the Home Office or state or municipal government, but is hired piecemeal as the need for his services arises.

The other problem concerns the meaning of the term 'executioner' and requires an explanation of who he is and what he does. Legally, the executioner is 'the official who carries into effect a sentence of death or inflicts capital punishment in pursuance of a legal warrant'.[64] However we have

---

[62] The City of Inverness, as hanging went out of fashion, discovered that they were paying their hangman £400 for each execution he performed: Atholl, *The Reluctant Hangman*, p. 32.

[63] Ibid.

[64] *Encyclopedia Americana*, 1962 ed., vol. x, p. 622.

indicated above that the person who actually performs the execution is not an 'official.' In the United States, although the official, i.e. legally pre-scribed, executioner varies among the states, it is always the sheriff of the county of trial, or the superintendent or deputy superintendent of the state prison.[65] In England the official is the Sheriff or Under-Sheriff.[66] What in-variably has happened, though, is that the legal executioner has preferred to execute the sentence rather than the man and accordingly has hired a real, honest-to-goodness hangman or electrocutioner to do the job. If for any reason the Sheriff, Under-Sheriff, warden, or deputy warden cannot secure someone to perform the work, he must assume the responsibility himself.

Upon reflection one realizes that the death penalty may take many forms and that the execution of a court judgment against a criminal is not neces-sarily the execution of the criminal himself. So it is that we find English 'hangmen' not only hanging their victims but beheading, burning, drawing and quartering, drowning, gibbeting them and killing them in every way imaginable and in some ways unimaginable but nonetheless real. English executioners were hangmen only in the sense that, with the abandonment of the more brutal techniques,[67] hanging was and continued to be Eng-land's favourite technique of capital punishment. In addition to inflicting the death penalty, hangmen were also charged with administering corporal punishment[68] and burning books.[69] There were even occasions when the hangman was expected to perform multiple operations on the same person, as witnessed by the following account: 'When Japhet Crook, alias Peter Stranger, was convicted of having forged deeds . . . he was condemned to stand in the pillory for one hour, to have both his ears cut off close to his head, to have both his nostrils slit and seared with a hot iron, to forfeit the issues of all his lands and tenements, and to be imprisoned for life. And it was (executioner) John Hooper's job . . . to see that the sentence was car-ried out.'[70] But John Hooper's responsibilities to law and order were in-significant compared to the duties of the French executioner in dealing

---

[65] The Sheriff of the county in which the trial occurs is held to be the proper officer if the matter is not otherwise regulated by statute. *Corpus Juris Secundum,* Brooklyn: American Law Book Co., 1962, section 2003.

[66] *Royal Commission of Capital Punishment, 1949–1953,* London: Her Majesty's Stationery Office, 1953, section 751, p. 261.

[67] By the first half of the nineteenth century hanging was the undisputed meth-od of legalized homicide, all other methods having been abolished. One exception was Scotland where, by an oversight, drawing and quartering was still in effect. Atholl, *The Reluctant Hangman,* p. 30.

[68] Andrews, *Old-Time Punishments,* pp. 156, 159, and Bleackley, *The Hangmen of England,* p. 97.

[69] Andrews, p. 101, and Bleackley, p. 95.

[70] Bleackley, pp. 60–61.

with traitors. As a punishment for inflicting a slight knife wound on Louis
XV, the executioner burned Robert Damiens' hand, proceeded to tear out
pieces of flesh from the prisoner's body onto which boiling oil and hot
pitch was poured, and finally harnessed four horses to his limbs in a beneficent gesture to end his suffering by quartering him.[71]

THREE FAMOUS EXECUTIONERS

An executioner may achieve fame—or infamy—for a number of reasons:
the status of his victims, his own personal characteristics, the distinction of
having killed the largest number of men or of having held the post for the
longest period of time, the uniqueness of certain of his experiences as an
executioner, etc. Aside from space limitations, the reasons for emphasizing
the three cases below will become apparent in the accounts themselves.

The most famous of all English executioners was Jack Ketch, whose
name remained the synonym for the hangman for two centuries.[72] According to Lloyd, the Manor of Tyburn, where executions traditionally took
place, was formerly held by Richard Jacquet, of which Jack Ketch is a cor-
ruption. Not much is known about Jack Ketch, and it is strange why, of all
hangmen he was selected by the public as the prototype, unless it was because his incompetence earned him the hatred of the masses. We can infer
that he was a self-important man, for he called himself 'Esquire' at a time
when that title meant something, but references to him were invariably
unfavourable. Ketch published an article defending himself against criticism which he received for bungling[73] the execution of Lord Russell in
1683, claiming that his lordship 'did not dispose himself for receiving the
fatal stroke in such a position as was suitable' and that his lordship moved
about too much. However, Ketch also bungled the execution of the Duke

---

[71] De Morgan, "Executions and Executioners," pp. 127–28.

[72] Along the same lines, 'William Boilman' was also used as a nickname for the
executioner. According to Macaulay, the name was derived from the practice of
publicly boiling the entrails of traitors after they had been disembowelled alive.
Arthur Koestler, *Reflections on Hanging*, New York: Macmillan Co., 1957, p. 3.

[73] There is a fascinating, if somewhat gruesome, literature on bungled executions. For bungled jobs see: Scott, *The History of Capital Punishment*, pp. 52 ff.,
175, 178, 191–92, 195–96, 211–12, 213 ff.; Raymond S. Thompkins, 'Notes on Hanging',
American Mercury, xxv (March, 1932), 286–87; Barnes and Teeters, *New Horizons
in Criminology*, pp. 418–19; Calvert, *Capital Punishment in the Twentieth Century*,
pp. 95–96; Palm, *The Death Penalty*, pp. 103–6; Atholl, *Shadow of the Gallows*, pp.
77–78, 119, 187–88, 191, 195; Laurence, *A History of Capital Punishment*, pp. 56–57,
65; Bleackley, *The Hangmen of England*, pp. 73, 75, 83–84, 141; Duff, *A New Handbook
on Hanging*, pp. 39–41, 104, 113–14, 119; Atholl, *The Reluctant Hangman*, pp. 128–37,
168; De Morgan, "Executions and Executioners," p. 129; Elliott and Beatty, *Agent of
Death*, pp. 29–30, 56–57.

of Monmouth two years later. At the place of execution Ketch became un-
nerved and cried 'I can't do it.' It was only at the Sheriff's insistence that
Ketch forced himself to continue, taking five strokes to behead the Duke.
After twenty-three years as an executioner Ketch was turned out of office
for impertinence towards the Sheriff and died toward the close of 1683.[74]

William Marwood's place in the annals of British executioners was
earned on two interrelated counts, his contribution to hanging[75] technique
and his character. The evolution of hanging, which began with the use of
trees as gallows,[76] reached the stage in which a short 'drop' from a scaffold
left the victim suspended in air. This free fall of a few feet shortened the
victim's struggle and was more humane than any previous device. However, the short drop was still insufficient to produce immediate death by
dislocation of the vertebrae. It was in connection with a solution to this
problem that William Marwood found himself a permanent place in the
hearts of all Englishmen. Although the inventor of the 'long' drop is unknown,[77] it was Marwood who first put its principles into practice. He used
the long drop systematically and deliberately, with the object of producing
painless and instantaneous death. Hanging had at last become revolution-

---

[74] Atholl, *Shadow of the Gallows*, pp. 144–45.

[75] Though the origin of hanging is obscure, it may be presumed that it was
invented for its deterrent effect rather than as a more efficient way of administering
the death penalty. Hanging displayed the victim to the onlookers in the most
humiliating and degrading of positions, and was therefore considered a dishonoring type of execution. *Royal Commission on Capital Punishment*, section 246, p. 701.

[76] This was accomplished by making a slip-knot at one end of the rope, tossing
the other end over a heavy branch and hauling up; this method continued to be
used for many centuries. The first advance in technique was the use of a ladder to
transport the victim to the branch of the tree. The free end of the rope was then
secured and the prisoner was thrust from his foothold on the rung of the ladder
by the hangman, or left to remain on the ladder until the hangman reached the
ground and then withdrew the ladder. With small variation, this technique of
hanging persisted until the the eighteenth century. It was customary to leave the
body hanging for an hour to insure death. Under these conditions death resulted
from strangulation, loss of blood supply to the brain, or shock. The next significant change after the introduction of the ladder was the use of the cart. The cart
was simply driven under the gallows, the rope adjusted, and the horse whipped,
leaving the victim suspended by the neck. Although considered humanitarian at
the time, it was actually less so than the ladder technique, for greater time elapsed
before death. But the cart did provide an advantage for th hangman and crowd in
that it avoided the problems involved in getting an uncooperative or physically
and mentally broken prisoner up the ladder. The next technical improvement was
the use of the 'drop'. The prisoner stood on a collapsible platform, the rope was
adjusted, and the platform was depressed when all was ready, leaving the victim
suspended. Atholl, *Shadow of the Gallows*, pp. 98–102.

[77] It has been suggested that although the invention of the long drop may have
been made on a purely theoretical basis by Irish surgeons, it was more likely the
result of observing the effect of unintentionally long drops. Moreover, the introduction of the long drop was seriously delayed by the conservatism and clumsi-
ness of Calcraft, who reigned as executioner from 1829–74. Ibid., pp. 111–12.

ized to the point where it was no longer hanging, for death was now instantly caused by rupture of the spinal cord instead of by strangulation. Marwood was a transition figure among English hangmen in other ways too: he was the first whose work had never been witnessed by the public[78] and also the first to give the explanation of 'service to society' as his reason for becoming a hangman. There could be little doubt of his sincerity, for he conducted himself both publicly and privately unlike any executioner before him. Taking great pride in his work, he never referred to himself as a 'hangman' but rather as an 'executioner'; attesting to this was his business card, which read: William Marwood, Public Executioner. Noted for his sense of humour, he was also convinced that his work was religiously inspired. A true credit to the English community of hangmen, he died in Horncastle in 1883, after serving for nine years as executioner.[79]

If Marwood represented a transition figure between the 'old-guard' hangmen and the new, James Berry was the first full-fledged member of the latter group. He was both literate and communicative, and though his position as executioner was relatively short (1884–92), it was highly eventful. Moreover, it was during Berry's period that the new technique of the long drop was officially noticed and examined scientifically. Berry had no small part in this undertaking.

As a shoe salesman[80] James Berry was unable to support his wife and three children. His personal acquaintance with Marwood undoubtedly impressed him with the financial possibilities of the position of hangman. Although Berry had no taste for the work, he did not consider it degrading and felt that he could 'somewhat improve the lot of those appointed to die'; weighing his family's needs against his personal inclinations, he decided in favour of the former.[81] As executioner he conducted himself with dignity and attempted to make the position one of respectability, including in his book a chapter on 'Hanging: From A Business Point Of View.' Whereas professionally Marwood was a link with the days of public strangulation, Berry never hanged anyone by strangulation except accidentally. Like Marwood, Berry led an exemplary personal life.

[78] Atholl, *The Reluctant Hangman*, p. 80.

[79] Account based on Bleackley, *The Hangmen of England*, pp. 231–46, and Laurence, *A History of Capital Punishment*, pp. 114–20 and Major Arthur Griffiths, *Fifty Years of Public Service*, London: Cassell & Co., Ltd., 1904, pp. 340–43. There is some disagreement over how Marwood was accepted by the people. See Laurence, p. 115, and Bleackley, p. 233.

[80] Prior to this, in 1874, he was a member of the Bradford Police Force.

[81] James Berry, *My Experiences as an Executioner*, London: Percy Lund and Co., no date, pp. 16–19. When Berry first applied to the Sheriffs of London and Middlesex, in September of 1883, he was turned down. He applied again in March 1884, writing the magistrates of the City of Edinburgh a humble but convincing letter which won him the position.

Berry's contributions to the art of hanging are manifold. Marwood may have 'invented' the long drop, but it remained for Berry to give the technique some degree of reliability and precision by varying the length of it in accordance with the physical characteristics of the criminal.[82] The ideal which Berry strove for in his work was dislocation without mutilation. More than anyone else, Berry recognized the importance of the rope in the drop. Realizing that the stretch of a rope under great force can be considerable and distort the estimation of the calculated drop, he made it a practice to stretch his ropes before using them on a victim. Berry was equally sensitive to the psychological discomforts of the doomed man; he noted that few men were able to mount the steps of the scaffold without difficulty and suggested to the authorities that the steps should be replaced with a gently sloping gangway. This suggestion was acted upon in the execution of William Chadwick in 1890.[83]

Three factors had completely revolutionized the type of person required as a hangman by the time that Berry was a member of the team: the abolition of capital punishment for all but a few crimes, the development of the long drop by Marwood, and, perhaps most important, the abolition of public executions in 1868.[84] This last-mentioned[85] is emphasized because

[82] Nonetheless, nearly eighty years of experimentation have not reduced the problem of the length of the drop to exact mathematical solution. Many other factors based upon experience and not the laws of numbers must apparently be taken into account. Atholl, *Shadow of the Gallows*, p. 119.

[83] Atholl, *The Reluctant Hangman*, pp. 108–11.

[84] Ibid., p. 103.

[85] Strictly speaking, the Capital Punishment Amendment Act of 1868 did not make hanging entirely private. The Act ordered that hanging would occur inside of the prison instead of outside of it. But it was still possible to view the execution if one were willing to pay the price of a good window overlooking the scaffold. Moreover, in addition to those entitled and required to witness the proceedings, the Sheriff or Governor of the Prison could admit 'such persons as they thought fit'. One class of spectators generally admitted in the early days of private executions were newspaper reporters. However, after the Aberdare Committee report in 1888, the Home Office resolved to exclude reporters from executions, and this decision has been strictly enforced to this day. Atholl, *Shadow of the Gallows*, pp. 86–89. The exclusion of these representatives of the people and the consequent aura of secrecy engendered by such government action have been bitterly resented by more than a few persons writing on the subject. The 'secret' aspect of modern-day English execution is further accentuated by the Official Secrets Act which prohibits those concerned with the execution from providing any information to outsiders. In addition, a confidential Home Office Instruction to Prison Governors concerning their behavior at hangings orders them to be as brief as possible in any references to the way in which they were performed and even suggests certain standard responses, e.g., 'It was carried out expeditiously and without a hitch.' If the Governor is pressed for details concerning time, he is directed to say that 'a very short time elapsed' or some general expression to the same effect. Scott, *The History of Capital Punishment*, p. 214, and *Executions* (a pamphlet for private circulation only, issued by the National Council for the Abolition of the Death Penalty), pp. 1–2.

while the death penalty continued to be conducted as a spectacle it was impossible for the executioner to be respected or respect himself, or experiment with ways to alleviate the suffering of his victims. It was more than coincidental that the 'breakthrough' in hanging occurred after public executions were prohibited. All three factors, of course, interacted with one another, for once the long drop was perfected it was no longer necessary for the authorities to be content to locate a man sufficiently strong and brutal to strangle his victim to death in front of a potentially dangerous crowd. They now sought men of good character, capable of employing the rope with efficiency and humanity. The reduction in capital charges meant that it was increasingly difficult—indeed, impossible after Berry—to earn a living exclusively from killing; in turn, the changed public attitude towards the hangman in the twentieth century made it possible for him also to obtain normal employment in society. The position of the hangman, in fact, has become so attractive that there seems to be an unlimited supply of people ready to undertake it for a reward which scarcely compensates them for their time and effort.

To return to Berry, despite his contributions to the profession, he was not temperamentally suited for it. A sensitive[86] man, Berry found it increasingly difficult to 'hang on.' A series of mishaps[87] had shaken him badly and the last execution at which he officiated proved too much for him. The condemned man had attempted suicide by cutting his throat, and there ensued a horrible scene when he was hanged, all the large blood-vessels of his neck being lacerated. This execution sickened Berry to the point of resignation. At the same time, Berry's decision to resign was strongly influenced by the possibility of earning a living by other means. An American had approached Berry and suggested that he could make a small fortune by coming to the United States to lecture against capital punishment. Accordingly, he announced to his public that he had given up the gallows and would henceforth devote himself to combating capital punishment, which he had always opposed 'in principle'—this from a man who hanged 135 people.[88] But Berry was not destined for American audiences while there were still English audiences to be conquered. The lecture tour in America was superseded by his entrance upon the British world of entertainment, his debut being made at the Westminster Aquarium. Pathetically, his lec-

---

[86] Berry started legal action against newspapers which had republished an article about him that suggested that he was in the habit of dressing in woman's clothes to avoid recognition on his way to an execution. Atholl, *The Reluctant Hangman*, p. 98.

[87] Ibid., pp. 124–39, 168–70.

[88] American electrocutioner Robert Elliott, after having thrown the switch on 387 electric chair occupants, reveals himself as an opponent of the death penalty in the last chapter of his book, *Agent of Death*.

ture-series against the death penalty turned into a farce, and he became an actor upon a stage, catering to the sensation-seeking public. As the 'lecture' engagements became less frequent Berry turned to various occupations, none very lucrative. Then an episode occurred in his life which resulted in his religious conversion and his decision to carry on the work of God by converting others. He proceeded to tour at a series of revivalist meetings all over the country and continued his evangelistic work until his death in October 1913.[89]

SOCIETY AND THE EXECUTIONER

The status of the executioner in England, as well as in America, has changed considerably over the years. Whereas at one time the community would not condescend to offer a thirsty executioner water, today it is the executioner who supplies an admiring and friendly public with drink.[90] Nevertheless, a subtle but real conflict exists between society and the executioner. Somehow society can not understand how an honourable citizen would deliberately kill for hire. And if financial compensation were not the major motivating factor, the individual accepting this task would appear all the more despicable. Given some of the outward signs of respectability, society may be able to tolerate the executioner, but this should not be taken for acceptance and true respect for his work. The people know, however, that the government now maintains certain standards concerning the selection of executioners and that therefore the man hired cannot be without merit as an individual. Yet, society's revulsion and guilt at the thought of plunging a helpless creature into eternity persists. Unable to displace their guilt and loathing upon the executioner, as they have in the past when his class and conduct invited social condemnation, there is an artificial attempt to justify the executioner's work and integrity by suggesting that someone must do the job and that the executioner is merely the final link in the chain of justice—as though his relation to the unpleasant business of legalized homicide was neither greater nor lesser than anyone else's. The executioner, we are told, does not really kill the victim; he is simply acting in the name and place of society. Consequently, if there is any personal degradation attached to the infliction of capital punishment, society must stand ready to assume responsibility for it. The executioner therefore is exonerated of the charges of insensitivity, inhumanity, and sad-

---

[89] Atholl, *The Reluctant Hangman,* pp. 167–84.

[90] Top hangman Albert Pierrepoint was mine host of Help the Poor Struggler, a public house at Oldham, Lancashire. Scott, *The History of Capital Punishment,* p. 146.

ism and becomes a man like all men, performing a job as we all do, motivated by the universal incentives of financial reward, social obligation, and
satisfaction from the efficient performance of one's occupation. Unfortunately, this reasoning is totally specious. Deny it as it will, society instinctly
recognizes the executioner as a man apart and places his contribution to
capital punishment in its proper perspective. In all forms of interaction
among persons there is a direct relationship between active physical proximity to a phenomenon and individual responsibility for its occurrence.
From the police who apprehend the criminal to the lawyer who prosecutes
him, from the jury who finds him guilty to the judge who sentences him,
an increasing burden of personal responsibility for the destiny of the criminal is assumed. In this respect, no one stands closer to the execution of an
offender than the executioner. Obviously the criminal is not killed *because*
of the executioner, but he certainly is killed *by* the executioner; and all the
words in the world can not distribute his participation in the event to his
fellow men.

SELECTED BIBLIOGRAPHY

BOOKS

ANDREWS, WILLIAM. *Old-Time Punishments*. London: William Andrews & Co.,
1890.

ATHOLL, JUSTIN. *The Reluctant Hangman*. John Long Limited, 1956.

ATHOLL, JUSTIN. *Shadow of the Gallows*. London: John Long Limited, 1954.

BARNES, HARRY ELMER, and TEETERS, NEGLEY K. *New Horizons in Criminology*.
New York: Prentice-Hall, Inc., 1943.

BARNES, HARRY ELMER. *The Story of Punishment*. Boston: Stratford Co., 1930.

BENTLEY, WILLIAM G. *My Son's Execution*. London: W. H. Allen, 1957.

BERRY, JAMES. *My Experiences As An Executioner*. London: Percy Lund & Co., no
date.

BLEACKLEY, HORACE. *The Hangmen of England*. London: Chapman and Hall,
1929.

BLEACKLEY, HORACE. *Some Distinguished Victims of the Scaffold*. London: Trubner and Co., Ltd., 1905.

BRUCE, PHILIP ALEXANDER. *Institutional History of Virginia*. London: G. P. Putnam's Sons, 1910.

CALVERT, E. ROY. *Capital Punishment in the Twentieth Century*. London: G. P.
Putnam's Sons, 1928.

CANTOR, NATHANIEL F. *Crime and Society: An Introduction to Criminology*. New
York: Henry Holt and Co., 1939.

DUFF, CHARLES. *A New Handbook on Hanging*. Stratford Place, London: Andrew
Melrose, 1954.

EARLE, ALICE MORSE. *Curious Punishments of Bygone Days.* New York: Book League of America, 1929.

ELLIOTT, ROBERT G., and BEATTY, ALBERT R. *Agent of Death: The Memoirs of an Executioner.* New York: E. P. Dutton & Co., Inc., 1940.

GRIFFITHS, ARTHUR. *Fifty Years of Public Service.* London: Cassell and Co., Ltd., 1904.

JOYCE, JAMES AVERY. *Capital Punishment: A World View.* New York: Thomas Nelson & Sons, 1961.

KOESTLER, ARTHUR. *Reflections on Hanging.* New York: Macmillan Co., 1957.

LAURENCE, JOHN. *A History of Capital Punishment.* New York: Citadel Press, 1960.

MENCKEN, AUGUST. *By The Neck: A Book of Hangings.* New York: Hasting House, 1942.

PALM, ANDREW J. *The Death Penalty.* New York: G. P. Putnam's Sons, 1891.

Royal Commission on Capital Punishment Report, 1949–53. Presented to Parliament by Command of Her Majesty, September 1953. London: Her Majesty's Stationery Office, 1953.

SCOTT, GEORGE RYLEY. *The History of Capital Punishment.* London: Torchstream Books, 1950.

SEMMES, RAPHAEL. *Crime and Punishment in Early Maryland.* Baltimore: Johns Hopkins Press, 1938.

SHERIDAN, LEO W. *I Killed for the Law.* New York City: Stackpole Sons, 1938.

PERIODICALS AND OTHER SOURCES

'A Neglected Art', *Nation.* cxxix (16 October 1929), 402.

'A Night's Work for Mr. Ellis', *Time,* lv (6 March 1950), 38.

BROWNE, WALDO R. 'A Word with Robert Elliott', *World Tomorrow,* xii (May 1929), 230–31.

'Capital Punishment—Execution by Electricity—The Kemmler Case', *Public Opinion,* ix (16 August 1890), 432–35.

Corpus Juris Secundum. Brooklyn: American Law Book Co., 1962.

DE MORGAN, JOHN. 'Executions and Executioners', *Green Bag,* xii (1900), 125–35.

Encyclopedia Americana. New York: American Corporation, 1962.

'Executions by Electricity', *Spectator,* lxi (21 April 1888), 540–41.

Executions. (For private circulation only: published by the National Council For The Abolition Of The Death Penalty, 23 Charing Cross, London, S.W. 1.)

FARGA, F. 'Lord of the Guillotine', *Living Age,* cccxxxiv (15 March 1928), 532–35.

GOINS, CRADDOCK. 'The Traveling Executioner', *American Mercury,* liv (January 1942), 93–97.

'Hangmen's Diaries: The Gallows at Close Range', *Living Age,* cccxx (28 August 1926), 467–71.

'Hangman's Turn', *Newsweek,* xlvi (25 July 1955), 40–42.

'In the Good Old Days', *Catholic World,* cxxix (May 1929), 217–19.

LEWIS, PETER. '*An E*xecution', *New Statesman,* lxi (21 April 1961), 620–22.

MARTIN, H. H. 'Hanging Is His Trade', *Saturday Evening Post,* ccxx (5 June 1948), 12.

MARTIN, R. E. 'Electric Shocks: Do They Really Kill?', *Popular Science Monthly,* cxxxiii (July 1938), 44–45.

MEGROZ, PHYLLIS. 'The Executioner', *Living Age,* cccxi (10 December 1921), 674–76.

NELSON, FREDERIC. 'The Executioner-Impresario', *New Republic,* lv (4 July 1928), 171–72.

REPPLIER, AGNES. 'The Headsman', *Harper's Magazine,* cv (September 1902), 569–72.

REYNOLDS, REGINOLD. 'A School for Criminals', *New Statesman and Nation,* xlviii (7 August 1954), 152–53.

REYNOLDS, REGINOLD. 'The Pierrepoint Papers', *New Statesman and Nation,* li (21 April 1956), 409–10.

RONNENBERG, H. A. 'America's Greatest Mass Execution', *American Mercury,* lxvii (November 1948), 565–67.

SHANE, S. M. 'Window on a Gas Chamber', *Nation,* cxciv (24 February 1962), 170–71.

'The Executioner's Bill', *Literary Digest,* cxxiv (13 November 1937), 30.

TOMPKINS, RAYMOND S. 'Notes on Hanging', *American Mercury,* xxv (March 1932), 280–88.

'Twenty-Two States Use Electric Chair As Means of Death Penalty', *Newsweek,* xvi (19 August 1940), 46.

6
social
institutions

LOUIS A. ZURCHER, JR., and ARNOLD MEADOW

On Bullfights and Baseball: An Example of Interaction of Social Institutions[1]

Los toros dan y los toros quitan.—Mexican proverb
The typical American male strikes out the Yankee side before going to sleep at night.—James Thurber

A "social institution," typically considered, is "a comparatively stable, permanent, and intricately organized system of behavior formally enforced within a given society and serving social objectives regarded as essential for the survival of the group."[2] Four major social institutions are found very widely in human society: 1) economic, 2) familial, 3) political, and 4) religious. Through these the society strives to achieve material well-being, an adequate population, organization, and some feeling of control over the unknown or unexpected. As a society becomes more urbanized, more "highly developed," it may evolve additional institutions, such as the recreational, the educational, and the aesthetic, which take over functions no longer adequately performed by the basic four.

Since individuals have overlapping roles in a number of the society's institutions, and since each institution is a functional segment of the total, ongoing society, the interaction of institutions presents itself as a fruitful area for study. This interaction is a key variable in the process of social change and highlights cultural themes running through the structures of a society.

The central institution of a society and its primary agent of socialization is the family—which interacts in various degrees with other institutions. Whiting and Child, for example, have described the impact of values

Reprinted from the *International Journal of Comparative Sociology*, 8, 1 (1967), 99–117, E. J. Brill, Leiden, Holland, by permission of the publisher.

[1] This research was supported by Public Health Service Mental Health Project Grant 5-R11-Mh-544-2, Arnold Meadow, Director.

[2] G. A. Lundberg, L. C. Schrag, and O. N. Larsen, *Sociology*, New York: Harper and Bros., 1958, 757.

learned in the family upon behavior in other social institutions.[3] Kardiner has written of the ways in which the religious institution is shaped by family patterns.[4] Tumin has described the interaction between the family and the economic institution.[5]

In this paper the authors will focus their attention on some aspects of the interaction between two social institutions: 1) the family and 2) the institutionalized recreation form known as the "national sport." It is hypothesized that the national sport symbolizes in its structure and function the processes in the modal family that both engender and restrict hostility toward authority, and that it also exemplifies a socially legitimized means for the expression of that hostility.

As Dollard has described it, the socialization process itself engenders hostility toward authority. The demands of socialization, which of course have their focal point in the family, conflict in many instances with the child's own behavioral choices. The child is thus frustrated and desires to move against the restrictive figure but does not do so because he fears punishment. This fear acts as a catalyst, inciting further aggressive feelings toward the frustrating agent. Repression of this aggression is not complete and the individual seeks sources for its legitimized expression.[6]

Hostility toward authority is especially generated in the authoritarian family milieu, or when some characteristics of the parents create for the child an uncertainty of or rejection of his or the parent's familial role. Situations such as this not only arouse keen hostility but are also usually unyieldingly restrictive and harshly punitive of any demonstration of that hostility.

From another view, it is quite possible that hostility toward authority is a lesson *of,* as well as a reaction *to,* socialization. That is, the characteristics of the society may be such that a general distrust for or hatred of authority has become part of the cultural value system. This is particularly the case in those societies which have undergone long periods of manipulation and oppression under a tyrannical or exploitative power structure.

Since every society depends, from the family up, on authority to maintain relative consistency of behavior, and since not all the members of the society will take well to that restrictive authority, it follows that the society must provide as a further means of control some outlet for the resultant hostility toward authority—not only that incited in the family situation or

[3] J. W. Whiting and I. L. Child, *Child Training and Personality: A Cross Cultural Study,* New Haven: Yale University Press, 1953.

[4] A. Kardiner, *The Individual and His Society,* New York: Columbia University Press, 1939.

[5] M. M. Tumin, "Some Disfunctions of Institutional Imbalances," *Behavioral Science,* July, 1956, 218–23.

[6] J. Dollard, "Hostility and Fear in Social Life," *Social Forces,* 42, 1938, 15–25.

learned in socialization, but also the generalized forms of hostility that are re-awakened and intensified by the demands of interpersonal relations. The provisions for such expression, as well as the degree to which it is controlled, vary from society to society. As Dollard points out, "Each society standardizes its own permissive patterns, and differs from the next in the degree to which hostility may be expressed."[7]

In the terminology of modern dynamic psychiatry, it can be said that the defense processes which societies employ to channel hostility differ from culture to culture. These defense processes will be differentially manifested not only in the families of different societies, but also, as we hypothesize, in their "national sports," since both are institutions of these societies.

PLAY, THE GAME, THE SPORT

Play has been considered by a number of social scientists to be of major importance in the socialization and personality formation of the individual. Other writers have seen the various forms of play as reflecting the particular traits, values, expectations, and the degree of social control in a given culture. In addition to the foregoing functions, play is a "permissive pattern," a "channel" serving as a legitimized means for the symbolic demonstration of hostility toward authority figures.

There is a hierarchy of play extending from seemingly purposeless, repetitive movements in the crib, through games (with competition, an "ethic" of some sort, elaborate rules and regulations, mutual player expectations, and an ostensible purpose), up to the highest level of complexity, the "organized sport" (with schedules, painstaking record keeping, large audiences, governing bodies supplying officials and dispensing rules, "seasons," recruiting, training, and if professional, the paying of participants). The "national sport" is an organized sport that has been adopted by a nation as its own special "home-owned" variety. When, for example, the "American Way" is alluded to, it implies, among other things, apple pie, hot-dogs, mother, Disneyland, and *baseball.*

It is hypothesized, then, that the national sport, as the epitome of institutionalized recreation, maximally reflects that aspect of the "social character" of a society which establishes the degree of tolerance for the expression of hostility toward authority. Furthermore, it is hypothesized that the national sport replicates, on the playing field or in the arena, the family processes which engender, exacerbate, or restrict that hostility, and will manifest the "societal ideal" for its expression.

Baseball is the national sport of the United States of America. Its coun-

---

[7] Dollard, "Hostility and Fear in Social Life," 16.

terpart in the United States of Mexico is the *corrida de toros,* the bullfight.[8] An analysis of baseball and the bullfight, and of the modal family patterns in their respective societies, should reveal, especially with regard to the dynamic of hostility toward authority, a facet of the interaction between the social institutions of family and recreation. In addition to the formation and legitimized expression of hostility, the analysis should reveal, as they appear in both the family and the sport, some of the characteristic defense mechanisms, values, and social relationships shared by members in each of the two societies.

ANALYSIS OF FAMILY PATTERNS

The Mexican family typically is described as a proving ground for the dominance needs of the father. Though the family structure is essentially mother centered, the father compulsively strives to maintain his *macho* (manly) role and to prove that he has *huevos largos* (large "eggs"), *muy cojones* (abundant testicles) or "hair on his chest" by playing the role of the emotionally detached but severely authoritarian head of the household. He overtly disparages the achievements of, violently disapproves of any show of independence in, and physically punishes any demonstration of hostility by his wife or children. Often, the children are punished by their father for sins (especially sexual) projected upon them from his own guilt-ridden repertoire. Drunkenness, promiscuity, and abandonment, as components of *machismo,* further compound the overpowering image of father. This pattern of behavior has been detailed in the literature by Lewis, Gillin, Meadow et al., and Diaz-Guerrero.[9]

The question then arises, how do the children, especially the males, handle the hostility that they cannot direct against the mitigated feudalism of such an unyielding socialization figure as the Mexican father? It appears that the son attempts to recoup his identity by emulating the father's exam-

---

[8] It should be mentioned here that the *aficionado* (dedicated fan) would object to the association of the bullfight with the term "sport", and there are good arguments in support of his opinion. For the sake of parsimony, however, and since the bullfight approaches the criteria established in this paper, it will be considered, for analysis, the equivalent of a national sport.

[9] Oscar Lewis, *Children of Sanchez,* New York: Random House, 1961; John P. Gillin, "Ethos and Cultural Aspects of Personality," in Yehudi Cohen (Ed.), *Social Structure and Personality,* New York: Holt, Rinehart, & Winston, 1961; Arnold Meadow, Louis Zurcher, and David Stoder, "Sex Role and Schizophrenia in Mexican Culture," *International Journal of Social Psychiatry,* In Press; Rogelio Diaz-Guerrero, *Estidios de Psichologia del Mecicano,* Mexico: Antigua Libreria Robredo, 1961; Rogelio Diaz-Guerrero, "Socio-Cultural Premises, Attitudes, and Cross-Cultural Research," Invited Paper, Section 17, Cross-Cultural Studies of Attitude Structure and Dimensions. Seventeenth International Congress of Psychology, Washington, D.C., 1963.

ple, but he does so in other quarters (dominating his younger sisters and brothers, fighting, being sexually promiscuous). The wife and daughters seem to develop a solidly female "mutual protection society," adopt a passively controlling "martyr" role, and wait patiently to seize control whenever the father's dominance falters. Thus exists a climate which fosters overcompensating sons, with ambivalence (passive-aggressive) toward the father, and daughters who, because of hostility toward a punishing father, distrust all men.

A safe but indirect manner for the Mexican male to express hostility against his father, then, seems to be one of "showing the old boy that I am as much, or more, man than he is." This, however, cannot be done in direct confrontation. Rather it is done in spheres away from the father's bailiwick —away from his watchful eye. As Jesus Sanchez puts it, "to grow up away from your parents helps you to become mature."[10] The son can't compete with the father directly, so he acts out his hostility guided by his father's example, but on his own terms in his own battle field.

The family is, of course, a reflection of and the basis for culture. Mexican culture is, as is the family, authoritarian and hierarchial in structure.[11] Though Mexican citizens have a general distrust of and disregard for the "officials" in government, church, and other large-scale organizations, they are most hesitant to directly or overtly criticize them. This passiveness in the face of authority has, as the passiveness to the father, an aggressive counterpart. As a matter of fact, Meadow et al.,[12] in depth studies of Mexican psychopathology, cite different degrees of passive-aggressiveness as a central feature of the modal personality of the Mexican. Does this aggressive component demonstrate itself in a socially acceptable manner in a Mexican institution? The premise here is that the bullfight will relive aspects of the frustration engendering conflict and provide an outlet for the resultant aggression. It would be expected, from observations of the Mexican family and from examination of the symptom-formation in Mexican psychopathology, that the legitimized expression would be of a type allowing "acting out" of hostility. But first, before considering the bullfight itself, let us examine by contrast the situation in the Anglo-American family.[13]

---

[10] Lewis, *Children of Sanchez*, 8.

[11] *Ibid.,* xxiii.

[12] Arnold Meadow and David Stoker, "Symptomatic Behaviour of Mexican-American and Anglo-American Child Guidance Patients", Unpublished paper, University of Arizona, Tucson, Arizona.

[13] Family dynamics are most certainly influenced by socio-economic class. Mexico generally is viewed by social scientists to be a "poverty" culture, and the United States to be a "middle class" culture, though interpretations always must allow for cultural heterogeneity. The present authors wish to utilize the concepts "modal family" and "model personality" as bases for discussion, but with caution against over-generalization and stereotypy.

If the Anglo-American father were to attempt to follow the dominance pa ern of his Mexican counterpart, he would posthaste be imprisoned, divoiced with the condemnation of the court, or at best, socially ostracized.

In the Anglo nuclear family, as in the Anglo culture, the ideological byword is equality. Mother, father, son and daughter are "members of the group" and have a *right* to be heard, to voice their opinion, and to register their vote around the family conference table. Everyone "shares the responsibility" and "pulls his weight" in the "togetherness" of the family.

The Anglo ethic, loaded as it is with the popular meaning of "democracy," encourages an unrealistic muting of authority as it exists in the society. Fathers and mothers are not supposed to be authority figures but "pals," "buddies," "good heads," and "regular guys." They are still, however, expected to be the prime socialization agents of Anglo society, and as such, must impress upon the child an awareness of behavior which is accepted and expected by that society. This cannot be done without the exertion of authority. Socialization makes demands that often are contrary to the child's own preferences. Thus, the frustration-aggression cycle is manifested. But how can the child demonstrate overt hostility to a "pal," a "buddy," or an equal? Furthermore, the vagueness of the parental role in the Anglo family presents the child with a mercurial identification model. Should he be dependent upon or independent of his parents—and when? Mother preaches togetherness, but usually agrees with the television and movie stereotype of the well-meaning, bungling father who needs her subtle domination.

Authoritarianism from people who are not supposed to be authoritarian, vagueness of or conflict in role expectations, obscure role models, plus the restrictions of socialization set the stage for hostility toward authority in the Anglo family. Typically, however, this hostility, and in fact most familial conflict, is intellectualized and abstracted into elaborate displacement and double-bind communications.

The Mexican child seems to have clear reason for hostility, but can't reveal it to the father because he may be beaten. He can't be hostile to the mother because she was a "saint." The Anglo child has difficulty showing overt hostility in his family because, first, he has a hard time tracing the basis for his frustration, and second, he can't be aggressive to two "buddies." But the hostility from socialization and role conflict is still there and needs expression.

The Mexican is forced to be passive to the frustrating agent, but along with this passiveness rides an aggressive component. If the Mexican has been shaped into a passive-aggressive, then it seems feasible to posit as a central feature of the Anglo modal personality the defense mechanism of intellectualization. The Anglo child learns from his parents to intellectual-ize conflict, to abstract hostility, to disengage it from painful affect, and to deal with it in a symbolic, ritualistic fashion. Whereas the Mexican acts out his hostility, the Anglo rationalizes it and elaborately disguises it with verbal repartee. Manuel Sanchez observed "life in the United States is too abstract, too mechanical. The people are like precision machines."[14]

As does the Mexican family in the Mexican culture, the Anglo family reflects and maintains the Anglo culture. Anglo society has been characterized by a plethora of writers as being abstract, universalistic, materialistic, impersonal, unemotional, and bureaucratic. One would expect, then, the ideal legitimized outlets for hostility to be similarly complex, elaborately diffuse, and intellectualized, impersonalized and de-affected after a bureaucratic fashion. The national sport of the United States, baseball, we have hypothesized, should fully reflect this pattern.

THE BULLFIGHT

Aficionados who are of a mind to describe the essence of the bullfight do so in terms that parallel the *corrida* with a Greek drama. Robinson writes that the theme of the bullfight lies "somewhere between the themes of fate and death."[15] Allen proclaims the bullfight to be "the last drama of our times that has death as an immediate object."[16] In *The Brave Bulls,* two of Lea's Mexican characters discuss the *fiesta brava* as follows:

> ". . . It is a form of drama as certainly as the works of Sophocles. But what a difference between the happenings on a stage or in a poem, and the happening in a plaza!"
> ". . . The festival of bulls is the only art form in which violence, bloodshed, and death are palpable and unfeigned. It is the only art in which the artist deals actual death and risks actual death that gives the art its particular power. . . ."[17]

Who, then, do the principals in this drama represent? Who is killing and who is being killed? We have hypothesized that the events in the bullfight will provide a socially legitimized, symbolic vehicle for the aggression toward authority which has been developed mainly in and by the Mexican family situation.

[14] Lewis, *Children of Sanchez,* 338.

[15] C. Robinson, *With the Ears of Strangers: The Mexican in American Literature,* Tucson: University of Arizona Press, 1964, 173.

[16] J. H. Allen, *Southwest,* New York: Bantam, 1953, 113–14.

[17] T. Lea, *The Brave Bulls,* Boston: Little, Brown and Co., 1949, 199–200.

Since the reader may be unfamiliar with the structure of the bullfight, we shall undertake here a brief description before proceeding to the analysis.

Prior to the appearance of any of the principals in the *corrida,* the *alguacil,* a mounted bailiff, rides across the bull ring and, with a bow and a flourish, renders his respect to the *Presidente* (a national, state, or local official, who is in charge of the conduct of the bullfight). The *alguacil* will thereafter be the courier for the *Presidente,* and will transmit orders from him to the principals in the *corrida.* Thus is the hierarchial nature of Mexican society represented in the bullfight. No major shift in action, no new sequence is attempted without first gaining the nod of the *Presidente.* It is he who will pass final judgment upon the performance of the *matador.* He, and only he can decide that the bull shall live (on rare occasions), or die. In essence he has the power of life and death. It is interesting to note that, though disapproval in the highly emotional framework of the *corrida* may incite the crowd eloquently and thoroughly to curse and insult the *matador,* his assistants, his mother, father, *compadres,* lovers, children, and future children, there is seldom a harsh word directed toward the sacrosanct *Presidente.* This respect remains, ironically, while symbolically authority is about to be murdered in the ring!

Upon receiving the nod from the *Presidente,* the *alguacil* rides out of the ring to lead back the *paseo,* or parade, which consists of in splendid order the *matadors,* their *banderilleros* (assistants), the *picadors,* the ring attendants, and the harnessed team whose task it will be to remove the dead bull from the ring. The *matadors* halt directly beneath the *Presidente* and bow their respect. Following this, all the principals, usually with the exception of a *banderillero,* leave the ring. The *Presidente* gives permission for the bull to be released, and the assistant receives the bull.

The bullfight itself consists of three major parts (*Los Tres Tercios de la Lidia*). In the first, the *banderilleros* work the bull with the cape, thus allowing the *matador* to observe the *toro's* idiosyncracies (direction of hook, favored eye, and straightness of charge). Then the *picadors* pic the bull, this to demonstrate the bull's courage (by his charge to the horse) and to lower his head. Following this, the ring is cleared—the bull remains, having "conquered," for a moment, all his antagonists. The *banderilleros* (sometimes the *matador*), in the second major part, place the *banderillas* (barbed sticks), these to correct for the bull's tendency to hook in one or the other direction. The third part consists of *brindis,* or formal dedication of the bull to the *Presidente* (then to anyone else in the crowd the *matador* chooses), the work with the *muleta* (small red cloth), and, finally, the sword.

Since there are two bulls for each *matador,* and two or three *matadors* in each bullfight, these three segments are repeated from four to six times in an afternoon.

Such is the bare structure of the bullfight. This tells nothing of the key to, the vitality of, the drama in the ring, the feeling in the crowd, or the symbolic expression of hostility.

Perhaps a discussion of this can best be introduced by quoting the *matador* protagonist in Ramsey's *Fiesta* as he describes, when facing the bull, "a fear that never quite left him, and that encompassed others too indefinite for him to understand or even name, a fear of authority, of the powerful, the patron . . ."[18]—of the *father*! Freedom from this authority is granted, he contends, in those rare moments when fear is combated and overcome.

Characteristically, the Mexican son profoundly fears his father. Manuel Sanchez testifies that in order to become a man, the individual must escape his father. Yet it was not until he, himself, was twenty-nine years old that he smoked in his father's presence. At that time, Manuel, though fearful, felt himself to be acting most bravely by showing his father that he was a man —*at twenty-nine years of age*!

This need for "manhood" (courage, domination, sexual prowess) which we have mentioned many times above is crucial enough in the Mexican culture to claim a syndrome entity all its own—the *machismo. Macho* connotes maleness—demonstrable and blatant maleness. The individual who is *macho* is *muy hombre* (much man), abundantly endowed with sexual organs, and fears nothing. The most grave and threatening insult to the Mexican male is one that challenges his masculinity.

What more natural pre-occupation could one expect from a son who has been subject to an emasculating father—to a father whose own fear of male competition has led him to use his physical size to dominate his son? We have mentioned that one way the son can compensate for his subordinate role is to emulate his father in another sphere, and later in his own home with his own wife and children. But through the bullfight another compensation is offered. As a spectator (or better, a principal) he can compensate symbolically, uninhibitedly, with all the hate, insult, and invective that he can muster. What clearer representative of the father than the bull with his flagrant masculinity, awesome power, and potential to maim and kill? What clearer representative of the son than the delicate, almost fragile, *matador* whose protection obviously cannot be strength but must be courage? See how the bull charges the *banderilleros*! See how he hurls himself against the pic and the horse! How can the *matador* stand up to the bull? How can the son stand up to the father? Aha! *Toro*! Aha!

The *matador* provides the spectator with an amazingly flexible psychological figure. He can identify with the *matador's* courage, with his expertise, with his kill, and yet he can project upon the *matador,* especially in a bad performance, accusations of cowardice and powerlessness he has experienced himself in the constantly losing battle with his father. It is interest-

[18] R. Ramsey, *Fiesta*. New York: John Day, 1955, 24.

ing that many bullfighters take nicknames with diminutive denotations—Joselito, Armillita *Chico*, Amoros *Chico*, Gallito, Machaquito, etc. Similarly, well over three hundred *matadors* whose names have been entered in the records have somewhere in their nickname the word *nino* (child)—El Nino de la Palma, etc. Thus is emphasized their smallness, their fragility *vis-a-vis* the bull. Thus is emphasized symbolically the helplessness of the child *vis-a-vis* the father. Strength is not nearly so valued an attribute of the *matador* as is demonstrable courage. The great *matadors* are not remembered for their muscle, but for their *macho*. Belmonte was sickly, Maera had wrists so fragile that he often dislocated them in a *faena* (series of passes), Manolete was painfully thin. In fact, size and strength may be a disadvantage. Joselito, a tall, athletic, and graceful man, often complained that he had to take more chances with the bull than the physically struggling Belmonte in order to make his *faenas* appear as difficult. When asked how he developed strength for the *corrida*, Gallo is said to have replied, "I smoke Havana cigars," adding that one cannot possibly match the bull for strength, but he can for courage. The *matador* must, then, appear finite when facing the awesome power of the bull. A sign of fear is acceptable, even desirable, if the *faena* is good. Thus is highlighted the fact that the *matador* has in spite of his fears faced, dominated, and killed the bull. A too calm, too nonchalant, too perfect *matador*, without the emotion of fear (and pride in controlling that fear), who cannot convey to the crowd that his is in fact a struggle in which he has faced, averred, and administered death to an over-powering force, may be viewed as a *matador* without *salsa* —without "sauce." The fact of the matter is that the Mexican father *is* threatening, does physically hurt, and *does* strike fear in the heart of his sons. To dominate and destroy him *would* be a remarkable feat. If the bullfight is to provide symbolically a resolution of this one-sided affair then it must be representative of its acts, events, and especially of its emotions.

We have mentioned earlier that the passive role forced upon the Mexican child brings with it an aggressive component—a dynamic seen again and again in the Mexican personality structure. This interaction is beautifully manifested in the three commandments for the *matador's* conduct in the bullfight—*Parar! Templar! Mandar!* (Keep the feet quiet! Move the cape and *muleta* slowly! Dominate and control the bull!) The central feature is, in the modern bullfight, the domination of the bull.[19] But domination is expressed in the *bonita corrida* with a studied parsimony of movement, with a deliberately slow tempo. Boyd writes that "the *matador* gains

---

[19] Based upon records from cases under intensive psychotherapy, Meadow reports the recurrently expressed need of the Mexican-American patient to dominate during interpersonal relations. A person who is easily dominated is considered by the Mexican-American to be *cobtrolado* (controllable). The same word is used to refer to manageable horses.

mastery by his cunning awareness of the power of the absence of movement."[20] The most valued placing of the *banderillas* and the most honored kill both consist of the *matador* performing these tasks while passively standing his ground and receiving the charge of the bull. The *matador's* knees may knock together with fright, and the crowd will understand—as long as he continues to *parar*.

Kluckhohn sees this passive element in another Mexican institution, religion. She describes the Mexican's dependence upon the Saints and submissive and accepting attitude toward the supernatural.[21] Since the basic cultural values run through all of a society's institutions, it is not surprising to find this same passivity modifying the legitimized expression of hostility toward authority in the bullfight.

The *matador* demands submissive behavior from his own assistants. Traditionally, the latter have not been allowed to eat at the same table with the *matador,* must obey his orders immediately and without question and, regardless of the amount of the *matador's* income, are paid very poorly. Hemingway writes ". . . a *matador* feels that the less he pays his subordinates the more man he is and in the same way the nearer he can bring his subordinates to slaves the more man he feels he is."[22] Thus, out of the ring as well as in, the *matador* perpetuates the *machismo*. This is also observed in the sexual exploits of *matadors*, and highlighted especially by their blatant disregard for and high incidence of syphilis. "You cannot expect," Hemingway says, "a *matador* who has triumphed in the afternoon by taking chances not to take them in the night."[23]

Often the *matador* will single out a woman in the crowd and dedicate the kill to her, expecting, of course, some token of appreciation in return. One of the authors witnessed a *matador* leaving the *Plaza de Toros* after a successful corrida survey a bevy of adoring females, make his selection with a toss of the head and beckoning gesture with his blood-stained arm, and walk off hand-in-hand with the amazed and grateful girl to her car.

It would seem from the *matador's* point of view that the crowd is symbolically female. The *matador* (son) looks for approval to the crowd (mother) when he demonstrates his domination, his superiority over, the bull (father). The crowd continually calls on the *matador* to work closer to the bull. It *demands* that he take chances and promises in return to give him manifestations of approval. In his study of Mexican psychopathology,

---

[20] G. Boyd, in M. Wright (Ed.), *The Field of Vision*. New York: Harcourt-Brace, 1956, 192.

[21] Florence Kluckhohn and F. L. Strodbeck, *Variations in Value Orientations*. New York: Row, Peterson, 1961, 235.

[22] E. Hemingway, *Death in the Afternoon*. New York: Scribner's and Sons, 16, 1945, 82.

[23] *Ibid.,* 104.

Meadow has observed that the Mexican mother subtly encourages the son to compete with the father, thus providing her an added element of control. It is not surprising, then, to see this dynamic represented in the *corrida*. The crowd (mother) calls for the *matador* (son) to challenge, to dominate, the bull (father), and offers love as a reward. *Matadors* who have been gored when responding to the crowd's urges have been reported to turn to the crowd, blaming it, shouting, for example, "See what you have done to me! See what your demands have done!" It may well be that the females in the crowd would enjoy seeing both the *matador* and the bull destroyed, thus expressing the generalized hostility that Mexican women have toward men. For the Mexican female, the *corrida* may be a legitimized way of acting out aggression towards dominating husbands, fathers, and lovers.

A famous breeder of *toros* writes that ". . . certain of their (the fighting bulls) number will stay home to take care of the cows and carry on the breed with those formidable sacs that swing between their legs. But not our fighters to the death. They are virgins. It is a curious thing, our festival."[24] The bull has not experienced mating, and never will, because the *matador* will kill him. Perhaps the son will have dominated and killed that symbolic father before he can mate with the mother (the matador prays before each fight to the *Virgin* Mother).

In *capeas*, or informal street bullfights, the bull may be slaughtered by many people (if the town can afford the loss) and often the testicles will be cut off, roasted, and devoured. At one time it was customary in the *corrida* to remove the testicles (*criadillas*) of the first killed bull of the afternoon and serve them as a prepared meal to the *Presidente* during the killing of the fifth bull. Thus with one symbolic move were expressed and satisfied two needs—to dominate and render forever impotent the father and to incorporate the "source" of his strength. In the same vein, small children are often seen flooding the ring after the last kill, dipping their fingers in the fallen bull's blood and licking their fingers of this fluid of courage. If the *matador* has performed well and is acclaimed by the crowd the *Presidente* may award him the bull's ear, two ears, or two ears and a tail, in that ascending order of honor.

Thus through the *corrida* does the Mexican spectator, identifying with the matador and re-enacting the family situation, not only symbolically dominate and destroy the unyielding and hated authority figure, but he captures some of that figure's awesome power.

The bullfight itself has undergone considerable change. What exists now, as "modern bullfighting," began with Belmonte in the early 1930's,

---

[24] Lea, *The Brave Bulls*, 87.

and according to the *aficionado,* is considerably different from its earlier stages. Hemingway writes,

> As the *corrida* has developed and decayed, there has been less emphasis on the form of the killing, which was once the whole thing, and more on the cape work, the pacing of the *banderillas,* and the work with the *muleta.* The cape, the *banderillas,* and the *muleta* have all become ends in themselves rather than means to an end. . . .[25]

A bullfighter is now judged, and paid much more on the basis of his ability to pass the bull quietly and closely with the cape than on his ability as a swordsman. The increasing importance and demand for the style of cape work and work with the *muleta,* that was invented or perfected by Juan Belmonte; the expectation and demand that each *matador* pass the bull, giving a complete performance with cape, in the *quites*; and the pardoning of deficiency in killing of a *matador* who is an artist with the cape and *muleta,* are the main changes in modern bullfighting.[26]

Pre-Belmonte, then, the "kill" was the focal point of the bullfight. The *matador* who could kill with lust and enjoyment was admired and loved. The earlier phases of the *corrida* were to demonstrate the bull's courage and power and to prepare him for the kill. The essence of the bullfight was the final sword thrust, the actual encounter between man and bull where for an interminable moment they became one figure and which was called the "Moment of Truth." Now, to accommodate the emphasis on the cape and *muleta* work, the bulls are smaller and killing is barely a "third of the fight"[27] and anticlimactic to the cloth work. As Boyd points out, the "Moment of Truth" is now at the highlight of domination with the cape and *muleta,* not at the kill.[28] Hemingway agrees, writing that the emphasis in the modern *corrida* is upon dominance rather than killing and that this has gone hand-in-glove with the padding of the horses, the smaller bulls, and the changing of the *picador's* function from lowering the bull's head and showing his courage to weakening him.[29] There are, say the older *aficionados,* no longer *matadors,* but now only *toreadors.*

Mexico has been gradually evolving from the feudal social structure and caste system imposed by the *Conquistadors* toward urbanization and industrialization. The reference group emulated in this transition is, of course, the "advanced" Western world, especially the United States. The trend to-

---

[25] Hemingway, *Death in the Afternoon,* 67.
[26] *Ibid.,* 175.
[27] *Ibid.,* 180.
[28] Boyd, in *The Field of Vision,* 192–93.
[29] Hemingway, *Death in the Afternoon,* 176.

ward urbanization brings with it more emotionally restrictive patterns of socialization and more abstract channels for the expression of hostility.[30] Western Europeans and Anglo-Americans are usually "shocked," for example, by the "brutality" of the bullfight and tend to dub cultures of which it is a part as "primitive." The more urbanized cultures do not, however, deny the need for legitimized expression of hostility. Kemp, a leading opponent of the bullfight, writes: "One of the functions of civilization is to direct the expression of one's desires by early training and social pressures so that, ideally, we will receive the minimum harm and maximum value from that expression."[31] He admits to the need for satisfaction of the appetite for violence in all members of society but thinks that they must be satisfied less grossly than in the bullfight.

The general disapproval of Western Europe and the United States concerning the "barbarism" of the bullfight certainly must have had considerable influence on its conduct. (The padding of the horses was instigated by the English-born wife of a King of Spain, following promptings from her own country.) Since the institutions of a society reflect its culture, since the culture is influenced by the demands of other more powerful societies, and since urbanization itself accounts in part for change in cultural patterns, we would expect to see corresponding changes in all of the subject society's institutions, including the bullfight. Thus is seen the shift in emphasis from the "primitive" killing of the bull to the more abstract, more aesthetic, and certainly more "acceptable" domination with the cape and *muleta*. Thus is seen the complete elimination of the kill in Portugal and Switzerland, and in Spain and Mexico, its secondary, almost apologetic status.

Urbanization not only demands more intellectualized dealing with hostility but also brings with it a need for task specialization. This too is reflected in the modern *corrida*. The well rounded "generalist" *matador* is rare. Most are specialists—cape men, *muleta* men, and a few who are known for their work with the *banderillas*.

The shift in emphasis in the bullfight (some say, the emasculation of the bullfight) has not affected the average American spectator's reaction of being revolted, disgusted, even sickened by the *corrida*. In sounding the reactions of some American college students to their first (and usually last) attendance at a bullfight, the authors have noted the recurring theme: "It's too much," "too blatant," overpowering." Robinson writes "the bullfight allows the American, protected from reality all his life by the palliation of

---

[30] The position of father in the Mexican family has, with urbanization, also begun to shift toward the "advanced" Western model. It might be said that as the father figure becomes less fearsome, less overpowering, there is less need to "kill" him symbolically—domination alone is an adequate expression of hostility.

[31] L. Kemp, *The Only Beast*. New York: Pocket Books (Discovery #4), 1954, 46–56.

modern American society, to face up to the real thing."[32] And the "real thing" is "too much."

No doubt the highly "civilized" Anglo-American is threatened by such a direct acting out of hostility and violence as is manifest in the bullfight. But in addition to this he is very likely frightened by such a direct confrontation with death. Americans tend to deny death, even avoiding it in their speech (he "passed away," was "laid to rest," etc.). In Mexico, according to Robinson, "the bullfight spectacle is only one of the forms through which Mexicans make their obeisance to death."[33] Brenner noted that concern for death is "an organic part of Mexican thought."[34] The possibility of early or violent death is much greater for the average Mexican than for the average Anglo. To see death averted by the matador is pleasing to the Mexican, giving him some feeling of control over an event that he witnesses, not atypically, taking place in the streets. To the American the drama is a grim reminder of the inevitability of an event he seldom sees and chooses to deny. Hemingway writes, "We, in games, are not fascinated by death, its nearness and avoidance. We are fascinated by victory and we replace the avoidance of death by the avoidance of defeat."[35] The symbolic "victory" over another team is certainly at a higher level of emotional abstraction than the symbolism of the domination of and bloody killing of a bull.

Anglo-Americans, the authors have observed, tend to "root" for the bull during a *corrida*. The *picadors* are soundly hooted (Mexicans only demonstrate disapproval if the bull is "ruined"), and a tremendous barrage of invective pummels the *matador* if it takes him more than one sword to make a kill (even if all his swords are perfectly "over the horns"). This may be the result of the proclivity of the American to identify with the underdog, or the revulsion at seeing an animal (who, in the American ethic, is also a "buddy") killed. This seemingly irrational preference to see the man rather than the bull killed may also be influenced by a degree of prejudice in the ethnocentric Anglo toward the Mexican *matador*. It may also be that the *corrida* does not present to the Anglo a perception of two "evenly matched" antagonists. The opponents are not "equal"—few *matadors* are killed, but the bull rarely lives. This may run counter to the "fair play" ethic of the Anglo.

If the bullfight's overt display of hostility with its over-riding components of inevitable death, animal suffering, and inequality, is not acceptable as a suitable means for the expression of aggression to the Anglo, what does he prefer? As mentioned earlier, the Anglo, too, is subject to socialization, and he, too, experiences conflict situations which engender hostility

[32] Robinson, *With the Ears of Strangers,* 250.

[33] *Ibid.,* 257.

[34] Anita Brenner, *Idols Behind Alters.* New York: Payson and Clarks, 1929, 21.

[35] Hemingway, *Death in the Afternoon,* 22.

toward parents and parent surrogates. How, then, as reflected in the Anglo national sport of baseball, is the expression of hostility toward authority legitimized?

BASEBALL

It was presented above that the Anglo child is prevented from directly manifesting hostility toward parents by their representation as "good guys" and "pals." Verbal aggression, elaborately intellectualized, is usually the most overt form of hostility allowed to the child. Whereas the Mexican seems painfully aware of conflict, hates his father, and acts out his hostility (displaces, projects), the Anglo appears hopelessly ambivalent toward the vague "buddy" father, and represses the fact that conflict exists. A good part of his psychic life is spent sustaining this repression compulsively and obsessively. In general, the legitimized means of expressing hostility are just as subtle as is the subtlety of the hostility generating conflict situation —this muteness is manifest as we shall see in the national sport.

The matador's servile bow to the *Presidente* is an obvious and undisguised move of deference. In the prelude to a baseball game, however, the players line up, facing the flag, and stand quietly during the playing of the National Anthem. Tribute to authority here certainly is less direct than in the bull ring. A flag is a considerably more abstract and less threatening symbol than the pompous gentleman in the privileged box. The government official who, as *Presidente*, attends the *corrida*, controls its conduct, and can directly interfere in the performance. Government officials who attend baseball games are in no way able to interfere with play—at most, they throw in the first ball.

While the observer need only take a quick glance at the "barbaric" *corrida* to see a dramatically overt display of violence and aggression, he is hard pressed, after considerable observation, to see any marked degree of hostility in the structure of the "good clean sport" of baseball. He looks out over the field and sees two teams (composed of an equal number of similarly uniformed men), patiently and systematically taking an equal number of turns (innings) in the attempt to score. The field is elaborately chalked, demarking those areas of "fair" from "foul" play, and an elaborate system of rules dictates when a player can get a "hit," take or advance a base, score a run, be "safe" or "out." The observer becomes aware of the game's dramatic emphasis on numbers (the most abstract of symbols)—the scoreboard, the batting averages, the earned-run averages, the team win percentages, and even the players, who are granted relative impersonality by the numbers on their backs.

Unlike the *matador*, who constantly communicates with the crowd, the baseball players are seen to remain distinctly aloof from them. The player's allegiance is to the team, and he who performs ostentatiously for the crowd is ostracized as a "grandstander." Contrast, for example, the baseball player's downcast eye and turf-kicking toe after an outstanding move with the *matador's* haughty glance and proud posture following a good series of passes. Contrast the convertible or television set given ritualistically by the crowd to the ball player on "his day" with the immediate, spontaneous, and extremely emotional reaction of the crowd following an appreciated *corrida*—they clamor for the *Presidente* to give him awards, throw him wine flasks, sombreros, and often rush into the ring to carry him about on their shoulders. It might be said that in baseball, the crowd is expected to observe, in a relatively detached way, the spectacle being performed for them on the field. At the bullfight, however, the crowd is expected to be one with the *matador*, to participate, fully, in the emotions of the fight.

There is, by contrast to the *corrida,* a noticeable lack of heterosexuality in the game of baseball. While the *matador* often dedicates his bull or tosses an ear to a senorita, the baseball player, on the field anyway, limits his interaction to male teammates, chattering to them, shaking their hands in success, slapping their buttocks in encouragement, and mobbing and hugging them for superlative feats of play.

There is, of course, competition taking place in the game—but nothing that can parallel the direct, individual confrontation of the *matador* with the bull. In baseball, two "teams" meet and the more evenly matched they are, the better the "contest" is. There are fans for both sides, each rooting for his team, hoping that it will win the "contest." After the game is over, there will be a winner, and a "good loser." (It is interesting that the participants in baseball are called "players." The matador is not "playing" at the *corrida*—it is a *fight*. The aggressive component that one would expect in competition is muted by the rules governing the conduct of play and by the expectations of the crowd. There are occasional emotional outbreaks between rival players, between players and umpires, and between managers and umpires, but these "rhubarbs" are ephemeral and seem somehow distant and artificial. The shouts and jeers of the crowd, with an occasional "murder the bum," lack the emotional punch and especially the personal reference of the venomous insults hurled by the displeased Mexican *aficionado*.)

Some psychoanalytically oriented behavioral scientists have written vividly of the symbolic castration represented in the baseball games. Stokes, for example, calls baseball "a manifest exercise in phallic deftness."[36] Petty sees the contest as a safe re-creation of the battle between father and son for the sexual favors of the mother.[37]

---

[36] A. Stokes, "Psychoanalytic Reflections on the Development of Ball Games." *International Journal of Psycho-Analysis,* 1956.

[37] T. A. Petty, Address to the American Psychoanalytic Association, 1963.

However, if hostility generated in a father-son competition is manifested here, how safe, how muted, is its expression. Its release is legitimized only under the restrictions of elaborate rules, omnipresent umpires, and with the insistence that each team systematically take turns playing one role or the other. It is diffused throughout a "team," no one man taking full responsibility and is submerged in a morass of batting and pitching rituals and superstitions that are unsurpassed by the most extreme of religion and the military. Batters will use only certain bats, stand a certain way, pound home plate a certain number of times, spit, rub dust, rub resin (or all three) on their hands, pull their clothing into a certain position before batting, wear lucky numbers, lucky charms, lucky hats, lucky sox, or use a lucky bat. Many pitchers have elaborate series of movements before delivering the ball—touch cap, rub ball, grab resin bag, scuff dirt, adjust glove, retouch hat, re-rub ball. . . . Professional pitcher Lew Burdette has taken as long as a full minute to complete a series of irrelevant gestures, ticks, clutches, and tugs before throwing the ball. Similarly, an observer would be hard pressed to find a baseball player who doesn't ritualistically chew gum.

Furthermore, the conduct of the game, and therefore any expression of hostility, is closely scrutinized by at least three umpires. Interestingly enough, the word umpire is derived from the Latin, meaning not equal. Thus, on a playing field where equality is a central ethic, the umpires are unique. They are the only personnel on the field who even during inning intermissions cannot sit down or relax. Like the "super ego" theirs is an unrelenting vigilance. Their word is law, and disrespect for them can bring an ousting from the game. But how different is the player-umpire relationship from that of the *matador-Presidente*. The *Presidente* is treated with deference, and the interaction between authority and *matador* is seen to be personal and direct. As in the Mexican society at large, the authority figure, though he may be hated, is shown the utmost respect.[38]

The umpire, on the other hand is an impersonal figure. How many "fans" know the names of big league umpires? So abstract is the black-suited authority that "kill the umpire" can be vociferously and safely shouted. How nonthreatening is the typical reaction of the umpire to the complaints, admonishments, and verbal aggressions of the players and managers—he turns his back and slowly walks away. Authority is challenged—and with impunity![39]

Another phenomenon, certainly cultural in nature, is the ritual hypo-

[38] Mexican patients have described their fathers as drunkards, brutes, etc., but always add that they "respect" them. Tucson, Arizona school teachers often report that the behavior of the Mexican-American students *vis-a-vis* the teacher is exemplary, though their drop-out and absentee records indicate a low value for education.

[39] There is, however, a carefully defined limit to the amount of abuse the umpire is expected to endure. Physical violence, and certain profanities bring not only

chondriasis of baseball players. *Matadors* traditionally disregard wounds (the *macho* does not fear, avoid, or show disability because of pain), and have even fought with assistants who tried to carry them out of the ring after a serious goring. Baseball players leave the field for a simple pulled muscle. Yards of tape, gallons of ointment, heat treatments, vitamin pills, "isometrics," "training rules," arm warmers, whirlpool baths, and rubdowns pamper the ball player. Pitchers are carefully protected from the wind, rain, and cold "dugout" seats, and can ask to be relieved if they are feeling tired.

As the conduct of the bullfight has changed with the increasing urbanization in Mexico, so also has the conduct of baseball changed with the increasing bureaucratization in the United States. In the early 20th Century, fines for insulting (or even striking) the umpire were non-existent. The crowd very often displayed displeasures by throwing bottles and cushions at specific individuals in the field. In general, the level of expression of hostility was more direct and involved somewhat more acting out. The farm club system, its scouting ties with organized collegiate athletics, and the bureaucratic "front office" were far less expansive. Rules and regulations were less restricting, and the tobacco chewing, swearing, sweating player was typical as contrasted with the "gentleman players" who grace our fields and television commercials today. Nine innings then took about two-thirds the time they do now, the ball was "dead," and the number of players on the team's roster was smaller. There were fewer substitutes, and pitchers as a rule stayed in for the entire game.

In the present situation even the abstract "team" concept has been made obsolete by increased bureaucratization. The authors witnessed members of the winning (1963) Los Angelos Dodgers speaking proudly of the "Dodger Organization," and the good job the "front office" had done.

In a television interview, Bill Veeck, an ex-professional manager, expressed dismay with the unnecessary "dragging out" of the game by prolonged warm-up pitches, drawn-out sessions of verbal haranguing, "long" walks to the dugout, and summit meetings of the pitcher, catcher, and manager. He complained about the time-wasting rituals of motion indulged in by both pitcher and batter. Veeck thus testifies to the increasing obsessive quality in the game, as its emphasis shifts to more and more diffuse, indirect, and disguised means for expressing hostility.

One wonders, in fact, if the restrictions in baseball are too many, if the fans aren't growing dissatisfied. The increasing public attendance at professional football games, reaching a point where some sports analysts pre-

---

a removal from the game, but severe fines to the offender. Since there are fixed fines for specific obscenities, angry players will often turn to the umpire and, escaping the fine by ascending a rung on the abstraction ladder, declare, "You're that five hundred dollar word!"

dict that it will replace baseball as the National sport, may be an indication of the demand for a less abstract expression of hostility in spectator sports. Nevertheless, from the point of view of social control, baseball masterfully mutes aggression behind its reciprocity, rules, records, and rituals. It duplicates the vagueness and intellectualization of the conflict situation in the American family and provides a markedly abstract and controlled expression of hostility toward authority. Macoby, et al., write that baseball represents the *ideal* of American society.[40] It remains to be seen whether or not this ideal can, in the face of a need for a clearer expression of hostility, remain intact.

SUMMARY

The passive-aggressive component of the Mexican modal personality can be traced to the dominant and harshly punitive role of the father and to the general authoritarian nature of the Mexican culture. This passive-aggressiveness is perpetuated in the *macho* pattern of the Mexican male, and in the "martyr" pattern of the Mexican female. Any acting out of the resultant hostility to authority must be carried out in spheres safely distant from that authority's immediate control.

The bullfight is seen to depict, symbolically, the power of the father, the subtle demands of the mother, and the fear of the child. Unlike the family situation, the awesome authority does not prevail, but rather is dominated and destroyed through the courage and daring of the *matador*. He, however, acting for the spectator, must accomplish this hostile act in a framework of "respect" for authority, and with a studied passiveness in and control of movement.

By contrast, the "intellectualization" component of the Anglo modal personality can be traced to the superficial ethic of "equality" among family members and to the general intellectualized nature of highly urbanized societies. The attempt to mute authority by a pseudo-philosophy of togetherness, when authority is in fact assumed by the father, the mother, and by the society, engenders a vagueness in role definitions, confusion in behavioral expectations, and an intellectualization of the resultant conflict. Hostility toward this intangible yet frustrating authority figure is expressed by the individual in a manner as abstract and as ritualized as its causative factors.

The national sport of baseball is set in a framework of equality. Hostility toward authority takes the symbolic form of competition and desire to

[40] M. Macoby, Nancy Modiano, and P. Lander, "Games and Social Character in a Mexican Village." *Psychiatry*, December, 1964, 50–61.

win, and is smothered under a covering of rules, regulations, and player rituals. Guided by the authority of umpires (who are sufficiently impersonal to be challenged with relative impunity), and protected in the safety of numbers as a member of a team, the players systematically alternate roles, allowing each to have an equal opportunity to "be aggressive."

Spectators of the baseball game view two similarly uniformed teams consisting of the same number of players vying for an abstract "victory." The spectators' emotional participation in the game is distant and safe—"murder the bum" or "kill the umpire" does not have enough of a personal referent to arouse guilt or anxiety. They can take sides in occasional and severely regulated conflicts on the field, because such conflicts have "meaning" only in the game, and are forgotten when the game is over.

Since 1920, the bullfight has gradually been modified to accentuate domination rather than the kill. Paralleling this, the position of the father in the Mexican family has, with gradual urbanization, come more closely in line with that of the "advanced" Western model. He is less threatening, less fearsome, and can be dominated to a degree sufficient to reduce the importance of his symbolic destruction.

Baseball, since 1920, has similarly undergone significant changes. With the increasing bureaucratization of Anglo society, and with the increasing emphasis upon "equality" and impersonality in the family have come the more complex bureaucratization and the more elaborate ritualization of baseball.

The family, and the institutionalized recreation form known as the national sport, mutually reflect, as they appear in Mexico, the cultural centrality of death, dominance, "personal" relationships, respect for and fear and hatred of authority, and the defense systems of the passive-aggressive character structure.

In the Anglo culture, these two institutions mutually reflect the cultural importance of equality, impersonality, and the defense mechanism of intellectualization.

Both national sports provide a socially acceptable channel for the expression of hostility toward authority. This channel is modified by other cultural values and expectations, and is framed in an activity which duplicates, symbolically, aspects of the hostility generating familial situation.

ROBERT D. HERMAN

Gambling as Work:
A Sociological Study
of the Race Track

This article examines a single type of gambling institution, the large, commercial horse race track. Three comments are in order concerning the social relevance of horse racing in comparison with alternative gambling enterprises. First, horse race gambling is an enormous industry. Almost $4 billion was wagered legally and openly at race tracks in the United States in 1963. Fifty-seven million persons attended horse races that year,[1] a greater number than the total for major league baseball, professional football, and collegiate football combined.[2] No estimates of the size of *illegal* horse playing are trustworthy, but one which is often cited states that $16.50 is wagered "off track" on horses for every dollar wagered legally.[3]

Second, in contrast to Nevada-style casinos, most of which are removed from major population centers and have the general features of resorts, race tracks are primarily identifiable with conventional urban culture. They are normally located well within the physical embrace of the metropolis itself. For example, "Aqueduct" (the largest race track in the New York area) enjoys the benefits of its own station on a subway line.[4] Los An-

The research for this report was supported by the National Institute of Mental Health, Grant #MH 08040-01.

[1] *The American Racing Manual* (Triangle Publications, Inc., 1964). In 1963, wagering increased 6.7 percent over 1962.

[2] Attendance at horse races increased 8 percent while the U.S. population 21 years of age and older increased 1.1 percent. *Statistical Abstract of the United States, 1963* (Washington, D.C.: U.S. Department of Commerce.)

[3] John Scarne, *Scarne's Complete Guide to Gambling* (New York: Simon & Schuster, 1961), p. 32. A more moderate estimate was reported by Robert Kennedy to Congress that $7 billion was gambled in the U.S. in 1960. See, *Hearings*, Subcommittee on the Judiciary, House of Reps., 87th Congress, Washington, 1961, "Legislation Relating to Organized Crime," p. 24.

[4] The "Big A" had an average daily attendance of 33,120 in 1964 with an average daily handle of $3,236,086. Hollywood Park (Los Angeles) had an average daily attendance of 34,081 that year and an average daily handle of $2,885,795.

geles has two major tracks, both located within a few minutes travel time from the center of the city. In fact, of the ten largest cities in the United States, only Houston has no horse race track within half an hour's reach. While the racing industry often celebrates its connections with the elegance of old Saratoga and the romance of the blue grass, it is clear that the realities of modern horse racing bring it closer to the model of the supermarket than to that of the vacation spa or the county fair.

Third, many precise data of interest to students of social behavior are readily available without dependency upon questionable and troublesome detective work. A variety of records are kept (and many are published) both because state governments have economic interests in the revenues of track operations and because tracks have almost no reason to hide their records—but every reason to encourage publicity. Exact tabs are maintained on attendance and wagering, even to the point of recording where and when every bet is made. In contrast, there is no way of computing, from the data available to the public, exact amounts wagered in casinos or card parlors. Of course casinos appear to do a very impressive business, but the size of that business is harder to pin down in exact terms. The Nevada Gaming Commission says that the reported gross revenue (taxes) from all gambling establishments in that state in 1963 was $260 million.[5] Still, the amounts actually wagered in that state remain unknown. While it is tempting to focus attention on the more bizarre and colorful world of casinos, the present study is an attempt to appreciate the more routine case of the "local neighborhood race track."[6]

The data for this study were collected in Los Angeles in 1962 and 1963 at Hollywood Park. Although it is one of the largest tracks in the United States (Santa Anita, across town is slightly smaller), Hollywood Park may be considered "typical" of major thoroughbred race tracks. This study should be considered to apply primarily to gambling behavior at thoroughbred races, which presently account for 74 percent of all wagering on horses

---

[5] Nevada Gaming Commission, *Legalized Gambling in Nevada* (Carson City, Nevada: Gaming Policy Board, 1963).

[6] Except for articles in this volume by Zola and Frazier, the following are the most important publications by sociologists on gambling in the last two decades: The best treatment of horse racing is Edward C. Devereux, Jr., "Gambling and the Social Structure—A Sociological Study of Lotteries and Horse Racing in Contemporary America," (unpublished PhD. dissertation, Harvard University, 1949). As this book goes to press, a second doctoral dissertation on the sociology of horse racing is being prepared by Marvin Scott, University of California, Berkeley. Soccer pools are studied by Nechama Tee, *Gambling in Sweden* (Totawa, N.J.: The Bedminster Press, 1964). Herbert A. Bloch has contributed two essays: "The Sociology of Gambling," *American Journal of Sociology*, 57 (1951), pp. 215–22; and Chapter 23 of *Crime in America*, edited by Bloch (Philosophical Library, New York, 1961). A few sociologists have, of course, examined issues related to gambling, especially racketeering, organized crime, and gambling among ethnic minorities.

in this country. Attendance figures, total amounts wagered, and a few other statistics are published in city newspapers and do not require special collection techniques. Some of the details of these figures are recorded by the management of the track for administrative purposes, and I am indebted to the Hollywood Turf Club for access to them. The management also cooperated in giving me and my student assistant the run of the entire establishment in order to make direct observations of patrons' gambling behavior supplemented by the spending of long hours simply counting the numbers of people of each sex as they appeared in various betting lines, as they came through track entrances, or as they purchased programs, tip sheets, or *Racing Forms*. Also included in this study were large numbers of structured and unstructured interviews. Our observations in general became relatively more quantitative as we learned more about the business.

THE SETTING

For the reader who is unfamiliar with a typical commercial horse race track, this may serve as a guided tour. The physical layout is functional and direct. The running track itself is usually an oval a mile in circumference with a grandstand situated along one side. Horses are walked to the track from nearby stables shortly before the races in which they are to run; they then parade in front of the crowd to the starting gate whose position may be varied to permit races of from ¾-mile (requiring about 1 minute, 12 seconds) to 1-½ miles (2 minutes, 24 seconds). An afternoon of racing consists of nine races spaced about one-half hour apart. Significantly, there is no prepared entertainment between races.

Exhibited in front of the crowd, in the infield, is a "tote" board, a large scoreboard showing, among other things, the payoff amounts for the first three horses in the preceding race and the "odds" against each horse entered in the following race. The odds are actually the payoff prices determined by the relative amounts wagered on each horse. Because these odds change as betting proceeds (betting on one race starts within a few minutes after the conclusion of the preceding one but increases in volume as the starting time approaches), the tote board commands the thoughtful attention of a majority of the crowd.

A major race track draws its patrons from a socio-economic cross-section of the city, a fact that is reflected in the division of the grandstand into three or four stratified zones. The largest is a section (for which the term "Grandstand" is usually reserved) that includes a large ramp for standees. At Hollywood Park, 77 percent of the crowd is accommodated within this area. An area, usually called the "Clubhouse" offers somewhat more elbow room and better conveniences for its patrons, but it seems primarily to serve to segregate the $1.00-extra customers from the crush of the main crowd. Twenty percent of the total attendance is contained in the Clubhouse. A more luxurious and expensive area, called the "Private Turf Club" contains 3-½ percent of the total crowd—but they bet about 10 percent of the money!

Almost all members of the Private Turf Club attend the races in the company of friends or family. In contrast, from 35 to 40 percent of the crowd in the Grandstand attend as loners, while 33 to 35 percent of the Clubhouse attendees are loners. On Saturdays and holidays when the size of the total crowd almost doubles that of ordinary weekdays, a somewhat greater proportion of the patrons attend with companions. The loners, although they number considerably less than half the crowd, are a major factor in its appearance. Casual observers are often impressed by the somber, even gloomy, expressions of horse players; win or lose, they seem withdrawn and joyless. However, this atmosphere is largely an artifact of the absence of conversation with companions. Animation normally requires company. It seems heedless to presume, as many commentators have, that some sort of pathology is indicated by the fact that many horse players wear serious expressions.

A more important element in the calm between races is that most patrons are kept quietly but actively engrossed in the demanding tasks of selecting horses on which to bet. Only a small proportion are "hunch" bettors or are willing to act blindly on the advice of public handicappers.[7] Most people indeed *play* the game; in risking their money, they attempt to select their own betting options by the deliberate application of rational criteria. The task is immensely complex, the list of factors which ought to be considered is very large, and the amount of information which is made available is overwhelming. There is so much, in fact, that most or all players must rely on simplifications and rules of thumb.

The most important source of information is a newspaper, the *Daily Racing Form*, purchased by approximately 40 percent of the Grandstand patrons and 60 percent of the Turf Club members. (We estimate that, at Hollywood Park, 89 percent of *Racing Form* purchasers are men, although

[7] In "hunch betting," a horse is selected on arbitrary grounds having nothing to do with the horse's ability. Hunch players usually agree that their actions are not objectively based, but other complex motives may be involved. For a discussion of "psychological probability," see John Cohen, *Chance, Skill and Luck: The Psychology of Guessing and Gambling* (Baltimore, Md.: Penguin Books, 1960).

The term "handicapper" formerly referred to the person, now called the racing secretary, who assigns racing conditions and weights carried by horses. The term now has been extended to include anyone who makes a calculated attempt to determine the winning probabilities of horses in a given race. Many city newspapers publish "selections" which are of some aid to novice bettors. For monthly ratings of major public handicappers, see the magazine, *Turf and Sports Digest* (Baltimore, Md.: Montee Publishing Co., Inc.).

two-thirds of the attendees are men.) This document provides three main types of material: (1) A few pages contain feature articles about important horses and their owners, trainers, and riders—of interest primarily to box holders and Turf Club members; (2) A couple of pages consist of ordered selections by the *Form's* handicappers along with equivocal comments on horses thought likely to be "in contention"; (3) The largest section, and most important for the individual bettor, is called simply, "Past Performances." Past performances are published for horses entered in each of the day's races at the local track and, interestingly, for *other* major race tracks across the country, in spite of the fact that betting on races is illegal (except in Nevada) where one cannot be present in person. Here are tabulated in astonishing detail the racing histories of each horse entered in each race. Among other particulars, the following information is offered *for each horse:* the weight he must carry in the present race, his age, color of his coat, sire, dam, dam's sire, the names of his owner, breeder, and trainer, the amounts of money he has won for his owner in the last two or three years, his speeds for his last few workouts, the dates, locations, and "conditions" of his last dozen races—and then *for each of those races:* his jockey, weight carried, running position relative to the leader at each quarter of the race including the finish, the names of the first three horses to finish, the weights *they* carried, etc.

Of course, a few important considerations receive no comparable publicity. Obscured, for example, are the subtleties of health and emotion of each horse just before racing and the trainer's strategy and instructions to the jockey (e.g., whether to press for victory under any condition or perhaps merely to engage the horse in training and exercise). However, even here, experienced bettors are sometimes able to draw inferences from clues in the *Form* or elsewhere.[8]

As might be expected, many "textbooks" on uses of the *Form* and methods of handicapping and betting are available to the public. These consist mainly of expositions on the asserted significance of a relatively limited number of variables (speed, consistency, post position, experience, etc.). A few books examine not so much the past performances of the horses but rather the possible opportunities afforded by the betting behavior of the crowd (favorites, prices, shifts in odds, etc.).[9] Yet both types of books are

[8] Marvin Scott gives special attention to the fact that the act of a trainer's giving final instructions to the jockey occurs in full view of the crowd—but out of earshot. *Op. cit.*

[9] Among the most highly regarded *Form*-oriented books is Robert S. Dowst, *The Odds, The Player, The Horses* (New York: Dodd Mead & Co., 1959). Two examples of crowd-oriented texts are Burton P. Fabricand, *Horse Sense* (David McKay Co., 1965); E. R. DaSilva and Roy M. Dorcus, *Science in Betting* (New York: Harper & Row, 1961).

likely to call for the application of considerable skill and effort. One recent volume directs its readers to *memorize* at least two tables, one with 42 cells, the other with 56, to be able to read and understand the *Racing Form*, and to be able to apply several complicated rules rapidly and on the spot.[10] More will be said below of those persons who, with the help of the *Form*, attempt to make independent choices; but it may be noted here that gambling at the race track is seen by most participants, and this writer, to require genuine mental effort. It is therefore quite unlike gambling in such casino games as craps, roulette, or slot machines, which depend almost entirely on chance.

THE "ACTION"

The actual operation of placing bets is simple enough. Since the 1930s, American race tracks, by state law, have prohibited private bookmakers from operating openly at tracks and have required that all wagering be pooled and held by the track for subsequent redistribution—the system called parimutuel betting. The bettor tells the "seller" (at a window of the desired denomination—$2, $5, $10, $50, $100) the program number of the horse on which he wishes to bet. The clerk presses a key on a machine (a form of cash register) which prints out an appropriately numbered ticket which is taken by the bettor. As the machine issues the ticket, it simultaneously telegraphs that information to a central computing station, which then, in turn, sends new totals and payoff odds information to the tote board in front of the stands. (Payoff information is corrected for the fact that, from each betting pool, the track withdraws about 15 percent of which about half goes to the state as taxes. The proportion to be returned to the winners, then, is 85 percent of the total bet.) Should the bettor's horse subsequently win, the bettor cashes the ticket at another window; both sellers' and cashiers' windows are distributed throughout the plant and are within a few steps of any potential bettor. Marketing studies have shown that virtually every person in attendance bets on at least one race during the afternoon and a majority bet on half the races or more. It seems that almost no one visits the race track merely to watch horses.

In addition to straight, or "Win" bets, other types of wagers may be made. "Place" bets (in the same denominations as Win bets) pay a return if the horse in question finishes either first or second; "Show" bets pay if the horse is first, second, or third. Payoffs for Place and Show bets are

[10] Fabricand, *Horse Sense*. This book purports to have been based on analyses of races performed by a high-speed digital computer. One is reminded of an analysis of blackjack ("21") gambling also based on computer analysis. See E. O. Thorp, *Beat the Dealer* (New York: Vintage Books, 1966).

smaller in consequence of the lower risk involved. Increasingly race tracks have also provided opportunities for people to bet on more than one race at a time. For example, a "Daily Double" ticket, sold before the first race, is printed with two numbers representing win selections in both the first and second race; thus the risks and the payoffs are greater than for single races. Other more elaborate betting opportunities are presently being introduced at some tracks which account for occasional news items reporting record payoffs when successions of long shots win.

The horse betting behavior of men is different from that of women. This can be seen in Table 1 which shows the proportions of attendees and bettors who are women in three areas of the stands and in four major types of betting situations. (Women tend to avoid risking larger stakes, hence we made no precise counts of the very few women at $10, $50, and $100 windows. The proportions of women who make Place bets are between the fig-

Table 1 Women as Percent of All Attendees and Bettors in Three Areas of Hollywood Park, by Denomination of Bet, 1963

Total in Attendance	Turf Club 47%	Clubhouse 33%	Grandstand 26%
Denomination of Betting			
$2 Win	48%	30%	18%
$2 Show	50	61	34
$5 Win	31	19	9
Daily Double[a]	39	29	22

[a] Two sizes of Daily Double bets are sold, $2 and $10; these data refer to $2 size only.

ures given for Win and Show.) Notice should be made, for later reference, of the relatively high percentage of women betting at $2 Show windows and the relatively low percentage making the more expensive bets. Pari-mutuel clerks and racing habituees are well aware of these differences in gambling behavior, and they are usually accounted for by such explanations as "Women bet defensively," or "Women try to keep from losing, but men try to win." It will be seen that the interpretation presented at the conclusion of this article is an alternative to these propositions.

The socioeconomic identities of race track patrons are difficult to determine accurately, except those of the 3-1/2 percent of the crowd who are members of the Private Turf Club who are upper-middle class and above. We must distrust responses to interview questions asking respondents to classify themselves, given sensitivities to traditional, critical judgments of gambling shared by an unknown proportion of attendees. Loners, in particular, are often timid about revealing their important affiliations in this context. (It may occur to some readers that identities of gamblers could be traced through income tax records even though these are not normally made available to the public. Tracks make a practice of requiring only winners of very large amounts to sign special income tax reports before collecting, but generalizations from such a sample would be inappropriate.) As an alternative to direct questioning, we exploited the fact that 90 percent of Hollywood Park attendees travel to the track by automobile (in contrast to the heavy bus and rail patronage of tracks in many other cities). By recording the license numbers of a sample of 604 cars entering the parking lot, while also recording the number and sex of the occupants, we were able to identify the street addresses of the owners of the cars (with the assistance of the California Department of Motor Vehicles).

Then census tract maps were used to indicate the socioeconomic characteristics of the neighborhoods in which the owners resided. Table 2 presents a summary of this information. The data from car licenses suggest that Los Angeles neighborhoods of each social rank contribute Hollywood Park attendees in approximate proportion to their percentage in the county. We have no way of determining whether track attendees are truly representative of their own neighborhoods nor can we judge, from these data, whether the proportionate attendance from middle-class areas is a recent development. Devereux believed most horse players were middle-class people. When he studied race tracks in the late 1940s,

> . . . The vast throngs that fill the stands at the modern race courses and that pour their money into the pari-mutuel machines . . . are for the most part middle-class laymen, out-groupers from the perspective of the race track society, who still take satisfaction in a day at the races.

It is also known by the management that Hollywood Park's Clubhouse attendance is now increasing at a faster rate than is Grandstand attendance, but this fact may represent either an increasing affluence among attendees generally or an increasing participation in horse playing by more affluent strata of the urban population. In any case, the data in Table 2 show that track habituees are correct when they say that racing patrons "come from all over."

MYTH AND EVIDENCE

Gambling is popularly believed to ensnare its participants in a system involving (a) the reckless expenditure of scarce resources on events of great risk in the naive hope of (b) "making a killing," and gambling is presumed to be (c) an escape from rationality, even where pathological addiction is

Table 2 Neighborhood Social Rank of Hollywood Park Patrons by Type of Group Attending, Compared with Los Angeles County Population

Number and Sex of Group	Social Rank[a]						Total	%	Mean Rank[b]
	I	II	III	IV	V	VI			
Lone, Male	26	37	63	79	68	36	309	54.3%	11.05
Group, Males	3	13	15	15	19	9	74	13.0	11.42
Lone, Female	2	5	8	4	8	6	33	5.8	11.48
Group, Females	3	7	7	4	6	4	31	5.4	10.55
Group, Mixed	5	20	23	17	39	18	122	21.6	11.75
Sample Total	39	82	116	119	140	73	569[c]	100.1	11.246
Sample %	6.85	14.42	20.40	20.92	24.54	12.84			County Mean = 11.308
L.A. County %	5.00	12.98	24.27	21.12	22.80	13.8			

[a] Rank I represents highest status, Rank VI, lowest status. The "Social Rank" index is a composite of three characteristics of census tracts; median family income, percent of population over 24 having completed 1 or more years of college, and percent of employed males in white collar occupations. This index was developed by Meeker for use in the Los Angeles Area. See Marchia Meeker, *Background for Planning* (Los Angeles: Welfare Planning Council, 1964), p. 81.

[b] The six ranks are actually combinations of sixteen levels, ranging from 3 to 18. The Mean Rank column refers to this continuum; a score of 10.5 is on the dividing line between Ranks III and IV.

[c] Original sample, 604. The remainder were eliminated from consideration as having untraceable addresses, address of businesses or auto rental services, or addresses outside Los Angeles County.

not at issue. However, an examination of race track data fails to confirm these impressions. In order to clear the way for alternative interpretations, these popular views are considered in the next few paragraphs.

RECKLESSNESS AS HEAVY BETTING ON HIGH-RISK ALTERNATIVES

1. The evidence is that the larger the amount of a given bet, the more likely it will be wagered on a favorite—the horse with the statistically *smallest* risk. Approximately 50 percent of the money wagered at $100 Win windows is bet on favorites, while about 29 percent of all smaller bets is wagered on favorites. Hollywood Park has two $100 sellers windows which account for 7 percent of the total handle but 16 percent of the total amount bet on favorites.

2. At one point in our investigation, we interviewed 100 men about the way they bet. (These were mostly loners drawn as a quota sample from the Grandstand and Clubhouse areas.) Among the questions asked was, "When you win, do you usually rebet all of your winnings right away or what . . . ?" Eleven percent of the respondents said they rebet all winnings immediately; 3 percent do so eventually; 34 percent rebet a fixed amount or a fixed ratio only; and 41 percent simply answered "No" to the question. If these responses can be believed, it appears that these men (probably the most likely to be "reckless" of anyone at the track) handle their money fairly "conservatively."

3. A relatively small proportion of all bets made costs over $50. The figures showing the amounts of *money* (not numbers of tickets) wagered by size of bet are presented in Table 3. In interpreting this information, note

Table 3   PERCENT MONEY WAGERED BY DENOMINATION OF WAGER, HOLLYWOOD PARK, 1963[a]

Denomination	Percent Money
$100	6.7
$ 50	14.6
$ 10	21.2
$ 5	12.5
$ 2	22.8
$ 15[b]	5.2
$ 6[b]	9.4
Daily Double	7.2
Total	100.0

[a] First 48 days of 1963 program ($126,791,000).

[b] These are "Combination" or "Across the Board" bets in which a single ticket is purchased betting that a given horse will win, *and* place *and* show, the payoff varying with the horse's actual performance.

should be given of the fact that about half of the $100 bets are made by Turf Club members, and it is very doubtful that any substantial part of the remaining large bets are placed by people without financial means. Most people buy reasonably inexpensive tickets.

4. Dividing the total handle for the tracks in the United States by the number of attendees, the average amount wagered per day was found to be $77 in 1964 ($85 at Hollywood Park, California; about $98 at Aqueduct, New York). Even when the disproportionate influence of wealthy bettors is subtracted, the average still seems sizable. However, these figures are misleading when taken out of context because they include both rebet winnings and fresh money. It is possible to compute the minimum amount of fresh money that must be invested by supposing that *all* winnings are immediately reinvested, and under these fictional circumstances, about 25 percent of the total handle would have to be fresh money. It would be more accurate to accept Scarne's estimate that half of the total handle consists of fresh money.[11] When this is further divided by the number of races per day, the average amount of fresh money wagered per bettor per race turns out to be about $4.70 at Hollywood Park and $5.45 at Aqueduct.[12]

"MAKING A KILLING" AS BETTING ON HIGH-PAYOFF CHOICES

People tend, in fact, to bet on horses whose odds are relatively low with no possibility at all of paying large returns. At Hollywood Park in 1963, only 6-$\frac{1}{2}$ percent of the total Win bets were on winning horses ranking lower than fourth choice (and even less was wagered on losing horses ranking that low). Fifty-seven percent of the money was wagered on the first two public choices—36 percent on favorites alone, a statistically "proper" amount in terms of winning probabilities.[13] Long shots capable of reward-

---

[11] Scarne, *Scarne's Complete Guide to Gambling*, p. 57.

[12] For further discussion of the daily pattern of betting at race tracks, see William H. McGlothlin, "Stability of Choices among Uncertain Alternatives," *American Journal of Psychology*, 69 (1956), p. 406.

Of the total handle, an unknown proportion consists of bets made by nonattendees who send money to the track by two main channels. Often attenders are given money by friends to bet on horses previously selected; bookmakers occasionally send "layoff" money by way of professional couriers. In layoff betting, the bookmaker places a bet with another bookmaker or at the track at which a race is to be run so as to hedge his losses to his customers should their heavy favorite in that race win. Layoff networks are illegal, and they are periodically the objects of Congressional scrutiny. See *Gambling and Organized Crime*, Hearings before the Permanent Subcommittee on Investigations of the Committee on Government Operations, United States Senate, 87th Congress, 1961.

[13] Derived from R. C. Evenson and C. C. Jones, *The Way They Run* (Los Angeles, Cal.: Techno-Graphic Publications, 1964), p. 55. The average win payoffs of first, second, third, and fourth choices were (for $2 wagered): $5.75, $8.90, $11.80, and $15.83.

ing their backers with large payoffs must, by definition, rarely be selected by bettors. The existence of high-risk, high-payoff alternatives is, of course, a statistical necessity; observers of gambling should not assume that the fact that some people play long shots means that the practice is widespread.

ESCAPE FROM RATIONALITY

The rationality of the betting public may be inferred from the wisdom of its choice. (Rationality may be considered by some to apply mainly to the *prior* choice of whether or not to take any risk at all or even to play a game, an issue touched upon in the final section of this article. However, once the game has been chosen by the player, the efficiency of his play may be treated as a separate index of rationality.) While any individual race is an exception to the perfect operation of the rule, data from any large number of races show a perfect rank-order correlation between the average popularity of horses and their ability.[14] In other words, for the crowd as a whole, betting behavior is consistent with actual probabilities of winning.

In summary, the data suggest that horse playing is more characteristic of self-control and caution than of recklessness, more a participant sport than a spectator sport, and, as we shall argue below, more ritualistic than innovative.

INTERPRETATION

Several interpretations of gambling have appeared in the sociological literature which consider gambling to be a form of deviancy or a cultural aberration reactive to a context of *deprivation*. Four examples may be identified.

1. An "escape hatch" interpretation of gambling has been proposed by a number of observers. Gambling is thought to provide an "escape from the routine and boredom of modern industrial life in which the sense of creation and the 'instinct of workmanship' has been lost. 'Taking a chance' destroys routine and hence is pleasurable. . . ."[15] Bloch goes on to say that the "chance element" is fostered by certain types of social systems, namely those which base status on competitive, pecuniary standards.

2. A related view is that gambling represents a "safety valve." Here ". . . instead of turning against the original source of their deprivations and un-

---

[14] Literally any race could serve as an example of a violation of the general rule, but to take a prominent instance, the 1965 Kentucky Derby: the fourth choice won, and the favorite placed tenth. Fabricand, a mathematician, is so taken with the correlation between wagering and winning, that he devotes an entire chapter of his "textbook" to extolling the public's wisdom. Fabricand, *Horse Sense*, Chapter IV.

[15] Bloch, "The Sociology of Gambling," pp. 217–18.

fulfilled aspirations, bettors are relieved through gambling of some of their frustrations and, hence, are less likely to attack the existing class structure."[16]

3. Another interpretation is that gambling keeps alive a hope for social betterment among people "who are least capable of fulfilling their mobility aspirations through conventional avenues. . . ."[17] (This, by the way, is the only theory mentioned here which has been subjected to tests against quantitative, empirical data.)

4. Zola, in his study of lower-class clients of a tavern bookmaker, proposes that gambling occasionally allows bettors to "beat the system" through rational means and thus permits them to demonstrate to themselves and their associates that "they *can* exercise control and that for a brief moment they *can* control their fate. Off-track betting . . . denies the vagaries of life and gives these men a chance to regulate it."[18]

While these interpretations attempt to place gambling into appropriate social contexts, they treat rather lightly the differences in gambling behavior among various types of players. In the following discussion, we shall distinguish between the actions of middle-class and lower-class men (Grandstand and Clubhouse), middle-class and lower-class women, and upper-class attendees (members of the Turf Club).

MIDDLE-CLASS AND LOWER-CLASS MEN

I have suggested that a primary characteristic of horse playing is the intellectual exercise of selecting horses on which to wager. It may not be an overstatement to argue that, for middle- and lower-class men, it is the *central* element in the attraction of gambling. The exchange of money, of course, is essential, but not central. If the acquisition of money were the main goal, then gambling must be judged inefficient in comparison with other ways that are easier, faster, and more certain. The evidence suggests that most horse players concur in such a judgment: they tend to avoid high-risk horses; they do not invest much money per race (although it is not possible to determine from our data how seriously gambling may drain individual financial resources); they admit, when asked, to the uncertainties involved. I suggest that *the function of money,* in the context of the gambling institution, *is primarily to reify the decision-making process.* Money establishes the fact of a decisive act, and in its being lost or returned, it verifies the involvement of the bettor in the "action." Thus the player, even

[16] Tee, *Gambling in Sweden,* p. 108.

[17] *Ibid.*

[18] Irving Kenneth Zola, "Observations on Gambling in a Lower-Class Setting," *Social Problems,* 10 (1963), p. 360.

the "little guy," is brought into meaningful association with processes beyond himself. The impression of involvement and participation in events of importance is facilitated by the presence of large numbers of people, the bustle of general activity, the color and drama of the race, and the movement of money. This is why the more important races, measured in terms of purses and quality of horses, attract relatively more wagering. It is difficult to determine the conditions under which money is primarily an end in itself or a means to other ends—undoubtedly it is usually both. In any case, tote boards give prominence to the total amounts of money wagered in addition to information concerning the odds, and in casinos, the raw cash itself is conspicuous everywhere.[19]

Decision-making requires of players that they study the past performance records, ponder the tote board, consider reasonable lines of action, estimate probabilities, risk money, and collect the fruits of their action. Though on a smaller scale, *they emulate traditional, entrepreneurial roles* —weighing alternatives, making decisions, and signalling these decisions by attaching money to them.[20] Gambling is a game. It has many of the social psychological qualities which have been identified in other games by such observers as Piaget and G. H. Mead who point to the socializing and integrative functions of many forms of play. Horse players demonstrate to themselves their self-reliance and rationality by engaging in decision-making games made up primarily of conventional roles. Gambling, by this view, is less dysfunctional than it appears to be to those who judge it solely by standards linked to the production of goods.[21]

But, in indicating the conventional quality of much horse gambling, we have not accounted for its growing attraction for large numbers of middle-class and lower-class men. The answer appears to lie in the fact that opportunities to demonstrate self-reliance, independence, and decision-making ability are less and less available in other roles in which these men are involved. Occupational deprivations are usually assumed to be more acute among lower-class men, but with the development of white-collar industrial bureaucracies and the more recent emergence of automation, middle-

---

[19] Some experimental attempts have been made to investigate the "utility of money" apart from the "utility of gambling." See Halsey L. Royden, Patrick Suppes, and Karol Walsh, "A Model for the Experimental Measurement of the Utility of Gambling," *Behavioral Science* 4 (1959), pp. 11–18.

[20] Gregory Stone has written that some sport modes, "mark transformations of the play form into work—professional and otherwise subsidized athletes. . . . Second, there are sports that are transformations of work form into play." These latter are engaged in by "amateurs." See Gregory P. Stone and Marvin J. Taves, "Camping in the Wilderness," in Eric Larrabee and Rolf Meyersohn (eds.), *Mass Leisure* (Glencoe, Illinois: The Free Press, 1958), p. 296.

[21] That such standards are obsolete is suggested by John Kenneth Galbraith, *The Affluent Society* (Boston: Houghton Mifflin Co., 1958).

class men may also be increasingly separated from traditional sources of self-esteem.[22] If horse playing fills a decision-making void in a social system increasingly unable to supply alternatives, the future of gambling may be hypothesized to follow changes in the supply of alternative devices for affirming personal autonomy.

MIDDLE-CLASS AND LOWER-CLASS WOMEN

The gambling behavior of women must be explained differently. As shown above, women are more likely to make Show bets and are less likely to study the past performances in the *Racing Form*. It appears that the search for independence through decision-making activities is not the attraction here. A look at some characteristics of Show betting should provide a basis for interpretation.

Show bets pay a return, of some sort, a large percent of the time! Show bets on favorites pay 63 percent of the time—though in insufficient amounts to be profitable over a large number of such bets ($2.93 is the average payoff). Even horses ranking as low as fourth choice pay a return to Show bettors 36 percent of the time.[23] To appreciate the meaning of this, we may turn to studies of working-class women by Rainwater, who describes his subjects as leading dull, sparkless, unfulfilled lives in routinized settings bereft of social-emotional rewards but heavy with responsibility.[24] If this is an accurate picture of even a substantial portion of lower-class women today, we may link their gambling behavior to their particular deprivations. Thus in attending the races and in playing horses to Show, women experience frequent "rewards." The rewards may be small (too small to make up for the losses) and financial (rather than personal), but they can be symbolic and meaningful nevertheless. Show payoffs are frequent sparks against a background of dreariness.[25]

But what of *middle-class* women who appear to gamble in the same manner? As Komarovsky has shown, middle-class women are brought up to be

[22] For a prediction of the ways in which automation may be separating middle managers from the traditional decision-making satisfactions of supervision, see Harold J. Leavitt and Thomas L. Whistler, "Management in the 1980's," *Harvard Business Review*, Vol. 36 (Nov./Dec., 1958), p. 46. For evidence that their predictions are correct, see Jack B. Weiner, "Cutbacks in Middle Management," *Dun's Review and Modern Industry*, Vol. 84 (July, 1964).

[23] 1963 data reported in Evenson and Jones, *The Way They Run*, p. 55.

[24] Lee Rainwater, Richard P. Coleman, Gerald Handel, *Workingman's Wife* (New York: MacFadden-Bartell, Inc., 1962), Chapter III, "Inner Life and the Outer World." "In comparison with the middle-class wife, *reality is, in its ordinary presentation to her, flat, unvarnished and not highly differentiated.*" p. 52.

[25] Betty Friedan (*The Feminine Mystique*, New York: W. W. Norton & Co., 1957), has described middle-class women as suffering from many of the same deprivations as those of their lower-class sisters. If she is correct, their similar gambling behavior could be accounted for by the same factors.

more dependent than men on the authority of their parents. "Competitiveness, independence, dominance, aggressiveness, are all traits felt to be needed by the future head of the family . . ." while middle-class girls are sheltered and given fewer opportunities for independent action.[26] It is to be expected, then, that middle-class women will gamble in ways consistent with their training. They will make low-risk (Show) bets and will follow the "authority" of public handicappers rather than choices based on their own independent selection. As it happens, their gambling behavior is roughly similar to that of lower-class women, but for different reasons.

PRIVATE TURF CLUB MEMBERS

These people suffer few of the deprivations just discussed. As a group, they bet large amounts of money, they are the prime supporters of favorites, and their gambling occurs in a setting of conviviality, sociability, and exclusiveness. Both their gambling behavior and their sociality are consistent with Veblen's notions of "conspicuous leisure" or "conspicuous consumption." "In order to gain and to hold the esteem of men it is not sufficient merely to possess wealth or power. The wealth or power must be put in evidence, for esteem is awarded only on evidence."[27] Clearly, heavy wagering in the exclusive gathering of the Turf Club is wealth put in evidence. However, while it is important to spend money lavishly, it is easier and less disruptive to spend it in ways which suggest conformity to the choices of fellow Club members rather than a rejection of them—hence the tendency to support favorites. Furthermore, since conversation with companions precludes all but a relatively superficial examination of the *Racing Form* during the periods between races, the simplest choice available to the Club member is to "play the favorite!" (It is also true that because favorites win more often than other horses, bettors of large stakes may hope to reduce their "down-side risks," to borrow a phrase from Wall Street.)

Thus, difficult decisions, symbolic of independence, are *avoided* by the Club member, they are *irrelevant* to middle-class and lower-class women, and they are *pursued* by middle-class and lower-class men.

SUMMARY

The functions served by gambling have been described in terms of the social contexts relevant for three different categories of horse players. By an analysis of this sort, the issue of the desirability of gambling for urban soci-

[26] Mirra Komarovsky, "Functional Analysis of Sex Roles," *American Sociological Review*, XV (August, 1950), 508–16.

[27] Thorstein Veblen, *The Theory of the Leisure Class* (New York: Macmillan Co., 1899), p. 36.

ety becomes less one of blanket approval or disapproval but rather one of the evaluation of alternatives. What other cultural devices are available to middle-class and lower-class men that can be as effective in bolstering a sense of independence and self-determination and that so compellingly exercise mental skills and rational powers? What else might be done to brighten the lives of working-class women? How else might the wealthy engage in the open consumption of leisure in ways that would be as "harmless"?

In short, commercialized gambling offers to many people efficient means of enhanced self-esteem and gratification in a culture in which satisfactions are increasingly likely to be found in enterprises of consumption rather than production.

LUCILLE HOLLANDER BLUM

The Discothèque and the Phenomenon of Alone-Togetherness: A Study of the Young Person's Response to the Frug and Comparable Current Dances

If one were to characterize the middle sixties, an applicable term would be "speed." There are our satellites and jets. Less removed from day-to-day living are the technological wonders which enable even the evening meal to appear quickly through plug-in or push-button arrangements. There is the cocktail hour with atmosphere conducive to on-the-spot friendships. The pre-school child has accelerated by years the academic knowledge he is destined to acquire; while frequently youth, insofar as his numerous adult experiences are concerned, becomes in a sense father to the man.

Needless to point up, the countless scientific contributions—and thus advancements—have effected a society which is a stronghold of security. Paradoxically, however, the individuals within the society often appear beset with insecurities.

Compatible with and an apparent emergent of the tempo of the time is the discothèque. The discothèque may be defined as a night club where in-

Reprinted from *Adolescence*, 1, 4 (1966/67), 351–66, by permission of the publisher.

dividuals, gyrating to phonograph records, while away the hours. In the discothèque the live band is usually not part of the scene. The popularity of the discothèque has, in a sense, become so pervasive that its influence has reached into the world of fashion and even women's facial make-up.

In a somewhat recent popularly written article, Grafton[1] indicates that the motto of the "new age" is "Where's the action?" But more significant than the drive for action, dancers of the frug and related dances appear to reflect a feeling of loneliness. Grafton goes on to say, "The people of the new Jazz Age seem curiously alone even when they are in crowds—as they usually are."

The present writer has been similarly impressed by the conspicuous air of detachment with respect to individuals on the discothèque dance floor. It was in fact a chance occasion of observation of a group of young people dancing that suggested the present undertaking.

THE STUDY

The study is an attempt to determine elements of the discothèque which account for its widespread popularity. The study raises questions such as, What are some of the possible factors that motivate expressive behavior on the dance floor of the discothèque? What is there about the frug and its relatives that particularly appeals to the adolescent and young adult? What are some of the feelings experienced by participants during the dance?

METHOD OF COLLECTING DATA

A questionnaire was developed with intent to furnish answers to the aforementioned questions. The questionnaires were distributed personally to the would-be respondents by individuals who were briefly oriented in regard to the study. It was felt that personal distribution would insure greater return than distribution through the mails.

Approximately half of the questionnaires were distributed in discothèques frequented principally by young people. The other half of the distribution was in an urban college setting. An addressed and stamped envelope was provided for return of the completed questionnaire.

THE SUBJECTS

A total of 52 questionnaires were returned out of a distribution of 215. In the light of the exploratory nature of the study, the return was considered

[1] S. Grafton, "The Twisted Age." *Look* (December 15, 1964).

Table 1 Respondent's Age, Sex, Occupation and Father's Occupational Status

		Questionnaire Sample (N = 48)*
Sex	Male	31
	Female	17
Age	Range	13–24
	Median	18
Respondent's Occupation	Student	36
	Clerical services	6
	Not employed	6
Father's Occupation	Professional	15
	Managerial	15
	Clerks & kindred workers	6
	Skilled workers	8
	Not stated	4

*Four of the 52 completed questionnaires had responses which were inappropriate to the line of inquiry and therefore could not be included in the statistical analysis.

sufficient for analysis. The background data of the sample are given in Table 1.

Table 1 shows that in the sample there were almost twice as many boys as girls. The median age of the total group was 18 years. The table further indicates that the majority of the respondents were students. On the basis of reported occupations for fathers, 31 per cent had professional status while 31 per cent were wholesale or retail dealers, or held executive positions of one kind or another.

DANCE PRACTICE AND DANCE PREFERENCE

One aspect of the study was an attempt to determine whether the dance that the young person engages in differs from what he might prefer. Thus the questionnaire asked for a statement of the individual's favorite kind of dancing. The questionnaire also provided a scale on which to indicate degree of enjoyment in current popular dances such as the frug. (In subsequent discussion, the frug is intended to encompass the whole constellation of discothèque dances and also refers to the monkey, fish, hitchhike, etc.)

Responses with respect to "my favorite kind of dancing" were studied and categories were developed from the data and defined in terms of them. All responses were found classifiable under three catgories. The first two categories reflected contrasting speeds—slow and fast—while the third suggested that speed of rhythmic movement was influenced by current affective factors.

Table 2 SUBJECTS' STATEMENTS CONCERNING THEIR FAVORITE KIND OF DANCE

Category with Illustrations		Male N* %		Female N* %		Total N %	
1. Enjoyment in dancing per se or in lingering quality of rhythmic movement							
Expressions which tend to reflect pleasure in general in a dance experience, or desire to slacken pace, and/or statements of specific dance preferences.	"I just love to dance." "Very slow." "Normal ballroom."	15	50	5	32	20	43
2. Enjoyment from frenetic quality in rhythmic movement							
Expressions which tend to reflect pursuit of heightened excitement, and/or statements of specific dance preferences.	"Mad." "Fast, real fast." "The kind that makes me feel horny all over." "The monkey."	11	37	11	68	22	48
3. Preferences in rhythmic movement circumstantial							
Statements which tend to indicate dance preference influenced by partner, and/or present mood.	"Fast or slow depending on the person I'm with and my mood." "Slow—then monkeying."	4	13	—	—	4	9

* In two instances (1 male, 1 female), dance preference was not stated.

The descriptive categories with comments to illustrate the categories and percentages, are presented in Table 2.

A somewhat pertinent finding is that 50 per cent of the boys indicated preference for unhurried and relaxed dancing in contrast to dances such as the frug. Another finding which seems worthy of mention is that 68 per cent of the girls expressed preference for dances enlisting highly accelerated movements.

Study of the data dealing with the degree of enjoyment of the frug and its counterparts showed that 77 per cent of the boys and 100 per cent of the girls liked these dances "moderately" or "very much." When the two categories described above were considered separately and in terms of sex differences, it was found that 53 per cent of the boys had only moderate liking for the dance and 26 per cent liked them very much.

With respect to the girls, a conspicuous reverse order occurred, in that 23 per cent of the girls liked the dances moderately well and 71 per cent liked them very much.

The findings suggest a sex difference when the data are considered from the points of view both of stated favorite dance and intensity of pleasure derived from the current popular dance. It appears that the boys incline to a greater degree than the girls toward dances which involve a somewhat easy, rhythmic movement.

Thus the findings indicate that boys may experience somewhat ambivalent feelings toward dances such as those performed in the discothèque. However, the girls' stated preference for speeded-up dances, regardless of the nature of the current popular dance, seems to indicate that it has a special appeal for female youth.

The abandon which is associated with dances such as the frug allows the girl or young woman to release with impunity a variety of strong feelings which our society might otherwise require her to suppress. The boy can give expression to these feelings through such sanctioned avenues as intensive sports. Henry,[2] in his discussion of differences between boys and girls in the United States, indicates that the faithfulness of boys to sports is a striking characteristic of American life.

Parsons,[3] in considering sex differences in our structure, states, "It seems to be a definite fact that girls are more apt to be relatively docile, to conform in general according to adult expectations, to be 'good' whereas boys are more apt to be recalcitrant to discipline and defiant of adult authority and expectations."

Again, Jersild[4] with respect to release of aggressive feelings points out that the differences between girls and boys are probably more apparent in their public behavior than in the privacy of their inner lives. "The common feeling (and expectation) is that boys are, on the whole, more openly aggressive than girls."

PARENTAL DISCIPLINE AND THE DANCE

The next step in study of the data was to attempt to determine the influence of parental discipline on the child's choice of a favorite kind of dancing. The respondents were requested to indicate the degree of discipline of each of his parents. A five point scale with categories ranging from "very strict" to "very permissive" was provided in the questionnaire.

It was found that 94 per cent of the subjects perceived at least one parent

[2] J. Henry, *Culture Against Man* (New York: Alfred A. Knopf, Inc. & Random House, Inc., 1965).

[3] T. Parsons, "Age and Sex in the Social Structure of the United States," *Personality* (New York: Alfred A. Knopf, 1953), 363–75.

[4] A. Jersild, *Child Psychology* (Englewood Cliffs, New Jersey: Prentice-Hall, Inc., 1960).

as "neither strict nor permissive," "permissive," or "very permissive." In 40 per cent of the cases, the respondents saw both parents in agreement as to disciplinary approach. Moreover, in instances of agreement, all responses came under the three aforementioned categories.

In 31 per cent of the cases, at least one parent was reported as "strict." There was only one response under the category, "very strict."

Analysis of the data indicated no difference between boys and girls in the way they perceived their parents. Further, no relationship was found between parents' disciplinary approach and the child's dance preference. The latter finding held for girls and boys in regard both to mother and father.

It might be concluded from the findings that the subjects tended to see both parents either in a kind of neutral zone of discipline or inclined toward permissiveness. It also appears that the young person's dance preference is influenced by factors other than the quality of discipline in the home.

RELEASE, LURE OF THE DISCOTHÈQUE

The questionnaire was further designed to yield an estimate of various feelings that the subject experienced as a participant of dances such as the frug. A check list was provided and the respondent was requested to mark all categories that described his feelings in connection with the dance.

Responses ranged from 0 to 4 per cent with a total of 77 responses for the group. Highest frequencies were found in regard to "Release or abandon" with 47 per cent of boys' responses and 28 per cent of girls' responses under the category. On the basis of the report, the feeling of release in discothèque dances made up 39 per cent of total responses.

It would seem that the boys' lead over the girls in actual *feeling* or release could stem from differences in sex roles. The earlier finding was that the girls designated dances with heightened movement as a first choice. However, society's expectation in regard to the girls' behavior in public might tend to be an inhibiting factor for certain feelings and not for others.

It was interesting to note that 25 per cent of the girls' total responses were under the category "Seductiveness" while only 2 per cent of boys' total feelings were thus characterized. That the present-day social structure gives the girl the green light, so to speak, in the aforementioned area of feeling is suggested by Parsons.[5] He points up a less sharply-defined feminine role than existed previously. "The rigidity of this line has progressively broken down through infiltration into the respectable sphere of elements of what may be called again the glamor pattern, with the emphasis on a specifically

---

[5] Parsons, "Age and Sex in the Social Structure of the United States."

Table 3   FEELINGS OF PARTICIPANTS DURING DISCOTHÈQUE DANCING

| | Male | | Female | | Total | |
Category	N	%	N	%	N	%
Release or abandon	21	47	9	28	30	39
Sexual arousal	8	18	5	16*	13	17
Conformity with world of young people	13	29	5	16*	18	23
Defiance of parental standards	—	—	—	—	—	—
Physical closeness to partner	2	4	5	16*	7	9
Seductiveness	1	2	8	25	9	12

* (15.6)

feminine form of attractiveness which on occasion involves directly sexual patterns of appeal. One important expression of this trend lies in the fact that many of the symbols of feminine attractiveness have been taken over directly from the practices of social types previously beyond the pale of respectable society."

There are two further findings of interest. Frequencies for boys under the category, "Conformity with the world of young people," were almost twice as high as frequencies for girls (29 per cent and 16 per cent respectively). Too, there were no responses for boys or girls under the category "Defiance of parental standards." Table 3 shows the group's responses in regard to the categories describing feelings in the questionnaire.

THE FRUG AND PRESENT-DAY REALITY

An optional section at the end of the questionnaire provided the subjects opportunity to make additional comments concerning the dances under consideration. Fourteen boys and 10 girls responded. The content of responses made to the open-end question was analyzed, and categories were developed from the comments, and defined in terms of them.

There was a total of 133 responses. However, where the comments by a respondent were a series and related to each other, the comments were treated as a single concept and counted as one response. Thus, the final categories emerged from a total of 70 responses.

Study of the data showed that the subjects' statements fell into four groups which were given titles defining the comments in each group. Further analysis indicated that the four specific categories could be placed under two major classifications. Headings which seemed most suitable were "The Frug and Withdrawal Response," and "The Frug and Approach Response."

The classification, "Withdrawal Response," related to all comments which reflected the subjects' attempt, in frugging, to shake off the accul-

Table 4 COMMENTS FROM OPEN-END QUESTION CONCERNING PARTICIPATION IN DISCOTHÈQUE DANCE

Category with Illustrations

1. *The Frug and Withdrawal Response*

Comments which tend primarily to reflect attempt to shake off the acculturated self and thereby to relax from societal stimuli.

  a. *Alienation from intellectual function and interpersonal relationship*

Comments which express search for temporary surcease of conscious thought, need to negate the mere presence of a partner, and/or to protect against specific involvement, and sexual arousal.

"The more we frug, the more South Vietnam, lung cancer and getting into your father's college fade into the distance."

"My mind is a blank. I feel a hundred million miles away."

"The feeling is of complete thoughtlessness. The Buddhists would have called it Nirvana."

"I am enjoying these dances because they are done without any contact with the partner, thus giving me complete freedom to move as I choose with the rhythms."

"When we dance to a slow record, we know that we will dance locked together and that we probably will be sexually aroused, but after the record is over, we calm down."

"Also there is no physical contact because you are at least five feet from your partner."

  b. *Defense against outside interference with climate conducive to release of physical response.*

Comments which indicate need for situation protective to expression of primitive behavior.

"To sum, I think that the society that was partly created for us, but is mainly our fault, is so tense that it is necessary for us to senselessly quiver in a steamed sweaty gym on Friday nights."

"Besides there is nothing I enjoy more than working up a sweat dancing."

"It exhausts any built-up strength due to anger or anxiety."

Table 4   (Continued)

"In other cases these dances imitate the movements of animals."

2. *The Frug and Approach Response*

Comments which tend primarily to indicate confrontation of society and exercise of intellectual faculties.

   a. *Critique: The dance*

Comments which assess the frug or its counterparts, and perceive it in disrepute, a gateway to the in-group and influenced by degree of partner acknowledgment.

"The dances you mention are only bad dances and will soon die out."

"I know I have commented when watching others that some people look like idiots when doing these dances (I guess myself included)."

"If one is to think later about the frug, etc., there is a wonderful perverted sense of security in knowing that all of your contemporaries frug."

"The slow dance brings partners closer together both physically and in the mind."

   b. *Perception: The authorities*

Comments which indicate that the young person sees the older adult as a "transgressor" too or as a non-constructive intruder, motivated by need to exploit, snoop and otherwise demean youth.

"Adults are looking for hidden meanings that are not present and never will be."

"The only conformity present is by old people doing the dances in order to feel young again."

"I do not believe these dances can be reasoned to be defiance of parents for not only teen-agers participate."

"Although children express sexual urges in-behind-the-bathroom-door, adults over 40 reveal them in lascivious glances on the beach."

"I can't see how anyone can find anything lewd or arousing about the dances and I think that those who look for such things are trying to find hidden meanings in places that don't exist."

turated self, so to speak, and thereby to relax from societal stimuli. "Approach Response," on the other hand, related to comments which tended to indicate the subjects' confrontation of society and thereby exercise of intellectual faculties such as perceiving and judging.

Description of categories used in classifying the comments and items to illustrate the specific categories are presented in Table 4. It was found that the combined frequency distribution for boys and girls was approximately equal in regard to the four specific categories.

Statements categorized under "withdrawal behavior," indicate that the young person has discovered a particular value inherent in dances of the discothèque. The data indicate that in a substantial number of instances the frug provides a kind of attenuated state of the faculties of cerebral function. There seems a delirious sense of freedom in the unrelatedness that was reported to occur when primitive feelings take over. One subject referred to his state of complete thoughtlessness as Nirvana. However, quite contrary to absorption with a supreme spirit, the data in the present study suggest a striving toward oneness with the self.

Grafton in his description of the "twisted age" notes the withdrawal aspect of the dancer on the discothèque floor. "Eyes appear to be turned inward. The partners, if they move their feet at all, may wander away from each other, lost in their private transports." Grafton adds, "They look as if their bodies are screaming."

More specifically, the data indicate that dances such as the frug offer temporary retreat from a complex environment with which youth seems to feel inadequately equipped to cope. For one thing, the young person seems confused by contradictions such as provision for permissiveness in an atmosphere where there are at the same time recognizable inherent rules concerning restraint.

The discothèque dance floor which affords distance—physically and affectively—between partners is a compromise adjustment in response to difficult day-to-day reality. One respondent with reference to the frug stated, "I feel free from the world of morals." Another said, "This basic self-expression offers young people an outlet for pent-up sexual energies that might otherwise take a more violent course." But, too, there were comments which reflect an ever-present threat of annihilation through atomic warfare, and felt pressures such as those of parents, for success through high grades, advanced education, and perhaps "getting into your father's college."

Statements which have been categorized as "approach behavior" reflect what the respondent saw when he moved closer to the conventional society and paused to assay it.

Objective judgment came to the fore. Thus, the individual appeared to recognize that acceptance in the "youth culture" is an important factor motivating his participation in the dance. He wants his contemporaries to consider him "a good Joe" and not "a square."

Also, with distance from the discothèque, the respondent was critical. He expressed disapprobation in regard to his "fun" world and his own role in it. But in an equal number of instances and in statements bearing a kind of vituperative quality, the subject communicated how he perceived the older adult. It might be mentioned that per cent of responses for boys under the category, "Perception, the authorities" was more than twice as high as that for girls (28 per cent and 12 per cent respectively of total responses). This finding appears in accord with society's expectation, namely that boys are more openly aggressive than girls and thus perhaps freer to air their grievances.

It was found that a considerable number of statements in the aforementioned category defended the young person's behavior by pointing up inappropriate behavior in the older adult. There were, for example, comments such as the one in Table 4 which acknowledges surreptitious sexual practices in the child and then reminds us that the over-40 adult casts "lascivious glances on the beach."

Moreover, the data point up that when interest on the part of the older adult is forthcoming, it tends to be of a negative kind. On the basis of their comments, it appears that the subjects perceive figures in authority as exploitative, prying, and, in general, relating to youth in a non-constructive or non-supportive way.

The following comments by a 20 year-old youth were written in the optional section of the questionnaire. "This year the dances young people do are the ones above, next year, it'll be some others. The teen-age market is the largest in this country and the opportunists in the entertainment field just are inventing some new music to dance a new dance to, so they will keep their profits high." He added, "I just do it for fun." This response seems to communicate an anticipation of change inevitable even in the "fun" world to which the young person must, from time to time, retreat.

RECAPITULATION

This study is exploratory and is designed to obtain information on factors which constitute the current appeal of the discothèque. The particular population focused upon in the study is the adolescent and young adult.

A questionnaire was developed in an attempt to obtain relevant answers. Approximately half of the questionnaires were distributed in discothèques frequented principally by young persons.

The sample consisted of 48 subjects. In the light of the exploratory nature of the study, the return was considered sufficient for analysis. The median age of the total group was 18 years.

One aspect of the study was an attempt to determine possible differences between dance practice and dance preference. Findings show that practically all the subjects participate in dances such as the frug and enjoy the experience "moderately" or "very much." However, a substantial number of the male respondents favor dances characterized by unhurried, easy rhythmic movement. Thus, it appears that boys may have somewhat ambivalent feelings in regard to the discothèque type of dance.

Girls, on the other hand, indicate strong preference for dances with highly accelerated movements. Therefore, the frug and its counterparts has special appeal to female youth. The findings suggest that the girl sees in the discothèque opportunity to release, with society's sanction, a variety of strong feelings which under most other circumstances she is required to suppress or repress.

A further step in the study was an attempt to determine parental discipline and its influence insofar as the subjects' favorite kind of dancing is concerned.

Analysis of the data showed that the respondents tend to perceive both parents either in a neutral zone of discipline or inclined toward permissiveness. It was further found that dance preferences were quite independent of home discipline.

Another line of inquiry was with respect to various feelings experienced by the individual as a participant of dances such as the frug. Findings show "Release or abandon" with highest frequencies. Study of the data in terms of sex differences pointed up a considerable lead in frequencies for girls in regard to "Seductiveness." Boys, on the other hand, feel more inclined than girls toward "conformity" with peers. "Defiance of parental standards" appears to figure negligibly in connection with discothèque dances.

A final step in securing data was an open-end question. The respondents were free to communicate thoughts and feelings beyond what was obtainable in the structured questionnaire. Categories were developed from the data and defined in terms of them. Responses fell into two major classifications, "The Frug and Withdrawal Response," and "The Frug and Approach Response." Comments in the category describing "withdrawal behavior" indicate essentially the young person's attempt to "shake off the acculturated self and thereby relax from societal stimuli." Comments categorized as "approach behavior" indicate the individuals' "confrontation of society and exercise of intellectual faculties." Subcategories define components of withdrawal and approach responses. Illustrations are presented. Findings in general suggest that the frug with its offshoots was shaped and is sustained by the needs of today's adolescent and young adult.

Several of the respondents in the present study pointed out that they do not differ from young people in years past in their participation in the dance currently popular. They state that earlier, for example, there were the Charleston and the Lindy Hop.

Observers with a professional eye, however, detect a difference between the atmosphere of the discothèque and the dance floor of an earlier period. Grafton,[6] for instance, states that the present jazz age is like one seen in "a distorting mirror."

Technological advances and industrial development have created differences in our culture since the days of the Charleston. And the difference has in turn, brought about changes in the individual. Henry,[7] in his description of contemporary America, indicates that an outcome of the "technological driven-ness," which characterizes our culture, is change in values. Henry indicates that increasingly the shift is from super ego values (the values of self restraint) to id values (the values of self-indulgence). "The loss of self and the rise of the values of the id have combined to create a glittering modern pseudo-self, the high-rising standard of living, waxing like the moon in a Midsummer Night's Dream of impulse release and fun."

Findings in the present study tend to indicate that the individual's self-indulgence and impulse release may at times serve to protect super ego values: The abandon which is experienced in dances such as the frug appears a remedy for pent-up tension which—as one subject indicated—might otherwise take a course incompatible with the "world of morals."

Henry[8] points up that psychoanalysis has come to the fore in America as an outcome of numberless selves being ground up by the technological system. On the basis of findings in the present study, the frug is also a therapeutic process—strenuous, speeded-up, and contrary to theories of psychoanalysis, inclined to effect ego withdrawal. It is the excursion away from the outside world that gives the individual the bearing of detachment and loneliness. It is perhaps his thought—however peripheral—of group relatedness that creates the phenomenon of alone-togetherness.

Finally, it would seem that some of the findings in the study have implications with respect to persons consciously beyond the adolescent and young adult periods, who have hitched on to youth's discothèque band wagon.

[6] Grafton, "The Twisted Age."

[7] Henry, *Culture Against Man.*

[8] *Ibid.*

7
problems and change

SIDNEY H. ARONSON

The Sociology of the Telephone

Amid the welter of recent writing on the phenomena of "modernization" and social change scant attention has been granted to technological innovations themselves as direct sources of new human needs and behavior patterns. Yet it seems apparent that the kind of modernization experienced by the Western world, and more specifically the United States, over the past century is intimately tied, both as cause and effect, to the availability of the telephone as an easy, efficient and relatively inexpensive means of communication. This may seem only to restate the obvious, yet how rarely is the telephone so much as mentioned in contemporary discussions of social change or modernization?[1] This is the more remarkable as the process of communication, generically considered, has come to be recognized as *the* "fundamental social process" without which society and the individual self could not exist. Communication-in-general (if such a thing can be imagined) has been much studied but the meaning and the consequence for individuals of being able to pick up something called a telephone and rapidly transmit or receive messages have been all but ignored. As with so many other aspects of social life that which we take most for granted usually needs to be most closely examined.

This inattention to the social consequences of the telephone is the more surprising still in light of the importance usually attached to the presence or absence of mass media of written communication in explaining differences among societies. It has become usual to distinguish between pre-industrial and industrial societies, each type manifesting distinctive characteristics partly attributable to the widespread dissemination and accessibility (by way of general literacy) of the printed word. It is surely conceivable that the presence or absence of a system of two-way oral-aural communication may account for equally important differences between types of societies, that the distinction between a society with and one with-

Reprinted from the *International Journal of Comparative Sociology*, 12, 3 (1971), 153–67, E. J. Brill, Leiden, Holland, by permission of the publisher.

I am grateful to Professor Richard Greenbaum of John Jay College for his considerable contribution to this article.

[1] The number of telephones present in a country is frequently used as an indicator of "modernization" by sociologists but the process by which telephone communications contributed to the changes implied by that term are not considered.

out a developed telephone system may be as great as that between one with and one without a developed system of printed media or even as great as that between a literate and a non-literate society. A necessarily brief examination of the history of the telephone in the United States will support these assertions.

Whether a matter of social structure or of "national character" American society not only fosters technological innovation but typically embraces it with alacrity once it occurs. The introduction and almost immediate acceptance of the telephone in the United States after 1876 is characteristic. That Americans at that particular moment in history wanted to or "needed" to communicate in new and faster ways facilitated the transformation of their behavior and the structure and character of their society.[2] The remainder of this paper will present a brief survey of some of the areas of American life where the "modernizing" impact of the telephone has been most pervasive and obvious. If the discussion that follows may seem, by implication at least, to give to the telephone an unwarranted primacy as an agent of modernization such an overstatement of the case can be justified as an understandable reaction to ninety-odd years of scholarly neglect, not to say disdain. The telephone, like modernization itself, has insinuated itself into even the most remote crevices of American life; the ubiquity of its ringing as an accompaniment to our daily lives can perhaps best be compared to the ever present tolling of church bells in a Medieval village or *bourg*. The railroad, the electric light, the automobile, even the bathroom —not to speak of the more dramatic radio and television—have all been granted their moment on the scholarly stage, to be examined more or less intensively, more or less dispassionately. The time seems overripe for a comprehensive examination of the slighted telephone. Nor is the story by any means all told. The recent development of a "picturephone" which adds the visual capability of television to the traditional telephone promises to make a new chapter in the history of Bell's creation as well as a new dimension to human communication.

THE TELEPHONE AND THE ECONOMY

What can be said regarding the most pervasive effects of the telephone on the organization and conduct of American economic life, aside from the obvious rise of the American Telephone and Telegraph Company itself as an economic monolith?

Perhaps the most conspicuous of these effects has been the dramatic con-

[2] This statement should not be taken as advancing a monocausal theory of social changes predicated on the idea of direct technological determinisms. Far from it. Mutual independence has always characterized technological and social change.

traction in the time needed to establish communication, transmit orders and consummate business transactions, what for the sake of brevity, may be called "transaction time." By bringing two or more persons, often separated by long distances, into direct and immediate communication the telephone eliminated much of the time which otherwise would have been spent in writing letters or traveling to meetings. Telephoning did not, of course, replace written communication and face-to-face meetings; it rather supplemented them and altered somewhat their character. The telephone greatly speeded the pace and the responsiveness of business at the same time that it tended to change the relations among businessmen from those between whole personalities to those between differentiated, functionally specific "roles," a fact which may help to explain the almost compulsive informality and conviviality that obtains when businessmen finally do come together face-to-face. This suggests that the increased efficiency of doing business may have been paid for, in part, by a decrease in the personal and emotional satisfactions of business activity. We are, for example, all aware that the insistent ringing of the telephone usually takes priority even over an ongoing face-to-face business conversation. The significance of this ordering of priorities needs to be examined as does the actual extent to which various kinds of businesses are dependent for their conduct on telephonic conversation.[3]

In addition the telephone made possible the efficient organization and operation of large-scale, integrated, mass production manufacturing enterprises. In the production of automobiles, for example, a single plant may comprise a hundred or more buildings sprawled over several hundred acres and employing thousands of workers. It is hard to see how the communications necessary for the effective coordination of such aggregates of men and machines could be arranged economically and efficiently without the use of the telephone. No previous mode of communication was able to combine the latter's speed with its simplicity and economy of operation. Had major industrial expansion come to an America lacking the telephone it would surely have resulted in physical arrangements very different from those we know today. It may be more than coincidence that Henry Ford's introduction of assembly line production in 1913 came at a time when telephone technology had already attained a sophisticated level.[4]

If each telephone were considered as a replacement for a human message

[3] On the extent to which American businessmen hastened to take advantage of the telephone see, American Telephone and Telegraph Company, *National Telephone Directory* (New York, October, 1894), (New York, October, 1897); Department of Commerce and Labor, United States Bureau of the Census, *Special Reports: Telephones: 1907* (Washington, 1910), 74–75; Herbert N. Casson, *The History of the Telephone* (Chicago, 1910), 204–11.

[4] Arthur Pound, *The Telephone Idea* (New York, 1926), 42–43.

carrier and further consider that the average number of telephone calls completed in the United States during 1968 was 426,200,000 *per day,* at least a vague idea can be gained of the effects of telescoping "transaction time" and of the extent to which the telephone system is the life-blood of the American economy.[5] Of course, not all these telephone calls were business calls and not all those that were were *necessary,* in a rational sense, to the conduct of business. The existence of a convenient, easy and inexpensive means of communication doubtless increases the perceived "need" of people to communicate with others as well as their opportunity so to do. This latter consideration raises the rather different question of the psychological as well as social functions served by the telephone, a question to be raised below.

The extent to which the telephone facilitated the consolidation of American corporate enterprise in the post–Civil War period should not be overlooked. The years from 1875 to 1914, during which telephone use spread rapidly, witnessed the growth of giant corporations and the formation of trusts, despite the passage of the Sherman Antitrust Act in 1890. The telephone possessed obvious superiorities over the telegraph in the planning and coordinating of business activity, especially where delicate and, at times dubiously legal manipulations were involved. It was far easier to use, required no intermediaries to encode and decode its message (thus necessarily making them privy to its contents and impairing the secrecy of the communication) and, perhaps most important, it left no written or printed record which might later prove embarrassing or incriminating.[6] Secrecy could be assured by face-to-face meetings but rail travel was far slower and more uncomfortable than a phone conversation and eventually phone lines connected many more points than rail lines.[7] It is suggestive that E. H. Harriman, one of the master trust-builders of the period, had

---

[5] These calls were distributed as follows: 330,200,000 were handled by the Bell System —American Telephone and Telegraph and its subsidiaries—and 96,000,000 by the Independent telephone companies. The figure does not include calls made between two extensions connecting through the same switchboard, but only calls between independent numbers. The total number of such calls in the United States in 1968 is in the trillions. *Statistical Abstracts of the United States* (Washington, 1969), 495.

[6] These advantages were stressed in advertisements appearing in the telephone directory: "'Despatch and Privacy' are among the important features of Long Distance Telephone Service. All subjects may be described without reserve." *National Telephone Directory* (1897), 733. Virtually every advertisement in that directory was directed toward educating businessmen of the benefits to be derived from using the telephone and especially the long distance lines.

[7] "To Omaha and return in five minutes by LONG DISTANCE TELEPHONE."; "The Mail is quick, the Telegraph is quicker but the LONG DISTANCE TELEPHONE is instantaneous and you don't have to wait for an answer."; "The Long Distance Telephone Furnishes the only satisfactory Substitute for a personal Interview." *Ibid.,* 565, 715, 723. This certainly implies that the use of the telephone during this period was substituted for much business-related rail travel. See also, *Special Reports: Telephones: 1907,* 75.

one hundred telephones in his mansion at Arden, New York, sixty of which were directly linked to long distance lines. An obviously naive magazine writer referred to Harriman's atachment to the talking machine by writing: "He is a slave to the telephone." Harriman replied, "Nonsense, it is a slave to me."[8]

Another major impact of the telephone on the business life of the nation may be seen in its effect on the development and expansion of the stock, bond, and commodity markets. The widespread use of the telephone probably added to the short-run instability of such markets, but at the same time, it permitted, for the first time, their development on a truly national scale and the widespread dissemination of stock ownership. The continuous spreading and the ever increasing efficiency (at least until the decade of the 1960's) of telephone communication (supplemented by the private wire system of brokerage houses) means that financial information is continuously available and that even the most modest order will be executed on the floor of a major exchange no more than a few minutes after it has been given by the customer to his broker. The history of the Wall Street market crash of 1929 only proves, among other things, that the telephone, as every other technological advance, can be a curse as well as a blessing, depending on the circumstances.[9]

By the same token the telephone eventually affected the buying and selling, both wholesale and retail, of almost all goods and services produced by the economy, although these effects have never been uniformly distributed. Even the most cursory examination of the first telephone directories illustrates that very soon after its invention much of American business took advantage of the new electronic wonder. Early directories facilitated the conduct of commerce by printing the kind of business or trade of the subscriber (a foreshadowing of the yellow pages). Indeed, a national telephone directory of 1894 which included all the customers of American Telephone and Telegraph in the United States who were connected by metallic circuit lines with its long distance system, is a summary of the nation's economic activities and gives evidence that virtually every product and service in the economy could be ordered by telephone.[10] Not only did the telephone stimulate trade by making buying and selling more convenient, it also

---

[8] Casson, *History of the Telephone,* 205–6.

[9] As early as 1910 Casson could write: "As for stockbrokers of the Wall Street species, they transact practically all their business by telephone. In their stock exchange stand six hundred and forty-one booths, each one the terminus of a private wire. A firm of brokers will count it an ordinary year's talking to send fifty thousand messages; and there is one firm which last year sent twice as many." *History of the Telephone,* 205. The even greater dependence of the stock market on telephone communications nowadays can be appreciated from the fact that daily phone volume on Wall Street in 1968 averaged 1,140,000 outgoing calls, to say nothing of incoming calls. *The Wall Street Journal,* March 3, 1969.

[10] *National Telephone Directory,* 1894.

furnished a medium for an incalculable but staggeringly large amount of mouth-to-mouth advertising, a most effective way of stimulating wants.[11] That telephone communication was a superb medium for advertising was because early users of the telephone tended to act exactly like those who later got their first radio or television receivers, that is they used the electronic wonder incessantly. Some critics of the telephone wrote of "telephone fiends," criminals, who stole time; others discovered the disease of "telephonics," a dread malady, which could visit an entire community.[12]

The central role of the telephone in commerce could also be seen in the custom in some businesses for contractual arrangements entered into over the telephone to have the same binding quality as written and signed contracts.

Professionals such as doctors and lawyers also listed occupations along with their names, addresses, and telephone numbers in the directories. A complete study of the impact of the telephone will have to include the question of the effects of the phone on the conduct of professional practice; for example, how did the use of the telephone affect the patterns of non-hospital medical care and the doctor-patient relationship? How did it affect the ways in which professional practitioners attracted clients and the size of the area from which they drew them?

The telephone and its related institutions summoned into being many novel services. The enterprising developer of the first central telephone exchange, George W. Coy, formerly a proprietor of a messenger service in New Haven, provided a free telephone to the United States Signal Service in that city and then advertised: "Anyone having a telephone can make inquiries as to the weather, temperature, and barometer."[13] The provision of time reports, answering services for businesses and individuals and wake-up calls for the indolent also became available in a number of cities.[14]

Changes in the occupational structure can be traced to the introduction and spread of the telephone and are not confined to those directly associated with the development, building, operation and servicing of the system itself. One occupational variant created by the telephone was, appropriately enough, that of "call girl," while that of messenger doubtless suffered serious attrition, though not total extinction.

[11] Pound, *The Telephone Idea*, 44.

[12] Minna T. Antrim, "Outrages of the Telephone," *Lippincotts' Monthly Magazine*, Vol. 84 (July, 1909), 125–26; Maude A. White, "Those Telephonics'. Have You One in Your Home?" *Delineator*, Vol. 96 (May, 1920).

[13] Fred DeLand, "Notes On The Development of Telephone Service," *Popular Science Monthly* LXX (January, 1907), 51.

[14] As early as 1909, for example, the Chicago Telephone Company had 60,000 requests per day for the time, the largest number coming in the hour between 7:00 and 8:00 A.M. In the same period, the New York Telephone Company was averaging 80,000 "Time please" calls. Katherine M. Schmitt, "I Was Your Old 'Hello Girl'," *The Saturday Evening Post*, Vol. 208 (July 12, 1930), 121.

Finally, no exploration of the likely economic effects of the telephone would be complete without suggesting that the instrument's services to illegitimate business enterprises have probably been as great (and as profitable to the phone companies) as its services to more legitimate activities.[15] The existence of organized, corporate crime as we are afflicted with it today, is just as inconceivable without the telephone as more morally acceptable corporate empires. Gambling of all types (but especially horse racing), prostitution (the "call girl" again) and drug dealing could probably not exist at their present levels of activity and profitability in the absence of the telephone. And if legitimate brokers and salesmen solicit customers over the telephone so do swindlers, "conmen" and "boiler-room" operators of all sorts. The telephone as an instrument of communication is morally neutral, though the uses to which it is put are surely not.

THE TELEPHONE AND MASS COMMUNICATIONS

From modest beginnings the telephone led ultimately to the development of institutions and instruments, most notably the radio, for the instantaneous dissemination of news, entertainment and "culture" to the masses. Institutions of mass communication are a defining characteristic of a modern industrial society and in America those institutions arose out of the uses to which the telephone was put and the new needs to which those uses gave rise. It often happens that a successful new means of satisfying an existing need gives rise in its turn to still further needs, the perception or even the existence of which were necessarily screened from awareness by the original unfulfilled need. To put the matter in epigrammatic terms we may say that a kind of Parkinson's Law operates in the matter of needs, as elsewhere in social life, that "needs" expand to equal the possibilities of satisfying them. The history of the telephone provides an example of the continuing cycle of social change that operates when the satisfaction of one "need" leads to the generation of new "needs" and new social arrangements for their fulfillment. Let us now look at some of the effects of the telephone on the institutions of communication in American society.

The perfection of the telephone represented a giant stride toward the goal of the immediate transmission of information, the virtual elimination of the time lapse between the occurrence of an event and public knowledge of it. The invention of the telegraph a generation before had been an advance toward that goal but by comparison with the telephone the older device was slow, expensive, involved and restricted in its use.

[15] J. Flynt, "Telephone and Telegraph Companies as Allies of Criminal Pool Rooms," *Cosmopolitan*, Vol. 43 (May, 1907), 50–57.

Mass communication by way of the telephone at first developed informally, rather as a by-product of its primary uses than according to any deliberate design, but in time those services became formalized and continuous and came to be deemed indispensable to the functioning of American society.

From an early period local telephone operators, who may be visualized as occupying the center of a more or less wide ranging communications network, took on the role of informal news broadcasters. They were able to play this role not only because of their central position in the communications network but because the demands of their job were still modest enough to leave them considerable free time during the working day. In the role of informal newscasters they provided information of general interest to people in their locality such as reports of fires and floods, police bulletins and missing-person reports, as well as specialized services to physicians, among others.[16] The end result of this informal practice was that many subscribers came to feel that they had the right to demand and receive such information from telephone operators. The public's interpretation of the phone company's "information" service so broadened that the latter eventually found it necessary to restrict that service to the narrow range it covers today.[17] But by the time public abuse of the information service had combined with the sharp increase in telephone traffic to end the informal newscasting role of the telephone operator (except perhaps in isolated rural areas, where she may continue to play that role even now) the direction of still newer communications arrangements was already becoming apparent.

These early informal applications of the telephone suggested to various imaginative and enterprising people the possibility of a more formal arrangement for satisfying the rising demand for information and for other messages of general interest and entertainment value. This thought led in time to the transformation of the telephone from an informal source of news into a new institution which, for a time, challenged the supremacy of the newspaper as a source of information and ultimately led to a completely new mode of communication.

It was Alexander Graham Bell himself who first demonstrated the tele-

[16] It was not unusual in the period to 1900 for operators to take calls for the service of physicians who were out on home visits. These doctors would then call in and be given their messages. Still later, doctors became so accustomed to using the phone to keep in touch with patients that a court held the Southern Telephone Company for damages when an operator failed to complete a call to a doctor sought for a sick patient who subsequently died. "Failure to Reach Physician by Telephone Responsibility of Telephone Company for Death of Patient," *American Law Review*, Vol. 46 (July 1912), 596–98. On operators as informal news broadcasters see, "When the Hello-Girl Tries Her Hand at Detective Work," *Literary Digest*, Vol. 195 (November 5, 1927), 52–54; Helen C. Bennett, "The Voice at the End of the Wire," *Ladies Home Journal*, XXXII (March, 1915), 8, 64; Schmitt, "I Was Your Old 'Hello Girl'," 121.

[17] Schmitt, "I Was Your Old 'Hello Girl'," 121.

phone's potential as a vehicle of entertainment. As early as 1879 he had transmitted music from the stage of Chickering Hall in New York City to a home in Yonkers. A few years later Alfred Ely Beach, editor of *Scientific American,* had Sunday sermons piped into his home via the telephone lines (shades of later radio preachers!) while during the '80's plays were similarly "broadcast" to private homes from the stage of a New York theater.[18]

But the crucial development came in 1898 when the first "telephone newspaper"—the precursor of the radio station—was established in Budapest, Hungary. Using telephone lines and receivers the telephone newspaper broadcast news reports from early morning until late at night. Nor did it restrict its offerings to news; it also provided concert and theatrical performances. In addition it distributed printed programs to its subscribers and alerted them to special bulletins with a loud whistle.[19]

Telephone-newspapers on the Budapest model were shortly established throughout the United States, although they varied widely in the services they offered. In some rural areas communication was two-way—unlike the Budapest system—and subscribers could question the "stentor" as the broadcaster was called. It is said that discussions similar to those heard today on radio "talk programs" often ensued between subscribers and stentors.[20] In Philadelphia the Bell System arranged with a newspaper, *The North American,* in 1903, to have special operators provide callers with news summaries at any hour of the day or night.[21] It is also reported that schools subscribed to a similar service so that students might learn of events as they unfolded, one of the earliest examples of an electronic teaching aid.[22]

THE TELEPHONE, THE COMMUNITY AND SOCIAL RELATIONSHIPS

The transformation of many aspects of urban life can be traced to the influence of the telephone either directly or in combination with other aspects of modernization. For the sake of convenience one can divide these effects into three classes: effects on the physical appearance of the commu-

[18] C. E. McCluen, "Hearing Operas by Telephone," *Scientific American,* Vol. 106 (May 11, 1912), 419; "Preaching Through the Telephone," *Literary Digest,* Vol. 52 (May 20, 1916), 1457.

[19] F. A. Talbot, "A Telephone Newspaper," *The Living Age,* Vol. 238 (August 8, 1903), 372–76; Thomas S. Denison, "The Telephone Newspaper," *World's Work,* I (April, 1901), 640–43.

[20] "American Telephone Newspaper," *Literary Digest,* Vol. 44 (March 16, 1912), 528–29; "The Farmer and the Telephone," *Independent,* Vol. 54 (March 13, 1902), 649.

[21] *The Philadelphia Directory,* 1902, 512.

[22] "Sociological Effects of the Telephone," *Scientific American,* XCIV (June 16, 1906), 500.

nity; effects on social interaction, and effects on patterns and models of communication among people.

The influence of the telephone on the design of urban and suburban areas has probably been minor compared to that of innovations in the realm of transportation (including the elevator) and the effects of building and zoning codes. But the telephone probably facilitated the separation of workplace from residence so characteristic of the American economy.

Far more important have been the effects of the telephone on the patterns and the quality of social relationships in urban areas. Those sociologists and social critics who studied the urban environment during the first thirty years of this century almost universally lamented the waning role in society played by primary groups and the declining solidarity of the neighborhood itself. They contrasted the impersonal, fragmented quality of contemporary urban life with an image of warm personal relationships believed to have characterized small towns and urban neighborhoods of an earlier age. (The degree to which this image corresponded to reality is not significant in this conection.) Earlier communities were thought of essentially as interacting groups of kinsmen and neighbors (who were also one's friends). In such communities all but the very wealthy were likely to confine their social contacts to members of their extended families and those living in close physical proximity; it was difficult and costly (of time if not always of money) to get to know others nor was it considered necessary. People's horizons were limited, in large part by the difficulties of other than purely local transportation and communication. The invention of the telephone, among other developments, helped to raise those horizons.

The breakdown of the earlier style of community life is regarded by most sociologists as the consequence chiefly of large scale industrialization and urbanization, of all that is connoted by the development of a "mass society." The extended family, the most important primary group, often disintegrated and dispersed as its consistuent units, responding to expanding economic opportunities, scattered over an ever widening geographical area. Although later studies have shown that the conjugal family is less isolated than once thought and although sociologists have discovered new types of primary groups in American life they have tended to see the latter as shifting friendship groups and cliques grounded either in the formal work situation or in informal associational activities rather than as stable groups on the model of the family. Completely overlooked has been the changing nature of the "neighborhood" made possible by the almost universal availability of the telephone.

With the spread of the telephone a person's network of social relationships was no longer confined to his physical area of residence (his neighborhood, in its original meaning); one could develop intimate social networks based on personal attraction and shared interests that transcended the boundaries of residence areas. It is customary to speak of "dispersed" social networks to denote that many urban dwellers form primary groups with others who live physically scattered throughout a metropolitan area, groups which interact as much via the telephone as in face-to-face meetings.[23] Such primary groups constitute a person's "psychological neighborhood." Modern transportation, of course, makes it possible for such groups to foregather in person but it is highly doubtful that they could long sustain their existence without the cohesion made possible by the telephone.

The nature, the structure and the functions of such psychological neighborhoods and telephone networks, whether or not they are considered to be "primary" groups are very obscure. The author has discovered one such network consisting of a group of elderly widows living alone who maintain scheduled daily telephone contacts as a means of insuring the safety, health, and emotional security of the group's members. The questions yet to be answered are, in brief, who talks to whom, often for how long, for what reasons and with what results?

By this circuitous route we return to the question raised earlier, that of what functions the use of the telephone serves for individuals rather than for the structure of the society as a whole or its consistuent institutions. This question requires detailed investigation but it may be suggested that among the most likely functions are the reduction of loneliness and anxiety, an increased feeling of psychological and even physical security and the already mentioned ability to maintain the cohesion of family and friendship groups in the face of residential and even geographic dispersion. Recent sociological inquiries have illuminated somewhat the role of the telephone in maintaining the cohesion of families in the face of pressures of industrialization but little is known about the variables (e.g., distance, degree of kinship, stage of the family cycle) associated with variations in these patterns.

Finally, it may not be amiss to suggest that, at least in the early years of its existence, the possession of a telephone may have served both to define and to enhance the social status of individuals, a function which, for a time, probably every consumer oriented technological innovation has served.

While the various questions and hypotheses we have examined above have been raised in relation to urban life they are no less valid when applied, *mutatis mutandis*, to the conditions of rural life. The rural, relatively isolated "folk" society (gemeinschaft) has frequently been idealized by nostalgic critics of contemporary "mass society" (gesellschaft) because such writers deplore the loss of those warm, primary-group relations and that sense of belonging to an organic, solidary community which they believe—

[23] On the notion of "social networks" see, Elizabeth Bott, *Family and Social Network* (London, 1957).

or imagine—to have characterized earlier rural and small town life. The type case of such a social order—as the origin of the idea in late nineteenth century German sociological romanticism immediately suggests—was rather the European peasant village or castle town of the High Middle Ages than the American farming community of the 1880's or 1890's. The typical American rural family of that period lived on its own farm, separated from any neighbors by distances ranging from a quarter mile to five miles or more. In consequence, the local town, which had to be within a few hours ride by horse and wagon, served chiefly as a trading center rather than as the scene of a richly textured organic community life. This is not to deny, however, that such towns served important socializing functions especially on those occasions—weekends and holidays—when all the families from the hinterland gathered there to renew acquaintanceships, buy provisions, compare experiences and entertain themselves and each other. The persistent theme of loneliness in accounts of nineteenth century American farm life suggests, however, that the "official" model of rural American society is closer to ideological fiction than to historical fact.[24] For these reasons it may be suggested that the increasing modernization of rural America, far from eroding primary group ties, actually strengthened them by expanding the area from which primary (and secondary) group members could be selected while simultaneously freeing people from social and psychological dependence on what may at times have been uncongenial neighbors. The telephone broke through the isolation of the rural family.

Moreover, the very construction of telephone lines in rural areas often gave impetus to social solidarity, as farmers frequently organized informal groups to string wires.[25] That these early farmers' mutual societies were organized so that all the farms in a given locality were on the same telephone line probably contributed further to the sense of shared communal identity. The whole area served by a telephone cooperative could intercommunicate simultaneously and, apparently, it was not unusual for all the families served by a single line to get on the phone at the same time to hear the latest news and discuss common problems. Since farmers' wives were especially susceptible to feelings of loneliness and isolation, the telephone here too helped to allay personal anxiety.[26]

The following statistic may illuminate both the importance of the tele-

[24] Pound, *The Telephone Idea*, 32; *Special Reports: Telephones 1907*, 75.

[25] United States Department of Agriculture, Farmers' Bulletin No. 1245, *Farmers Telephone Companies* (Washington, 1930), 5–6; Frank Gordon, "To Teach Farmers Telephone Repairing," *World Technology Word*, XXII (January, 1915), 722.

[26] H. P. Spofford, "Rural Telephone: Story," *Harper's Monthly Magazine*, Vol. 118 (May, 1909), 830–37; H. R. Mosnot, "Telephone's New Uses in Farm Life," *World's Work*, IX (April, 1905), 6103–4; "Spread of the Rural Telephone Movement," *Scientific American*, Vol. 104 (February 18, 1911), 162; Frederick Rice, Jr., "Urbanized Rural New England," XXXIII (January, 1906), 528–48.

phone on the farm and its rapid acceptance by the rural population (which is typically thought to be more tradition bound than urban dwellers): according to the special telephone census of 1907, 160,000 (73%) of Iowa's approximately 220,000 farms were already supplied with telephone service.[27] The major share in this development was the work of farmers' cooperatives. Assuredly, other factors such as the need for mutual aid and the economic advantages of being able to obtain up-to-date information on market conditions in the cities and towns played their part in the rapid spread of rural telephone service, but the importance of more strictly sociological and psychological factors must not be underestimated.[28]

If the suggestions thus far advanced are ultimately confirmed by additional research it may turn out that the extent to which rural life in America actually does or ever did exhibit the characteristics of a solidary, organic community so often imputed to it is primarily the result of modernization and specifically of the introduction and spread of the telephone. This would also help to explain the greater uniformity of values and attitudes among the rural population; for people who share common problems and interact frequently with one another tend to develop similar values and attitudes and to inhibit the expression of deviant sentiments. That rural areas have typically been served by party rather than individual lines has tended to make rural telephone conversations relatively public, thus facilitating both the reinforcement of dominant attitudes and the suppression of deviant ones.[29] This situation stands in sharp contrast to that prevailing in the heterogeneous urban residential neighborhood, with its mixing of people from many "psychological neighborhoods," within which no single set of attitudes or behaviors could easily be imposed. In urban areas telephone messages tended to be transmitted on one or two-party lines and even if one's physical neighbors took exception to one's expressed values or behavior a person could usually find support for his "deviance" within his psychological neighborhood. Urban "deviance" is thus but the Janus face of privacy.

A discussion of the social effects of the telephone would, however, be incomplete were reference to its relationship to other modes of communication omitted. In the absence of research one can only suggest these relationships through a series of questions: Does telephone communication lessen or increase total face-to-face communication? Does it supplement or replace

[27] *Special Reports: Telephones 1907,* 18, 23.

[28] *Ibid.,* 75–76. Access to the telephone was regarded as being so essential to life on the farm that the United States Department of Agriculture issued a bulletin in 1922 designed to assist farmers in establishing and improving telephone service. See *Farmers Telephone Companies.*

[29] Spofford, "Rural Telephone: Story," 830–37; Mosnot, "Telephone's New Uses in Farm Life," 6103–4.

the latter? How does telephone communication change the character of face-to-face and of written communications? What effects has use of the telephone had on the rate of use of the telegraph and on the letter writing habits of Americans? Has there occurred specialization within the media of communication wherein certain kinds of messages are considered appropriate for transmission by telephone while other kinds are transmitted by telegraph (e.g., the congratulatory message) or by letters? And if so, why? What is the effect—in political campaigns and direct selling—of a telephone message directed to a particular person as against a newspaper, radio, or telephone message addressed to a mass, anonymous audience?[30]

Although these questions have not as yet been subjected to systematic research, some of them have been the subject of discussion and study.

Among the first generation of Americans to use the telephone were those who were concerned about the ways in which people behaved while talking on the phone and the rules evolving to govern that behavior. Some objected to Bell's invention precisely because it seemed to generate new codes of conduct which were at variance with those governing face-to-face relationships. One can easily imagine the responses of men and women of social standing at discovering a social climber at the other end of the line. Other critics were shocked by the apparent absence of inhibitions when people spoke on the phone. One wrote of impulsive women who "say things to men and to each other over the telephone that they would never say face to face." Others complained about people who made calls at inappropriate times, or who phoned last minute invitations, or about the obligation to return a call if one was missed.[31]

An early, more scientific approach to the question of how people behave on the telephone consisted of a study of the words spoken. The study, conducted in New York City in 1931, analyzed 1,000 telephone conversations. Eighty-thousand words were spoken in that sample of calls. Only 2,240 (3%) different words were employed and 819 of these were used only once. Thus 1,421 of the total number were words used over and over again. The study demonstrated not only the diminutive character of the vocabulary of the average American telephoner but suggested, at least, the general contents of the conversations: the most frequently used words were "I" and "me."[32]

---

[30] For a discussion of some of these questions see, G. S. Street, "While I Wait," *Living Age*, Vol. 276 (March 15, 1913), 696–97; Antrim, "Outrages of the Telephone," 125; Andrew Lang, "Telephone + Letter-Writing," *The Critic*, XLVIII (May, 1906), 507–8; "Telephone and Telegraph Prospects," *The Journal of Political Economy*, XXII (April, 1914), 392–94.

[31] Antrim, "Outrages of the Telephone," *Lippincotts' Monthly Magazine*, Vol. 84 (July, 1890), 125–26.

[32] "The Frequency of Words Used Over the Telephone," *Science*, Vol. 74 (August .14, 1931) supplement, 11–13. Everyday conversations have more recently been studied by a

In recent years, it has been observed that for some time the telephone has come to be used as an instrument of aggression and hostility. Such uses for the phone can probably be traced back to its earliest days but the additional anonymity provided by automatic dialing no doubt greatly encouraged the use of the telephone for such purposes. The behavior ranges from the standard April Fool joke (i.e. calling the Zoo and asking for Mr. Wolf) to the sex deviants who call women unknown to them personally and whose conversational style varies from the use of seductive language to enormous obscenity. There is also a kind of "persecution" apt to occur between acquaintances and friends which consists of calling at intervals, letting the phone ring until it is answered and then hanging up. "Crank-calls" probably are akin to poison pen letters.

The opportunity to talk on the phone may also function to limit and to deflect the expression of hostility. Loud haranguing on the wire can mitigate situations that might otherwise lead to blows if the antagonists were face-to-face. The practice of screaming at the operator may serve as a safety-valve. Whether she is employed by the telephone company or handles the switchboard for a large firm, the operator can be a built-in victim or target for the caller.

Over the past century the telephone has been diffused throughout America. As it has done so it has helped to transform life in cities and on farms and to change the conduct of American business, both legitimate and illegitimate; it imparted an impetus toward the development of "mass culture" and "mass society" at the same time it affected particular institutional patterns in education and medicine, in law and warfare, in manners and morals, in crime and police work, in the handling of crises and the ordinary routines of life. It markedly affected the gathering and reporting of news and patterns of leisure activity; it changed the context and even the meaning of the neighborhood and of friendship; it gave the traditional family an important means to adapt itself to the demands of modernization and it paved the way both technologically and psychologically, for the thematically twentieth century media of communication: radio and television.[33]

---

number of ethnomethodologists. See Emanuel A. Schegloff, "Sequencing in Conversational Openings," *American Anthropologist*, Vol. 70 (December, 1968), 1075–95; *The First Five Seconds: The Order of Conversational Openings,* Unpublished Ph.D. dissertation, Department of Sociology, University of California, Berkeley, 1967; Emanuel A. Schegloff and Harvey Sacks, "Opening Up Closings," unpublished manuscript; Donald W. Ball, "Toward a Sociology of Telephones and Telephoners," in Marcello Truzzi, ed., *Sociology and Everyday Life* (Englewood Cliffs, N.J., 1968), 59–74.

[33] Virtually each topic deserves at least a chapter of its own. The following references are intended as a guide to subjects not discussed elsewhere in this paper. "Improvements in the Telephone," *Literary Digest*, Vol. 92 (January 1, 1927), 42–49; "Few Telephones Mean High Death Rate," *Ibid.*, Vol. 105 (May 24, 1930), 105; H. T. Wade, "Telephones Throughout the Fleet," *World's Work*, XV (March, 1908), 9991–92; "Battles by Telephone," *Literary Digest*, Vol. 50 (June 19, 1915), 1464; "Directing An Attack," *Scientific*

THE COMPARATIVE PERSPECTIVE

While this discussion has concentrated on the cumulative impact of the telephone on American society over the past century, there are obvious advantages to examining its effects both in other industrialized societies of differing cultural traditions and in newly industrializing areas. The consequences of the telephone in other industrial societies have not necessarily been identical to those in American society and may, in fact, have been quite different, for any number of reasons. Only a comparative historical approach can distinguish recurrent structural and psychological effects of the telephone (or any other technological innovation) from idiosyncratic ones, can delineate the range of varying cultural contacts in channeling the effects of technological innovation. Studying the consequences of the telephone as it is being introduced in developing nations is, on the other hand, analogous to observing an experiment, with history as the laboratory.

Furthermore, there are theoretical issues at stake which perhaps can only be resolved through comparative study. What degree of modernization in the American or Western sense is, for example, possible in the absense of a well-articulated telephone system? A reflection on Daniel Lerner's *The Passing of Traditional Society* (New York, 1958) may be pertinent here. Either there were no developed telephone systems in the Middle East in the mid-1950's (almost certainly not true in the case of Turkey) or the author overlooked their significance for, despite an incisive analysis of the role of mass communications in the modernization of such societies, he nowhere mentions the telephone in that connection. It may be that essential social communication in such societies emanates from a few strategic elite groups and is disseminated among the largely illiterate masses primarily by way of radio and television. Is an elaborate widely-dispersed telephone system necessary to successful modernization given the existence of the latter? The role of the transistor radio in the modernization of underdeveloped nations certainly cries out for analysis. These are more than idle questions for post-

---

American, Vol. 83 (March 17, 1917), Supplement, 166; M. B. Mullett, "How We Behave When We Telephone," *American Magazine,* Vol. 86 (November, 1918), 44–45; Dr. Alfred Gradenwitz, "A German Police Telephone: Scientific Aids for Patrol Service," *Scientific American,* Vol. 75 (January 25, 1913), Supplement, 61; "A Pocket Telephone," *Literary Digest,* Vol. 44 (March 30, 1912), 639; "Private Telephone System in School," *Journal of Education* (March 31, 1910), 355; William F. McDermott, "Emergency Calls," *Today's Health,* XXIX (November, 1951), 38; "Mine Rescue Telephone Equipment," *Scientific American,* Vol. 109 (November 1, 1913), 340; "Telephone in the Mississippi Flood," *Literary Digest,* Vol. 99 (August 20, 1927), 213; Alfred M. Lee, *The Daily Newspaper in America* (New York, 1937); A. H. Griswold, "The Radio Telephone Situation," *Bell Telephone Quarterly,* I (April, 1922), 2–12; S. C. Gilfillan, "The Future Home Theatre," *The Independent,* LXXIII (October 10, 1912), 886–91; W. Rupert Maclaurin, *Invention and Innovation in the Radio Industry* (New York, 1949).

prandial senior common room debate: governments for developing societies require a rational basis for assigning priorities and allocating resources
for the development of communications systems.

DENTON E. MORRISON and CARLIN PAIGE HOLDEN

The Burning Bra:
The American Breast Fetish
and Women's Liberation*

Blumer has recently pointed out that sociologists have largely
neglected to treat fashion seriously, including fashion in personal adornment (1969).[1] This neglect was never defensible either on intellectual
grounds or on grounds of social relevance, but today more than ever before
it is difficult to regard adornment fashions as epiphenomena, or their study
a trivial matter. In the past decade important changes in adornment patterns have been the focus of serious social concern and controversy. Secondary schools, in particular, have been torn, sometimes to the point of
temporary paralysis, by conflicts over dress and hair fashions and related
matters of personal adornment. In addition, business and industrial firms,
families, the military, religious orders, and even whole communities have
been strained by similar controversies over these changes. At a more abstract level, it is clear that adornment differences, changes, and conflicts are
often related to broader differences, changes, and conflicts involving age

Copyright © 1970 by Denton E. Morrison and Carlin Paige Holden. Reprinted by
permission.

* We wish to acknowledge the suggestions and encouragement of the following people
who read earlier versions of this paper: Mary Ellen Roach, Herbert Blumer, Donald
Zochert, Mario Bick, William Form, Joanne Eicher, Marvin Riley and Hans Gerth. We
are also grateful for the editorial assistance of Nancy Hammond.

[1] "Fashion" while used mainly in reference to personal adornment, refers to all consciously, more or less regularly introduced, and subsequently widely adopted changes in
culture and is thus not found in static, unchanging societies (Young, 1930:552 ff.). "Personal adornment" refers to all conscious alterations in the appearance of the human
body and is universal (Bick, 1968:1). Some exceptions to the general neglect of fashion
research in the area of adornment are reprinted in Roach and Eicher (1965), and other
exceptions are cited in their annotated bibliography.

groups, the races, the sexes, political groups, occupational groups, and status groups. Both sociology and society need a better understanding of these relationships, particularly those between contemporary changes in adornment and the broader changes involving social movements toward egalitarianism and individual freedom.

Changes in adornment are not new, of course, nor is the controversy over such changes. But the rate and radical character of these changes, the extent of their diffusion, and the degree of mass participation in them are greater than ever before. Thus, the scope and depth of the controversies such changes engender are of especially pressing significance. As with previous controversies over such changes, an important theme in much of the current discord centers on changes in the sexual aspects of dress, particularly the way in which zones defined as erogenous are displayed and emphasized, and the way in which dress tends or fails to differentiate the sexes. Some recent adornment fashions that have been the subject of controversy along these lines are: miniskirts, see-throughs, natural look and no-bras, bikinis, toplessness and other forms of partial nudity, and the uni-sex and mod looks as well as related styles, including long hair, perfumes, beards, and bright colors for men and slacks for women.

It is noteworthy that the bulk of the past as well as present controversy over erotic display focuses on women's adornment, and we shall be concerned with a specific aspect of this phenomenon in this paper. Clearly, the general trend of the last 50 years in the U.S. has been toward greater freedom in erotic display in female dress. This trend has, in itself, been controversial, but equally controversial have been recent organized protests of this trend by participants in the women's liberation movement who, paradoxically, see the trend as one of many threats to women's status, women's rights, and, implicitly, women's freedom. Although hardly an extreme example of erotic display, the 1968 Miss America Pageant was an early target for a dramatic protest by the movement, since the Pageant gets widespread publicity and stresses heavily the importance of female appearance, in particular the figure and its provocative display, as a desideratum for young American women. *Time* magazine (1968:36) reported the incident as follows:

"No more Miss America" announced the flyer from the Women's Liberation Force. The protest came from a group of angry ladies led by Robin Morgan, 27, poetess and housewife. As the Liberators see it, Miss America represents "racism with roses"; she is a "military death mascot" symbolizing "the living bra and the dead soldier." What's more, this "mindless boob girlie symbol" represents the "pop-culture obsolescent theme of spindle, mutilate and discard tomorrow." As the contest went on in Atlantic City's Convention Hall, the protesters outside rallied around a "Freedom Trash Can" into which they urged all good women to toss "bras, girdles, curlers, false eyelashes, wigs and representative issues of *Cosmopolitan, Ladies Home Journal* and *Family Circle.*

Although no special focus on brassieres may have been intended by the protestors, it is significant that in this and similar episodes the discarding of bras as well as references in the protest literature to de-emphasis of breasts as criteria for female attractiveness have been constant and prominent symbolic elements. There is, in fact, to our knowledge no concrete evidence that bras were ever actually burned; paradoxically, there is widespread belief that this occurred and there has been widespread reaction to this belief —again bearing out the old sociological adage that "things believed to be true are true in their consequences." The significant point, then, is that widespread belief in the protestors' interest in the discarding of bras was the element in these protests that caught press and public attention and created the initial public interest in and controversy over the protests and the movement. This is partly because bralessness motivated by a desire to de-emphasize the erotic aspect of the breasts constituted a great American heresy to many of those who made this essentially correct interpretation of the protests. To many others on both sides of the general morality-in-dress issue, the movement's seeming emphasis on bralessness was erroneously interpreted as endorsement of the general trend toward greater erotic display of breasts in women's clothes, a trend which included variations of bralessness both before and since the initial women's liberation protests.

Both of these types of reactions are understandable, since in the U.S. and elsewhere a major and more or less persistent feature of women's adornment has included an emphasis on the breasts as distinctive as well as distinctively attractive features of womanhood. In the last 40 years or so this emphasis has increased in this country to the point where it has been described by foreign observers as our "breast fetish" (Gorer, 1948:54ff.; Dingwall, 1958:165ff.): contemporary Americans more than others, particularly those outside the American sphere of influence, and more than Americans of previous times, regard breasts as objects of erotic awe, potency, and significance.

Several types of evidence for the existence of our breast fetish are available. Perhaps the clearest indicator is the development over the last two decades of a mass market for a host of men's magazines devoted largely to the display of photos of bare breasted women, and carrying such illustrated features as "The Bosom," "Annual Big Bust Issue," "Forty-Inch Club," and so on. (Compare, for instance, the number of their photos that display breasts with the number that contain legs and hips.) For several years prior to this men's magazines of this type emphasized "pin-ups" and "sweater girls" and exhibited a trend in which increasingly bared breasts eventually displaced legs and hips as the focus of interest. While partly these developments simply reflect changes in what can legally be shown in magazines (at least until recently), they also reflect what men in our culture have learned to find most exciting. Kinsey, from his investigation of American male sexual behavior, concluded that there "is reason to believe that more males in our culture are psychically aroused by contemplation of the female breast than by the sight of the female genitalia" (1948:575).

Women's magazines over the past few decades have contained an increasing array of methods and devices for enhancing the breasts, particularly means for making them appear larger. Indeed, we might more accurately speak of our "*big* breast fetish." Ample evidence of the extent of the American male's special responsiveness to large breasts was given in 1968 when national news was made by massive crowds that assembled in the Wall Street area to witness the stroll of an unusually buxom secretary (*N.Y. Times*, 1968). This could hardly have been news to Hollywood film producers, who for years have recognized that large breasts bring a good following. Raquel Welch, the latest of the film queens in this tradition, questions and describes the American breast fetish with considerable candor (*Playboy*, 1970:77):

> After all, sexuality isn't something that can be talked about. It's not on the surface of the body and, contrary to current fashion, it has nothing to do with the size of one's breasts; it exists in the mind and spirit. There's an unfortunate obsession in this country with the mammary glands . . . as an isolated symbol of sex. They're the softest, most vulnerable part of a woman and, because they stick out the farthest, they're the easiest part to grab. And the American male is too quick to do just that. He makes them synonymous with sex, which they're not.

With the advent of the mini-skirt and the general lessening of restrictions on body display in recent years, the breasts have perhaps lost some ground, relatively speaking, as the focal point of feminine pulchritude; there is also some evidence of a shift in the last few years from concern with breast size alone.   But there is little evidence that breasts will soon become unimportant ingredients in the cultural stereotype of an attractive woman in America.   Moreover, if the American breast fetish is now on the decline or is becoming only one aspect of our broader "figure fetish" or more broadly yet, our "female appearance fetish," the more general arguments in this paper remain substantially intact. But we think there are good reasons for focusing on the explanation of the American breast fetish and the basis for its real and perceived selection as a symbolic target for protest and concern by some elements of the women's liberation movement. We will approach these specific problems by first outlining some general notions on the social psychology of adornment and fashion and by making some observations on women's roles, women's status, and women's adornment.

REWARDS, ROLE AND STATUS SIGNS,
AND AMERICAN WOMEN

We assume, initially, that social interaction tends over time to be character-ized by the efforts of the participants to emit behaviors and seek responses that are rewarding. Rewards may range from goods and services to looks and glances that suggest respect and approval. To the extent that a person obtains rewards his self-esteem (how he evaluates himself) and his esteem in the eyes of others (how others evaluate him) are enhanced. Some roles (parts played in society) are, of course, more rewarded than others. It is gen-erally the differential rewards attached to different roles that we speak of when we refer to "status," and movement in a hierarchy of these roles that we refer to when we speak of "status mobility." However, differences in re-wards also exist by virtue of differential evaluations of performance within given roles; these differences often are the means for status mobility.

Where different statuses and roles exist they are typically indicated by well-understood differences in the signs and symbols[2] surrounding the actors: the observable cues that communicate roles and statuses to their pos-sessors and others, and which thus serve to generate the normatively appro-priate self-concepts and interpersonal responses. Particularly in affluent, "modern" societies such as the United States, consumption patterns, partic-ularly material possessions, tend to assume importance as signs of status, both in terms of the expense of particular items, and in the ability to have what is in fashion. In such societies, however, much of the interaction is impersonal and fleeting and hence puts severe limits on the type, range, and depth of contact most people can have with the status signs of others. This puts a special burden on clothes and other modes of personal adornment to serve as status signs, since they are the omnipresent characteristics of self-presentation in face-to-face interaction. As Veblen said, "our apparel is al-ways in evidence, and affords an indication of our pecuniary standing to all observers at the first glance" (1953:119).

Clothes are particularly prone to fashion because clothes are easily imi-tated and mass produced, and thus the signs of one's status are quickly usurped by those below, requiring a constant input of new styles at higher status levels if clothes are to indicate status at any level. Consequently, there is never a perfect relationship between the status sign value of cloth-ing and status *per se*. There is, however, enough tendency toward this rela-tionship to prevent gross counterfeiting while allowing some fraudulent gains in rewards by exhibiting signs that are not based on status. This is

---

[2] Status signs have meanings that are intrinsically connected with their referents (for instance, expensive clothes are signs of wealth). Status symbols have meanings that are arbitrarily connected with their referents (for instance, a lieutenant's bars symbolize his rank), or at least have meanings that have much broader connotations than what is in-trinsically connected with the symbol (see Banton, 1965:68–69).

only to say, then, that, while the material objects that money will buy, particularly clothing, provide convenient, concrete, and useful status indicators, status is not fully reflected in or based on wealth *per se*.

Status is more fundamentally based on a complex composite of factors related mainly to occupation and what leads to it, particularly education. In addition, factors such as family, ethnic and religious background and certain personal characteristics help determine educational and occupational opportunities and have other independent influences upon status. One such personal characteristic is race; another, which is of special importance for our analysis, is sex.

When other factors related to status are equal, women in the U.S. have lower status than men. Even when women have the same jobs at the same pay as men, women are likely to experience less status than men in the form of less promotions, responsibility, decision making power, control over others, etc. By far the more usual situation, however, is that women get lower status (and lower paying) jobs than men (even when equally qualified) and lower pay in the same jobs. Thus, it is very difficult for women to compete with men in the world of work for status or for pay.

Married women cannot completely share the status of their husbands; nevertheless, their status is substantially the reflection of the status of their husbands, and typically (often legally) they completely share his income. Thus, in general, women can obtain relatively more rewards in marriage, or in some combination of work outside the home and marriage, than they can by remaining single and working. However, at least within the same income levels, most women are relatively deprived of the more fundamental components of status as compared with their husbands, and relatively advantaged with regard to wealth. The same is generally true of single, dependent women in relation to single, dependent males in similar affluence levels. As Simmel suggested in his classic essay on "Fashion" (1957:550ff.), women compensate for and attempt to correct this imbalance by seeking rewards through the material signs of status, just as do others whose monetary resources are often relatively greater than the other, more fundamental components of their status, for instance, the dependent young, ethnic minorities, Blacks, and the nouveau riche. Additional considerations must, however, be brought to bear if we are to understand the special attention that women give to clothes and other aspects of adornment. These considerations have to do with the ways and means by which women obtain and maintain marriage.

In a society in which status mobility is valued and key rewards are best approximated by women (but only approximated) through marriage, women must turn to the kinds of behavior that involve gaining these rewards through a special kind of appeal to the opposite sex. Adornment plays a crucial part in this effort. The affluence indicated by dress and other aspects of adornment is rewarding to women for the same reason it is rewarding to all persons (as a status sign), but it is especially important to women. Since a woman's status will largely depend on her husband's status, a woman must get interaction with and appeal to men whose actual or potential status match her own aspiration, and moreover she must appeal to men partly on the basis of the way she can and will consume to express and enhance the man's status (Veblen, 1953:127; Sapir, 1931:142). In addition, such appeals must be made within the context of her willingness and ability to play a role that is defined first and foremost by her sex. Sex differences are, of course, everywhere defined and expressed in differentiated appearance through clothing and other aspects of adornment.

THE AMERICAN BREAST FETISH

The *general,* historical importance of breasts and other physiologically defining elements of the sexual differentiation of women in dress is explained, we think, by the fact that, where roles are sex-defined and women's status largely sex-linked to men through marriage, women will generally maximize their rewards by emphasizing their "fit" in this sex category, at least in so far as they accept the cultural definitions of such role and status arrangements. Although many of the criteria for "fit" are culturally defined (hair length, use of cosmetics, etc.), some, such as breasts and hips, are biologically determined and thus often—though not always—are enhanced or articulated in adornment for this purpose. Sex appeal, then, is in the first instance accomplished by making one's sex unequivocal: breasts are a role sign. The reason for the particular appropriateness of breasts as a role sign is, of course, related to the part they play in the biological attraction of the sexes: "From time immemorial the breasts especially have attracted Man, perhaps because they are the most obvious feature of Woman's body at the age when sexual instinct is strongest" (Cunnington, 1941:104–5). Particularly in Western cultures, sexual drives develop in the context of strong normative requirements for sexual modesty in dress, especially as regards emphasis and exposure of the genitals. By emphasizing their breasts women are able to achieve a modicum of erotic exposure without violating the cultural requirement for sexual modesty in dress (Flugel, 1931:108–10). Indeed, Flugel maintains that it is the diffuseness of woman's sexuality, in contrast to the genital focus of man's, that is related to the general tendency for women, more than men, to expose flesh and emphasize body shape in dress: "They can enjoy the pleasures of exposure without apprehending or intending any concomitant genital desire" (1931:109).

These notions about the general importance of breasts in sex-related interaction do not explain the generally *growing* importance breasts have come to have in America in the last 40 years or so, but these ideas do suggest that the explanation of our breast fetish may lie in changes that have increased the reward value of women's specifically sensuous appeals to men, as well as in changes that have tended to fixate these appeals on secondary rather than primary erotic zones.

FROM HOMEMAKER TO LOVER

By the 1920's American women had made important inroads on traditional male occupations and prerogatives, including voting, smoking, and drinking. Women's adornment of the period reflected these advances by being both less restrictive of movement than previously and by de-emphasizing the unique features of the female figure. Following World War I and until about 1929, "the female torso became a flattened tube, and the body was as wide at the waist as at the hips" (Laver, 1937:134). This was the era of the "flapper" fashions, and the bust disappeared altogether in an effort to achieve a "boyish flat appearance" (Dingwall, 1958:164). Women with large breasts were forced to wear correctors or flatteners in an attempt to conform to prevailing fashion (Laver, 1937:134). The eclipse of the traditional female figure was short-lived, however, and when curves re-appeared the emphasis had changed in an important way:

> The fundamental fact of feminine fashion of the 'thirties has been the frank re-emergence of the bust, or rather, to speak plainly, of the breasts, for the bust is no longer the unified protuberance which it was at the beginning of the century (Laver, 1937:135).

The emergence of breasts in the 'thirties was accompanied by the continued emphasis on smooth and narrow hips, and by the re-introduction of the tiny waist, which was in vogue in the first decade of the century (Laver, 1937:135). This general configuration has continued to dominate female figure fashion until very recently, but with increasing emphasis on the breasts, including emphasis on their size and cleft.

The Great Depression of the 1930's reversed many of women's occupational gains of the previous decade, and increasingly made the marriage route to status security and mobility the only one open for women during this period. Thus, competition for men increased, and at a time when the traditional family-maintenance roles of women in the home were declining in importance, a decline which has generally continued to the present. Specifically, the Depression brought the deferment of children as well as smaller families, and the period from 1930 to the present brought the general continuation if not the acceleration of other changes with special implications for women's role in marriage: the automation, commercialization, and simplification of household tasks such as cooking, cleaning, canning, and sewing, the displacement of many childrearing functions to the schools and other specialized organizations, and urbanization, with shifts away from the possibility of shared husband and wife work roles on farms. World War II opened up many job opportunities for women, but most were defined as temporary, since it was understood that the men returning from the war would get the jobs as well as the women as wives to provide the children and other emotional-expressive rewards, including sex, from which both parties had been long deprived. In short, there have been certain *structural* changes that have contributed directly to a decrease in the family-maintenance rewards exchanged by women in marriage, and, indirectly at least, to an increase in the emotional-expressive rewards provided by family, companionship, and sex. These changes have taken place during a period of initial decline and subsequently no increase, at least until the last decade or so, in the status opportunities for women outside marriage. In addition, both before and during the same period, there have been important *attitude* changes in the U.S. in the direction of more open recognition and sanctioning of sexual pleasure as an intrinsic goal of relations between the sexes, including marriage. In particular, attitudes have become favorable toward active female participation in and pursuit of such pleasure. Such attitudes were not a part of either the Puritan or subsequently the Victorian views of sex and marriage that prevailed in this country until about 50 years ago and that have only gradually declined—with certain important residuals remaining. Some appreciation of the magnitude and significance of this change can be obtained by noting the kind of advice commonly given women in the early part of the century:

> The best mothers, wives, and managers of households know little or nothing of sexual indulgences. Love of home, of children, of domestic duties, are the only passions they feel. As a general rule, a modest woman seldom desires any sexual gratification for herself. She submits to her husband, but only to please him; and but for the desire of maternity, would far rather be relieved from his attention (Kellogg, 1910:520–21).

FROM SUBMISSION TO PARTICIPATION

Far from the Victorian view, the idea of "submission" to men has been replaced by the notion that it is every woman's obligation actively to participate in producing sexual pleasure for the man and, in addition, to seek and receive such pleasure for herself as well. Indeed, the sexual relationship has increasingly become defined as less than completely satisfactory for either party unless the pleasure is mutual. In fact, an important criterion of male sexual status has become his ability to arouse and fulfill the female's sexual needs as well as his own. The emergence of such a criterion is a quite recent change in the definition of the sexual relationship, but it has been widely held in the U.S. in recent years.

Breasts have become important in this context for several reasons. One contributing factor may be that the decline of breast feeding has taken bared breasts from view, and thus increased their curiosity value for young American males.[3] More important, however, is the growing belief that female erogeneity is more diffuse than that of males, more in need of gradual, conscious arousal, and the associated belief that the breasts are key erogenous zones. There is a widespread belief, promulgated by sex and marriage manuals and reinforced in modern erotic literature, that breast stimulation is a necessary initial step in the sexual arousal of the female and, given the new definition of the sexual relationship, of the male as well. Thus, because males perceive the maximization of their own sexual pleasure as dependent on the arousal of the female, and female arousal dependent on breast stimulation, the breasts become sexually exciting to males.

Obviously these beliefs about female erogeneity have implications for the role of breasts in sexual behavior both prior to and during marriage, but the situation prior to marriage is somewhat more complex than simply male attraction to and interest in breasts for the purposes of accomplishing seduction. The norms surrounding courtship have increasingly emphasized the specifically sexual aspects of the relationship during the period of the declining Victorian moral code, but have continued to forbid sexual consummation in intercourse on moral as well as practical (VD, pregnancy) grounds, particularly for women (the familiar "double standard"). Consequently, given the growing, openly held and pursued belief in their erogenous significance, breasts have assumed an important role in the intermediary and partial sexual interaction short of intercourse that is involved in "necking" and "petting." Along with other, more daring features of the game of technical chastity described by Kinsey (1948:377–81), varying degrees of exposure and concealment of the breasts (Wax, 1957:589–90) as well as the granting to males of varying degrees of access to the breasts have been central to the themes of sexual attraction and experimentation that have characterized the provocative prudery expected of American girls.

This analysis is not intended to imply that our description of widely held *beliefs* about the diffuseness of female sexuality and the importance of breast stimulation for every woman's sexual arousal is necessarily valid in physiological terms. Indeed, the evidence suggests the opposite.[4] But clearly these beliefs have become an important part of twentieth century Ameri-

---

[3] Gorer (1948:54 ff.) suggests that the breast fetish has an unconscious infantile origin: rigid breast-feeding schedules have increased the breasts' scarcity value for certain generations of American men. Sewell's evidence (1952), however, makes us skeptical of this notion.

[4] Kinsey found that "In actuality, many females are not particularly aroused by such breast manipulation, but some are aroused" (1953:253). Masters and Johnson (1966) show that the breasts definitely change and react during sexual stimulation, and that some women can achieve orgasm by breast auto-manipulation alone, but the bulk of their evidence seems to indicate that breast stimulation is neither necessary nor sufficient for sexual climax for most women.

can sexual folklore. And it is also clear that, beyond the bed, breast size and emphasis have become associated with a woman's willingness, ability, and desirability as a sexual and marriage partner: her sexiness is in important measure, or at least *ceteris paribus*, indicated by her breasts.

Neither is our analysis intended to imply that the democratization of sexual or other relations between the sexes has been complete. The fact that a woman now theoretically receives sexual pleasure partly or initially through breast stimulation by the man does not mean that the empirically resulting pleasure is, in general, equal, since the male nearly always reaches orgasm in the sex act while, in general, the woman's climax is more problematic and dependent on the willingness of the man to approach the act in a particular way. Thus the claim that women are "sex objects" for men is still in some measure true, perhaps in a more invidious sense than in the past. For a woman is now increasingly supposed to receive only sexual pleasure in exchange for giving a man pleasure, rather than, as formerly, trade access to her body ("submit") for values such as status mobility that she could not obtain by her own efforts. But the sexual gains have proved incomplete and she still cannot obtain status gains on her own to any meaningful extent. These considerations allow the speculation that the female contribution to the various dimensions of the breast fetish may involve more her perception of what males want than what is in it for her, sexually at least.

In sum, sexual performance and the associated sensuousness in attracting males have become part of a woman's role expectations and a basis for her direct and indirect rewards: women get status directly (are regarded as attractive) in terms of erotic criteria, which, in turn, help to give them access to other rewards by attracting and keeping men. Breasts have assumed a special importance as erotic criteria because of the way female eroticism has been defined, and because of the cautious and partial way eroticism must be employed in the extended and extensive search for thrills in the context of the larger goal of status gain in courtship. Concrete evidence supporting these notions is available in Kinsey's finding (1948:369–71, 574; 1953:280, 399) that upper status persons practice various forms of breast stimulation both prior to and during marriage more than persons of lower status: upper status persons practice deferred gratification more than others and, in addition, are the ones most likely to first acquire the new beliefs about female sexual equality and erogeneity.

RECENT DIMENSIONS OF THE BREAST BOOM

While the breasts are only one component of the definition of female attractiveness in this country, and cannot be considered in isolation from the other components, breast concern, attention, and emphasis have ranked high if not highest in our priorities in the last few decades, and the breast fetish persists today. There is some evidence that, among some of the current generation of the young, breasts may be declining in importance, perhaps reflecting the continuing decline of the Victorian sex ethic and the reduced relative importance of the preliminary and intermediary functions of the breasts in courtship, but such a trend is far from clear or general at present, and may simply reflect a movement away from emphasis on breast size alone. In general, the breast fetish has incorporated the American penchant for equating size with quality and has been promoted with (though we think not fundamentally caused by [see Sapir, 1931:142–43; Blumer, 1969:280]) typical capitalistic fervor for the profits therein by technological ingenuity, including a full array of mass marketing techniques. (Indeed it is tempting to think that breasts have become a fetish partly because they lend themselves more readily than other parts of the female body to enhancement and development by technological means.)

In particular, the fashions of the '50s and '60s reflected the breast fetish. Waist cinchers and tight sweaters exaggerated the breasts, making even small ones seem large in comparison to tiny waists. Bras were designed and marketed that acted to "lift and separate," and thus "improve" the figure. Other bras added to the bust measurement or properly shaped the "immature" figure. Various plans of exercise promised larger bustlines. Silicone injections became available as a more drastic measure. Training bras and pre-bra bras started little girls toward the great American bosom before their dolls were cold on the shelf, and the dolls themselves grew up and gained hourglass figures. (It has been reported that nine-year-olds spend more than two million dollars annually on bras [Stern, 1970:89].) The extent to which women accept the breasts as a central part of their identity is seen especially in the wearing of padded bras by adolescents who are late in maturing, and in the esthetically-based trauma (in addition to the physically-based trauma) experienced by women in breast removal. Clearly the Playmate image has increasingly become the standard by which American women judge themselves and are judged by others. Breasts are no longer simply a role sign, but a status sign and an instrument for gaining other status signs as well.

BURNING BRAS AND THE WOMEN'S LIBERATION MOVEMENT

At the same time that the Playmate standard has become increasingly important, more women have been prepared to meet the standards of the world of work by receiving a college education, and a higher proportion of women have both gained and exercised skills in the paid labor force. Many women who have not entered the labor force (and some who have) have found the housewife-companion-lover-mother role relatively unrewarding, given their skills and education and the job demands that remove the husband from the home, and have found the Playmate standard unrealistically difficult to reach and a decreasing source of rewards as age increases (see Friedan, 1963). Women who have entered the labor market with career aspirations have found that to succeed they must also conform to the Playmate criterion, and nevertheless obtain poorer jobs, lower pay, and experience restricted mobility opportunities as compared with males of similar or inferior training and ability. These women in particular have come to realize that the barriers that exist to women are *structural* blockages,[5] i.e., the restricted opportunities for women are not ultimately a result of individual shortages of talent, motivation, skill, or luck, but the result of the way the system is organized into a pattern of institutionalized sexism. Increased awareness of sex-based discrimination has also come as a result of roles women have played in the civil rights and anti-war movements, where in the analysis and confrontation of institutionalized racism and imperialism they have come to see and understand the basis of their own oppression— aided in some measure by the subordinate and sex-defined roles women were forced to play in these movements (Dixon, 1970:60).

All of the above factors and others are involved in the articulation of an ideology and the organization of the current movement for women's liberation. It is not our purpose to describe or analyze this movement in detail, but a key strategy in its effort to eliminate institutionalized sexism is to create an awareness of and change the processes by which women come to concentrate their energies into obtaining the best they can obtain from men as subordinates in general and as sex objects in particular.

One of the tactics of some of the movement's participators has involved drawing attention to and symbolically destroying the Playmate standard. Bra burning has been an understandable choice for symbolic emphasis in these efforts (we do not necessarily use the term "bra burning" literally, but as a way to refer to all attempts to de-emphasize breasts by the movement). For breasts are key signs and symbols of women's passivity and reticence (sexual and otherwise), the belief that women must be aroused by men to be active, competent, and fulfilled, women's mystery and delicacy, the peculiar suitability of women for motherhood and childrearing, and, in general, all the ways women are commonly thought to be different from, dependent on, and of service to men.

In addition, the women's liberation movement shares both personnel and ideology with the recent and broader egalitarian, underdog, and contraculture movements. Generally these movements have denounced the es-

---

[5] See Morrison and Steeves (1967:427) for a discussion of the role of the perception of structural blockage in another movement.

tablished bases for awarding status. In particular, they object to making rewards contingent on contrived conformity to WASP appearance and behavior norms. Thus the burning of bras in the women's liberation movement has its cultural antecedents in the no make-up, no shave, casual hair, casual dress, and unisex looks first generated in other movements. While the ideology behind these behaviors is not fully compatible with all schools of thought within the women's liberation movement, bra burning has been partly motivated by broader ideological considerations, in addition to the way that it attempts to strike directly at the specific signs of women's role and status.

Unfortunately, the cultural meanings attached to these signs are so deeply inculcated that the broader symbolic meaning of bra burning has often been lost, and the acts have created considerable misunderstanding of the movement and the issues. Because the beginnings of a no bra and natural bra fashion trend were already underway at the time of the initial protests, many mistook the bra burning actions as simply another manifestation of the breast fetish, i.e., as a further step toward eroticizing of the breasts. This reaction has been widely promoted and exploited by the adornment industry, which has capitalized on the attention given to bralessness in various ways: from selling see-through garments, to developing breast make-up kits, to arguing that most women have a need for some sort of bra (obviously a new sort to conform with the new look [N.Y. Times Magazine, 1970]). Hence this type of reaction to bra burning has had an effect opposite to that intended by protestors.

Another type of reaction was to regard the burning of bras as silly or ridiculous, since the connection of bras and the oppression of women was anything but obvious to many observers. Indeed, many assumed that the burning of bras was a sour-grapes reaction by women who lacked erotic figures or other conventionally attractive features—a stereotype frequently expressed by those who lack sympathy with the movement. Similarly, many persons regarded the bra burnings as a variety of far Left or Hippie or other rejection of established cultural values, and regarded the protestors as both morally and politically threatening.

Still others who basically understood and even sympathized with much of the message of the bra burners were repelled because the protestors seemed to imply (and in certain instances fully intended to imply), by their actions and appearance, that the movement aimed substantively at reducing sexual differentiation in appearance as well as erotic attraction between the sexes. In particular, the burnings carried for some the implication that participation in the movement might require some sort of drastic de-eroticizing actions by each follower, an understandably difficult concept for most people to accept, given their long socialization and commitment to the contrary. Indeed, the questions of sexual differentiation in appearance and of sexual relations between the sexes have been hotly debated within the movement, but relatively few factions of the movement have suggested that renunciation of conventional patterns of personal appearance or of sexual relations with men must necessarily or at least immediately be a part of participation in the movement. However, if the bra burnings implied general agreement within the movement on the necessity of such renunciations they may have had an adverse influence on recruitment.

Obviously the de-eroticizing of women's adornment will not in itself be sufficient, nor perhaps even be necessary, to bring about the changes that will liberate women from reliance on sexual attraction to achieve rewards. These changes will, however, require a viable, power-oriented social movement of women, and acts such as bra burning have served such purposes as drawing meaningful attention to the movement and some of its issues, creating the polarization that gives the movement some concrete enemies to move against, creating the sense of camaraderie among participants that is a part of any movement, and preparing the participants for other radical actions. While bra burning has perhaps tended to fixate the public image of the movement at the level of the *signs* of women's role and status without creating an adequate understanding of their basic role and status problems, the growth of the movement since the initial bra burning incidents and the recent surge of increasingly thorough and sympathetic analysis by the mass media (particularly magazines) indicate that bra burning has not had a lasting negative impact on the movement.

The above is not intended to argue, however, that dress reform will not play an important part in the current women's liberation movement. The dress reforms of the earlier feminist movement—a crucial aspect of that movement—were aimed at giving women greater physical freedom (through bifurcated outer garments and less restrictive undergarments) so that more active roles in homes, communities, factories, and offices would be possible (Riegel, 1963). The clothing concerns of the present movement are, however, less with the physical and more with the sociological and psychological aspects of women's bondage in dress. Substantively, de-emphasizing the breasts and erotic de-emphasis in general are not an attempt to make women look like men (an accusation leveled at the earlier movement) or even an attempt to prevent women from looking like women. They are attempts to prevent women from looking the way men want women to look and the way women have come to want to look *in order* to extract favors from men rather than relate to men as equals.

Assumedly, if the liberation of women did away with the special need women now have to use adornment in general and eroticism in clothes in particular as instruments for gaining status through and in relation to men, women would still attempt to gain rewards through adornment in the same way that men make such gains, and would also want to continue to be sexually attractive to men. (Certain elements of the current movement are, however, urging complete sexual independence for women.) Thus, we would predict that, even if women were liberated, a general consciousness about fashion and adornment would continue to be an important part of their lives, though no more so than for men. Further, we would predict that equality for women will be accompanied by a relative decrease in the concentration of erotic emphasis in women's adornment and a relative increase in the eroticizing of men's adornment. To a limited extent, of course, these predictions are already coming true, particularly among the young. Women, particularly younger women, *are* partly liberated, but *only* partly so, which is probably why the time is ripe for a movement: it is seldom the totally deprived who rebel (see Morrison and Steeves, 1967).

SUMMARY, HYPOTHESES AND CONCLUSION

We have attempted to describe the nature and sources of the American breast fetish and to explain why bra burning has been connected with the women's liberation movement. Our explanation has involved bringing to bear certain facts about continuities and changes in the American social structure and moral code. These facts have been interpreted within a guiding explanatory framework of some general notions about status and role differentiation, and the part played by adornment as a sign that is instrumental in obtaining and increasing the rewards of various roles and statuses. What remains is to make a step toward systematically stating these notions as general hypotheses.

A slight modification of Bush and London's hypotheses (1960:365) has provided a general framework for our analysis (our changes are indicated in brackets):

1. Differences in modes of dress within a particular society are indicative of differences in social roles [, statuses] and self-concepts of members of that society.
2. Changes in fundamental or enduring modes of dress in a society are indicative of changes in the social roles [, statuses] and self-concepts of members of that society.
3. The greater the variability of clothing styles in a society, the less well defined and conflict free are social roles [and statuses] in that society.

Our hypotheses are mainly elaborations or sub-classes of theirs:

1a. The more differentiated and stable are roles and status according to sex, the greater and more stable are sex differences in adornment.

Within given income levels in societies where there is general participation in fashion and a theoretically open stratification system:

1b. those with lower status will show greater concern with and consciousness of fashion, including fashions in adornment;

1c. the more that superordinate status is concentrated in one sex in the society, the more will the subordinate sex emphasize adornment fashions, including the erotic in adornment;[6] and

2a. conscious de-emphasis of eroticism in adornment by the subordinate sex indicates an attempt to alter the subordinate relationship to the opposite sex.

We think that these hypotheses warrant refinement and testing by data better than the somewhat casual impressions we have offered. Thus, we both join with Blumer in his plea that sociologists take fashion seriously and hope that we have taken a step toward responding to his challenge. Given the present concern with environmental quality we must bear in mind that "clothes, in several important respects, are the frontiers of our environment" (Dearborn, 1918–1919:49). Clothes as well as other aspects of adornment in part determine and in part are determined by the quality of our lives as they provide the explicit and hinted communication of what we are and what we want to be (Stone, 1962).

REFERENCES

BANTON, MICHAEL, *Roles: An Introduction to the Study of Social Relations.* New York: Basic Books, 1965.

BICK, MARIO, "What's On, What's Coming Off? Notes on a Theory of Adornment," paper read at the Annual Meeting of the American Anthropological Association, 1968.

BLUMER, HERBERT, "Fashion: From Class Differentiation to Collective Selection," *The Sociological Quarterly,* 10 (Summer 1969), 275–91.

BUSH, GEORGE, and PERRY LONDON, "On the Disappearance of Knickers: Hypotheses for the Functional Analysis of the Psychology of Clothing," *Journal of Social Psychology,* 51 (May 1960), 359–66.

CUNNINGTON, C. WILLITT, *Why Women Wear Clothes.* London: Faber and Faber, 1941.

DEARBORN, G. V. H., "The Psychology of Clothing," *Psychological Monographs,* 36 (1918–1919), 1–72.

DINGWALL, JOHN, *The American Woman.* New York: New American Library, 1958.

DIXON, MARLENE, "Why Women's Liberation?" *Ramparts,* 8 (December 1969), 58–63.

---

[6] Bick's (1968:4) hypothesis is similar: "When economic resources can be gained through participation in the sexual market-place, as for example, through marriage, then the sex that controls those resources will act as the consumer in the market-place, and the other sex will provide the objects for consumption."

FLUGEL, J. C., *The Psychology of Clothes*. London: Hogarth Press, 1930.

FRIEDAN, BETTY, *The Feminine Mystique*. New York: W. W. Norton, 1963.

GORER, GEOFFREY, *The American People*. New York: W. W. Norton, 1948.

KELLOGG, J. H. *Plain Facts for Both Sexes*. Battle Creek, Michigan: Good Health Publishing Co., 1910.

KINSEY, ALFRED, et al., *Sexual Behavior in the Human Male*. Philadelphia: W. B. Saunders, 1948.

——, *Sexual Behavior in the Human Female*. Philadelphia: W. B. Saunders, 1953.

LAVER, JAMES, *Taste and Fashion*. London: George G. Harrap, 1937.

MASTERS, WILLIAM H., and VIRGINIA E. JOHNSON, *Human Sexual Response*. Boston: Little, Brown, 1966.

MORRISON, DENTON E., and ALLAN D. STEEVES, "Deprivation, Discontent, and Social Movement Participation: Evidence on a Contemporary Farmers' Movement, the NFO," *Rural Sociology*, 32 (December 1967), 414–34.

New York Times, "Ten Thousand Wait in Vain for Re-appearance of Wall Street's Sweater Girl" (September 21, 1968), 14.

New York Times Magazine, "In San Francisco on August 1, 500 Women Took Off Their Bras in Protest. Should You Have Been Among Them?" [Peter Pan International advertisement] (January 25, 1970), 53.

Playboy, "Playboy Interview: Raquel Welch," 17 (January 1970), 75–90.

RIEGEL, ROBERT E., "Women's Clothes and Women's Rights," *American Quarterly*, 15 (Fall 1963), 390–401.

ROACH, MARY ELLEN, and JOANNE BUBOLZ EICHER, *Dress, Adornment and the Social Order*. New York: Wiley, 1965.

SAPIR, EDWARD, "Fashion," *Encyclopedia of the Social Sciences*, Vol. 6. New York: Macmillan, 1931, pp. 139–44.

SEWELL, WILLIAM, "Infant Training and the Personality of the Child," *The American Journal of Sociology*, 58 (September 1952), 150–59.

SIMMEL, GEORG, "Fashion," *American Journal of Sociology*, 62 (May 1957), 541–58. [Reprinted from *International Quarterly*, 10 (October 1904): 137–40.]

STERN, PAULA, "The Womanly Image: Character Assassination Through the Ages," *Atlantic*, 225 (March 1970), 87–90.

STONE, GREGORY, "Appearance and the Self," pp. 86–118 in Arnold Rose, ed., *Human Behavior and Social Processes: An Interactionist Perspective*. New York: Houghton Mifflin, 1962.

Time, 92 (September 13, 1968), 36.

VEBLEN, T., *The Theory of the Leisure Class*. New York: New American Library, 1953. [Originally published in New York: Macmillan, 1899.]

WAX, MURRAY, "Themes in Cosmetics and Grooming," *American Journal of Sociology*, 62 (May 1957), 588–93.

YOUNG, KIMBALL, *Social Psychology*. New York: F. S. Crofts, 1930.

WILLIAM KORNBLUM and PAUL LICHTER

Urban Gypsies and the Culture of Poverty

We need more studies of the social attitudes of criminals, of soldiers and sailors, of tavern life; and we should look at the evidence, not with a moralizing eye (Christ's poor were not always pretty), but with an eye for Brechtian values— the fatalism, the irony in the face of establishment homilies, the tenacity of self-preservation.—E. P. Thompson, *The Making of the English Working Class*

The remarkable achievement of the gypsies in Western societies is that they have maintained their traditional cultures and social structures despite all the pressures to assimilate which industrialized, urban societies bring to bear on foreigners. In the cities of Europe and America, where so many ethnic groups have struggled to win access to the social and material rewards of assimilation, the gypsies have resisted any temptation to compete for education, jobs, or rectitude in local communities. The gypsies continue to speak the language of the Rom, they maintain nomadic occupations, and they hold intact a patrimonial corporate family economy and a social structure based on endogamy. Unlike other diaspora peoples, the gypsies have never developed any but the most instrumental attachments to their host cultures. As nomads, wandering for centuries throughout Asia and Europe, the gypsies were never hunters or herdsmen who adapted to a difficult physical environment. Instead, they have been traders, tinkers, fortune-tellers, entertainers, and amiable conmen in a most human environment. This aspect of gypsy culture has been detailed in rural settings, where gypsy families travelled through the peasant lands of Central and Southern Europe, but in the city the gypsies are princes of the lumpenproletariat, and it is this special adaptation of gypsy culture which is our concern here.[1]

In general we do not support the theory that there is a "culture of pover-

"Urban Gypsies and the Culture of Poverty," by William Kornblum and Paul Lichter is reprinted from *Urban Life and Culture*, Volume 1, No. 3 (October 1972) pp. 239–53 by permission of the Publisher, Sage Publications, Inc.

[1] The best general works on the gypsies, although they deal almost exclusively with rural, nomadic gypsies, are Clebert (1967) and Yoors (1967). Two journals chronicle the movement of European gypsies; they are *The Journal of the Gypsy Lore Society* (London), and *Etudes Tsiganes* (Bulletin de l'Association Des Etudes Tsiganes, Paris).

ty" which organizes the society of under-class urban people (Valentine, 1968). Different groups adjust to poverty with a wide range of adaptive strategies and world views, and no group values poverty itself or makes it a desirable condition to wish upon its children. On the other hand, the gypsies are an outstanding example of a people who have spent generations in a milieu of great scarcity and whose culture allows them to survive and even flourish in relatively impoverished human environments. In common with other under-class ethnic groups, the gypsy world view stresses values of individual and group survival above all others. Among the recurring themes in gypsy thought are these: (1) the outside society is corrupt and exploiting and should in turn be exploited whenever possible; (2) status pretensions of group members and outsiders should be deflated, virtue cannot be maintained, and trust should be based on intimate knowledge of personal biographies; (3) loyalty to the gypsy family must be maintained at all costs, for solidarity is essential to survival. Of course, in the gypsy world view, these themes are manifest in forms of expression and patterns of behavior which vary among culturally different gypsy subgroups in different urban situations. The present paper will describe how the main elements of the gypsy world view sustain gypsy society in the cities of France and the United States.

TWO GYPSY GROUPS: THE BOYASH AND THE KALDERASH

The authors conducted field research in two settings: the first was among gypsies living on the industrial periphery of Paris; the second was among gypsies living in working-class neighborhoods of Seattle, Washington.[2] In the first case, the gypsies comprised a four-generation extended family, numbering approximately 87 persons. They made their base in a large, migrant shantytown, and although the family rarely moved en masse, it maintained a nomadic life style. Family members lived in their vehicles, and groups of them took frequent long trips through the French countryside. In the second case, in Seattle, the gypsies were more sedentary, although this is a matter of degree. The Seattle gypsies lived in private homes and tended to develop more prolonged attachments to some urban institutions than did the Parisian gypsies. On the other hand, the Seattle gypsies travelled widely throughout the West Coast states and could hardly be considered a sedentary people when compared to nongypsies.

The Parisian gypsies, whom the senior author was fortunate to meet and live with, are members of the Boyash group within the European Rom

[2] Kornblum lived with the Boyash gypsies in Paris for two months during 1968 and has conducted interviews with informants on gypsy cultures since that time. Lichter worked in Seattle as a volunteer caseworker for gypsy families during 1971.

gypsies.[3] The Boyash are predominantly animal trainers and circus travellers who wander through Yugoslavia, Romania, and other Balkan countries. The Ivanovich family, the Boyash family with whom the senior author lived, included approximately 87 adults and children, almost all of whom were members of the extended family led by M. Ivanovich and his wife. Typical lodgings for the nuclear family units within the larger family were either traditional gypsy wagons or panel trucks and buses. These were grouped around separate courtyards which the family had appropriated in the migrant "bidonville." In addition to the actual gypsy family members, the Ivanoviches also offered their society and protection to a wide variety of hangers-on in the camp, including a number of superannuated prostitutes and French hobos (clochards). The latter were treated as servants who did much of the undesirable work around the camp, including cutting firewood for cooking stoves, and caring for the family's menagerie.

Animals are still the economic mainstay of the Boyash gypsies, and in large packing crates on the edge of their compound, the Ivanovich family housed a bear, two llamas, a pony, five monkeys, and assorted goats and dogs. Whenever money was needed, small groups of gypsy men and boys put on animal shows in the working-class market areas of Paris. In addition to these itinerant shows, family members also engaged in other economic activities, including some trade in gold, stolen auto parts, and used wagons. The Boyash women typically remain in the camp and do not go out to tell fortunes, as do the women of the Kalderash and other gypsy groups.

The Seattle gypsies, whom the junior author met as a welfare case worker, are members of the Kalderash group of Rom-speaking gypsies. The Kalderash are the largest of the Rom groups and comprise the majority of gypsies in cities of the United States. Perhaps the largest American gypsy colony is located in Brooklyn, N.Y., but other groups of Kalderash Rom live and travel in Chicago and Los Angeles and other large cities of the Southwest. The Seattle gypsies considered here belong to three extended families: the Stephens, the Millers, and the Georges. In Seattle, as elsewhere in the United States, the Kalderash gypsies do itinerant repair work on automobiles and some trading of autos.

Traditionally, the Kalderash were tinkers and repairers of metalware, and their ability to repair dented fenders is only one adaptation of this skill. In addition to metal-working, the Seattle Kalderash obtain much of their income by exploiting the welfare system. Since rather large numbers of related gypsies share the same name, it is easy to circulate children and otherwise claim larger benefits than are strictly due. Nevertheless, the Seattle gypsies live in one-family, rented houses and thus appear to their neighbors to conform to the American pattern of single-family dwelling and

---

[3] Lang (1966) provides a good summary of materials on gypsy ethnicity.

nuclear family organization. In reality, the gypsies associate exclusively with members of their extended family networks.

Neither the Parisian nor the Seattle gypsies encourage their children to attend school at all, and the adults insist that gypsy language be spoken in the home. In consequence of this, most of the children and adolescents are illiterate. Like their parents, they must depend on a limited number of gypsy individuals in the families who can read. Of course illiteracy itself is not as important in creating dependence upon the extended family as is the fact that the children are rarely allowed to develop roles or peer relations in the outside community.

GYPSY WORLD VIEW AND THE LARGER SOCIETY: PARIS AND SEATTLE

Gypsies everywhere refer to nongypsies as "gadjé," a term similar in its nuances to "goy" or "ofay." The gadjé may be dangerous, they may be stupid, or they may be dangerously stupid, depending on their position in the larger society with respect to the gypsies. The world of the gadjo is a corrupt one, in which human exploitation is the rule, and the misery the gypsies have experienced is attributed to the exploitiveness of gadjo society. Beyond these common elements of the gypsy world view, the Boyash and Kalderash gypsies must deal with different urban institutions in metropolitan Paris and Seattle, and this necessity brings out contrasting modes of thought and behavior in the two groups. The Boyash gypsies most often deal with community political institutions, and they have developed to a fault the picaresque political style of under-class people. The Kalderash, on the other hand, are rarely visible in the urban communities where they live. On a regular basis, they deal only with the welfare system, and become extremely adept at working that system for their own benefit without becoming any more visible to the larger society.

In European cities, the Boyash gypsies are likely to live among other immigrant groups, particularly the Yugoslav, Algerian, and Spanish laborers who inhabit the migrant camps. The gypsies commonly travel between migrant camps, although they may make a more permanent base in a particular one. In consequence, the gypsies often find themselves considered part of a larger "social problem" in the urban communities where the camps are located. The gypsies and other migrants in the camps are often the subject of local ordinances and repressive actions by the police.[4] In re-

---

[4] One of the many ironies of this political conflict is the fact that the industrial suburbs of Paris, such as Saint Denis and La Courneuve, are often administered by elected officials of the French Communist Party. Debates within local party organizations over the treatment of gypsies and other migrant groups often are reduced to ideological conflict between Stalinist and Maoist factions in local governments.

action to hostile community officials, and given the difficulties of getting along with other nationality groups in a congested camp, Boyash gypsies place even greater stress on the need for internal solidarity than do the Kalderash. The Boyash gypsies often respond to repressive ordinances by becoming public figures, and by taking their case to sympathetic listeners in the press and in local government.

The situation of the American gypsies is quite different. As a group which exists in the proletarian backwaters of major cities, they have become less visible in the larger society just as the urban proletariat itself has receded into the background of American consciousness. Indeed, American gypsies have succeeded in becoming an almost secret culture. Even the most knowledgeable observers of the urban scene in Seattle are unaware of the existence of a gypsy community in the city. It is true that welfare officials notice gypsies who appear on the public assistance rolls. Most hospital personnel have also had experience with groups of gypsies who descend on the hospital to supervise the care of some important gypsy personage, usually claimed to be a king or queen of the gypsies.

In these instances, the gypsies use the outsiders' ignorance of their culture for instrumental purposes. For example, the claim that a hospitalized patient is a gypsy king or queen is usually sufficient to ensure that the patient receives special attention. In reality, however, the gypsies have no such monarchy, and the device is an elaborate public relations ploy designed to win concessions from local welfare institutions without making any concessions to the ethic of assimilation. In Europe, on the other hand, the conditions of gypsy life are still more difficult, and it is often necessary for them actively to campaign for the right to maintain their traditional models of existence.

THE BOYASH STYLE OF PICARESQUE POLITICS

Since they lack power in urban communities, under-class groups develop political styles which rest on illusion and disarming attacks against conventional norms. To be "loud and wrong," to have "chutzpa," to "epater les bourgeois," are all statements of how to bluff and disarm the opposition when one is actually powerless. In the case of the Boyash gypsies, the politics of bluff and illusion are often carried to heights of the picaresque, as is apparent in the following episode from Parisian field notes:

> The Boyash believe that they can train almost any animal, although their experience is limited to bears, goats, and monkeys, and their knowledge of other large animals is slim. Nevertheless, the elder Ivanovich convinced his sons and sons-in-law that they could add to their income and to the prestige of the family if they could procure and train an elephant. After mailing inquiries throughout their extensive network of contacts in European cities, they located a baby

elephant for sale in Brussels. By calling in debts owed to them in the camp, and by selling some of their gold reserves, the family quickly raised the necessary cash. The senior Ivanovich and his three oldest sons left for Brussels at once to close the deal.

Once back at the camp on the edge of Paris, the elephant was installed in a large packing crate while the Ivanovich family congratulated themselves on the success of the venture. Other inhabitants of the bidonville—Algerians, Serbians, and Portuguese—flocked to the gypsy quarter to view this latest feat of the gypsies' ability to hustle and succeed. The elephant, along with the bear and other animals, was paraded through the camp regularly, and all other business came to a halt while the gypsies held center stage.

Three days later the elephant was dead, apparently the victim of careless worming by the former owner. Without delay the Ivanovich men armed themselves and rushed to Brussels to settle their debt. Before leaving, they and other members of the family dragged the elephant to an open space behind the camp. In their absence, it being the middle of a hot summer, the elephant began to cause serious concern among local health officials, who demanded that the gypsies bury the beast in a deep lime-filled pit. Since the adult men were gone, the gypsy women claimed that they would have to wait for their return, or else the township would have to dispose of the carcass. Four days passed, and this stalemate between the gypsy women and local officials continued. Photographers from *France-Soir* and other metropolitan newspapers brought the story to the attention of the larger city, while the mayor of the local township fumed and threatened to bulldoze the entire squatter settlement.

As the debate continued in the press and at the camp, the Ivanovich men made their second triumphal entrance, this time parading two adult llamas which they had accepted to make good on their loss. To inquiring reporters, the senior Ivanovich expressed concern that the township had not fulfilled its obligation to preserve the health of the community. He noted that he was in poor health and of advancing years. His eldest son had died the year before, leaving the family without its rightful heir, and his younger sons could not handle the job of digging a pit large enough to bury the carcass. All these interviews were conducted with a great deal of flourish and at such length as to make it difficult for township officials to speak with the gypsies alone. Usually the interviews climaxed with a parade of the new llamas, whose unique trait seemed to be a propensity to hiss and spit at admirers. By this time the story was being carried in "human interest" spots on the national television network, and the local officials were hardly in a position to carry out their threats.

In the end, the township sent a bulldozer to dig a large trench for the decaying elephant. The gypsies made a show of buying the lime and sprinkling it over the departed. It was only much later that M. Ivanovich discovered that his llamas were impossible to train for circus work. However, they did add another touch of the exotic for occasional parades.

The picaresque political style which the Ivanovich family has perfected seems necessary if their traditional corporate family economy is to remain intact. When travelling circuses were commonplace, the Boyash gypsies had little trouble showing their animals in city streets. Today, however, television and mass culture have made inroads into the audience for folk performances. More than ever before, the Boyash find it difficult to socialize their children into the traditional family occupations. Adolescent children feel shame at having to go into Paris with the older gypsy men to show the animals in the market places. They feel embarrassed at having to hold out a hat for donations and at being so often the object of laughter and scorn. But the Ivanovich world view reinforces their dependence on the extended gypsy family, and operates over time to bring the adolescents and young adults closer to the traditional gypsy values.

Within the family, shame and scorn are used to deflate illusions of personal status for the benefit of the entire group. For example, if a man or a woman is thought to be guilty of excessive pride, that person is upbraided in front of the entire family. If a protest is made, the common response from the senior Ivanovich couple is, for example, "Madame la Marquise, allez coucher dans ton chateau, ici nous sommes tous dans la misere"[5] (spoken in French rather than Rom for the added irony). This practice of using shame and cynicism to deflate illusions generalizes to all attitudes concerning the future. It is used in particular to describe the future of relations with the outside world, for family members believe the authorities will inevitably come to break up their camp, and therefore they must maintain their capacity to move out on short notice. They perceive the world of the gadjo as unstable and dependent for its order on arrangements among powerful actors. "Today we say vive le president," Madame Ivanovich explained. "Tomorrow we will say vive le roi, it's all the same to us."

Events in the gadjo world usually confirm the gypsies' cynicism and demonstrate to young gypsies the need to remain in the family. For example, during the abortive 1968 revolution in France, when Paris was crippled by general strikes and riots, the other migrant groups in the camp were forced to join the bread lines. The gypsies' major complaint was the difficulty of obtaining cigarettes. Years of travel through the political states of Europe had prepared them for such events. They had only to call out their gold reserves and find sources of food through their wide-ranging contacts in the city in order to do quite well in this period of crisis in the gadjo society.

KALDERASH GYPSIES AND WELFARE POLITICS

The Seattle Kalderash strike a quite different stance with regard to the gadjo world. They place great emphasis on accumulating the trappings of material respectability, while making only the most minimal commitments

---

[5] "Your highness the Marquess, you go sleep in your castle, here the rest of us are down and out."

to gadjo society. In part, this is possible because their traditional crafts more readily lend themselves to adaptation in American cities than would those of the Boyash gypsies. Also, opportunities abound in this society for the Kalderash gypsies to do well by seeming to the gadjé to do poorly.

Kalderash men engage in automobile body repairs, roofing, stove cleaning in restaurants, and other short-term jobs which do not result in any extensive personal or financial commitment between gypsy and employer. In almost all cases, the work is contracted and paid for by cash, so that the Seattle gypsy does not experience payroll deductions for Social Security or income tax, and no records of the transactions exist. This is particularly desirable for segments of the Kalderash families who are simultaneously receiving unemployment compensation or public assistance. Some Kalderash families also add to their level of living through the use or misuse of credit. If a family plans to move soon, they may have goods delivered to them at home under a false name, and large phone bills are accumulated in the process of communicating with far-flung kin. At times, it is possible to buy expensive items (color TVs, furniture, and the like) on time under false names and abscond with them after making the down payment. Housing, too, can be had cheaply if the family makes a deposit, moves in, and pays no more rent until they are evicted and move someplace else. These practices are not universal among Seattle's Kalderash gypsies; a large proportion pay their bills and conduct their business affairs quite conventionally. However, the instances of fraud cited here occur in a larger percentage of gypsy families than in most other ethnic groups. And it is the cultural premeditation of these activities which distinguishes gypsies from others who operate in terms of chance and opportunism.

These instances of conflict with gadjo society maintain the gypsy sense of community which, in turn, further isolates them from the respectable mainstream of American life. But the Kalderash do not perceive these situations as creating either personal or communal tension, for these are merely local adaptations of time-worn cultural practices. In the rural gypsy world view, as described by Yoors (1967: 34):

> stealing from Gadjé was not really a misdeed as long as it was limited to the taking of basic necessities, and not in larger quantities than were needed at that moment. It was the intrusion of a sense of greed, in itself, that made stealing wrong, for it made men slaves to unnecessary appetites or to their desire for possessions. Gleaning a little dry wood for the fire, from the forest, was no misdeed. There was so much of it, and anyway if they did not take it it was left to rot. Putting a few horses to pasture overnight in someone's meadow was not that bad. Grass grew without the owner's active contribution or effort.

Urban gypsies in the United States often take an equivalent position with regard to the bountiful social environment created by American welfare institutions. In a forest of bureaus and branch offices, with so many transient gadjé who want to give help in such small amounts compared to the great riches elsewhere in the city, it is almost impossible to resist the temptation to glean supplementary incomes from the welfare institutions. The welfare system is grounded in principles of egalitarian liberalism and functions according to a bureaucratic methodology that is designed to treat all clients in a similar manner. But the Kalderash do not relate to established authority like "all clients." Their approach to the welfare system involves the creation of situations of quiet chaos for administrators and caseworkers. Since job turnover among these officials is quite high, it becomes almost impossible to sort out the record of aid to gypsies who do not have birth certificates, marriage certificates, or Social Security numbers, and yet maintain extremely large, extended families. The Kalderash gypsies' relation to the welfare system on the West Coast is evident in the following correspondence from the general manager of a large office of public assistance in California to the director of the Seattle–King County Central Office.

Dr. Mr. M.——:

Enclosed please find Xeroxed copy of gypsy "family trees" recently compiled by this worker, who is presently responsible for all Aid to Families with Dependent Children Gypsy families in ——. It is believed this information may be useful to you and your Index office to forestall possible duplication of aid to these highly transient people.

Although almost all of the George families, underlined in red, are highly transient, worker is, at the moment, specifically concerned about the three children of Catherine George, presently sharing the same address. These are: Rachel (George) Mitchell, Case No. 533–038, mother of Jerry, date of birth 9/29/60; Tammy George, Case No. 624-152, mother of Baca, 9/29/60; Susie, 10/8/64; Peaches, 7/31/61; Ginny, 4/1/68; and Nana, 8/1/69; and Dina (Efram) Marks, Case No. 531-393, mother of Unda, 8/8/64.

The other families who have used the George residence temporarily while claiming aid, all of whom have left town within a week or two, are (see Xeroxed sheets), the Ruby George family, the Bobbie George family, the Lizzie Miller family, the Mary Miller family, the Rosie Miller family, the Steve and Ruby George family, the Tina George family and another Ruby George family. Actually almost all of the Miller-George families noted on the sheets attached, are, and have been highly transient. Please note, on page 9, the Steve and Marjorie George family and the Ron and Ann Miller family placed out of order on page 6. They are somehow related to the Rita Miller family, bottom of page 8, who is reportedly receiving aid at the present in Portland, Oregon.

Worker has no doubt that if the families are, as reported, moving up and down the Western coast, applying for aid, they will be returning within a week or so claiming never to have left town.

Thank you for any assistance you can provide in this matter.

The family trees which "worker" compiled demonstrate the futility of attempting to trace the movements of Kalderash gypsies in the United States. The documents are crammed with page after page of names, birth dates, last known addresses, and suspected kin ties. In general, they are so confused as to make it impossible to have any confidence in the records, and the project itself becomes another instance of the effectiveness with which the gypsies manage their relationships with gadjé institutions. Also, there is no mention here of possible causes for Kalderash abuses of the welfare system. For their part, the Seattle gypsies often justify abuses of the welfare system on the grounds that laws making fortune-telling illegal in most cities deprive their women of their traditional means of earning a livelihood. And to make matters more difficult for welfare caseworkers, gypsy dealings with offices of public assistance tend to increase the amount of feuding which normally exists between large gypsy families.[6]

The Seattle gypsies often attempt to displace pressure from welfare officials on other families with whom they are feuding. Such feuds are commonplace and may be due to quarrels over bride price, between competing fortune-telling shops, or other family rivalries. It is tempting to use the welfare system as a weapon in these quarrels by suggesting to caseworkers that another family may be abusing the system. These violations of in-group solidarity increase the level of bickering between gypsy families and in some instances act to increase dependence on the system itself. In general, the more the Kalderash gypsies struggle to retain their welfare benefits, the more they come to believe that the benefits are essential and must be maintained.

CONCLUSION

Of all the cultures which have encountered the assimilating pressures of modern, urban societies, the gypsy's has been perhaps the most self-sustaining. Rather than accept values from the dominant society, the tenacity of gypsy culture depends in large part on a specific rejection of those values. What Marcuse has called the "great refusal" of lumpenproletariat groups to become attached to the dominant institutions of the larger society has been a feature of gypsy culture for centuries. The Kalderash, the Boyash, the Lovara, and other Rom groups will continue to look with a cynical eye at the enticements Western societies offer to groups which assimilate. On the other hand, this research has demonstrated that the Boyash gypsies in

[6] The subject of feuding among gypsy families deserves more attention than can be given to it in this paper. Solidarity among gypsy subgroups usually does not extend very far beyond the patrilocal extended families and long-standing feuds between gypsy families of different or the same subgroups are common.

France and the Kalderash gypsies in the United States must cope with quite different urban institutions. Although assimilation itself may be minimal for both gypsy groups, contrasting urban environments in Paris and Seattle call forth different adaptive strategies which themselves should have lasting effects on the survival of gypsy culture and the gypsy world view.

The Parisian gypsies' style of bluff and illusion in dealings with urban political institutions readily lends itself to further political organization among gypsies in general. As the Boyash take on public political roles, they also begin to select leaders who can represent more than one extended family. These are usually men and women who have had experiences such as described for the Ivanovich family, and whose advice in similar situations is sought after by other gypsy families in the city. It is not surprising, therefore, that in Paris and other European cities the gypsies have begun to organize ethnic political organizations whose activities are designed to win concessions which allow the gypsies to maintain their traditional life style. In contrast to the growing nationalism of European gypsies, gypsies in the United States are quite reluctant to assume public political roles or to do anything which draws attention to themselves. Thus Kalderash gypsies in Seattle attempt to limit their dealings with gadjo institutions to the welfare system, while remaining largely unknown as a people elsewhere in the city. The ease with which funds can be had from offices of public assistance, and the dependence the relationship fosters may eventually be inimical to the traditional mobility and independence of gypsy cultures.

REFERENCES

CLEBERT, J. P., *The Gypsies*. Baltimore: Penguin, 1967.

LANG F., "Tsiganes, Gitanes, Romanichels et Autres Distinctions." *Etudes Tsiganes* 6 (June 1966), 11–22.

VALENTINE, C. A., *Culture and Poverty*. Chicago: Univ. of Chicago Press, 1968.

YOORS, J., *The Gypsies*. New York: Simon & Schuster, 1967.

GEORGE H. LEWIS

Capitalism, Contra-Culture, and the Head Shop: Explorations in Structural Change

If there exists a single word that would most aptly reflect the ethos of the new American youth culture—especially as this culture is articulated in both urban and rural youth ghettos—that word is *anti-capitalism*. As Rom Thelin, originator of the first head shop[1] in San Francisco's Haight-Ashbury district in 1966 put it: "Money people, the people who see through the eyes of money, cannot see any activity or human involvement unless they surround it with some kind of relationship with money. This is the most difficult thing to transcend . . . doing things for free instead of for money" (Von Hoffman, 1968: 124).

From this reactive stance was born the concept of the "free store"—that which was put into practice in 1966 by the street people of the Haight (Howard: 1969; Cavan, 1972: 49–55). Although the concept was not a new one, it had a new audience and was quickly spread up and down the West Coast by the youth underground.

The spring of 1967 saw the beginnings of the (not entirely unwelcome) media exploitation and rape of the Haight "contra-culture"[2] and the invasion of that territory by both tourists and upper-middle-class summer run-

"Capitalism, Contra-Culture, and the Head Shop: Explorations in Structural Change," by George H. Lewis is reprinted from *Youth and Society*, Volume 4, No. 1 (Sept. 1972) pp. 85–102 by permission of the Publisher, Sage Publications, Inc.

This is a revised version of a paper read at the 1971 American Sociological Association annual meeting, Denver, Colorado, August 29–September 3, 1971.

[1] The term "head shop" was originally used by members of the youth contra-culture to refer to shops that sold the necessary accoutrements for a successful drug trip—i.e., incense, posters, cigarette papers, water pipes, black lights, recordings, and so on. It is in this sense that the term is employed in this paper. The distinction is necessary because of the fact that the term has been appropriated by the general public to refer to *any* shops whose wares appeal to those of the youth contra-culture—health food stores are but one example that comes to mind. A shop of this variety would not be considered a head shop by this author.

[2] In this paper, the term contra-culture is used in the sense Yinger (1960:629) employs it: "Whenever the normative system of a group contains, as a primary element, a theme of conflict with the values of the total society, where personality variables are directly involved in the development and maintenance of the group's values, and wherever its norms can be understood only by reference to the relationships of the group to a surrounding dominant culture."

aways. The psychedelic or "head" shops, subjected to strong social and economic pressures, began to change. Although a very few remained close to the originating impulse, most began charging money and changing orientation—looking to the outsider as customer.

By the close of summer 1967, the head shops in the Haight were charging more for the same wares than shops in more commercial areas of San Francisco, such as along Market Street. And by middle fall of that year, with dying ideological support from the street, economic mismanagement, and a bursting of the "Hashbury" media bubble, shop after shop was pointed toward extinction. Most were gone by December.

One of the few shops that remained solidly in support of the originating anti-capitalistic ethic—that did not "rip-off the people"—was Ron Thelin's *Psychedelic Shop*. He closed his doors early in October 1967. "The mass media made us into hippies. We wanted to be free men and build a free community. That word hippy turned everybody off. . . . Well, the hippies are dead" (Von Hoffman, 1968: 238). And so, it seemed, was the concept of the "free store," operating within the structure of the most affluent nation on earth.

Was this breakdown inevitable? Or, put another way, can an organization based on values generally antithetical to those of the social structure within which it exists become and remain viable? This is the central question which this paper addresses. The first investigative step will be to examine in more detail entrepreneurial aspects of the Haight-Ashbury phenomenon.

THE HEAD SHOP: 1966–1967[3]

Perhaps the most important point to be kept in mind when examining organizations of the youth contra-culture is that their value structures are overarchingly anti-capitalist. This is a reactive framework—a rejection of the means, goals, *and* values of American society.[4] Although by no means

[3] The material presented in this section has been taken from empirical studies and published accounts of the experiences of those in the Haight-Ashbury district of San Francisco (Berger, 1967; Cavan, 1972; Davis, 1967; Hinkle, 1967; Howard, 1969; Karpel, 1970; Luce, 1969; Thompson, 1967; Von Hoffman, 1968; Wolf, 1968; Wolfe, 1968; Yablonsky, 1968), as well as the author's own observations and those of acquaintances—some of whom have been involved in conducting research in the area.

[4] Lewis Yablonsky (1968: 362), in analyzing the responses of dropped out youth to his open-ended question, "how do you feel about American society," found criticisms falling in three major areas: the lack of human interpersonal relationships, materialism, and hypocrisy. I have found that many of those with whom I have talked point to these three as symptoms of a a capitalist society, thereby isolating the cause—capitalism—against which they are reacting. John Howard (1969: 46) has aptly termed this reactive stance as one of an *inversion* of traditional American values. See Cavan (1972: 57–78) for a cogent discussion of hippie belief systems as articulated in Haight-Ashbury.

the first American social movement to reject the American social system,[5] the hippie phenomenon has emerged as one of the most emphatic and widely publicized of these movements.

With respect to economics, the reactive ethic takes the form of generalized reciprocity,[6] redistribution,[7] and the rejection of the use of money wherever possible. Confusion arises, however, as it does in situations of reactive value formations, as to how exactly to translate thought into action.[8] And so the philosophy: "Establish the social facts first, and the economics will follow" (Von Hoffman, 1968: 124). Thus, there was a great deal of "slippage" between ethic (or value) and behavior when the first of these shops opened.

The stores were, in general, of two types:[9]

1. The *exchange and redistribution model*, where goods and services were exchanged. These stores generally stocked used clothing, a few books, some food, and whatever bric-a-brac was offered for trade. This model rejected totally the medium of money as exchange, relying primarily on the concept of the redistribution of goods from a centralized location.

2. The *community-oriented model*, where accoutrements necessary for the playing of community roles could be purchased "at cost." These stores generally stocked books, incense, papers and pipes, jewelry, posters, and records. Community seamstresses and tailors operated from the community-oriented shops.

The exchange and redistribution model, as an ideal type, soon proved unworkable. It was recognized that the most important function of this type of shop was to provide basic necessities (such as food, clothes) for com-

[5] Polsky has argued that the *ideology* of the 1950 beats lay behind their absolute refusal to work within the "system," thereby refuting the traditional "double failure theory of retreatism." Examination of the youth contra-culture might lend further credence to Polsky's view that ideological refusals to perform within the range of establishment norms are largely cultural (or contra-cultural) in origin (Polsky, 1967: 154).

[6] The term is meant as Sahlins (1965) defined it—a form of exchange based on the assumption that returns will balance out in the long run.

[7] The term is meant as Polanyi (1953) defined it—the flow of goods and services into a central store, to then be redistributed throughout the system.

[8] According to Richard Rubenstein (1970), this lack of concrete designs for action is typical of American social movements, which usually take the form of reactions to territorial intrusions. Howard (1969: 45) sums up these reactions as attempts to transform the larger society by the *example* of doing one's own thing.

[9] In a rough sense, the distinction between these two types of stores (with respect to the wares they handled) parallels Nash's (1966: 48–53) distinction in non-monetary economies between the subsistence circuit of exchange and those of luxury and ceremony. Those operating stores of the exchange and redistribution type were primarily concerned with the redistribution of subsistence goods. Those operating community-oriented stores were more concerned with the exchange and redistribution of ceremonial (and to a lesser extent, luxury) goods.

munity members, and that this service would have to be financed in *some* way. This function was generally taken on by: (a) some community-oriented shops, (b) some charitable organizations that located in the Haight, and (c) organizations such as the Diggers, who operated as free-form mobile redistribution centers (Howard, 1969).

The community-oriented shops, then, evolved into what are known as head shops—serving the community by: (a) offering for sale "at cost" the accoutrements for community role performance—most especially drug "tripping," (b) acting as centers for the distribution of information concerning community activities, and (c) acting as centers for "rap sessions"— reaffirming community values (even as these were mainly reactive anti-values).[10]

As John Lofland (1967) has pointed out, the members of the youth contra-culture, seeking territorial autonomy, have voluntarily withdrawn into "youth ghettos," Haight-Ashbury being one of the first of these.[11] Historically, the sense of community within the ghetto has been necessarily high (Wirth, 1928) and leads to strong feelings of hostility toward members of outgroups that "trespass" on community territory, as well as to purposeful attempts to maximize the autonomy of the community social system (Rubenstein, 1970). Cavan (1972: 75) recounts a not uncommon incident from her field notes in Haight-Ashbury that illustrates this point well.

> The tourist approaches a cluster of Hippies lounging against one of the cars. Only a few minutes earlier, I had been listening to their conversation, which was essentially that love would set the "straight" world straight. The tourist, with deference and politeness, requests permission from the Hippies to take their photograph. One of the Hippies says to him, "I'd like to take that camera and bash it in your face." Two or three other Hippies nod in agreement; none of them protest the response.

Within the social structure of the Haight-Ashbury ghetto, then, the head shop fulfilled a number of primary community functions—being in a loosely analogous sense, a combination of church, community center, and public drinking place in the straight world.

There was, however, one major problem in the operation of these shops. Not being completely divorced from the larger social structure surround-

---

[10] As Sherri Cavan (1972: 109; 1966: 205–33) has pointed out, this use of the head shop is quite analogous to the use of public drinking places as informal gathering places for various collectivities.

[11] Other youth ghettos of 1971 being the Isla Vista area of Santa Barbara and Telegraph Avenue area of Berkeley. Rural ghettos have also been established, as youth are driven from the more accessible and blight-stricken urban ghettos, such as Haight-Ashbury. The Telegraph area of Berkeley is at present rapidly going the same route as the Haight.

ing them, shop operators found a need for money as a medium of exchange. Many of the goods offered had to be purchased from outside the community system, there were rents to consider, not all food was gratis the Diggers. Furthermore, although the community had rejected money as a medium of exchange, nothing had been set up in its place. The social facts, although not crystallized, were established. Economics *did* follow. As one member remarked: "This community is based on dope, not love" (Von Hoffman, 1968: 240). And dope can be translated into money.

During the spring of 1967, the highly visible Haight community became increasingly the target of the mass media. As members of the out-group invaded community territory, the owners of the head shops were faced with a dilemma—that of competing clientele. In most cases, this dilemma was resolved by means of a "Robin Hood rationalization"—that it was permissible to charge members of the out-group inordinately high prices for the accoutrements of community role performance, as the profits from these "rip-offs" would be injected into the community system. Much like earlier "Harlem slumming" behavior patterns as well as the 1959–1961 invasion patterns of Greenwich Village (Polsky, 1967: 148–49), the ethic is summed up by Dan, who owned one of the Haight shops:

> Our products exploit middle-class people who affect [sic] the idea of hip. I'm not against exploitation, you see. Everything's exploitation. You just have to be careful whom you exploit and for what reason. In the process of the rip-off, I want to come up with something in my pocket [Karpel, 1970: 277].

That "something in my pocket" began to take on more and more value in the cases of many shop operators. Profits from the rip-off were of a much lower risk content than those gained from dealing in drugs (especially with the increased visibility the mass media produced for the community). As many of the shops catered more to out-group clientele, new anti-values took root in the community. Possession of the accoutrements labeled one as an outsider—new role costumes evolved (flashy flower clothes gave way to faded mismatches . . . bells and beads were dropped).[12] The shops played less and less a role in the community system. As they became increasingly capitalistically oriented, with dying ideological support from the street community, shop owners found themselves hooked into the system they had originally fled.[13]

[12] This process, labeled by Goffman (1951) as the circulation of symbols and by Polsky (1967) as the stealing of signals is explained as an attempt on the part of a subgroup to create new symbols to replace those which laymen have appropriated. See also Simmel's (1950: 334–44) cogent discussion of the social significance of secrecy, adornment, and secrecy as adornment.

[13] By making this generalization I am not overlooking the few shops that chose not to close their doors rather than go this route, nor those that sprang into being with out-group ownership concerned only with exploiting the system.

As the excitement of the Haight as a media fad burned itself out (as it did within eight months), disappointment, economic mismanagement, and a slowing trickle of straight customers forced most of the shops that still remained open to close. The Haight, as a youth community, was dead. However, the anti-values expressed and acted out by those in the Haight of 1966 were diffused (even as they were romantically distorted) across America by both over- and underground media.

THE NORTHWEST CITY STUDY[14]

As word spread about the "death of Hippie" in the fall of 1967, the search for alternative youth territories intensified. This search, on the West Coast, involved locating other possible urban ghettos as well as the search for rural ghettos (communes).

Northwest City, a community of around 100,000, was the site in 1967 of the beginnings of one West Coast alternate youth ghetto, its inception facilitated no doubt by the preexistence of a sizable (although atomistic) college community. As in Haight-Ashbury, head shops arose as important aspects of this youth community. The following is an attempt to trace the natural history of these shops from their emergence in 1967 to the present (spring 1971). The data consist of interviews with those involved in founding the more important of these shops and running them since their inception, as well as interviews with "steady" customers. Artifact analysis was employed as a second means of data collection (in terms of those artifacts displayed in the shops). Lastly, participant observation was employed, as the author has been involved with the personnel of these shops during the four years of their existence.

PRESENTATION OF THE DATA

As was the case in Haight-Ashbury, the first (1967) generation of Northwest City shops (three in number) took the form of experimental community centers. Set up in the low-rent downtown business district of the city, these three served as meeting places and information dissemination centers. Their wares consisted primarily of contra-culture accoutrements for role performance (leatherwork, beads, incense, papers and pipes, posters, and so on). Each had a community bulletin board upon which announcements

[14] In presenting the Northwest City data, I chose to concentrate on a few shops rather than attempt a description of all. There were many reasons for this, not the least of which being the lack of available space in this paper in which to do an adequate job. The shops I did single out seemed not only typical of the processes I was studying, but were important in another sense, in that many exhibited a continuity of actors across generations of shops, thereby linking the processual cycles involved (see Table 1 for a chronological listing of all Northwest City head shops).

Table 1 Chronological Presentation of Northwest City Head Shops, 1967–1970 (by Quarter Years)

Year	Quarter	1st Generation	2nd Generation	3rd Generation	4th Generation
1967	2				
1967	3				
1967	4				
1968	1				
1968	2				
1968	3				
1968	4				
1969	1				
1969	2				
1969	3				
1969	4				
1970	1				
1970	2				
1970	3				
1970	4				
1971	1				

were tacked. In the main, these announcements were of two types: (a) declarations of group activities (picnics, be-in's, meditation sessions), and (b) appeals for transportation or home mates. In the beginning, announcements of salable goods, although in existence, were of a minimum.

Established during the early and middle spring of 1967, two of these three shops were nonexistent by early fall of that year. The remaining shop was closed early in 1968. There seemed to be four major reasons for the demise of these organizations:

a. The patrons of these shops viewed them more as community centers than as places to purchase goods. As a result, economic transactions were of a minimum nature—the stores became places to "hang out."

b. Again, as in the early days of the Haight, the primary exchange network set up was in terms of drugs (which could be translated into funds for rent, food, and the like).

c. The reactive economic ethic led to gross mismanagements of the small cash funds that were established.

d. The larger business community was hostile to the existence of these shops in their midst and continually pushed for their closure. Two of the three shops were closed when their owners were arrested on drug charges. The third closed as a result of outside community pressure (infractions of city noise ordinances led to revoking of the lease) and internal economic mismanagement.

In the late fall of 1967, the first of the second generation of shops was opened. The owner (Ted) was well aware of the reasons behind the demise of the earlier shops and vowed not to repeat their mistakes. "We made it by steering clear of dope which is the big bugaboo by which most counterculture stores are brought down. That and allowing the store to become a hangout for bikers and other scruffy types that intimidate would-be customers."[15] Although Ted also encountered the hostility of the larger business community, he was careful in managing his shop and steered clear of the drug network.

Ted began by stocking the same general goods as had the other shops. Yet his emphasis on the economic exchange network (as opposed to the drug network) and his management practices combined to make feasible his branching out, in early 1968, into the record market. Records, an increasingly important artifact of the youth contra-culture, were seldom stocked by the early head shops because of the cost involved. Ted felt he could afford to stock records and sell them more cheaply than the establishment stores in Northwest City were doing, while he expanded his stock gradually and at a relatively low cost per unit.

During 1968, as Ted's shop shifted emphasis more and more toward recording stock, there was a concomitant shift in clientele. High school and college youths, eager to purchase the accoutrements of contra-culture, began to make up more and more of the business. The community bulletin board reflected this change—more and more advertisements announcing cultural artifacts for sale, or music lessons for a price, appeared. Fewer announcements of contra-culture happenings were tacked up—although the proportion of "rides wanted" notices seemed to remain about the same.[16] By 1969, Ted was caught in the same dilemma as the Haight shops before him—that of competing clientele. As he continued to expand his record stock and cater to the out-group clientele, Ted was labeled more and more often an "outsider." Finally, in the summer of 1969, three of his long-standing employees left him to start (along with two others) a third generation shop. As Ted explained it:

> Carl [one of the employees], in association with two other employees, believed that I was making and stashing large amounts of money. . . . Their belief persisted even though I opened the books to them. . . . Also of importance was

[15] It is interesting to note the importance of *intimidation* in contra-cultural social systems. See Yablonsky's (1968: 181–98) discussion of Fillmore blacks in the Morningstar commune, Howard's (1969) and Von Hoffman's (1968) discussions of bikers in the Haight, as well as the performance of the Hells Angels at the Rolling Stones' free 1969 Altamont concert, as chronicled in the semi-documentary movie Gimmie Shelter.

[16] These data were obtained by asking shop operators, workers, and customers if they had perceived any changes in the content of bulletin board announcements during the time intervals specified. These data, more impressionistic as they applied to 1967 and 1968 and more systematic in their collection from late 1968 on, were compared with the author's own perceptions during this period, to arrive at the general conclusions as reported in the body of the paper.

the fact that many considered Carl as "one heavy dude." There was always constant conflict as to who really knew where it was at.

Carl explains it thusly: "Ted is an excellent businessman . . . but I thought he should start responding to the community that supported him. . . . We opened [the new shop] to give people an alternative store . . . righteous prices, etc."

Carl's shop, at its inception, bore a striking resemblance to Ted's shop in its early days—the main difference being that one of the owners had a fairly large amount of capital (an inheritance) which he sank at the outset into stock. Hence Carl's shop began with a fair supply of records and some musical instruments, as well as the traditional leather goods, candles, pottery, and incense. Located next to Northwest City College, Carl's shop began attracting the college crowd. Again, over the months, one could note bulletin board content changes similar to those at Ted's. More heavily into the drug scene (but careful not to allow the shop to become a distribution center), Carl and his associates became involved with the rock bands of Northwest City. This involved another change, as Carl began stocking the artifacts of rock band culture (largely, guitars and amplifiers). Again the classic clientele dilemma was posed, and economic considerations seemed to win out.

> I'd say we deal more with the "college hippie" and the straights. Yes, it's changed. When we were the underdog, everyone patronized us to see who we were and what way we were going. Now they sense the presence of a lot of money (guitars and amplifiers) and it makes them a little uneasy. As it does me. I think freaks only use our shop for musical needs.

Recently (fall 1970) an employee of Carl's (one of the original employees of Ted) has left and opened his own shop, dealing mainly in recording, candles, and leather goods. A more modest shop than Carl's, this heralded the inception of a fourth generation of Northwest City head shops. Whether it will be any more successful than its predecessors in resolving the dilemma of the contra-culture shop remains to be seen.[17] As Carl has put it:

> The store . . . any hip store, really . . . has to go one of two ways when it's clear it's making it. When money gets involved, naturally the owner moves onto another level . . . of income and philosophy. . . . He has to decide who he works for—himself or the people. It's kind of obvious which way he goes. Personally I don't think it can be done. . . . We're certainly copping out right and left.

---

[17] As of early 1972, this fourth generation shop, after a year of marginal operation, had closed its doors. The owner, determined not to sell out, as Ted and Carl had, in his eyes, refused to make similar concessions and clientele adjustment—opting for closure instead.

DISCUSSION AND IMPLICATIONS

As previously stated, the overarching question to which this paper is addressed is: can an organization based on values generally antithetical to those of the social structure within which it exists become and remain viable? I have noted the early failure in the Haight of those shops attempting to utilize exchange or redistribution of goods as an alternative. In both the Haight and Northwest City, those shops that attempted to utilize drugs as an alternative exchange network also failed. The shops that survived were those shops whose owners recognized the fact that, even though capitalism was abhorrent to them, they would have to work through established monetary exchange networks. This process of accommodation, of fitting into the established society while remaining apart from it, seemed to produce in the operators of these shops a great amount of ambivalence and ambiguity in attitude.

Table 2   TYPES OF HEAD SHOPS, CLASSED BY IDEOLOGY AND BEHAVIOR PATTERN[a]

Type of Head Shop	Values of Established Order	Behavior Patterns of Established Order
1. Shopping center plastic	accept	accept
2. Radical	reject	reject
3. Hip capitalist	accept	reject
4. Midnight hip	reject	accept

[a] I have deliberately set up this paradigm on the basis of acceptance or rejection of the patterns of the established social order (and not with respect to alternatives of the contra-cultural order) precisely because the values and behavior patterns of the contra-culture are, as Howard (1969: 46) has pointed out, inversions of established patterns.

According to Thomas O'Dea, there are three options a group has in establishing relations with the social order (not, for the moment, considering isolationism). The first possibility is to reject the social order, the second is to accept it, the third is to promote one's own ideology while behaving within the normative boundaries of the established order (O'Dea, 1966: 48). These options are useful in establishing a paradigm within which to classify the various forms of contra-culture head shop—for they point up the basic distinction one should make between the ideology, or values, of a social group and the behavior patterns of its members.[18]

[18] This distinction is similar to the one Cavan makes between "beliefs" and "practices"—a distinction she traces back to a theoretical problem first raised and explored by Max Weber. "While the problem raised by Weber is not forgotten in sociology, in contemporary sociological work we tend routinely to treat that relationship between beliefs and practices as a constant conjunction. That is, we tend to make use of the concept of 'culture' in a way which assumes there is a relationship between a people's beliefs and a people's practices. . . . For Weber, however, that relationship was always in part an open question" (Cavan, 1972: 11).

CATEGORIZATION OF SHOP TYPES

(1) Shopping center plastic. The values and the behavior patterns of the established order are accepted. This is the case of the shop that never did have anything to do with youth contra-culture. These shops sell mass-produced equivalents of contra-culture role accoutrements to middle-class straights—"shopping center plastic hip."

(2) Radical. The values of the established order are rejected, as well as the accepted behavior patterns. This is the radical option—taken by the exchange and redistribution shops and those utilizing drugs as an alternative exchange network.

(3) Hip capitalist. The values of the established order may be accepted, but the accepted behavior patterns are not. Although none of the shops focused on in this paper is of this type, they do exist—shops whose owners orient themselves toward the goal of being successful businessmen, yet effect the behaviors and postures of the youth culture (labeled by many as "hip capitalists"). Dan represents the owner of this type of shop: "Even if there's a depression, I'll survive. People will be buying necessities and freaks think anything they like is a necessity so they'll continue to buy anything they like and I know what those things are and I'll sell them" (Karpel, 1970: 277).

(4) Midnight hip. The values of the established order are rejected, but the accepted behavior patterns are followed. This is the route most of the successful shops have followed—even though the accommodation involved has produced a great deal of psychic ambivalence in the shop operators and has tempted many of them to come up with the "Robin Hood rationalization"—that which leads them further along the path toward acceptance of established values and institutionalization.[19] The instability in following this option, as O'Dea points out, is in the continual conflict between utopianism and conservatism.[20] When institutionalization looms too large, as in the Northwest City examples, utopians break from the established shops to form their own. Yet the utopian ideal is, in this case, more mythic than

[19] This, by the way, may shed light on Bryan's comment that many in deviant subcultures learn the ideology of the subculture but neither believe it, act by it, nor permit it to influence their other ideas (Bryan, 1966). Hip capitalists may follow Bryan's pattern, but those shop operators in this category of midnight hip may believe the ideology but not act by it, thereby throwing themselves open to severe attacks of psychic ambivalence. From my own observations, it seems that typically these shop operators are intensely paranoid, especially around members of the contra-culture—until some form of Robin Hood rationalization has been worked out.

[20] Howard terms those who subscribe to the utopian values of the movement, yet adopt establishment behavior patterns, *midnight hippies.* He does not, however, assume there is much psychic conflict involved in their stance (Howard, 1969: 50). I believe there is.

rational—mainly a reactive stance of *anti-capitalism*. As such, it is nearly impossible to utilize in building any viable alternative to the existing behavior and exchange networks. Hence these utopians are, in their turn, faced with the same dilemma as the shop owners they originally broke from.

The resolution of this dilemma has, in Northwest City, seemed to take one of three forms: (a) moving closer to institutionalization (which in turn generates another set of spin-off utopian idealists;[21] (b) adopting the radical stance (which seems to lead to extinction within the system);[22] or (c) in the isolationist case, retreating or establishing the territory of the youth ghetto (communes) and leaving the shops behind (as happened in the Haight-Ashbury instance, as well as in some more recent Northwest City occurrences).[23]

In closing, I would note that the dilemma of the head shop revolves around the twin concepts of dissemination and diffusion. The shop operator, in order to stock many of the artifacts of youth contra-culture, is locked into an established economic chain of artifact dissemination, and has to perform accordingly or be denied access to necessary wares (recordings, guitars, clothing, incense, and such). Attempts to break this dissemination chain on the part of the shop owners will be successful only to the extent that: (a) those within the contra-culture can produce their own artifacts, and (b) those artifacts produced outside the culture are defined as unnecessary by those within the culture (this happened in the Haight and, with respect to recordings, instruments, and such, seems to be occurring in the Northwest City youth ghetto).[24]

With relation to diffusion, as the artifacts of youth contra-culture are processed, watered down, mass-produced, and advertised by establishment institutions, a market is created. "Teenie boppers," and college and weekend hippies place demands upon the owners of the shops as they become a

[21] Much as the routinization of charisma creates new charismatic forms (Weber, 1947: 363–92).

[22] This, applied to the Diggers in San Francisco, is chronicled in Howard (1969). Howard further points out that radical stance of voluntarism and exchange can work out only when the actors involved *understand* the system.

[23] A process similar to *sect formation* (Troeltsch, 1931; Wilson, 1961, 1959).

[24] An important aspect of contra-cultural study would be now to study these new and, so far, more successful attempts to break the dissemination chain and to encompass production, distribution, and utilization of artifacts entirely within the institutions of contra-culture. A new wave of Northwest City shops, devoted to this orientation, is now springing up. Essentially, a large garage-type building is rented, and each person interested sets up a shop within the larger area. The shops involved "sell" only materials produced by members of the contra-culture, thereby breaking the dissemination chain. In the Northwest City case, however, sales are to anyone (not only to those members of the contra-culture), and rents have to be paid to Northwest City businessmen for the garage-type structures. It will be interesting to follow the directions these experiments will take.

competing clientele—the other horn of the dilemma—that which is so tempting to the shop owners as the object of the rip-off.

REFERENCES

BERGER, B., "Hippie Morality—More Old than New," *Trans-action* 5, 2 (1967), 19–20.

BRYAN, J. H., "Occupational Ideologies and Individual Attitudes of Call Girls," *Social Problems* 13 (1966), 441–50.

CAVAN, S., *Hippies of the Haight*. St. Louis: New Critics, 1972.

———, *Liquor License*. Chicago: Aldine, 1966.

DAVIS, F., "Focus on the Flower Children," *Trans-action* 5, 2 (1967), 10–18.

GOFFMAN, E., "Symbols of Class Status," *British J. of Sociology* 11 (1951), 294–304.

HINKLE, W., "A Social History of Hippies," *Ramparts* 5, 9 (1967), 9–10, 17, 18–19.

HOWARD, J. R., "The Flowering of the Hippie Movement," *Annals of Amer. Academy of Pol. and Social Sci.* 382 (1969), 43–55.

KARPEL, C., "Das Hip Kapital," *Esquire* 6 (1970), 184–88, 275–81, 288.

LOFLAND, J., "The Youth Ghetto," pp. 756–78 in M. Laumann et al. (eds.) *The Logic of Social Hierarchies*. Chicago: Markham, 1967.

LUCE, J., "Haight-Ashbury Today." *Esquire* 1 (1969), 65–68, 118–24.

NASH, M., *Primitive and Peasant Economic Systems*. San Francisco: Chandler, 1966.

O'DEA, T. F., *The Sociology of Religion*. Englewood Cliffs, N.J.: Prentice-Hall, 1966.

POLANYI, K., "Anthropology and Economic Theory," in M. Fried (ed.) *Readings in Anthropology*, Volume II. New York: Thomas Y. Crowell, 1953.

POLSKY, N., *Hustlers, Beats and Others*. Chicago: Aldine, 1967.

RUBENSTEIN, R. F., *Rebels in Eden*. Boston: Little, Brown, 1970.

SAHLINS, M. D., "On the Sociology of Primitive Exchanges," in M. Banton (ed.) *The Relevance of Models for Social Anthropology*. New York: Frederick A. Praeger, 1965.

SIMMEL, G., *The Sociology of Georg Simmel*. New York: Free Press, 1950.

THOMPSON, H. S., "The 'Hashbury' Is the Capital of the Hippies," *New York Times Magazine* (May 14, 1967).

TROELTSCH, E., *The Social Teaching of the Christian Churches*. New York: Macmillan, 1931.

VON HOFFMAN, N., *We Are the People Our Parents Warned Us Against*. New York: Quadrangle, 1968.

WEBER, M., *The Theory of Social and Economic Organization*. New York: Oxford Univ. Press, 1947.

WILSON, B. R., *Sects and Society*. Berkeley: Univ. of California Press, 1961.

———, "An Analysis of Sect Development," *Amer. Soc. Rev.* 24 (1959), 3–15.

WIRTH, L., *The Ghetto*. Chicago: Univ. of Chicago Press, 1928.

WOLF, L., *Voices of the Love Generation*. Boston: Little, Brown, 1968.

WOLFE, B. H., *The Hippies*. New York: NAL, 1968.

YABLONSKY, *The Hippie Trip*. New York: Western Publishing, 1968.

YINGER, S. M., "Contraculture and Subculture." *Amer. Soc. Rev.* 25 (1960), 625–35.

RICHARD L. HENSHEL

Ability to Alter Skin Color: Some Implications for American Society[1]

In light of advances in dermatology it has become pertinent to consider what the social consequences would be of an ability to change one's apparent race. Specifically, since social reaction to race often is determined by outward, visible manifestations, the effects of a capacity to alter at will the color of one's skin must be seriously examined.[2] It must be clear at the onset that this does not mean the application of superficial external dressings or stains to the skin but to controlled alterations of its color. In view of the importance that so much of the world attaches to skin color, it is mystifying how it should have escaped widespread attention that crude techniques to change skin color already exist and that these techniques are probably improvable. This paper reviews briefly the work that has been done before discussing possible social implications.

DESCRIPTION OF BIOMEDICAL ADVANCES

The color of human skin can be changed by known methods. It can be made significantly lighter or darker, using different approaches. The altera-

Reprinted from *The American Journal of Sociology*, 76, 4 (1971), 734–42, by permission of The University of Chicago Press. Copyright 1971 by The University of Chicago Press.

[1] Earlier versions of this paper were presented at the Seventh International Conference on Cell Pigmentation, Seattle, September 1969, and the Southern Sociological Society meetings, Atlanta, April 1970. I am indebted to Norval Glenn and Aaron Lerner for their helpful suggestions. Naturally the analysis and the conclusions remain my responsibility.

[2] The writings of John Howard Griffin (1960), who disguised himself as a Negro, provide excellent clues to the psychological effects of one form of color change. Recently, Grace Halsell has emerged from a similar journey (Halsell 1969), managed solely by changing skin color. Halsell never altered intonation or vocabulary. In addition to factual experience, the 1960s also witnessed considerable fictional treatment of pigment change.

tion is very marked and quite dramatic: interested readers can examine several color photographs in Stolar (1963), Lasker (1968), and—if frogs suffice—Lerner (1961).

Skin *darkeners*, excluding stains, are of two types: those that stimulate the creation of melanin pigment and those that stimulate the tanning process from exposure to ultraviolet radiation. The drug psoralen will cause light skin to tan deep brown—strikingly dark—upon exposure to the sun or ultraviolet light. John Griffin used psoralen treatment prior to his experiences as a "Negro." Psoralen is sometimes used, in smaller doses, as a treatment for vitiligo, a skin disorder in which patches of skin turn deadwhite, leaving the individual more or less disfigured by blotches of different color. Treatment of vitiligo has also played a role in the study of skin lightening.

A second technique for darkening skin uses a hormone known as MSH (for melanocyte-stimulating hormone) to stimulate the production of melanin in the skin.[3] The operation of MSH is still imperfectly understood, but it is clearly effective. MSH has now been synthesized, and in mass production its price would probably be modest. It can be applied only through injection. Human subjects given large injections of MSH begin to darken within twenty-four hours; daily doses increase darkening until discontinued. The skin returns to its normal color three to five weeks after the last injection. The skin of Negroes shows a more marked and more rapid response to MSH than that of whites (Lerner 1961, p. 102). Psoralen and MSH constitute the known effective means of darkening human skin.[4]

Of greater social interest, however, in view of the state of the world's prejudices, are means of rendering human skin *lighter* in color.

Monobenzyl ether of hydroquinone (MBEH) lightens skin and, since the late 1940s, Dr. Robert Stolar has used it to treat Negro patients who have vitiligo. He has used MBEH to make some of his patients "white."[5]

---

[3] All human skins except those of albinos contain melanin, a brown-to-black pigment which forms the basis of skin color. Color difference among races stems from the amount and spatial distribution of melanin in the skin.

[4] In addition to those agents, estrogen is now recognized as a marginal skin darkener, which explains why some pregnant women become slightly darkened. Artificial use of estrogen also produces darkening.

[5] The treatment has consisted of daily application of MBEH to the skin in ointment form. After four to eight weeks, skin depigmentation becomes apparent. Hair and eye color remain normal. In some patients, depigmentation occurs in skin areas distant from the sites of application. It has also been noted that depigmentation may continue even after treatment with MBEH is discontinued (Spencer 1961). No patient has failed to respond in at least some degree of depigmentation. In fifty-five patients (Lasker 1968), Stolar has continued his treatment to virtually total depigmentation, a process requiring from two to three years (Stolar 1963). Depigmentation proved permanent among those with vitiligo, although exposure to sunlight would sometimes produce brown spots on the areas exposed.

On nonvitiliginous subjects, depigmentation of various degrees also occurred, but repigmentation occurred spontaneously if the ointment was not continually applied.[6]

There are obviously drawbacks that cast doubt on the efficacy of MBEH in mass usage, although its present limited application on vitiligo sufferers has evidently been a great success. But, of the drawbacks, some are clearly hypothetical, some can be eliminated, and some depend simply on individual conscientiousness.

It is impossible to predict future development in this or any field, but one can detect enthusiasm among research dermatologists.[7] The skin darkener, MSH, now synthesized, is a naturally occurring hormone from the pituitary gland. There are, in fact, two natural varieties of MSH, both of which produce the darkening effect. Theoretically, there should also be one or more hormones that lighten human skin; that is, there should be at least one natural mechanism that works in each direction.[8] Since persons with vitiligo are born with normal-appearing skin, there *must* be a natural mechanism to produce the white patches later. There may, in fact, be more than one such mechanism, in view of the possibility that there are several forms of vitiligo (Stolar 1963, p. 72). There is widespread feeling that the medical exploration of enpigmentation and depigmentation has only begun to bear fruit.

THE QUESTION OF MASS ACCEPTANCE

A new technology can be examined at three levels: Will it work? Will it be used, and by whom (mass acceptance)? What are the direct and indirect consequences—social, economic, political, psychological? The latter questions are, for the most part, both dependent upon and more uncertain than the earlier questions. The first question is already answered for both skin darkeners and lighteners (if MBEH is regarded as an acceptable technical solution). Some years ago, the question of mass acceptance might also have been readily answerable: "no" for the darkener and "yes" for the lightener. Today, the issues of mass acceptance are much more problematic. The question of usage is intricate and, at the same time, critical to the entire examination: indeed, by addressing this topic systematically, many of the social issues which may confront American society are brought out.

[6] Throughout his experiments, Stolar kept close track of any adverse reactions to the treatment. Reactions were generally good, with little or no irritation reported. Those few that did experience irritation were able to continue on reduced dosage.

[7] While presenting a paper, I benefited from informal conversations at the Seventh International Conference on Cell Pigmentation (Seattle, September 1969).

[8] Personal communication from Aaron Lerner, Yale University School of Medicine, February 1, 1969.

ACCEPTANCE OF SKIN LIGHTENERS

The rise of "black militancy," the search for black identity, and the stress placed upon Black Pride have had myriad implications over the past few years—from widespread rejection of the word "Negro" to promotion of the idea that "black is beautiful." That mass acceptance of anything so destructive of these new concepts as a truly effective skin lightener is unlikely might appear to be self-evident.[9] But the analysis is not so straightforward; for example, *Ebony* and many other Negro-oriented magazines still carry advertisements for skin creams, hair straighteners, and similar blandishments.[10] In spite of the marginal usefulness of these products, manufacturers are still making money or hope to do so.[11]

As Cruse (1968) illustrates, the polar themes of integration and separatism have for years been a burning question among black intellectuals. Disputes about criteria of beauty—whether to be as close as possible to whites or as far removed as possible—have reflected parallel questioning on the part of the black masses. The question of mass acceptance of a skin lightener, therefore, defies easy solution.

The complexity of the question can be illustrated by examining the critical variables involved. Prominent among these are contemporary attitudes, prior to public announcement, toward the phenomenon of passing. The analogy between contemporary passing and the situation which would ensue under a technique to alter skin color may, in some respects, be a close one, so that these "pre-announcement" attitudes provide a useful first step in our inquiry.[12]

---

[9] It is widely known that "black beauty" is promoted to eliminate a hopeless attempt to emulate white appearance standards. But Grier and Cobbs (1968) equally stress the psychological significance (and detrimental quality) of the hair-straightening process which all Negro women used to endure. Thus, in addition to obvious psychological attractions, the stress upon blackness and naturalness reaps less recognized benefits.

[10] The ads which promise to lighten skin are not so blatant or direct as in earlier years; the reader must read between the lines: "Helps to clear away unnaturally dark areas." The recent issues of Negro magazines contain advertisements for both "natural" or "Afro" hairstyles and the more traditional ones. The word "natural" has become such a good word that even ads which obviously offer the traditional styles (pictorially) usually use it.

[11] *Ebony* itself, a mass-circulation magazine with some 3 million readers, far surpasses in volume of sales any other single medium of black expression. It is obvious that the old market is still alive. Lasker (1968) quotes a figure of $14 million for sales in 1968 of marketed bleaches (relatively ineffective) and hair straighteners.

[12] Estimates of the volume of permanent passing in the United States vary from 25,000 to 300,000 per year. These are estimates only; the real figure is not only unknown but essentially unknowable, given the delicacy of the matter. For an excellent discussion, see Drake and Cayton (1962, pp. 159–73).

Even a skin lightener of unparalleled effectiveness, however, would obviously not remove secondary racial characteristics, which might impede passing for certain individuals. Stolar's vitiligo patients are quite instructive, for they were just ordinary-looking Negroes whose only unique characteristic was their common affliction, and later their common depigmentation, while their secondary racial characteristics did not change. Stolar reports that "almost all the patients I worked with, even the ones with very Negroid features, pass easily, because there are whites walking around with comparable features" (Lasker 1968, p. 65). This was especially likely if the patients dyed their hair. One patient was able to move among her friends without being recognized, and each patient evidently changed social status; many obtained better jobs. And of course the experience of John Griffin and Grace Halsell shows that whites will be taken for blacks if they are black. Nevertheless, one must be cautious in extrapolating such findings, since increased public knowledge of the technique would presumably make a decided difference in the acceptability of those with marked Negroid features.

Assuming for the moment an analogy to traditional passing, it is important to note that passing itself is complex, and several forms may be distinguished. "There are various degrees of passing, accompanied by different degrees of estrangement from the Negro group and emotional identification with the white community" (Drake and Cayton 1962, p. 160). Many Negroes will occasionally pass just for convenience, to get better service; some develop the practice of passing just for amusement. Since it is at the whites' expense, this behavior apparently generates no feeling of guilt or disloyalty to the race. This may be true also of passing for economic necessity, in which case the individual gains better employment but returns to the black community for social contacts. Finally, a light-skinned Negro may turn his back on the race and cross the color line completely, associating only with whites. As Drake and Cayton put it, "For a Negro to pass socially means sociological death and rebirth" (1962, p. 163).

Whether or not other Negroes protect the identified passer may depend upon whether the acquaintance feels he is being slighted or whether he understands that the passing is for economic reasons. While passing for social reasons (for the company of whites) almost invariably arouses deep hostility, passing for economic reasons may be treated with understanding or at least acceptance.[13]

Attitudes today are in flux due to the emergence of militant perspectives. The time of introduction would be a major factor because, especially

[13] Parenthetically, it is significant that we know virtually nothing about the psychological effects of racial passing. It should also be noted that our information on passing in the United States has become dated.

among the younger blacks, the trend is running strongly toward acceptance of cultural pluralism.[14] With only modest extrapolation of these trends, it seems clear that the later such an innovation is introduced, the greater the hostility to passing may be.[15] There are numerous indications that attitudes are changing; cultural manifestations of Black Pride are becoming widely accepted.[16] Just how successful this search by American Negroes for a new identity will be is crucial; it can provide a psychological anchor for the individual, notwithstanding the economic inducements of passing. If, on the other hand, passing affords only temporary respite, then the appearance of a true skin lightener should be received by at least inward rejoicing and a concomitant strain toward acceptance.[17]

Analysis of pre-announcement attitudes, instructive though it may be, is insufficient to forecast the degree of mass acceptance. Response to an innovation of this magnitude would be based not only on preexisting attitudes; the innovation would generate new attitudes in its own right, and the very announcement of such an epochal innovation would demand reconceptualization. Presumably, a fundamental reappraisal of racial questions would occur by black and white, militant and integrationist.[18] Preexisting attitudes cannot be ignored in the reformulation, but they will provide only one component of the emerging post-announcement orientation.

[14] Several recent studies have shown that, in spite of militant urging, a strong majority of the black community still supports structural assimilation (as opposed to, say, a black state). But the studies also show growing support for cultural pluralism (or cultural nationalism) with separateness in clothing, music, and concepts of beauty. (William J. Wilson presented a substitute paper on this topic: Session 65, 1969 ASA meetings.)

[15] For further substantiation of recent attitude change in Negro college students, see Morland and Williams (1969, p. 110).

[16] Along with other observers, Glenn (1963) concluded that the importance of skin color as a basis for status is diminishing; from data of a study published elsewhere in this issue of the *Journal*, Udry, Bauman, and Chase conclude that the traditional advantage of light-skinned Negro men in mate selection has declined, although no change is found for women.

[17] Some doubts about the ultimate efficacy of Black Pride are raised by a limited study of Philadelphia black preschool children. For his undergraduate thesis at Princeton, James A. Floyd, Jr., ascertained the strength of parental beliefs in Black Pride and Black Power concepts. Using Morland's picture test, he examined racial awareness in their children ("Self-Concept Development in Black Children," 1969). He found the only significant relationship between parent beliefs and children's responses was: "the stronger the parent's support of 'Black Power,' 'Black Pride,' and the 'Black Revolution' in general, the more the child wants to be white." The study is reported in Morland (1969, p. 373).

[18] A voluminous and sophisticated literature exists on the topics of attitude change and acceptance (diffusion) of innovations, both of which appear relevant to the question at hand. For an overview of the literature on the diffusion of innovations, see Katz, Levin, and Hamilton (1963) and Rogers (1962). For attitude-change theories, see Cohen (1964).

For post-announcement attitudes, the nature of the perfected technique itself, its strengths and drawbacks, would inevitably be significant. This refers not only to such evident factors as cost and availability, ease of application, or toxicity, although these have obvious implications for usage, but most clearly in those variables specific to the problem of skin color change: the rapidity of change from a single dose, the "naturalness" of appearance, the evenness of the change across body surfaces. Significantly, of the three existing techniques, only MSH comes out successfully on most of these dimensions. The lightener does not perform at all well.

The nature of white reactions should be of great significance. Indeed, the reaction among Negroes in America might depend to a considerable degree upon the reaction among American whites. This is paradoxical not only because of the strong thrust for black cultural independence; the reaction might perhaps be strongest by the militants who regard themselves as most independent of white demands. If white racists passed laws against color change in a last stand against "defilement," the black reaction, even by militants, might be extensive use as a measure of defiance. They would be mightily tempted to "singe the king's beard." At the same time, perceptive individuals would recognize that the technique precipitates a crisis for black identity.

Widespread popular adoption of skin lighteners would undoubtedly engender efforts to transfer prejudice to such secondary racial characteristics as lips, nostrils, and hair. Whites possessing one or more Negroid characteristics, however, would greet such attempts with rage.[19] It is questionable whether such efforts to transfer prejudice would be entirely successful.

POPULAR ACCEPTANCE OF SKIN DARKENERS

As with skin lighteners, mass adoption of a skin darkener would raise both aesthetic and ideological issues. On the one hand, we have the long-standing paradox that it is considered aesthetically attractive for a person to be dark (or "tanned"), yet if the natural color is too dark the person encounters racial prejudice. The fashions of bodily aesthetics are wonderfully changeable; the question may be raised whether a drug which turns one dark under the bathing suit as well as elsewhere could become fashionable. The question is impossible to answer in its entirety, but certain conclusions are clear. To begin with, technology for turning light people dark is more

---

[19] Many dark-skinned persons do not have these secondary features. Those that do could make use of the widespread availability of hair straighteners, hair dyes, and similar mechanisms, or, as John Griffin did, simply, shave their hair and pretend to be bald, or wear a wig. The devices are legion, and they would be aided by powerful men who consider themselves truly "white" but happen to have nonwhite features.

effective than that for turning dark people light. It is clear that the technical characteristics of a skin darkener would affect popular acceptance, and it is interesting to note that on most criteria MSH comes out very well. Thinking, then, of a decade after introduction (perhaps conservative), the adoption of skin darkeners for beauty purposes is entirely possible.

That this estimate may be conservative is clear when the recent history of the "natural" hairstyle is examined. What started as a symbol of black militant protest was ultimately absorbed by many in the Negro middle class. The latest stage has been adoption of the "kink" by white fashion. In certain metropolitan centers, fashionable boutiques and even department stores have carried "natural" wigs for whites in all colors from black to blonde.[20] Fashion, then, which can lead white men and women to broil for hours under the sun, and which can steal the militants' "thing," may ultimately be capable of making darkness under the bathing suit fashionable.

The possibility of an ideological use of a skin darkener must be seriously considered within the near future. The idealism and direct-action orientation of youth today provide fertile ground for a movement of reverse passing. Analogies with the southern Freedom Riders come quickly to mind. The alienated segment today easily outnumbers previous cohorts. The desire to throw off parental bonds, the moral admonition to "do one's own thing," the enthusiasm to expose hypocrisy, even a desire for "voluntary servitude" in the black cause—all could be served by reverse passing. This suggests that the experiences of Griffin and Halsell may be repeated by hundreds, perhaps thousands, and that the use of skin darkeners for serious ideological purposes (or for psychiatric adjustment) must be considered as a possibility.

CONCLUSION

Although parts of the preceding analysis were of necessity highly speculative, certain points are unmistakably clear. Techniques to alter skin color exist, and efforts to improve them are both feasible and well advanced. The possibility definitely exists that the advent of such techniques on a production scale would lead to widespread usage by segments of the black and/or white populations. Such wide acceptance would undoubtedly produce massive alterations in racial attitudes within both races—alterations of such magnitude as to be of fundamental importance to American society.

The material presented has covered only selected implications for Amer-

[20] *Women's Wear Daily*, often regarded as the trade's bible, has noted the trend and given its seal of approval (*Ebony*, January 1969, pp. 104–9).

ican society, omitting discussion of the possible use of a pigmentation technology by other racial groups—"Chicanos" or American Indians, for example. Its possible effects on interracial marriage have not been explored here, nor the possible impact of the technique in other societies such as the Union of South Africa. Internationally, this is not strictly a black-white problem, for skin color and class or caste are closely aligned in many societies.

REFERENCES

COHEN, ARTHUR R., *Attitude Change and Social Influence*. New York: Basic, 1964.

CRUSE, HAROLD, *The Crisis of the Negro Intellectual*. New York: Morrow, 1968.

DRAKE, ST. CLAIR, and HORACE R. CAYTON, *Black Metropolis*. New York: Harper, 1962.

GLENN, NORVAL D., "Negro Prestige Criteria: A Case Study in the Bases of Prestige," *American Journal of Sociology* 68 (March 1963):645–57.

GRIER, WILLIAM H., and PRICE M. COBBS, *Black Rage*. New York: Basic, 1968.

GRIFFIN, JOHN HOWARD, *Black Like Me*. New York: Signet, 1960.

HALSELL, GRACE, *Soul Sister*. Cleveland: World, 1969.

KATZ, ELIHU, MARTIN L. LEVIN, and HERBERT HAMILTON, "Traditions of Research on the Diffusion of Innovation," *American Sociological Review* 28 (April 1963): 237–52.

LASKER, LAWRENCE, "A Whiter Shade of Black." *Esquire* 70 (July 1968):62–65.

LERNER, AARON B., "Hormones and Skin Color." *Scientific American* (July 1961), pp. 99–108.

MORLAND, J. KENNETH, "Race Awareness among American and Hong Kong Chinese Children," *American Journal of Sociology* 75 (November 1969):360–74.

MORLAND, J. KENNETH, and JOHN E. WILLIAMS, "Cross-cultural Measurement of Racial and Ethnic Attitudes by the Semantic Differential," *Social Forces* 48 (September 1969): 107–12.

ROGERS, EVERETT M., *Diffusion of Innovations*. New York: Free Press, 1962.

SPENCER, M. C., "Hydroquinone Bleaching." *Archives of Dermatology* 84 (July 1961):131–34.

STOLAR, ROBERT, "Induced Alterations of Vitiliginous Skin." *Annals of the New York Academy of Sciences* 100 (February 1963):58–75.

UDRY, J. RICHARD, KARL E. BAUMAN, and CHARLES CHASE, "Skin Color, Status, and Mate Selection." *American Journal of Sociology* 76 (January 1971):722–33.

MARCELLO TRUZZI

The Occult Revival
as Popular Culture:
Some Random Observations
on the Old and the Nouveau Witch

In his classic article on fashion, Edward Sapir noted that:

There is nothing to prevent a thought, a type of morality or an art form from being the psychological equivalent of costuming the ego. Certainly one may allow oneself to be converted to Catholicism or Christian Science in exactly the same spirit in which one invests in pewter or follows the latest Parisian models in dress (Sapir, 1937:143).

Although religion holds a somewhat exalted position in many of the prominent macro theories of societies (e.g., those of Durkheim, Weber, etc.), it is often a rather mundane phenomenon, satisfying a wide variety of idiosyncratic needs for society's many groups and their members. The functions of a religious phenomenon will often vary for its different actors and audiences, and they need not necessarily reflect a single fundamental fact or crisis of social life. This point is nicely exemplified by Ogden Nash's delightful poem describing the sequential religious affiliation of Mrs. Marmaduke Moore. He reminds us that her changes in religion might result from causes other than those of some set of central social-structural origins (e.g., anomie, status inconsistency). Describing her many conversions from Methodism to Bahai, he concluded:

> When seventy stares her in the face
> She'll have found some other state of grace.
> Mohammed may be her Lord and Master
> Or Zeus, or Mithros, or Zoroaster.
> For when a woman is badly sexed,
> God knows what god is coming next (Nash, 1945:12).

The revival of interest in the occult and the supernatural is a current example of religious events that some have seen as being of great cultural significance and as reflecting serious social conflicts and strains of macroscopic import. (For good examples of this alienation-argument, see Staude, 1970; Greeley, 1969. For a somewhat similar view, see Harris, 1970.) A wide variety of indicators shows that we are in the midst of a widespread boom of things occult. As *Time* magazine (1968:42) noted: "A mystical renaissance is evident everywhere, from television to department stores." In late 1969, the *Wall Street Journal* reported that the boom continued and "mysticism is becoming a big business. A New York book store specializing in the occult says sales have zoomed 100% in the past three years" (Sansweet, 1969:1; for the British counterpart, see Williams, 1970). In 1968, 169 paperback books dealing with occult topics were in print [see *Paperbound Books in Print* (June 1968), under the headings "Psychology: Occult Sciences," "Parapsychology," and "Astrology,"] and, by 1969, the figure had jumped to 519 books (see *Paperbound Books in Print,* October 1969). In 1969, 364 hardback volumes dealt with occultism, which represented an increase both from 261 volumes in 1968 and from 198 volumes in 1967 (Prakken and Shively, 1967, 1968, 1969). A final indicator of this boom has been the sales of Ouija boards. After some forty years of poor sales, companies reported over two million sold in 1967 (Pileggi, 1970:63), thereby outdistancing the sales of *Monopoly* (Buckley, 1968:31). (An excellent history of the Ouija and its family can be found in Jastrow, 1962:129–43. For a discussion of the mechanisms involved, see Rawcliffe, 1959:134–51; and for an interesting case study, see Wenger and Quarantelli, 1970. On the earlier Ouija board fads, see Sann, 1967:139–44.)

The revival of occultism has been heavily touted as (and, in large part, certainly does represent) an important part of the current youth culture (see Greeley, 1969; Levin, 1968; and Gams, 1970; and on the concept of "youth culture," see Berger, 1963). Certain facts and assumptions, however, indicate that a broad spectrum of persons has been involved in this boom. My own teaching experiences[1] and the wide variety of magazines now giving space to this subject (from *McCall's* and *The Ladies Home Journal* to *Playboy* and *Esquire*) show that many persons outside the youth culture are interested in the occult. A 1969 survey of *Fate* magazine readers, which then had about 94,000 monthly readers, showed that 88 percent of them were over 34 years old, 37.9 percent being over 55 years old (Consumer

---

[1] In the fall of 1969, I offered an evening class for the Adult Education Center on "Witchcraft, Black Magic and Modern Occultisms." The course drew 225 registrants from a wide spectrum of age and background characteristics which, I think, reasonably represented the middle-class population (those able to afford the course-fee).

Communication Corporation).[2] A 1963 Gallup Poll showed that one in five persons reported some sort of sudden or dramatic "religious or mystic experience." The study further showed no relationship between the respondent's experience and his level of education (Gallup, 1963; for a detailed analysis of this report, see Bourque, 1969; and Bourque and Back, 1968). It is safe to assume that even though they were not sudden or dramatic, a great many other Americans have had comparable religious experiences. It is also likely that even though today's social scientists have only superficially examined the subject, a vast reservoir of magical and superstitious thought exists in the American population. (Such studies of magic in modern America would include Henslin, 1967; Hyman and Vogt, 1967; McCall, 1964; Lewis, 1963; Blumberg, 1963; Whitten, 1962; Vogt and Golde, 1958; Roth, 1957; Vogt, 1956; Simpkins, 1953; Levitt, 1952; Zapf, 1945–1946, and 1945; Belanger, 1944; Weiss, 1944; Passin and Bennet, 1943; Caldwell and Lundeen, 1937; Dudycha, 1933; Hurston, 1931; Grilliland, 1930; Wagner, 1928; Park, 1923; Conklin, 1919; and Shotwell, 1910.) These facts and assumptions plus the well-known concern held by the elderly about occultisms relating to healing and survival of bodily death (see Buckner, 1968)[3] indeed indicate that interest in the occult is not an unique phenomenon with the youth culture.

Despite the widespread interest in occultism throughout the population, this current revival seems to be primarily a youth phenomenon. Some facts support this claim. The mass media portray youth as adherents of occultism. Occult bookstores have emerged around the academic campuses. Even many institutions in the nation, including so-called Free-Universities, have offered numerous courses dealing with occult topics.

Empirical research on the prevailing attitudes of the occult among youths is nearly non-existent. During the past three years, my investigations of the national occult scene reveal four rather distinct foci of interest, foci sometimes intersecting but basically quite separate. Three major sources of data provided the basis for my interpretation of the integrated pattern of existing occult belief-systems: extensive readings in the available literature, interviews with hundreds of students, and interviews or exchanged communications with numerous major occult figures, writers, and publishers. The four major foci of occult interest currently dominating the youth culture are (1) astrology, (2) witchcraft-satanism, (3) parapsychology and extra-sensory perception, and (4) Eastern religious thought. Classified as a

[2] *Fate's* circulation in 1969 was approximately 120,000 (Fuller, 1970).

[3] The demographics of the readership of *Fate* magazine, a pre-revival periodical, indicate an older population. The publisher attributes this to the belief that "as people grow older, they become more interested in survival" (Fuller, 1970).

"waste-basket variety," a fifth category encompasses a large number of esoteric items of occult interest, including among others, prophets (Edgar
Cayce, Nostradamus, etc.), strange monsters (sea serpents, snowmen, were-
wolves, vampires, etc.), unidentified flying objects,[4] and many others.[5]
Because the interests in the fifth category either have small scope and influence or are in an actual state of decline,[6] the interests in the four major
categories represent the dominant factors or motifs currently in fashion. At
times, these four interest-areas do intersect among some believers. (For example, some witches, like Sybil Leek, also believe in astrology.) This, however, is not necessarily the case and indeed is relatively uncommon.

Of the four major foci of occult interest, the first two are most clearly
central in the current revival. Parapsychology does not seem to be undergoing any significant increase in popularity.[7] Interest in Eastern religious
thought seemingly passed its peak as a topic of mass interest when interest
in Zen Buddhism, which the so-called "beat-generation" writers of the
1950's made popular, began to decline (for sociologically relevant works
on this subculture, see Rigney and Smith, 1961; Moore, 1960; and Feldman and Gartenberg, 1958). Both parapsychology and Eastern religious
thought act not as central values in the youth occult world, but as *bolsters*
or legitimizing linkages to the broader and more generally accepted cultural areas of science and religion. One becomes receptive to an analysis of
witchcraft-satanism with their generally unacceptable magical elements if
he remembers two facts. First, the current limits of scientific understanding
have been highlighted by the parapsychologists conducting "respectable"
laboratory investigations. Second, in the process of establishing their own
identity, some proponents of Western philosophical naturalism may have
become rather parochial in their own views toward the older and more
mystical traditions of the East. I will now devote the rest of this paper to an
analysis of these two major foci of occult interest currently dominating the
scene—astrology and witchcraft-satanism.

[4] A massive literature and following exist for the "flying saucer" phenomenon. (For
two sociological investigations, see Buckner, 1968; and Warren, 1970.)

[5] The variety of occult offerings is immense. A Delphic Society in California proposes
the revival of the ancient pantheon. (An excellent survey of these esoteric groups is
Mathison, 1960.)

[6] An interesting decline of interest in unidentified flying objects would appear to have
followed the lunar landings and the Condon report (Fuller, 1970.)

[7] Although scientific interest in ESP continues, a decline, at least in the United
States, seems to be occurring in this area of occult interest; J. B. Rhine's departure
from Duke University may have precipitated this decline. (For an excellent survey of the
literature, see Hansel, 1966. For critical responses by parapsychologists to this very negative evaluation, see Eysenck et al., 1968.)

ASTROLOGY

Certain existing indicators of occult preferences clearly reveal the predominant interest in astrology. In 1969, 252 or 68 percent of the 373 books printed on occultism dealt with astrology (Prakken and Shively, 1969).[8] In 1969, 33 of 40 articles dealing with occultism covered the topic of astrology [in *Readers Guide to Periodical Literature* (New York: H. W. Wilson Co.), for January 17, 1969, to January 29, 1970]. Paperbound books on astrology increased from 35 in 1968 to 102 in 1969 (see *Paperbound Books in Print,* October 1969, June 1968). Even the popular press (*Time,* 1969; Jennings, 1970; Robinson, 1970; and Buckley, 1968) has widely reported the phenomenal growth of interest in this ancient pseudo-science (for good reviews of the scientific repudiation of astrology, see, Bok and Mayakkm, 1941; Thorndike, 1955; Hering, 1924:18–37; de Camp and de Camp, 1966:20–31; Lewinsohn, 1962:90–114; and, especially, Gauquelin, 1970); such interest has become a marketing bonanza. Twenty years ago only about 100 papers carried horoscope columns, but today 1200 of the 1750 daily newspapers regularly carry such columns (Buckley, 1968:31; and Jennings, 1970:104). Because of their public endorsement of astrology, a wide variety of celebrities, which range from Hollywood stars (e.g., Marlene Dietrich, Robert Cummings, Susan Hayward),[9] to members of the political (e.g., Ronald Reagan)[10] and intellectual (e.g., Marshall McLuhan)[11] communities, have added to its attractiveness to their admirers. The popular musical *Hair* with its hit song of *Aquarius* and its own well publicized company-astrologist gave special impetus to the movement (Buckley, 1968:136). The Dell publishing company alone had some 49 horoscope publications in press and sold over 8,000,000 copies of its annual astrological dopesheet in 1969 (Jennings, 1970:104). About 10,000 full-time and 175,000 part-time astrologers in the United States serve some 40,000,000 persons in their American audience (Jennings, 1970:154). One only has to look around at the shops in any semi-urban community to see astrological recordings, calendars, ashtrays, hairstyles, sweatshirts, and thousands of merchandised items linked to the zodiac. As one leading figure in the occult world, who himself does not endorse astrology, succinctly put it: "The stars may affect no one, but astrology affects everyone" (LaVey, 1968).

[8] Of these 252 volumes, 4 were astrology dictionaries and bibliographies and only 5 related to the early history of astrology.

[9] Hollywood has long been a center for astrological counselors. (For an excellent survey of this phenomenon, see Abramson, 1969.)

[10] Because of the advice of astrologer Carroll Righter, Governor Reagan reportedly set his inauguration time at 12:30 A.M. (Jennings, 1970:154).

[11] "McLuhan . . . believes that for various reasons astrology may have worked better in antiquity than it does now" (Buckley, 1968:138).

How, then, are we to account for the renewed popularity of this ancient and scientifically discredited belief system? No one who is familiar with the rules of scientific evidence or with the history of both astrology and astronomy over the centuries can accept the interpretation of the manifest functions of astrology, that it represents a scientifically true explanation and predictive framework for understanding man and his actions. Of course, some followers of astrology claim acceptance of their "science" for just such reasons. Such rigid scientific justification, however, is rare among the practitioners. Most astrology-believers place their credence in their system for reasons, at least partly, beyond what they themselves see as a legitimate science. To them, the heart of the matter is not that they use science as the basis for their acceptance of astrology as truth but that science must catch up with their truth. We, thus, might look at the latent functions of astrological beliefs, both for the social system (group) in which they exist and for the needs of the social actors involved in the system.[12] One must, however, recognize that the involvements of those "into" astrology are quite varied. One can meaningfully speak of at least three, somewhat over-simplified and "ideal typical," levels of involvement. Each level of involvement manifests somewhat different consequences for the actors.

At the first, most superficial level of involvement, we find the occasional reader of the newspaper and magazine astrology-columns. This person knows next to nothing about the "mechanics" of astrology. From my interviews and preliminary explorations, I found that most of the middle-aged (over 35 years old) population who follow astrology fall into this category. These astrology-followers were largely present before the astrology-revival of these past five years. Because horoscopes do not normally take into account the subject's (client's) exact time and place of birth, those more advanced than are others in astrology perceive this level of astrology-believers as highly superficial. Even the noted newspaper-astrologer, Sidney Omarr, was quoted as conceding that "daily columns provide entertainment rather than enlightenment" (Buckley, 1968:31). The overwhelming majority of astrology-believers fall into this first level. Consideration of the latent functions for the individual involved at the first level would have to take into account the following factors: (1) the familiarity with astrology, its ancient and pervasive character; (2) the quasi-scientific character of astrology that acts as legitimating astrology to those not scientifically critical

---

[12] I am here making the distinction between sociological functions (after Durkheim and Radcliffe-Brown) and social-psychological functions (after Malinowski), that is, between the fulfillment of the needs of the social system and the fulfillment of the needs of the individual personalities within that system. The two can and do exist simultaneously. I will argue, however that, depending upon the degree of involvement of the astrology-believers, the functions of astrology will vary on these two levels. Instead of a detailed explanation of the functions of the current astrological boom, only an adumbration of its functions is given in the paper.

but personally concerned about the present explorations of the heavens; (3) the usually positive character of astrological advice that makes it ego-boosting; (4) the ego-directed attention of the advice; (5) the element of mystery, of the esoteric that makes the advice exciting and entertaining; (6) the ambiguity of the message that makes it amenable to interpretation and difficult to falsify; and (7) the self-fulfilling nature of many astrological predictions. (This phenomenon may operate in the following way: a person who reads that he is in good spirits becomes so, or a person who reads that he should be cautious acts so and then finds a justifying event.) Some latent functions on the group (societal) level might include the following factors: (1) tension-management of anxieties within the social system; (2) fulfillment of economic goals that the mass merchandising of an astrology-fad affords; and (3) the availability of a cognitive belief-system that transcends science and is "safe from the sanctions of or overt conflict with the major religions. (This is true today, but it was not always so.)

At the second level of involvement with astrology, we find those people who have some knowledge of the "mechanics" of astrology. These people usually have their own personal horoscopes cast. They do this through a variety of ways, ranging from personal visits with a consulting astrologer to a computer-analysis of their horoscopes.[13] Unlike those in the first level of involvement, the astrology-believers in the second level have some knowledge of the special language and of the astrological reasoning; they are able to speak about other people astrologically. Like those in the first level, most astrology-believers in the second level seek advice and predictions from their excursions into astrology.[14] I have observed that *the astrology-believers in the second level primarily represent those of college-age, and this level has had the greatest relative increase during the current revival.* Some latent functions for the individual involved at the second level might include the following factors: (1) all functions available to those involved at the first level; (2) the enhancement of the *personal* and ego-gratifying character of the involvement; (3) an increased commitment to astrology [by means of the expense and trouble of getting a personal horoscope, by means of a direct interpersonal relation with the astrologer, and by means of a personal investment (dissonance) strongly motivating the person to act upon the belief-system]; and (4) the enhancement of the believer's self-esteem among his friends and colleagues. (This phenomenon operates in the following way: because of its special language, astrology is an excellent

[13] At this writing, Time Pattern Research Institute, Inc., in New York City, will run off a 10,000 word-horoscope in two minutes for twenty dollars.

[14] This advice is often surprisingly good (Sechrest and Bryan, 1968). Apparently unknown to Sechrest and Bryan, mail order "astrologers" systematically churn out much of this "astrological" advice by means of rules that they find in a variety of privately published manuals made available to professional mentalists.

topic of conversation; because the believer can direct the substance of astrology to another's ego as well, he gains great interpersonal merit in his interactional process.) Some latent functions on the group (societal) level might include the following factors: (1) all functions available to those involved in the first level; (2) the creation and maintenance of an in-group cohesiveness and an out-group exclusion by means of the special language of astrology; and (3) the presence of a highly interpersonally binding conversational framework that often centers around a highly personal and egocentric discourse. (Astrology and psychoanalysis both share this and many other common features.)

At the third level of involvement with astrology, we find those people who have become really involved in the literature of the field and usually cast their own horoscopes. Until relatively recently, this level was composed of only a very small number of elderly people; it now consists of many youthful advocates. Persons involved this deeply in astrology are still comparatively few. (For example, the approximately 30,000 students at the University of Michigan have enough interest in astrology to support an occult-astrology bookstore; yet only about 20 such serious adherents are reportedly around that campus.) Unlike those in the first two levels of involvement, the astrology-believers in the third level are not primarily concerned with advice or prediction. For them, astrology represents a highly complex and symbolically deep conceptual scaffolding which offers them a *meaningful* view of their universe and gives them an *understanding* of their place in it. They use astrology as a means of establishing their identity (Klapp, 1969). They usually acknowledge the great difficulties in establishing any predictive statements from astrology. To them, astrology represents a world-view far more reminiscent of religion than of science. In fact, they most likely speak of their belief-system, not as a science like physics or astronomy, but as an art or as one of the "occult sciences." The latent functions for the individual involved at the third level may well include many of the features found in the first two rather superficial levels of involvement. The major latent function, however, is that the adept astrologer obtains an ideological integration of his self with his perception of the universe. Of course, other benefits may occur. He may, for example, become a leader in his astrology-oriented circle of friends. He may even become a professional astrologer and earn his living from his involvement; for the social actor, however, the central function is that the astrological belief-system operates as a grand conceptual-philosophical scheme. (Because the actor is aware of the consequences of his belief in astrology, this central function may now become manifest, not latent.) On the group (societal) level, this intensity of involvement may well act as a "sacred canopy" (see Berger, 1967) for the social group. Composed of only a few thousand astrology-believers, this level of involvement clearly follows the depiction of the astrological belief-system as a social reaction against the normlessness of modern life. It is at this level of involvement that we see the search for identity and for new sacred elements. We should, however, see these relatively extreme astrology-believers in their true perspective: they represent a very small minority of those involved in the massive revival of interest in astrology. I would argue, in fact, that the vast majority of those involved with astrology, those at the first two levels, take a highly irreverent, almost playful attitude toward astrology. To most of these people, astrology is fun; it is a non-serious, leisure-time element of popular culture, *not* a spiritual searching for Karmic meaning.

WITCHCRAFT AND SATANISM

Witchcraft and Satanism follow astrology as the second most popular focus of current attention in occultism. The large number of recent popular books and articles dealing with these subjects attests to this upsurge of interest in them.[15] (Often these publications are reprints of much older volumes.) Although witchcraft and Satanism are commonly linked together, they actually represent very different belief-systems, and each has an existing variety of forms.

The alleged difference between so-called *white* versus *black* magic is one major distinction discussed in much of the occult literature. While white

---

[15] A sample of the best of these articles would include Rascoe (1970); Newsweek (1970); Ward (1970); Bloxham (1970); Weir (1970); St. Albin-Greene (1969); Freedland (1969); Pageant (1967); Kobler (1966); Thomas (1966); Graves (1964); and Bone (1964).

This variation is not surprising because broad differences over the question of the existence of the Devil do exist among Christians. While 66 percent of the Roman Catholics in the United States apparently believe in the actual existence of the Devil, only 6 percent of the Congregationalists, 13 percent of the Methodists, and 31 percent of the Presbyterians believe in his existence. The Southern Baptists (92 percent) are the only major group that seemingly remain solid in their belief in an actual Devil. (See Glock and Stark, 1965: 10).

Some of the better (more informative) popular-audience or mass-market books on witchcraft and Satanism include Huson (1970); Crow (1970); Rohmer (1970); Steiger (1969); Robson (1969); Martello (1969); Holzer (1969); Seth (1969); Tindall (1967); Wallace (1967); Daraul (1966); Maple (1966 and 1965); Glass (1965); Valiente (1962); Wedeck (1961); Parrender (1958); and Hole (1957).

Recent books by witches include Leek (1968); Heubner (1969); and Gardner (1954 and 1959). A great many of these books and articles consist of interviews with witches (e.g., Holzer, 1969). Most of the above works dealing with contemporary witchcraft are notoriously unreliable. Many are apparently published as merchandise for a highly interested market. One of the best (worst) examples of such a work is Johns, 1970.

The major academic works on the West European witchcraft traditions would include Lea (1957); Kittredge (1956); Murray (1921); Lethbridge (1968); Baroja (1964); Michelet (1939); Rose (1962); and Robbins (1959).

magic is supposed to be the use of magic for socially beneficent ends,[16] black magic is supposed to be the use of magic for malevolent ends. Even though some ritual forms of black magic clearly involve calling upon such malevolent forces as the Devil or his demons, most magicians basically view magic as a value-free "technology-of-the-supernatural" (or *super-normal,* a term preferred by many magicians). They believe that their own motives really determine whether their use of magic is for good (white), or for evil (black). Most contemporary witches stress that they perform only white magic (e.g., Leek, 1968:3–5; or Holzer, 1969:19) as an attempted antidote for the stereotypes usually portraying them as evil workers of the devil. The distinction between black and white magic is essentially a matter of the user's intent rather than of his technique.[17]

Contemporary witches usually do not consider themselves to be Satanists. Satanism is basically a worship of the Judaeo-Christian Devil, which is, at times, only a symbol and, at other times, very literally real. (Varying degrees of fundamentalism exist among Satanists. For these varieties, see Truzzi, in press; and Lyons, 1970.) Practitioners in witchcraft do not usually view themselves as an heretical off-shoot of Christianity, but Satanists do view themselves, either literally or symbolically (since many Satanists are atheists), as members in league with the Christian's Devil. Most witches perceive witchcraft as a folk tradition of magical beliefs. Many, if not most of them, further perceive it as an ancient, pre-Christian fertility religion[18] that the Christian churches sought to suppress: primarily through the Catholic inquisitions and the Protestant witch trials.[19] They believe that their religion became misrepresented and distorted as an heretical worship of the Devil. [For the early Catholic image, see Kramer and Sprenger, 1948. Most Catholics no longer accept the orthodox picture of the witch, but

---

[16] This conception that magic is directed toward social, beneficial ends is at odds with the common, anti-social definition of magic found among many sociological theories (e.g., Durkheim, 1961:58–63). Wax and Wax (1963) outline well the difficulty facing most current sociological and anthropological theory in dealing with empirical cases of magical practices.

[17] As one of my traditional white witch informants put it: "Magic is like a knife. A surgeon can use it to perform an operation to save a life or a madman can use it to murder someone." The expression "white magic" became widespread after the journalist William Seabrook (1940) first used it. (For a fuller discussion of this subject, see Truzzi, in press.)

[18] The major exponents of the view were Murray (1921) and Gardner (1954). This is the dominant view among the non-Satanic, organized witch groups (covens) today.

[19] Sociologists who have recently published studies on these trials include Erikson (1966), Curie (1968), and Macfarlane (1970). In his new appraisal of the celebrated Salem cases, Hansen (1969) repudiated the traditional histories of these trials. While he argued for the real existence of witchcraft in Salem, Erickson and Curie did not believe a real foundation existed for witchcraft in Salem (and, by implication, in other areas). Thus, he indirectly raised some serious questions about the accuracy of some elements in their sociological studies.

some Catholic scholars do; e.g., see Pratt, 1915, and Cristiani, 1962. The leading writer presenting the strictly orthodox (medieval) Catholic viewpoint in recent years was the late Montague Summers (1946, 1956, and 1958).] On the other hand, Satanists do often constitute a kind of inverted Christian sect. (Most of the presently vast literature on Satanism is quite unreliable. Some reliable sources include Hartland, 1921; Spence, 1960: 123–24; Carey, 1941; and Murray, 1962. For the official views of the Church of Satan, centered in San Francisco, see LaVey, 1969. For good historical commentaries, see Carus, 1969; Langston, 1945; Coulange, 1930; and Garcon and Vinchon, 1929. And for the classic occult view on Satanism, see Huysmans, 1958; and Waite, 1896.) Oddly enough, most of history's Satanisms seemed to be direct outgrowths of the Christian churches' misrepresentations of early witchcraft practices. The inquisitors so impressed some individuals with the fantastic and blasphemous picture of Satanism that they apparently decided that they also would "rather reign in hell than serve in heaven."

Several different varieties seem to depict the non-heretical, non-Satanic or white witches. The major division of great importance to the sociologist is between those witches who are individual practitioners and those who belong to organized witch groups or *covens*. Most frequently encountered, the former variety represents the independent or solitary witches. This variety can be further subdivided into two, somewhat oversimplified, classes: (1) one represents those who, having learned the secrets of the art through some special kinship-relation to another solitary witch,[20] practice witchcraft as a culturally inherited art from kin; (2) the other represents those who, having invented their own techniques or having obtained their practices from the occult literature, practice witchcraft as self-designated witches. My investigations show that the vast majority of witches are in the second class: they belong to no organized group and have obtained their knowledge from their readings and conversations with others uninitiated into coven-held secrets. The typical person of this class is a young high-school or college-age girl who, for a variety of reasons, self-designates herself as a witch to her peers; because her status is attractive to her friends but elicits fear in her enemies, it produces many social rewards for her. Yet this type of witch is "illegitimate" in terms of the very criteria that she herself may accept for being a witch. Most of the major works on witchcraft state that before one becomes a true practitioner of the craft, he must obtain initiation into a coven and learn the group (coven) secrets. These

---

[20] This pattern is most often associated with rural areas, especially in the South. The "inherited" witchcraft usually consists of the acquisition of magical recipes or technology rather than the acquisition of a general religious belief-system. A common example would be the "inheritance" of dowsing abilities by a "water witch." (Cf., Vogt and Hyman, 1959; for typical cases, see Randolph, 1947:266.)

secrets, however, are not available in such public works as the occultism-volumes in most public libraries or occult bookstores.[21]

A number of varieties exist among the organized white witch groups. A rather clear division seems to exist between the witch covens formed before and after the 1951 repeal of witchcraft-laws in England or, especially, after the 1954 publication of the late Gerald Gardner's first book on witchcraft (also, see Gardner, 1959, and Bracelin's biography on Gardner, 1960). Gardner's works were very influential in British occult circles, and many contemporary witches, sometimes called Gardnerites, received their credentials through Gardner's Witchcraft Museum on the Isle of Man.[22] The question of legitimacy among British witches is still raging, each accusing the other of concocting his own rituals. *Pentagram: A Witchcraft Review,* the publication of the Witchcraft Research Association in London, prominently featured this debate in its first five issues (for an example of a lively exchange, see issue number 5, December 1965:18–19). The much publicized witch, Monique Wilson, who with her husband inherited Gardner's museum, has stated that she holds a secret register of covens existing around the world (Wilson, 1968). This, however, seems to include only the Gardnerite covens, which, according to Mrs. Wilson, numbered several hundred at that time. In 1969, another well publicized witch, Mrs. Sybil Leek, estimated to me that approximately 300 covens were then operating in the United States. The facts are that covens, especially those in existence before 1951, have little communication with one another. Members sometimes migrate from an area and join or begin a new coven, but no central hierarchy or witchcraft-organization actually exists. Except for Mrs. Wilson and Mrs. Leek, most witches know little about those in the other parts of the country. These women are somewhat unusual because their extensive publicity and travel about the world have brought them into contact with a great many witches wanting interaction with them. It is, therefore, impossible to obtain any sort of accurate estimate of the number of covens now in operation. Because a great number of new covens did begin after 1951, they certainly appear to represent the bulk of the *known* witchcraft-groups about which we read today. Even though more could exist, I did locate

---

[21] Of course, numerous books allege to give such group secrets. All coven witches whom I have interviewed and whose interviews I have read deny this.

[22] From his museum, Gardner apparently ran some sort of diploma-mill for witches. He either initiated or was associated with many of the "Professional" British witches who have been greatly publicized in the United States. (For some very enlightening articles that suggest some of the financial motivations behind Gardner's efforts in reviving witchcraft, see Graves, 1964; and Weir, 1970. For a critical examination of Gardner's writing, see Rose, 1962.) Because of Gardner's success, at least five other witchcraft museums now exist in Great Britain and the United States. An American Gardnerian witch-anthropologist runs one of these, the Buckland Museum of Witchcraft and Magick (Buckland, 1970).

three pre-1951 covens in Michigan. I thus estimate that at least 150 such traditional covens probably exist in Great Britain and the United States.

According to Murray, the maximum number of persons in a coven is thirteen: Thus, Great Britain and the United States probably can claim no more than 1,950 coven members. These cultists represent a rather small part of the mass market currently devouring the many marketable witchcraft items and books. Coupling the number of coven members with that of the solitary witches (many of whom are really not very serious about witchcraft) still leaves us with a relatively small number of witches in the United States, the maximum being probably less than 3000. Like their interest with astrology, the popular interest of the general public toward this form of occultism is very superficial. From my observations of many people's reactions toward witches during public occasions,[23] I know that most people show interest in meeting a witch for the novelty rather than for any occult enlightenment. Like astrology, witchcraft also represents a play-function for the major portion of its current popular audience.

Like the witches, the Satanists also represent two distinct types of individuals: those acting as solitary agents and those operating in groups. We know next to nothing about the former. If some individuals in the world believe that they have made contractual arrangements with the Devil, then they probably would prefer that this not be widely known: this seems likely, especially if they are really doing evil things. Much diversity exists among the Satanic groups; these groups have at least four major varieties. Probably the least frequent, the first variety represents Satanic groups who follow some non-heretical (to them) interpretation of Christianity in which Satan is perceived as an angel still to be worshipped. These may represent some sort of Gnostic tradition which the members claim to follow.[24]

A second variety about which one can read a great deal in the "soft-core" pornographic literature (e.g., Moore, 1969) consists of sex clubs that incorporate Satanism and some of its alleged rituals. Here we find, as an attraction or embellishment, the celebrated but usually artificial "black mass" (for the best work on this topic, see Rhodes, 1954). Many of these groups are sado-masochist clubs or flagellation societies.

Probably more frequent than the previous two, a third variety of Satanic group is an outgrowth of the current narcotics or "acid-culture" now found in various parts of the country [even though the author seems to confuse it with traditional Satanism, Burke (1970) presents a good description of one

---

[23] Often I take a witch with me when I lecture, and I have accompanied them when they lectured and met the public. I generally found this reaction during my own promotional talks for the sale of my witchcraft-cookbook (Truzzi, 1969).

[24] A good example of this sort of "white-Satanism" is a small group in Toledo, Ohio, who practices this under the leadership of Herbert A. Sloane. (See Eckman, 1969; St. Albin-Greene, 1969; and in Steiger, 1969:16–21, a lengthy interview with Sloane.)

of these groups]. Epitomized by the much publicized Charles Manson group that allegedly killed Sharon Tate in 1969, this sort of group has received much publicity. It is, however, much more rare than the newspaper headlines would imply. More importantly, most of these groups are almost completely untraditional, and they make up their brand of Satanism as they go along (Burke, 1970; and Kloman, 1970). Like the sex club, their central focus is not occultism at all; in their case, it is narcotics. Ironically enough, many traditional Satanists commonly complain that the sex and acid cultists give a "bad name" to "real Satanism."

Clearly dominant today, the fourth variety of Satanic group consists of members of the Church of Satan in San Francisco. High Priest Anton Szandor LaVey[25] founded this church, which is, in fact, a church, not a cult.[26] Only LaVey knows the exact number of members in the Church of Satan, but on numerous occasions he has stated that over 7000 were contributing members.[27] He gave this figure before mid-1969: since then, LaVey's book *The Satanic Bible* has had national circulation (125,000 copies in its first of now four printings), and two movies that prominently feature the Church of Satan have been released nationally. The figure of 7000 appears reasonable, if not conservative,[28] for several reasons; because LaVey does remarkable public relations work and because *Rosemary's Baby*, the movie with

[25] Founded in 1965, the church claims that it really represents a direct connection with the authentic Satanic traditions of the past. Some do not believe that this authentic tradition reflects the history of Satanism. Like the white witches, Satanists also complain that their enemies (generally, the Catholics) have published wild distortions about them.

In the "introduction" to *The Satanic Bible*, Burton H. Wolfe (LaVey, 1969:13–19) describes well the origins of the Church of Satan and the background of Anton LaVey. LaVey gives his views on a variety of topics not only in *The Satanic Bible* but also in his weekly column, "Letters from the Devil," which appeared until 1970 in *The National Insider* and now appears in *The Exploiter*. In addition to these public-policy statements, the Church of Satan produces for its membership a variety of information-bulletins and a newsletter, *The Cloven Hoof*.

[26] Four sociological criteria determine that the Church of Satan is not a cult but a church: (1) it is very large; (2) it is bureaucratically organized and hierarchically governed; (3) people become members of the church only through complex testings and initiations; and (4) the success of the church no longer centers around its founder's charisma. The government also has given the Church of Satan legal recognition of its church status for tax and other purposes. (For an excellent discussion of the distinction between cult and church, see Nelson, 1968.)

[27] Contributing members belong to the lowest membership-level in the Church of Satan. Although they receive their membership-card, they are not involved in the rituals or ceremonies of the church. The six hierarchical levels of membership in the church include (1) Contributing Member, (2) Active Member, (3) Witch or Warlock, (4) Wizard or Enchantress, (5) Satanic Master or Sorcerer or Sorceress, and (6) Magus (High Priest). (Cf., LaVey, 1970.)

[28] During my visits to the headquarters in the summer of 1970, I observed that they receive a large volume of mail. Even if only a small percentage represented mail from new persons seeking membership, the volume itself reinforced my opinion of the accuracy of the figure.

which he was associated, has been a great success, the Church of Satan has received vast international publicity over the past five years.

The church has been remarkably successful during its short life. Although it still depends heavily upon the charisma of its founder, it is hierarchically governed[29] and now has two other churches (Grottos) in the Bay Area plus a number of still secret (to the general public) branches scattered around the country. By the end of 1971, LaVey hopes that Grottos will exist in every state of the Union. At the current rate of growth, achievement of his goal is not impossible. Because contributing members pay an initial fee of twenty dollars for their life-time membership, the church has a relatively prosperous economic beginning.

Although the Church of Satan believes in the practice of magic, it simply defines magic as "obtaining changes in accordance with one's will."[30] The church perceives magic not as supernatural (i.e., forever scientifically inexplicable), but simply as supernormal (i.e., not yet fully understood by science but amenable to eventual scientific explanation). The church actively rejects spirituality and mysticism of any sort; it espouses an elitist, materialist, and basically atheistic philosophy. Satan constitutes a worship of one's own ego. Unlike most atheisms, the position of the Church of Satan is that these symbolic entities are powerful and indispensable forces in man's emotional life and that these forces are necessary conditions for the success of greater (Ritual) Magic.

In its major features, the Church of Satan takes the position of extreme Machiavellianism and cynical-realism toward the nature of man. It has many philosophical parallels with philosophies as divergent in sophistication as the Superman views of Friedrich Nietzsche and the Objectivist ideals of Ayn Rand.[31] Its major feature, however, is its emphasis upon the importance of myth and magic and upon their impact in a world of people who can still be manipulated through such beliefs and emotions. This Satanist, then, is the *ultimate pragmatist*.[32]

This predominant form of Satanism does not represent a new mysticism at all. It not only denies the existence of anything supernatural or spiritual, but it even condemns any narcotics, hallucinogens, or other agents that might act to separate rational man from his material environment. This

---

[29] The secret governing body of the Church of Satan is called the Order of the Trapezoid. Pastors or priests of the Church of Satan are called Magister Cavernus or Master or Mistress of the Grotto. (Cf., LaVey, 1970.)

[30] This agrees with the definition of the well-known 20th Century magician, Aleister Crowley, whom others often mistakenly accused of being a Satanist. (Cf., Crowley, 1929: xii.)

[31] Because of its positivistic stance and of its emphasis on ritual, the Church of Satan is remarkably parallel with the Positive Religion begun by Auguste Comte.

[32] It is not insignificant that a magical ritual is usually termed a *working*.

Satanist does not seek escape from reality; he wishes full control of reality and is even willing to use all forces—including irrational elements—that help him in achieving his desired ends. Unlike the acid-culture Satanist who seeks identity through mysticism and other levels of "consciousness," this Satanist is very much opposed to the hippie culture of acid and altruism.[33]

Thus, I argue that, like those interested in astrology, the major followers of Satanism represent not a search for a new spiritual meaning, but only a disenchantment with religious orthodoxy.

CONCLUSION

How are we to assess this rising tide of interest in the occult? I have shown three major facts in this paper. First, the interest in the occult is multidimensional, and it is not the simple, integrated, and consistent "bag" that many, especially the writers in the popular press, have described it to be. Second, many persons involved in the following of today's occultisms are not the simple identity-seeking variety that some have portrayed them to be; these occultisms serve a variety of functions quite apart from offering new normative structures as an escape from alienation for the anomic. Third, most of those involved in supporting the current occult revival have a relatively superficial connection with it, a connection that is usually more one of play than one of seriousness. For most Americans, the involvement in the occult is a leisure-time activity and a fad of popular culture rather than a serious religious involvement in the search for new sacred elements.[34]

Dr. Donald Kaplan has made a very insightful observation about astrology:

> It's pop science . . . It has the same contempt,
> in a playful way, for science that pop art
> has for academic art (Quoted in Buckley, 1968:133).

---

[33] As a result, many conservative, anti-hippie persons have been strongly attracted to Satanism. The Church of Satan is elitist, but it has no political ideology or preference for a particular economic system. Some authoritarian personalities are especially attracted to the Church of Satan; in some of the recent church literature, a rising note of appeals to patriotism has occurred.

[34] We can find an interesting parallel between this debate and the popular interpretations of the recent folksong revival (late 1950's and early 1960's). Many commentators interpreted this revival as the alienated modern youth's search for traditions and for roots in our historical heritage. For most persons, it was nothing of the sort; it simply reflected some of the special functions that are very much like those of astrology today. In fact, the folksong revival and the ukelele fad of forty years ago bore marked similarities.

I believe that we may even go further and refer to the mass version of occultism as *pop religion*. I would argue that it shows a playful contempt for what many once viewed seriously (and some still view thusly). I further would argue that the current mass interest in occultism represents, in fact, a kind of victory over the supernatural. What we are seeing is largely a demystification-process of what were once fearful and threatening cultural elements. Most significant is the very playfulness in the attitudes of most of the people involved in the occult revival. What were once fearful and awe-inspiring dark secrets known only through initiation into arcane orders are now fully exposed to the eyes of Everyman.

I illustrate this point by the example of the probable contemporary reaction to the allegation that a house in the neighborhood is haunted. Years ago, few would dare enter the house; all would whisper in fear about it. Now, such an allegation would bring a rush of inquisitive teen-agers who desire to spend the night there just to see the ghost. Would it be proper to interpret this direct interest as a renewed belief in ghosts? It is precisely because we no longer believe in the fearsome aspects of the occult that we are willing to experiment with them. Most of those who would willingly draw a proper pentagram on the floor to invoke a demon would do so precisely because they do not really believe that some Devil's emissary who might just pluck their souls down to Hell would possibly ever visit them. If we fully believed in demons, we certainly would not want to call them up.

This assessment does not deny that a growth has occurred in the number of true believers in the occult. It also does not deny that other non-occult phenomena, which indicate a growing number of persons seeking new religious meanings, have occurred. Certain factors, however, would alone cause an expected increase in occult activity: (1) the increase in our general population, (2) some disillusionment with the dominant religions, (3) our lack of fear of the occult or an involvement with it; (4) the present lack of social sanctions against involvement with the occult, and (5) the increased saliency of the occult resulting from the revival itself. *I must stress that I am concerned more with the mass character of the occult than with its small but significant minority of serious advocates.* As long as these *mass* phenomena represent a playful and non-serious confrontation with the supernatural elements, they then represent a possible cleansing or purging of the old fears and myths still present in our society. The more we eliminate these old fears and myths, the more we develop a naturalistic rationalism, a scientific view of the universe.

REFERENCES

ABRAMSON, M., "Have You Consulted Your Friendly Astrologer Lately?" *TV Guide* (4 October 1969), 6–8.

BAROJA, JULIO C., *The World of the Witches*, O. N. V. Glendinning, trans. Chicago: University of Chicago Press, 1964.

BELANGER, A. F., "An Empirical Study of Superstitious and Unfounded Beliefs," proceedings of the fifty-seventh meeting of the Iowa Academy of Science, 51 (15 April 1944), 355–59.

BERGER, B. M., "On the Youthfulness of Youth Cultures," *Social Research*, 30 (Autumn 1963), 319–42.

BERGER, PETER, *The Sacred Canopy*. Garden City, N.Y.: Doubleday and Co., 1967.

BLOXHAM, P., "The Devil and Cecil Williamson," *New York Times* (19 April 1970), 5.

BLUMBERG, P., "Magic in the Modern World," *Sociology and Social Research*, 47 (January 1963), 147–60.

BOK, B. and M. W. MAYALL, "Scientists Look at Astrology," *Scientific Monthly*, 52 (March 1941), 233–41.

BONE, R., "We Witches Are Simple People," *Life* (13 November 1964), 55–62.

BOURQUE, L., "Social Correlates of Transcendental Experience," *Sociological Analysis*, 30 (Fall 1969), 151–63.

BOURQUE, L. and K. W. BACK, "Values and Transcendental Experiences," *Social Forces*, 47 (September 1968), 34–38.

BRACELIN, J. L., *Gerald Gardner: Witch*. London: Octagon Press, 1960.

BUCKLAND, RAYMOND, *Ancient and Modern Witchcraft*. New York: H. C. Publishers, Allograph Books, 1970.

BUCKLEY, TOM, "The Signs Are Right for Astrology," *The New York Times Magazine* (15 December 1968), 30.

BUCKNER, H. T., "The Flying Saucerians: An Open Door Cult," pp. 223–30 in Marcello Truzzi, ed., *Sociology and Everyday Life*. Englewood Cliffs, N.J.: Prentice-Hall, 1968.

BURKE, T., "Princess Leda's Castle in the Air," *Esquire* (March 1970), 104.

CALDWELL, OTIS W., and GERHARD E. LUNDEEN, *Do You Believe It?* Garden City, N.Y.: Garden City Publishing Co., 1937.

CARUS, PAUL, *The History of the Devil and the Idea of Evil*. New York: Land's End Press, 1969.

CASEY, R. P., "Transient Cults," *Psychiatry*, 4 (November 1941), 525–34.

CONKLIN, E. S., "Superstitious Belief and Practice Among College Students," *American Journal of Psychology*, 30 (January 1919), 83–102.

CONSUMER COMMUNICATIONS CORPORATION, *Dimensions of the Fate Magazine Audience*. Highland Park, Illinois: Fate Magazine, n.d.

COULANGE, LOUIS, *The Life of the Devil*, S. H. Guest, trans. New York: Alfred A. Knopf, 1930.

CRISTIANI, LEON, *Evidences of Satan in the Modern World*. New York: Macmillan, 1962.

CROW, W. B., *A History of Witchcraft, Magic and Occultism*. North Hollywood, Calif.: Wilshire Book Co., 1970.

CROWLEY, ALEISTER, *Magick in Theory and Practice*. Paris: Lecram Press, 1929.

CURIE, E. P., "Crimes Without Criminals: Witchraft and Its Control in Renaissance Europe," *Law and Society Review,* 3 (August 1968), 7–32.

DARRAUL, AKRON, *Witches and Sorcerers.* New York: Citadel, 1966.

DE CAMP, LYON S., and CATHERINE C. DE CAMP, *Spirits, Stars and Spells: The Profits and Perils of Magic.* New York: Canaveral Press, 1966.

DUDYCHA, G. J., "The Superstitious Beliefs of College Students," *Journal of Abnormal and Social Psychology,* 27 (January–March 1933), 457–64.

DURKHEIM, EMILE, *The Elementary Forms of the Religious Life,* Joseph Ward Swain, trans. New York: Collier Books, 1961.

ECKMAN, B., "Witch Sounds His Trumpet for Satan," *The Detroit News* (19 October 1969), 18-B.

ERIKSON, KAI T., *Wayward Puritans.* New York: John Wiley and Sons, 1966.

EYSENCK, H. J., D. J. WEST, J. BELOFF, I. STEVENSON, C. E. M. HANSEL, E. SLATER, R. C. B. AITKEN, D. H. W. KELLEY, C. J. S. WALTER, S. M. CANNICOTT, and R. H. ARMIN, "Correspondence," *British Journal of Psychiatry,* 144 (November 1968), 1471–83.

FELDMAN, GENE, and MAX GARTENBERG, eds., *The Beat Generation and the Angry Young Men.* New York: Citadel Press, 1958.

FREEDLAND, N., "The Witches Are Coming!" *Knight* (October 1969), 12.

FULLER, C. G., Personal communication, 1970.

GALLUP, G., JR., "The Gallup Report on Religious Experience," *Fate* (April 1963), 31–37.

GAMS, JAN, "From Astrology to Witchcraft: Occult on the Rise on Campus," *Wisconsin State Journal* (Madison) (18 January 1970).

GARCON, MAURICE, and JEAN VINCHON, *The Devil: An Historical Critical and Medical Study,* S. H., trans. London: Victor Gollancz, Ltd., 1929.

GARDNER, GERALD, *The Meaning of Witchcraft.* London: Aquarian Press, 1959.

———, *Witchcraft Today.* London: Rider and Co., 1954.

GAUQUELIN, MICHEL, *The Scientific Basis of Astrology: Myth or Reality.* New York: Stein and Day, 1969.

GILLILAND, A. R., "A Study of the Superstitions of the College Student," *Journal of Abnormal and Social Psychology,* 24 (January-March 1930), 472–79.

GLASS, JUSTINE, *Witchcraft: The Sixth Sense and Us.* London: Neville Spearman, 1965.

GLOCK, CHARLES Y., and RODNEY STARK, "Is There an American Protestantism?" *Trans-action* (November-December 1965), 8.

GRAVES, R., "Witches in 1964," *Virginia Quarterly Review,* 40 (Autumn 1964), 550–59.

GREELEY, A. M., "There's a New-Time Religion on Campus," *The New York Times Magazine* (1 June 1969), 14.

HANSEL, C. E. M., *ESP: A Scientific Evaluation.* New York: Charles Scribner's Sons, 1966.

HANSEN, CHADWICK, *Witchcraft in Salem.* New York: George Braziller, 1969.

HARRIS, T. G., "Religion in the Age of Aquarius: A Conversation with Harvey Cox and T. George Harris," *Psychology Today* (April 1970), 45.

HARTLAND, SIDNEY E., "Satanism," pp. 203–7 in James Hastings, ed., *Encyclopedia of Religion and Ethics*, Vol. 11. New York: Charles Scribner's Sons, 1921.

HENSLIN, J. M., "Craps and Magic," *American Journal of Sociology*, 73 (November 1967), 316–30.

HERING, D. W., *Foibles and Fallacies of Science*. New York: D. Van Nostrand, 1924.

HOLE, CHRISTINA, *A Mirror of Witchcraft*. London: Pedigree, 1957.

HOLZER, HANS, *The Truth about Witchcraft*. Garden City, N.Y.: Doubleday, 1969.

HUDSON, PAUL, *Mastering Witchcraft: A Practical Guide for Witches, Warlocks and Covens*. New York: G. P. Putnam's Sons, 1970.

HUEBNER, LOUISE, *Power through Witchcraft*. Los Angeles: Nash Publishing Co., 1969.

HURSTON, Z., "Hoodoo in America," *Journal of American Folk-Lore*, 44 (October–December 1931), 317–418.

HUYSMANS, JORIS-KARL, *Down There*, Keene Wallis, trans. New Hyde Park, N. Y.: University Books, 1958.

HYMAN, R. and E. Z. VOGT, "Water Witching: Magical Ritual in Contemporary United States," *Psychology Today* (May 1967), 34–42.

JASTROW, JOSEPH, *Errors and Eccentricity in Human Belief*. New York: Dover, 1962.

JENNINGS, C. R., "Swinging on the Stars," *Playboy* (March 1970), 103.

———, "Cultsville USA," *Playboy* (March 1969), 86.

JOHNS, JUNE, *King of the Witches. The World of Alex Sanders*. New York: Coward-McCann, 1970.

KITTREDGE, GEORGE L., *Witchcraft in Old and New England*. New York: Russell and Russell, 1956.

KLAPP, ORRIN E., *Collective Search for Identity*. New York: Holt, Rinehart and Winston, 1969.

KLEMESRUD, J., "Some People Take This Witch Business Seriously," *The New York Times* (31 October 1969), 50-C.

KLOMAN, W., "Banality of the New Evil," *Esquire* (March 1970), 115.

KOBLER, J., "Out for a Night at the Local Caldron," *Saturday Evening Post* (5 November 1966), 76–78.

KRAMER, HEINRICH, and JAMES SPRENGER, *Malleus Maleficarum*, Montague Summers, trans. London: Pushkin Press, 1948.

LANGSTON, EDWARD, *Satan, A Portrait*. London: Skeffington and Sons, 1945.

LAVEY, ANTON SZANDOR, "Letters from the Devil," *The Exploiter* (14 February 1970), 5.

———, *The Satanic Bible*. New York: Avon Books, 1969.

———, Personal communication, 1968.

LEA, CHARLES HENRY, *Materials Toward a History of Witchcraft*, 3 Volumes, A. C. Howland, arr. and ed. New York: Thomas Yoseloff, 1957.

LEEK, SYBIL, *Diary of a Witch*. Englewood Cliffs, N.J.: Prentice-Hall, 1968.

LETHBRIDGE, T. C., *Witches*. New York: Citadel Press, 1968.

LEVIN, J., "The Magic Explosion," *Eye* (October 1968), 24.

LEVITT, E. E., "Superstitions: Twenty-Five Years Ago and Today," *American Journal of Psychology*, 65 (July 1952), 443–49.

LEWINSOHN, RICHARD, *Science, Prophecy, and Prediction*, A. J. Pomerans, trans. Greenwich, Conn.: Fawcett Publications, 1962.

LEWIS, L. S., "Knowledge, Danger, Certainty and the Theory of Magic," *American Journal of Sociology*, 69 (July 1963), 7–12.

LYONS, ARTHUR, *The Second Coming: Satanism in America*. New York: Dodd, Mead and Co., 1970.

MACFARLANE, A. D. J., *Witchcraft in Tudor and Stuart England*. London: Routledge and Kegan Paul, Ltd., 1970.

MAPLE, ERIC, *The Domain of Devils*. New York: A. S. Barnes, 1966.

————, *The Dark World of Witches*. London: Pan, 1965.

MARTELLO, LEO L., *Weird Ways of Witchcraft*. New York: H. C. Publishers, Allograph Books, 1969.

MATHER, B., "Witchcraft and Satanism Are Alive and Well in Michigan; Meet Bill Who Believes," *The Detroit Free Press Sunday Magazine* (15 June 1969), 8–11.

MATHISON, RICHARD, *Faiths, Cults and Sects of America*. Indianapolis, Ind.: Bobbs-Merrill, 1960.

MCCALL, GEORGE J., "Symbiosis: The Case of Hoodoo and the Numbers Racket," pp. 51–66 in Howard S. Becker, ed., *The Other Side*. New York: Free Press, 1964.

MICHELET, JULES, *Satanism and Witchcraft*, A. R. Allinson, trans. New York: Citadel, 1939.

MOORE, HARRY T., "Enter Beatniks," pp. 376–97 in Albert Parry, *Garrets and Pretenders: A History of Bohemianism in America*. New York: Dover, 1960.

MOORE, MARTIN, *Sex and Modern Witchcraft*. Los Angeles: Echelon Book Publishers, Impact Library, 1969.

MURRAY, H. A., "The Personality and Career of Satan," *Journal of Social Issues*, 18 (October 1962), 36–54.

MURRAY, MARGARET A., *The Witch Cult in Western Europe*. London: Oxford University Press, 1921.

NASH, OGDEN, *The Selected Verse of Ogden Nash*. New York: Modern Library, 1945.

NELSON, G. K., "The Concept of Cult," *The Sociological Review*, 16 (November 1968), 351–62.

Newsweek, "The Cult of the Occult" (13 April 1970), 96–97.

Paperbound Books in Print. New York: R. R. Bowker Co., October 1969, June 1968.

PARK, R., "Magic, Mentality, and City Life," *Papers and Proceedings of the Eighteenth Annual Meeting of The American Sociological Society*, 18 (December 1923), 102–15.

PARRINDER, GEOFFREY, *Witchcraft*. Baltimore, Md.: Penguin, 1958.

PASSIN, H., and J. BENNETT, "Changing Agricultural Magic in Southern Illinois: A Systematic Analysis of Folk-Urban Transition," *Social Forces*, 22 (October 1943), 98–106.

PILEGGI, N., "Occult," *McCalls* (March 1970), 62.

PRAKKEN, SARAH L., and RUTH P. SHIVELY, eds., *Subject Guide to Books in Print*. New York: R. R. Bowker, 1969, 1968, 1967.

PRATT, ANTOINETTE MARIE, *The Attitude of the Catholic Church towards Witchcraft and the Allied Practices of Sorcery and Magic*. Washington, D.C.: National Capital Press, 1915.

RANDOPH, VANCE, *Ozark Superstitions*. New York: Columbia University Press, 1947.

RASCOE, J., "Church of Satan," *McCalls* (March 1970), 74.

RAWCLIFFE, D. H., *Illusions and Delusions of the Supernatural and the Occult*. New York: Dover, 1959.

RHODES, H. T. F., *The Satanic Mass*. London: Rider and Co., 1954.

RIGNEY, FRANCIS T., and L. DOUGLAS SMITH, *The Real Bohemia: A Sociological and Psychological Study of the "Beats."* New York: Basic Books, 1961.

ROBBINS, ROSSELL H., *The Encyclopedia of Witchcraft and Demonology*. New York: Crown, 1959.

ROBINSON, S., "Maurice Woodruff: Astrology's Brightest Star," *McCalls* (March 1970), 76.

ROBSON, PETER, *The Devil's Own*. New York: Ace Books, 1969.

ROHMER, SAX, *The Romance of Sorcery*. New York: Paperback Library, 1970.

ROSE, ELLIOT, *A Razor for a Goat*. Toronto, Ontario: University of Toronto Press, 1962.

ROTH, J. A., "Ritual and Magic in the Control of Contagion," *American Sociological Review*, 22 (June 1957), 310–14.

SANN, PAUL, *Fads, Follies and Delusions of the American People*. New York: Crown, 1967.

SANSWEET, S. J., "Strange Doings: Americans Show Burst of Interest in Witches, Other Occult Matters," *The Wall Street Journal* (23 October 1969), p. 1.

SAPIR, EDWARD, "Fashion," pp. 139–44 in *Encyclopedia of the Social Sciences*, VI. New York: Macmillan, 1937.

SEABROOK, WILLIAM, *Witchcraft: Its Power in the World Today*. New York: Harcourt, Brace and Co., 1940.

SECHREST, L., and J. M. BRYAN, "Astrologers as Useful Marriage Counselors," *Trans-action* (November 1968), 34–36.

SETH, RONALD, *Witches and Their Craft*. New York: Award Books, 1969.

SHOTWELL, J. T., "The Role of Magic," *American Journal of Sociology*, 15 (May 1910), 781–93.

SIMPKINS, OZZIE N., *Magic in Modern Society: A Situational Analysis.* University of North Carolina: Unpublished Ph.D. dissertation, 1953.

SPENCE, LEWIS, *Encyclopedia of Occultism.* New Hyde Park, N.Y.: University Books, 1960.

ST. ALBIN-GREENE, D., "There May Be a Witch Next Door," *National Observer* (13 October 1969), 24.

STAUDE, J. R., "Alienated Youth and the Cult of the Occult," paper read at the Annual Meetings of the Midwest Sociological Society, April, at St. Louis, Missouri. Mimeographed, 1970.

STEIGER, BRAD, *Sex and Satanism.* New York: Ace Books, 1969.

SUMMERS, MONTAGUE, *The Geography of Witchcraft.* New Hyde Park, N.Y.: University Books, 1958.

——, *The History of Witchcraft.* New Hyde Park, N.Y.: University Books, 1956.

——, *Witchcraft and Black Magic.* London: Rider and Co., 1946.

THOMAS, V., "The Witches of 1966," *Atlantic* (September 1966), 119–25.

THORNDIKE, L., "True Place of Astrology in the History of Science," *Isis,* 46 (September 1955), 273–78.

Time, "Astrology: Fad and Phenomenon" (21 March 1969), 47–56.

——, "That New Black Magic" (27 September 1968), 42.

TINDALL, GILLIAN, *The Handbook of Witches.* London: Panther, 1967.

TRUZZI, MARCELLO, "Towards a Sociology of the Occult: Notes on Modern Witchcraft," in I. I. Zaretsky and M. P. Leone, eds., *Pragmatic Religions.* Princeton, N.J.: Princeton University Press, in press.

——, *Caldron Cookery.* New York: Meredith Press, 1969.

VALIENTE, DOREEN, *Where Witchcraft Lives.* London: Aquarian Press, 1962.

VOGT, E. Z., "Interviewing Water-Dowsers," *American Journal of Sociology,* 62 (September 1956), 198.

VOGT, E. Z., and P. GOLDE, "Some Aspects of the Folklore of Water Witching in the United States," *Journal of American Folklore,* 71 (October–December 1958), 519–31.

VOGT, EVON Z., and RAY HYMAN, *Water Witching, U.S.A.* Chicago: University of Chicago Press, 1959.

WAGNER, M. E., "Superstitions and Their Social and Psychological Correlatives Among College Students," *Journal of Educational Sociology,* 2 (September 1928), 26–36.

WAITE, ARTHUR E., *Devil Worship in France.* London: George Redward, 1896.

WALLACE, C. H., *Witchcraft in the World Today.* New York: Award Books, 1967.

WARD, H. H., "Can Satanists and Christians Talk Together," *The Detroit Free Press* (27 June 1970), p. 4-A.

WARREN, D. I., "Status Inconsistency Theory and Flying Saucer Sightings," *Science,* 170 (6 November 1970), 599–603.

WAX, M. and R. WAX, "The Notion of Magic," *Current Anthropology,* 4 (December 1963), 495.

WEDECK, HARRY, *Treasury of Witchcraft*. New York: Philosophical Library, 1961.

WEIR, W. W., "The New Wave of Witches," *Occult* (January 1970), 24–37.

WEISS, H. B., "Oneirocritica Americana: The Story of American Dream Books," *Bulletin of the New York Public Library*, p. 519.

WENGER, D., and E. L. QUARANTELLI, "A Voice from the 13th Century: A Study of a Ouija Board Cult," paper presented at the Annual Meetings of the Ohio Valley Sociological Society, 1 May 1970, at Akron, Ohio. Mimeographed.

WHITTEN, N., "Contemporary Patterns of Malign Occultism Among Negroes in North Carolina," *Journal of American Folklore*, 75 (October–December 1962), 311–25.

WILLIAMS, P., "There's Money in Myths and Magic," *The Sunday Telegraph* (12 April 1970).

WILSON, MONIQUE, Interview with Johnny Carson on NBC-TV, the Tonight Show, 31 October 1968.

ZAPF, R. M., "Comparison of Responses to Superstitions on a Written Test and in Actual Situations," *Journal of Educational Research*, 30 (September 1945), 13–25.

———, "Relationship Between Belief in Superstitions and Other Factors," *Journal of Educational Research*, 38 (April 1945), 561–79.

further readings[1]

RE ACADEMIC GAMESMANSHIP

ROBERT SOMMER, *Expertland*. Garden City, N.Y.: Doubleday, 1963.

OTTO N. LARSEN, "Sociological Gamesmanship in the Professorial Role-Set of the Ultramultiversity," *Pacific Sociological Review*, 12, 2 (1969), 65–74.

C. WRIGHT MILLS, *The Sociological Imagination*. New York: Oxford University Press, 1959.

RE THE COFFEE BREAK

DAVID RIESMAN, ROBERT J. POTTER, and JEANNE WATSON, "The Vanishing Host," *Human Organization*, 19 (1960), 17–27.

RE WORD FREQUENCIES

ROGER BROWN and MARGUERITE FORD, "Address in American English," *Journal of Abnormal and Social Psychology*, 62 (1961), 375–85.

RE CARD GAMES

IRVING CRESPI, "The Social Significance of Card Playing as a Leisure Time Activity," *American Sociological Review*, 21 (1956), 717–21.

BRIAN SUTTON-SMITH and JOHN M. ROBERTS, "Game Involvement in Adults," *Journal of Social Psychology*, 60 (1963), 15–30.

HUGH GARDNER, "Bureaucracy at the Bridge Table," in George H. Lewis, ed., *Side-Saddle on the Golden Calf: Social Structure and Popular Culture in America*. Pacific Palisades, Calif.: Goodyear, 1972, pp. 138–53.

[1] The references listed here in order of the article to which they apply are meant to supplement the bibliographies cited by the authors. Refer to the authors' citations for most of the primary works dealing with each topic.

RE QUEUES

Leon Mann and K. F. Taylor, "Queue Counting: The Effects of Motives upon Estimates of Numbers in Waiting Lines," *Journal of Personality and Social Psychology*, 12, 2 (1969), 95–103.

————, "The Social Psychology of Waiting Lines," *American Scientist*, 58, 4 (1970), 390–98.

Erving Goffman, *Relations in Public: Microstudies of the Public Order*. New York: Basic Books, 1971.

RE PRIVACY

Robert A. Stebbins, "Modesty, Pride, and Conceit: Variations in the Expression of Self-Esteem," *Pacific Sociological Review*, 15, 4 (1972), 461–81.

Michael A. Dorsey and M. Meisels, "Personal Space and Self-Protection," *Journal of Personality and Social Psychology*, 11 (1969), 93–97.

RE GRAFFITI

Paul D. McGlynn, "Graffiti and Slogans: Flushing the Id," *Journal of Popular Culture*, 6, 2 (1972), 351–56.

G. Legman, *Rationale of the Dirty Joke: An Analysis of Sexual Humor*, First Series. New York: Grove Press, 1968.

RE HIPPIES

Sherri Cavan, "The Class Structure of Hippie Society," *Urban Life and Culture*, 1, 3 (1972), 211–38.

Nathan Adler, "The Antinomian Personality: The Hippie Character Type," *Psychiatry*, 31 (1968), 325–38.

Warren Hinckle, "A Social History of the Hippies," *Ramparts*, 5 (March 1967), 9–12, 17–20, 24–26.

John Robert Howard, "The Flowering of the Hippie Movement," *Annals of the American Academy of Political and Social Science*, 382 (March 1969), 43–55.

RE PLAYBOY MAGAZINE

Dennis Brissett and R. P. Snow, "Vicarious Behavior: Leisure and the Transformation of *Playboy* Magazine," *Journal of Popular Culture*, 3, 3 (1969), 428–39.

Charles Winick, "Some Observations on Characteristics of Patrons of Adult Theaters and Bookstores," *Technical Report of the Commission on Obscenity and Pornography, Vol. 4, The Marketplace: Empirical Studies*. Washington, D.C.: U.S. Government Printing Office, 1970, pp. 225–44.

RE THOUGHT REFORM

J. A. C. BROWN, *Techniques of Persuasion: From Propaganda to Brainwashing.* Baltimore, Md.: Penguin Books, 1963.

JACK BALSWICK, "The Jesus People Movement: A Sociological Analysis," paper presented at the Annual Meetings of the American Sociological Association, New Orleans, La., August 28–31, 1972.

DONALD W. PETERSEN and ARMAND L. MAUSS, "The Cross and the Commune: An Interpretation of the Jesus Movement of the 1960's and 1970's," paper presented at the Annual Meetings of the American Sociological Association, New Orleans, La., August 28–31, 1972.

RE JEALOUSY

NENA O'NEILL and GEORGE O'NEILL, "Open Marriage: A Synergic Model," *The Family Coordinator,* 21, 4 (1972), 403–10.

RE ODORS

HARRY WIENDER, "External Chemical Messengers. I. Emission and Reception in Man," *New York State Journal of Medicine* (December 15, 1966), 3153–70.

ROY BEDICHEK, *The Sense of Smell.* Garden City, N.Y.: Doubleday, 1960.

RUSSELL C. ERB, *The Common Scents of Smell: How the Nose Knows and What It All Shows.* New York: World Publishing Co., 1968.

RE HOMOSEXUALITY

MARY McINTOSH, "The Homosexual Role," *Social Problems,* 16, 2 (1968), 182–92.

EVELYN HOOKER, "The Homosexual Community," in J. O. Palmer and M. J. Goldstein, eds., *Perspectives in Psychopathology.* New York: Oxford University Press, 1966, pp. 354–64.

RE TRANSSEXUALS

ROBERT J. STOLLER, "Passing and the Continuum of Gender Identity," in Judd Marmor, ed., *Sexual Inversion.* New York: Basic Books, 1965, pp. 190–210.

ESTHER NEWTON, *Mother Camp: Female Impersonators in America.* Englewood Cliffs, N.J.: Prentice-Hall, 1972.

RE AUTOEROTICISM

R. H. MacDONALD, "The Frightful Consequences of Onanism: Notes on the History of a Delusion," *Journal of the History of the Behavioral Sciences,* 28 (1967), 432–41.

WILLIAM GUY and MICHAEL H. P. FINN, "A Review of Autofellatio," *Psychoanalytic Review,* 41 (1954), 354–58.

RE SALES BEHAVIOR

F. WILLIAM HOWTON and BERNARD ROSENBERG, "The Salesman: Ideology and Self-Imagery in a Prototypic Occupation," *Social Research,* 32, 3 (1965), 277–98.

T. E. LEVITIN, "Role Performance and Role Distance in a Low Status Occupation: The Puller," *Sociological Quarterly,* 5, 3 (1964), 251–60.

RE DANCE TEACHING

ELON H. MOORE, "Public Dance Halls in a Small City," *Sociology and Social Research,* 14 (1930), 256–63.

RE SCATOLOGICAL RITES

LAWRENCE WRIGHT, *Clean and Decent: The Fascinating History of the Bathroom and the WC.* Toronto: University of Toronto Press, 1967.

RE EXECUTIONERS

FINN HORNUM, "The Executioner: His Role and Status in Scandinavian Society," in Marcello Truzzi, ed., *Sociology and Everyday Life.* Englewood Cliffs, N.J.: Prentice-Hall, 1968, pp. 126–37.

RE BULLFIGHTS

JACK R. CONRAD, "The Bullfight: The Cultural History of an Institution," Doctoral dissertation, Duke University, 1954.

RE HORSE RACING

MARVIN B. SCOTT, *The Racing Game.* Chicago: Aldine, 1966.

OTTO NEWMAN, "The Sociology of the Betting Shop," *British Journal of Sociology,* 19, 1 (1968), 17–33.

RE DANCING

D. DUANE BRAUN, *The Sociology and History of American Music and Dance, 1920–1968.* Ann Arbor, Mich.: Ann Arbor Publishers, 1969.

WARREN T. MORRILL, "Ethnoicthylology of the Cha-Cha," *Ethnology,* 6 (1967), 405–16.

RE THE TELEPHONE

FREDERICK F. STEPHAN, "Some Social Aspects of the Telephone," M. A. Thesis, University of Chicago, 1926.

RE WOMEN'S LIBERATION

JOAN HUBER, ed., *Changing Women in a Changing Society*. Special Issue of the *American Journal of Sociology*, 78, 4 (1973).

RE GYPSIES

MARNA F. FISHER, "Gypsies," in A. M. Rose and C. B. Rose, eds., *Minority Problems*. New York: Harper & Row, 1965.

PATRICIA LYNDEN, "The Last Holdouts," *The Atlantic*, 220, 2 (1967), 42–46.

RE THE HEAD SHOP

LAWRENCE J. REDLINGER, "Dealing in Dope," Doctoral dissertation, Northwestern University, 1969.

RE SKIN COLOR

GUSTAV ICHHEISER, "Sociopsychological and Cultural Factors in Race Relations," *American Journal of Sociology*, 54 (1949), 395–401.

RE OCCULTISM

EDWARD A. TIRYAKIAN, "Toward the Sociology of Esoteric Culture," *American Journal of Sociology*, 78, 3 (1972), 491–512.

ROBERT GALBREATH, ed., *The Occult: Studies and Evaluations*. Bowling Green, Ohio: Bowling Green University Popular Press, 1972.